Robert Griffin

BERNARD SHAW'S LETTERS TO
SIEGFRIED TREBITSCH

George Bernard Shaw, 1905.

BERNARD SHAW'S LETTERS TO SIEGFRIED TREBITSCH

Edited by Samuel A. Weiss

Stanford University Press 1986
Stanford, California

Published with the assistance of the
National Endowment for the Humanities

Stanford University Press, Stanford, California

CIP data appear at the end of the book

For Rana

PREFACE

W<small>HEN HE MET</small> Siegfried Trebitsch, Shaw's German-language translator, in Austria in the summer of 1922, Robert Beecher, American correspondent and would-be playwright, was intrigued by Trebitsch's wistful reflections on his many years of service to Shaw. The following autumn, Beecher visited Trebitsch in his villa in the fashionable Viennese suburb of Hietzing and there was shown a number of letters from Shaw revealing the early history of the Shaw-Trebitsch collaboration. Besides showing the importance of Trebitsch's "Great Adventure" in placing Shaw on the German stage, the letters were a dazzling display of a supremely confident Shaw—irreverent, brilliant, lavishing counsel, declaring himself emperor of a stage that he had yet to conquer.

With Trebitsch's aid and Shaw's consent, Beecher selected 27 early letters and embedded them in narrative commentary. The resulting article, even after editing by Shaw, was so long that no magazine would touch it. Years later, much shortened and reduced to ten letters, it appeared in *Plain Talk* (February–March 1930). Subsequently, Archibald Henderson reprinted two of Beecher's letters in his biographies of Shaw (1932, 1956), and later still Dan H. Laurence, in the second volume of the *Collected Letters of Bernard Shaw 1893–1910* (1972), published 37 Shaw letters to Trebitsch (out of a possible 136), more than to any other correspondent during that period. Shortly before, a proposal for the present edition had been accepted by the Shaw Estate with the generous concurrence of Mr. Laurence.

The prospects were large and mainly uncharted. Over six hundred letters, covering almost fifty years of collaboration and friendship (1902–50), had survived. Begun when Shaw was forty-six and virtually unknown as a dramatist on the continent, the correspondence spanned Shaw's rise to fame, the momentous events of the first half of the twentieth century, which raised the friendship to new planes of loyalty and concern, and the final years of Shaw the world celebrity. Over a thousand letters must have passed between the two men. Thanks to Trebitsch's foresight and care, the great majority of Shaw's letters—616, including postcards, wires, and notes—remain.

After his flight from Austria in 1938, Trebitsch succeeded in rescuing his collection of Shaw's letters and secreting them in Paris until after the war. Thereafter he continued to guard his treasure: "I have not the intention to sell Shaw's letters during my life-time," he wrote to Archibald Henderson in June 1953, "if I shall not be compelled to do so one day." And again, the following month: "Why should I ruin my collection by selling a few out of it and make the rest more or less worthless?" He estimated the value at $100,000 and added in a postscript: "I may be *forced* one day to sell, not to let my wife pennyless [*sic*]." Yet some sixty known items did escape the collection, mostly clustering around 1938–40 and 1949–50, when perhaps Trebitsch, pressed for ready funds, disposed of them. Fortunately, all but five of the strays ended up in the Hanley Collection, purchased by the University of Texas. Roughly a dozen more items alluded to in the letters have not surfaced, including the letters written immediately after Trebitsch's marriage in 1907 (Trebitsch translated and published one in his memoirs, *Chronik eines Lebens* [Chronicle of a Life], 1951), although Shaw's claim to have written "dozens" of letters that eluded Trebitsch's attention during his honeymoon is wildly exaggerated. How many other letters may be missing one cannot say.

In 1953 Trebitsch read through his collection in search of the original English version of Shaw's preface to the German edition of his plays "Was ich der deutschen Kultur verdanke" ("What I Owe to German Culture," 1911), which had been requested by Henderson. During his reading, Trebitsch added a note to one of the letters (16 January 1936) and presumably also on that occasion crossed out several embarrassing passages in other letters. Finally, in 1956, two years after the death of his wife and shortly before his own death, Trebitsch sold his collection, which is presently owned by the Berg Collection of the New York Public Library.

The loss of Trebitsch's side of the correspondence has immeasurably complicated an editor's task. Allusions and misreadings that the other half of the correspondence would have instantly made clear demanded great effort or serendipitous luck to decipher. Moreover, as the handful of Trebitsch's letters that somehow did survive show, Trebitsch's bumbling English and sentiment carry their own amusing charm and are an index to his personality. Nor was Shaw remiss. After his death, his file of Trebitsch's letters was deposited with the British Museum (Library), which later assigned them along with his other business papers to the Library of the London School of Economics. By then Trebitsch was dead, and litigation arose over Trebitsch's sale of his rights in Shaw to publisher William Heinemann Ltd. To determine what agreements had existed between the collaborators, a representative of the Public Trustee, then the executor of the Shaw Estate, in 1960 removed the file of Trebitsch's letters and turned it over to the law firm handling the case. In time the file was forgotten, and, whether misplaced, lost, or carelessly discarded, it was never returned to the Public Trustee or the London School of Economics and has vanished. (I am indebted for this information to the indefatigable Dan Laurence, who discovered the loss and traced its history.)

The task of tracking Shaw's German dealings was further complicated by the fact that in 1929 Shaw asked Alma von Bank, who helped translate Shaw's German correspondence, to go through a file of old German business letters and destroy those no longer current. Yet seventeen letters from Trebitsch to Shaw (including postcards and wires, some with Shaw's shorthand replies and notes) found their way into the Hanley Collection, and five surfaced elsewhere. Eighteen of substantive interest are included in this edition and add some contrasting spice.

Of Shaw's letters, some seventy brief items have been omitted from this edition as irrelevant or inconsequential. These consist of business notes, wires, acknowledgments, train schedules, fragments, and the like, or anticipate matters dealt with more fully in subsequent letters. The remaining 531 letters have been reproduced in full, except for repetitious matter and distracting minor details. As a general rule, cuts have been avoided within paragraphs. Within letters, deletions are indicated by ellipses; omitted postscripts are noted in the bibliographic data preceding the notes.

In transcribing the letters, I have basically followed the principles of the *Collected Letters of Bernard Shaw*: headings have been regularized (and are supplied in brackets where necessary), salutations and complimentary closes follow Shaw's holograph style of punctuation and capitalization and are omitted when Shaw omits them—typically in postcards and notes. When, however, the beginning or end of a letter that almost certainly had a salutation and closing is missing, or when a closing has been cut off, Trebitsch's name in a salutation obliterated, or a letter typed by Shaw's secretary mailed inadvertently without Shaw's signature, the missing elements have been provided in brackets. Periods are dropped after abbreviated titles (Mr, Mrs, Dr), and commas and periods are placed inside quotation marks. Otherwise, the body of a letter is meticulously reproduced, including Shaw's idiosyncratic orthography and punctuation (e.g., his typical omission of apostrophes in contractions, odd capitalization of titles, and combined substantives), and his inconsistencies and misspellings of names. Where lapses may confuse the reader, corrections have been added in brackets, as have translations of Shaw's divagations into German and his sprinkling of unfamiliar foreign phrases. Mere typos have been silently corrected. The same principles apply to the letters of Trebitsch, with their Germanized English, misspellings, and solecisms. An indication of the nature of the manuscript (e.g., whether autograph or typed) appears in a bibliographic byline preceding the notes to each letter. Unless otherwise stated there, all letters are owned by the Henry W. and Albert A. Berg Collection, New York Public Library.

Needless to say, no work of this scope could be completed without the cooperation of many persons and institutions. Happily, no curtain divided East from West in my quest for information. Not only was I granted immediate

and full access to the indispensable state and university libraries in East
Berlin (and during a briefer stay in Prague), but all my queries to collections
in Leipzig, Budapest, Warsaw, Cracow, Zagreb, Prague, and Moscow were
promptly and fully answered. For use of German newspaper, theatre, and reference materials, I am indebted to the Deutsche Staatsbibliothek, East Berlin,
and its neighboring Humboldt Universitätsbibliothek, to the Österreich-
ische Nationalbibliothek, Vienna, and its splendid Theatersammlung, the
Wiener Stadtbibliothek, the Haus-, Hof-, und Staatsarchiv, Vienna, the Institut für Zeitungsforschung, Dortmund, the Landesarchiv Berlin, the Theater-
historische Sammlung Walter Unruh, the Max Reinhardt-Forschungsstätte,
Vienna, and the Stadt Verwaltung, Hamburg.

Additional German data were provided by the Artemis Verlag, the Bay-
erische Staatsbibliothek, Munich, the Dumont-Lindemann-Archiv, Düsseldorf, the Institut für Theaterwissenschaft der Universität Köln, the
Niedersächsische Staats- und Universitätsbibliothek, Göttingen, the Rat-
hausbücherei, Stuttgart, the S. Fischer Verlag, the Stadt- und Universitätsbibliothek, Frankfurt, the Suhrkamp Verlag, the Theatermuseum der Clara-
Ziegler Stiftung, Munich, the Theatersammlung, Universität Hamburg, and
the Universitätsbibliothek, Leipzig.

Other institutions that generously contributed materials and information
were: Arkhiv i Muzej Hrvatskog Narodnog Kazalista, Zagreb; the BBC;
Biblioteca Nazionale, Milan; Biblioteca Nazionale, Venice; Center for Re-
search Libraries; Central State Theatre Library of the U.S.S.R. Ministry of
Culture; Gabrielle Enthoven Theatre Collection; Leo Baeck Institute; Muzeum Historyczne Miasta Krakow; Muzeum Teatralne Warszawe; Narodni
Muzeum, Prague; Nationalbibliothek Szechenyi, Budapest; Panstwowy
Instytut Sztuki, Warsaw; Schiller-Nationalmuseum; Universita Karlova,
Prague; University Center at Binghamton; and the Wiener Library. I am also
obligated to the Research Board of the University of Illinois at Chicago for
two domestic travel grants and a third grant that allowed me to obtain photo-
copies of Shaw's letters to Trebitsch.

For access to important collections of Shaviana, I am indebted to the British Library, whose reference and newspaper holdings were essential as well,
to the British Library of Political and Economic Science, London School of
Economics, the New York Public Library, the Harry Ransom Humanities Research Center, University of Texas, Cornell University Library, and Yale
University Library.

Special thanks and acknowledgments are due to the following owners of
the Shaw-Trebitsch letters for permission to publish them: the Henry W. and
Albert A. Berg Collection, New York Public Library, Astor, Lenox, and
Tilden Foundations, whose collection of Shaw's letters to Trebitsch form the
main body and soul of this edition; the Harry Ransom Humanities Research
Center, University of Texas, which contributed 39 letters by Shaw and 14 by
Trebitsch; the Bernard F. Burgunder Collection of Bernard Shaw, Cornell
University Library, and the Mugar Memorial Library of Boston University
Library, which provided one letter by Shaw each; the National Trust, which

supplied one letter by Shaw and another by Trebitsch; and the National Library of Ireland, which provided one letter by Trebitsch. My thanks as well to the Southern Historical Collection, Library of the University of North Carolina at Chapel Hill, for permission to cite brief passages from the letters of Trebitsch to Archibald Henderson.

For use of copyrighted materials, I am indebted to the Society of Authors as executors of the Estate of George Bernard Shaw; to King's College, Cambridge University, and the British Library for excerpts from a letter by Gertrude Kingston to Shaw; and to the Trustees of the Will of the late Mrs. Bernard Shaw, by whose kind permission the letters of Mrs. Bernard Shaw to Trebitsch are printed. The portrait of Shaw in 1905 is by permission of the British Library; that of 1914 by courtesy of the Victoria and Albert Museum, Theatre Museum; that of 1947—as well as Shaw's holograph drawings—by courtesy of the Henry W. and Albert A. Berg Collection, New York Public Library, Astor, Lenox, and Tilden Foundations; and that of the Grand Stairway of the Burgtheater by courtesy of the Bild-Archiv der Österreichischen Nationalbibliothek, Wien (Vienna). The photograph of Elisabeth Bergner is from *Max Reinhardt; 25 Jahre Deutsches Theater*, edited by Hans Rothe (1930), and is reproduced by permission of R. Piper & Co. Verlag.

Of those who personally aided by sharing materials and information, my greatest debt is to the prince of editors and model Shavian Dan H. Laurence, who, drawing on his incomparable knowledge of Shaw, unfailingly, promptly, and zestfully answered my innumerable queries, provided copies of stray letters and items concerning this edition, and graciously undertook to read proofs. For his encouragement, generosity, and consideration, my warmest thanks. To Mrs. Lola L. Szladits, Curator of the Berg Collection, whose magnanimous cooperation opened the door to this undertaking, my sincere gratitude. Others to whom I owe thanks for courtesies and shared information are: Maria Becker, Dr. G. Bermann Fischer, David Farmer, Sir Michael Kerr, Lesley Macdonald, Dr. Sybil Milton, the late Ivor Montagu, Helene Ritzerfeld, the late Adolf Scharf, A. Seabrook, Eric Trebitsch, Dr. James Tyler, the late Dr. Friedrich Witz, Roma Woodnutt, and Katharina Wyler-Salten. To the many unheralded reference librarians, whose knowledge is a pillar of research, to the cart pushers, interlibrary loan staffs, and unmentioned others who contributed to this work, my appreciation and thanks.

Finally, to editors Norris Pope and Helen Tartar, for friendly, cogent, and exemplary supervision ot the manuscript, and to Shirley Taylor, who, fascinated by the letters of Shaw, brought to her usual sharp-eyed, meticulous editing a constructive enthusiasm that enhanced the edition and spared me more than one error, my felt thanks and commendation.

S.A.W.

CONTENTS

ILLUSTRATIONS

ABBREVIATIONS

The following abbreviations of descriptions and sources have been used in this volume:

Als.	Autograph letter, signed.
Ans.	Autograph note, signed.
Apcs.	Autograph postcard, signed.
Ayot	Shaw's Corner, Ayot St. Lawrence, The National Trust.
B.L.	British Library.
Boston	Mugar Memorial Library, Boston University.
Cornell	Bernard F. Burgunder Collection, Cornell University Library.
L.S.E.	British Library of Political and Economic Science, London School of Economics.
Pcs.	Postcard, signed.
Texas	Harry Ransom Humanities Research Center, University of Texas.
Tls.	Typed letter, signed.
Tpcs.	Typed postcard, signed.

Where signatures are missing, the *s* in the abbreviation is of course omitted. Incomplete and dictated letters are appropriately indicated.

PART ONE

Conquering the German Stage

26 June 1902 through 4 August 1914

O NE AFTERNOON in mid-March 1902, a young Viennese author, with a letter of introduction from the English critic William Archer, stood before Bernard Shaw's London residence at 10 Adelphi Terrace. "In London," he recalled years later (1928), "because of the huge distances, one easily has time to become irresolute and to turn back half-ways. An inner voice still held me back as I extended my hand to the knocker. I must have dimly sensed that a turning point in my life had struck. Then I remembered some infinitely beautiful poetic words of Eugene Marchbanks [in *Candida*], which I had already translated into German. These quickly silenced all my hesitations, and I knocked at the door."*

The young man was quickly ushered into the presence, not of Shaw, but of Shaw's wife, Charlotte, who set her guest at ease while quietly sizing him up. Suddenly Shaw appeared and offered his hand. Charlotte vanished, and the young man burst into praise of Shaw's plays, which he had recently discovered. "Lord knows," Shaw interrupted, "you've made a pretty thorough study of my works. What are you really aiming at? What do you intend for me?" To which the visitor replied that he was determined to translate Shaw's plays and had set himself the goal "of conquering the German stage for him" (1926, 1928, 1931, 1951). At this, "Shaw leaped up and hurried like a flash up the staircase. I heard him call out: 'Charlotte, here's a young lunatic whom I

*Trebitsch's basic account of how he became Shaw's translator is his lecture "Der deutsche Aufstieg Bernard Shaws," delivered in honor of Shaw's seventieth birthday and published, somewhat shortened, in *Weltbühne*, XXII (1926). Essentially the same account, with some omissions, additions, or embellishments also appears in "Wie Bernard Shaw nach Deutschland kam," S. Fischer Verlag, *Almanach*, 1928; "How I Discovered Bernard Shaw," *Bookman*, April 1931 (a condensation of the *Almanach* article with some refinements); *Bernard Shaw dem Neunzig-jährigen*, Zurich, 1946; and *Chronik eines Lebens*, Zurich, 1951 (Engl., *Chronicle of a Life*, trans. Eithne Wilkins and Ernst Kaiser, London, 1953). A variant account, which differs in language but not in basic substance, is "Als Shaw noch unbekannt war," *Neue Freie Presse*, 10 March 1929. In addition, there are Trebitsch's interviews with the *Observer* ("The Vogue of G. B. S.," 7 November 1920) and with the BBC ("Bernard Shaw's Translator," *Listener*, 27 October 1938). References to these sources are by year of publication. Where slight differences distinguish successive accounts I have chosen the earliest version.

can't bring to his senses; you try to calm him down; perhaps you will succeed.'" Mrs. Shaw reappeared, and the would-be translator explained his project to her. Charlotte nodded approvingly and called up to Shaw: "The young man seems uncommonly sensible. Come and listen to him." Shaw returned. "He's perfectly right," Charlotte began. "Why shouldn't the German theatre, which has turned Shakespeare into a German poet, bring you the satisfaction that is still denied you at home?" Incredulously, Shaw cried out: "So you want to become my Schlegel-Tieck?" and launched into the matter of copyright (1946, 1951).

Thus began the lifelong collaboration of Bernard Shaw and Siegfried Trebitsch. Trebitsch's account of meeting Shaw first appeared in 1926 and was later revised and embellished. The premonitory hesitation before Shaw's door does not appear in the earliest version, although Trebitsch mentions starting out with a "very heavy heart." Shaw's springing up and calling to Charlotte to rescue him from the "young lunatic" is first hinted in a BBC interview in 1938 and written up in 1946. By then Shaw was ninety, Trebitsch seventy-eight.

Shaw's version, written less than a year after the event, on the eve of his introduction to Vienna, only tangentially corroborates Trebitsch's account. Shaw mentions two visits. "It may be asked," he wrote, addressing the Viennese, "why I, a foreigner, should trouble Vienna with my plays. . . . I can only say in reply that I am quite guiltless in the matter. One day when I was away from home a Viennese gentleman called on my wife with an introduction from my friend William Archer. . . . He demanded an authorization to translate my plays into German. My wife politely explained that there were difficulties—difficulties raised by the copyright laws and the course of business. The impetuous Trebitsch replied that he was surprised to hear a woman of sense talking in such a manner; that such excellent plays as mine were wasted in the foolish English theatre; that Vienna alone could do them justice; that he must, could, should and would translate them; and that he had not come all the way from Austria to listen to quibbles about the copyright law. My wife was crushed. To propitiate him she invited him to lunch. He came, and crushed me." ("Ein Teufelskerl. Selbstkritik," *Die Zeit*, 22 February 1903; English version, B.L.)

Years later, Shaw merged the two visits into one. Trebitsch appeared with an offer to become Shaw's "interpreter and apostle." "I attempted to dodge his visit by asking my wife to see him and to explain politely that a proposal to translate could be entertained only when made by the responsible manager of a theatre with a view to immediate production. The evasion failed ignominiously. My wife came to me and said that the young gentleman . . . had swept aside her excuse with explosive contempt, and would take no denial. If I was to get rid of him . . . I must go down and do it myself. I came down; and the result was that the young gentleman carried the citadel by storm as successfully as he had carried the outworks. I did what I could to dissuade him from what seemed a desperate undertaking; but his faith in my destiny was invincible. I surrendered at discretion." ("Translator's Note,"

Jitta's Atonement, 1925.) This much is certain: on 17 March 1902 Mrs. Shaw wrote to Trebitsch in London from Adelphi Terrace:

Dear Sir,
My husband has been thinking over your proposition and we shall be very glad if you will come to lunch here tomorrow (Tuesday) at 1.30 and talk it over with him.

Yours sincerely,
C. F. Shaw

At the time of his first meeting with Shaw, Siegfried Trebitsch was thirty-three years old, unmarried, and modestly started on a literary career. He was born in Vienna on 22 December 1868 (Trebitsch, who had a morbid horror of what he regarded as the convention of birthdays, claimed 21 December 1869) into a wealthy, assimilated Jewish family of silk manufacturers, who had emigrated from Moravia. Appropriately, he was early under the care of governesses and tutors and learned English and French. In time, he also learned to ride, skate, dance, and fence. He was also a fine swimmer and shared his family's passion for chess. As a youth, he joined the whirling social life of upper-middle-class Vienna and, being a skilled rider, served his military duty in the cavalry and became a reserve officer.

The Vienna recalled by Trebitsch as an old man was, despite its darker aspects, a gay city, full of talent. Public and private balls abounded; but even more compelling—the passion of the affluent—was the theatre, above all the imperial Burgtheater, cynosure of Vienna's would-be dramatists, among them the young Trebitsch.

Yet Trebitsch, even as a child, was gloomy and melancholy. An older brother had died at the age of one, and his father died at the young age of thirty-three (when Siegfried was four). These two deaths haunted the boy. At twelve, Siegfried began suffering from migraine headaches, which were to plague him all his life and send him in search of cures. The remarriage of his mother to her brother-in-law, Leopold Trebitsch, was unhappy, although Siegfried became very fond of his stepfather. And sexual repression and outward proprieties took their toll. (As a writer, Trebitsch was almost morbidly concerned with sexual lapses and guilt.) Moreover, disaster could strike in adolescent affairs of honor (Trebitsch was seriously wounded before he was twenty), and among certain wealthy families, especially Jewish ones, there was tension between the business-oriented or professional older generation and younger scions like Siegfried Trebitsch, Stefan Zweig, Felix Salten, Arthur Schnitzler, and Hugo von Hofmannsthal, who dreamed of artistic achievement.

As writers, they gathered, under author-critic Hermann Bahr, as Jung Wien (Young Vienna) or Die Moderne (The Moderns). Trebitsch, intended for a business career, did not go to the university but during his twenties reluctantly worked in the family firm while publishing theatre reviews, a short story, and a slim volume of poems (*Gedichte* [Poems], Vienna, 1889), which made no impression. A second volume of verse was rejected by the eminent Berlin publisher S. Fischer. But in late 1901 Fischer issued Trebitsch's novella *Genesung* (Convalescence). Book in hand, Siegfried approached his stepfather and declared his intention to be a full-time author. Some months later, he was in London offering to become Shaw's translator and herald.

This odd diversion of energies was noted by critics after Trebitsch had become best known as "Shaw's translator." It may also explain why Trebitsch later insisted that he did not, on discovering Shaw, intend at first to become Shaw's interpreter and made no effort to meet Shaw until a year had passed, during which he tended largely to his own work and vainly tried to interest German agents and translators in Shaw: "Only . . . the cool dismissal of my enthusiasm, and the resultant exasperation that rose up in me turned me into Bernard Shaw's translator" (1928, 1946, 1951; also 1920, 1926). But Trebitsch is inconsistent. In his 1938 interview he maintained that he had "by accident" obtained Shaw's plays in London, read them on his return to Vienna, and been so impressed that he "actually returned at once to London to try to get in touch with Mr. Shaw."

The "accident" was William Archer, whom—if Trebitsch recalled correctly (1951)—he met after the appearance of *Genesung*, or at the earliest in late 1901. But (except for his 1946 account) Trebitsch persists in giving November 1900 as the date of meeting Archer, which allows a year to pass before he reluctantly comes to Shaw's door. (In *Chronicle*, Trebitsch omits the year and changes the season to spring.)

That Trebitsch did not delay or approach Shaw with a "heavy heart" is suggested not only by Shaw's version but also by Trebitsch's having already become the translator of two other contemporary writers, the French playwright Georges Courteline and the Belgian symbolist poet and dramatist Georges Rodenbach. "I was evidently born with an unusual delight in discovering men of genius," the aged Trebitsch ruefully confessed. "In the moment of making such a discovery I have never thought of the consequences. . . . No sooner had I succeeded in paving the way to my own career than I created new difficulties for myself by the discoveries, or . . . translations, that I myself put between myself and my work." (*Chronicle*, p. 77.)

At their meeting, Trebitsch found that Archer shared his low estimate of London's commercial theatre, but Archer also reproached him for assuming that English theatre consisted solely of the West End: "I want to draw your attention to an author," Archer reportedly said, "who is almost as unknown in our country as in yours." And Archer named Shaw.

Returning by train to Vienna, Trebitsch leafed through the three volumes of Shaw's plays, which he obtained with effort, and attracted by the title *Candida* began to read: "Never had the long journey seemed so short to me. I enjoyed the strange fairy-tale of this poetic work as one of the most exquisite gifts of a new and individual poetry" (1928, 1931, 1946, 1951). And when, at home, he read the remaining plays, he felt like a "gold prospector who unexpectedly strikes an inexhaustible vein" and foresaw that the unknown Shaw would promptly "conquer the world stage" (1929).

Shortly thereafter, if we are correct, Trebitsch met Shaw. No more disparate personalities could have conjoined; but Trebitsch was captivated by the contrast between his own Viennese melancholy and Shaw's high spirits: "Never . . . had so much heaviness and sentimentality been lifted off me, had I found such a counterweight to my youthful troubles. . . . Mr. Shaw's brilliant, witty and lively art is the very antipodes to me. . . . Well, *les extremes se touchent"* (1920).

The gentleman's agreement reached in Shaw's flat was ratified—at Trebitsch's request—on 10 April 1902 as follows:

Dear Mr. Trebitsch

I will undertake and do hereby agree to refer any manager or publisher who may apply to me before the first of April 1903 for permission to translate, publish or produce any of my published plays in Germany or Austria to you, and I will not before that date sanction the publication or performance of a translation or adaptation by any other hand than yours.

G. B. Shaw*

Trebitsch's task during the probationary year was to select and translate three plays and get them produced or published. If he failed, translation rights were to revert to Shaw, but there was no agreement that if Trebitsch succeeded he would necessarily continue as Shaw's exclusive German translator. Trebitsch later claimed that he had not at the time been aware of the extent of his undertaking and fully intended continuing with his own original work. Yet his limited creativity, which he attributed to his migraines, apparently settled his choice.

The plays chosen for translation were *Candida, The Devil's Disciple,* and *Arms and the Man* (the last two, alone among Shaw's plays, had achieved some measure of success). Working rapidly under the pressure of time, Trebitsch would pencil question marks next to English idioms that he did not understand, later consulting dictionaries, and where still baffled or puzzled by a Shavian paradox would guess at its meaning or adapt the German to make some kind of sense. The end products, though adequate for conveying plot and character and serviceable for the stage, were often careless and inaccurate and shortly embroiled Trebitsch in controversy.

Trebitsch's immediate problem, however, was to interest German producers in an unknown foreign playwright who had yet to conquer his native stage. Only two of Shaw's ten plays had been performed publicly in London. Small wonder that German managers concluded: "There's no money in his plays, otherwise they would be done in England" (1920). Yet the German theatre, with hundreds of repertory companies, was open to foreign drama. Reverence for the theatre as a temple of high art was, despite middle-class preference for light, sentimental, or sensational fare in tandem with the classics, deeply rooted, albeit more as ideal than reality. Court theatres were a distinct minority by the turn of the century, and the municipal theatres (*Stadttheater*), which existed in every city of any size, were now mostly

*Copy in letter by Trebitsch to Cotta Verlag, 11 October 1902, Cotta Archiv, Schiller Nationalmuseum Marbach a.N.

leased to private managers. Privately owned theatres proliferated—especially in Berlin and Vienna where they predominated—and some of them, notably the Deutsches Theater in Berlin, ranked among the most outstanding in contemporary theatre art.

Trebitsch's ambitions in Vienna centered on the resplendent, if conservative, imperial Burgtheater and in Berlin on the Deutsches Theater. But he energetically pursued theatres throughout Germany. His first nibble came in June 1902 from the civic Deutsches Volkstheater, Vienna, which waffled over *Devil's Disciple*. By July he had tentatively interested the Burg in *Candida*, but to his "great sorrow" (1926) he was turned aside by the commanding Otto Brahm of the Deutsches Theater in Berlin. Nor was Paul Lindau of the Berliner Theater ready to commit himself. There remained Ernst Gettke of the Raimund Theater, Vienna, who "to get some rest" from Trebitsch agreed to risk *Devil's Disciple* if Trebitsch could get the aging Karl Wiené to play Dick Dudgeon. Trebitsch did, and Gettke, in early August, yielded.

Meanwhile, Trebitsch was negotiating with the publisher Cotta of Stuttgart (S. Fischer avoided unknown foreign dramatists as unprofitable) for his three translations, and toward the end of August, as he prepared to go to England, Trebitsch thought he had a second triumph and so informed Shaw. But Cotta returned the manuscript. Embarrassed, Trebitsch offered to forgo all royalties in favor of sharing any profits. Cotta agreed, and a contract arrived in London in time to be presented to Shaw. Only six months had passed since Trebitsch first met Shaw.

Two months later, Shaw publicly granted the "Viennese author Siegfried Trebitsch exclusive authorization" to translate his plays and serve as his agent (see 18 November 1902). No contract passed between the two men. (In 1907, after Shaw almost drowned while swimming off the coast of Wales, he secured Trebitsch's rights formally.) "Shaw was deeply impressed that I had kept my word and carried through my designs," Trebitsch later wrote. "He overwhelmed me with signs of his confidence. Yet I did not have an easy time with him. We both had the same objective: his recognition. But he was impetuous, and I persistent. He wanted to demand, and I to persuade" (1926, 1931, 1946, 1951). On 5 December 1902, Trebitsch sent Shaw a copy of *Drei Dramen von Bernard Shaw* (Three Plays of Bernard Shaw) inscribed, "To Mr. Bernard Shaw, I dedicate his works with a thousand hearty greetings and wishes for ever. Berlin, 5–12–1902, Siegfried Trebitsch." The following February *Devil's Disciple* opened at the Raimund. It was Shaw's first entrance onto the German stage.

Almost from the start, Trebitsch's translations were criticized. At first, Rudolf Lothar praised Trebitsch as "poetically knowing and linguistically adept" (*Neue Freie Presse*, Vienna, 11 January 1903). But very soon, Leon Kellner, a Viennese Anglist who had met Shaw some years earlier and had written the first general article in German on Shaw in 1899, set Vienna laughing by deriding half a dozen or so blunders in the German stage directions to *Candida*: the "greensward" sprouted vegetables, *Fabian Essays* was

Siegfried Trebitsch as a lieutenant in the dragoons in 1899, three years before meeting Shaw.

by the author Fabian, character descriptions were distorted so that "the painful sensitiveness that very swift and acute apprehensiveness produces in youth" became "the painful sensitiveness that marks the very swift and suddenly matured youth," and more of the same. Trebitsch's version was a "ridiculous caricature" and Shaw "not yet translated into German" ("Eine verunglückte Uebersetzung" [A Wretched Translation], *Neues Wiener Tagblatt*, 22 January 1903).

Shaw, who knew of Trebitsch's indifference to "little things," was amused. But Trebitsch was outraged and induced Hermann Bahr to publicize Shaw and dispute Kellner by insinuating the scholar's undue concern with literalness while Trebitsch artistically captured Shaw's spirit and provided easy, natural dialogue as attested to by Shaw and confirmed by Bahr ("Bernard Shaw," *Neues Wiener Tagblatt*, 7 February 1903).

Then on the eve of his Raimund debut with *Devil's Disciple* (*Teufelskerl*; lit., Devil of a Fellow), Shaw intervened. In a superb Shavian puff that appeared in *Die Zeit* he presented himself as a fascinating playwright, above Schiller and Goethe, a plagiarist, whose *Candida*, called "sublime" by Bahr, was "snivelling trash," and warned "romantic and artistic" Vienna that he might not suit its tastes since he cared neither for happiness nor beauty but only for life. Then turning to Trebitsch, Shaw posited that "Like all really able men, I am congenitally incapable of acquiring foreign languages; but I have been so steeped in German music, and consequently in German poetry, all my life (having indeed learned more of my art as a writer for the stage from Mozart than from Shakespear, Molière or any literary dramatist) that I cannot help believing that I know German." Good translation is a matter not merely of knowledge but also of "divination," and only one who can conceive the original and write dialogue can translate another man's plays. Trebitsch by "divination and dramatic faculty" had assimilated and reproduced Shaw. But there is one play, *Candida*, that "wallows in domestic sentiment" and fatally affects Germans: "there is a pastor and a poet and an ewigweibliches Hausfrau [eternally feminine housewife] and everything that a good German loves. When it is produced at the Burg Theater—as I have no doubt it will be; the irresistible Trebitsch adores Candida—all Vienna will smell of kerosene and onions; and the women will erect a monument to Trebitsch and trample on their husbands forever after." Even the "strongminded" Kellner succumbed to Candida, and when Trebitsch was beforehand in translating her play, he took "a hideous revenge": "I shudder to think what will happen when all the German speaking peoples . . . become acquainted with Candida. Hermann Bahr has already declared his infatuation; and Schnitzler will certainly go into holy orders when he comes under its spell. Trebitsch, I hope, will grow out of it: I am doing my best to cure him of it." ("Ein Teufelskerl. Selbstkritik," *Die Zeit*, 22 February 1903; original in B.L.)*

*Three years later, Shaw recalled the controversy to William Archer, to whom Kellner had complained of his treatment by Shaw. Shaw noted Kellner's "slashing attack on poor Trebitsch, who was held up without mercy as an ignoramus & impostor," and added: "Trebitsch has no power of

Kellner responded with a shrewd and intriguing portrait of Shaw the satirist and personality but dismissed Trebitsch as an "idle Fifth-former" ("Bernhard Shaw. Eine Charakteristic," *Frankfurter Zeitung*, 17 March 1903). Yet eight years later, when a revised collected edition of Shaw's plays appeared (*Dramatische Werke*, Berlin, 1911), Kellner returned to the *Neues Wiener Tagblatt* ("Der verdeutschte Shaw," 6 July 1911) and acknowledged that Trebitsch's persistence, despite "hostile, . . . openly malicious criticism," had led to a "certain command" of his craft so that readers would find in the amended versions a "very acceptable substitute" for the original. Still Trebitsch could be more colloquial and less literal. As for lists of errors: "that would be as tasteless as vulgar; I don't . . . feel any inclination to feed the malicious joy of barren literati at the cost of a diligent author who deserves well of the theatre."

In dissociating himself from the "barren literati" with their lists, Kellner no doubt was alluding, above all, to Max Meyerfeld, translator of Oscar Wilde. Meyerfeld had quickly seconded Kellner's attack on *Drei Dramen* ("Bernard Shaw," *Literarische Echo*, 1 May 1903) in what became an increasingly mordant polemic against Trebitsch. While dropping journalistic references to the German versions of Shaw as "truly defective" and "disgracefully mishandled" ("G. B. S.," *National Zeitung*, 14 May 1903; "Uebersetzer-Elend," *Frankfurter Zeitung*, 10 December 1903), Meyerfeld had prepared a full-scale onslaught that provided lists of errata, added a charge of plagiarism against Trebitsch, whose introduction to *Drei Dramen* borrowed from Shaw's prefaces, and ridiculed Trebitsch's innocence in English literature ("Bernard Shaw und sein Dolmetsch," *Englische Studien*, 33 Bd., 1904). He could cite even more blunders, Meyerfeld contended, "But I would be as shamefully abusing my time as Trebitsch the English language, if I were to inflict an additional 42 wounds on a corpse."

Ironically, Meyerfeld had mentioned his forthcoming piece to Trebitsch, who, schooled by Shaw, thanked his critic and requested a copy. Disarmed, Meyerfeld remained silent for four years. Then in a review of Shaw's *Dramatic Opinions and Essays*, he noted Shaw's rise to European fame and Trebitsch's role in "being hitched to Shaw's triumphal chariot." But "we commiserate with Shaw," Meyerfeld added, "that, obliged to be grateful, he must deal charitably with this steed," whose blunders are unmatched, yet whose versions appear in leading journals and are praised by critics, whose editors, eager to get articles from Shaw, curry favor with Trebitsch, while Shaw "wraps his apostle in the broad mantle of his socialistic altruism and laughs up his sleeve at the trade he enjoys abroad despite his steed. But for once the bolt must be slammed in the face of this corruption." (*Literarische Echo*, 1 January 1908.)

defending himself against attacks of this kind; but he has fought 3 duels. He declared Kellner was an infamy, & that he must give him an ear-box; & Kellner would probably have fallen beneath his avenging sabre if I had not pacified him by declaring my satisfaction with his translations." Shaw admitted that he might have been made "very uncomfortable" about Trebitsch's translations had he not been warned by the attacks on Archer's versions of Ibsen and ascertained for himself that Trebitsch's mistakes did not matter (*Collected Letters*, edited by Dan H. Laurence, 1972, II, 7 June 1906).

A week later, a Dr. Ernst Groth of Leipzig informed Trebitsch that Meyerfeld's motives were being questioned especially since his translation of Wilde contained "serious errors" and that if Meyerfeld was dishonorable it would be well to "put a spoke in his wheel" (B.L.). Emboldened, Trebitsch wrote to *Literarische Echo* mocking his foe as an obscure, envious, uncreative pedant, who, for all his literary airs, left it to Trebitsch to discover Shaw and whose version of Wilde contained "numberless" mistakes that dismayed Wilde's admirers ("Zuschriften," 15 February 1908).

In a rebuttal printed in the same issue of *Literarische Echo*, Meyerfeld pointed to his years of forbearance as Trebitsch's "comb swelled higher and higher" and no one appeared to challenge this "shameful stain" on German translation, and he added examples of Trebitsch's mistakes before dropping this "cruel game." In turn, he demanded that Trebitsch produce those alleged dismayed Wildeans or be branded a "base slanderer."

Shaw, revolted by the exchanges, sketched a letter that he urged Trebitsch to write deploring the lack of German collegial ethics and renouncing an attempt to discredit Meyerfeld (see 9 March 1908).* Instead, on 9 April, Trebitsch published in *Die Schaubühne* an article, "Zur Schulmeisterethic" (On Schoolmaster Ethics), in which he dismissed Meyerfeld as vulgar and malicious and listed a dozen slips in Meyerfeld's translation of Wilde's *De Profundis*. Appended to the article was Shaw's suggested draft, which Trebitsch presented as a letter from Shaw on the controversy. Unknown to Trebitsch, Meyerfeld had worked from a variant typescript of *De Profundis*, and thus Meyerfeld was promptly vindicated (*Schaubühne*, 16 April). Then, on 15 May, *Literarische Echo* attacked the purported letter from Shaw on the grounds that one who accused his translator's critics of spiteful envy without naming names had forfeited the privilege of commenting on German literary ethics. And so Shaw, trying to guide Trebitsch into more fruitful battle, ironically came under fire himself.

Two years later, in a special preface to Shaw's *Dramatische Werke* entitled "What I Owe to German Culture" ("Was ich der deutschen Kultur verdanke"), Shaw offered his strongest defense of Trebitsch by reducing his critics to absurdity and declaring himself "hopeless on the subject of Herr Trebitsch . . . for there is no man in Europe to whom I am more deeply indebted or with whom I feel happier in all our relations, whether of business, or art, or of personal honor and friendship" (original Engl. in *Adam*, 1970). But Meyerfeld, reviewing *Dramatische Werke*, pointed to the corrections in the new edition based on his exposures and repeated that Shaw's support of Trebitsch was commercially motivated: "[Shaw's] remark that Trebitsch puts a hundred pounds annually into his purse is, when all is said and done, not just a joke" ("Shaw resartus," *Literarische Echo*, 10 October 1911).

Meyerfeld then disappears until years later when he resurfaces anonymously to defend a young colleague, Hans Rothe, who had reviled Tre-

---

*In a letter to the *Athenaeum* on 4 April, Shaw also criticized the "shameless" conduct of German and French professional translators toward rivals and cited insane attacks on Trebitsch by men who wanted to translate Shaw and "make no secret of their disappointment."

bitsch's version of *Saint Joan* ("Die geschändete Jungfrau," *Das Tagebuch*, September 1924). Rothe was rebuked as envious by Shaw (*Observer*, 2 November), and retorted, "Not all your exertions on your Siegfried's behalf will erase the incredible blunders which he has utilized for many years to make your works incomprehensible to us" (*Berliner Tageblatt* and *Leipziger Neueste Nachrichten*, 30 November). Meyerfeld* seconded Rothe in an unsigned open letter to Shaw (*Roland*, 15 January 1925): "You were informed time and again fifteen years ago from the most competent sources that your plays were not translated but Trebitsched."†

Above all, Trebitsch had trouble with English idiom. In *Devil's Disciple*, for example, "a most ungodly allowance of good looks" became "a most worldly [ungodly] delight in goodlooking clothes." Idiom was part of a larger problem of colloquial dialogue, modulating levels of speech, and dialect. The last Trebitsch simply avoided. Errors crept in when he mistook less familiar words for more familiar ones—for example, "revered head" for "severed head" (*Caesar and Cleopatra*)—or when an English word was confounded with an apparent German cognate, "taps" becoming "tappt nach," that is, "gropes towards." Careless use of the dictionary or wrongly associating a word with a related meaning led to translating *castor* (of a chair) as *beaver* and "you have lost the last scrap of my regard" as "you have lost me up to the whites of my eyes" (*Philanderer*). At times, Shavian paradox nonplussed Trebitsch, so that the clergyman who was kept from promotion although he was "not a bit more religious" than Morell became "not a bit less pious."

But that Trebitsch's early blunders placed Shaw in a false light or prevented his popular acceptance is doubtful. German critics and audiences showed no greater misapprehension of Shaw than their English counterparts, and their initial befuddlement was due more to the unfamiliar Shaw than to Trebitsch, whose accuracy improved in successive editions and who, all along, was praised as well as criticized. With the revised collected edition (1911), those who were not in Meyerfeld's camp granted that the new versions were "very acceptable" (Kellner) or "serviceable" (Caro). "There are now plays [by Shaw]," wrote Estella Maas, "that are well translated and some that are excellently translated and capture the spirit of Shaw" ("Der deutsche Shaw," *Süddeutsche Monatshefte*, 1912).

Withal, what was to be almost fifty years of devoted service to Shaw by Trebitsch was an extraordinary if imperfect achievement, covering major segments of Shaw's prose as well as drama and earning the translator well-deserved kudos, not just criticism. In an obituary tribute to Trebitsch, the London *Times* wrote: "Trebitsch's inspired and faithful translations . . . [are]

---

*So identified by Rothe in a private letter to the editor.
†The foregoing treats the journalistic cases in which Shaw intervened. The philologists' quarrel with Trebitsch included: Katharina von Sanden, "Shaw und sein Übersetzer," *Süddeutsche Monatshefte*, 1909; Eiserne Maske, "Eine Musterübersetzung," *Standarte*, 1907; J. Caro, "Die autosierte Shaw-Uebersetzung," *Englische Studien*, 1917–18, 1921, and "Die neueste Shaw-Übersetzung," *Die neueren Sprachen*, 1921; Hermann Stresau, "Mit dem süssesten Anstand," *Deutsche Universitäts-Zeitung*, 1953.

indubitably, one of the most perfectly accomplished transfers of thought and form from one language into another, without loss of the author's very particular characteristics" (4 June 1958).

Trebitsch was more modest. "I am quite aware," he wrote in *Chronicle of a Life*, "of what German literature owes to me. By this, however, I am far from asserting that the Irish master might not have succeeded in finding a better exponent of the art of translation if he had the choice in time, instead of being dependent on a writer who was led to him only by his own enthusiasm and intense impatience to see an intellectual wrong righted, a writer to whom he then—perhaps to his disadvantage—who knows?—doggedly and with unswerving loyalty kept faith throughout a long life."

Although Shaw the Fabian was known to active German socialists, Shaw the playwright was virtually unknown in turn-of-the-century Germany. Leon Kellner's pioneer article, "Ein Humorist unserer Zeit" (*Nation*, 16 January 1899), gained so little attention that two years later, in the same journal, M. Handl, apparently unaware of Kellner, announced his wish to introduce a "most remarkable" dramatist, Shaw, whom it would be "laudable" to win for the German stage. No such attempt was made, however, until Trebitsch's "discovery" of Shaw. Then the situation rapidly changed: *Drei Dramen* appeared; Vienna was astir with articles by Kellner, Bahr (who hailed Shaw as the potential savior of the German theatre), and Shaw himself; *Arms and the Man* was censored in Vienna; a controversy arose over rights to its production in Berlin; and productions of *Devil's Disciple* and *Candida* were pending. All proved, Shaw informed a journalist (Golding Bright), that Trebitsch's translations had created a "sensation" and a Shaw "boom" in Germany (see letter of 1 March 1903). It was not that the Germans were more receptive to originality than the English, explained Shaw, correcting an interview, but rather that the German repertory system, unlike the English single-play system, could risk short runs (*Westminster Gazette*, 28 February 1903).

Shaw's use of the term "boom" was not mere self-puffery. On 15 March 1903, the socialist *Die Freie Volksbühne* predicted that German theatre would be "swiftly opened" to one of the "most wittily original" dramatists, and by the end of the year Felix Heilbut noted that both literary and practical theatre managers were seeking rights to Shaw's plays, which would soon inundate Germany ("Der Dramatiker Shaw," *Die Gegenwart*, 5 December 1903). A year later, J. T. Grein, founder of the Independent Theatre and a Shavian proponent, declared that Shaw in Germany was the "object of a cult" (*Sunday Times*, 6 November 1904), and the *Berliner Tageblatt* (9 December 1904), noting that four of Shaw's plays had appeared that year in Berlin, exclaimed: "Shaw, Shaw and again Shaw! The witty Irishman, whose name but two years ago was known only to a very small circle of German literati, has now become a monarch of our stages."

The facts were modest. But by the second year of Shaw's arrival, all his translated plays were in production (Trebitsch had added *Man of Destiny* and *Caesar and Cleopatra*, and an unauthorized *Mrs Warren's Profession* was privately produced), and the number of theatres presenting Shaw went from three to twelve, with a total of 45 performances. The next season, 1904–5, the number increased to twenty-two theatres and 135 performances, including 36 performances of *Arms and the Man* and 21 of *Devil's Disciple* in Berlin alone. Yet Shaw's growing presence was no popular success.

"There is a Shaw boom on in Germany," Shaw wrote to Forbes-Robertson, "because four of my plays have been produced in Vienna, Leipzig, Dresden and Frankfurt; and they have failed so violently, and have been hounded from the stage with such furious execrations, that the advanced critics proclaim me the choice and master spirit of the age and no manager respects himself until he has lost at least 200 marks by me" (21–22 December 1903, *Collected Letters*, II). The slow acclimation of Germans to Shaw was not lost on Trebitsch or others, who attributed it to the "incomprehension" of the public, for whom Shaw was "too superior" (Fritz Telmann, *Literarische Echo*, March 1906), or to Shaw's ignoring theatrical taste and dramatic form (*Wiener Abendpost*, 19 March 1906). In *Chronicle* (p. 171) Trebitsch cites an anecdote, which if correct belongs to 1908, concerning the Berlin opening of *Doctor's Dilemma*: a colleague explodes to Trebitsch's wife, Tina, "Your husband really might have spared us this disgusting stuff," whereupon Tina urges Siegfried: "Do drop this Irish friend of yours now! People simply don't want him, and you can't force them to share your taste."

Something of a Shaw "cult" did exist, as the already-cited Grein and the *Berliner Tageblatt* pointed out. In 1906, the right-wing *Berliner Lokal-Anzeiger* dismissed *Caesar and Cleopatra* and declared that if the tedious production "dampens the exaggerated Shaw-cult of recent years," it will have been worthwhile (1 April). And later, in an unfavorable review of *Man and Superman*, the leading left periodical, *Die Schaubühne* (13 December), suggested that in choosing so "exceptionally worthless" a play by an otherwise very considerable author Max Reinhardt "went along with the [Shaw] boom" and tried to exploit "a fashionable movement." By 1909, Karl Frenzel could observe that for "some years" Shaw had belonged "half-ways among German authors" (*Deutsche Rundschau*, May 1909). "Make no mistake about it. Bernard Shaw is a Berlin author," wrote the *Neue Freie Presse* on 30 November 1909. And the next year, Granville Barker reported from Berlin: "Shaw's plays come to Berlin with the same regularity that Sardou's came to England thirty years ago" (*Times*, 21 November 1910). And indeed no season had passed since Shaw's appearance on the German stage without a production of Shaw in Berlin.

A satiric response to Shaw's incursion was a doggerel playlet by Julius Knopf in the conservative *Bühne und Welt* (1909–10), "Der rettende Engel aus Engelland" (The Delivering Angel from "Engelland"). In this playlet, a producer is complaining of bad times to his dramaturge, when in walks a Foreign Author, who declares himself the "literary savior" of Germany and proffers a thick volume of plays. When the irate dramaturge demands to know who he is, the author replies:

> Of the German stage I am the Czar
> And Czarevich as well.
> I need but mention S. Trebitsch
> My identity to tell.
> You look as if the anti-Christ
> Had suddenly appeared
> Before you in disguise
> With upturned brows and beard.
> But you, the Germans, are, I know
> My faithful convertees,
> And so I tender to your care
> My latest acting piece.
> I am Shaw!

The producer and dramaturge leap with joy, fall at Shaw's feet, kiss his hands, press his book to their hearts, and stand on their heads "like a Shavian paradox."

Briefly, by the end of the decade, although general popularity lay some years ahead, Shaw was an expanding presence on the German stage, having gone from three productions in 1902–3 to 54 in forty cities in 1909–10. By the outbreak of World War I, 11 of Shaw's plays had been produced in Germany, including all the full-length plays with the exception of *John Bull's Other Island.*

Shaw's growing recognition in Germany led to comparisons with relative English neglect, not least by Shaw himself, for whom his prior acceptance in Central Europe over that in England was a lifelong conviction. Even as he approached ninety, Shaw, accused of ingratitude to England, bitterly observed: "when I came to England I got nothing for nothing, and very little for a halfpenny; . . . I was abused, vilified, censored, and suppressed to the limit of possibility until my successes in Germany and America convinced my detractors that there was some money in my evil doctrine" (*Melbourne Age,* 23 March 1946). His international reputation, Shaw declared earlier, owed more to Germany, where he was employed when English theatres were "contemptuously" closed to him, than to any other country ("Shall Roger Casement Hang?" *Manchester Guardian,* 22 July 1916). At times, Shaw unwittingly or polemically exaggerated his early theatrical and financial success in Central Europe. But during his first three seasons in Germany, Shaw's plays earned more than in England, and only with the experimental venture of Vedrenne and Barker in 1904 into "the desert air of Sloane Square," featuring Shaw at the Royal Court Theatre, did the latter's English theatre royalties move up and in 1905–6 exceed his German earnings. (Shaw's declared German income was half the actual sums that he shared with Trebitsch.) For the next seven years (excepting 1910–11, if one includes Trebitsch's share), Shaw's plays earned more in England than they did in Germany. Then in

1913–14 Shaw yielded a world premiere to Trebitsch and the Burgtheater. With the opening of *Pygmalion* on 16 October 1913, a watershed in Shaw's German popularity was reached. Hitherto, openings of Shaw's plays were chancy (and one to four years separated productions of Shaw's new plays in London from those in Germany, except for *Fanny's First Play*, which was a great success in London). But now, Trebitsch recalled, "financially interested circles suddenly discovered that this English dramatist whom they had once avoided so nervously could write sensationally successful plays." And so, "I was at last out of the wood, and Bernard Shaw, the hero of so many wanderings, had reached firm ground" (*Chronicle*, p. 175).

Ten years had passed since Trebitsch had placed the obscure Shaw on the German-language stage, and on the evening of 16 October 1913, he no doubt savored a triumph in the making. Shaw, informed of the success, refused to be impressed and declared *Pygmalion* his "last potboiler."

Maybury Knoll. Woking
26th June 1902

My dear Trebitsch

I am amazed at your industry. But why dont you write plays of your own?

You must tell the Volkstheater[1] people that you quite agree with all their suggestions, and that you regret greatly that I am so unreasonable a man. But you must assure them that unless they will perform the play exactly as it is written, the negotiation must drop at once. If they know how plays should be written let them write plays for themselves. If they dont, they had better leave the business to those who do. I wont have the two last acts run into one. I wont have a line omitted or a comma altered. I am quite familiar with the fact that every fool who is connected with a theatre, from the callboy to the manager, thinks he knows better than an author how to make a play popular and successful. Tell them with my compliments that I know all about that; that I am fortysix years old; that I know my business and theirs as well; that I am quite independent of tantièmes and do not care a snap of my fingers whether they produce my plays or not; that I shall give my plays titles thirtyfive words long if I like: in short, that I am a pigheaded, arrogant, obstinate, domineering man of genius, deaf to reason, and invincibly determined to have my own way about my own works.

Say the same thing to all the managers the moment they begin to sing that old song about alterations & modifications. Tell them it is no use: if my plays are too advanced for them, they can let them alone: they need not add stupidity & vandalism to Dichtersbeleidigung.[2] But say how delighted you would be to meet their wishes if only I would let you. Let all the agreeable things come from you, and the disagreeable things from me.

I write in great haste on the eve of a journey. Next week I will answer the other points in your letter.

Once more, dont neglect your own work. Translation will not teach you half so much as original composition.

yrs sincerely
G. Bernard Shaw

Als.

1. *The Devil's Disciple*, among the three plays Trebitsch translated under his year's probationary agreement with Shaw, was offered to the Deutsches Volkstheater, Vienna's privately sponsored municipal theatre. The Volkstheater, although committed to contemporary drama, vacillated over the unfamiliar Shaw.

2. Crime against the author: Shaw's play on *Majestätsbeleidigung* (lese majesty).

Maybury Knoll. Woking
1st July 1902

My dear Trebitsch

The following information may be useful to Hermann Bahr.[1]

I am an Irishman (like Goldsmith & Sheridan), born in Dublin on the 26th July 1856. I came to London in 1876. I wrote 5 novels; but nobody would publish them. I was equally unsuccessful in my attempts to get work as a journalist: no editor would touch my articles. Early in the eighteen-eighties there was a revival of Socialism in England. I plunged into the movement, having been greatly impressed by Das Kapital, which I read in the French translation. However, I soon challenged the soundness of Marx's economics, and threw over the traditions of the revolutionary party of 1848–71. The English Social-Democrats were as much horrified at my heresy against Marx as the German Social-Democrats now are at the similar heresies of Bernstein.[2] In 1884 a society of middle class Socialists—mostly journalists and civil servants—was founded under the title of The Fabian Society. Of this society I became a leading member. Sidney Webb, Sydney Olivier (now colonial secretary in Jamaica) and Graham Wallas were my colleagues;[3] and we set to work to find a perfectly constitutional and parliamentary formula for Socialism, and to free it from the Marxian dogmas and from the old fashioned revolutionary street fighting foolishness. Bernstein was in exile in London at that time; and it was by us that he was won over from his Marxian orthodoxy to his present position. For twelve years [1883–95] I was very active as a public speaker and agitator, delivering addresses from all sorts of platforms, sometimes to the British Association or the literary societies, sometimes to the passers by in the streets and parks.

In the meantime I had at last (from 1885 onward) obtained work as a critic, first of literature and then of music. My mother had been a distinguished amateur of music in Dublin; and I had acquired a good deal of knowledge of music in this way in my boyhood. I used my musical feuilletons as vehicles for political & social satire, and soon began to be known by my signature "G. B. S." I still call myself a pupil of Mozart in comedy much more than of any of the English literary dramatists. Later on I criticised the theatre, and fought for Ibsen as I had already fought for Wagner. I also criticised pictures. The dates are, roughly, 1885 to 1889, literature in the Pall Mall Gazette & painting in The World; 1888 to 1890, music in The

Star; 1890 to 1894, music in The World; 1895 to 1898, the theatre in The Saturday Review—practically ten years of criticism. In 1898 I got married.

The story of my plays is in the prefaces to Plays, Pleasant & Unpleasant; so I need not repeat it here. Besides my novels (the best known of which is "Cashel Byron's Profession") and the plays, I have published "The Quintessence of Ibsenism" and "The Perfect Wagnerite," both of them rather philosophical than critical. Some of my Socialist writings, especially those in "Fabian Essays" (of which I was the editor), have been translated into German.[4]

If there is anything else you want to know, write me a catechism & I will answer all your questions.

When the theatres come to business about the plays we can agree as to the division of the royalties. Shall we share half & half?[5] But we must agree for each play separately, as you must always be able to tell the managers that you can do nothing without my consent and that the royalty must be enough for two. I will not promise to take half what they offer; *but you must insist on their giving double what I will take.* My rapacity will be your excuse for pressing them to give the full market price. By the way, what is the usual price? We must not try to get too much; but then we must not err in the opposite direction either.

In haste,
yrs sincerely
G. Bernard Shaw

Als.

1. In publicizing Shaw, Trebitsch approached the writer Hermann Bahr (1863–1934), leader of Vienna's "Moderns" and theatre critic for the democratic *Neues Wiener Tagblatt.* Bahr did not use the biographical materials until the next year in "Bernard Shaw" (*Neues Wiener Tagblatt,* 7 February 1903), which hailed Shaw on the eve of his German-language stage debut. Instead, Trebitsch incorporated the sketch into "Bernard Shaw" (*Neue Freie Presse,* 7 December 1902) and used it as the introduction to *Drei Dramen.*

2. Eduard Bernstein (1850–1932), German socialist theoretician, leader of the revisionist wing of the German movement, denied the increasing polarization of society, stressed moral appeal and education over class struggle in achieving socialism, and attacked the economic emphasis in Marxist historiography.

3. Shaw, Sidney Webb (1859–1947), Sydney Olivier (1859–1943), and Graham Wallas (1858–1932) were the Fabian "Big Four." Webb, in celebrated partnership with his wife, Beatrice, was the leading Fabian organizer, eminent social historian, influential reformer, and later a member of the first Labour governments. In 1895, the Webbs founded the London School of Economics, and in 1913 the *New Statesman.* Olivier went on to become Governor of Jamaica. Wallas, political scientist and psychologist, lectured at the London School of Economics and later at London University.

4. Shaw's "The Illusions of Socialism" ("Die Illusionen des Socialismus") had appeared in the liberal-left *Die Zeit* (24 and 31 October 1896); a German edition of *Fabian Essays* (*Englische Socialreformer: eine Sammlung* "Fabian Essays") was published in Leipzig in 1897.

5. For an unknown foreign dramatist to share royalties with his translator-representative was not extraordinary, although generous. German theatre royalties varied from about 5 to 10 percent.

Maybury Knoll. Woking
7th July 1902

My dear Trebitsch

"Das Capital" has been translated into English since I read it—at least the first volume has; but nobody ever read the second & third volumes, either in

England or Germany. In 1882 there was nothing but the French version and the original, which I could not read.

Excuse my asking you a personal question? Are you dependent on your pen; or have you an independent income?[1] My reason for asking is this? There are more ways than one of sharing half & half. We may say that we shall divide the royalties of every performance. Or we may agree that you shall take the first £50 and I the second, and, after that, share in the ordinary way for each performance. In that case if the play only produced £50 I should get nothing; if it produced £75 you would get £50 and I £25; if it produced £100 we should get £50 each; but you would get your £50 first. You would thus get some sort of payment for your trouble if the play were not successful; and I should not get my half unless there was enough to prevent you from being absolutely out-of-pocket by the time spent in translating. My wife says you must be a millionaire because you stayed at one of the most expensive hotels in London; but I tell her that you are perhaps only a man of genius, in which case you had better protect yourself by some such arrangement as I suggest.

Candida is too sentimental for the Burgtheater. Tell Dr Schleuther [Schlenther] to produce "Caesar & Cleopatra," with Britannus changed into an echt Wiener [true Viennese] bourgeois, and a splendid *mise en scène.*[2] Candida would do better in Berlin, would it not?

Make them give you 10%, as it has to be shared. Sardou[3] gets £30 (600m.) per performance for plays from the principal theatre here, though the mounting is enormously expensive and the translator has to be paid also. Making all possible allowance for lower prices of admission, the Burgtheater should not insult us by offering us less than half what Sardou gets.

My latest play [*Man and Superman*] is *very* unlike Candida. You must not translate it, as you would get six years in a fortress for the preface alone.

yrs ever
G. Bernard Shaw

Als.

1. Trebitsch was independently wealthy. Besides his inheritance from his father, which was held in trust, he had inherited a sizable fortune from a childless uncle, which was "well invested" and allowed him to be "very comfortably situated" (*Chronicle*). He had a fashionable bachelor apartment in central Vienna and a personal servant.

2. Vienna's conservative, imperial Burgtheater was directed by Paul Schlenther (1854–1916)— Shaw trips on Trebitsch's writing *n*'s like *u*'s—formerly of the progressive Freie Bühne (Free Stage) in Berlin. *Caesar and Cleopatra*, which required spectacular staging, had yet to be produced professionally.

3. Victorien Sardou (1831–1908), popular French playwright disdained by Shaw as the master of "Sardoodledom."

Victoria Hotel. Holkham
3rd August 1902

Your card & portrait have just reached me. I am at the seaside, swimming, and quite indifferent to plays and theatres und so weiter.

The Raimund people seem to consider the D's D a short play, not worth

10%.[1] Tell them that if they wait long enough between the acts it will fill up a whole evening.

However, do the best you can: I leave the matter in your hands. Only, do not make any permanent and irrevocable agreement.[2] Let us bind ourselves for no longer than is necessary to guarantee the theatre the use of the play long enough to recoup it with a fair profit for its expenditure on scenery, costumes &c.

Dr Heinrich Kanner, the editor of Die Zeit, is pressing me to write articles in his paper.[3] He tells me he hopes shortly to make Die Z a big daily paper. I can easily write him an article if it would help to make my name known in Vienna. Would this be wise in your opinion?

G.B.S.

Apcs.
    1. After failing to place *Devil's Disciple* with the Deutsches Volkstheater, Trebitsch turned to the privately owned Raimund Theater, Vienna's third-ranking house.
    2. Shaw never surrendered copyright but licensed producers or publishers for a limited period.
    3. Dr. Heinrich Kanner (1864–1930), Austrian political economist and journalist, was co-founder of the liberal-left weekly *Die Zeit*, which shortly became a daily.

Victoria Hotel. Holkham
9th August 1902

Ausgezeichnet! Ganz vorzuglich! Furchtbar nett! Famos! Colossale! Wiené ist—wie heisst es?—Gastspieler, nicht wahr? [Excellent! First rate! Awfully nice! Capital! Colossal! Wiené is—how do you say?—guest star, right?][1] Well, it does not much matter whether he can act or not: *anybody* can play the title part in the D's D. The most important part to cast well is Burgoyne, who must be both a fine comedian and a distinguished "père noble." It is also very important to get the last scene well stage managed, with a big surging crowd. Unless both Burgoyne and the crowd are well handled the last act will collapse as mere opera bouffe. However, time enough to think about all that in October.

I suppose Wiené will try to get other theatres to take up the play if he makes a success in it.

We look forward to seeing you next month; but do not come to London too early in September or you will find everybody away at the seaside.

GBS

Als.
    1. Trebitsch had persuaded Karl Wiené (1852–1913), popular actor of the Hoftheater, Dresden, to play Dick Dudgeon. Wiené was too old for the part, but the production of *Devil's Disciple* was secured.

Victoria Hotel. Holkham
29th August 1902

Here I am still, enjoying the primeval simplicity & inaccessibility of this unerhörtes [unheard of] place (that adjective is not Viennese but Wagnerese).

When I heard about Candida I was too disgusted to reply: the Burgtheater ought to be ashamed of itself for such a sentimental choice. Why dont they do Caesar & Cleopatra & leave little Candida to the amateurs? However, since you are pleased, I shall not positively forbid the performance; but you may tell Dr Sch[l]enther that a man in his position ought to have a more robust mind. You are young and a poet, so I forgive you; but as for Sch[l]enther, he is wasting his subvention in producing a play that has been successfully performed in London for a charity by a couple of hospital nurses, a doctor, an idiot (who played Eugene) and an actor (who played the old man).[1] It is mere child's play.

I hope to get back to London before the 20th Sep^r; but my movements are not yet decided on.

G.B.S.

Apcs.

1. *Candida* was first publicly performed in London on 15 February 1902 by the amateur New Stage Club at the Cripplegate Institute, a nursing facility.

10 Adelphi Terrace W.C.
16th October 1902

Dear Trebitsch

I have received your letter with the enclosed cheque safely.[1] Will you be so good as to get me a copy of the [Raimund] agreement to keep by me. As soon as I receive it I will have a proper form of receipt printed for future use. Charge the cost of typing the copy to me. I will then send you a formal stamped receipt. Nothing terrifies a manager more than a Dichter who is businesslike.

I positively forbid you to waste another moment in talking to managers about the production of my plays. Their proposals and compliments over a cigar are only their ways of building castles in the air—Alnaschar dreams which they cannot realize. They like talking to you: it makes them feel literary and intellectual; but you need never give a second thought to their promises: when they really mean business they will come to look for you with a cheque in one hand and an agreement in the other.

Dont wait for the Burg or any other theatre. If the manager of a marionette show offers to produce Candida next week, and Schlenther says that he admires the play enormously and will produce it at the Burg as soon as he can cast it in a manner worthy of its merits, give it to the marionettes without a moment's hesitation. Remember, le mieux est l'ennemi du bien. Keep writing: that is your business—your own stories first, and the translations when you are tired of original invention. If I had troubled my head about managers and wasted my time and energy hawking my plays from stagedoor to stagedoor, I should have ruined myself, and probably died of mere worry. Give up all anxiety about those plays: we two can live without the managers; so why should we put ourselves at the mercy of their caprices and their difficulties and risks and tastes and follies?

Tell Schlenther that you have heard from me, and that I say that he has no right to waste public funds on kinderspielen like Candida. The play I want produced at the Burgtheater is Caesar & Cleopatra. If Kains can act Caesar, let him.[2] And the Cleopatra must not be over fortyfive or heavier than 4,000 kilos. If Vienna is not ready for Caesar, then it is not ready for me. I am quite in earnest about this. If Schlenther now offered to do Candida on the first of November, I should refuse to let him have it. Aut Caesar, aut nullus.

Have you any theatrical "trade paper" in Vienna, like the London Era or the New York Dramatic Mirror. If so, I could put an advertisement in it referring inquirers about my plays to you. But if any manager questions your *locus standi* in the matter, give him my address and tell him to write to me; and I will send him a credential for you that will make him wish he had never been born.[3]

I have engaged a German lady to read your stories to me.[4] Kanner has sent me the first numbers of Die Zeit. Tell the Raimund director that now I have got his money I dont care a (what is the German for a damn) whether he produces the D's D. or not.

Give up *wanting* to have the plays produced if you value your happiness as a man and your dignity as an artist.

yours ever
G. Bernard Shaw

Tls.
  1. Shaw had received an advance of 300 kronen (£12.10) from the Raimund.
  2. Joseph Kainz (1858–1910), celebrated classical German actor, was less suited for naturalistic drama.
  3. Trebitsch, having placed Shaw with the Raimund and also with a publisher, had asked Shaw to publicly declare him his official translator-representative.
  4. Trebitsch was preparing a volume of his stories, to be called *Weltuntergang* (End of the World).

10 Adelphi Terrace W.C.
22nd October 1902

Dear Trebitsch

The agreement of which I want a copy is not between you and me, but the one with the Raimund Theater for the Devil's Disciple. I am bound by that agreement; and there should be a copy of it among my papers not only for my own information, but for that of my executors if I chance to die unexpectedly.

If I send you a letter undertaking to agree with every arrangement you make, I deliver you bound and helpless into the hands of the managers. You must always be in a position to say:—"My dear Schlenther (or whoever it may be): I think your offer most reasonable, je, most generous, most noble. It breaks my heart to be unable to accept it at once with my warmest thanks. But this cursed scoundrel of a Shaw, ein Grobian vom Hause aus [a ruffian, born and bred], will neither let me arrange matters for him nor deal with anyone except through me. He *will* have his own way. I blush for him; but what can I do?"

Of course Troilus & Cressida was a failure: nobody in England would ever dream of producing it except as a curiosity. It is a very remarkable Shakespearian *jeu d'esprit*; but it is not popular, and Schlenther must be a co-lossal Esel to have supposed it ever could be popular.[1]

As to Caesar, we must make them do it. If it fails, they can fall back on Candida; but they must begin with Caesar. If you have not translated it, they must wait for you. Why are you in such a hurry to see your Liebling [favorite; i.e., *Candida*] murdered, as it will be on the Burg stage, no matter how clever the actors are—indeed the cleverer they are the worse they will handle it.

I have read the first three pages of Hilsekil![2] The effort is fearful; but the story is interesting. Why dont you write your stories in English—a much easier language. I want Genesung in German: I am resolved not to be beaten.[3] I have bought a devil of a big dictionary, also a grammar.

Cashel Byron is a boyish affair.[4] If Die Zeit would publish it as a feuilleton I should not object; but translating it would be an abominable waste of time: any German novelist could write as good a story.[5]

yours ever
G. Bernard Shaw

Als.

1. Shakespeare's anti-Homeric *Troilus and Cressida* was rarely staged in Germany. The Burg's production of the play opened on 18 January 1902, with Kainz and Lotta Witt, and lasted only nine performances. Schlenther apparently had used its failure as an argument against Shaw's anti-romantic *Caesar*.

2. Hilsekil is the hero in Trebitsch's story "Weltuntergang," which was shortly to appear in the Fischer collection of Trebitsch's stories.

3. *Genesung* (Convalescence; Berlin, Fischer, 1902), Trebitsch's first novel, was to be translated into French, and Trebitsch had apparently suggested that Shaw, whose German was limited, wait for the French version.

4. *Cashel Byron's Profession*, Shaw's fourth novel (first serialized in *To-Day*, published in book form in 1886), was written when Shaw was 26.

5. Trebitsch did not translate *Cashel Byron*.

Maybury Knoll. Woking
18th November 1902

My dear Trebitsch

If your nerves are overtaxed, go to bed for a fortnight, and read nothing but the silliest stories you can find. Never eat meat or drink tea, coffee, or wine again as long as you live. Dont take any exercise; and do exactly the opposite of what the doctor advises. If you are very bad, hire yourself out as a laborer and live on your wages for a month or so. If you are very very very bad, become religious, and go every day three times to the nearest Roman Catholic Church. Go round all the Stations of the Cross on your knees, and pray incessantly. When you begin to feel sceptical you will be getting well.[1]

I read 10 pages of Genesung three times a week with a Fraülein who acts as my dictionary. It must be a most scandalous book; for she refuses to translate most of it.[2] I read a sentence and ask her what it means. She blushes and says it is nur dumme Zeug [just nonsense]; and my wife tells me to go on to the next paragraph. I am much more interested now that Böhlau is getting tired of Lea and beginning to take a serious view of his profession. You should give up literature and take to politics. I owe all my originality, such as it is, to my determination not to be a literary man. Instead of belonging to a literary club I belong to a municipal council.[3] Instead of drinking and discussing authors and reviews, I sit on committees with capable practical greengrocers and bootmakers (including a builder who actually reads Carlyle) and administer the collection of dust, the electric lighting of the streets, and the enforcement of the sanitary laws. You must do the same. Keep away from books and from men who get their ideas from books; and your own books will always be fresh. I notice in Genesung that you are genuinely concerned about the political and philosophical bearing of people's lives, and are much more than a mere romancer.

For the Erklärung[4] the Genossenschaft [Association] demands M3.60, and Bühne & Welt M30!! I have paid these sums, the smaller one as a matter of business, the latter as a bribe. The editor suggested M100 for a whole page; but I thought M30 for a quarter page was quite enough.

Entsch[5] had better tell all the people who want to wait for the Wiener production that if the play is a success our terms will go up next day to 20%; so they had better secure a 10% contract at once. . . .

I was much alarmed when I read in your letter of the 6th that Cotta had "behaved against us."[6] To do anything *against* one means in English to do something hostile. "Towards" is the right word. Your English has only two faults. One is "against" for "towards": the other is "included" for "enclosed." Otherwise you write better English than most Englishmen. However, as to Cotta, you see what a good effect it has on a publisher to tell him that the author totally disapproves of his proposals and proceedings. It is very noble of him to advance the 900 books (send me 3—one of each); but bless you! it is the printer who will really advance them: Cotta wont pay him until the book is on the market; and when your half-profits account comes in you will find that it shews a huge loss on the edition, and we shall have to pay half the loss as well as the 320 marks. *Timeo dona ferentes* [I fear those bearing gifts]. I shall be quite disappointed now if Cotta behaves well; but perhaps he will for your sake.

Do not bother about business until you are well. You carry Caesar and his fortunes, not to mention your own as well.

Who is Doctor Buzzi?[7] Is it starvation cure, or overfeeding cure, or water cure, or grape cure, or faith healing, or what?

yrs ever
G. Bernard Shaw

Als.

1. Trebitsch's persistent migraines led him in search of "cures."

2. Trebitsch's novel *Genesung*, partly autobiographical, concerns Richard von Böhlau, who is seduced by Lea Miller, is wounded in a duel, suffers sexual guilt, and is spiritually rejuvenated. The erotic passages, mostly things like "her close-pressed lips, hot and soft, fired kisses at his mouth," are, in fact, brief and infrequent.

3. Shaw's six years as Vestryman (later Borough Councillor) for St. Pancras, London, began in 1897.

4. A formal announcement ("Erklärung"), appointing Trebitsch as Shaw's translator-representative, appeared in December 1902 in *Bühne und Welt*, organ of the Deutscher Bühnen Verein (Association of German Stages).

5. A. Entsch, a leading Berlin theatrical agent whom Trebitsch had retained.

6. The firm of Cotta, in Stuttgart, had agreed to publish Trebitsch's translations of Shaw after Trebitsch offered to forgo a royalty in favor of one-half of profits. Shaw disapproved of the contract but accepted it for Trebitsch's sake. To mollify Shaw, Cotta offered to advance 300 prompt copies of each of the three plays. *Drei Dramen von Bernard Shaw*, including *Candida, Teufelskerl*, and *Helden (Arms and the Man)*, appeared in December (dated 1903).

7. Dr. Fausto Contone-Buzzi (b. 1858) maintained a sanatorium in Berlin that specialized in diet and massage cures.

10 Adelphi Terrace W.C.

10th December 1902

My dear Trebitsch

Your letter has just reached me. As to the Man of Destiny, you must by no means say that you do not want anything for the performances in London.[1] On the contrary, when London is concerned, *you* must be stern and inflexible and I conciliatory and regretful. Entsch must conduct the business just as if it were a German transaction.

As to the title, is there no well known phrase attached to Napoleon corresponding to our Man of Destiny? Der Schicksalskerl would hardly do, I am afraid.

Now as to your translations. You are thinking about nothing but the artistic side of the business. About that I never concern myself: it is in the hands of Providence. As a work of art, your translations seem to me better than the originals in several ways, and to have a certain charm of style and character that cannot be purchased for money or contrived by corrections & the like. But all this we may leave to the critics & the public. There is a mechanical side to the business that can be mastered only by experience and by drudgery. Now there is no need for doing that drudgery twice over. I know ten times as much about all those *dramatis personae* as you do, or as you ever will. I could write you the whole history of Richard Dudgeon from his boyhood. I know all about Burgoyne, all about the war, all about Anderson's position & salary and religion. I remember every word they say, and keep alluding to these sayings pages after you have forgotten them. My stage effects are based on that. Let me give you an example. Look at page 94. Swindon says "Die englischen Soldaten (it should be in the singular) werden dann schon zeigen, was sie können." On page 131, Burgoyne says to Swindon "Ihr Freund, der britische Beamte &c &c." There is no sense in this: Swindon has never said a word about the britische Beamte. Burgoyne's exit speech, which brings down the house in England, is made quite pointless. Now in England the audience first hear Swindon utter his conventional brag about "the British soldier" (not soldiers). Attention is specially called to it by Burgoyne's retort, and by its value as shewing the man's character. Consequently when Burgoyne afterwards says "Your friend the British soldier &c," the audience takes it at once. But suppose Swindon first said unrhetorically "the English soldiers," and Burgoyne afterwards said, "your friend the British official," there would be no point, no sense, no fun in it. You see, I have the whole thing in my head: you have only read it and made a version of it; and though you remember the poetic connexion and course of the feelings and the more

touching ideas of the characters, you cannot remember the mechanical con-
nexions nor the comic incongruities. You are like my wife, who thinks that
making people laugh is an unworthy and vulgar practice; but laughter is my
sword and shield and spear.

Now you must make up your mind to undergo a most tedious and miserable apprenticeship to the stage over my plays. You are a sensitive & fastidious young poet: I am a sordid and disillusioned old charlatan. But I have
built up these plays out of atoms of dust bit by bit, and planned them for the
stage and corrected them for the press and rehearsed them for performance;
and the result is that I can see at a glance these little oversights that seem
trifles to you. Siegfried Trebitsch: I tell you it is the trifles that matter when
you are a man of genius. You go right by instinct when you are on the top of
the mountain; the avalanches that scare smaller men away have no terrors
for you; but when you get back safe and triumphant to your hotel you trip
over the umbrella stand and break your nose. And remember, the "heavy
minded public," as you call it, can always be depended on to know when you
break your nose, and to laugh at you, but you cannot go far up a mountain
before they lose sight of you. The moment you are off the mountain you
think nothing matters. You talk of "a few little things" (48 appalling errors
& ruinous oversights in the D's D alone—I'll send you a marked copy tomorrow or next day)! You tell me not to be anxious about my stage directions
(Good God!) because your directors & actors are much cleverer than English
ones. Madman: *all* actors are idiots: *all* "directors" are impostors. Even if
they were not, would you copy out Wagner's orchestral parts carelessly &
omit a bar here and there because Austrian players have such virtuosity in
fingering? Do not be deceived by reputations: unless you tell people exactly
what to do, as if they were little children, and persuade them at the same
time that they have thought of it all themselves, you will never get anything
done properly. You and I have to teach all Europe; and you must learn how to
do it in my plays so that you may know how to do it in your own. You must
never trust anybody, never leave to chance anything you can arrange beforehand, no matter how distasteful & prosaic it may be. Caesar's rule must be
our rule: provide for every contingency you can foresee & then remember
that Fate will decide. I have no room for more; but this is only the beginning
of your troubles. When you are my age, you will have acquired a taste for
trouble as other men acquire a taste for brandy. And now one question more.
How often have you read your versions aloud to a circle of friends? You
should do that *10* times before going to press. Even I, who cannot speak German, have read your version aloud to a German[2] before writing you about it.
How is your neuralgia? Immer Muth! [Courage!]

GBS

Als.
    1. The German Theatre, London, was negotiating for the German version of *The Man of Des-
tiny*, which had been delayed by Trebitsch's illness.
    2. The "German" to whom Shaw read Trebitsch's translations was H. A. Hertz, a founder of the
German Theatre.

10 Adelphi Terrace W.C.
18th December 1902

My dear Trebitsch

Good: we can do no more now as to the text.

Now as to the general philosophy of the thing. I know that the transfer of any work to the professional stage means desecration, prostitution, sacrilege and damnation. It means this *at best*. At worst it means mere ignorant rascality, lies, cheating, evasion, and interpolation of obscenities and idiocies. But you must never admit this, or make any truce with it, or allow anybody to tell you that it is the custom. When old actors grumble at my stage directions, I point out to them that an actor is not a mechanic to be ordered to cross right or left, sit, stand, or exit left upper entrance, without understanding why, but an artist who is entitled to demand that an author shall address himself to his taste, fancy, intellect, imagination, wit &c &c &c &c. This crushes him utterly: his self-respect compels him to agree with you; and when he returns to the greenroom he says to the first actor he meets there, in a loud voice, "You know, my dear Kainz-Barnay-Schulz,[1] I dont agree with you about these stage directions of Shaw's. In my opinion he is quite right, because an actor is not a mechanic to be ordered to cross left and right, but an artist &c&c&c&c&c&c&c&c." In a theatre you must always assume that the noblest aims, the highest artistic integrity, the most scrupulous respect for artistic considerations, the most strenuous fidelity to the poet's text, are the law in that particular house, and that it is only in third rate places and among the lowest class of actors that malpractices occur and liberties are taken. Never let them put you in the position of a novice who does not know what theatres are really like: put *them* in the position of having to act up to your high estimate of their conscience and respectability. It is quite possible to do this pleasantly and familiarly if you have the requisite social tact; but you will find that even the people who are not in that fortunate position are forced to do the same thing pompously and arbitrarily. The pompous author or manager is disliked and laughed at behind his back; and the author who has social charm gets liked and respected; but both get the work done in the same way, by insisting on a high standard of artistic scrupulousness and intellectual character. The actors are not scrupulous and probably have no character at all: no matter: they cannot come to you and tell you that: they must pretend to be as good as you take them for; and the few good ones know the value of your respect and support you. Even opera singers, the most demoralized class of artists in existence, accustomed to perform under conditions which absolutely forbid honest and thorough work, were persuaded by Wagner to take unheard-of pains with his works at a time when they could hardly recognize them as music at all. The truth is, theatrical people, with all their insane vanity and lack of any positive element of character, are for that very reason easy to manage by anyone who thoroughly learns the business of the theatre. They are so susceptible that you can put anything you like into their heads, and finally work them up to believing that the production of the piece they are rehearsing is the most important event in the history of the world. The first thing is to read the piece over and over again to all your friends until you have learnt to do it effectively. Then read it to the cast and make a good impression to begin with. Then work out all the stage management and mark a copy to work from. This is very troublesome; but it is indispensable; for it makes you master of the situation at the first rehearsal. The stage manager never prepares his work as he should: he trusts to chance, and tries to invent the positions as he goes along, stopping and altering and disputing and wasting time. If you are ready to do his work for him, he will not dare to interfere with you. I always come to the first rehearsal with the whole stage business cut and dried. If the scenery is not ready (it never is in England) I seize chairs, forms &c. with my own hands, and arrange them to mark doors and objects of furniture. (The stage manager waits until he can order a carpenter to do it, as such manual work would compromise his dignity). I open the prompt-book; seize the actor or actress who begins; lead them to their entrance in my pleasantest and busiest and friendliest manner, and say, "Here you are: this is your entrance—now down here and across to here" letting them read the words just as they please, and simply piloting them through the movements. At the end of the first act, I say "Now we'll go through that act again"; and the repetition of the act ends the rehearsal. Next day I go twice through the second act in the same way. Next day twice through the third act. I take care, of course, that Burgoyne (zum Beispiel) is not called for the first two days. On the fourth day I go straight through the whole play. By that time the movements are settled. I then apologize for interfering and pretend that I am withdrawing to allow the stage manager to stage manage the play. Of course he does nothing, as the whole thing is virtually settled by that time. I then do not interfere for a day or two, because the actors are all trying to "swallow" their words, and until they have done that it is useless to try to get any expression out of them. When they get familiar with the play, then I take notes during the scenes—never actually interrupting if I can help it—and at the end explain the point and get the passage repeated. The great difficulty to a beginner is to refrain from saying too much. For instance, you will note, say, twelve points that the leading lady misunderstands or misses or spoils. If you tell her all the twelve on one day, you will worry her out of all loyalty to you. Tell her two at most, and save up the rest for the following rehearsals. You will find that she will correct some of them herself before you come to them.

At first you will have to depend on careful preparation and forethought to gain authority, as nothing but experience will teach you all that the actors themselves know; so that at first they will know better than you on certain points. But when you have rehearsed half a dozen plays you will have mastered the artistic business as well as the mechanical business; and then you will be able to double the value of every actor (except the *very* best) by coaching him in points that he would never think of himself. Then your authority behind the curtain will be as undisputed as that of Sardou. Remember: the actor is very jealous, and trusts neither the professional stage manager (who is generally an old actor) nor any of the other actors. But he knows that the author really wants to make the best of everybody; and consequently the author has only to take trouble enough to become an expert (and if he doesnt he will become a nuisance) to be more powerful on the stage than any other person in the theatre.......[2] Who is to translate my new volume—a masterpiece? It contains, among other things, a most wonderful play, and a set of aphorisms which eclipse Larochefoucauld's.

yrs ever
G. Bernard Shaw

PS My wife screamed with laughter at your telling me to "be quiet." It is what one says in England to a naughty child or a dog that barks too much!!!

Tls.

1. Ludwig Barnay (1842–1924), co-founder of the Deutsches Theater, Berlin, and later founder of the Berliner Theater; Antonie Schulz, an actress at the Burgtheater.
2. Shaw's ellipsis.

Maybury Knoll. Woking
26th December 1902

My dear Trebitsch

I send you a corrected copy of "Helden" [*Arms and the Man*]. It is full of hideous and devastating errors, but not so full as Candida, which I will send you as soon as I have gone completely through it.

No doubt some of the passages I have marked cannot be done in my way without spoiling their effect in German; but some of them are the crimes— the unashamed, intentional crimes—of a classically educated Viennese litterateur. If you took to painting & made a portrait of me, you would give me the leg of Apollo and the torso of the Farnese Hercules, and if I complained you would think me an ignorant Philistine. Now all that—everything romantic, everything classical, everything that is academically de rigueur or romantically artistic, is just what I have come into the world to trample on, laugh out of countenance, and finally slay. However, I will say more of this when I send Candida.[1]

In Arms & The Man the chief errors are due to your not acting the play over and over again until you know it by heart & then retiring for six months to the mountains to realize it right through to the bone. The way in which you translate every word just as it comes and then forget it and translate it some other way when it begins (or should begin) to make the audience laugh, is enough to whiten the hair on an author's head. Have you ever read Shakespear's Much Ado About Nothing? In it a man calls a constable an ass; and throughout the rest of the play the constable can think of nothing but this insult and keeps on saying "But forget not, masters, that I am an ass." Now if you translated Much Ado, you would make the man call the constable a Schaffkopf. On the next page he would be a Narr, then a Maul, then a Thier, and perhaps the very last time an Esel. And if Shakespear's ghost came to you to remonstrate, you would smile a superior smile and tell him that all accomplished litterateurs made it a point of style to vary their expressions and never repeat a word if they could help it. Whereupon Shakespear would place the pillow over your mouth and sit on it, and serve you right too!

But now I have something serious to say. What about my new book. Who is to translate *that*? This translating of old plays is all very well; but it is baby's work. I want my new book translated & published by Cotta simultaneously with the English edition.[2] It will be a frightfully difficult task; and the publisher & printer will probably be sent to prison for it. But I want the Germans to know me as a philosopher, as an English (or Irish) Nietzsche (only ten times cleverer), and not as a mere carpenter of farces like Helden and nursery plays like Candida. Besides, I want to complete *your* education. You must begin where I leave off & surpass me as far as I surpass Goethe & Schiller & Shakespear and Strindberg & Ibsen & Hauptman[3] & Sudermann[4] & Tolstoy *et hoc genus omne* [and all of this kind]. Genesung is not bad; but all that book will only make a sentence in your future work. And it is not lighthearted enough; you must learn to laugh, or, by Heavens, you will commit suicide when you realize all the infamy of the world as it is. You must avoid literary people & go into public life. I avoid literary and artistic people like the devil: the greengrocers and bootmakers and builders and publicans (Gasthauswirths) with whom I sit on committees in the Borough Council are far better company. What is the use of people whose heads are full of the very same books you have read yourself? Keep with people who never read anything. Wagner said that to devote yourself to Art is to make it certain that you will at last wake up and find that you have let life slip by you. The people at Buzzi's now—are they amusing?

I am glad your Hamburg man has promised to do Helden.[5] Probably he wont (no play is ever done until the curtain falls on the last act—NEVER count on a promise or even an agreement by a theatre); but it rejoices me when you are pleased. As for me, Helden has no charms for me: it is past & done & gone & over. Wait until you see my new play: the third act alone will send you back to Buzzi's raving & struggling.

My wife sends you her hochachtful regards. The people in the foreign bookshops run to her with your translations in great excitement whenever she goes into them.

yrs ever

G. Bernard Shaw

Als.

1. Trebitsch corrected *Helden* and *Candida* for the single-play edition of 1905.

2. Shaw wanted simultaneous publication in England and Germany so that he could compare the reception in the two countries. Trebitsch's translation of *Superman* was laid aside while he concentrated on the earlier plays, whose prospects for staging appeared brighter. The translation was published in 1907 by S. Fischer.

3. Gerhart Hauptmann (1862–1946), foremost German playwright of his day, had established naturalism on the German stage with his stark portraits of workers and peasants.

4. Hermann Sudermann (1857–1928), popular rival of Hauptmann, adapted naturalism to essentially well-made, middle-class "problem" plays.

5. The premiere of *Helden* took place at the Deutsches Schauspielhaus, Hamburg, on 16 April 1904; only two other performances were given there. Trebitsch was also negotiating for a production by the Deutsches Theater in Berlin.

Overstrand Hotel. [Cromer.] Norfolk
7th January 1903

My dear Trebitsch-Spiegelmann

Why do I call you Spiegelmann? Look at the corrections to Candida and you will understand. What is a Spiegelmann? A Mirrorman. A Looking Glass man. What is a Looking Glass? A thing that reflects what is before it with exquisite fidelity, but that has neither Rücksicht [hindsight] nor Vorsicht [foresight], neither memory nor hope, neither reason nor conscience. And that is what you are as a translator. You translate a sentence beautifully, but you do not remember the last sentence, do not foresee the next sentence, and when you finish the play it goes out of your head just as your head vanishes from your mirror when you have finished shaving.

Nearly all your mistakes are Spiegelmanly mistakes. But two are worse. One of the two is dishonorable; and the other is stupid.

The dishonorable one is Candida's *white* hand.[1] Now "white hand" is not a *chose vue*. It is a commonplace of romantic literature. It is a "reach-me-down," a "*décrochez moi cela*," a thing said by people who either cannot see things at all, or else admire women made up with *blanc de perle*. Now this crime of picking up secondhand phrases & sticking them into work that professes to be your own original work is the one crime that an author cannot commit without dishonor. You may do anything else: you may lie, you may steal, you may run away from the field of battle, you may poison your whole family, you may combine the vices of Nero & Peter the Great with the hypocrisy of an archbishop; but you must not be insincere and unoriginal. You must be prepared to guarantee every word as the record of an accurate observation or of a fancy suggested by a real experience. To write a word because some idiot has written it before, is the quintessence of folly and sin; and if you do it you will go to hell when you die.

The stupid mistake is your making Eugene revile Morell as heftig and unmännlich [violent and unmanly].[2] That makes him a real Naseweis [impertinent fellow] at once. Now the whole point of the play is the revelation of the weakness of this strong and manly man, and the terrible strength of the febrile and effeminate one. Morell is always strenuously acting the strong and manly part. Eugene never acts at all. Morell thinks that he must be strong & manly to be worthy of Candida's respect; and, what is more, he *is* strong & manly, and *is* worthy of her respect. Eugene never denies this, never disparages it, never belittles it; but he throws into the scale against it his weakness, his "horror," his loneliness, his Herzensnot [heart's need]. Morell cannot understand why Eugene is so determined that he shall tell Candida how strong & manly he (Morell) was, and how weak & helpless he (Eugene) was. And you, unhappy Siegfried, did not understand it either. You thought it was a misprint. Now that is what I call stupid. You didnt understand the play: you only wallowed in it. The fact is, you are young and still sentimental. You are on the Morell plane: you still want love and happiness, as Eugene thought he did until Candida's quiet description of their happy home opened his eyes to the fact that "life is nobler than that." Now if you

are to translate me you must give up this bourgeois craving for happiness &
love and all the rest of the petty consolations of the people who do routine
work in the world. Like Napoleon in The Man of Destiny you must learn to
say "Should I be what I am if I cared for happiness?" Like Dick Dudgeon you
must be able to look around the parson's home & see that it is beautiful—
"almost holy," and yet know that you yourself have something bigger in hand
than domestic joys. You can never dramatize anything until you get above it.
Your Genesung [convalescence] must cure you not only of Lea but of Marie[3]
& of much more besides, especially of art and romance [and] all the other
commonplaces of Soirées de Vienne.

When I read in your letter that Raïna could not say "Das arme Ding"
["poor thing"] because that was only said to children, I tore out large hand-
fuls of my hair and uttered screams of rage.[4] Why, that is exactly why I chose
it. It is just the same in English. The moment a woman applies to a man a
word that fits a child, it is all over: she is in love with him. Did you give
a second thought to my careful stage direction that Raïna, in worshipping
Sergius's portrait, should do nothing körperlich [physical] with it? Did you
notice that though Sergius is her hero, her Lord & her God, he is never her
Ding or her Wurm—that she never wants to stuff *his* mouth with pralines,
as she wants to stuff Bluntschli's? The moment Das arme Ding is out of
Raïna's lips every experienced man & woman in the theatre knows what has
happened, and that her hero may go whistle for his heroine. She has adopted
Bluntschli as her baby; and that settles the matter. In Candida Morell is
Candida's "boy," *her* Jakob. Now though she pities Eugene's youth and immaturity, he is never her boy. She knows that he is beyond them and will grow
out of them (we talk of a boy "growing out of" his clothes when he grows too
big for them); and the relation that grows up between them—the relation
that is even closer than that between herself & Morell—is the relation between two clever people who understand certain things that others, far
dearer to them, do not understand. You, being a clever man, will often meet
married women who, being cleverer than their husbands, will be able to talk
to you in a way that they cannot talk to their husbands; but dont ever suppose, or encourage *them* to suppose, that they love you better.

When I read also in your letter that in the passage about Raïna buckling
on Sergius's sword, "als" would mean that she did it only once, I plucked up
my beard by the roots and threw it after my hair.[5] Of course she only did it
once—on the great occasion when all Bulgaria rose to maintain its independence and every Bulgarian maiden buckled on the sword of her lover. Good
Heavens! do you suppose that he wore a sword in peace time and that she
buckled it on every day for him?

Your last letter had to follow me round the country, as I am taking a week's
holiday at the seaside. So, having kept Lindau[6] waiting so long, I decided to
keep him waiting a little longer. I certainly should not undertake to wait
until 1904 unless we get a contract which will compel Lindau (or whoever
else takes his place if he dies) to produce the play whether he has cooled
down about it or not. I should think, however, that the present man [Otto

Brahm] will try to anticipate him now that the papers are puffing us. At all events dont be in a hurry.

I received a press cutting the other day from a Swiss paper—very complimentary, but mostly following the lead of your preface. I have written too many reviews myself to attach such importance to them. I have inquiries from the National Theatre of Christiania [Oslo], probably as a result of your translation & the notice it has attracted.

You shall translate the new book by all means if you will. What does Cotta say? It will be no good for the theatre, as it is too long to be acted & too philosophic to be read. But it is a great work.

When I return to town I must send you Haig's "Diet & Food in Relation to Strength & Power of Endurance."[7] Your neuralgias & headaches may be amenable to his treatment.

No room for more today
G. Bernard Shaw

Als.

1. Trebitsch had translated "the lilies in her hand" as in her "weissen Hand."

2. In Act I, Marchbanks actually characterizes his rival as "strong and manly." Trebitsch also reduced Morell's scornful dismissal of Marchbanks as a "snivelling cowardly whelp" to "Naseweis" (impertinent fellow), apparently associating "snivelling" with "nose" (*Nase*).

3. Lea and Marie: contrasting images of illicit and virginal love in Trebitsch's *Genesung.*

4. Where Raina in *Arms* exclaims over the exhausted Bluntschli "The poor dear," Trebitsch had used "Mein armer Freund" (My poor friend).

5. Trebitsch used the conjunction "wenn" (whenever) instead of "als" (when) for Raina's remark: "When I buckled on Sergius's sword."

6. Paul Lindau (1839–1919), the prominent German author and producer, was to take over the Deutsches Theater, Berlin, from Otto Brahm (1852–1912) for 1904–5 and was negotiating for *Helden.* Trebitsch had also approached Brahm, but Brahm found Shaw uncongenial and did not produce any Shaw until 1910: *Getting Married (Heiraten)* at the Lessing-Theater, which failed.

7. This book (1898) by the British physician Dr. Alexander Haig (1853–1924) recommended vegetarianism.

Overstrand Hotel. Cromer
10th January 1903

My dear Trebitsch

Thanks for the Man of Destiny. I am writing by this post to H. A. Hertz, the financier of the German Theatre here, to tell him that you have finished & sent over the translation, and that any delay that may occur will be my fault & not yours. At the same time I will read & return it as soon as possible. Already some little delay has been caused by my absence from London. I am down here by the sea until the morning of Wednesday the 14th.

Der Schlachtenlenker [Ruler of Battles] is a perfect title for the Man of Destiny. So *that's* settled. The Strange Lady would not do at all. You will find some difficulty in getting the play performed unless the German playgoer tolerates a longer program than the London playgoer. Here it is too long for a "curtain raiser" or for an afterpiece, and not long enough for a principal piece.

As to Wiené, take the part away from him at once & tell him he can take the money at the doors on Shaw nights, and play Schiller & Shakespear on the other nights.[1] I know exactly & precisely what he wants to do; and if he does it our ruin is certain. Good God! imagine the idiot whispering & crying out and "springing about," with the sergeant & the soldiers & the woman standing round admiring him like a Donizettian opera chorus! Tell him with my compliments that he is a Schafkopf [blockhead]. Also that the principal people in the scene are the woman & the sergeant, upon whom he is to play, and that all he has to do is just what he is told. I wrote it for a good but quite brainless actor who was assassinated shortly afterwards.[2] Tell him, in particular, that from the moment the sergeant arrests Richard a deadly suspense and silence must fall on that *little* room (I dont care how big the stage is: it is a little room). On that silence Richard's words must fall with frightful *quiet* distinctness: everyone of them must strike on Judith's heart with a pang of terror. The sergeant stands with his back turned & his head bent down as if at church; and at a certain point he must raise his head; at another point later on he must turn his head; and when Richard turns away, he must find himself confronted with a face full of suspicion. And then must come the great effect of Richard getting the quaint notion of removing the sergeant's suspicion by making Judith kiss him. All that will be utterly ruined if the damned scoundrel *acts*. He will want to act—to agonize, to make convulsive movements & play tricks with his voice. Dont let him. Tell him I say that he shall not act. He may pray and fast and weep and go to confession; but *act*, by God, he shall not. I will have no monkey tricks in my play.

I write in great haste: a party[3] is waiting for me to read my new play to them.

yrs ever
G. Bernard Shaw

Als.
1. *Teufelskerl*, with Wiené, who was known for his intense character acting, was in rehearsal at the Raimund.
2. The popular melodramatic actor William Terriss (1847–1897) had offered to collaborate with Shaw but was fatally stabbed by a madman.
3. Beatrice and Sidney Webb and the Graham Wallases.

10 Adelphi Terrace W.C.
15th January 1903

Dear Trebitsch

I will write to Forbes Robertson's brother, who played Burgoyne, to ask whether he has any photographs of his uniform.[1] There should be no difficulty, however, about the military costumes, as the period is definite and well known. The other dresses were far too pretty: they spoiled the play; so I want them to be forgotten.

I will try to get you a good print of one of my photographs for reproduction.

Die Sch[l]acht bei Tavazzano [The Battle of Tavazzano] will not do, because it is absolutely essential that the name of the play should proclaim it a Napoleon piece.[2] It would be better to call it simply "Bonaparte" than to give it the very wittiest title that did not mention him. The Schlachtenlenker is just what you want: why not let it stand?

How can you possibly conclude that "in some things I am wrong." My dear Trebitsch, *I am never wrong.* Other people are sometimes—often—nearly always wrong, especially when they disagree with me; but I am omniscient and infallible. The friends with whom you have deliberated simply dont understand the art of writing for the stage. I tell you again and again, most earnestly and seriously, that unless you repeat the words that I have repeated, you will throw away all the best stage effects and make the play unpopular with the actors. When you study my corrections in the Man of Destiny, you will understand this better. Half the art of dialogue consists in the *echoing* of words—the tossing back & forwards of phrases from one actor to another like a cricket ball. I have never objected to your varying a word or phrase when it doesnt matter. You will find that I have passed over dozens of variations without comment because I considered them either improvements or indifferences. But when you make Burgess forget the word that Morell has branded into his astonished brain as with a red hot iron, and then tell me that one can do that in German (as if it were a question of language) then I tear my hair & ask God why he has forsaken me. And when you spoil Candida's retort "Oh, the worse places arnt open on Sundays"—when you make it sound like this: MORELL—"Why dont they go to worse places on Sundays?" CANDIDA—"Oh, the less desirable places of entertainment are not available," and then tell me that a council of your friends has decided that this is permissible in Germany (Good God: as if we were arranging the conditions of a duel!), then my feelings go beyond all expression.

And now you tell me that "weisse Hand" is "Sprachgebrauch" [usage] out of Goethe, Schiller, Heine &c. Of course it is. That's what I meant by calling it a "décrochez-moi-cela." That's just why I object to it. I never write Sprachgebrauch; and neither must you. And remember that though we may be no bigger men than Goethe and Schiller, we are standing on their shoulders, and should therefore be able to see farther & do better. And after all, Schiller is only Shaw at the age of 8, and Goethe Shaw at the age of 32. This, by the way, is the highest compliment ever paid to Goethe.

All your business news is excellent. Go on and prosper.

Later on I will say a word about your preface.[3] The new play is too bulky to send you in typescript. I will send you proofs as soon as I have arranged for its publication here. Meanwhile, do you think Cotta would care to publish it in Germany simultaneously with its appearance in England? He would be imprisoned for Majestatsbeleidigung [lese majesty] for six months or so;[4] but I shouldnt mind that in the least: it would be an excellent advertisement.

yrs ever
G. Bernard Shaw

Als.

  1. Ian Robertson, brother of the actor-manager Johnston Forbes Robertson (1853–1937), played Burgoyne to his brother's Dick Dudgeon in *Devil's Disciple* at the Coronet Theatre (7 September 1900).

  2. Trebitsch, still struggling for a German title to *Man of Destiny,* suggested the play's setting, "The Battle of Tavazzano," but ultimately settled for *Schlachtenlenker.* He changed it to the literal *Der Mann des Schicksals* for the collected edition of 1911.

3. Trebitsch's essay "Bernard Shaw," written for *Drei Dramen*.
4. The "Revolutionist's Handbook," appended to *Man and Superman*, contained several thrusts at monarchs.

Maybury Knoll. Woking
19th January 1903

Dear Trebitsch

Miss Margaret Halstan, the Strange Lady, has been engaged by Forbes Robertson to play in his new piece, an adaptation of Rudyard Kipling's "Light that Failed." Her father, who finances the German Theatre, offers to go on with the Man of Destiny nevertheless, substituting a German actress for his daughter. But the German actress is not so young & pretty as Miss Margaret, to whom, besides, I have already taught the part. So I have declared my readiness to wait until The Light that Failed fails again (as I quite expect it will) so that Miss Halstan can play the part later on. I have, however, said that it is as much in your hands as in mine. But it will be better to wait; so there is no hurry about the "scrip" (stage slang for the prompt book).[1]

One of my reasons for advising you not to call the Man of Destiny Sch[l]acht bei Tavazzano is that it is not likely to be played unless some actor takes a strong fancy to the part of Napoleon. Now you will find that there is nothing an actor loves more than a "title role." If Sarah Bernhardt played it (which God forbid) she would call it The Strange Lady.[2] If Wiené played it he would call it Der Schlachtenlenker, or Bonaparte, or something of that sort. One often has to resist these actor-vanities; but in this case a "role title" is desirable both from our point of view & the actor's. The Battle of Tavazzano is a good title only to those who have seen the play. To those who havnt, it is misleading and not specially tempting. I myself think Der Schlachtenlenker an ideal title.

I agree as to the advisability of not glutting the market with translations of my stage plays. My new volume, however, is rather an exceptional one. Although the play which forms a small part of it is technically a stage play, and could be actually performed, yet nothing of the kind is likely to happen, because the first act is much longer than the Man of Destiny; the third act, with the interlude in hell, is a little longer than the whole of Arms & The Man; and the second and fourth acts are of the full length customary in three-act plays: that is, much longer than in five act plays. So it will be as much out of the question as Ibsen's Peer Gynt or Emperor or Galilean. On the other hand it ought to raise a good deal of literary, political & philosophic discussion. However, it can wait. You must get on with your own work.

Do not be anxious about Archer's astonishment that Brandes does not appreciate my Shawishness.[3] Archer knows me so well personally that he cannot understand how anybody can read my books without seeing that it is "only Shaw talking," and not literature. I dont think he has seen your translation. [Better wait for the second edition before sending it to him . . . be conscious . . . would set Archer laughing . . .][4]—as I think—great excellence of the translation. I have told him that it is in many places superior to the original.

If you make a tour in Provence, do not be misled by the guide books into wasting time on Carcassonne. Pass it by and see Toulouse. Instead of Carcassonne, see Aigues Mortes, after which Carcassonne is a wretched pasticcio. When you are at Arles, let nothing tempt you to miss Les Baux. Take it on your way to St Rémy, which is on your way to Avignon. Nimes is a prosaic place, in spite of its antiquities: were it not for the trip to the Pont de Gard, you might pass it without any great loss. Vaucluse is sentimental & romantic and certainly very pretty; but it is not really worth taking much trouble to see. Marseilles, like Genoa and all the great Mediterranean sea-ports, is magnificent. Les Saintes Maries, on the coast near Arles, barren & desolate as it is, is worth 50 Vaucluses. Avignon is a venemous hole; but the Pope's palace has a chapel in which you can see what the early frescoes in the Santa Croce in Florence were before they were spoiled by repainting in coarse outlines. Dont forget Les Baux, which is like nothing else in the world, and Aigues Mortes (for medieval fortifications); and go boldly on to Toulouse: you will not be sorry. And dont be seduced by Carcassonne & Vaucluse unless you have plenty of time & money to *waste*.

GBS

Als.

1. Margaret Halstan (1880–1967), the Strange Lady in the first London production of *Man of Destiny* (Comedy Theatre, 29 March 1901), was the daughter of H. A. Hertz of the German Theatre, where she also performed. *The Light That Failed*, in which Miss Halstan shortly opened at the Lyric, was a great success and precluded her performing in the German Theatre.

2. As drama critic for the *Saturday Review*, Shaw had specifically criticized Bernhardt's monotonous intoning of her lines, her shallow characterizations, and her superficial roles.

3. Georg Brandes (1842–1927), eminent Danish critic and friend of Ibsen, published "Bernard Shaw's Teater" (*Politiken*, 29 December 1902), based on *Drei Dramen*. Brandes named Shaw the most original contemporary British playwright and urged that he be produced. Shaw's friend and fellow critic William Archer (1856–1924) responded in "The Two Georges" (*Morning Leader*, 10 January 1903), deploring the "monstrous" failure of commercial London managers to produce Shaw but disputing Brandes's claim that Shaw grasped different epochs and races. On 12 January Shaw wrote to Archer agreeing with Brandes and mentioning Trebitsch, "whose translations, apart from the mere mistakes, which are mighty ones and millions, are so good that I prefer them in many respects to the originals" (*Collected Letters*, ed. Laurence, II).

4. Segment canceled by Trebitsch but partly legible.

10 Adelphi Terrace W.C.
26th January 1903

Dear Trebitsch

Do not think me unfeeling—but I have laughed myself almost into hysterics over Kellner's onslaught.[1] I quite expected that this would happen, though, oddly enough, I never thought of Kellner. He spent a day with me in 1898, and was one of the first German Shawites. As he wrote about me in the German press long ago, he is probably indignant at your entry on the scene as my discoverer.

And now, what is to be done? Well, first, let this experience cure you of your excessive sensitiveness to reviews. When you were so pleased at the favorable ones, you were preparing yourself for the penalty of being kept awake at night by the unfavorable ones. If I bothered about such things I should go mad three times a week, and die on the alternate days.

A reply to Kellner is impossible, because he is perfectly right on the points which admit of argument. You cannot *prove* that your translation is artistically good, any more than you can prove that Rembrandt was a great painter. Artistic qualities are a matter of taste. Now Kellner, on the other hand, *can* prove that you dont know County Council English, and dont know what the Hackney Road is like, whereas he knows both. A letter to the paper will give him just what he wants: that is, an excuse for writing a second article in which he will pour out all the mistakes that he had not room for in the first one. Besides, a letter from the author would be alluded to and quoted in other papers; and the result would be a big advertisement of a literary controversy instead of a simple review passed by in silence. The truth is, you are very lucky to get off so easily. Suppose he had read The Devil's Disciple as carefully as he has read his pet Candida, and had gone on to make fun of your translation of civilian as civilized person, and all your other slips! And he will do that if you give him the smallest excuse for writing another article on the same subject. There is nothing to be done but turn over and go to sleep like a philosopher, saying "Serve me right."

Now shall I tell you what I should do myself in your place? I should write straight away to Dr Kellner, hochundwohlgeboren [the Hon.], offering him ten guineas for a copy of the plays with all the blunders noted and corrected in the margin, and promising him to add to the preface in the second edition a paragraph like this: "I am indebted to Dr Leon Kellner, who was the first to draw the attention of the German readers to the works of Bernard Shaw, and whose knowledge of contemporary English local life and political organization is unrivalled, for several important corrections in this edition, especially in those technical references to the political structure of English suburban life which are intelligible only to one, who, like Dr Kellner, is an expert in English sociology as well as in English literature."

This is the grand style of fighting. It is just what any ordinary writer wouldnt do, and therefore it is what you should do at once. Remember, it is perfectly true and perfectly becoming and handsome for you to acknowledge as true. You made the mistakes, and you made an enemy at the same time. To remedy this you must not lie awake and get neuralgia: you must correct the mistakes and disarm the enemy. That will instantly cure your neuralgia and give you a sense of having compelled Kellner to respect you, as well as pleasing him. You must not bluntly offer him the ten guineas, as he might resent it as a bribe; but you may quite well ask him to correct the whole volume and ask him to allow you to negotiate with Messrs Cotta for a fee for the literary work involved.

One thing that comes out of it all is the uselessness of depending on me for technical corrections. If you call a Zunft [trade union] a Vogel [bird] or a Steuerzahler [taxpayer] a Pferd [horse], I can correct that; but when you call them Gewerbeverein [tradesman union] and Ratenzahler [installment payer], naturally I am satisfied. That is where Kellner's special knowledge comes in; and since he has got it, there is no use rebelling against fate: the man who knows is master of the situation.

I will go shares in any fee that Kellner may be paid for corrections. Of course he will offer artistic corrections as well; but these you need not bother about: it will be easy enough to pay him the compliment of adopting a word or two here and there (when it makes no real difference) to spare his feelings. He will be delighted at being consulted; for as he is the editor of a paper he could not possibly find time to make a translation himself: otherwise he would no doubt have offered to do so long ago.

I have finished Weltuntergang, and dont at all approve of the end of it.[2] What do I care about a man who hangs himself from his window! You must learn to walk down a whole street of houses with a man hanging from every window without the least emotion. Anybody can write a pathetic story by killing a baby in it; anybody can write a tragic story by making the hero or heroine commit suicide in a thunderstorm; and when people are tired of these you can always rouse them by a duel. But that is all romantic postiche. I am interested in what Hilsekil does whilst he is alive; but when you make your Sontagskind into a Werther hero and try to persuade me that he committed suicide, I can think of nothing to say except a German word which I dont understand, but which the Fräulein at Woking uses when I talk Shaw philosophy to her. That word is "Schnack" [twaddle]! However, it is all right: one gets tired of a story and kills the hero when one is young simply to save trouble. When you are my age you will make a big volume or a long play out of your Sontagskind.

Meanwhile dont worry; be magnanimous with Kellner; sleep well; and do not neglect your work to grieve over your mistakes. Even I—I, Bernard Shaw—make mistakes sometimes.

yrs ever

G. Bernard Shaw

Tls.

1. Leon Kellner (1849–1928), who had met Shaw through William Archer in 1898 and had written the earliest general article on Shaw in German, had published an article, "Eine verunglückte Uebersetzung" ("Wretched Translation," *Neues Wiener Tagblatt*, 22 January 1903), in which he derided Trebitsch's translations of Shaw as a "ridiculous caricature" and cited some half-dozen howlers, drawn largely from Trebitsch's careless handling of the stage directions to *Candida*.

2. In Trebitsch's story "Weltuntergang" Hilsekil, oppressed by Sundays (as was Trebitsch), gambles his money away and hangs himself.

Maybury Knoll. Woking
14th February 1903

You will have to make the bow yourself: I am far too busy to come.[1] Besides, it is just as well not to divide the interest of the occasion too much. Let Wiené & Thaller have it all to themselves.

This morning I sent an article to Die Zeit of the most Shawish description, full of the most insufferable egotism, and warning the Viennese against Candida.[2] Also explaining that the Teufelskerl is all stale melodrama. I have also made merry at the expense of Kellner & talked about you in the most indelicate manner. You will tear your hair when you read it.

How are the rehearsals going?

GBS

Apcs.

1. *Teufelskerl* (*Devil's Disciple*), staged by Arthur Raeder, was to open at the Raimund on 25 February, with Wiené as Dick Dudgeon and Willy Thaller (1854–1941), popular comic actor, as Burgoyne.

2. In this brilliant puff, "Ein Teufelskerl. Selbstkritik" ("Devil of a Fellow. Selfcritique," *Die Zeit*, 22 February), Shaw set himself above the German classics, mocked Viennese taste, dismissed *Candida* as "snivelling trash," laughed at Kellner, and called translation a matter of "divination."

Maybury Knoll. Woking
17th February 1903

Tell Judith[1] that the effect of the third act will depend largely on her acting. At the end of the first scene she must cry in a really heartrending way; and all through the court martial she must not let the audience lose the sense of the horror with which she listens to the deadly jesting of Burgoyne & Richard. All the rest is easy.

I hope you have a good man for Anderson.[2] He should be a thoroughly sympathetic person, but capable of suggesting great reserves of strength. The stupid people will all make the same mistake as Judith about him at the end of the 2nd Act unless he says "Du kennst selbst den Mann nicht, mit dem du verheiratet bist" ["You dont know the man youre married to"], very cleverly.

Do not let them give the part of the sergeant to a third rate actor.[3] It is most important. Tell the actor that I regard it as the part which, more than any other in the play, depends on the skill of the actor. The others have capital dialogue to help them: the sergeant must make all the effect by his acting.

Dont send me any wires:[4] I am not impatient. But subscribe to a press cutting agency & send me the notices.

GBS

Apcs.

1. Hedwig Lange, playing the role in the Raimund production of *Teufelskerl*.
2. The role was played by Arthur Raeder.
3. Robert von Balajthy played the Sergeant.
4. On 19 February, Charlotte Shaw wrote to request Trebitsch to wire "if the great first night" is "really a success" (Berg).

Maybury Knoll. Woking
17th February 1903

I shall get into a nice mess over the Freie Volksbühne.[1] As I knew nothing about Lindau's contract I wrote to Bloch[2] that I had much rather be introduced to Germany by the F. V. than by any other theatre in the world. Now my plays will be denounced by the court papers because I am a Socialist, and by the Socialist papers because I have betrayed them for Lindau's sake.

However, it cannot be helped. But I assure you it is enormously important not to offend the Social Democrats, because all the clever journalists who become influential later on begin by being enthusiastic Socialists.

I wrote the Zeit article with a view to its being published at once. It is full of Kellner. Let the affair be forgotten when we have had the last word, but not until then. There is no harm in letting him know that my arm is long enough to reach Vienna if there is to be a newspaper war. The more we are written about the better. In such matters there is always the consolation that your enemy must either let you alone or advertize you.

GBS

Apcs.
1. Freie Volksbühne (Independent People's Theatre), formed in Berlin in 1890 as a private working-class subscription theatre affiliated with the Social Democratic Party. Its repertory inclined toward social realism (Ibsen, Hauptmann, Zola, etc.), and it performed on Sunday afternoons in leased theatres (until 1914, when it occupied an imposing new building, financed by its members).
2. J. Bloch, one of the F. V.'s directors. On 10 February he wrote to Shaw of the F. V.'s plan to introduce Shaw to Germany with *Arms and the Man* (*Helden*). Shaw gave the undertaking his fraternal blessing, but he hadn't reckoned with Paul Lindau, who had acquired *Helden* for the Deutsches Theater and was concerned about being anticipated by the F. V.

Maybury Knoll. Woking
21st February 1903

Dear Trebitsch

The Freie Volksbühne have just sent me the enclosed press cutting.[1] I enclose a copy of my reply to their letter. I hope you will be able to decipher it: it has been very badly duplicated.

I have no objection to being taken seriously. What ruins me in England is that people think I am always joking.

Yes: that article will be awful. I was in a mischievous humor when I wrote it.

Dont wire: send me a letter giving your own impression of the performance; and be sure you write it *before* you read the newspapers.

As to success, the box office, and not the press notices, will decide that.

In haste to catch the post.

yrs ever
GBS

Als.
1. From the *Berliner Tageblatt*, 18 February, reporting the dispute between Lindau and the F. V. over *Helden*. The article noted that although it was not formally possible to interfere with the private F. V., Lindau stood to lose much by the planned production of *Helden*. Then in a statement that bears the hallmark of Trebitsch, the paper declared that it would find the F. V. "loyal only if it respects the moral prior-rights of Director Paul Lindau and withdraws its earlier production."

10 Adelphi Terrace W.C.
23rd February 1903

Dear Trebitsch

I am delighted at the misunderstanding in Berlin: nothing could be more fortunate for us. It means advertisement, advertisement, advertisement. Your second telegram has just arrived; but by this time Bernstein has the letter of which I sent you a copy—or at least he will get it today or tomorrow at latest.[1]

The consent which has been published is, I presume, the letter I wrote to Bloch in reply to his letter to me telling me that the performance was about to take place. He said nothing about any difficulty; and I of course assumed that he had arranged all the business part of the affair with Entsch, and that nobody had made any objection. All I knew about Lindau at that moment was that he had proposed to produce Helden at the Deutsches Theater when he entered on his duties there as director next year (or next season); but I did not know that we had actually concluded a contract with him. . . .

Now as to my attitude, you must understand that Bernstein expressly claims in his letter to me that as the performance is technically a "private" one, we have no control over it, and that there is no question of law involved, but solely one of courtesy. In this he is right according to English law; but this would not shield him in England from an action for damages if we, the authors, could shew that the performance by the F. B. had prevented our getting the piece accepted at other theatres, or if the Deutsches Theater had a failure with the piece and could shew that this failure was due to its having been discredited by the way in which the F. B. handled it. Therefore, though the Stage Society[2] here is exactly on the same legal footing as the F. B., I have no doubt whatever that I could prevent the Stage Society producing a play of mine against my will, although I could not get an injunction from the courts forbidding the Stage Society to proceed with their performance. If you give the F. B. notice through Entsch, or directly from yourself, that you object to the performance, and that you will hold them responsible for any damage that may ensue to you through the refusal of the play at the German theatres or elsewhere in consequence of their producing it, or through the repudiation of the contract by Lindau, they will surrender, because such an action for damages would certainly be decided against them.

My own position is rather a delicate one. My position in the Socialist movement here obliges me to extend every possible courtesy to the German Social-Democrats. I could not countenance for a moment the notion that my play could be discredited by being connected with a Socialist organization: on the contrary, I am bound to assume—and do actually hold—that such a connection is a distinction. My only ground for objection would therefore be the common opinion in the theatrical world that performances of this class spoil the novelty of a piece and interfere with its chances of success. But this, as it happens, I dont believe. I have listened to that sort of thing here for years. I have been more or less connected with every experiment of the Freie Bühne type that has been made in London since 1885 or thereabouts; and I am convinced, as a matter of practical experience, that such experiments are not only useful but indispensable, and that no play has ever suffered from being connected with them, although many young authors (and old ones) have lost valuable chances by allowing themselves to be frightened away from them by the talk of the regular theatrical people, who are utterly ignorant of the world outside the Garrick Club. If I were in Lindau's position I should help the Freie Bühne instead of hindering it. If I were in your position I should do the same. Consequently all I can say to the

F. B. people is that as far as I am concerned there is no objection to the performance either from a political, personal or business point of view. I dont believe it will do any of us any harm. But the dispute now raging will no doubt do us good by making the affair more widely known; so let Lindau and Bernstein fight away as hard as they please: the more they hammer one another's skulls the better for us. As to the play being ruined for all German stages, do not trouble about that. When you have been ruined as often as I have, you will find your reputation growing with every successive catastrophe. Never ruin yourself less than twice a year, or the public will forget all about you. . . .

I sympathize with you over the rehearsals. How I should like to drop in at the last one and stand them all on their heads!

Do not let Entsch[3] bind us to wait for Dresden unless the Hoftheater people bind themselves under penalty to produce by a certain date.

It is very desirable that the action of the Censor over the Macedonian question & Helden should get into the newspapers.[4]

If you know any London correspondents in Vienna, make them come on the 25th.

GBS

Tls.

1. On 22 February, the *Berliner Tageblatt* cited a letter from the Freie Volksbühne (Shaw's references to the "F. B."—Freie Bühne—are misleading since the two organizations were distinct), noting the appeal to its "loyalty" and responding that it had not known of Lindau's interest in *Helden* and that it would be disloyal to its audience and to Shaw to withdraw his play. The F. V. then quoted Shaw's letter to Bloch preferring the F. V. to all German stages. Shaw confirmed his consent to Eduard Bernstein, who interceded for the F. V., but indicated that it did not affect the legal situation. The Volksbühne production of *Helden*—the first staging of Shaw in Germany—opened on 15 March at the Metropol Theater for five matinees. The party organ *Vorwärts* (17 March) reported "stormy applause," but to placate Lindau no reviews were permitted. Lindau's production of *Helden* followed two seasons later on 8 December 1904 for 36 performances.

2. The Stage Society, founded in 1899 as a private society to produce serious plays that were avoided by commercial managements, had introduced four of Shaw's plays to London.

3. A. Entsch, the Berlin agent, was negotiating for *Candida* at Dresden's Hoftheater (Königliches Schauspielhaus), where the play had its premiere the following 19 November.

4. The Burgtheater had turned to *Arms*, but the censor, to whom the play was submitted, advised against its performance because of the tensions between Bulgaria and Macedonia.

Maybury Knoll. Woking
1st March 1903

Dear Trebitsch

I had no idea that there was any secrecy about the action of the Censorship. When you first told me of it I mentioned it to Archer and to another journalist. This other man promptly published it (I meant him to); and the enclosed cuttings are the result. I hope no harm will come of my indiscretion.[1]

Reuter's telegram about the production appeared in nearly all the papers except the Daily Chronicle, which came out with a paragraph which I suspect was sent by Kellner himself.[2]

I have not had time to read the notices from Vienna yet.[3] I have, however, got through Bahr's feuilleton. Has he written any plays? He knows more about the business than most critics do. I guess from it that he is disgusted

Preis dieses		Preis dieses
Zettels		Zettels
20 Heller.		20 Heller.

Mittwoch, den 25. Februar 1903.

Raimund=Theater.

Gastspiel des Herrn

Carl Wiene
königlich sächsischer Hofschauspieler, und

Willy Thaller.

Zum 1. Male:

Ein Teufelskerl.

Schauspiel in 3 Akten von Bernard S h a w, deutsch von Siegfried T r e b i t s ch.

Regie: Arthur Raeder.

Frau Dudgeon		Frl. Rucker
Richard Dudgeon, } ihre Söhne		* * Hr. Lackner
Christof Dudgeon, }		
William Dudgeon, } ihre Brüder		Hr. Krug
Titus Dudgeon, }		Hr. Kirschner
Effie, ihre Pflegetochter		Frl. Reingruber
Anthony Anderson, Pastor		Hr. Raeder
Judith, seine Frau		Frl. Lange
Hawkins, Advocat		Hr. Heller
General Burgoyne		**Willy Thaller**
Major Swindon		Hr. Popp
Ein Korporal		Hr. Balajthy
Kaplan Brudonell		Hr. Dürrer
Frau William Dudgeon		Fr. Hirschhuber
Frau Titus Dudgeon		Fr. Wagner
Ein Mann		Hr. Zeigenhofer

Offiziere, Soldaten, Volk.

Ort der Handlung: Eine kleine Stadt in Nordamerika. Zeit: Das Jahr 1777.

* * * Richard Dudgeon — Hr. **Carl Wiene**, kgl. sächs. Hofschauspieler als Gast.

Zwischen dem 2. und 3. Akt ist eine größere Pause.

Cassa=Eröffnung ¹/₇ Uhr.   Anfang 7 Uhr.   Ende gegen ¹/₂ 10 Uhr.

Donnerstag, den 26., Abends halb 8 Uhr, bis inclusive **Samstag**, den 28., Gastspiel des Herrn Carl Wiene, königl. sächsischer Hofschauspieler und Willy Thaller: **Ein Teufelskerl**. — **Sonntag**, den 1. März, Nachmittags halb 3 Uhr bei Abendpreisen, Gastspiel des Herrn Carl Wiene, königl. sächsischer Hofschauspieler und Willy Thaller: **Ein Teufelskerl**. — Abends halb 8 Uhr, Hansi Niese — Willy Thaller: **Der Herr Gemeinderath**. — **Montag**, den 2. und **Dienstag**, den 3., Abends halb 8 Uhr, Gastspiel des Herrn Carl Wiene, königl. sächsischer Hofschauspieler und Willy Thaller: **Ein Teufelskerl**.

F. Brukka & Comp. Wien.

Playbill of *The Devil's Disciple*, Raimund Theater, Vienna. Shaw's first appearance on the German-language stage.

with Es lebe das Leben, which seems to me like a play written by Sardou in the style of Sudermann.[4]

It is very dangerous to judge by newspaper notices; but it seems clear that Wiené was a complete failure, and that the play would have collapsed altogether but for Thaller. The Raimund people should try again with another Dick, another Judith, another Anderson & another Essie, since none of these seem to have made any impression. However, you may tell them that in England a play is rehearsed every day for three weeks, and that every rehearsal is a general rehearsal.[5] In my boyhood I saw the results of the "stock company & star" plan at the Dublin theatre; and it was quite hopeless. If they had played the D's D, Dick would have been a convention called "the juvenile lead," Anderson would have been "the heavy father" complicated with the stage clergyman, Essie would have been "the singing chambermaid," Christie "the joskin," Judith "the leading lady," Swindon "the utility," and so on and so forth, all playing exactly as they would play in every other piece from Shakespear to the latest melodrama, and all personally known by every tone of their voice & every trick of their gait to an audience deadly weary of the whole lot.

—A visitor has just interrupted me. I must break off.

GBS

Als.

1. On 23 February, Shaw wrote to William Archer of the ban on *Arms* in Vienna and its vindicating the play's "verisimilitude" (*Collected Letters*, II). He also wrote to Golding Bright, a young journalist, about the ban, the dispute over *Arms* in Berlin, and the pending production of *Candida* in Dresden, all indicating a "Shaw boom" in Germany (*Advice to a Young Critic*, ed. E. J. West, 1955). Bright placed the news with the *Daily Express* ("'G. B. S.' Censored," 25 February); interviews with Shaw followed.

2. Reuter's reported that *Devil's Disciple* at the Raimund was "on the whole very well received" despite the audience's puzzlement and "indifferent" acting, but the *Daily Chronicle* (26 February) reported "some applause" and predicted failure: "It is badly translated, and the cast was by no means a strong one."

3. Viennese reviewers agreed that Wiené was too old and old-fashioned for Dick Dudgeon and criticized the portly Lange as Judith, but praised Thaller's Burgoyne.

4. Sudermann's *Es lebe das Leben* (English title, *Joy of Living*, 1902) had just opened in London's German Theatre. From Bahr's review of *Devil's Disciple* (*Neues Wiener Tagblatt*, 26 February), which deplored German pseudo-Ibsenism, Shaw deduced that Bahr—who indeed was a playwright—disapproved of *Es lebe*.

5. "General rehearsal," Trebitsch's literal English for *Generalprobe* (actually "dress rehearsal"), misled Shaw.

10 Adelphi Terrace W.C.
6th March 1903

Dear Trebitsch

I am very sorry you have had neuralgia over this business. Dismiss it from your mind now: there is no use bothering about a commercial failure. You have done everything that the oldest hand could have done: the interest was worked up to the utmost; and you contrived to send all the impressionable critics to the theatre quite determined to see something very remarkable, and to imagine they appreciated and enjoyed the play. All this is excellent so far as it gives the failure the air of being like the failure of Tannhäuser in the forties at Dresden: we can say that it is the public that has failed. But still a failure is a failure; so instead of getting neuralgia over it, let us laugh and try again.[1]

I have a heap of press notices; but I have not had time to read more than two or three of the long ones. By far the best was a Viennese one—I forget the name of the paper just now, and I have left the cutting at Woking—in which the writer said that listening to the play was like eating oysters and pretending to like them because it was fashionable.[2] The play, he said, was clever; but it was not kunstlerich [artistic], and did not convince you that the author really had any consistent intention. Now that is the truth. That is what a capable theatregoer ought to feel when confronted with my work and my style for the first time, without having read the play beforehand, as Hermann Bahr no doubt did.[3] It is what I think I should say myself of my own plays if I suddenly came across a performance of them for the first time. You cant feel at home with anything that is strange, no matter how open-minded you may be. Until the critics get used to me, they will feel exactly as this writer felt. As to the public, we cannot even guess whether I shall ever hit their fancy.

You must be charitable to poor Kellner and people like him. When a man has had ardent literary ambitions, and has worked very hard to equip himself with plenty of information, it always seems to him unjust when younger men, in whose work he can see nothing but a handful of mistakes, should suddenly get in front of him, and take from him the place he has aimed at as an original writer. Your contemporaries will never forgive you for being a genius until they are old and broken enough to accept the verdict of the world and to forget the time when you were to them only a damned young fool with whom they went to school. Your elders will never be able to understand it at all, unless they have themselves achieved so high a position that they can afford to make much of you as Haydn made much of Mozart. There is no use in resenting this. Be inexhaustibly patient; and things will gradually change. The older men will die out; the contemporaries will surrender; and the generations of boys to whom you are a literary hero will grow up and fight for you as enthusiastically as they will abuse their own contemporaries and poohpooh those who come after them. Meanwhile say all the nice things about Kellner you can; and never let the world see you angry.

If Schlenther [director of the Burgtheater] hears about the English papers, tell him that the Fabian Society knows everything that happens in Europe. I am still in difficulties as to the publication of the new book [*Man & S*]; but I am afraid it must not wait until October. It is important that when people go away for their holiday in August & September they should take my book with them. I will send you an early set of proofsheets. The translation will be a fearful job: the plays are child's play in comparison.

yrs ever

G. Bernard Shaw

Tls.

1. *Teufelskerl*, Shaw's first staging in the German language, failed. Announced for ten performances, it was withdrawn after four.

2. An allusion to the *Wiener Allgemeine Zeitung*, 27 February: "It was like eating oysters"; no

one dares admit he doesn't like them: "So he swallows them, makes a delighted . . . face and when alone confesses . . . that the stuff doesn't agree with him at all." Several critics mentioned the audience's bewilderment as well as their own.

3. Bahr, elaborating his view that Shaw might revive true Ibsenism in Germany, praised "this devilishly cunning play" (*Neues Wiener Tagblatt*, 26 February). Felix Salten predicted that Shaw, "a remarkable writer," would not soon disappear from the German stage (*Zeit*). The socialist *Arbeiter-Zeitung*, hailing Shaw as perhaps the best living comic writer, laid the play's failure to faulty translation, poor acting, and Shaw's dialectical approach to character and truth.

10 Adelphi Terrace W.C.

20th March 1903

Dear Trebitsch

I havnt time to write an article for the Easter Monday Zeit; but I have sent Salten an article which has been already printed in England, with permission to use it if he likes.[1]

His notice of the D's D. was a very competent one, and was—as well as I can judge—the best criticism of the acting that appeared.

As to the position of Die Zeit, I am not at all in the dark about that. I wrote for Dr Kanner long before the daily Zeit was thought of.[2] However, I shall not write many feuilletons for German papers. They pay me £4; and I have applications from American magazines for articles at £40; so you need not fear my taking to German journalism except when there is something special in hand like the D's D.

I hope you did not go to Berlin to see Helden. It was not worth while. I would not go ten miles myself to see it.

As to the order in which you take the translations, all I can suggest is that if we have any success in Berlin you are much more likely to have demands for You Never Can Tell and Captain Brassbound's Conversion than for such a big & expensive affair as Caesar & Cleopatra. But perhaps that is all the better reason for getting Caesar done before the demand for the others begins.[3]

I have no personal preference in the matter, except for the English order of the plays with their prefaces. As that has been departed from, the rest is really a question of your own convenience and of the requirements of the managers. Besides, I am so occupied with my new volume that the others seem to me to be ancient history.

They have sent me a picture of Wiené, Judith & Anderson.[4] Wiené is just what I expected: a majestic ruin, looking like Possart's[5] grandfather. Anderson a wooden stage person without a ray of humor or geniality. Wiené would have done excellently for Anderson. Judith is prettier & younger than I expected. I took it for granted that she would be 50 & very fat.

When do you start for Provence? I must take a holiday at Easter, myself.

yrs ever

G. Bernard Shaw

Als.

1. Felix Salten (1869–1945) was literary editor of *Die Zeit*; his fame as novelist and playwright lay ahead.

2. Shaw did not appear in *Die Zeit* during the Easter season: his "Illusions of Socialism" had appeared in *Die Zeit*, co-founded by Kanner, in 1896.

The Devil's Disciple, final scene, Raimund Theater, 1903. Central figures (left to right) are: Karl Wiené (Dick Dudgeon), Hedwig Lange (Judith), Arthur Raeder (Anderson), Willy Thaller (Burgoyne), Wilhelm Popp (Swindon).

3. After *Man of Destiny* Trebitsch turned to *Caesar* before the earlier *You Never Can Tell*.
4. Photographs of the Raimund *Teufelskerl* appeared in *Bühne und Welt* in April.
5. Ernst von Possart (1841–1921), actor-director in Munich, belonged to an earlier generation of declamatory performers and was even older than Wiené.

Maybury Knoll. Woking
24th March 1903

Dear Trebitsch

I have not seen Kellner's article:[1] no doubt it will be sent to me presently. But in the mean time you must not move a muscle. There is no getting over the iron fact that the play has failed; and now it is Kellner's turn to amuse himself at our expense and to revenge himself for my article. We must take our defeat without flinching, and without the slightest sign of ill humor. If you meet Kellner you must not box his ears: you must smile from ear to ear and drag him off at once to the best restaurant in Vienna and give him a first-rate luncheon. Make him drunk if possible, and give him better cigars than he has ever been able to afford for himself. Whether in this affair or in any other, you must never exhibit yourself to the public as a man with a grievance. Never admit that anything that any mortal man can say or write could make the smallest difference to your reputation or to your personal serenity. Remember that of all earthly spectacles the most ridiculous and the most unpitied by the public is that of an author smarting and raging under criticism.

There is only one way of confuting Kellner, and that is by a successful production in Berlin. Until that comes Kellner can enjoy himself to his heart's content; and you must admit, with enchanting politeness, that Dr Kellner is fully entitled to his opinion, and is no doubt perfectly honest in it.

I quite expect that when the Frankfurter Zeitung arrives I shall be delighted with the article. A failure is half a success when it leaves a controversy behind. It is better to be attacked than to be forgotten; and critics are so fond of contradicting one another that the moment Kellner attacks us, all the people who dislike Kellner will attack him. We shall thus find plenty of defenders without condescending to defend ourselves.

Kellner writes and speaks English quite as well as you do, and probably a great deal better. Kellner is exactly the sort of man to master a foreign language: that is why you call him a schoolmaster. Now you are the sort of man that never masters a foreign language; and for the life of me I cannot understand how you have forced yourself to learn as much as you know. The correct attitude for you to take on such points is to say with a great appearance of humility, "I do not profess to be a linguist or a mathematician: I am merely a man of genius; and if these three plays which I have translated are really original inventions of my own, all I can say is that I think they reflect great credit on me and that Shaw ought to be greatly obliged to me for letting me [him] have the fame of their authorship."

yours ever
G. Bernard Shaw

Tls.

1. On 17 March, Kellner appeared in the *Frankfurter Zeitung* with "Bernhard Shaw. Eine Charakteristik," in which he gloated over the failure of *Teufelskerl* as proof of Trebitsch's incompetence, which he condemned in even more offensive terms.

[Maybury Knoll. Woking]
31st March 1903

Dear Trebitsch

You are the most ungrateful man alive. Kellner's article is ausgezeichnetissimus [superexcellent]. That is what has got us the offer from Frankfurt to do the Sch[l]achtenlenker[1] (which will be a worse failure than the Teufelskerl, as it requires Virtuosen of the first order to act it). It is true that he calls you a Sekundaner [fifth form pupil]; but then he tells the Frankfurt managers that all the literary people in Vienna took the Shaw boom up and swore that your translations were masterpieces and that he was only a Philologer; and he also tells them that you organized the réclame to perfection, which will impress them more than if he said that I was Goethe & Shakespere & you Tieck & Schlegel[2] rolled into one. He flatters me to the skies just as I flattered him: all that description of me is calculated to make people far more curious to see the plays than any ordinary favorable criticism.

Your article is totally, utterly, completely, ausserordenlicherly,[3] insanely out of the question. To begin with, it is a defence of yourself; and you must NEVER defend yourself. Worse than that, you reply to a thrust clean through the body with a pin prick. He says the piece ran for two nights only. You reply that he is a liar: it ran *three*!!! Good Heavens! does that matter? Everybody will forget the two nights until they hear about your triumphant three; and then they will laugh so much that it will be remembered forever. As to the spelling of my name, he is quite right to Germanise it. In England I do not write Michelagnolo or Händel, but Michael Angelo & Handel. You mustnt pick up *little* stones to throw at your adversaries: they dont hurt & they always get thrown back. Besides, you are wrong about my references to Kellner in Die Zeit. I meant to praise him: it would be in my eyes the most horrible crime against "altirischer Gastfreundlichkeit" [old Irish hospitality] to say that my guest had bored me with his billiards & his conversation. In fact you are all wrong, because you are not accustomed to be shot at in the newspapers. As for me, I am all over bullet marks; and I have come to enjoy the noise of the fusillade: it advertises me.

Bahr ought to be much obliged to Kellner, who does not disparage him, or say he is unknown, or that I am a libertine. On the contrary, it was Bahr who disparaged Kellner as an old pedant.

I must take poor Kellner under my protection, I see. I think his abuse of your slips in translation is wildly exaggerated; but there is no effective reply to that except perfect goodhumor & imperturbability. If you want me to see the depth of his villainy, you must induce him to abuse *me*.

Shall I put your letter in the fire? I want you to forget Kellner & go to

Provence & cure your neuralgia. Dont bother about Frankfurt: they will cut the Schlachtenlenker & spoil it and worry you out of your life. Go straight to the Rhone & forget all about Drei Dramen von

> yrs ever
> G. Bernard Shaw

Als.

1. Trebitsch had placed *Man of Destiny* (*Schlachtenlenker*) with the Neues Schauspielhaus, Frankfurt. In "Bernhard Shaw," Kellner had quoted admiringly from *Man of Destiny* and offered an intriguing portrait of Shaw as first-rate satirist, while contesting Bahr's defense of Trebitsch in "Bernard Shaw," *Neues Wiener Tagblatt* (7 February).

2. Ludwig Tieck (1773–1853) and August von Schlegel (1767–1845), collaborators in the classic German translation of Shakespeare.

3. "Extraordinarily," another Shavian humorous coinage.

> 10 Adelphi Terrace W.C.
> 12th June 1903

Dear Trebitsch

Ouf!!! I have been nearly killed by the rehearsals of my greatest play— "The Admirable Bashville." [1] However, I got an admirable cast (for nothing) and it went with a roar from beginning to end. The policeman made himself up like me; and my aunt firmly believes that I actually played the part. It was hard work; and writing letters, except to the cast, was out of the question.

Yes: Caesar & Cleopatra is too long; but the only remedy is to omit the third act—the lighthouse act. It is a pity; but it would be a still greater pity to mutilate the rest.

I shall send you a Perfect Wagnerite presently. [2] I am waiting for a new & correct edition.

The new book [*Man and Superman*] is now *printed*—not published. As soon as I can spare a complete set of proofs I will send it to you.

> In haste
> ever
> G. Bernard Shaw

Als.

1. The first professional production of Shaw's "literary joke," *The Admirable Bashville*, by the Stage Society at the Imperial Theatre, London, opened on 7 June, with Ben Webster and Henrietta Watson. C. Aubrey Smith (1863–1948), who later had an outstanding film career in Hollywood, was the policeman.

2. Shaw's *The Perfect Wagnerite* (1898), reissued with minor revisions in 1902, was about to be reprinted with a brief new preface.

> [Maybury Knoll. Woking]
> 21st June 1903

Dear Trebitsch

You know all about "The Admirable Bashville," or at least you would know if you ever read my books. Surely I gave you a novel of mine entitled Cashel Byron's Profession [revised ed., 1901]. At the end of it you will find a dramatic version in Shakesperean blank verse—pure tomfoolery. It was performed by the Stage Society here as a joke to wind up the last evening of the season. I had a very good cast; and there was great laughter, and as many press notices as if it had been Caesar and Cleopatra at Drury Lane. It would be impossible to translate it, first, because it would be necessary to raise Tieck and Schlegel from the grave to write the blank verse, and second, because the hero is a prizefighter, and Germans know nothing about English Prizefighting, and would not enjoy a burlesque of it.

As to going through Caesar in 3 or 4 days, I suppose that was a slip of the pen for three or four months. I will do my best; but I am overwhelmed just now with business connected with the publication of the new book; and I am much more likely to keep Caesar six weeks than three days.

As to your suggestion of a preface by Brandes, I can only say that if the publisher is fool enough to spend his money on it, I shall not stand between Brandes and the job.[1] But if you will read the middle section of my own preface to Three Plays for Puritans, you will see what I think of these silly prefaces which are nothing but publishers' advertisements. What I want for Caesar is either my own preface—the section entitled Better than Shakespear?—or else the sort of preface that you wrote to the Drei Dramen that is to say a general biographical introduction of myself to the German public.

I got a tremendous heap of Press notices of the Frankfort performance.[2] I tried to wade through them all, but broke down at the end of the first half dozen or so. However I read sufficient to gather that the result was a hideous failure. I have seen the Schlachtenlenker performed twice. Once, when I stagemanaged it myself,[3] it was bearable, and even passed for a success. On the other occasion,[4] when I had nothing to do with the rehearsals, it was so unendurably dull that I could hardly sit it out without hissing, and was amazed at the patience of the audience. Still, that will not harm us. Of course it would put a stop to everything if actors and managers had any sense. But as it is, they cling affectionately to failures, and are afraid of nothing but strength and success.

Nobody will be in London in the first week of September. We shall be at the seaside from the end of July to the beginning of October; but we have not yet decided on the particular place. Anyhow, we must contrive to see you.

Give my love to Kellner if you meet him.

yrs ever
G. Bernard Shaw

Tls.

1. Trebitsch sent his version of *Caesar* to Shaw for correction; it appeared the next year without a preface by Brandes.

2. *Schlachtenlenker*, staged by Emil Claar, opened at the Neues Schauspielhaus, Frankfurt, on 20 April as part of a triple bill, with Richard Kirch and Marie Laue, and ran only two nights. The *Frankfurter Zeitung* (21 April) found Shaw clever and original but negligent of stage demands and denigrating of Napoleon.

3. A performance at the Comedy Theatre, London, on 29 March 1901, with Granville Barker and Margaret Halstan.

4. At the Grand Theatre, Croydon, on 1 July 1897.

10 Adelphi Terrace W.C.

20th July 1903

Dear Trebitsch

I havent answered a private letter for months. The business of getting my new book through the press and arranging for its publication has been overwhelming, as I have changed publishers both in London & America; and I have been full of my ordinary work, both literary & political, into the bargain.[1]

Caesar & Cleopatra will take me some time to correct. The dialogue is, as usual, excellent; [but the descriptions and stage directions are full of the . . . disastrous errors . . . , which would make Kellner . . . with joy].[2] However, you will see when I return your copy all scrawled over with notes, how much remains to be done.

I got the Schlachtenlenker safely, but have not had time to read Bahr's dialogue.[3] Schnitzler[4] must be a very sensible man: his remarks on C & C. seem to me to be in the best possible taste.

As to the director of the Neues Theater [Max Reinhardt], I am sorry for the poor devil, as the play will probably fail—in fact it certainly will unless he can find an extraordinarily able and interesting actor for Caesar.[5] However, nothing succeeds like failure. You must have read it very well to capture him so promptly.

I suppose we had better go halves, as usual, in the payments by the Rundschau & other magazines—that is, if you are satisfied with such very slender remuneration for your trouble. For my part I am quite willing to depend on the tantièmes [royalties] alone, and leave magazine articles entirely to you.[6] But for Heaven's sake be careful about the copyright. In this unhappy country a magazine article cannot be republished for 23 years without the consent of the magazine proprietor, unless the copyright is specially reserved by the author.

I shall go to Scotland at the end of next week for a two months holiday. We have chosen a place on the west coast, about four hours journey from Glasgow westward, near the Kyles of Bute. Rather a long way from Cromer, I am afraid; but perhaps you will come to Scotland.

yrs ever

G. Bernard Shaw

Als.

1. For *Man and Superman*, Shaw had sought to replace Grant Richards and H. S. Stone, his English and American publishers, respectively. After considerable difficulties, Shaw printed the work at his own expense and arranged with Constable of London to serve thereafter as his publisher on commission. In America, Shaw settled for formal copyright.

2. Segment canceled by Trebitsch but partly legible.

3. *Schlachtenlenker* had just appeared in the leading Berlin journal *Neue Rundschau* (July 1903), which also contained Bahr's "Dialog vom Tragischen," a cultural and psychoanalytic study of tragedy.

4. Arthur Schnitzler (1862–1931), Vienna's leading playwright and author of *Anatol, Reigen,* and *Liebelei,* was a friend of Trebitsch and either saw Trebitsch's translation of *Caesar* or attended the reading of the play.

5. The Neues Theater, Berlin (seating 890), had been acquired by the rising star Max Reinhardt (1873–1943), Austrian-born actor-manager, who also managed the Kleines Theater. His young

company was on summer tour in Vienna where Trebitsch met Reinhardt, aroused his interest in *Candida*, and invited him to a reading of *Caesar*. Reinhardt, gravitating toward spectacle, contracted to do the play.

6. Trebitsch did not accept Shaw's offer to forgo sharing the meager German magazine fees.

[Maybury Knoll.] Woking
26th July 1903

Dear Trebitsch

The very utmost I can do now is to send you the first act [of *Caesar*]. It is not possible for me to skip the dialogue; for though Schnitzler is quite right as to its excellence, yet here and there you have made a little slip which would prove very puzzling to the actors. Sometimes you make an improvement without considering its consequences or its antecedents; and although the sentence, taken by itself, is better than my sentence, it does not belong to the chain of thought and does not lead to the answer.

Certain words always set you wrong. [Sentence canceled by Trebitsch.] And you do not read your Bible. However, you will find this all explained in detail on the scrip.

As to the stage directions it is impossible to be too particular. With all my care—and I worked the whole thing out carefully on a model stage with a map of Alexandria before me—I forgot to get Apollodorus off the stage in the fourth act. The great difficulty is to give all the necessary directions for the stage management without spoiling the book for the reader by using technical terms.

As to Fischer,[1] everything depends on the terms of his contract. It *must* be a terminable one: nothing will induce me to bind myself to any publisher for more than five years, even if I have to print the prompt copies myself. And a half-profits agreement is out of the question. Do not listen to the advice of your friends: all authors are duffers in business: and all publishers are sharks. Remember that if the play is produced with any success we can make better terms than we can now; and we must not pay too dearly for the convenience of having the books printed. Fischer must not put the agency into the publishing contract as a condition. He may be a failure as an agent; and in that case we must be free to hand the play over to Entsch without disturbing the publishing arrangement.

Is it possible that I received a cheque from you and forgot to acknowledge it? What a shame! When I return to London on Wednesday I will send you a formal receipt.

I have just met the most beautiful Shavian I have ever seen.[2] She is the wife of one of our diplomatic staff, who is joining the British Embassy in Vienna very soon. I think I will ask her to correct your translations: you can make mistakes on purpose.

yrs ever
G. Bernard Shaw

Als.

1. Samuel Fischer (1859–1934), founder of the S. Fischer Verlag, Berlin, leading publisher of modern authors, including Ibsen, Tolstoy, Dostoevski, Hauptmann, Schnitzler, Bahr, etc., had re-

cently founded a theatrical agency and offered to become Shaw's publisher and agent for those new translations not placed with Cotta or Entsch.
2. She remains unidentified.

[Springburn. Strachur]
2nd July [August] 1903

Dear Trebitsch

My work on C & C has been interrupted by the journey down here; but I will resume it tomorrow.[1] It is a slow business, because I dont know the language: in fact, I have not yet got to the end of the second act. The dialogue is very good; but there are misunderstandings enough to make it necessary that I should go through every sentence carefully lest Kellner should return to the charge. . . .

yrs ever
G. Bernard Shaw

Als.
   1. The Shaws left for Scotland on 1 August.

Springburn. Strachur
4th August 1903

Trebitsch, Trebitsch, du bist ganz und gar unverbesserlich [you are altogether incorrigible]. I tell you you are utterly, totally, completely and absolutely wrong about the stage directions, and I am u, t, c & a right about them. What you must do is this. Write a translator's preface; and explain all your departures from custom. Explain that one of the most important things I have done in England is to effect a reform in the printing of plays. Say that the English people had for a whole century absolutely refused to read plays, although they had been free from the ridiculous French convention of Sz [scene] 27—Die Vorige und ein Diener [the same with servant]—two lines and then—Sz 28, Die Vorige, ohne [without] der Diener. Mention the fact that, curiously enough, in the first play I ever printed [*Widowers' Houses*, 1893] I introduced this silly fashion myself, and, in doing so, cured myself for ever of such folly. Nobody bought that play: the English people have too much imagination to tolerate these conventions. I then set to work to make plays readable. I abolished the list of characters at the beginning. I introduced them as they entered by descriptions as elaborate & far more concise than those of Tolstoy and Turgenieff. I never made any reference to the stage technically, never used the words "enter" or "exit," never shattered the reader's dream by the smell of the footlights, and yet concealed in my apparently purely poetic directions a technical specification for the stage manager far more detailed and complete than any author has ever given before.

Now *you* think me an old ass, and coolly propose to undo all my work and reduce my reformed drama to the old silly prompt book. "Not at all important" you call it. It is *all*-important. You say that every manager will alter for his stage as he likes & that you will only be present at Berlin & Vienna. Infant that you are! I tell you that managers are the most slavish copiers of the metropolis in the world. What is done at Berlin & Vienna will be reproduced without a single original idea everywhere in Germany, Austria, Poland, Switzerland & probably Russia. And of what use will your presence be in Vienna or Austria unless you have the whole stage business at your fingers' ends? An author who is not thus prepared is paid a few empty compliments & pushed into a corner at rehearsal. I get the command of my rehearsals, not because I am the author, but because I stop all the compliments & introductions by rushing at the work, placing the chairs to mark the entrances &c, and leading on the actors to their right places, which they presently find to be the most effective places for themselves. I get through the first act and say "Now let's run through that act again" before the stage manager has finished staring at me. I never assert my authority, and never give an order: I simply tell them what to do; and when they see that I know my business they leave it all to me & appeal to me whenever they are in doubt. Mind! it is hard work: I have to slave at it the night before like a schoolboy until I have learnt my lesson; but the result is well worth the trouble. All this you will have to do; and unless you make the directions clear you will not be able to do it. You are young & have plenty of time for this. I am old—47—and can ill afford to waste a moment. Yet I think it important enough.[1]—Historisches Schauspiel [Chronicle Play] is the right term [for *Caesar*].[2]—I do not object to the book giving the *cast* of the first performance, provided it is not made part of the play. See Mrs Warren z.b. [e.g.].

GBS

Als.

1. Henceforth in his translations Trebitsch discarded the convention, followed in *Drei Dramen*, of numbering each entrance and exit as a scene change, but he continued to supply lists of characters and ended each act with "Curtain."

2. Shaw's subtitle for *Caesar* was "A Page of History" (later "A History"); Trebitsch settled for "Eine historische Komödie."

Springburn. Strachur
10th August 1903

Dear Trebitsch

You are perfectly mad—mad as a hatter. You were as anxious as possible about that Raimund Theater affair, at which we could do nothing but send poor old Wiené back to his grandchildren, a ruined man; and now that this Berlin performance, on which our whole fate depends, is coming on, you calmly tell me "not to be too careful about Caesar." I am working like a slave at it; and you must not omit the smallest detail, or neglect the most trifling precaution, to ensure a good performance. When you have provided for every possible contingency, and left your part of the work as good as your utmost faculty can make it, then it will be time to trust to luck & leave the management to lose its 20,000 marks [£1,000; c. $5,000] (it should be 120,000—20,000 is not half enough) or double them, as the gods may decree.

Now first—and this is most important and must be done within the next ten minutes. Write to the manager [Max Reinhardt] to stop the designing of the scenery &c until he has our plans & sketches. If they get the scenery

wrong—and they cannot help doing so if they work from your stage directions, which are DISASTROUSLY inaccurate—the whole play will be thrown
into confusion, and the stage business will be found impracticable. If the
scenes are right, it will be as easy as possible; and we shall save a month of
changing and disputing & mangling the play to suit the mistakes of the
painters & machinists.

Will you find out for me *at once* what the mechanical resources of the
Neues Theater are. All I want to know is, 1 Have they an electric turntable?
2 Have they hydraulic bridges? 3 Have they hydraulic clutches—that is,
ropes to draw up weights from above—or is everything pushed up by a
piston from below?[1] 4 What is the depth of the stage from the footlights to
the back wall & what is its width from side to side? Promise them drawings.
I cannot draw; but I can make the painters and carpenters understand what I
mean. . . .

yrs
G.B.S.

Als.
   1. All these devices were designed to speed scene changes and had already appeared in Germany,
which had pioneered the turntable stage. Reinhardt ordered a turntable stage built for the Neues
Theater—the first in Berlin—where it went into manual operation the following year. The Neues
also had clutches, but they were apparently not hydraulic; nor did the theatre have hydraulic
bridges.

Springburn. Strachur
16th August 1903

My dear Trebitsch

Your letter arrived yesterday—Saturday evening—too late to post the IV &
V acts [of *Caesar*] to you. Today is Sunday; and in Scotland nothing can be
done on Sunday except go to church. So I cannot post this & register it until
tomorrow. Perhaps you will get it on Wednesday.

As to Fischer, there is only one thing I really care about; and that is the
time limit of the agreement. It must be limited either to a definite number of
copies or to a term of years. The royalty[1] is a very good one—the same as I
get in England; but the main thing is that if Fischer turns out badly, if he
does not advertize & push the book properly, if he takes to drink, or goes
mad, or files a petition in bankruptcy, we must not be tied helplessly to him
for ever and ever. I have just paid £60 to secure the American copyright of
my new book [*Man and Superman*] by printing it in America at my own
cost sooner than let the Macmillan Company have it without a time limit.

By the way, if Cotta reproaches you for giving this book to Fischer, you
may tell him that I was so dissatisfied with the half-profits agreement that I
would not hear of any further dealings with him.

And now as to C & C. The corrections are very important, because the production in Berlin, whether successful or not—but especially if successful—
will not crush Kellner: it will, on the contrary, give him a much better
chance than he had before of taking your scalp. His article in the Wiener
Tagblatt did not matter outside Vienna; and even in Vienna it was possible to
counter it by the Zeit articles, my own, Bahr's &c &c. But a Berlin produc-

tion at the Neues Theater will create a demand for magazine articles on me, just as the production of Cyrano here created a demand for magazine articles on Rostand[2] in England & America. Kellner, who lives, I suppose, by his pen, is pretty sure to seize the opportunity to earn the price of a magazine article. And if Kellner sets the fashion of saying that there are blunders in the translation, all the others will follow suit; for 99 out of a 100 of them cannot read English; but all of them will have to pretend that they speak & read it like natives. The bigger the success the more articles there will be. Therefore now is the time to give no chance to the enemy. This is why I have brought down a huge Muret-Sanders dictionary here and spent a month revising a translation in a language that I have never learnt. In future I will make the translation and you shall revise it. The dialogue seems to me to be just as good as the original and sometimes better; but still there are lots of mistakes. Mistakes dont matter: they can always be corrected, and they dont kill a play even if they are left uncorrected; but they are just what Kellner wants for a slashing review. For instance, he could write ten pages about Rufio swearing by Zeus instead of by Jove; and as to the centurion's cudgel being changed into the Dionysiac Thyrsusstab, you would never hear the end of it. You race recklessly through these things, which dont interest you. You care for nothing but the drama. That is just as it should be, as the drama is the main thing. But you give yourself away to the people who are interested in Roman history, Roman politics & Roman institutions. And indeed you ought to be interested in them. A true dramatist should be interested in everything. Kellner would write ten pages of the most erudite Roman history to shew that only the most ungebildeter Uebersetzer [uneducated translator] could possibly make Lucius Septimius call the Okkupationsarmée "rebels," or indeed mention such a delicate subject as rebellion to Caesar at all. So be very careful to set all these little things right. I should not have sweated over them all these days if I were not convinced that they would get you into trouble.

Barbarous as my drawings of the scenery are, a great deal depends on them. Even an ordinary modern play like [Sudermann's] Es Lebe das Leben, with drawingroom scenes throughout, depends a good deal on the author writing his dialogue with a clear plan of stage action in his head; but in a play like Caesar it is absolutely necessary: the staging is just as much a part of the play as the dialogue. It will not do to let a scenepainter & a sculptor loose on the play without a specification of the conditions with which their scenery must comply. Will you therefore tell the Neues manager that we will supply sketches. I will not inflict my own draughtsmanship on him; but I will engage a capable artist here to make presentable pictures.

Now as to all this obsolete powder & pigtail—Szene VIII—Die Vorige &c &c—! There is no point in the Schlachtenlenker or in the Drei Dramen at which these silly interpolations are positively insufferable; but in the 4th act of C & C. there are two places at least in which they are simply an outrage. Believe me, nobody will miss them. If their disappearance would incommode anybody I should not be so cocksure about omitting them; but I am so certain that they will die unlamented and even unnoticed that if I were you I should not even mention the matter in a preface. I only suggested that, in order to break the innovation to you as gently as possible. When you meet a foolish superstition, dont stop to remonstrate or argue or apologize: walk straight through it as if it didnt exist. As the American poetess (Charlotte Stetson) says in her poem "The Prejudice"[3]—

> "I simply walked straight through it
> As if it wasnt there."

and that is what we must do with this nonsensical pedantry. If anybody points out that we have affected an audacious reform, so much the better for us; but I am afraid the blow will be so completely in the water—in the sense that there will be no resistance to it—that we shall have to do without that useful advertisement.

As to waiting for a success, do you realize that if Caesar fails we shall never have another chance? You must never wait for anything. We must plank everything on this production. We must do everything on the assumption that it is going to be a triumph, and that its failure will be the end of all things. As to thinking twice as to such a trumpery affair as this "Die Vorige &c" business, that would be absurd. Of course the play *may* fail. Very likely it will; for as you, being an Austrian, very well know, the Germans are as stupid as any people under the sun, and are not a bit likely to treat me better than they treated Wagner—except that they adore foreigners & despise themselves. But what then? We shall simply begin again, & treat the next production in the same way, as if it, too, were the crisis of our destiny. That is the way things are done in this world. Meanwhile be as peculiar & as affected & as conceited & as bizarre as you possibly can about the trifles whose importance exists only in the imaginations of the journalists & *flaneurs*. Reserve your seriousness for the real things of which they know nothing. If the play fails, I hope they will say that my plays are only good to read; for then the public will buy them from Fischer.

I do not object to the cast being published. You will find it in Mrs Warren. But there must not be an idiotic list of nameless characters, ending with "soldiers, citizens, boatmen, performing dogs &c &c &c."[4]

If Hauptamme wont do, let Ftata call herself Kronamme or Königlichamme or Reichs Amme or something pretentious & prahlerisch [boastful].

Now as to Pilum. Mommsen's[5] "Wurfspiess" is *vieux jeu* [old fashioned]: it dates from 1871, when Bismarck & the Germans affected an extravagant Nationalism and called the telephone the Fernsprecher. Nowadays Nationalism has expanded into Imperialism; and ancient Rome is fashionable. The Kaiser will see himself as Caesar; and when Britannus says "Only as Caesar's slave have I found true freedom" he will give an enthusiastic Hoch & decorate you with the Iron Cross. I have carefully considered all this before recommending you to call the Pilum by its Roman name; and I am still of that opinion—more than ever, in fact.

If Bahr disagrees with me on this or any other point, it shews that he needs a holiday. The work of the season has been too much for him.

Yes Du der Du is all right: I became resigned to it after the 6th or 7th time.

I never heard of Rodenbach.[6] The Sold Smile[7] suggests women & love—the most tedious subjects on earth. However, I am delighted to find that you have not been sacrificing your own work to mine. When is the Verkauft[e] Lächeln to appear?

I forgot to say that you have not translated the notes to C & C. This is a fearful insult to me. I cherish those notes beyond all the rest of the play. You must translate them. . . .

And now as to your visit. It sounds inhospitable; but I seriously advise you not to come unless you make up your mind to take a Scotch holiday. It would be easier for me to go to London than to Scarborough or Cromer, because the railway journey from Glasgow to London is much faster than the cross-country journeys to intermediate places off the main line. As to meeting you in Glasgow, that would be very dismal indeed. If you come so far, you may as well take the rest of the trip by steamer from Gourock. You would, by leaving Glasgow at 8:45 a.m., go to Gourock by train (a short journey) and then go on board the Lord of the Isles (you can get a reasonably good lunch on board), go through the Kyles of Bute and up Loch Fyne, and land at Strachur at about 2 in the afternoon. Most likely it will rain—it has rained almost continuously since we came here on the 1st Aug. To do this for one day would be absurd: you had better come for a week, or for as long as you can bear it. I can imagine no place more dreadful to a Viennese. There is no railway, no town, no shops, no society, no music, no entertainments, no beautiful ladies, absolutely nothing but fresh air and eternal rain. Our house is primitive; our food is primitive; we do nothing but wander about, cycle against impossible winds, or pull a heavy fisherman's boat about the loch when the weather is fair enough. If you like this sort of thing, come by all means: you can write as much as you like—indeed there is nothing else to do. But if you dont like it, let nothing induce you to come; for you can get away only once a day, and you would commit suicide in twelve hours at most.[8]

I must now positively stop: everything is said.

> yrs ever
> G. Bernard Shaw

P.S. One more thing I forgot to warn you of. Wine is unknown here: whiskey is the only beverage. Charlotte says that if I tell you all these things you will think I dont want you to come; but as a matter of fact I dont: the expense & fatigue of the journey are far too great for a one day visit. Except for this we should both be delighted to see you; and, after all, the place is very pretty.

Als.

1. Fischer agreed to a 20 percent royalty and the next year issued *Schlachtenlenker.*

2. Edmund Rostand (1868–1918), French playwright and author of the popular *Cyrano de Bergerac* (1898).

3. The correct title is "An Obstacle." Charlotte Stetson Gilman (1860–1935) was an American feminist, poet, and socialist.

4. Trebitsch corrected his version of *Caesar* as Shaw suggested but retained a list of characters and *Wurfspiess* for "Pilum."

5. Theodor Mommsen (1817–1903), distinguished German historian, whose study of Caesar was used by Shaw.

6. Georges Rodenbach (1855–1898), French-Belgian playwright, whose *Le Mirage*, translated by Trebitsch (*Trugbild*), was soon to open at the Deutsches Theater, Berlin (12 September).

7. *Das verkaufte Lächeln* (The Sold Smile), Trebitsch's latest tale, concerned an inwardly pure woman who declines into prostitution. It was rejected by Fischer but published by the Wiener Verlag (1905).

8. Trebitsch did not visit Shaw that fall but instead went on "cure" to Dresden.

Strachur. Argyllshire
18th September 1903

Dear Trebitsch

Forgive my not writing to you; but—as usual in holiday time—I am heavily occupied politically. The whole country here is convulsed by Chamberlain's proposal to abandon Free Trade.[1] He is to open his campaign by a great speech in Glasgow on the 6th Oct. Well, *I* am going to make a great speech in Glasgow on the 2nd on the same subject; and I am up to the neck in statistics & blue books in consequence.

I received Archer's article[2] & Terra Cotta's a/c safely. Thanks for both. I will return the latter as soon as I have made a memorandum of it to put among my London papers.

We can leave the Perfect Wagnerite aside for the moment. Of course a great deal of it has been said before; but some of it is at present being fiercely disputed by the Bayreuth people, not à propos of my book, but of Ellis's translation of Glasenapp's Life of Wagner.[3]

I feel sure you are spoiling the dialogue of Caesar with your revisions. It was admirable as it stood except for a mere mistake or two. Correct it by all means; but dont *polish* it: why perfume the sea air? a little roughness is all the better. Translate the notes instead. They are of *enormous* importance: the one on Caesar's character has in it the foundations of a whole philosophy. Or better still, get back to something of your own. . . .

I am greatly mortified by your saying that you dont know 10 works as good as Caesar published within the last 15 years. It reminds me of the Suisse at the Haymarket Theatre, who said to Beerbohm Tree[4] "I dont suppose, sir, there are more than six actors in London who could play Hamlet equal to you." Who are these 9 imposters who pretend to have written anything comparable to my masterpiece?

Meyerfeld[5] has extracted from my publisher a review copy of the Superman, which has made a considerable sensation here.

I have stupidly mislaid your Berlin address & must send this to Vienna.

yrs ever
G. Bernard Shaw

PS What is Dr Lahmann's special sort of quackery.[6] Is it cotton wool, or chopped meat & hot water, or vegetarianism, or what?

Als.

1. Joseph Chamberlain (1836–1914), leader of the Liberal Party, called for a protectionist policy—a position Shaw supported.

2. William Archer's "Das moderne Drama in England" (*Die Zeit*, 2 September) blamed the low level of English drama and Shaw's failures in England on the commercial London system of theatre and its fashionable audience.

3. Shaw's *The Perfect Wagnerite*, recently reprinted, stressed Wagner's revolutionary activities in 1848 and interpreted the *Ring* as anticapitalist allegory. Volume III of Carl Glasenapp's *Life of Richard Wagner*, in Ashton Ellis's English version (1903), dealt with the years 1849–1853 and the composition of the *Ring*.

4. Herbert Beerbohm Tree (1852–1917), the noted English actor-manager, collected anecdotes, real and invented.

5. Max Meyerfeld (1875–1952), German Anglist and translator, had reviewed *Drei Dramen* and seconded Kellner against Trebitsch (*Literarische Echo*, 1 May 1903).

6. Dr. Heinrich Lahmann's Sanatorium, Dresden, was patronized by many Fischer authors and specialized in "metabolism, reducing, rejuvenation, and diabetes cures."

10 Adelphi Terrace W.C.
7th October 1903

Dear Trebitsch

Here I am back in London, with a mountain of dull correspondence to deal with. I shall have time for only a line or two.

My exploits as a mob orator in Glasgow were highly successful;[1] and I have hardly yet quite recovered from the self-loathing which such triumphs produce. I am an incorrigible mountebank; but I always suffer torments of remorse when the degrading exhibition is over. However, the thing had to be done; and there was no use doing it by halves. I was in good training, and delivered two harangues of ninety minutes each, besides a roaring quarter hour oration at another meeting, where I was invited to the platform and yelled for by the intelligent Scotch proletariat. I am not at all ashamed of what I said: it was excellent sense; but the way I said it—ugh! All that prodigious expenditure of nervous energy—that assumption of stupendous earnestness—merely to drive a little common sense into a crowd, like nails into a very tough board—leaves one empty, exhausted, disgusted.

And now the worst of it is that I shall have to set to work to write a Fabian Manifesto on the subject instead of setting to at a new play—or rather at the abominable book on Municipal Trading that I have to finish first.[2] That is the secret of the greatness of my dramatic masterpieces: I have to work like a dog at the most sordid things between every hundred lines.

My rage about the Caesarian cuts did not hurt me much. I always get into a rage very carefully and conscientiously when it is necessary, because it saves a lot of time and makes people realize my opinion vividly and promptly; but my indignation, as you probably guess, is purely histrionic—mere mountebanking! I knew you would not find C&C cuttable. I cut everything out of it that could be spared before I published it—including, by the way, a lovely scene in which Caesar received four ambassadors in succession and humbugged them all.

The Superman play, with a big cut in the scene between Ann and Tanner in the first act, and the omission of the dream, would make an amusing comedy: perhaps I may try it at the Stage Society. But it would suffer greatly in German, because the Irishman and his American son would be much stranger and less interesting than in England.

If you ever try your hand on Brassbound, let me know before you begin, as the part of the cockney is absolutely unintelligible to anyone who has not lived twenty years in London and included several costermongers among his personal friends. I will have it copied out for you in normal spelling. I think you are wrong in dismissing it as an impracticable play. In some ways it is unique. Take your Austrian actress Odilon,³ for example. She is getting too old to stand the competition of pretty young women side by side with her on the stage. But in Brassbound she has a great part, and no other woman in the play, the want of bright costumes (usually supplied by the women's dresses) being supplied in Brassbound by the costumes of the Arabs. It is a tremendously effective part for a comedy actress of the first order, though no use at all for a second rater. Therefore, though until you find your Odilon the play is worthless, yet when you do find her it is the only one of my plays that she is likely to want—and to want very badly. Widowers' Houses, ugly as it is, is a very effective stage play, especially for Berlin audiences, who are trained not to mind a little squalor. The part of Lickcheese is one of the best for a character actor in my whole repertory: it made the reputation of James Welch here in London even at a desperately shabby performance in 1892. The Philanderer I cannot answer for, as it has never been played; but I suspect it would make money if properly handled. It is the little plays that pay for the great ones in actual theatrical business.⁴

I am somewhat perplexed as to what I should do in view of the long arrears of my works that you propose to translate. How old are you? everything turns on that. You may easily be led into a frightful waste of your life on another man's work; and my conscience is not quite at peace on the subject. Can you not arrange to set aside only a part of your time to translate?

I have thought of Cromwell, and may perhaps do him someday. But my next play is to be an Irish one [*John Bull's Other Island*], not, I am afraid, of much use for Germany.

I must break off now, and go back to Free Trade, and preferential duties and exports and Chamberlain &c. &c. &c. &c.

GBS

P.S. Are you sure that your eyes are not partly the cause of your neuralgia? Have you had them carefully tested for astigmatism? I have very slight astigmatism of my right eye; but slight as it is it has probably a great deal to do with my occasional headaches.

Tls.

1. On 2 October, Shaw spoke before Fabians in Glasgow on Free Trade and contended that labor is rightly protectionist. On 4 October he spoke before the Independent Labor Party on "Socialist Unity."

2. Shaw's *The Common Sense of Municipal Trading* appeared in February 1904.

3. Helene Odilon (1864–1939), popular Viennese actress, known as the "Austrian Duse."

4. Trebitsch, dubious of *Captain Brassbound's Conversion*, did not translate it until 1907; nor did he undertake *The Philanderer* until then. Instead, he turned to *Mrs Warren* and *Widowers' Houses* and then to *Man and Superman*.

10 Adelphi Terrace W.C.
22nd October 1903

My dear Trebitsch

I was in earnest about Anne Leete; [1] but exquisiteness is a quality that gets lost in translation. Barker has a curious delicacy of style which could be reproduced in another language only by a writer with exactly corresponding qualities. I used to think that this quality would not travel across the footlights; but when I saw Anne Leete performed under Barker's own management (he is a born stage manager) I had to confess that he had succeeded. His style is so difficult that most of his plays are unintelligible at the first reading or hearing; and Archer always describes Anne Leete as a play written down to his comprehension, as it is much more perspicuous than the others. There is a sort of dainty strangeness about it that fits its eighteenth century period and costumes; and the curious way in which it begins in a garden at midnight takes it so effectually out of the Philistine key that its quaint fantastic conversation, consisting mostly of hints and inuendoes, seems to belong to it naturally. But all this, as I said, is untranslateable. A translation would make it much clearer than it is in English, and destroy its charm in doing so. The last scene is very moving and effective if it is properly played: the actor [C. M. Hallard] who played the gardener for Barker astonished everybody by coming out as a great artist, though nobody ever thought anything of him before; and this says a good deal for the part. However, I quite agree that it is an unpromising play to translate. You would probably do it better than anyone else, as you have (as far as I can guess with my very small knowledge of German) a certain individuality of touch with your pen that would suit Barker's style better than anybody else that Barker is likely to find. No doubt, as he is very young—only 24—he will do something later on that will be much better fitted for a voyage across the frontier.

I have been too busy to struggle through all the Leipzig notices; but those which I have deciphered are even more abusive than the London notices of 1894.[2] I perceive that there was some division of opinion in the audience; but the press seems tolerably unanimous. We shall be hissed into celebrity if this goes on.

Meyerfeld sent me his article, which I have not yet had time to wade through.[3] I am frantically overworked, and am writing this at the end of a devastating headache. I must now break off to rush to a meeting of the committee of the Fabian Society.

Has Dr Lahmann done you any good? You must really stop eating meat and drinking tea and coffee.

My wife sends you always some kind messages; but I generally forget to give them to you.

GBS

Tls.

1. *The Marrying of Ann Leete* by Harley Granville Barker (1877–1946), then at the beginning of his career as actor-playwright-director, opened at the Royalty Theatre on 26 January 1902.

2. *Helden* opened at the Altes Theater, Leipzig, on 11 October 1903 with Gertrud de Lalsky, Arnold Hänseler, and Ferdinand Schuy, staged by Bruno Geidner, and ran only one night—Shaw's third successive failure in Germany. According to the *Leipziger Zeitung* (12 October), which expressed bewilderment at the play, the audience laughed and clapped, but the evening was not a true success, and "hisses were not absent, especially at the end." The *Leipziger Tageblatt*, which quar-

reled with Shaw's use of history and satire of the heroic, reported a "complete fiasco." Reviews of the English production of *Arms* in April 1894 had accused Shaw of cynicism and sneering.

3. Meyerfeld's review of *Man and Superman* ("Der wahre Don Juan," *National-Zeitung*, 18 October) presented Shaw as incomparable essayist but faulty dramatist.

Maybury Knoll. Woking
24th November 1903

Dear Trebitsch

"Candida" is, I presume, withdrawn by this time.[1] If it is not, then I give the German nation up as hopeless. People who cannot understand Arms & the Man or the Devils Disciple, but are ready to wallow in domestic piffle like Candida, are past praying for.

The postponement of Caesar to February will probably be followed by a further postponement to August, after which the sphinx will be sold by auction & the production finally abandoned.

I have no press notices from Dresden yet—only the telegraphed Viennese ones, with a couple from Berlin. Except one which speaks of the second act attaining to something like success, they are pretty cool. Assuredly the second performance will be the last.

There is as yet no cut version of the Superman. But the Superman must be published just as it has been in England, with prefaces and postfaces and everything complete. For that reason I hardly like you to face the fearful drudgery of translating it; for it will probably never be performed on the stage; and so there will be no fun and no pay. You must not waste your years on secondhand work.

I have not yet finished Sokrates;[2] but I like it immensely. I, too, have had to fight these old Liberals all my life; and I am so delighted by the way Sudermann pitches into them that I am half tempted to translate the play and make the Stage Society perform it.[3]

In haste, & in the worst of tempers
GBS

Als.

1. *Candida* had its premiere in Dresden's Königliches Schauspielhaus (seating 1,400) on 19 November, with Karl Wiené as Morell, Clara Salbach as Candida, and Otto Gebühr as Marchbanks. Ernst Lewinger directed. The *Dresdner Nachrichten* (20 November) reported "a partial success" for a "meagerly entertaining" play; the more favorable *Dresdner Neueste Nachrichten* noted that it could not claim loud applause but was a "succes d'estime." The play closed after three performances.

2. Sudermann's *Der Sturmgeselle Sokrates* had opened at the Lessing-Theater, Berlin, on 3 October. Its caricature of political idealism associated with the revolutions of 1848 alienated many of Sudermann's admirers.

3. The Stage Society—Shaw was on its Executive Committee—did not produce *Sokrates*.

10 Adelphi Terrace W.C.
5th February 1904

On the 5th March the election for the London County Council will take place. I am a candidate. My colleague is a baronet, formerly Attorney General on the Gold Coast.¹ He knows nothing of local politics; and I shall have to do everything. To make things worse, the publishers of my new book, The Common Sense of Municipal Trading, have just gone bankrupt; and I have had at a moments notice, to find new publishers & rush the book through the press in time for the election.² Result: I am distracted with work, and until after the 5th March I shall have no time for anything. I hope I shall be defeated.

GBS

Apcs.
1. Shaw and Sir William Geary were put up for the London County Council by the Progressive Party in a constituency that they had given up as lost.
2. Grant Richards, Shaw's earlier publisher, had gone bankrupt; *The Common Sense of Municipal Trading*, drawing on Shaw's experience as Vestryman, was issued by A. Constable.

10 Adelphi Terrace W.C.
16th February 1904

My dear Trebitsch

I live a dog's life: cursed be all elections for ever and ever! Nothing is worse than giving your whole attention to things that do not really interest you at all. Even the chicanery ceases to be amusing after the first few *coups*.

I enclose you my receipt for the M 336. I am sending Fischer a receipt for the M 75. I leave the checking of the accounts to you.

I have not had time to read the notices. I am told that the Berlin papers scorn the Schlachtenlenker as mere stage trickery—an *English* play. They are, for once, quite right.¹

Candida is sending New York into transports.² The poor devil who is playing Eugene is in the seventh heaven—everybody talking about him and me, and his money vanishing in bucketsful.

I enclose some prints of photographs. The newspaper people like these sticky looking silver prints: they are the best to make blocks from. I am looking as like Rodin & Tolstoy in them as possible.

Get me a photograph of Sorma if you can.

In wildest haste—your distracted
G. Bernard Shaw

Als.
1. With *Caesar* postponed, Reinhardt put *Schlachtenlenker* and *Candida* into production at the Neues Theater, with himself as Napoleon—his only Shavian role—and Agnes Sorma (1865–1927), most admired of German actresses, as the Strange Lady. Richard Vallentin directed. *Schlachtenlenker* opened on 10 February on a double bill with Maeterlinck's *Sister Beatrice*. The press, while flattering to Sorma, was cool to the play, which the *Berliner Tageblatt* (11 February) faulted for disrespect to the great man and which *Vossische Zeitung* found less original than Maeterlinck's. The production ran only six times.
2. Arnold Daly (1875–1927), struggling American actor-manager, had produced *Candida* with limited funds for a special matinee at the Princess Theatre, New York, on 8 December 1903, with himself in the role of Marchbanks. Notices were so favorable that Daly extended the run, which continued to the following April, after moving to several theatres before moving to the Vaudeville Theatre.

10 Adelphi Terrace W.C.

14th March 1904

My dear Trebitsch

I have been defeated—wiped out—annihilated at the polls, mostly through the stupidity of my own side.[1] Consequently I am perfectly furious. It is no use sending me congratulatory telegrams about that silly old Candida.[2] To the devil with Candida! Agnes Sorma is an idiot, Reinhardt a duffer, Kerr an impostor, Gold an imbecile, Duesel a humbug, Heimann a bounder, Holländer a noodle, Morgenstern an ass, Osborn a dolt, Zieler a booby, Frisch a fool, Stucken a driveller, Kayssler an oaf, and Kahane a dunderhead.[3] I tell you I got only 1400 votes and my opponent got 1900. And everybody is delighted—openly and indecently delighted—at my discomfiture. What is Candida to me at such a moment? Away with Candida! "Verehrung" [adoration] indeed! I wanted 500 more votes. I am convinced that the performance was execrable, ridiculous, disastrous. It has been described by English correspondents in the papers here—Mill as a comic curate with misfitting clothes, Morell as a Tyrolese pastor of the XVIII century, Heaven knows what not! I have not had time to read the German notices: they are all lies. Reinhardt ought to be ashamed of himself. The theatre ought to be closed, and all the actors sent to a fortress for six months.

However, the election is over now; and time will restore my peace of mind.

Why the devil did not Sorma send me her photograph instead of a silly telegram?

I have received an application for authorization from the Freie Bühne [Volksbühne] people. They say the censorship will not allow a public performance of Mrs Warren's Profession. I have replied that I can give no authorization to translate or perform any play of mine, as I have made arrangements with you which would be contravened by such authorization. I have also referred them to you, saying that you might possibly allow them to perform the play if the press were excluded, and that I should not object in that case. The play would make a great effect among the Social-Democrats, and would start a good deal of talk about it. You can judge best whether to allow the performance or not.[4] Did the performance of Helden do any harm?

Tomorrow I shall go up to town & execute the Power of Attorney to enable you to deal with the Budapest people.[5] Do not let them involve us in a costly lawsuit if you can help it.

Granville Barker is going to give six matinees of Candida here in April as an experiment.[6] Why not come over & soothe your nerves by attending the rehearsals?

yrs ever

G. Bernard Shaw

Als.

1. Beatrice Webb thought Shaw was "hopelessly intractable" as a candidate, but Shaw blamed his defeat on the clergy, who opposed his support for public aid to sectarian schools.

2. *Candida*, staged by Felix Holländer, opened at Reinhardt's Neues Theater on 3 March, with Agnes Sorma, Emanuel Reicher, and Max Eisfeldt. Trebitsch was delighted with the notices: "a triumph of poetic individuality" (*Vossische Zeitung*, 4 March), "a worthy subject for discussion" (*Berliner Tageblatt*); but the play was more a literary than popular success: "caviar for the general" (*Berliner Tageblatt*), and ran only eight times.

3. Shaw's string of names—presumably signers of congratulatory cables—embraces the progressive theatrical literati of Berlin: Alfred Kerr (1867–1948), Alfred Gold, Friedrich Duesel, Christian Morgenstern (1871–1914), Max Osborn (1870–1946), and Gustav Zieler were critics; Moritz Heimann (1868–1925), reader for S. Fischer, was an author-critic; Eduard Stücken (1865–1936) was a playwright; Felix Holländer (1867–1931), Efraim Frisch (b. 1873), Friedrich Kayssler (1874–1945), and Arthur Kahane (1872–1932) were with Reinhardt's literary staff.

4. Trebitsch, who had not yet translated *Mrs Warren*, consented to the Volksbühne's private performance of the play in a version by one of its members. The press was barred, but despite precautions Fritz Mauthner of the *Berliner Tageblatt* attended the opening on 3 April at the Metropol Theater and reviewed the play, leading to recriminations by Trebitsch.

5. On 17 February, an unauthorized production of *Arms* (*Hősök*) at the Király Theatre introduced Shaw to Budapest where despite a good press it ran only two times.

6. The Granville Barker–J. E. Vedrenne experiment at the Court Theatre, London, which opened on 26 April, ran three seasons and presented eleven plays by Shaw, who rehearsed his own works.

10 Adelphi Terrace W.C.

28th March 1904

My dear Trebitsch

Your careful arrangements to die in Spain shew the most praiseworthy forethought; but on the whole it would be more convenient to me if you could be prevailed on to survive.[1] Who the devil is Hugo von Hofmannsthal?[2]

I cannot meet you in Paris on the 25th April, because I shall just then be working at the final rehearsals of the accursed Candida, of which Barker is giving half a dozen matinees beginning in that very week. You had better come over & give us some notions from the Berlin performance.

How do you manage to knock your nerves to pieces as you do? Is it overwork, or romantic attachments to women?

. . . We are at present looking for a new house in the country. Candida will prevent my going for a trip at Easter; but in May my wife will insist on going off with me somewhere.[3]

I have begun a new play [*John Bull's Other Island*]; but as it is for the Irish Literary Theatre, and will deal with Irish-English politics, I am afraid it will be of no use to you.[4]

Paris is the dullest town in the universe. Better come to London: we should much like to talk to you.

yrs ever

G. Bernard Shaw

PS What is the best season for a trip to Vienna? I have never been there.

Als.

1. After attending the opening of *Candida* in Berlin, Trebitsch proceeded to Vienna and thence to Spain to rest his nerves.

2. Hugo von Hofmannsthal (1874–1929), Austrian poet-playwright, perhaps best known for his later collaboration as librettist with Richard Strauss, had written a number of verse playlets and a free adaptation of *Elektra* (1903) and was shortly to publish his adaptation of Otway's *Venice Preserv'd* (*Das gerettete Venedig*, 1904).

3. The Shaws rented the Old House at Harmer Green as a country home. On 1 May they left for Italy where they remained until 10 June.

4. The Irish National Theatre Society, led by Augusta Lady Gregory (1852–1932) and William Butler Yeats (1865–1939), had requested a play from Shaw for their new theatre in Abbey Street, Dublin. The resulting *John Bull's Other Island* turned out to be too long and demanding for the Abbey Theatre.

32 Via Porta Pinciana. [Rome]
15th May 1904

Dear Trebitsch

The Times critic is Walkley, to whom Man & Superman is dedicated. I shrieked with laughter over your comment on his notice, & promptly sent it on to him.[1]

I now send you Archer's notice.[2] I wonder will you like it any better.

I have been to Bayreuth either three or four times: I forget which. Charlotte has never been; so perhaps she might be induced to come, though she hates Germany & romantically adores Italy. As for me, the truth is, I hate travelling: that is why I always want you to come to London instead of going half way to meet you. I used to go to Bayreuth because I was, from 1888 to 1894 by far the greatest musical critic in Europe; and I went because it was my business to go. I used to write feuilletons between the acts.

Archer has been studying your Schlachtenlenker & is horrified at the liberties you have taken with my historical introduction. He says you translated Napoleon crossing the Alps as Napoleon following the custom of the ancients, and that you perverted my allusion to Marengo in the interests of Austria.[3] I daresay you did; but I must have concluded that your variations didnt matter or were improvements. Archer admits that the dialogue is more faithful.

yrs ever
G. Bernard Shaw

Als.

1. A. B. Walkley (1855–1926), drama critic for the *Times*, had reviewed *Candida* in the *Times Literary Supplement* (29 April) and characterized Shaw as a "fantasist" who travesties life by removing everything from it but intelligence, and *Candida* as a "mathematical demonstration," a "joke." Trebitsch had exploded to Shaw: "Who is that desperate impostor, who wrote all this frightful nonsense? Not even his grand-children will be able to understand this deep and poetic work. I did not finish to read that writing: it would have caused me neuralgics."

2. On 12 May Shaw wrote to Archer: "Trebitsch's howlers are certainly mighty ones and millions, though I think I got them driven out of the dialogue of the Schlachtenlenker. But how can I reproach him when he sends me the following, which I am sending on to Walkley?" Shaw then quoted Trebitsch, adding, "I shall send him your criticism in the hope of extracting some further blossoms from him." (*Collected Letters*, II, 417.) Archer's review (*The World*, 3 May) found *Candida* the "most human" of Shaw's plays.

3. Shaw's stage directions to *Man of Destiny* read: "Napoleon has therefore approached the Alps in command of men without money." Trebitsch translated this as: "Napoleon musste es daher den Alten gleichtun" (Napoleon had therefore to do like ["approach"] the Ancients). He also patriotically changed "handicapped by Austrian statesmanship" to "led by." The errors were subsequently corrected.

10 Adelphi Terrace W.C.
16th June 1904

My dear Trebitsch

I got back to London last week, but found such a mass of letters and business waiting for me that I had no time to make enquiries about Wilde until yesterday afternoon.[1]

There is no "daybook," or diary, as it is called in English (a daybook is one of the account books kept in a merchant's office).[2] Wilde was quite incapable

of keeping a diary, or doing anything systematically. The only personal documents he has left are his letters, which have never been collected. Unluckily
I did not see his friend Robert Ross yesterday, but only his friend's partner,
who, however, probably knows everything that Ross knows.[3] You may take it
that there are no secret memoirs of any kind. If you care to undertake the
article yourself I can tell you all that you cannot get from his books—rather
more than is fit for publication. . . .

In Rome I met Anatole France:[4] we had a private view of the Sistine
Chapel from a scaffold which enabled us to see the prophets and sybils at
close quarters; but I have not time to tell you all about it: my letters are still
lying unanswered in heaps.

[yrs ever
G. Bernard Shaw][5]

Tl.

1. Strong interest in Oscar Wilde (1854–1900) had been aroused in Germany the previous year
by the translation of Robert Sherard's *Oscar Wilde,* and Max Meyerfeld, Trebitsch's antagonist,
was interested in translating hitherto unavailable Wilde materials.

2. The "daybook" and rumored memoirs, whose existence Shaw doubted, was the unpublished
De Profundis.

3. Robert Ross (1869–1918) was Wilde's literary executor and, with More Adey, partner in the
Carfax Gallery.

4. Anatole France (1844–1924), prominent French satirist, critic, and social reformer, elected to
the Académie Française in 1896.

5. The closing and signature have been cut off.

10 Adelphi Terrace W.C.
23rd June 1904

Dear Trebitsch

There has always been a persistent rumor that Wilde left a sort of "Apolo-
gia pro sua Vita" in MS; and various publishers & journalists have tried to
get at it. But I cannot get any authoritative confirmation of this; and in any
case it is clear that if such a thing exists, it is inaccessible.[1] For my own part
I dont believe it does exist. When Wilde came out of prison he had energy
enough left to write a very good article on prison life which was published
in the Daily Chronicle, and also the Ballad of Reading Gaol. But after that, if
he had had any real literary energy left, he would have used it to write plays.
As it was, he tried to get advances of money for plays that were never written—at least there has been gossip to that effect among London managers,
which may or may not be true—and a fashion arose of declaring that every
new play that had the least attempt at wit in it had been written or touched
up by Wilde; but the truth seems to be that he simply went under and loafed
about cafés in Rome & Paris until he died. An autobiography requires more
energy to write than almost anything else; and had Wilde been capable of
writing one he would also have been capable of rehabilitating himself.[2] He
was not, like Verlaine,[3] habitually squalid in his habits: on the contrary, he
was fastidious, luxurious, and even snobbish.

Have you got Sherard's book about him?

I cannot undertake the article [on Wilde] now: I have a year's work on hand—in fact I have ten years work on hand; but at least a year of it is pressing. You had better do the job yourself. . . .

> In haste
> ever yrs
> G. Bernard Shaw

PS. Wilde's parents are both dead. "Parents" in English means always father & mother only: the rest—the brothers, sisters, cousins, aunts &c, are "relatives." The French use of "parent" and "parenté" is quite unknown in England.

Als.

1. Wilde had given the manuscript of *De Profundis* to Ross, who secreted it after having a typescript and carbon copy made. Meyerfeld, whose translation of Wilde's *Duchess of Padua* was to appear in October, had persuaded Ross to allow him to translate *De Profundis*. Meyerfeld's version, along with four letters from Wilde to Ross, was published in *Neue Rundschau* (January and February 1905), preceding the English edition. Both editions were heavily expurgated.

2. Shortly after his release from Reading Prison on 19 May 1897, Wilde published "The Case of Warder Martin: Some Cruelties of Prison Life," in *Daily Chronicle* (28 May); *The Ballad of Reading Gaol* appeared the following February.

3. Paul Verlaine (1844–1896), French lyrical poet, was notorious for his debauched life and for his affair with his protégé, Arthur Rimbaud.

> Rosemarkie—a hole on the
> N.E. coast of Scotland—
> 9th September 1904

Dear Trebitsch

I have just finished a new play [*John Bull's Other Island*], and am almost fit for Dr Lahmann in consequence. Unfortunately it is no good for Germany, as it is about England and Ireland; and the chief figure is a typical Englishman surrounded by typical Irishmen & discussing English-Irish questions which would have no interest abroad. It is a pity; for it is a very good play of its sort.[1]

Whilst I was finishing it I had to stop for four days to write a short play to go before the Schlachtenlenker. I enclose a copy. Its only use is that it gets over the old difficulty about the Schl. being too short to occupy a whole performance and too long to be a *lever de rideau*. Arnold Daly, who made a great success last winter in New York as Eugene in Candida, will play the Schl. and this new "comediettina" together, and so have a complete Shaw bill.[2] . . .

Meyerfeldt's "one existing exemplaire" of the Duchess of Padua[3] is a mare's nest. A bookseller named Frank Hollings, 7 Great Turnstyle, Holborn, London W.C., will sell you a dozen copies if you want them: he has reprinted all the trash that Wilde discarded as immature & worthless. The Duchess of Padua is a youthful attempt at a romantic cape-and-sword play, of no importance, except that it contains the first form of Wilde's favorite epigram (used in Lady Windermere's fan) that "experience is the name men give to their mistakes." It is not in verse. And this reminds me that I may be quite wrong, and that Wilde may really have written a romantic play in verse at the end of his life. But I dont believe it: first, because it is wildly improbable in itself;

second, because Mary Anderson retired from the stage many years before Wilde died; third, because I think I remember that the name of the early play of which I speak was The Duchess of Some place or other. However, if Meyerfeldt can turn an honest penny by persuading Berlin that he has unearthed a unique classic, let him do so. It wont hurt anybody; and it may benefit him. Let him alone.

I never heard of Hermann the Cherusker.[4] What the devil is a Cherusker? I have not written a Cromwell drama:[5] an American paper started that *canard*. But I intend to write a short play called "The Death of Cromwell" which might go with the Schlachtenlenker, or even make a big triple bill of

"How He Lied to Her Husband"	1
"Schlacht" or "Cromwell"	2
"The Admirable Bashville."	3

I await your book & play[6] & am dusting my German dictionary in anticipation. But if they have a great success, goodbye to translation. You will never catch up with me. Remember: a book must be translated within *ten* years of publication to secure copyright; and the years are running out. I wish I had caught you younger.

I have not examined Cotta's account. I know too well that the half-profit system is hopeless. The edition has, as you say, served its turn; but the sooner we get a revised edition into Fischer's hands on a proper royalty basis, or on a commission basis, I paying for the printing, the better. I wonder what Cotta would sell his "remainder" for—I mean all the copies he has left. However, we can settle that later on.[7]

I doubt if Caesar will draw me to Berlin or Candida to Vienna.[8] Life is short (I am 48) and it is better to write new plays whilst I can than to gad about after the old ones.

Hayden-Coffin[9] is our most popular light opera baritone here—an American by birth & a very nice fellow.

Your nerves (not nerfs) will never get right until you give up Wein, Weib und Fleisch—the Gesang you can keep.

Our seaside holiday has been a horrible failure; and we are both out of sorts & exhausted.

yrs ever

G. Bernard Shaw

Als.

1. Trebitsch did not translite *John Bull* until 1909, and it was not produced in Germany until 1917 (see 22 August 1919).

2. The play was *How He Lied to Her Husband*, written at Daly's request as a curtain raiser to *Man of Destiny*.

3. Wilde's early verse-prose tragedy, commissioned by Mary Anderson (1859–1940), American actress, and privately printed (1883). Copies were rare, but a transcript survived with Robert Ross and was used by Meyerfeld for his scheduled translation in October, three years before the English edition. Doubts of its authenticity arose, and Trebitsch, smarting from Meyerfeld's attack in "Bernard Shaw und sein Dolmetsch" (*Englische Studien*, 1904), wanted to expose his rival's incompetence.

4. Hermann the Cherusker (of the tribe of Cherusk), Germanic hero of the first century, known as Arminius.

5. Gustav Kobbé in "A Personal Sketch of George Bernard Shaw" (*Harper's Weekly*, 27 August) had alleged that Shaw was writing a play on Cromwell for Daly.

6. Trebitsch's new novella *Das verkaufte Lächeln* and his play *Ein letzter Wille* were not yet published.

7. The edition of *Drei Dramen* had not sold out, but Trebitsch, anxious to correct his translations, negotiated with Cotta for revised single editions of the plays, which appeared the next year.

8. Reinhardt's *Caesar* was still pending; *Candida*, with Lili Petri, opened at the Deutsches Volkstheater, Vienna, on 8 October, and ran only five times.

9. C. Hayden Coffin (1862–1935), English actor-singer, whom Trebitsch had met. Coffin's wife, Adeline, did translation from the German.

North British Station Hotel. Edinburgh

15th September 1904

Dear Trebitsch

Dr Lahmann will have to cure your arithmetic. Why do you send me M232/45? The half of M462/45 is M231/22.5. And what am I to do with a florin and five nickels? In future I propose that you keep all odd sums like this to pay for postage, registration &c, as there is no reason why all the office expenses should fall on you.[1] . . .

yrs ever

G. Bernard Shaw

Als.

1. Trebitsch remitted royalties for productions of *Man of Destiny*, *Candida*, and *Arms* in ten theatres.

10 Adelphi Terrace W.C.

[after 1 November 1904]

. . . John Bull made a sensation. Divided opinions, some furiously unfavorable, others insanely enthusiastic.[1]

GBS

Ans.

1. *John Bull* opened at the Court Theatre on 1 November and became Shaw's first fashionable success in England. Archer thought it Shaw's best play, but the *Times* found it a "Shavian Farrago," and the *Daily Mail*, a "nightmare . . . a tract gone mad."

[Trebitsch to Shaw]

Hotel Saxonia. Berlin

22nd November 1904

My dear Mr. Shaw!

Mr. Slivinsky,[1] the great compeater of Entsch, offered me 750 Marks for "How he lied," which he wants to buy once for ever. I asked 2000 M. [£100]. Please tell me by a *dispatch* as soon as you get these lines, if you consent, even with 800; I hope to bring him to 1000 M. which would be a very decent price for this act; I don't believe that we could make more out of it; and this man would do his best then of course, to have the act performed as much as possible; quite a good wip for Entsch.

I am tired rehear[s]ing "Teufelskerl"; Friday is the first night![2] The cast is not very good. "Wherlin" plays the title-roll, just a *young Wiené*! We shall see.

Monday morning "How he lied" will apear in the "Berliner Tageblatt."[3] Thats all for the present. Thanks for your thorough receipt.

I am in a great hurry.

Good bye, dont forget to wire at once

Yours ever

Siegfried Trebitsch

Als.; Texas.

1. Adolf Sliwinski, proprietor of Felix Bloch Erben, Berlin.

2. *Teufelskerl* opened on 25 November at the Berliner Theater, with Arthur Wherlin (b. 1863), who was some ten years younger than Wiené of the Raimund premiere.

3. *How He Lied* (*Wie er ihr Mann belog*) appeared in the *Berliner Tageblatt* on 28 November, the first instance of a Shaw play being published in Germany before England.

10 Adelphi Terrace W.C.

26th November 1904

Dear Trebitsch

I write in great haste, as this is the day on which we revive Candida for ten more matinées.

Never under any circumstances or for any sum—even a million—sell a play out and out. Ten years ago, when I had not ten pounds in the world, I was offered £160 for the German rights of Helden. I refused it, fortunately for both of us. Tell Slivinsky two things. 1. That he is an ass to offer M750 for a play so very doubtfully worth it. 2. That he evidently thinks me an ass to suppose that I am in the habit of selling my rights in this way to speculators.

However, you may not agree with me. You may be willing to take M500 for your half share of the play. In that case, I—moi qui vous écrit—will buy your half share for M600 baares Geld [cold cash], so that you shall not lose by my obstinacy. But when you come to deal with your own plays, be prepared to die in the streets of starvation sooner than part with your rights for ever. To sell a play for a lump sum for a definite period—not more than five years— may sometimes be good business; but to sell it for ever is only admissible in the case of plays which will be dead and rotten eighteen months after their first production.

I conclude from what you say of Wherlin that the D's D. will fail, unless Anderson is really good and Burgoyne very fine.[1] It is a pity: a Berlin failure just now will spoil everything. But it cant be helped. Oh, if only I could speak German as I speak English, I would go over and make your German actors jump out of their old fashioned skins.

Hideous weather here. And I also am tired of rehearsing Candida.

yrs ever

GBS

P.S. Make them understand, if you can, that the 3rd act is NOT comic opera. A great deal depends on Judith, as she alone can keep up the underlying tragedy of the court martial scene.

Als.

1. The cast of the Berliner Theater production of *Teufelskerl* also included Ida Roland (Judith), Leo Connard (Anderson), and Ernst Pitschau (Burgoyne). Only Pitschau was unreservedly praised by the critics, but the play was well received as witty and original and ran 21 times, the first respectable run for Shaw in Germany.

10 Adelphi Terrace W.C.
13th December 1904

My dear Trebitsch

. . . If you knew how they have been imploring me to go to America for the first night of You Never Can Tell,[1] offering me big sums to lecture, special state rooms in Atlantic liners, begging it as "a personal favor" &c &c, you would laugh at the idea of my going to Berlin. I am simply desperate in the face of all the work before me. Tell them the longer they postpone Caesar the greater will be my relief.

A translation of the stage version of the Superman only, is quite out of the question. We must have the whole book—a terrible task, but a great literary sensation.

I have great bundles of newspaper notices [of *Helden*], but havnt had time to read one of them.[2] A few have been translated in the London papers—enough to shew, by what they say of the dialogue, that your translations produce all the effect of the original.

In England a reviewer always complains of a translation, because it makes his editor & the public think he knows the original language very well.

GBS

Als.
   1. The Daly production opened at the Garrick Theatre, New York, on 9 January 1905.
   2. With the production of *Helden* at Lindau's Deutsches Theater on 8 December, four of Shaw's plays reached Berlin in one year, which led the *Berliner Tageblatt* (9 December) to remark that the "witty Irishman . . . has now become the monarch of our stages." The *Vossische Zeitung* was ecstatic. Yet audience applause was mingled with some hisses (*Lokal-Anzeiger*), and *Vorwärts* (11 December), noting that the theatre was not filled on the second night, urged the public to attend or be disgraced. *Helden*, with Adele Hartwig, Julius Strobl, and Otto Sommerstorff, ran 36 times, a record for Shaw to that point.

10 Adelphi Terrace W.C.
20th December 1904

. . . I have given up attempting to keep pace with my correspondence just now. But I am quite impenitent as to Lindau. No doubt the success of our piece is a great surprise to him; but it is of no interest to me. I intended it to be successful. He might as well telegraph to say that the sun had set that evening.

I never bow before the curtain now. I used to come out & make speeches, when the battle still raged over "the new drama"; but that is all over.

G. Bernard Shaw

ps I am [in a] very bad temper. I hate Christmas.

Apcs.

[Harmer Green.] Welwyn
16th January 1905

Dear Trebitsch

All I can tell you about Helden is that it was written under the following circumstances.[1] In 1894, Miss Florence Farr, an actress whom I knew very well, and whom I had persuaded to produce Ibsen's Rosmersholm in the early days of the Ibsen boom here, and who had also played Blanche in Widowers' Houses for me in 1892 (my first appearance as an author), this Fräulein Farr, I say, was entrusted with a handsome sum by a lady[2] to open a high class modern theatre in London. She took the Avenue Theatre and produced a play called "A Comedy of Sighs" by a well known Irish poet, Dr John Todhunter, with, as *lever de rideau*, a little play in verse called The Land of Hearts Desire, by a much younger and now well known Irish poet, William Butler Yeats. The playbill was designed by Aubrey Beardsley; and copies of it are now worth a few pounds apiece.

The first performance was a failure; and Florence Farr sent for me the next day and begged me to let her perform Widowers' Houses. Instead of doing so I went out into the Embankment Gardens & hastily set to work to finish Arms & The Man, which I had begun some time before with no particular object. In little more than a fortnight it was produced. The first night was wildly successful; but the net result was as stated in the preface to the Pleasant Plays.

The first version of the play had no geography—nothing but a war with a machine gun in it. It was Sidney Webb who suggested the Servo-Bulgarian war. However, I adapted it to the historical & social facts of the time very carefully. I first consulted Stepniak;[3] and he introduced me to the Russian officer who commanded the Danube fleet for the Bulgarians during the war. This officer gave me a great deal of information, thanks to the accuracy of which you have had all this trouble with the Censor.

In London in 1894 the play was received, except by a few people, as an *opera bouffe* without music. The notion that soldiers ate chocolate was taken as a silly joke; and it was not until the South African War reminded the English of what war was really like, and Queen Victoria presented all the troops with boxes of chocolate, that Arms & The Man was justified. Some military details came from a German staff officer who had served in the war of 1870–71: the description of a cavalry charge in the first act is his.

The name Arms & The Man is Virgil's "Arma virumque cano," the first line of the first canto of the Aeneids, which in Dryden's famous translation run[s]

"Arms & the man I sing, who first by Fate,
And haughty Juno's unrelenting hate" &c &c &c.[4]

> In wild haste, yrs ever
> G. Bernard Shaw

Als.

1. Trebitsch was preparing the single-play revised edition and sought information for a translator's note.

2. Miss Annie Horniman (1860–1937), who later subsidized the Abbey Theatre, Dublin.

3. Sergius Stepniak (Sergei Kravchinskii, 1851–1895), Russian artillery officer who turned revolutionary and assassinated the head of the Russian secret police in 1878. He fled to Switzerland and later lived in England, where he wrote and lectured on Nihilism.

4. Shaw misquotes. The line is: "Arms, and the man I sing, who forc'd by fate."

10 Adelphi Terrace W.C.

19th January 1905

Dear Trebitsch

Why am I silent![1] Um Gottes Willen! Am I ever silent? Here with me it is jabber, jabber, jabber, scribble, scribble, scribble, from breakfast to bed. My literary career is at an end: I no longer have time to do anything but attend to other people's business.

At Alexandria get your health back, and buy me some photographs for use by the scenepainters [for *Caesar and Cleopatra*].

Come & see us: we will teach you how to get rid of your neuralgia. . . .

yours ever

G. Bernard Shaw

Als.

1. Trebitsch was on holiday in the Middle East and had not received Shaw's last letter.

[Trebitsch to Shaw]

[Egypt]

postmarked 11th February 1905

I am correcting all the time G.B.S. on the Nile-steamer.[1] Wonderful are the excursions here to the grand antiquities! I just have read, that "Helden" were tremendously successful in *Munique*.[2] . . .

Yours ever

S.T.

Apcs.; Texas.

1. Trebitsch was correcting *Drei Dramen* for single-play editions.

2. *Helden*, Shaw's introduction to Munich, opened at the Schauspielhaus on 1 February and ran 13 times. The *Allgemeine Zeitung* (3 February) remarked on Shaw's tardy appearance in Munich, the electric atmosphere in the theatre, and the stormy applause at the play's end.

10 Adelphi Terrace W.C.

18th March 1905

My dear Trebitsch

. . . You must have an unusually nice father to be so attached to him still.[1] Most men are prepared—even eager—to lose their fathers with complete resignation. But I hope he will pull through this time. Where is the tumor? Weak hearts are all nonsense—mostly indigestion. *My* heart plays all manner of tricks; but I have undergone two operations and had three teeth out under nitrous oxide gas without being any the worse. So dont be in a hurry to bid the devil goodmorning: matters may not be so serious as you fear. And even if they are, you cannot expect your poor father to live for ever merely to amuse you: at 63 a man begins to be entitled to some rest. Whilst he lives, rejoice in his life; when he is dead, rejoice in his memory; and away with melancholy!

In haste (it is close on post hour)

yrs ever

G. Bernard Shaw

PS I wrote the Wilde article[2] in mad haste: it is probably very bad; but I depend on you to polish it up a little in German.

Als.
  1. Trebitsch traced his affection for his stepfather, Leopold Trebitsch, to the latter's devoted concern when Siegfried fell ill with scarlet fever. Leopold lingered until the end of 1906.
  2. "Oskar Wilde," Shaw's first contribution to Vienna's leading *Neue Freie Presse*, appeared on 23 April.

> [Harmer Green.] Welwyn
> 11th April 1905

This is horrible news. I was hoping that your confounded play would fail.[1] *Now* you must go on writing plays, and stop translating; and I shall have to fall back on Kellner & Meyerfeldt. . . .

Titus & William Dudgeon [in *The Devil's Disciple*] are Mrs Dudgeon's brothers-in-law. There is no blood relationship between them. Uncle William addresses her as "sister" in a sentimentally religious moment, but she is Schwägerin, not Schwester.

GBS

Apcs.
  1. Trebitsch's *Ein letzter Wille* in fact was given only one performance in Hannover's Residenz Theater on 6 April. Later that year it was performed twice in Leipzig and twice in Vienna.

> The Old House. Harmer Green
> 30th May 1905

My dear Trebitsch

It is no use: you *must* take it;[1] or I will put an end to our partnership & take on Meyerfeldt. If once we begin trying to calculate on each separate job how much you have done and how much I have done, and dividing the money proportionately, life will become unbearable & dishonorable for both of us. The agreement is that we are partners, sharing half & half. I take my half when you have had a lot of trouble and I have had none. You must take your half when—as happens much seldomer—I have had more trouble than you. So take your cheque and pay me instantly my 30 kronen. You also owe me twopence-halfpenny, the postage of this letter, as you have made me send the cheque twice over.

There are no photos of You Never Can Tell, except an album of American ones weighing about 10 tons. The Court scenery is too cheap & shabby for the Burgtheater to copy.[2] I can send you rough plans & sketches to work from as soon as the scenery seems likely to be put in hand. At present I am too hard pressed to spend a moment on them until we know that Schlenther really means business.

GBS

Als.
  1. Trebitsch had remitted the full fee paid by *Neue Freie Presse* for Shaw's Wilde article—250 kronen (c. £11)—while keeping only the translator's fee of 60k.
  2. The Burgtheater was now negotiating for *You Never Can Tell*, which had been revived in London's Court Theatre on 2 May.

The Grand Stairway and foyer of the Burgtheater, Vienna.

10 Adelphi Terrace W.C.

8th June 1905

My dear Trebitsch

I hereby acknowledge receipt of 30 kronen, being my half of your fee for translating my article on Wilde for the Neue Freie Presse. I note that you will never feel comfortable until I take back my remittance of £5. This is sad news, as you will be uncomfortable all your life. The 30 kronen do not make me uncomfortable: quite the reverse. You will get used to the £5 after a month or two.

The only name I can suggest instead of Crampton is McNaughtan, pronounced Maknawtn (the aw as in English). It would suit the character as well as Crampton, and would be sufficiently like Gichtknoten [gouty knots] to make the joke pass in German.[1]

The name Bohun is pronounced Boon (Bun in German) in England. It is a highly aristocratic name, indicating descent from one of the Norman invaders of the Conquest of 1066. The name Boon is also an English name, but much commoner. McComas tells the waiter that he expects a Mr Bohun. Then, recollecting that the gentleman will probably give the waiter a card for Mrs Clandon, and thinking that William will not know that the name Bohun on the card means Boon, he warns the waiter that the name is spelt that way. The waiter replies that he knows that very well, as his own name is Bohun, though he thinks it best to spell it Boon, so as not to appear pretentious. We have several of these ridiculously spelt names in England. Thus the Scotch names Hume and Kerr are pronounced Home and Carr; Eugene Marchbanks would spell his name Marjoribanks; Colquhoun is called Cohoon; my wife's sister, Mrs Cholmondely, is called Mrs Chumly; Cockburn is pronounced Coburn, Bourchier Bowcher, Geohegan Gaygun, Claverhouse Clayvers, Beaulieu Bewly &c, &c, &c. If your ancestors had come over with William the Conqueror, you would probably be called Trabbs. And if you were a waiter with a barrister for a son, your son, as a parvenu and "rasta" would take care to put Trebitsch on his visiting card, whilst you would be content to spell yourself humble Trabbs.

Tell Schlenther that the play is going to be called Man kann nie Wissen and nothing else.[2] If he does not like it he can get a play with a nice name from Schonthan[3] or somebody else. If the Viennese are not accustomed to names like that, the sooner they become accustomed to them the better. My plays are not like anybody else's; and I will call them what I like, and not what Schlenther or Plappart[4] like. Man kann nie wissen is a first rate title: that is why Schlenther wants to spoil it. Tell him that if he finds fault with my names or my plays, I will refuse to have anything to do with the Burg Theater; and then he will have to shut it up. . . .

yours

G. Bernard Shaw

Tls.

1. Trebitsch altered the name of this character in *You Never Can Tell* as suggested by Shaw.

2. The play was produced (and published, 1906) as *Der verlorene Vater* (The Prodigal Father), and the literal *Mann kann nie wissen* was only adopted for later productions and the collected edition of 1911.

3. Franz von Schönthan (1849–1913), an Austrian writer of light popular comedies.

4. August Freiherr Plappart von Leenheer, the court-appointed General-Intendant of the Burgtheater.

[Harmer Green.] Welwyn
14th June 1905

My dear Trebitsch

You will be the death of me with your confounded titles. Meyerfeld came to Adelphi Terrace the other day in his nicest new frock coat, with a heap of flowers for my wife. I told him your so-called translations of my works were excellent original plays, and that if they had been in the least like mine they wouldnt have succeeded. He said you were a very keen man of business, but that you had cut him. Also that the Perfect Wagnerite was a disgraceful book, because it did not praise Meyerbeer.[1] From which I conclude that Meyerfeld is a Jew.

What am I to do with this beast of an agreement? It is not even in Lateinischschrift; so I will have to learn the German alphabet before I read it. This will take me at least a month; for I am fearfully busy; and when I have at last made out the sense of the document I shall probably refuse to sign it.

And I positively will not stand any of Schlenther's nonsense about the stage directions, or about Scene 1, Scene 2 &c &c. I know exactly what that means—treating the actors at the Burg as if they were gasmen or carpenters who were paid to learn their words & do as they are told, and not to think. They must read the play exactly as I wrote it, long directions and all. I am determined to educate them up to my standard and not stoop to theirs. I have been through all this lazy foolish nonsense here; and I have never given in to it, and wont begin now. It is bad enough to have the play called The Prodigal Father [Der verlorene Vater]; but that does not matter so much, because it is not altogether a bad title, though it will strengthen the hands of the people who disparage your translations. But as to having my stage directions interfered with, or my text broken up in numbered scenes, I wont hear of it; and if Schlenther pesters me with such impertinences I will tear up his agreement and write four letters, one to him, one to his Hofamtmann [i.e., court official], one to Plappart, and one to the Emperor, that will send them into apoplectic fits. I am conferring a great honor on his miserable theatre by condescending to let him have my name on his affiches; and I am half disposed to withdraw my consent: in fact, it is only because it amuses you that I submit. If he had accepted a play *before* Berlin, or chosen a big one like Caesar, I should have said "Thank you" to him: as it is, I shall very reluctantly consent to stand on his neck & give him my orders, which he must obey unquestioningly. Tell him, to begin with, that I object to his name, and that in future he must call himself Schulz. . . .

The hot weather makes me extremely irritable. Damn the Burgtheater!!

G.B.S.

Als.; postscript omitted.

1. Giacomo Meyerbeer (1791–1864), popular German opera composer of Jewish descent.

10 Adelphi Terrace W.C.
2nd July 1905

My dear Trebitsch

Heaven evidently has me under its especial protection. In spite of your protestations about Formsache [mere formality], I felt all my instincts warning me not to sign that agreement before I had read it. When you asked me reproachfully why I treated you as a child, I said to myself "He IS a child—a child of five; and this Schlenther is an old serpent." Now I have mastered the agreement: and I find it to be one of the most infamous documents ever set before an author. Tell Schlenther that in vain is the net spread within sight of the bird. I will see him damned to the deepest hell before I will sign it.[1]

Under the Berne Convention my copyright lasts as long as in the country of origin: that is, for 42 years, or until seven years after my death, whichever period may be the longer. Under this rascally agreement if I die this year (which I fully expect to do from overwork) you would find your tantièmes stop in fifteen years instead of forty. Nothing is said about your interests at all.

The agreement gives Schlenther the power to keep the play locked up for two years and a half and then to throw it back on our hands without a farthing of payment of any kind, a thing he is quite capable of doing merely to prevent any of the other theatres getting it. The clause undertaking to perform the play between the 1st October next and the 1st April next is waste paper, because there is no penalty. . . .

Schurkerei [villainy], lieber Trebitsch, reinstes Schurkerei!

I now suspect that his readiness to give the 10% meant merely that he did not intend to pay anything at all, but only to get the power to stop the other theatres for 32 months.

Fortunately, like all theatrical swindlers, S. has not sense enough to draw up an agreement properly. I am not a party to the agreement: therefore my signature would have no sense. And having got hold of the signature he entrapped you into giving him, I shall keep it tight. Schlenther will never see that agreement again until the Recording Angel presents it on the Day of Judgment, when S. will be calling on the mountains to hide him and the hills to fall on him.

I will dictate an agreement myself; and if Schlenther does not accept it on his bended knees the Burgtheater shall never have Caesar[2] or any other play of mine.

By the way, in discussing the production of Caesar here with Forbes Robertson, he objected so strongly to the omission of the third act that we went into the length of it more carefully, and ended by convincing ourselves that there would be plenty of time for the whole play. So Reinhardt and Teddy Craig[3] had better design two more scenes; and the jeune premier can be given the part of Apollodorus to study.

I have no objection whatever to killing the old man who writes out the rolls at the Burgtheater. He has lived quite long enough. I am also perfectly willing that you should be sent to prison; so that I may have a clear field to

deal with Schlenther myself. As Lord Clanricarde said, "If you think you
will intimidate me by shooting my agent, you are very much mistaken."[4]
Can Reinhardt read English? And can Schlenther?
Siegfried: you will be the death of me with your contracts.

You cannot supply Schlenther with reproductions of the scenery at the
Court Theatre. Such reproductions do not exist; and if they did I should expect the Burgtheater to do much better. However, I hear that they have been
making some flashlight photographs; and I will try to get a set for you.

As to You Never Can Tell I will try to read it when I go to the south of
Ireland next week—or perhaps at the end of this week—meaning the week
in which this letter will reach you.[5] I am nearly dead with overwork; and the
reason I have delayed reading your translations so long is that I can only do
thirtysix hours work every day. I am sorry that you should be worried; but
my own troubles make me callous. The theatres must wait: that is all.

After you left[6] I had a visit from [Gerhart] Hauptmann,[7] to whom I took a
great fancy. My efforts to converse in German were excruciating.

your hochachtungsfully ergebenst
G. Bernard Shaw

Tls.
1. Schlenther's agreement with Trebitsch provided for a 10 percent royalty but stipulated that
the Burg have exclusive rights to *You Never Can Tell* for fifteen years.
2. Schlenther had also expressed interest in *Caesar*, which was still delayed in Berlin.
3. Edward Gordon Craig (1872–1966), brilliant designer son of Ellen Terry (1848–1928) and the
architect Edward Godwin. Reinhardt had engaged him to design the scenery and costumes for his
production of *Caesar*.
4. Lord Herbert Clanricarde (1832–1916), the "cruelest landlord in Ireland," was a bitter foe of
land reform. One of his agents had been assassinated.
5. Charlotte Shaw had prevailed on her husband to visit Ireland, which Shaw had not seen since
leaving it at the age of nineteen. They left England on 6 July and returned on 29 September.
6. Trebitsch had been in London to see *Superman*, which opened at the Court on 23 May.
7. Hauptmann had come to England to receive an honorary doctorate from Oxford.

Derry. Rosscarbery
[c. 20th July 1905]

My dear Trebitsch

On the subject of the Burgtheater, you are simply a dangerous lunatic.[1]
You are prepared to sell your soul and mine—to concede any terms—to commit any crime—for a production at this foolish fashionable playhouse. Now
I am quite willing to allow the Burgtheater to produce my play on honorable
terms. I have drawn the agreement so as to include all the admissible points
of the official agreement—quarterly payment of royalties, no advance &c &c
&c. I will even go further. If the Emperor finds that the ordinary payments to
authors burden his theatre too much, I am quite willing to signify my own
royal pleasure that he may perform the play at his theatre without any payment to me at all, and leave you to make what terms you please for the use of
your translation. But if any attempt is made to impose on me the terms of
the agreement you sent me, I shall not only refuse to allow *any* of my plays
to be performed at the Burgtheater, but I shall publish my reasons in a letter

to The Times and do what I can to induce the Vienna papers to quote my letter. I can quite understand that it is difficult for German & Austrian authors to resist being blackmailed out of their rights by royal theatres; but it is all the more incumbent on me, who am in no such difficulty, to fight their case for them. I should enjoy such a fight more than ten productions in the Burgtheater and my statue erected in the vestibule. If my conduct makes your position difficult, repudiate me, blush for me, assure Plappart-Schlenther that the Emperor has no more devoted subject than Siegfried Trebitsch, but that I, unfortunately, am an Impossibilist and will not listen to reason. I shall win in the end because I do not care a snap of my fingers whether I win or not. I can do without the Burgtheater; but the Burgtheater cannot do without me. If Caesar does not succeed in Berlin, the B.t. will not produce it anyhow. If it *does* succeed in Berlin, the B.t. can no more refuse it than they could refuse Lohengrin because Wagner was an 1848–9 revolutionist.

Remember: you will never be able to bargain unless you are prepared to refuse the deal unless you get your price. All the arguments you use would apply equally if Sch[l]enther were demanding a bribe of a thousand kronen a night and the exclusive right to all our plays. I consider that I am treating Schlenther very handsomely; and so I am; but my terms are my terms: c'est à prendre ou à laisser.

You tell me that if the plays had been in my hands all along I should never have had them produced at all. You forget that if I had acted on your principle of consenting to anything rather than lose a production, the plays would never have been translated by Siegfried Trebitsch. Take one case, typical of all the rest. In 1894 I was offered £160 for the German rights of Arms & The Man. If I had taken it (and the sum was a large one to me then) I should immediately have had the play pushed into half the theatres in Germany. That sort of thing was always happening. And when I said no, the poor refused creatures—Jews mostly—remonstrated with me just as you do, and used all your arguments. They might as well have argued with a stone wall. And the result is that we are now sharing the royalties of Helden. I shall treat the Emperor exactly as I treated the Jews; and if the customs of the B.t. do not suit me, they must be altered: that is all. So go to Schlenther as my ambassador and tell him exactly what the agreements mean, and that he must sign them or deprive the B.t. of all hope of ever being in the European movement.

So much for Schlenther and your Kaiserchen! Now let us deal with matters of importance.

I am sincerely remorseful for my apparently heartless neglect of your translations [of *You Never Can Tell* and *Mrs Warren*]. But the fact is, my situation here has been made quite desperate by the success of John Bull & Man & Superman. The moment I became the fashion, and money was openly made of me, the managers, maddened by the spectacle of rows of carriages & regiments of footmen outside the Court Theatre, made a rush. Business, or the refusal of business, was heaped on me—all the business of thirteen years of playwriting. At the same moment the bankruptcy of my publisher [Grant Richards] threw my books into confusion, and forced me to set my wits to work to get my stereo-plates and photogravure blocks out of the hands of the printers, binders &c &c, who were holding them as security for my publishers debts to them. Then, too, came pressure from America, where my publisher [Brentano] forced me to revise, preface, & see through the press an old novel written in 1880 [*The Irrational Knot*], which was not copyright in the U.S., and would have been pirated if I had not at once supplied an "authorized edition" with copyrighted preface, revisions &c. I had also, of course, to find a new English publisher, and incidentally to change my whole method of publishing. And yet I had to rehearse, rehearse, rehearse, at the Court Theatre as if I had nothing else to do. The result has been that for six months past I have been able to do nothing that could possibly be postponed. My French translator[2] is howling for his MSS back again; and he howls in vain. Your translations lie there heavy on my conscience; but I have never had a chance of reading them. I came here to rest and avoid a breakdown; but the only rest I shall get is the clearing off of some arrears of business and the writing of my new play [*Major Barbara*]. Therefore, O Siegfried, be patient: I have not been lazy nor indifferent, but simply overwhelmed with impossible labors.

I have received the play [Trebitsch's *Ein letzter Wille*] safely. When I have read it, I will consider whether anything can be done with it in London. I have no hope of anything beyond a Stage Society production, or at best a trial by the Court Theatre; but either of these are as good, as far as publicity and press honors go, as a production at the Burgtheater. Only, there is no money at all in the Stage Society, and very little in a Court production for a few matinees. . . .

In haste—I am always in haste now— yours ever

G. Bernard Shaw

Als.; private.

1. On 6 July, Shaw sent Trebitsch copies of an agreement for the Burg's production of *You Never Can Tell*, exclusively licensing the Burg for a period of two years to produce the comedy in Vienna in return for a 10 percent royalty on gross intake. If the Burg failed to produce the play, they were to pay damages.

2. Augustin Hamon (1862–1945), prominent Socialist writer, whom Shaw induced to become his translator despite Hamon's limited knowledge of English.

Derry. Rosscarbery
27th July 1905

[My dear Trebitsch]

. . . Now as to the penalty. There is no penalty in the agreement. You and I, as private people, have no power to impose a penalty on anyone, whether he be Emperor or booth-showman. Now suppose you sign an agreement without a penalty, and the other party breaks it! Your remedy is to take action against him for damages (auf Schade Klagen). . . . You must explain to Schlenther very diplomatically that the Burgtheater is in a different position to other theatres because as an action against the manager would be an action against the Emperor, and as "the King can do no wrong," and no jury would give a foreign author damages, the author has no remedy at all by this method.[1] We are therefore acting with the greatest consideration and forethought as far as the damages are concerned.

If anything is said about Hauptmann, Bahr &c &c accepting the 15 years infamy, you might say delicately that if I were an Austrian or even a German you would not hesitate to appeal to me to make this concession as a matter of loyalty and patriotism, but that you feel that the Emperor himself would not approve of a foreign author being asked to give up his international property to any monarch but his own.

If you master these arguments you will at least be able to talk Schlenther's head off; so that for ever after he will sign anything rather than face you in a discussion.

I have read Frau W's Gewerbe [*Mrs Warren's Profession*], and find it, as far as I can judge, so expert a piece of work that I have taken a good many of the words I dont understand on trust. I hope to post it to Zurich tomorrow. [Passage crossed out by Trebitsch.] There is a famous English novel called Sense and Sensibility by Jane Austen, which you ought to keep on your desk to remind you that an empfindlich [sensitive] person is the very opposite of a vernunftig, verständig, gerade [sensible] person who thinks all empfindlich people wahnsinn [mad]. Vivie is sensible (full of common sense); McNaughtan [i.e., Crampton] is sensible; Anderson in the Teufelskerl is sensible; Bluntschli in Helden is sensible; *I* am sensible. *You* are sensitive (empfindlich); Eugene is sensitive; Sergius is sensitive; Judith is sensitive; all poets & heroines are sensitive.

The name of the new unfinished play (keep it a dead secret) is "Major Barbara." "Passion, Poison & Petrifaction, or The Fatal Gazogene" was performed over and over again (it lasts quarter of an hour) at the Actors' Orphanage Bazaar [in Regent's Park, London, on 14 July], and drew £250 for the orphans. It is gross tomfoolery—not fit for Kladderadatsch,[2] much less the N[eue] R[undschau]. Translating it would be a waste of time, unless there is a German Actors' Orphanage that gives bazaars.[3] Tomorrow, when sending Mrs Warren, I shall send you a line or two for the preface;[4] but you will find all that there is to be said about it in the preface to Plays Unpleasant. I once spent a week in Zurich.[5] Twice a day I took a long swim in the lake: the rest of the time I sweltered in an International Socialist Congress [1893].

yrs ever
G. Bernard Shaw

Als., incomplete; published in catalogue of T. R. G. Lawrence & Son, 23 October 1969.

1. Schlenther objected to "liquidated damages" of 500 kronen if the Burg did not produce *You Never Can Tell* within two years.

2. A political-literary humor magazine published in Berlin.

3. The next year, after a pirated translation appeared (see 28 August 1906), Trebitsch published his version ("Leidenschaft, Gift und Versteinerung") in *Berliner Tageblatt* (8 October).

4. Trebitsch's "Vorwort" to the translation *Frau Warrens Gewerbe*, published in 1906, gave the history of the play's suppression in England and declared that such a ban would be incomprehensible in Germany.

5. Trebitsch was on holiday in Zurich.

10 Adelphi Terrace W.C.

2nd October 1905

Dear Trebitsch

I have just been at a monster meeting of the Salvation Army, singing hymns with enormous fervor, and making notes for Major Barbara.

I enclose receipt for the Revolutionist's Handbook fee.[1] I have glanced at a sentence or two: the translation seems excellent. Your versions are getting devilishly good.

I think it would be a mistake to attempt Bashville. You would find it excessively troublesome to burlesque Tieck & Schlegel in blank verse; and the public would not understand the joke when it was done. It was played in Manchester the other day [22 September]; and the archaic phrase "hight Paradise" (geheisst Paradise) was mistaken for a name, and printed in the program "Hight Paradise," as who should write "Siegfried Trebitsch."[2] As to the prizefighting essay,[3] what interest has that in Germany, where nobody boxes? . . .

yrs ever

G.B.S.

Als.

1. "Der Katechismus des Umstürzlers" ("The Revolutionist's Handbook") appeared in *Neue Rundschau* (October 1905) and earned Shaw £6.

2. Trebitsch did not translate *Bashville* until 1909.

3. "A Note on Modern Prizefighting," which appeared as a preface to the 1901 edition of *Cashel Byron*.

Edstaston. Wem. Shropshire

6th October 1905

Dear Trebitsch

Shropshire is not in Ireland.[1] I have returned from my native land, and now find that I must rewrite the last act of Major Barbara,[2] as the moist Irish climate quite spoiled it.

As to Schlenther, I greatly doubt that you have heard the last of his demands. I am doing what I can to protect you in the matter, because, as you have set your heart on a production at the B.T. [Burgtheater] they can do what they like with you unless I interpose with all the strength I derive from not caring one single solitary individual damn whether I am played at the B.T. or not. I do not in the least care whether the agents & managers refuse to deal with you or not. In that case they will have to come to me; and I shall simply send them back to you. In the case of Y.N.C.T. it does not greatly matter if Sch[l]enther will proceed on the understanding with you. But it is as likely as not that they will start a red tape entanglement on us; and then all the fat will be in the fire. But provided you take care to sign nothing fresh (for they will try to trap you if they cannot trap me), I shall of course not apply to the courts for an injunction to stop the performance. So if it can be managed without any further formalities, nothing need happen except the performance of the play.

In future, however, I advise you very strongly to make yourself appear as foolish (as you call it) as possible. When a manager or agent asks you are you empowered to negotiate, reply "Not at all. Shaw is a personal friend of mine. I translate his plays. He insists on my arranging for production in Germany without giving me any powers. And he is as obstinate as a pig." MANAGER: "Then, my dear sir, I really cannot negotiate with you. I must go direct to the author." TREBITSCH—"Do so by all means. His address is 10 Adelphi Terrace, London W.C. Count on me always. Good morning." A week elapses. The manager requests another interview. MANAGER. "Herr Trebitsch: your thrice accursed Schafkopf of an author refers me to you—says you will arrange everything. Why did you tell me you had no powers?" TREBITSCH "I havn't, I assure you. The man worries the life out of me. He dislikes having his plays produced. He insists on impossible agreements. What can I do for you?" MANAGER. "I want the play." TREBITSCH: "Well, I will do my best for you. Here is the sort of agreement he demands. If you sign this, it will be all right." MANAGER. "Sign this! Never! Monstrous! The man is a gottverdamte English thief." TREBITSCH: "Just so. Well, whats to be done? I can do nothing. He owns the copyright." MANAGER. "Herr Trebitsch: your position is ridiculous. Your demands are unreasonable. You tell me you have no powers; and yet I find that I can do nothing without you. You are trifling with me. You are a conspirator. You are probably the real author of the plays. You are a traitor, selling your country to the English. I will not bear it. I dont care whether I get the play or not. I have my desk full of plays. I can play Schiller instead, or von Schonthan. You are a very foolish young man. You are acting against your own interests. Your translations will never be played. It is a piggery. Leave my office. Never dare enter it again. My seconds shall wait on you. I will give 5%, not a penny more; & the rights must be assigned to me for ever. I ask you to consider my position & be reasonable. I appeal to you as a gentleman, as a friend, as a patriot. What are you taking up your hat for?" TREBITSCH. "My heart bleeds for you, my dear friend; but I assure you you will have to play Schiller unless you give Shaw his terms. The man has a forehead of brass & bowels of stone." MANAGER. "Very well. I will sign, but under protest, mind, under protest." TREBITSCH. "I will tell Shaw so: it will perhaps make him blush. When is the first rehearsal to take place?" And so weiter.

yrs ever

G. Bernard Shaw

Als.; Boston.
  1. The Shaws were visiting Charlotte Shaw's sister, Mrs. Mary Cholmondeley, in Shropshire.
  2. Since returning to England, Shaw had read *Major Barbara* to Granville Barker and Gilbert Murray, the model for Cusins, and had come away feeling that the last act was a "total failure."

10 Adelphi Terrace W.C.
25th October 1905

Dear Trebitsch

. . . There has been an appalling row here in consequence of the article in Die Neue Freie Presse.[1] I wish I could get a copy of the German translation, to see whether it really corresponds to my MS. All day yesterday I was besieged by interviewers; and when I appeared at a public meeting in the afternoon an attempt was made to prevent me from speaking. Today I have a letter in The Times. I expressly told the editor of the N.F.P. to get you to translate it; and if I find that he has made a hash of it I will give him a piece of my mind on the subject. A stupid translator might easily have bungled it frightfully.

John Bull's Other Island seems to have failed in America.[2]

GBS

Als.

    1. On the death of Sir Henry Irving (13 October), *Neue Freie Presse* (Vienna) requested an article from Shaw. "Sir Henry Irving" appeared in a non-Trebitsch translation on 20 October. It was then retranslated into English with serious distortions reflecting discredit on Irving and published in the English press. In the ensuing furor, Shaw, attacked by Stephen Coleridge in the *Times* (24 October), defended himself on the 25th. The *Neue Freie Presse* exonerated Shaw (26 October), and, in turn, Shaw, on the 28th, apologized the paper of a false translation. During the fracas, Shaw attended the London Shakespeare League; a move to silence him was voted down when a member wittily called out, "Why, let us hear Bernardo speak of this."

    2. *John Bull*, produced by Arnold Daly on 10 October at the Garrick Theatre, New York, ran only two weeks.

[10 Adelphi Terrace W.C.]
17th November 1905

[Dear Trebitsch]

Your religious education has been badly neglected. Get a Bible and look at Ev. Matthae XXIII, 14. "Weh euch, Schriftgelehrte und Pharisaer, ihr Heuchler, die ihr der Witwen Hauser presset . . ." [Woe unto you, scribes and Pharisees, hypocrites! for ye devour widows' houses . . .]. The play should be called "Witwen Hauser"[1] or "Weh euch, ihr Heuchler," or something else out of the Bible.

I have received Das Haus am Abhang[2] safely, and hope to read it before I die. Alas! I have not read the Last Will yet. . . .

Craig usually promises to be ready in a week and devise beautiful effects which cost only twenty pounds. The effects *are* beautiful; but he keeps you waiting six months; and the cost is £50,000,000,000 or thereabouts. You must be careful that his system of lighting does not ruin the play. Remember that a comedy scene in the dark is impossible. Unless the faces of the persons on the stage are well lighted, the dialogue will fall flat. If Craig makes beautiful mysterious silhouettes of the speakers, all will be lost. "Caesar and Cleopatra" must not be two ghosts; they must be vivid personalities. For the rest, you may trust Craig, who is a real artist.[3] Outside the art he is probably as unscrupulous as most artists; so he will probably cost the management more than they bargain for. He is a son of Ellen Terry, who is going to play in "Brassbound."

The Irving article was not actually mistranslated, except in two places. The use of the word Fahigkeit [ability] suggested that I was accusing Irving of failing as Romeo for want of skill, whereas what I meant was that it was physically impossible for him to look like Romeo. And my attempt to describe him as living in a dream, an imaginary figure in an imaginary world, was spoiled by turning world into "Pose," which changed the description into an insult.

In haste inconceivable,
rehearsing "Barbara."
G.B.S.

Als.; published in catalogue of G. A. Van Nosdall, August 1945.

1. *Widowers' Houses.* Trebitsch had rendered the title as *Heuchler* (Hypocrites). He later changed it to *Die Häuser des Herrn Sartorius*, and in performance it was sometimes called *Zinsen* (Rents).

2. *Das Haus am Abhang* (House on the Slope), Trebitsch's new novel, which concerned a young doctor who succumbs compassionately to a dying patient with disastrous results.

3. A theatrical visionary, Gordon Craig proposed a kinetic theatre, in which actors were subordinated to lighting and scenery.

10 Adelphi Terrace W.C.
13th December 1905

My dear Trebitsch

I promised the Neue Freie Presse that they should have their article ["Ellen Terry"] on the 15th; and I now hurry it off to you without getting it typed, as I should lose the post & break my word if I waited.[1]

If you have not time to translate it, send it to them & let them translate it themselves. But it is a very delicate article & might be made very offensive by a slight mistake.

I call myself an unsuccessful lover of Ellen's: if they mistake that for "successful," heaven knows what will happen.

In haste
GBS

Als.

1. In "Ellen Terry," Shaw, for the Viennese readers, stressed the woman rather than the actress and contrasted her with Henry Irving. The article appeared on 24 December.

Edstaston. Wem. Shropshire
NOT IN IRELAND[1]
23rd December 1905

I shall be here until the 28th. I am sorry the article was so hard to read. I had intended to send you a typed copy; but at the last moment there was no time for this. Jiacomo should be IACHIMO, the male-star part in "Cymbeline." You must not despise Pinero and Sudermann.[2] Remember what Dumas *fils* said: "It takes a great deal of merit to make even a small success."[3] And S. knows a good deal more than P[inero] or J[ones],[4] neither of whom could have written Heimat. The Superman continues to succeed colossally in New York & at the Court—full houses always & no sign of a decrescendo.[5] If we can get a sufficiently beautiful & fascinating Ann in Berlin & Vienna, it will support us for the rest of our lives.

G.B.S.

Apcs.

1. "NOT IN IRELAND" is underlined three times. For the pointing finger that Shaw draws to add still greater emphasis, see the illustration on p. 92.

81

Odstastor. Wem. Shropshire
NOT IN IRELAND 23/12/05.

I shall be here until the 28th.. I am sorry the article was so hard to read. I had intended to send you a typed copy; but at the last moment there was no time for this. Giacomo should be IACHIMO, the male star part in "Cymbeline". You must not despise Pinero and Sudermann. Remember what Dumas _fils_ said: "It takes a great deal of merit to make even a small success." And S. knows a good deal more than P or J, neither of whom could have written Heimat. The Superman continues to succeed colossally in New York & at the Court — full houses always, & no sign of a decrescendo. If we can get a sufficiently beautiful & fascinating Ann in Berlin & Vienna, it will support us for the rest of our lives.

G. B. S.

Postcard to Trebitsch, 23 December 1905.

2. Shaw in "Ellen Terry" alluded to the moderns as the "Ibsens, Hauptmanns, Sudermanns and their English imitators." Trebitsch, a partisan of Hauptmann (and Shaw), objected to the inclusion of Sudermann and, by implication, of his English counterpart, Arthur Wing Pinero (1855–1934), popular writer of farces and sentimental comedies, who responded to Ibsenite influence in his social dramas but remained a conventional, middle-class playwright.

3. Alexandre Dumas (1824–1895), French dramatist and novelist, had evolved the well-made play into the "problem play" and scored his first success with *La Dame aux camélias*.

4. Henry Arthur Jones (1851–1929), English playwright and critic, wished to broaden the moral and social scope of the drama but was essentially superficial and melodramatic.

5. *Superman* was revived at the Court on 23 October and ran nine weeks. In New York, it opened on 5 September at the Hudson Theatre, with Robert Loraine as Tanner, and ran 192 performances. The third act was omitted in both productions.

10 Adelphi Terrace W.C.
10th January 1906

My dear Trebitsch

I have been bellowing speeches to enormous crowds of Lancashire working men every night for a week past & have just returned to London to bellow again in the suburbs.[1]

I never complain of any publication or performance that does not infringe my copyright.[2] In New York a play founded on my novel "Cashel Byron's Profession" has been performed with—it is reported—great success.[3] My agent in America wanted me to protest. I instructed her to tell the papers politely that I wished the actor & manager every success, but that I had nothing to do with the adaptation.

What on earth does Pipper taust mean?[4] . . .

yrs ever
G. Bernard Shaw

Als.

1. From 4 to 11 January, Shaw spoke on behalf of radical candidates, including the Marxist H. M. Hyndman and labor leader John Burns.

2. *Aus fremden Zungen*, Berlin monthly, edited by Richard Schott, began a serialization of Shaw's *Cashel Byron's Profession* in an unauthorized translation by Alfred Brieger, as *Ein seltsamer Beruf.* The original edition of 1896 was out of copyright.

3. The stage version, by Stanislaus Stange, opened on 8 January with the boxer James J. Corbett as Cashel and, contrary to Shaw's expectations, ran only two weeks.

4. "Pipper taust": Shaw's misreading of *Pippa tanzt*, Hauptmann's new play that was about to open in Berlin.

10 Adelphi Terrace W.C.
30th January 1906

Dear Trebitsch

Will you read the enclosed & return them to me. It might be well to warn the editors of Aus Fremden Zungen and the Vossische Zeitung that any translations they print will be carefully watched, and that if they include a single sentence from the later editions which are still copyright, we will at once proceed against them.[1]

Does Entsch understand that he must not deal with my plays except in the German versions? I was told the other day that he had done some business with Sweden for a Swedish translation from the German of Helden. We must not do this. I deal with Scandinavia & with France &c quite separately, and will not recognize any contract made by Entsch for Swedish, Danish, French, Italian or Spanish versions.

I am not at all surprised about Craig. It is impossible to hold him to anything. Reinhardt is well out of his hands; for with all his artistic genius, he is ruinously expensive & uncertain. The new artist will do his best to shew that he is as good as Craig. Probably he isnt; but Craig might easily have sacrificed the play to the picture.[2] . . .

I will try to send back your versions in good time. But I am hard pressed by my French translator & a thousand other things. I dont do my best—nobody does—but I do as much as my weakness & laziness will let me.

In haste—ever
G. Bernard Shaw

Als.
   1. Shaw thought that the revised 1901 edition of *Cashel* was still copyright and presumably enclosed draft letters warning editors away from it. *Vossische Zeitung* did not publish the novel.
   2. Craig, finding that he was not going to be in control of the entire production of *Caesar*, had withdrawn. Reinhardt had given in on Craig's demands to design not only sets and costumes but also lighting and movement, but he could not permit him to act as stage director, which Craig (as he explains in *The Art of the Theatre*, 1905) considered his role. Karl Walser and Hans Olden took over the designing.

10 Adelphi Terrace W.C.
5th February 1906
My dear Trebitsch
   . . . Please cherish your typist as a wise counsellor. The man who stops to fight every fool & rascal he meets never gets to his own destination. In future I think I will send you every letter I get about you. Do you know that for years I have had letter after letter from German literary hacks, all wanting to translate my works, and all assuring me that you write the most infamous German, that you are an Austrian foreigner, that you have been in prison six times for disgraceful conduct, that you murdered your first wife and are now living separated from your second with three mistresses, that my plays would be far better known in Germany if I had a reputable translator, and that you are well known to be the illegitimate son of the Crown Prince and a notorious ballet dancer. You must get accustomed to these common incidents of public life.

At the election, the day after I made a great speech in Rochdale, the candidate [S. G. Hobson] told me that a man had refused to vote for him because he was supported by that blackguard Shaw, who left his wife to starve 20 years ago & has since been living with two women *on their earnings.*

Do not be angry with poor Brieger.[1] The poor devil must live—at least he thinks so.

I begin rehearsing Brassbound at the Court on the 19th.[2]

Is the whole of Mensch & Ubermensch [*Man and Superman*] really translated! I am amazed at your industry. Magnificent! The third act is cut out chock-a-block (ganz und gar).[3] Also, in the 1st Act, from the middle of p 31 to near the end of p. 38. It runs thus—*Tanner. It is over: let me forget*

it. Ann. I am sorry you thought my influence a bad one.—The Perfect
Wagnerite is still copyright.[4] It has a few years to run still.

yrs ever

G. Bernard Shaw

Als.
   1. Trebitsch was incensed with Alfred Brieger for undertaking the translation of *Cashel Byron.*
   2. *Captain Brassbound's Conversion,* with Ellen Terry, opened at the Court on 20 March 1906.
   3. Shaw is speaking of cuts in production, of course, not of the printed version.
   4. Trebitsch's translation, *Ein Wagnerbrevier,* appeared in 1908. A selection appeared earlier in
Neue Rundschau, 1907.

10 Adelphi Terrace W.C.

1st March 1906

My dear Trebitsch

As to Brieger personally, you may challenge him and cut him in small
pieces with a sabre if you like;[1] but that will not settle the question of Aus
Fremden Zungen. These people have begun their translation; and they must
either finish it or make themselves ridiculous in the eyes of the public. To
finish it they must do one of two things. 1. Get somebody in London to go to
the British Museum, and copy out the old edition of Cashel Byron's Profession from end to end, so as to find out what parts of Brieger's translation are
copyright. 2. Purchase our consent to the appearance of Brieger's translation
in the paper only, without allowing it to be reprinted or used again in any
way. I suggested £200; but it would be cheaper for them to send to London—
in fact, if they were clever enough to offer a London bookseller £10 for a
copy of the original edition (or any edition earlier than 1896) they would
probably get it. They are now very close to the chapter in which I made the
first alteration for copyright purposes. The last number sent to me is Heft 4.
Perhaps you had better send me the paper as soon as it appears; so that I may
know at once if they have overstepped the mark, when I will go to the Authors' Society[2] here and get the name of a German lawyer to set at them. We
must make them pay: otherwise they will do it again. Meanwhile if they
open negotiations with you, say you simply wish to know what they offer
for the right to complete their publication of the novel.

My wife insists on dragging me to Paris for twelve days at Easter so that
Rodin may make a bust of me!!!!![3]

There are really no pictures of the scenery of You Never Can Tell available;
and if there were I should not send them, as the Burgtheater does not need to
copy the second hand makeshift of a little repertory theatre like the Court.
Give them the plans and let them paint really good scenery and send pictures of it to me for use when the play is revived next autumn.

yrs ever

G. Bernard Shaw

Als.; postscript omitted.
   1. As Shaw knew, Trebitsch as a youth was involved in several duels.
   2. The Society of Authors was founded in 1884 to promote and defend the rights of writers.
Shaw joined in 1897.

3. Auguste Rodin (1840–1917), celebrated French sculptor, had been to lunch with the Shaws that day, during which Charlotte arranged for her husband to sit for Rodin. The Shaws left for Paris the following month.

[Harmer Green.] Welwyn
28th March 1906

My dear Trebitsch

At last I snatch a moment to write to you.

Aus Fremden Zungen has at last reached the chapter in which the first new passage of the 1901 edition occurs. You will by this time have received from the Authors Society a copy of the statement they have placed in the hands of Justizrath [King's Counsel] Bohun Jonas.[1] We must make them pay us through the nose for their piracy. But what is more important than the money is that whatever terms we make, we must get from them all rights in Brieger's translation; so that if you use it as a text to correct later on, there may be no question of his interfering with us.

Hjaltar (Helden) has been a success in Sweden.[2] I broke Entsch's contract by paying £16 to the manager; and my translator Hugo Vallentin got £8 of it back. I have already got royalties enough to clear me, and my footing is established in Sweden; so that is all right. And of course I got a higher percentage than Entsch asked.

I will not deal with Eirich.[3] Complaints of him have been received here by the Authors Society; and I am not sure that he has not collected royalties which he has never sent to the authors he pretends to represent. A London agent named Mayer, representing Felix Erben, offers to negotiate a Hungarian treaty for me; and I think I shall consent.[4] Charley Musek[5] translates me into Bohemian; but I havnt got anything out of him yet.

Several accounts of Y.N.C.T. were telegraphed to the London papers, chiefly to the effect that the play was too English & unfamiliar for Vienna, and that the hissing was as vigorous as the applause.[6]

If you cross the Mediterranean to Africa, look out for any photographs that would be useful for Brassbound. There is money in Brassbound if you can find an Austrian Ellen Terry to make it for you.

I have not read your scripts yet, I am ashamed to say. I am struggling with a mountain of French, Swedish, Italian, American & English business, all thrown frightfully into arrear by the rehearsals of Brassbound. Brassbound goes into the evening bill on Easter Monday: you must come over and see Ellen Terry in it. She is immense, though she is 58, and cant remember half my words.

On that same Easter Monday I sit for the first time to Rodin. He undertakes to complete the bust in 12 days of two sittings each; so I shall perhaps get back to London by the beginning of May.

Though I have neglected your translations I have wrestled with Die Letzte Wille, and got through three quarters of it *à coups de dictionnaire*. I wish I knew German. I cannot say what I think of the play until I see how it ends; but it seems to me to have a peculiar quality that will pull it through. As far as I can judge Austro-German seems to be as much superior to Berlin-German as Irish-English to London-English. There is a certain intensity about the theme and about your grip of it which makes me disposed to believe that you have the energy of imagination which makes the dramatist; and the characters are real. On the other hand, it is melancholy; it is all about women and love; and I have a presentiment that it is going to end unhappily. In that case I shall write a new last act in which, after a lively interview with Markstein's ghost, Heda shall divorce Lecher and marry the lawyer.[7]

I shall finish reading it this week & then reopen communications with Mrs Hayden Coffin. If she makes a rough translation I shall make Barker read it. He does not know German. If he doesnt like it, there is always the Stage Society to fall back on.

I note that you are to be in London about the 12th May.

Do they ever photograph the scenes at the Burgtheater by flashlight? If so, I would buy a set of pictures of Y.N.C.T.: such things are useful when planning the *mise-en-scène* for revivals.

yrs ever

G. Bernard Shaw

Als.

1. Paul Jonas, a German lawyer recommended by Trebitsch; Shaw rechristened him "Bohun" after the counselor in *You Never Can Tell*.

2. *Hjältar* opened in Stockholm on 17 March to 23 curtain calls and ran 35 times.

3. Otto F. Eirich, Viennese agent, wanted to represent Shaw in the Austrian empire for all non-German languages.

4. Ernst Mayer, acting for the Berlin agency Felix Bloch Erben, had informed Shaw of an offer by the Comedy Theatre (Vigszinhaz), Budapest, to produce *Devil's Disciple* and *Caesar*.

5. Karl Musek (d. 1924), Shaw's Czech translator and agent, introduced Shaw with *You Never Can Tell* on 16 January 1906 at the National Theatre, Prague.

6. *Der verlorene Vater* (*You Never Can Tell*), the Burg's first production of Shaw, opened on 17 March, staged by Ernst Hartmann, with Lotte Witt, Arnold Korff, and Hugo Thimig. Ill prepared and severely cut, it baffled the audience, which "hissed and applauded" (*Neue Freie Presse*), and was coolly received as lesser Shaw. The play had only eight performances.

7. In Trebitsch's *Ein letzter Wille* von Merkstein, from beyond the grave, compromises Heda Lecher for rejecting his advances in favor of her lover. Heda abandons her home, but in the end yields to her husband's plea to return to her child.

Harmer Green. [Welwyn]
28th [29th] March 1906

My dear Trebitsch

I have at last finished Die Letzte Wille. It will be a difficult play to place in London. You know that our audiences are pretty childish. They like heroines who are in their first youth—or pretend to be. They like some fun, and a happy ending. No ordinary manager or actor-manager would produce it; but an actress touring with a repertory—Miss Olga Nethersole, for instance[1]—might take it if the part of Heda fascinated her. That, I should think, is the only chance for it beyond a few matinees at the Court (where, however, I do not at present see the right woman for it), and a performance by the Stage Society.

I find the play interesting all through; and though it is rather a string of duets, I dont dislike duets. There is no hero except Markstein, who dies early. Rudolph[2] is an elusive character. He leaves the impression that he is going to desert Anna, not because he dislikes her or is uncomfortable with her, but because he has come to the conclusion that a comfortable life is unscientific, old fashioned, & impossible. The whole play is really morbid & depressing because none of the people have any will: they are all flies on the wheel of Fate & Circumstance, like the people in George Eliot's novels. But you save the situation by making the main struggle poetic and dramatic. Still, your philosophy is nothing but nerves; and I must cure you of it. Human will and purpose *do* count for a great deal in the making of human destiny. Really vital people are always knocking the inevitable into a cocked hat, and achieving the impossible. *Your* fate was to be either a man of business or a military duel-fighting officer. There was nothing whatever but your own will to save you. Well, it *did* save you; so let the people in your next play have a little will and a little victory, and then you will begin to enjoy yourself and write your plays in the Shavian Key—D flat major, vivacissimo.

I shall convey my opinion to Mrs Hayden Coffin and confer with her as to the play's chances of finding a market here.[3]

If you can secure any pictures of the dresses & scenery in Caesar,[4] from the illustrated papers or otherwise, let me have them, as they will be useful here.

I wrote to you yesterday about the other matters.

yrs ever
G. Bernard Shaw

Als.

1. Olga Nethersole (1870–1951), English actress-manager, toured widely in popular repertory.

2. Heda's brother; he openly lives unmarried with Anna but smugly preaches the sacred duties of motherhood.

3. On 15 April Mrs. Coffin wrote to Shaw that *Ein letzter Wille* would be hard to place with producers, since it lacked clear purpose and had an unattractive heroine. The play was never translated into English.

4. Reinhardt's long-delayed production in Berlin was about to open.

Harmer Green. Welwyn
13th April 1906

My dear Trebitsch

Your Bohun-Jonas man will not reply to the letters of the Authors' Society. It is essential that instant action should be taken, as the threat of stopping the publication of Brieger's piracy will be far more effectual than any threat of an action for damages later on, when the publication is finished. Do you know whether he is doing anything? A man who will not answer business letters must be either a genius or a nincompoop.

The Devil's Disciple has had a huge success at Budapesth; but the whole affair, production translation & all, was a flat piracy. I never authorized it. A London agent, Ernest Mayer, says they "misunderstood" some letters of on earth does he not induce the Kaiser to pay a visit. Wilhelm would see himself as Caesar, and perhaps write an additional act or play the part himself some night. And then Reinhardt's fortune would be made. He should also set his press agents to work to emphasize the fact that the play owes its inspiration to Germany, as my Caesar is Mommsen's Caesar dramatized.

However, it is a shame to bother you with all this on your holiday. I feel, myself, that if I write another letter or think out another sentence I shall go stark mad. On Sunday I start for Paris – Hotel Palais d'Orsay. Rodin has influenza; but he thinks he can at least make a beginning. I have the greatest doubt of the bust being ever finished.

Final page of letter to Trebitsch, 13 April 1906.

his, *and sent him £40 in advance on account of royalties*(!!!!), and that he greatly regrets their stupidity.[1]

I am sorry Caesar was not more successful in Berlin.[2] It would have been better to omit the third act: the play is too long. Was the Caesar able to rise to the grander moments of the part in Act IV and in the scene with Septimius in Act II? What I dread is that they played it as a comedy all through—five acts of Bluntschli in a bald pate instead of Caesar. However, if Reinhardt is so anxious to secure Man & Superman he can hardly have had a complete disaster with Caesar. Why on earth does he not induce the Kaiser to pay a visit. Wilhelm would see himself as Caesar, and perhaps write an additional act or play the part himself some night. And then Reinhardt's fortune would be made. He should also set his press agents to work to emphasize the fact that the play owes its inspiration to Germany, as my Caesar is Mommsen's Caesar dramatized.

However, it is a shame to bother you with all this on your holiday. I feel, myself, that if I write another letter or think out another sentence I shall go stark mad. On Sunday I start for Paris—Hotel Palais d'Orsay. Rodin has influenza; but he thinks he can at least make a beginning. I have the greatest doubt of the bust being ever finished.[3]

                                                                        GBS

Als.

   1. *Devil's Disciple* (*Az ördög cimborája*), directed by Sándor Goth, opened in Budapest on 28 March and was "eminently successful," its political allusions evoking "thunderous applause" (*Glasgow Evening Citizen*, 31 March). Dr. Mihály of the Comedy Theatre wrongly believed that Shaw had accepted a suggested 4 percent royalty and £40 advance, but Shaw sued the theatre and aborted the run at 15 performances.

   2. Reinhardt's *Caesar*—its first professional production—opened on 31 March with Albert Steinrück and Gertrude Eysoldt at the Neues Theater, staged by Hans Olden, and was coolly received: "A few strong-voiced faithful shouted their approval," but most left "confused and silent" (*Berliner Tageblatt*, 1 April). Critics faulted the play's episodic structure and uncertain tone but praised the production, which ran 18 times.

   3. For Shaw's accompanying drawing, see the illustration on p. 99.

Hotel Palais d'Orsay. Paris
1st May 1906

We are still alive. We spent the afternoon in the crowd on the Place de la Republique, close to the Bourse du Travail; and Charlotte enjoyed for the first time in her life the sensation of seeing a crowd charged by cavalry. She got very angry and wanted to throw stones. She rather enjoyed being part of the revolution and having to run out of danger from time to time. We finished up in the evening with a very stirring performance of Beethoven's 9th symphony at the Opera; so the day was a pretty full one.[1] It was pleasant to see you in Paris:[2] we hope to hear of your safe arrival after a bearable journey.

                                                                        G.B.S.

Apcs.

   1. Police and troops were mobilized in expectation of massive May Day demonstrations in the Place de la République by striking workers demanding an eight-hour workday. The feared uprising

did not occur, but violence broke out when troops charged the crowd, which responded by over-
turning buses and building barricades. Many workers were injured and over a thousand were arrested. Troops guarded the Bourse and the jewelry district, but at the Opéra and the State theatres
performances went on as usual.
   2. The previous evening the Shaws and Trebitsch attended the Grand Guignol.

                                           Hotel Palais d'Orsay. Paris
                                           7th May 1906
My dear Trebitsch
   The secret of Caesar's failure is out at last; and never again shall Reinhardt
have a play of mine to ruin. Barker[1] has seen it and told me all about it.
   They have cut out the first scene of the 4th act!!! Of course that meant
utter failure. It is in that scene that the change in Cleopatra's character is
shewn, and the audience prepared for the altered atmosphere and deeper seriousness of the later scene. To omit it is such a hopeless artistic stupidity
that the man who would do it would do anything. I will not trust him with
the Superman or with anything else after that. Write to him and tell him so.
If you dont, I will write myself, not to him, but to the Berlin papers.
   He has also cut out the burning of the library, which must make the end
of the second act unintelligible. In short, he has done everything that a
thoroughpaced blockhead could do to achieve a failure; and he has achieved
it accordingly. If he has advanced any money on the Superman, send it back
to him at once; and tell him that I protest against any further performances
of Caesar with his abominable mutilations. I told him what to do—to omit
the third act. He was too clever to do that; so he spoiled the 2nd 3rd & 4th
acts instead, and wrecked the play. May his soul perish for it!
   It is always a mistake to trust to these people to alter a play. They see the
effects, but they dont see the preparation of the effects—the gradual leading
of the audience up to them. They cut the preparation out, and then are surprised because the effects miss fire.
   Barker presented your introduction to Reinhardt, and sent him two letters
& a telegram. Reinhardt took not the smallest notice of either your letter or
Barker's. Barker naturally regards this as a Schweinerei [piggishness] of the
first order.
   Please challenge him (R) to a duel with redhot sabres at once.
   I give Rodin a final sitting tomorrow (Tuesday the 8th) and leave for London by the 4 o'clock train, arriving at midnight.

                                                         GBS

   PS. Barker says that the Roman army consisted of about half as many men
as the crew of Captain Brassbound's ship at the little Court theatre. But that
I could forgive. It is the cutting of the 4th act that rouses me to an implacable,
vindictive fury. My play has been deliberately murdered.

Als.
   1. Granville Barker, recently wed to Lillah McCarthy, was on honeymoon in Germany, where
he saw Reinhardt's *Caesar* and wrote Shaw about it.

10 Adelphi Terrace W.C.

30th May 1906

My dear Trebitsch

In case anybody wants to know my opinion about Ibsen's influence in England, I send you a proof of an article which will appear tomorrow in The Clarion, a Socialist paper. Perhaps the Neue Freie Presse might like it.[1]

I met Meyerfeldt at a dinner given to celebrate the opening of the exhibition of pictures by German artists. [R. B.] Haldane, our Minister for War, presided; and there was great speech making and *entente cordiale* u.s.w. [and so on]. Haldane proposed the toast of the Drama; and I responded.[2] We all did our best to cry Hoch in the proper German way.

Later on, Meyerfeldt called on me. He has been asked to write a preface to Brieger's piracy, which extends, it appears, to all my novels.[3] He said, of Brieger & Schott (the editor of Aus Fernem [Fremden] Zungen) that, after all, they were gentlemen. I overwhelmed poor Meyerfeldt with the energy of my very contrary opinion. I told him I had no objection at all to their using their legal rights over the early editions of my novels, and that I should not quarrel with him if he accepted the job of writing a preface, but that I would pursue them with the utmost vengeance of the law if they touched the new matter in the later editions. I explained to him that if Schott's claim that the lapse of a copyright applied to all later editions of the book, it would follow that the latest edition of the Encyclopedia Britannica, or of Webster's Dictionary, would not be copyright—sooner than admit which, the English & American publishers would carry the case through every court in Germany. The matter is now in the hands of the Society of Authors & of Jonas, whose instructions are to smash the pirates rather than attempt to come to terms with them.

I strongly advise you not to be in a hurry to dispose of Man & Superman. I greatly dislike the system of locking up plays for the sake of advances. Managers who care very little about plays care very much about preventing other managers from getting them. If you wait, the Burgtheater is bound to produce Man & Superman. Schlenther will presently realize the extent of the American success, which has been colossal.[4] He must take, not what he wants, but what we think good for him. *Refuse him Die Heuchler [Widowers' Houses]*. Tell him it will do very well for a small theatre, but that the next Shaw play at the Burg must be either Caesar or Man & Superman. If you feel too modest to say these things for yourself, tell him that those are my orders—that I do not deal with Imperial theatres for Guignol plays.

Fischer has sent me M382.50, which he says is a Garantie of 500 kronen from Budapesth for the Verlorene Vater [*Y.N.C.T.*].[5] I do not understand this. . . . I am just now up to my neck in legal proceedings in Budapesth;[6] and if, after instructing the lawyers that I have authorized no one to deal with my Hungarian rights, it turns out that Fischer or Entsch have been making contracts for performances in Hungarian or Bohemian, there will be no end of a mess. Do all you can to make them understand that they must not touch any language except German. The complications of my foreign business are already enough to drive me mad; and it is only by keeping the different languages from becoming entangled that I can make any headway. . . .

As to Reinhardt, I wish he had not the Superman. If he made a mess of Caesar he will make a worse mess of the other. As for you, O Siegfried, you are capable of anything in the way of cutting a play, because you never really believe in my opinion. My instructions were to cut out the third act. I knew perfectly well that it would be enormously popular; but I knew also that it would kill the sequel. And I was quite right. As to the reduction of the crowd and the other outrages, you say that these things happen on all German stages. They happen on all the stages in the world *if you let them*. The way to prevent them is to refuse the next play to the manager who does them. You should have given Reinhardt my undying curse instead of letting him capture the Superman. I do not remember getting any money direct from Die N.F.P. lately; but I may be mistaken: as my account books are in London.—Barker is still in the Tyrol.—Sorma should do Brassbound: it is evidently the very thing for her.[7]

yrs ever

G.B.S.

Als.; postscript omitted.

1. Trebitsch's translation of Shaw's obituary article on Ibsen ("Ibsen in England"), who had died on 23 May, was published in *Neue Rundschau* (1906).

2. At a banquet in honor of the German Art Exhibition in London, Shaw spoke of his debt to German drama and music and contrasted German recognition of his works with English neglect (*Standard*, 22 May).

3. Brieger had let it be known that he intended to translate all of Shaw's novels.

4. *Superman* ran six months in New York and then toured.

5. *Der verlorene Vater* was not produced in Budapest that year.

6. The Comedy Theatre was defending their production of *Devil's Disciple* by claiming that they believed the play was American and not subject to copyright in Hungary, and moreover that they had bought rights from Mihály.

7. Agnes Sorma did play Lady Cicely in *Brassbound* the following year at Barnowsky's Kleines Theater.

Harmer Green. Welwyn

2nd June 1906

My dear Trebitsch

I find that there is a clause in the copyright treaty between England & Austro-Hungary which says that unless a foreign author complies with all the formalities required of a Hungarian author he loses his copyright. I am greatly afraid this means a checkmate for me in my battle with the Budapesth pirates.[1] But there is one chance left. If *you* have complied with all the formalities (whatever they may be) your Drei Dramen &c may be copyright in Hungary; and I may be able to claim on the strength of it. You are a citizen of the Austro-Hungarian Empire, and may have common law rights over and above those created by the treaty for foreigners. Have you registered your translations in Hungary? . . .

yrs ever

G.B.S.

Als.

1. Shaw's attorney confirmed that Shaw had forfeited copyright in Hungary by not registering a translation within six months of publication. The Comedy now refused to pay anything.

10 Adelphi Terrace W.C.
13th June 1906

My dear Trebitsch

Your letter, for which we have waited anxiously, destroys our hopes. You have not grasped the situation. There is no question of quarrelling about royalties: what has happened is the discovery that I have no copyright at all in Hungary because I did not register my plays there within a year of publication with all the formalities which a Hungarian author has to go through.

There is only one chance left; and that is that though my plays are not copyright, your translations may be; and in that case you may be able to claim that the piratical performances are violations of *your* rights. Therefore what we want to know is whether your translations have been registered in Hungary with all the proper formalities, or whether, as a subject of the Austro-Hungarian Empire you are exempt from formalities. In short, have you copyright or have you not? Did Cotta register the Drei Dramen? Has Fischer registered Caesar & Y.N.C.T.? If not, and there is still time, make him do it.

Do you realize that I am in the middle of a lawsuit, and that the question is not one of royalties but of copyright. I am beaten; but you may be still master of the situation.

In haste—yrs ever
G.B.S.

Als.

10 Adelphi Terrace W.C.
18th June 1906

My dear Trebitsch

Believe me, I am not heartlessly indifferent about Übermensch [*Superman*], Heuchler [*Widowers' H.*] & Co., but the pressure on me has reached the limit of human endurance. I have gone through Heuchler and the first act of Übermensch, and noted several places that need revision, especially in the Superman. But to take a dictionary and explain and write down all the corrections will take time. I had hoped to give my evenings to it this week. But yesterday I arranged for the production of Caesar in America;[1] and one of the conditions is that I start rehearsing it in London tomorrow. In the evenings I must prepare the stage business and write dozens of speeches, exclamations, whispers &c &c for the crowds (it is the only way of getting a natural effect); and in the mornings I must rehearse. Meanwhile, the press is waiting for the prefaces to John Bull & Major Barbara at which I have been slaving; and the text of them corrected for the printer. And there are dozens of other things turning up every day without mentioning the frantic appeals of Hamon for his French versions. What can I do?

I wish I could convince you that you are spoiling these theatrical people by sending them texts. They dont read them; and they would not understand them if they did. Send them a circular to say that the translation of Man &

Superman, the greatest of my successes in England & America, will be ready in time for production next season. That is quite enough. And mind you dont let the Viennese rights go. Tell Schlenther that I have made up my mind that Man & Superman shall be produced at the Burg, and that he shall get nothing else of mine until he has agreed to that. I must earnestly beg you not to dismiss this as a joke & sell the thing to Jarno [of the Theater in der Josefstadt] or the first comer. Your plan of catching the bird in the hand on the principle that le mieux, c'est l'ennemi du bien, is all very well; but a man who cannot say NO is lost in the theatrical world. Schlenther is in a weaker position than Jarno, not in a stronger one. He *must* have Caesar & The Superman whether he likes it or not, in the long run. If you let these men worry you, you will die before your time. They must wait for you; and it is absurd to wear yourself out as if they could pick up Shaw plays in every street.

The Hungarian business is a serious loss for us; and I dont quite know what to do. My own course is clear: if I have no copyright I have nothing to sell, and cannot employ Eirich & Co to extort money from Hungarian theatres on false pretenses.[2] I had intended to notify the Hungarian managers that my plays, so far, are not copyright, and to warn them not to pay any sums to anyone for rights which do not exist. But I have to consider you in the matter. There must, I should think, be still time to copyright the Verlorene Vater, in which case you are entitled to the enclosed money. As to the Devil's Disciple, I think you will find that the Budapesth people are now thoroughly alive to their advantage, and will refuse to pay anything.

In haste for post—yrs ever
G. Bernard Shaw

Als.; postscript omitted.

1. *Caesar* opened at the New Amsterdam Theatre, New York, on 30 October—the first professional staging of the play in English—with Forbes Robertson, for whom the play was created, and Gertrude Elliott.

2. Because Trebitsch's translations were not registered in Hungary, Shaw had no claims to the 382.50 marks remitted by Fischer for the prospective *You Never Can Tell* in Budapest.

10 Adelphi Terrace W.C.
25th June 1906

My dear Trebitsch

If you allow Reinhardt to depart by one millimetre from the strict letter of my instructions, the Superman will [be] a disastrous failure.[1] I have been through all this clamor in London. All the wiseacres there were equally convinced that the play was unfit for the stage, especially without the third act. Nobody was such an utter idiot as to propose to play the dream with heads only visible; but they were quite sure that the play without the dream and the brigands would be uninteresting.

Tell Reinhardt that I will pay him £50, to surrender his contract and let us have the Superman back again. If he refuses, tell him that this time I will take steps to protect myself from having my work spoiled as he spoiled

Caesar. I am making the acquaintance of the German editors who are now visiting London, expressly that I may be able to use the press to appeal against any attempt to mutilate my play. My conditions are clear. The cuts will be made by me. They will include the whole third act, and a large part of the second half of the first act, just as I explained to you. Mendoza will not appear at all: his lines at the end of the fourth act will be spoken by Straker. There will be no cutting of the long speeches of Tanner: they must be spoken at full length not only on the first night but on every other night. I will not have this rascally chicanery of giving a play properly on the first night to secure good press notices, and then cheating the public with short-ened and spoiled performances later on. It is no use telling me that it is al-ways done in Germany: you might as well tell me that pockets are always being picked in Germany. If Reinhardt does not like my ideas of art and busi-ness he can write plays himself or go to other authors.

I most earnestly beg you not to put this aside as what you call a Shawish answer, and smooth over things with Reinhardt. If you do not like to deal with him in my fashion, tell me so; and I will write to him direct. I can easily get my letters translated here if he does not know English. I know that it is rather difficult for you to behave as if you were fifty, and were thoroughly practised in the way of handling managers; but it is still harder for me to throw away my advantages and let these people muddle my plays as if I were a beginner with no position and no experience of the stage. Besides, I am doing it as much for your sake as mine. You must learn to say No, and to throw money in the faces of the managers: otherwise they will go on be-lieving that they have only to hold out and you will give in. You thought Schlenther would not give in about the agreement for Y.N.C.T. Well, he did give in. You threw away the Superman on a minor theatre because you thought—in spite of my assurances—that Schlenther would never do it at the Burg.[2] He would have done it next year.

When you see Reinhardt, the FIRST thing to do is to offer him whatever money he advanced us on the Superman (I forget whether he advanced any) *and* £50 down to break the contract. If he accepts, I will pay the money at once. The effect of that on Reinhardt will be worth £100 to me. If he wants to know why, say that his violation of my instructions by performing the light-house scene in Caesar, and thereby sacrificing the fourth act and turning a success into a failure, has convinced me that he has not the necessary grasp of theatrical conditions to handle my plays, and that his monstrous proposal to do the dream with cuts and four heads has completed my disillusion. If he refuses the offer and sticks to the play, let it be clearly understood that he does so on my conditions, which are as I have stated them above. I shall also ask him to put upon the program a statement that the stage version has been made by the author; that the omission of the third act is in accordance with my instructions; and that the management placed themselves at my dis-posal in the matter and are not responsible for the cuts except in so far as they have had to admit that some cutting was necessary, as the play in its entirety would take nearly eight hours to perform.

You need not fear the result. I know what I am about, and the sort of people I am dealing with; and you, O Siegfried, are far too amiable to be left in the hands of these sharks. They take advantage of your inexperience. I dont want you to bully them. Be as nice as you like; but be inexorable. I am afraid I have lost the post after all, confound it!

GBS

Tls.

1. Reinhardt had succeeded to the management of the Deutsches Theater, Berlin's preeminent playhouse, which he now purchased and to which he added an intimate "chamber theatre"—the Kammerspiele—seating 300, which he intended for contemporary playwrights and to which he typically assigned premieres of Shaw.

2. Trebitsch, despite Shaw's instructions, had given *Superman* to the Deutsches Volkstheater in Vienna, not to a "minor" theatre, rather than wait for the Burg.

Pentillie. Mevagissey
19th July 1906

My dear Trebitsch

You are giving yourself the most horrible worry and trouble for nothing at all. You are trying to fight the whole battle of my life over again, and to make it a series of surrenders instead of victories. Germany & Austria & the Viennese-Palace-Theatre-Chamberlain [Plappart of the Burgtheater] are all going to do just what I choose & not what they choose. Man & Superman will have the same title all over the world. Mensch und Übermensch is precisely right. Such a title as Der neue Don Juan, or Donna Juana, would mislead the public & create furious disappointment. Die Jagd nach dem Mann [The Manhunt] would belittle the play & drag it down to the level of the silliest & vulgarest of the critics. Mensch und Übermensch affirms its essentially philosophic quality & dignity. It has been so enormously successful merely as a title that the phrase has become a proverb in England & America; and so it shall in Germany.

Why, oh why, do you devote your life to translating me if you dont believe in me, and are ready to throw over my most carefully considered plans whenever some blockhead mentions the first objections that come into a fool's head in the first five minutes? You are too modest—too diffident. Well, as Drinkwater in Brassbound says, "If you want to be modest, be modest on your own account, not on mine." And when you find how successful my policy will be, you will try it on your own account too.

Jonas is an utter imbecile. That point about copyright passages in new editions is *the most important of all the points of copyright law*, because millions of money invested in encyclopedias, gazetteers & dictionaries, depend on it. I have instructed the Society of Authors to engage another lawyer at once: we can get a trustworthy one through the British embassy.[1] Write privately to Jonas that he has utterly disgraced himself, and that he had better look for employment as a railway porter; for he will never succeed as a lawyer. Where did you pick up the idiot?

There is a violent controversy going on about me in Berlin because I told the German editors that the Social-Democrats are too old fashioned & reactionary to dare print my articles in their papers.[2] . . .

yrs ever
G. Bernard Shaw

PS. The publication of the hell scene in the Rundschau is impossible:[3] it is far too long; and it must not be mutilated. You will utterly ruin me by throwing my works in crumbs to the dogs instead of publishing them complete. And what is this Kleines Theater to which you are giving Y.N.C.T.?[4] Why not the Grosses Theater?

Als.

1. Paul Jonas, Shaw's Berlin lawyer, was replaced by the firm of Schneider and Jablonski.

2. A feud between left German Social Democrats and the Fabians was exacerbated by an interview with Shaw in *Die neue Gesellschaft* in which Shaw derided the Social Democrats as "too reactionary" and cited the refusal of *Vorwärts* to publish his May Day article. The Social Democrats retorted (12 July) that the article had been rejected as too bourgeois. Shaw responded in the liberal *Berliner Tageblatt* (25 July) because, he explained, *Vorwärts* would mishandle his views, which were too advanced for their Party ("Bernard Shaw über die deutsche Sozialdemokratie"). The next day, *Vorwärts* scornfully reprinted Shaw's letter as "megalomaniac literary socialism."

3. Despite Shaw's wishes, Trebitsch published the hell scene from *Superman* in *Neue Rundschau* (November 1906).

4. The Kleines Theater (seating 400) passed from Reinhardt to Victor Barnowsky (1875–1952), who, next to Reinhardt, was to lead in premieres of Shaw's works in Berlin. *You Never Can Tell* (*Man kann nie wissen*) opened at the Kleines on 24 September for 25 performances with Harry Walden, Marietta Olly, and Guido Herzfeld.

10 Adelphi Terrace W.C.
24th July 1906

My dear Trebitsch

Lowenfeld[1] was formerly well known in London as what is called an "outside stockbroker." He made a lot of money by a lucky railway speculation, and with it launched out into theatre management—mostly musical comedy of the vulgarest kind, though he began with light operas. He built the Apollo Theatre and shortly afterwards came to grief and vanished, much discredited. I knew him a little, as he used to offer me £500 a year & a third of his profits if I would write librettos for him.

You had better not have anything to do with him in the way of business. He is not a manager; and his Bankgeschäft [bank business] is simply a "bucket shop." In fact he is just exactly what he appears: you can take his measure at sight. But I never got virtuously indignant with him: I let him talk & make me offers, and told him he was born to play Napoleon in my Man of Destiny. I rather liked him, in fact.

If you have a spare copy of Die Letzte Wille by you, send it to me and I will send it to Dr Wheeler,[2] who is interested in the Austrian theatre (he translates Schnitzler) and would perhaps translate your piece for the Stage Society, as he has just joined the committee. I am so full of work for years ahead that there is no use waiting for me, though I will collaborate with Wheeler if he needs my help. I think the S.S. ought to do the play: there is a certain quality about it that is significant & attractive.

I am plodding through the hell scene slowly but surely.

Send me the Wagner book: there may be some technical mistakes in it that only a professional musician could avoid. For instance, there is a fearful mistake in the Superman: you make the statue a baritone instead of an Alt.[3] . . .

In haste

G.B.S.

Als.

1. Henry Lowenfeld (1859–1931), an Austrian-born impresario and speculator.
2. Dr. C. E. Wheeler, a homeopath; along with Granville Barker, he translated Schnitzler's *Das Märchen*.
3. Shaw was correcting Trebitsch's translation of *Superman* while Trebitsch worked on *The Perfect Wagnerite*.

[Pentillie.] Mevagissey
18th August 1906

My dear Trebitsch

The Hungarian business has entered into a new phase. When I instructed my solicitor to inform the Budapesth theatres that my plays had fallen into the public domain, and might be performed without fees, he discovered that the Hungarian courts had decided that the right of representation was *not* forfeited along with the right of translation. I then told him to proceed against the Vigsinhas for the full profits of The Devil's Disciple, which, if his view of the law is right, are forfeited to me. If I am successful, I shall exact full terms for Caesar & Cleopatra [from the National Theatre].[1]

You must constantly bear in mind the horrible unfairness of the position of dramatic authors in small countries like Hungary, Poland, Denmark &c. Here am I, with half the world open to me, getting huge sums from England & America for a successful play. It seems the easiest thing in the world to take 4% or some small sum down for such trifles as the Hungarian or Danish rights. But think of how that runs the market down for the wretched native author. It would be hard enough for him to live on 10%; and yet the manager offers him 4% & says, "If you dont take it I can easily get an English play for the same figure." I therefore make it a rule to ascertain, if I can, the highest terms paid to native authors, and demand *more*. In Denmark they told me that no Danish author ever got more than 6%; and they offered me 5. I said 7½. They said it was utterly impossible. I stuck to it like a mule. They gave in; and now the Danish authors bless me for putting up prices. As to Hungary, a Hungarian agent [Ernest Mayer] followed me about with a cheque for 4% on The Devil's Disciple receipts as my "moral" right. If I had accepted it I should never have discovered that I still have legal rights.

I tell you all this lest you should think my No simply unreasonable. Remember that agents always make bad bargains, because, as I explained to you in Paris, it pays them better to make 20 bad bargains quickly than to make 5 good ones slowly.

The Superman dream has been very troublesome because it requires exact translation. You have in several places thought I was writing poetry when I was writing the most rigidly scientific psychology. I have just come to a place where you translated the bob of a pendulum as a "triple bob major" rung on a peal of church bells. This makes a sort of glorious nonsense suggestive of the music of the spheres; but as I was carrying out the mechanical idea of the pendulum with the most careful exactitude, it knocks the whole argument to pieces. Again, what Don Juan says about the evolution of the brain may be a rather transcendental sort of physiology; but it *is* physiology and not poetic metaphor, and should be translated as if it were a scientific treatise. It is quite amazing how well you have succeeded; but it is still more amazing that, understanding it so well, you should have let one or two passages pass as sheer nonsense. I rub this into you because you must not underrate the importance of my corrections. I often have to go behind the popular use of a word into its etymology to get it quite right; and though you may think it mere pedantry on my part to reject "unbedeutungsvoll" as an equivalent for "irrelevant," I dont do so without good reason. I never alter anything merely because it says the thing in a different way to me: only when it alters the meaning or risks an ambiguity do I question it. And of course I may sometimes be quite wrong, owing to my ignorance of German usage. When I am, disregard my corrections.

I am sorry to say that my unfortunate French translator has become desperate, as he will lose a production at Brussels unless I immediately send him back Candida & You Never Can Tell (which I have had for months) with my corrections. Also I have begun a new play which must be ready at the Court Theatre by the end of October. I have received the Wagner Brevier safely. The copyright is safe: I wrote it in 1898; so 1892 is impossible. I hope you have the corrected English edition instead of the American one, which is a mass of errors.

Yesterday I had to stop working through a colossal headache.

ever

G. Bernard Shaw

Als.

1. With his newly discovered rights in Hungary, Shaw demanded from the National Theatre, which planned to stage *Caesar*, $1\frac{1}{2}$ percent more than the best royalty paid in Hungary.

Pentillie. Mevagissey
27th August 1906

My dear Trebitsch

I am paralyzed at the presumption of Oscar Bie. He will probably write the greatest nonsense. However, to please you, let him do the preface.[1] I shall certainly not write to him until I have read his stuff; and if it is all wrong I shall tell him so. But if it is all right, why, desto besser [all the better].

I am trying to get through the last act of the Superman; but it is slow work. My new play is going ahead fast: it is to be called "The Doctor's Dilemma" (Der Artztesdoppelschluss), and is full of medical stuff. Most of the characters are doctors; and it will make the medical profession shriek.

yrs ever
GBS

Als.
1. Oscar Bie (1864–1938) was a noted Berlin music critic and editor of the *Neue Rundschau*, in whose August issue selections from Shaw's *Perfect Wagnerite* ("Aus dem Wagner-Brevier") appeared with a brief editorial introduction, presumably by Bie. Apparently, Bie wished to write a preface for the forthcoming German edition of the work, but did not.

Pentillie. Mevagissey
28th August 1906

My dear Trebitsch

Can you get a copy of the Prague paper with the piracy?[1] I must set a lawyer at them at once. It will cost time & money (I already have the Hungarian & Schott-Brieger affairs on my hands); but the only way to make them afraid to meddle with us is to attack them every time & fight them to the end. This is a gross case, as the playlet has not yet been published a year. I must have dates & copies of the paper for the lawyers.

I have received Bab's magazine; but it is as much as I can do to work my way through the Superman & Heuchler [*Widowers'Houses*] without starting on his article just now.[2] I have read as much of the marked passages as I can without a dictionary. Later on I will study it: his magazine looks interesting.

I hope to finish the Superman 4th act this evening or tomorrow. Every night, when you say your prayers, [remainder of sentence canceled by Trebitsch].

It is true that the early edition of Widowers Houses [1893] is out of copyright; but it is very different from the one in Plays, Pleasant & Unpleasant [1898]. However, I am alive to the importance of getting it through the press in October. Wagner is safe—1899.

I am writing the new play [*Doctor's Dilemma*] at hurricane speed. It springs into existence impetuously with leaps & bounds: the only trouble is to get it inked.

GBS

Als.
1. On 19 August, the *Prager Tagblatt* published an unauthorized translation of Shaw's farce *Passion, Poison, and Petrifaction* (*Leidenschaft, Gift und Versteinerung*), which had appeared in *Harry Furniss's Christmas Annual*, 1905.
2. Julius Bab (1880–1955), young Berlin theatre critic, was a contributor to *Die Schaubühne* (later *Weltbühne*), leading cultural-political journal on the left. His "Philosophie der Schauspielkunst" appeared there on 16 August with a passage on the "life lie" in Ibsen and Shaw.

Castle Haven Rectory. Castle Townshend
27th September 1906

Please tell Reinhardt to look for an intelligent sheep and exchange heads with him: it will be a good bargain for him, though a bad one for the sheep.

Tell him that he made a disgraceful failure of Caesar by disregarding my instructions, and that if he does it again he shall never have another play of mine. The third act is to be omitted totally—not one word or syllable of it is to be performed. There is to be no Mendoza, no brigands, NOTHING. The play, as cut by me, is as long as any audience can endure: if the Mendoza scenes were done, they would create roars of laughter, and the fourth act would fail just as the serious part of Caesar failed after that tomfooling with the lighthouse. This is final and peremptory. My word has gone forth: let Reinhardt tremble and obey. . . .

                                                                    G.B.S.

Apcs.

                                                    Ayot St Lawrence. [Welwyn]
                                                    11th November 1906
My dear Trebitsch
    You had better translate the enclosed & send it to the press as your own. It must not appear until the 20th, because the play is not to be produced until the afternoon of the 20th. You will thus get ahead of the people who actually see the play; but there will not be time for the English papers to copy your article. It is most important that the article should not be quoted in England, as in mentioning Sir Almroth Wright I am giving you away a secret of the greatest importance.[1]
    This is all I can do for you. I am worked almost to death. . . .

                                                                    In haste
                                                                    GBS

Als.
    1. Shaw's article, puffing *Doctor's Dilemma* as profound and sparkling and proving that Shaw is indeed a "poet," appeared in *Neue Freie Presse* ("Bernard Shaw und die Aertzte," 20 November) under Trebitsch's name and revealed that Ridgeon was modeled on the noted physician Sir Almroth Wright (1861–1947).

                                                    10 Adelphi Terrace W.C.
                                                    14th November 1906
My dear Trebitsch
    . . . There is not a seat left in the house for the first performance of The Doctor's Dilemma. It will go into the evening bill for six weeks in January. Just now we shall give only the customary six matinees which are *de rigueur* at the Court Theatre.[1] It is not worth your while to come unless you have other business. The weather is dark, cold, raw & foggy; and Barker & I are worked to rags: we could do nothing to make you happy. On the whole, I advise you to stay at home, or in Berlin. It is too late to come for the rehearsals, which are the really important part of the business for you.

                                                    In horrible haste—I am really
                                                    worked to death
                                                    GBS

Als.
    1. The production of *Doctor's Dilemma* ran nine matinees before transferring to evening performances on 31 December.

10 Adelphi Terrace W.C.
6th December 1906

My dear Trebitsch

I now send you receipts for your October remittances, Charlotte having dug them out of the letter on my desk after a long tidying-up. I am sorry for the delay; but I can hardly describe the time I had in October & November. I had ten months work to struggle with in those two.

One consequence was that I had to neglect my lawsuits. Today, however, I am going to try to get my German lawyer to work. . . . he demanded copies of the different editions of Cashel Byron to compare & study; and this was a matter of difficulty; so I had to postpone it. Now at last I have got the copies; and perhaps with these, Schneider will wake up and become a little Schneidig [cutting].[1]

I was rather horrified at your planting Passion, Poison &c on a theatre.[2] I hope it wont be taken as a serious play.

Caesar has had a success in New York.[3] Do not forget that the Burgtheater is to have nothing of mine until it produces Caesar.

Another trouble is my Budapesth lawsuit. The theatre, hoping that I was a penniless author, had the action stopped until I gave security for costs. I offered to deposit a million in court instantly; so that game was stopped. I have heard nothing of Man & Superman from Berlin yet.[4]

yrs ever
G.B.S.

PS. I have just found the original edition of "Socialism for Millionaires." Alas! its date is 1896; so Landauer[5] cannot be touched. He waited until the ten years expired.

Als.

1. Franz Ledermann, bookdealer-publisher, had taken over *Aus fremden Zungen* and refused to withdraw the issue that used the revised edition of *Cashel.*

2. *Leidenschaft, Gift und Versteinerung,* "mad theatre" to the *Neue Freie Presse,* opened at the Kleines Schauspielhaus, Vienna, on 17 November for eight performances.

3. Forbes Robertson's production opened in New York on 30 October and ran 49 times.

4. Reinhardt's production, *Mensch und Übermensch,* opened that day at the Kammerspiele.

5. Gustav Landauer (1870–1919), independent German socialist author, assassinated after World War I, had just published his unauthorized translation of "Socialism for Millionaires" (*Sozialismus für Millionäre,* Berlin, dated 1907).

London
8th December [1906]

IMMER MUTH [Courage!] ONE REJOICES IN THE DEATH OF AN HONORABLE MAN AS IN HIS LIFE SO NO SNIVELLING SIEGFRIED BUT LET THE DEAD MARCH BE PLAYED TRIUMPHANTLY[1] SHAW

1. Telegram sent in reply to the news that Trebitsch's stepfather, Leopold Trebitsch, had just died.

Ayot St Lawrence. Welwyn
11th December 1906

I sent off all the letters;[1] but I had to strike out the clause about "illoyales Vorgehen" [disloyal proceedings], as I have made it a rule never to claim more than my legal rights. By the way, I am not at all sure that I cannot make a claim; for though anyone can translate after ten years, the copyright is still mine—a legal dilemma which has never been solved. . . .

If M[ensch] & U[bermensch] fails, it *must* be because Ann is 50 and Tanner a bad actor.[2] Come! Hand aufs Herz! how old is Ann?

Success to Die L[etzter] W[ille]!

G.B.S.

Apcs.; postscript omitted.

1. Trebitsch had drafted a letter (in German) to be sent by Shaw to editors protesting unauthorized translations and stating: "I consider this procedure, although it cannot be stopped legally, as disloyal proceedings."

2. *Mensch und Übermensch*, which had opened on 6 December at the Kammerspiele and was staged by Rudolf Bernauer, had a young cast, including Lucie Höflich, who was not yet 24, Paul Wegener, 32, and Tilla Durieux. It was not well received, and ran only eleven times. The *Schaubühne* (13 December), reporting a unanimously poor press, asked what led Reinhardt to so "worthless" a play and answered that Reinhardt "went along with the [Shaw] boom, and sought to exploit a fashionable movement."

10 Adelphi Terrace W.C.
3rd January 1907

My dear Trebitsch

. . . Now about this Freie Volksbühne affair.[1] On receiving your telegram, I wired at once to Schneider & Jablonski . . . to stop the performance of Widowers' Houses. They wired back that it had already taken place last Sunday. They also asked for your address and whether they might communicate with you. I have wired it to them, and asked them to write to you.

The affair stands thus. It is possible that the translation was made from the old edition of Widowers' Houses, which was published in 1893, and is thus lost to us as far as the translation rights go. But it is almost certain that they used the 1898 edition, which is still copyright. In any case the lapse of the translation right does not carry with it any lapse of the performing right.

My own position requires a little study. I cannot very well refuse a Socialist Theatre the right to perform my plays as long as they are in my own hands. I have always said to them that they must obtain your consent; and that if they got it, I should not interfere with them. But they have not said anything to me for a long time; and I knew nothing about this Widowers Houses affair, or of course I should have stopped it. They may however claim that they had reason to believe that I would not enforce my own rights against them. In this they are right; for I do not think that Arms & the Man was much the worse for their meddling; and in any case I should have let the matter pass, as I have the whole world to draw on for tantièmes. But your case is different. You have only Germany; and there can be no doubt that you have suffered serious damage by the anticipation of Heuchler [*Widowers' H.*]. I suggest therefore that Schneider & Jablonski should claim damages for you, and that you should be a party to the proceedings—the principal, in fact. I will pay any costs that may be incurred in the proceedings up to, say, £100: beyond that, I should like to reconsider the matter before I go in any deeper.

The letters to the papers are no use this time. When we put the matter into lawyers' hands, we must not take any step without consulting them. Complaints are no use: we must hit them in the pocket. Now that the mischief is done, and cannot be undone, we must concentrate ourselves on making it clear to everyone that every time we are attacked we will fight. The proceedings against Brieger & Co will help. Schneider has at last waked up to the importance of my legal point in that case, and is going ahead with an action unless they formally acknowledge that their piracy was illegal, and pay the costs. Success in the proceedings is after all a secondary consideration. If it is known that a man will fight every time he is hit, very few people will hit him, even though he may be beaten in every fight. I have just sent off a long letter to Schneider & Jablonski, telling them all this. It has taken so long to write that I have missed the post with this letter; but that cannot be helped.

I have received copies of Mensch & Übermensch. I quite forget how much of it I revised. Did I ever do the preface or the Revolutionist's Handbook? I think I remember doing the hell scene. The small book with the stage version must not on any account be sold to the public. It would kill the sale of the large book, and get into German literature as the real original Man & Superman.

As to Wagner and the Philanderer and the rest, God only knows when I shall be able to do them for you. The truth is I am desperately overworked, or would be if I did everything that is waiting for me. I will do my best by working at night at the translations. The French ones are heaped up beside yours. Thank God I dont know a word of Danish, Swedish or Hungarian, or I should be utterly lost. . . .

Has your father's death made any difference to you in money matters? Can I be of use to you in any way?

yours ever

G. Bernard Shaw

Tls.; postscript omitted.

1. The Freie Volksbühne had given Shaw's *Widowers' Houses* (*Die Häuser des Herrn Sartorius*) in an unauthorized version at the Berliner Theater on 30 December 1906. Because of its past difficulties with Trebitsch (see 14 March 1904), the Freie Volksbühne did not ask for Trebitsch's translation, which was being considered by the Kleines Theater.

10 Adelphi Terrace W.C.

10th January 1907

My dear Trebitsch

. . . I learn from Schneider and Jablonsky that the Freie Volksbühne actually proposes to give eight performances of "Widowers' Houses" on successive Sundays. This is beyond all reason: no play would be worth sixpence in any capital in the world after such an exploitation. Yesterday I made a

Statutory Declaration and sent it to Schneider. He wanted a second Statutory Declaration from somebody else in confirmation; but I told him he had better get one from you. You should declare that you are my sole authorised translator for the German language; that a share of the *tantièmes* on "Widowers' Houses" is part of the consideration for which you have agreed to translate my entire works; that you receive no other remuneration except your share of the *tantièmes* for the arduous work involved by such translation; that you have already finished your translation of "Widowers' Houses" which has been read and approved by me; that you have met with no difficulty in disposing of the performing rights in your translations in Berlin in the case of plays which were new to the Berlin public and the Berlin press; that on the other hand it is practically impossible to induce the managers of the Berlin theatres with whom you are accustomed to deal to produce a play that has already been performed in Berlin and criticised by the Berlin press; that the performances by the Freie Volksbühne are being given from an unauthorised translation without your knowledge or consent; and that they cannot fail to cause you serious pecuniary loss and to discredit your just pretension to be my sole authorised translator and literary representative in the German speaking countries.

As to the comparative failure of the first performance of "Man and Superman," I am not much concerned about that. As you say, the public did not know what to expect. When they have forgotten their expectations and become familiar with the piece, it will probably do very well, especially as you say that Ann is young and beautiful. The second Act will always be a difficulty unless a very clever comic actor takes the part of the chauffeur, and frankly makes him a racy bit of Berlinese character. Otherwise Straker must be an intolerable bore.

I have been thinking over what you told me concerning the failure of "Die Letzte Wille" after the second Act. The truth is that the first two Acts create much greater expectations than the end of the play fulfils—I mean, of course, expectations of startling events. You must either wait until the public are cured of their foolish habit of looking forward to pistols and poison on such occasions, or else find a little more of a story for the second half of the play. But on the whole I advise you to write another one and not bother about the fate of this one. Later on I will read it myself over again, and see what I think of it the second time.

God only knows what you and Doctor Redlich have made of my "Revolutionist's Handbook"![1] I shall make no attempt to go back on that until I have been through Wagner. It is all very well to say that my French translations do not matter; but unfortunately the business connected with the forthcoming performances of "Candida" in Brussels and "Mrs Warren's Profession" in Paris do matter very much.[2] Besides, my French translator Hamon, who began life as an Anarchist, and tried to write a History of France year by year, besides fiercely attacking the Army in a book "Military Psychology" and totally ruining himself with a confounded review called "L'Humanité

Nouvelle," has to be much more carefully coached than you. No doubt I shall succeed in the end in training him to behave like a reasonable man of the world; but for the present he is to all intents and purposes about 20 years younger than you are. And then the Italian question is very pressing. Rome is pining for "Candida." I sometimes wish "Candida" were at the bottom of the sea.

yours ever
G. Bernard Shaw

Tls.

1. Trebitsch, not trusting his own knowledge of sociology and politics, had enlisted the aid of Dr. Josef Redlich (1869–1936), a distinguished Viennese jurist and minister, in the translation of *Revolutionist's Handbook*.

2. *Candida* opened in Brussels on 7 February—the first production of Shaw in French translation—as one of the "matinées littéraires" at the Théâtre du Parc. The projected production of *Mrs Warren* in Paris did not take place.

10 Adelphi Terrace W.C.
15th January 1907

My dear Trebitsch

I enclose receipt for your cheque. What right has Entsch to hold over our fees for three months? confound him! It doesnt matter to me; but it does matter to poorer authors a good deal.

Schneider has extorted 500M [£25] from the V.B. I have wired to him that you must decide whether to take it or stop the performances; but I strongly advise you to take it.[1] If we could have stopped *all* the performances I should say stop them & refuse the money; but as two have actually been given and cannot be ungiven, and as the payment is a substantial one, I say by all means take it. . . .

Do not compromise me by being too haughty with the F.V.B. [Freie Volksbühne] people if they ask you again to perform my pieces. Remember, I also am a Socialist, and am bound to treat them with distinguished consideration, especially now that I write letters to the Berliner Tagblatt to say that they are out of date & not revolutionary enough.

The failure of Man & Superman is all nonsense. Reinhardt must make it a success by playing it until it comes right. A play that *cannot* be exhausted in America & England can fail in Berlin only through a bad performance or mismanagement of some sort. Did he explain on the program that *I* made the cuts and that the play at full length would last 7½ hours? Anyhow, tell R. that he is a duffer and that he shall have no more of my plays. Let him stick to von Schonthan & Co.

In haste for post
GBS

Als.

1. Although the Freie Volksbühne claimed immunity as a private theatre, Shaw's attorney, Schneider, argued that the ease of attending the theatre made it public. He therefore demanded M500 [£25], in return for which the Freie Volksbühne could complete its eight matinees of *Widowers' Houses* but would bar the press and obtain Trebitsch's consent to future productions of Shaw. The Freie Volksbühne agreed. As will appear, Shaw miscalculated the value of M500.

10 Adelphi Terrace W.C.

22nd January 1907

My dear Trebitsch

Your last postcard nearly killed me. "Please name me all the articles of any importance you have written and send them to me."

Listen to me. I was born in the year 1856. Everything that I wrote between that date and 1896 is out of translation right in Germany. Just think of it. Omit my years of early struggle and the five novels I wrote then. Take only the eleven years from 1885, when I gained my footing as a critic, to 1896. Say I wrote at least one article a week during that time, and made three or four reputations, as literary critic, as musical critic, as dramatic critic, and as political pamphleteer and agitator. 11 times 52 is 572. Do you seriously ask me to name you all those 572 articles?

You will simply die of nervous exhaustion if you allow unauthorized translations to worry you. If you estimate the 572 articles, mostly signed feuilletons, at 2000 words each, which was the usual length of them, you get a total of one million words, all waiting for the Landauers and Briegers to fall on them and turn them into bad German. Only the other day my dramatic criticisms were collected into two fat volumes and republished in America [*Dramatic Opinions and Essays*]. They contain 114 flashing, scintillating, brilliant articles on Shakespear, Ibsen, Echegaray,[1] Hauptmann &c. &c. &c. Two thirds of them are out of translation right already: the other third will be out of it at the end of this year. There is nothing to prevent a steady stream of unauthorized Shaw coming from the German press for years to come. That is why I take it so coolly. If the pirates only knew how much plunder here was ready to their hand! I am only too thankful that they have discovered so little.

I think we have done very well over the Freie Volksbühne. We have got £100 [£25] for eight performances, with our costs in Berlin, and a pledge that the FV will let us alone in future. And this in respect of a play which was published in 1893. We should not have done much better if we had had it produced in the ordinary way: in fact, we might not have done so well. Schneider seems to have done his work very well. If he deals as successfully with the Fremden Zungen pirates we shall have established a Reign of Terror. Of course we shall get no money out of them, because they haven't any; but I have told Schneider that I am prepared to spend 2000 marks [£100] if necessary, in order to convince the pirates that they will have to fight every time they touch you, no matter how sure they may be of their rights. Can I do more?

The one thing I wont do is, complain. Never complain. The world hates a man with a grievance. Strike when you can: if you cant, smile. The man who loses his temper loses everything else as well.

Which Chamberlain do you allude to in your postcard—Joseph the politician or Houston the writer?[2] I have no doubt mentioned both in my writings; but I have written nothing of any importance about either. . . .

I am busy rehearsing The Philanderer for a series of matinees at the Court Theatre.[3] It is a first rate acting play.

You will be shocked when you see me in April. I have worked so constantly this winter that I am an old whitehaired bentbacked man.

G.B.S.

Tls.
1. José Echegaray (1832–1916), Spanish dramatist, mathematician, economist, and politician, winner (with Frédéric Mistral) of the 1904 Nobel Prize for literature.
2. Houston Chamberlain (1855–1927), English racialist philosopher and Germanophile, was living in Vienna where Trebitsch met him. A cheap edition of Chamberlain's *Grundlagen des XIX Jahrhunderts* (1899), an "Aryan" view of culture, had recently been issued.
3. *Philanderer* opened at the Court on 5 February and was coolly received.

10 Adelphi Terrace W.C.
29th January 1907

My dear Trebitsch

I made a hideous mistake about the F.V. I was up to the neck in American business just then; and I calculated 500 Marks as 500 dollars! However, it cant be helped.

William Archer is going to Italy next Saturday for a short time. You had better write to him direct.[1] His address is Kings Langley, Herts, or c/o The Tribune, Bouverie St, London E.C. He knows who you are, and will probably pay you more attention than he will pay me, as I know him so well that he stands on no ceremony with me. . . .

In haste
ever yrs
GBS

Als.
1. Trebitsch's business with Archer perhaps bore on the Foreword to the pending German edition of *Widowers' Houses* (*Heuchler*), in which Trebitsch recounted the early collaboration of Archer and Shaw in that play.

10 Adelphi Terrace W.C.
6th May 1907

My dear Trebitsch

I wonder how you can bear life in Vienna. All your friends appear to be the stupidest men in Europe; they are always giving you bad advice. *Der Liebhaber* [The Lover] is not at all a bad title for "The Philanderer"; *Der Schmetterling* [The Butterfly] is perfectly idiotic. You had better take your friend Heimann to the nearest hospital for imbeciles and leave him there. Philanderer is certainly a very difficult word to translate; as far as I know, there is neither a French or German equivalent. It means a man who cannot help making love to women and making them fall in love with him, but who will not go any further—who always retreats in time when there is any question of marriage or of serious relations. *Liebler* would be wrong, because it means a serious lover. *Liebhaber* appears to me to be as right as you can get it; because it suggests an actor, and therefore a man whose love-making is not quite real.

You had better let me go through Ibsen,[1] as some of it is very subtle and difficult: in fact I dont believe it would be possible for any human being to avoid mistakes without the help of the author. On the very first page of "The Wagner Book," I have found a sentence in which you have given the exact contrary of my meaning; and yet I dont see how you could possibly have avoided it: I should have made the same mistake myself in your place.

I quite forget the article which you call "The Moral of Music."[2] I advise you to send a postcard to my wife with a list of all the things I promised to send you.

I congratulate you on the high spirits you are in after your tour. You are now much madder than I am; for I could not possibly send the telegram that you drafted for me. In private, you may abuse Reinhardt as much as you like; in fact, I am quite ready to write you a letter of the most abusive character to transláte and send to him. But in public we must treat him with the most distinguished consideration. The one thing that is utterly unpardonable is for an author whose play has failed to attempt to blame the actors or the manager or anybody else but himself for the failure. He may, however, recompense himself for this delicacy by informing the manager and the actors and everybody else concerned in private that the failure is entirely due to their infamous incompetence and stupidity, so as to encourage them to do better next time. Personally I always confine my reproaches to the Manager, and do my best to persuade the actors that they have achieved an artistic triumph which has been unfortunately spoiled by a commercial failure.

What I advise you definitely to do is to write to Reinhardt proposing that he should invite the entire Viennese Company to visit Berlin and show the Berlinese how "Man and Superman" should be played.[3] That may make him sit up.

As to your being accused of mutilating the play. Why did you not carry out my suggestion, which has been acted on both in England and America: that is, to put a statement in the playbill that the Management has placed the resources of the theatre without reserve at the disposal of the author, and that all the omissions have been made by his direction. I actually once sent you a copy of the statement which I drafted for the American production, but you must have forgotten all about it.

yours ever

G. Bernard Shaw

Tls.

1. Trebitsch's version of *The Quintessence of Ibsenism* (*Ein Ibsenbrevier*) appeared in 1908; a selection was published in *Schaubühne* (30 October 1907).

2. "The Religion of the Pianoforte" (*Fortnightly Review*, February 1894).

3. The Viennese premiere of *Man and Superman* at the Deutsches Volkstheater, on 27 April, staged by Richard Vallentin, with Leopold Kramer and Elsa Galafrés, was warmly received: "Never before has Shaw been so unanimously applauded in Vienna" (*Neues Wiener Tagblatt*, 28 April); but the *Neue Freie Presse* noted that the audience's mood waned. The production was praised as a

"true triumph" (*Neues Wiener Journal*), but the omission of the third act was deplored, the *Wiener-Zeitung* referring to the "cruelly mutilated Shaw in this disgraceful translation." Despite the favorable opening night, *Man and Superman* ran only eight times.

10 Adelphi Terrace W.C.
22nd May 1907

My dear Trebitsch

I am delighted to find that Meyerfeld has fired off that joke of mine at last. I told it to him most carefully, fully intending him to publish it. I want it to become the stock joke in Germany about your translations. What you must do is to keep it up by pretending that you dont know English, and that you produce your versions by sheer inspiration. If people express any doubt as to the truth of this, refer them at once to Meyerfeld and Kellner. In this way you will easily put a stop to the whole controversy. The more you keep on protesting your ignorance, whilst your translations are being played all over the country, the more people will believe you to be a perfect devil of a translator and a very clever fox into the bargain. You must make it a rule in life, not only in this matter but in every other, never to deny an accusation. Always confess to twice as much as you are accused of. If Meyerfeld says that you have picked my pocket, assure everybody that you have robbed the Bank of England. If he says that you beat your wife, declare that you have murdered your mother-in-law. You will never get through life if you allow yourself to be stopped in your business and annoyed by every fool who chooses to say an ill-natured thing about you.

. . . Tell Kanner that even if I had time to write him an article, I do not know the Austrian situation well enough to handle it competently.[1] I can only suppose that all the newly elected Socialists will make unmitigated donkeys of themselves until they become accustomed to Parliament and public life.

The worst of trying to conceal the antiquity of my Bernhardt-Duse Critique is that Duse has now for some years taken to wearing a wig and making up her face, and doing all the things that I then praised her for not doing: consequently the article will seem ridiculous to those who have seen her lately.[2]

One of the pieces I am rehearsing is the Hell scene from Man and Superman.[3]

yours ever
G. Bernard Shaw

Tls.

1. Kanner, of *Die Zeit*, wanted Shaw to do an article on the results of Austria's first general election under universal male suffrage, which had brought the Christian Socialists and the Socialists to the fore and aroused hopes—unrealized—for economic reform.

2. Shaw's celebrated essay "Duse and Bernhardt," contrasting the natural Duse with the flamboyant Bernhardt, appeared in the *Saturday Review*, 15 June 1895. Trebitsch's translation had just appeared in *Neue Freie Presse* (17 May).

3. "Don Juan in Hell" along with *Man of Destiny* opened for eight matinees on 4 June at the Court.

10 Adelphi Terrace W.C.

4th June 1907

My dear Trebitsch

Fischer has made a mess of the whole business. He is like all the rest of the agents: the moment any speculator offers him an advance of twenty pounds he will sell the author's body and soul for the sake of grabbing the commission on it. Don't allow him to put the blame on you; on the contrary, tell him that you assured me that I might depend on his taking care of my interests, and that you would never have done so if you had imagined that he would throw away one of my principal plays for the whole term of the copyright for a 5% royalty, without reserving to me even the choice of a translator. Tell him it is perfectly monstrous, and that you do not wonder at my repudiating such a contract.[1] And make these agents, Entsch and Fischer and all the rest, understand that they must keep their hands off other countries. It cost me £8 to get out of a contract which Entsch made with Sweden; and I shall think myself very lucky if I get out of the Hungarian contract for £20. I am writing to Fischer telling him to offer the Hungarian man that sum to tear up the contract and get rid of the matter. I have also given Fischer my opinion of his efficiency as an agent very frankly.

There is one passage in Fischer's letter to you about which I beg you to attack him at once with all the indignation of which your pen is capable. That passage is "Es ist der übliche Vertrag" [It is the usual contract]. Ask him how dare he make an übliche Vertrag about our works. Ask him does he suppose that we are manufacturers of ordinary farces and vaudevilles, and that a contract that is üblich for such works is quite enough for us. Heap insults on him. Don't consider this waste of time: it will make him much more careful in future.

I have had a tremendously busy time for the last month. I had to rehearse Man and Superman with a new Tanner [Robert Loraine]; and at the same time I had to rehearse the hell scene and the Man of Destiny, it will be produced this afternoon. The hell scene is the most wonderful thing ever seen. A well-known artist here named [Charles] Ricketts, has designed the dresses. You really ought to come over and see them. Unfortunately one consequence of all this work has been that I had to give up all idea of working at the translations. I hope now to be able to turn my hand to them.

yours ever,

G. Bernard Shaw

PS—The hell scene has been a huge success. The audience listened to it breathlessly for an hour and forty minutes.[2]

Tls.

1. S. Fischer had sold rights in an unauthorized Hungarian translation of *Mrs Warren* for production in Budapest, with no time limit and for a 5 percent royalty as against Shaw's usual 10 percent. (Fischer could not understand why Shaw objected to 5 percent when that was all he received after sharing his 10 percent German royalty with Trebitsch. What he failed to grasp was Shaw's concern to set decent floors below authors' fees in small countries for the sake of native writers.)

2. Press reaction was generally hostile, however.

Hafod y Bryn. Llanbedr
25th July 1907

My dear Trebitsch

. . . I have made a few alterations & omissions [in *The Philanderer*]. They are very slight; but if you think they will expose you to press attacks, you can publish the play with a prefatory note to say that as your version does not correspond exactly with the English edition, you had better explain that your version is a new edition revised by the author expressly for Germany.[1] You might add that this is the explanation of many of the mare's nests which have been discovered by German critics in your translation.

I am quite aware that I have neglected you most monstrously for a year past; but I have had a fearful time of it. A revolt in the Fabian Society led by H. G. Wells came quite unexpectedly on me, and gave me work enough for one man during a large part of the winter.[2] Then I have all Europe on my shoulders in the matter of translations. The 10 years from the publication of Plays, P & Unp, expires next March; and I have had this year to find translators in Hungary, Italy & Spain to save my rights.[3] The correspondence & trouble involved have been very heavy. Hungary has been the very devil— lawsuits, piracies, and at last this Fischer business. And on top of Hungary came Bohemia, with the exasperating discovery that in spite of all my warnings to Entsch & the rest not to meddle with any language except German, Eirich, acting for Entsch, had collected royalties of 5% on the Bohemian translations, and paid half of them to you, leaving Charles Musek, my unfortunate Bohemian translator, with nothing for his work.[4] It is quite impossible for me now to disentangle the accounts and identify the Prague performances which were in Bohemian & not in German; but I should be durchaus [quite] indebted to you if you would write strongly to Entsch and Eirich telling them that they must not touch my works in any language but German, and that they have actually put you in the position of taking the fees of my Bohemian translator and compromising your honor with me & Musek &c &c &c &c &c. I do not think Fischer needs any fresh warning; but I wonder whether he is taking any further steps to cancel that bargain he made. There will be a good deal of trouble about it; for I have at last got the Hungarian pirates fairly by the throat and secured a decent translator; and if any attempt is made to produce "Mrs Warren" on the strength of that outrageous agreement made by Fischer I will have to fight it at law. Forgive my worrying you with these details; but you can see what it means for me. I am at the centre of the European & American web and have to keep nine languages separate. When Entsch, Fischer, Eirich begin to entangle them it means that I have to spend in correspondence & in lawsuits the time I might otherwise devote to correcting the translations.

Thank God I have no rights in Russia & Holland! And thank God I dont know Spanish, Danish or Swedish!

And the endless rehearsals for Vedrenne & Barker, and my literary work on top of it all! Judge how much time I have to write little articles on Liebermann[5] &c &c. Tell all applicants that my desk is full of applications for articles, some of them offering me 2000 Marks, and that if they will pay you that in advance you will try to get something from me. Remember that these requests pour in on me from all the civilized world now & that I could spend my whole life six times over in complying with them. As to Liebermann, I have seen too few of his pictures to be able to say anything really valuable about them; and I never make merely ceremonial utterances.

This letter is all grumbling: I am very sorry; but I want to excuse myself for my delays & silences.

yrs ever

G.B.S.

Als.

1. *Liebhaber* (*Philanderer*), published that year by Fischer, contained the prefatory note suggested by Shaw.

2. The previous year, H. G. Wells (1866–1946), then a Fabian, attacked the society's organization and policies and, in effect, demanded the removal of the Executive Committee, which included Shaw. At a special meeting in December, Shaw outmaneuvered Wells. Wells resigned from the society two years later.

3. Shaw's translators for Hungary, Italy, and Spain were, respectively, Alexander (Sándor) Hevesi (1873–1939), Antonio Agresti (1866–1926), and Julio Broutá (d. 1932).

4. Karel Mušek, Shaw's Czech translator, was now authorized to collect and remit Shaw's Czech royalties. Meanwhile, S. Fischer tried unsuccessfully to buy back the rights sold in Budapest.

5. Max Liebermann (1847–1935), leading German impressionist painter, was celebrating his 60th birthday.

Hafod y Bryn. Llanbedr

30th July 1907

My dear Trebitsch

All right: send me Brassbound; and I will make a heroic attempt to grapple with it and Ibsen. But you should hear my Frenchman shrieking for my revision of his Arms & The Man & Man & Superman.

I will also try to correct The Doctor's Dilemma for the printer, and send you proofs. It is a sort of play that ought to be performed soon, before the scientific part of it gets stale.

It is useless to protest about poor Musek. We have robbed that excellent Bohemian—STOLEN his money—spent it in Paris, London, Engelberg &c &c &c &c. Eirich collected tantièmes on all the performances at Prague (at least Musek says so) on behalf of Entsch. Entsch sent them to you. You divided them with me. We are simply a pair of thieves.

The Philanderer translation seemed to me excellent—nothing wrong about it except the real unavoidable mistakes, such as calling the casters of a chair beavers,[1] & one or two other things that you would never have found out except at rehearsal.

GBS

Als.; postscript omitted.

1. The stage directions to *Philanderer* (Act III) mention a "chair on castors," Shaw using the later *-or* spelling, which initially meant *beaver*. To assist Trebitsch, Shaw here uses the *-er* spelling.

Hafod y Bryn. Llanbedr
2nd August 1907

Dear Trebitsch

I send you by this post the remainder of Brassbound, and will now set to work on Wagner. I am also writing to London pressing for immediate proofs of the Nordau Essay,[1] which I shall take care not to make public here until your translation is out in Germany. It is rather long for a magazine article. However, if Marz will print it in full, and will pay decently, let it appear there by all means.[2] Be very careful, by the way, in giving receipts for payment to magazines, to acknowledge the money as for the serial right only— that is, for permission to print in one number of the magazine only. Editors have a trick of trapping authors into signing receipts for the full copyright.

The other day, when bathing here on a rather rough day, I was swept out by a tidal current and very nearly drowned.[3] For five minutes I was swimming simply to put off the unpleasantness of drowning as long as possible, without the least hope of getting back to shore. Luckily I got carried on to a sandbank, and escaped. But while I was in the water I was thinking of certain alterations I had intended to make in my will, and also about the unsettled state of my arrangements as to translations. Suppose I had been drowned, you might have had all sorts of trouble with my executors. If you died also, your mother—or whoever would inherit your copyrights—would probably find it impossible to ascertain what our relations really were, or to prevent other translations being made & substituted for yours. You had better have a proper agreement.[4]

I send you the form of agreement I use for the other countries. Read it carefully, and suggest any alterations you think necessary. Dont be delicate about it. Remember that I may at any moment take to drink, or go mad, or fall into the hands of some unscrupulous woman, or quarrel with you, or do any of the disastrous things that men do every day. It is only by both parties insisting on the fullest protection for themselves that a satisfactory agreement can be reached.

I must stop now—I have one of my headaches today.

yrs ever
G. Bernard Shaw

ps. In Brassbound you translated Redbrook's nickname "the Kid" as der Schwindler [the Swindler]. It has only just occurred to me that you must have been misled by our slang verb "to kid": that is, to humbug, to deceive. But this is quite another use of the word. "A kid" in slang is a child: z.b. "How many kids has he?" = "How many children has he?"

Als.

1. Max Nordau (1849–1923), Austrian art critic and physician, was author of *Entartung* (*Degeneration*, 1893), a psychiatric study that attacked modern art, including Tolstoy, Ibsen, Nietzsche, and Wagner, as degenerate. Shaw's rebuttal, "A Degenerate's View of Nordau" (*Liberty*, 27 July 1895), was soon to appear revised with a new preface and title: *The Sanity of Art*.

2. Trebitsch's translation, "Wie Shaw den Nordau demolierte" (How Shaw Demolished Nordau), appeared in *März* (October, November).

3. Shaw's brush with death occurred while he was swimming with his actor friend Robert Loraine in the sea off Merionethshire.

4. Shaw's arrangements with Trebitsch up to this point had been for the most part largely gentlemen's agreements.

Hafod y Bryn. Llanbedr

3rd August 1907

In dealing with the Kleines Th. [for *Brassbound*] make it a condition that Sorma shall play Lady Cicely, and withdraw the play if they refuse. Without a star of the first magnitude failure is certain.

You may be sure E[irich] collected *everything*, whether he sent it on to us or not. Musek has made no claim for payment. He considers it natural that Bohemia should be robbed by Austria. He said positively that Eir. had collected 5% on behalf of Entsch.

I will send you a copy of the Nordau essay before it is published here. I have written a preface to it. It must not be published as something new: that would be unfair & discourteous to Nordau, whose Entartung appeared about 1894. My essay was written in 1895.

You may pitch into the Rundschau as hard as you like for omitting your name.[1] I set great store by the constant association of our names in Germany. . . .

G.B.S.

Apcs.

1. The *Neue Rundschau* published excerpts from *Wagnerite* ("Aus dem Wagner-Brevier," August 1907) without mentioning Trebitsch as translator, but such omissions were common.

Hafod y Bryn. Llanbedr

4th August 1907

My dear Trebitsch

In a book about me just published, the author makes public the date of the Nordau essay & the name of the American paper it was published in.[1] There is therefore no time to lose about it, though the American paper will be difficult to get. This morning the first proofs of the forthcoming reprint arrived. I send you one, and shall send you the successive instalments as they come.

Can you get me a copy of the N.F.P. containing Nordau's comments on Rodin. If so, do; and I will make special reference to them.[2] Has he said anything about Richard Strauss?[3]

You ought to dedicate your translation of the Wagner book to Richard.

yrs ever

G. Bernard Shaw

Als.

1. Holbrook Jackson's *Bernard Shaw* (London, 1907), the first book-length study of Shaw in England, cited Shaw's article on Nordau in *Liberty*.

2. Nordau, since *Entartung*, had added Rodin as a degenerate artist dealing in decadent mysticism and sexual pathology ("Auguste Rodin," reprinted in *Von Kunst und Künstlern*, Leipzig, 1905). Shaw did not mention Nordau on Rodin in *Sanity of Art*.

3. Richard Strauss (1864–1949), leading German composer and conductor, influenced by Wagner, and, at this time, known more for his tone poems than operas, most of which lay ahead. Nordau did not write on Strauss, to whom Trebitsch, at Shaw's suggestion, dedicated the *Wagnerbrevier* (*The Perfect Wagnerite*; Berlin, 1908).

Nordau struck back in an open letter to Shaw in *Frankfurter Zeitung* (24 November), ironically using Shaw's title: "Wie Shaw den Nordau demolierte" and professing surprise at being destroyed. He then accused Shaw of anti-Semitic bias in referring to him as "one of those remarkable cosmopolitan Jews" who attack modern civilization. Shaw, in the *F.Z.* on 14 December, regretted the misunderstanding and explained that his reference was not pejorative, that in England one's Jewishness aroused favorable interest, and that the existence of Marx, Lasalle, and Nordau supported Shaw's concept of cosmopolitan Jews opposed to modern civilization. The main passages of Shaw's letter appeared also in the *Jewish World* (20 December) with a note expressing Shaw's sensitivity to being called anti-Jewish since he never supported such prejudice. The complete text was published in *New Age* (18 January 1908).

Hafod y Bryn. Llanbedr
25th September 1907

My dear Trebitsch

The enclosed has been sent to me for correction & return.[1] Is your name in it? If not, it ought to be. I still get heaps of ridiculous applications for authorizations to translate from people who say that they have just discovered me and will undertake to introduce me to the German public &c. . . .

I doubt if it is good policy to enlarge the third edition of Wagner: it infuriates the buyers of the first edition. If it is announced nobody will attempt piracy, because the announcement of a translation revised by me and with specially written chapters for Germany would make the sale of a rival edition hopeless. And we could be ready by the 1st Nov. It is not a bit too late to hold back the publication. No doubt Fischer doesnt want his arrangements upset; but the upset is for his own good & ours. He can wait a year if necessary. He ought to be overwhelmed with gratitude at my offering to make his edition copyright without demanding 2000M. for my trouble.[2] . . .

G.B.S.

Als.
    1. The item corrected by Shaw was for *Wer ist Wer* (Who's Who), which included Shaw in 1906 and, updated, in 1908.
    2. For the *Wagnerbrevier*, Shaw added a preface and a chapter, "Why Wagner Changed His Mind," later revised and included in the third English edition (1913).

10 Adelphi Terrace W.C.
13th November 1907

Great Heavens, no: Strauss wird furchtbar beleidigt sein [will be terribly offended].[1] Bashville is far too trivial. I wish he would compose the incidental music for the Hell Scene in Superman—a Mozartian fantasia by Richard would be magnificent. But I should like enormously to do a new libretto for him.

An.

1. Trebitsch had suggested that Richard Strauss compose incidental music to *The Admirable Bashville.*

10 Adelphi Terrace W.C.
16th November 1907

My dear Trebitsch

I had no idea that these Munich performances[1] were piracies, and dash me if I submit to them without any more effectual protest than an ironic letter to the papers! We must take proceedings at once, as we did in the Freie Bühne case. I made a fool of myself in that because I was so full of American business at the time that I calculated the sum offered to us at four times its actual amount by mistaking marks for dollars. Nevertheless we extorted the undertaking that there should be no piracy of this kind in future; and I see no reason why we should not do the same now. By this post I am instructing Schneider and Jablonski, Leipzigerstrasse 101/102, Berlin, to proceed against the Munich Verein. Will you please call on them and give them the necessary particulars, as far as you know them. I have told them that you will call, and have formally instructed them to see you on my behalf. I daresay it will cost a little money and a little trouble; but unless we fight like devils every time an unauthorized hand touches a play of ours, we shall be pirated in all directions.

Can it be that there is no Society of Authors in Germany to resist this sort of aggression?[2] If there is, we ought to join it, and act through it. If not, the sooner one is formed the better. Can you not stir up some of your German colleagues to take the work in hand?

yours faithfully
G. Bernard Shaw

Tls.

1. On 5 November the Neue Verein, Munich, a private society, gave an unauthorized performance of *Mrs Warren* at the Residenz Theater. Shaw learned of the performance from his Fabian colleague Ashley Dukes, who described it as a "libellous caricature," with a screeching Kitty Warren, a preposterous Reverend Gardner with a red nose, little hat, and falsetto voice, and a small nervous Crofts with bright red hair and glasses (L.S.E.).

2. Shaw apparently forgot that Trebitsch had floated the idea of a German Society of (Stage) Authors in *Schaubühne* the previous year (22 March) and that among the respondents was Shaw with a supporting comment (17 May). When such a society was formed in 1911—Verband Deutscher Bühnenschriftsteller und Bühnenkomponisten (V.D.B.B.)—both Shaw and Trebitsch joined.

10 Adelphi Terrace W.C.
21st November 1907

My dear Trebitsch

The Irrational Knot did not appear in an American magazine: it appeared in an English one (obscure & difficult to get) [*Our Corner*] much more than ten years ago [1885 – 86]. About two or three years ago [1905] a new edition, with a very interesting preface, was published. If your pirate touches that, he is a lost man: Schneider will have his life. If he has really got hold of the old version, you can tell him that it will be immediately denounced as unauthorized and shorn of the famous preface &c. There is a chapter purposely so altered in the new edition that an attempt to pirate the new edition under cover of the old can be immediately detected & proved, as in the case of Cashel Byron's Profession.[1]

I send you a 2 mark stamp which cannot be sold here.

In haste—full of rehearsals
G.B.S.

PS What happened to Sorma & Lady Cicely?[2] Was it a dead failure? It was practically a failure at first with Ellen Terry; but now that she has at last actually *become* Lady C, and *lives* the part, saying just what comes into her head without bothering about my lines, she is very successful in it.[3] Can Sorma read English?

Als.

1. A first hearing in Shaw's case against *Aus fremden Zungen* found the revised 1901 edition of *Cashel Byron* essentially the same as the original. A second hearing was set, but Ledermann announced that he would publish Shaw's other novels beginning with *The Irrational Knot*.

2. *Kapitän Brassbounds Bekehrung*, with Agnes Sorma and Erich Ziegel, staged by Barnowsky at his Kleines Theater, opened on 24 October. Although Sorma personally triumphed, the play, criticized as too English, was withdrawn after six performances: "the actress was celebrated, the author politely rejected" (*Berliner Tageblatt*, 25 October).

3. After the London run in *Brassbound*, Terry took the play to America and then to the English provinces.

10 Adelphi Terrace W.C.
18th December 1907

My dear Trebitsch

I have written you dozens of letters; but you have been so absorbed in your honeymoon[1] that you either have not read them, or have forgotten all about them.

Can you tell me what are the exact terms on which you accepted that money from Oscar Strauss's librettists?[2] As I understood it, they said they only wanted to use the situation from the First Act. But paragraphs are now appearing in the English papers to the effect that Strauss is setting the play to music, and that his opera will be practically a musical setting of the play. This would never do. Such a musical version would simply drive the play off the boards. Let me know, if you can, the exact wording of the authorization you gave them.

I am sorry to say that I cannot find a copy of the Oscar Wilde article among my papers. I have just searched carefully, but without success.[3]

yours ever

G. Bernard Shaw

Tls.

1. Trebitsch, aged 39, had just married Antoinette (Tina) Keindl (1869–1954), a native Viennese and Catholic, widow of the Russian Grand Duke Engelitschew, who was killed in the Russo-Japanese War. According to Trebitsch's *Chronicle*, Shaw wrote (retranslated from the German): "Good God! What have you gone and done? Heaven knows whom you've married and what in the world is going to happen to you now! Why at least didn't you show me your wife first and get my verdict, advice and blessing?" The Trebitsches were honeymooning in Paris.

2. Trebitsch had accepted £40 from Rudolf Bernauer (1880–1953) and Leopold Jacobson (1878–1949), German librettists, for rights to adapt the idea of *Arms & the Man* into an operetta-libretto for the popular Oscar Straus (1870–1954). Shaw agreed to the burlesque use of the "idea" but strictly forbade use of his dialogue or name.

3. Trebitsch was preparing a collection of Shaw's *Essays* and presumably wanted to check his version of the Wilde essay (see 18 March 1905) against the English original.

10 Adelphi Terrace W.C.

20th January 1908

My dear Trebitsch

You make the greatest mistake in the world in thinking that you are going to Durand's.[1] You still talk as if you were a bachelor. Madame will have you out of the Place de la Madeleine and into the Place Vendome or the Palais d'Orsay before you can say Jack Robinson.[2] Also she will come to London with you and be greatly disappointed to find me an old man.[3]

The agreement you signed about Arms and the Man is perfectly appalling. The only thing in it that saves us from utter ruin is the word operetta. I think we can prevent them from going beyond one act by that blessed word. But what a reckless ruffian you are to go and sign an agreement for all countries and all languages and all time! Do you realize that there are seven other translators in Europe with whom I am under solemn contract that they shall have the exclusive rights to deal with my works in their country and in their language? I am happy to say that the Hungarian affair seems to be settled satisfactorily. I had a long correspondence with poor Fischer,[4] who complained bitterly of the wounding expressions in my letters. He pointed out to me that if I took proceedings against the Hungarian [Ludwig Valentin] with whom he had made the contract, the Hungarian would proceed against him. I said the Hungarian was quite welcome to proceed against him as much as he liked, but that I must defend my translator [Hevesi]. I am greatly afraid that poor Fischer got the contract cancelled at last only by paying through the nose. It serves him right; for the contract he made was a most monstrous one.

When do you expect to arrive in London? You must see the present production of Helden at the Savoy Theatre:[5] the cast is extraordinarily good, and you will be able to see how it comes out under my stage management.

yours ever

G. Bernard Shaw

Tls.
1. A famous restaurant on the Place de la Madeleine in Paris.
2. Place Vendôme and Palais d'Orsay are fashionable shopping quarters in Paris.
3. Tina Trebitsch did not come to London.
4. For Fischer and Hungary see Shaw's letters of 4 June and 25 July 1907.
5. Vedrenne-Barker had transferred to the Savoy Theatre, where *Arms* opened on 30 December 1907, with Barker, Robert Loraine, and Lillah McCarthy.

Ayot St Lawrence. Welwyn
9th March 1908

My dear Trebitsch

I have been so furiously busy working at my play [*Getting Married*], getting my 1898 French translations into print to save the copyright, and delivering heroic orations up & down the country, that Meyerfeldt has gone clean out of my head, which is just as it ought to be, because Meyerfeldt does not matter.[1]

You must not publish that list of errata in De Profundis. That is the sort of thing that Meyerfeldt does. Why should you do it? How can you complain of his doing it if you do it yourself? You say he will be ruined. He wont—no more than you are ruined by his attack; but suppose it were so, why would you ruin him? The poor devil has as much right to live as anyone else. Murder is not justified by misconduct on the part of the victim.

You really have no grievance. You have the monopoly of Shaw for Germany; and every play that you translate & that he doesnt translate drives your car over him. By stopping to quarrel with him you waste time, rack your nerves, and lose dignity. Squabbling weakens a man: work builds him up.

I should like to write a letter to some leading literary paper in Germany calling attention to the absence of a Society of Authors, Germany being thus behind all the other European Powers of the first rank, except, I suppose, Austria. I should give as an example of the absence of *esprit de corps* and even ordinary professional decency, the attempts that have been made by professional translators to get my works to translate by attacks on you. But you can anticipate me by writing the letter yourself, and pointing out how helpless you are with no court of honor in your profession to appeal to. Point out that when you present a translation of one of my plays, revised by myself expressly for the German edition, and embodying all my interpolations, alterations & omissions, the changes are misrepresented as errors of translation by professional translators who have applied to me for authorizations to translate my works, and failed to secure them. Say that I have expressed to you my astonishment that such breaches of professional etiquette should be practised in Germany without, apparently, exciting any reprobation. Say that it would be easy for you to retaliate, since your friends, indignant at the attacks on you, have placed in your hands long lists of blunders made by your assailants in translating the works of English authors who, being dead, cannot have authorized the discrepancies between the English & German texts of their works, but that your object is not to follow the example of your critics, but to set one of professional decorum.

Then you can "let yourself go" about the absence of any business co-operation. Here again you can quote me as surprised at having to defend my copyrights against the most impudent piracies by my individual action and at my own sole cost, whereas any German author, by subscribing 21 marks a year to the Society of Authors here can have his rights protected in England without any further cost to himself. We have taken cases even up to [the] House of Lords, at enormous expense, in the interests of the literary profession both at home & abroad. You need not mention M's name once in all this; and if you succeed in getting a Society founded, you will become a representative man of letters in Germany.[2] As to Llandauer I can do nothing to stop him if he does not infringe my copyright.[3] And my Socialist pamphlets are the common property of the human race.

yrs ever
G.B.S.

PS. I enclose a remittance from the N.F.P. What does it refer to, & why do they send it to me instead of to you?[4]

PPS. Oscar Strauss announces Arms & The Man as an opera; and a three act work of his just produced here [*Waltz Dream*] is described as "an operetta." There will be trouble about this. I am writing to him to warn him that he is not authorized to use A & The Man as a libretto.

Als.

1. After four years, Max Meyerfeld resumed his attack on Trebitsch in "Shaw als Theaterkritik" (*Literarische Echo*, 1 January 1908). Rancorous exchanges followed in which Trebitsch challenged Meyerfeld's translations of Wilde, Meyerfeld drew up lists of Trebitsch's errors, and the two traded charges of "base slanderer" (*Literarische Echo*, 15 February, 15 March).

2. Trebitsch, in *Schaubühne*, 9 April, listed some alleged errors by Meyerfeld in *De Profundis* and adapted Shaw's suggestions for a letter into a purported statement by Shaw ("Zur Schulmeisterethik"; see also *Schaubühne*, 16 April and *Literarische Echo*, 15 May).

3. Gustav Landauer now planned to translate and publish Shaw's "The Impossibilities of Anarchism" (1893).

4. The *Neue Freie Presse* remitted £5 for "Die Gruel von Denshawai" ("The Denshawai Horror") from the Preface to *John Bull*, which attacked Britain's mistreatment of Egyptian prisoners. Shaw's agitation for their release (*New Age*, 24 October 1907) had recently succeeded.

10 Adelphi Terrace W.C.
11th April 1908

My dear Trebitsch

I have read Mr Jacobsen's letter. The difficulty is that he does not know the law and is not in possession of the facts. The agreement should have been made with me, not with you. I never saw it until quite lately; and then, as you know, I at once protested against it. It was represented to me that you had had an offer of 1000 crowns for permission to use "the idea" of the first act of Arms & The Man for an operetta: that is an opera in one act. I was very doubtful about it at the time, not being able to see what they were paying for; but I did not like to deprive you of 500 crowns; so I let the thing pass on the understanding that the bargain was to be limited as above. My receipt, drawn by my secretary, was a mere matter between you and me: it was not a receipt to Mr Slivinski,[1] and cannot imply any contract with him.

However, it is no use now wrangling as to the facts. The question is, how to get out of the difficulty we are in. The first thing to do is to return the 1000 crowns. You obtained them by going beyond your legal powers; and since I refuse to confirm the contract (to do so would be to violate my own contracts in other quarters) you cannot honorably keep the money. I enclose a cheque for the amount, as it is really my fault—or rather the fault of the heavy pressure of business which compels me to let so many matters pass without sufficient attention—and there is no reason why you should suffer for my negligence. When the money is returned and the contract torn up, then the position will be as follows.

The opera, as performed, must not be called Helden, nor announced as a musical setting of it. None of the names of my characters must be used. None of my dialogue must be used. There must be no possibility of a foreign manager attempting to stop performances of my play on the ground that they violate his rights in the opera. Further, there must be no possibility of an attempt to stop a performance of a real attempt to set Arms & The Man to music, if I should at any future time authorize a composer to do it. This is not likely to happen; but it is possible that if Elgar or Richard Strauss were to propose to set the play—not paraphrased into a string of waltzes, but just as it stands—I might not refuse. This would not interfere with the Oscar Straus–Jacobsen paraphrase. You will note that these conditions are just as important to Herr Straus as to me: more so, in fact, as he could not claim an infringement against me without admitting the identity of his libretto with my play. If the similarity went beyond the limits of a general similarity of subject, he would be liable to an appeal to the courts to stop the performance in every copyright country in Europe. In France, where my translator is a member of the powerful Societé des Auteurs, which under its *traité générale* with the theatres, can stop a performance at will, a contract signed *ultra vires* [in excess of granted power] by a German in violation of a Frenchman's rights would not be of much use to him. I should have to publish the warning I have already sent privately to Herr Straus in all the countries; and immediately a cloud of difficulties would arise, costly and troublesome to Herr Straus, costly and troublesome to me, very unfavorable to Herr Slivinski's international reputation as a careful man of business, and profitable to nobody but the lawyers.

On the other hand, if the libretto complies with my conditions, or is altered so as to comply with them, Herr Jacobsen is quite welcome to any suggestions or ideas he has taken from our play. If he or Herr Oscar Straus had applied directly to me (as I applied directly to Herr Strauss) without relying on these men of business who are regarded as men of business only by artists and as artists by real men of business, there would have been no trouble: I should have pointed out at once the limits within which my work could be used. I have no right to be generous at your expense; but now that I return the 1000 crowns, Herr Jacobsen gets his borrowed ideas for nothing. It may be that the borrowing is so obvious that the critics will accuse him of plagiarism, especially if he has done nothing very brilliant before. In that case he can put a note in the program as follows:—"One of the scenes in this operetta has been suggested by Herr Siegfried Trebitsch's translation of one of Bernard Shaw's best known plays." But it would be much better to say nothing, as it is hard to devise a formula that is legally unobjectionable. At all events, any such statement must be submitted to us and agreed upon before publication. It must not convey the impression that the operetta is an authorized musical version of Helden or that I have disposed of any rights.

The next step is to get from them a copy of their libretto. Until I see that, I can give no undertaking in the matter. Any suggestions I may have to make about it are far more likely to be in the nature of improvements than otherwise. I am probably as clever a dramatist as Herr Jacobsen; and I know a good deal about music, and of the situations that musicians can handle effectively.

I consider that Herren Straus & Jacobsen will now have no reason to suspect me of any intention to act unreasonably or to make money out of them. I shall get nothing whatever out of the business except the loss of a good deal of time in which I might have been earning money with my pen. I have made no attempt to make them the butt of my wit. The difficulty has not been of my making. It would have been obvious to anyone in the world except a theatrical agent that your powers did not extend beyond the German language, and that an agreement for international rights should be made with the author.

I write this letter with great difficulty, as I have had a severe attack of influenza—in fact, I am in the middle of it, and am unfit for any sort of business.

Please lose no time in returning the money & getting a copy of the libretto. Impress on Herr Jacobsen that the matter is of great importance, as even if he could make his case good against me in Germany, he would still have to deal with seven translators throughout Europe who have exclusive rights of unquestionable validity in the text of Helden in their respective languages.

yours ever

G. Bernard Shaw

P.S. Morgen has just arrived, like a bombshell.[2] Oh Siegfried, Siegfried, what have you done? Here is my best and most useful piece of economic analysis mutilated so as to appear like a strong defence of Anarchism & revival of Bakunin,[3] and presented to the German public as an authentic work of mine. What on earth am I to do? You have utterly ruined me. Llandauer would have translated the whole thing. Have you gone stark mad? Or has the influenza given me hallucinations? Is the Morgen affair a piracy, or is it yours? It reads like yours. But to—oh Lord! oh Lord! This is the VERY WORST thing that has ever happened since the world was created. Do you realize that Anarchism is a serious thing? Heaven forgive you!

Als.

1. Adolf Sliwinski, theatre agent, represented Oscar Straus, Bernauer, and Jacobson.

2. To forestall Landauer, Trebitsch had rushed through a drastically cut version of "The Impossibilities of Anarchism," which appeared in *Morgen* on 10 April ("Die Unmöglichkeiten des Anar-

chismus"] without Trebitsch's name as translator. The cut version was weighted against state violence and hypocrisy and appeared to support the anarchist view of the state. Moreover Shaw's economic strictures against anarchism—the heart of his argument—were only briefly alluded to.
3. Mikhail Bakunin (1814–1876), Russian revolutionary and leading exponent of anarchism.

Ayot St Lawrence. Welwyn
18th April 1908

My dear Trebitsch

I am too seriously out of health to write all that about the Straus opera over again: it nearly killed me to write it before. You are a baby; and you dont understand anything & dont care for anything except getting beforehand with Llandauer & getting kronen out of editors. If you cant bring yourself to give back that cheque, send it back to me. I will send it to Schneider with instructions; but I wish there had not been all this delay. Anyhow, remember that every farthing we have had for that opera must be at once returned; and no solitary pfennige or kreutzer must be retained or accepted on our side. Already difficulties may be arising: they may be making contracts based on the right to use my name. Do, I beg you, wire to me the moment you receive this if you decide *not* to carry out my instructions. I would have willingly paid another 1000 kronen to save this delay. I have to begin rehearsing my new play [*Getting Married*] on Tuesday;[1] and I can only do it without a second relapse (which would finish me) by getting every moment of absolute rest I can until then. The money is no consequence to me: the instant settlement of the affair may save me £1000's worth of trouble later on. You have no notion of the seriousness of it: you write to me like a blessed child of three years old.

The Impossibilities of Anarchism must be translated word for word from the latest English edition without omitting a line.[2] Good God! do you think the thing is a literary *jeu d'esprit* to amuse a few dilettanti? Of course nobody knows Tucker[3] in Germany: do you suppose they know him in England? What sort of *pays de Cocagne* are you living in that you behave in this raving mad fashion? Has marriage turned your head?

The maddest of all your proposals is to publish The Doctor's Dilemma with the last act cut out. Am I Brieux, to cut out a vital limb of my play because a few newspaper men complain of it?[4] Also, you must find a title that really means The Doctor's Dilemma.[5] The whole point is that the doctor, having to choose deliberately between saving a man & killing him, kills him.

I am getting a relapse already & can write no more. Regard yourself for the next month as a hopeless lunatic and do nothing but what I tell you—and even I am hardly sane, with this cursed poison in my blood.

In haste & fury
GBS

Als.
1. The Vedrenne-Barker venture at the Savoy had collapsed and the partners had joined forces with Frederick Harrison at the Haymarket Theatre, where *Getting Married* was to open in May.

2. Trebitsch now prepared a complete translation of "Impossibilities of Anarchism," for *Essays von Bernard Shaw*, published that year.

3. Benjamin Tucker (1854–1939), American anarchist publisher of *Liberty* and one of Shaw's targets in this essay.

4. Eugène Brieux (1858–1932), leading French naturalist playwright, had just defended rewriting the third act of his latest play, *Simone*, after the dress-rehearsal audience objected to it (*Times*, 14 April).

5. Trebitsch chose the title *Der Arzt am Scheideweg* (Doctor at the Crossroads).

Ayot St Lawrence. Welwyn
20th April 1908

My dear Trebitsch

Cash the cheque at once. Then send, *per registered letter*, your own cheque for 1000 kronen, to Jacobsohn or Slivinski or whoever paid you the money, with a letter to say that since you have failed to obtain my ratification to the agreement, you return the "consideration."* Say that any attempt on their part to force a payment on me will be regarded by me as a refusal to settle the matter in a friendly way. They may pay you a million kronen for your trouble if they like; but under no circumstances will I accept a single farthing. The matter will be one of courtesy between us: there will be no consideration, and no contract—nothing but a permission in any points on which they may have exceeded their legal rights. . . .

I await the libretto. Everything will turn on that. They need not waste time sending an agreement with it. When I read the libretto I will tell them what to do.

I am sorry to give you so much trouble about this; but I have no alternative. The matter is a very serious one, which might involve me in endless international disputes.

There was a row in Budapesth over the Hebbeltheater & Mrs Warren's Profession.[1] My Hungarian translator, Hevesi, was naturally very indignant at his translation being anticipated by a German performance without asking his permission; and he demanded that I should stop it. However, I persuaded him that two performances, if they were as good as the Berlin ones, would advertize the play instead of damaging it; and he consented to let them pass. It now turns out that the performance was not very successful. Do you know whether they had the same actress for Mrs Warren? If not, we should not have consented to the performance. The affair is of no great importance; but I mention it to shew you how difficult it is for me to drive my nine (9) foreign languages round the European arena without getting the reins entangled. . . .

I shall have to get a Schlegel & Tieck & pick out the lines quoted in the D[octor]'s D. They are a mosaic of lines & half lines from Macbeth, Hamlet & Othello.[2]

You had better let me see your translation of the Aerial Football story. There are bits from the Bible which you—atheist that you are—will not recognize, and at least one utterly untranslatable pun—that about Tellus. By the way the price I got for the story in America was £200; and later on they sent me another £200, as a prize for the best story of the year(!), which I indignantly flung back at their heads. So do not let it go too cheap.[3] The Pianoforte essay is a rotten little thing, hardly worth republishing.[4] It is not the 5th act of the Doctor's D. that kills the play: it is the 4th. Everything will depend on whether Dubedat can make an acting success of this. Barker made it ghastly: people used to go out & faint & ask for brandy at the Court Theatre: he missed the peculiar softness & prettiness that gives pathos to the death, and made it hard & frightful. Of course the critics did not know what was wrong: they never do. Lots of people thought the 5th act the gem of the play: others thought it spoiled everything.

G.B.S.

*In English law there can be no contract without a "consideration"; and their object in refusing the return of the money is to be able to plead that I have accepted the consideration & therefore am bound by the contract.

Als.
1. The Hebbel, directed by Eugen Robert, had successfully produced *Mrs Warren* in Berlin (16 November 1907) and then toured the play with the original cast—Rosa Bertens and Maria Mayer as Kittie Warren and Vivie—opening in Budapest on 10 April for four performances at the Hungarian Theatre.
2. Trebitsch needed aid in unpuzzling B.B.'s scrambled Shakespeare in *Doctor's Dilemma*.
3. Shaw's short story "Aerial Football" appeared in *Collier's* on 23 November 1907; Trebitsch's version ("Luftfussball," *Neue Freie Presse*, 19 April) earned Shaw £11.
4. "The Religion of the Pianoforte" ("Ist das Klavier ein musikalisches Instrument") was placed with the *Oesterreichische Rundschau* (1908).

Ayot St Lawrence. Welwyn
20th April 1908

My dear Trebitsch

In the matter of that confounded Munich Verein which pirated Mrs Warren, I have been hammering away at them through Schneider; and they now offer a solemn undertaking never to perform again without my permission. But they deny that their performance was a *public* one; and they refuse to pay any damages, alleging that I have sustained none.

Can you give me any particular case in which the play was refused by a Munich manager on the ground that the Verein had already performed it. You understand—I want to *prove* actual damages—to shew that but for the Verein I should have been able to make some money out of the play in Munich.[1]

Oh these lawsuits, these lawsuits!

Also, what does the deduction from the Hebbel-Warren gross receipts of M3650.80, representing a percentage of M365, for "Prog. u Garderobe" mean? Does it mean that the program & cloak room fees were included in the returns, or that the Hebbeltheater charges no fees, and makes a deduction against the author for their value? In the latter case, I should object.

yrs ever
G.B.S.

Als.
1. Lacking evidence for damages, Shaw eventually dropped his case against the Neue Verein (see 16 November 1907).

10 Adelphi Terrace W.C.
29th June 1908

My dear Trebitsch

I have ordered the books you mentioned to be sent to Julius Bab.[1] As to the enormously comprehensive question as to what literature he ought to read about Irish civilization, it is quite unanswerable. My advice to him is to read the preface to John Bull's Other Island and be content with that. The alternative is to spend the next twenty years in a Public Library reading everything he can find there on the subject of Ireland.

On Saturday next, the 4th, I start for Stockholm by sea, via Gothenburg and the Gotha Canal. As my wife has never been to Bayreuth, we shall go there at the end of July. Our present intention is to hire a motor car and do our travelling in that way. This might conceivably take us even as far as Vienna; but I am not quite sure as to that. However, I must break away from my work and have a good holiday, as I am pretty nearly at the end of my tether. You can judge of the extent to which I have been pressed by the impossibility of getting a letter out of me.

As to the title of the Doctor's Dilemma, tell Reinhardt that if he wants a play called Der Arzt und der Tod [The Doctor and Death] he had better write it himself: I simply wont have it. Der Arzt am Scheideweg [Doctor at the Crossroads] exactly expresses my title; and unless Reinhardt can find an alternative which is equally correct as well as more effective, I shall vote for the Scheideweg.

Bad as the press notices of The Doctor's Dilemma were, they were nothing to the torrent of denunciation that burst over Getting Married.[2] The effect is of course very bad in Germany; but here the reaction produced by the fact that the play has not been a failure after all, has been rather useful to me. Many of the notices declared that though the first act was tolerably well received, the play was received at the end with hisses. As a matter of fact, I heard a solitary hiss at the end of the first act; but at the end of the play there were six curtain calls, although the great length of the play must have made it most exhausting to the audience. I believe it will prove a money making play.

As to the Ledermann piracies, it is quite useless writing petulant letters to the papers, claiming rights that I do not possess. I have already sustained a defeat in the Court of First Instance because I could not persuade my lawyer to put my case properly. Instead of claiming, as I instructed him, copyright in the *new* portions of Cashel Byron's Profession only, and admitting that the old edition had fallen into the public domain, he claimed that the whole story was copyright; and of course the Court decided against him. The defeat brought him to his senses: then for the first time he applied his mind to the case; and I believe I shall win it on appeal. Indeed, he is now getting quite enthusiastic about it, seeing at last that the interests involved in it are enormous, and that the case will be a leading case in copyright law, instead of a dirty little squabble on my part for money.[3] But while these proceedings are going on I cannot write letters to the papers.

As to Landauer, unless you wish to die of nervous irritation, you must make up your mind to allow the German nation to enjoy the copyrights which have actually and irrevocably fallen into the public domain. Landauer has a perfect right to translate anything of mine that is not copyright in Germany; and so has Ledermann. It is only when they represent their editions as being authorized by me, that I have any reason to complain.

Meyerfeld is in London; but he has made no attempt to see me this time, though he has been stuffing Archer, and I presume everybody else, with stories of your horrible incapacity as translator.

Now as to Jacobson. First, will you tell him that if he wishes to make any impression on me by his letters, he must write in Latin script. I cannot decipher those infernal German characters. I have read his libretto. With the exception of certain passages which can easily be altered or removed, and which are simply translations of my dialogue and therefore violations of the rights of my translators in other countries, there is nothing I need object to, provided it is not implied in any way that I am responsible for the operetta, and provided especially that a stop be put to the statements in the press that the managers who have acquired the rights of the operetta have acquired also the rights of Arms and the Man. The libretto should be announced frankly as parodierte nach Bernard Shaw's Helden. The first act is an allowable and amusing parody. The second and third acts may succeed if the music and the actresses are pretty enough. Of the passages to which I object, the principal one begins on page 24 of Act 3 with the words "Wie viel Pferde haben Sie?" This is not a parody of the situation in my play, but a literal translation of it. Again, on page 40 of the second Act, the first eight speeches, about the pawning of the coat, must be left out, because they also are practically translated straight out of the original. A good deal of the act, especially the passages about the chocolate, the cavalry charge, and the portrait, are really open to the same objection; but we can let them pass, partly because we should make the whole libretto impossible if we objected, and partly because the first Act is a genuine parody, and genuine parody is quite allowable.

My conditions then are as follows. The passages I have marked with blue pencil . . . must be omitted. I have made the cuts in each case so that it will not spoil the scene: it will only shorten it and make it play closer. The operetta may be announced as parodierte nach Bernard Shaw's Helden von Rudolf Bernauer and Leopold Jacobson. The title used in England and America must be The Chocolate Cream Soldier, a musical parody of Arms and the Man (with apologies to Mr Bernard Shaw).[4] Further, the English version must be a bona fide translation of the German of Messrs Bernauer and Jacobson, and must not reproduce verbatim any sentence in Arms and the Man. There must, in short, be no greater use made of my play in England and America than in Germany. Now as to the advance of a thousand kronen. The return of this sum must be accepted. The entire sum must be returned by you, and returned on the express ground that you find, on referring to the exact terms of your agreement with me, that you went beyond your powers in signing the letter dated 13th October 1907. That letter must be returned to you in exchange for the thousand kronen and for a letter setting forth the conditions I am now making. (If they refuse this—if they persist on standing on this agreement and maintaining its validity, then all negotiations are at an end; and I hold myself free to take legal action in England and America the moment a performance is announced.) There is, however, no reason why you should not accept any payment they choose to make you for your trouble in the matter. Only, it must be clear that I get none of it.

If these conditions are accepted, I shall take no steps to hinder the production either in English or German. Also, I will not suggest any hostile proceedings in other countries; but it must be distinctly understood that my translators, under my agreement with them, have the right, not only to take proceedings themselves, but to make me a party to those proceedings if they choose, and that in the event of their doing so, I am bound to stand by them. The purchaser of the rights can, however, guard himself by employing my translators to translate the libretto. Still, I repeat that I cannot guarantee their consent.

yrs ever
G. Bernard Shaw

PS As to boycotting *März, Morgen* &c &c, because they publish unauthorised translations, that is unreasonable & ruinous.[5] An Unsocial Socialist, of which there is no edition less than 10 years old, has lapsed into the public domain in Germany; and both the translators & editors are perfectly within their rights in translating & publishing them. There is nothing whatever improper or dishonest in the transaction: the law is the law; and you have no right to treat people as dishonest because they dont respect rights that you dont possess. An author has nothing to sell but his copyright—that is, his power to protect the purchaser against competition: when he has no copyright he has nothing to sell. If they touch the copyright matter in the new editions of Cashel Byron & The Irrational Knot, I shall fight them as I am fighting Ledermann, whom I think I shall finally vanquish. But I shall not go an inch beyond my legal rights; and neither must you. You cannot be too exact & scrupulous in these matters: artistic anarchism does not pay in the long run.

Tls.

1. Julius Bab, the Berlin social-democratic theatre critic, was preparing the first book-length study of Shaw in Germany.

2. The Vedrenne-Barker production of *Getting Married*—their last—opened on 12 May at the Haymarket to a poor press and ran 54 times. Shaw's previous play, *Doctor's Dilemma*, had a divided press, with those opposed rejecting the work as tasteless, disgusting, tedious, etc.

3. A second court hearing on the Shaw-Ledermann case again held that the 1901 edition of *Cashel* was essentially the same as the original. Shaw appealed, but Ledermann promptly issued Shaw's other novels in translations by Alfred Brieger and Wilhelm Cremer.

4. Jacobson met Shaw's terms, and *Der tapfere Soldat* (English title, *The Chocolate Soldier*) opened in Vienna on 15 November 1908 and in Berlin the following February. The subsequent English version did not adhere strictly to the German text, and Shaw demanded changes before approving the London production, which opened on 10 September 1910 at the Lyric Theatre.

5. Shaw mentions *März* and *Morgen* for illustrative purposes; neither journal published piracies.

The Railway Hotel. Mallaranny[1]
16th September 1908

My dear Trebitsch

I take so little interest in Jacobsohn's nonsense that I cannot invent any better expression than the one he proposes.[2] Tell him to go ahead & not bother us about it. No agreement is necessary: the correspondence will be enough if he carries out the understanding faithfully.

[Leon] Kellner is now Professor of English at the University of What's-itsname (somewhere in Austria) [Czernowitz]; and he is greatly pleased with himself—as big as blue beef. He wrote me rather a guarded letter, as if not quite sure of his standing with me, asking for Archer's address. He wanted to interview Archer. So I arranged a lunch, and invited Archer, and treated Kellner as my oldest & dearest friend. He was in prime condition and apparently enjoyed himself very much. He assured me that nothing but my utter ignorance of German could lead me to approve of your translations, which had prevented my plays becoming known in Germany. He repeated to Archer all his old examples from the Candida stage directions of your lack of even a rudimentary knowledge of English. I encouraged him as much as possible; for he evidently takes a keen interest in you: you are one of his favorite topics. Why dont you ask him to lunch and get him to correct a few difficult passages for you and tell him that the second edition of the Drei Dramen owes all its merit to his invaluable criticisms.[3] Now that you are becoming famous, he would at once adopt you as his literary godson & play Dr Johnson to your Goldsmith. I like Kellner: he knows more English than I do, and sticks to his guns like a man. Whenever you meet an enemy of mine in Austria, ask him to lunch at once: then he will be only half an enemy, and will go about saying that all the merit of the boasted Shaw plays lies in the translation—that Shaw is an illiterate pig who owes all his reputation to Trebitsch. . . .

It is raining cats & dogs. The west of Ireland is the most beautiful of all places on earth; but oh Lord! the rain! After six weeks of Germany it is clearing my head amazingly.

My compliments to Madame. Will she come to England next year?[4]

GBS

Als.

1. The Shaws had gone to Ireland after returning on 4 September from their two months in Sweden and Germany.
2. The proposed "expression" for *Tapfere Soldat* was: "with use of motifs" from *Arms*.
3. Trebitsch did not befriend Kellner, but in 1911, in a review of the collected edition of Shaw, *Dramatische Werke*, Kellner praised the revised versions as "very acceptable" ("Der verdeutschte Shaw," *Neues Wiener Tagblatt*, 6 July 1911).
4. Tina Trebitsch and the Shaws did not meet until 1910, in London.

10 Adelphi Terrace W.C.
15th January 1909

My dear Trebitsch

In Getting Married the curtain falls immediately before the first entrance of Hotchkiss, at the conclusion of the Bishop's speech. When it rises again the people are in exactly the same position on the stage; and the play goes on as if there had been no interruption. The second time is immediately after the first entry of Mrs George. As she appears on the stage, and before she has spoken, the curtain goes down again. When it rises she is in the same position; and the play proceeds as before just as if there had been no interruption. These intervals must not appear in the printed version; and the play must not be announced as in three acts on the programme. Instead, the programme must contain a notice that though the play is not divided into acts, the management, for the convenience of the audience, and with the consent of the author, have decided to lower the curtain twice in the course of the performance; but the two intervals thus created are not part of the author's design. . . .

I return you the cheque for two pounds ten (£2:10:0). If you had been paid anything for the translation [of "Das Interview des Kaisers Wilhelm"], I should have dunned you for half of it. It is not a question of exactly how much you do or I do: there is hardly a single transaction which involves exactly equal work for you and me. The sensible thing to do is to share the proceeds of the business equally. Sometimes you will get a windfall; sometimes I will: the thing will average itself out in the long run.

I quite understand that the reason there was such a fuss in Germany about the Kaiser's communication to the Daily Telegraph was that the Germans are thorough-going Pro-Boers, and were infuriated to find that the Kaiser sympathised with Roberts and not with Kruger. They think I misunderstood because I did not say the thing they wanted to have said, but the thing that it was good for them to hear.[1] As that happened to be also what the Kaiser himself probably wanted to have said, I think the Kaiser ought to have come to the Doctor's Dilemma in state, and crowned my bust with laurels. But kings were ever ungrateful.

Of course I never read that confounded contract. Why should I? It is much easier to assume that it is all wrong, and complain to you about it. Then you read it yourself for the first time, and are able to correct me, besides learning something about it yourself.

John Bull's Zweite Insel seems to me as good a title as you can find.[2] The English title grew out of a book written by a Frenchman who called himself Max O'Rell, (since dead), which was much spoken of here some years ago. It was called John Bull and his Island; so I called my play John Bull's Other Island. I was afraid that you would have had to find a new title altogether, as I did not know that the Germans were familiar with the name John Bull.

I do not think it likely that Fischer took any steps to secure the American copyright of the Doctor's Dilemma. Unless he were expressly warned to the contrary he would have assumed that publication had already taken place in England. However, I am not very anxious about it, as no American publisher of any standing is likely to bring out a hack translation from the German as my original work. I am rehearsing The Admirable Bashville for His Majesty's Theatre just now, and have no time to do anything; so the corrections for the Doctor's Dilemma must wait a little longer. You evidently don't understand my explanations about the error in the medical theory. It is my solemn belief that you don't know what the circulation of the blood means. You can, however, find out by a very simple experiment. At dinner this evening take the carving knife and give yourself a good deep slash across the wrist, or ask your wife to drive it into your neck just under your ear. You will then discover that your heart acts as a force-pump and drives your blood to the tips of your toes and sucks it back again about 60 times a minute when you are in a condition of calm, and about 135 times immediately after you have received a letter from me.

This is the circulation of the blood; and it has nothing whatever to do with the positive and negative phases. Nevertheless, you have applied the word circulation—Blutkreislauf—to this alternation of the positive and negative phases in the secretion of opsonin.

Are the performances still going on?[3]

What the deuce is the good of making your will if you have not insured your life? The will is no use unless you have something to leave.

I have several times considered very seriously the question of having my next play produced for the first time in Germany. It would be quite useful to the pioneers of the dramatic movement here to be able to point to an English author driven to Berlin by the attacks of the English Press. Besides, now that the Vedrenne and Barker enterprise is suspended, my plays are no longer wanted for immediate use in London.

I have several remittances from you which are still unacknowledged. My secretary [Georgina Gillmore] has gone to bed for a month; and my new secretary [Mabel W. McConnell] does not yet know how to spell your name; but you will have all due acknowledgments in the course of a year or so.

yours ever

G. Bernard Shaw

Tls.

1. On 28 October 1908, the London *Daily Telegraph* reported a private exchange in which the Kaiser professed peaceful intentions toward Britain despite German public opinion and pointed to his secret refusal to support the Boers against Britain. The Kaiser's pro-English sentiments amazed the German imperialist press, while the liberal-left press denied that the middle and lower classes in Germany were anti-British. Shaw's "Das Interview des Kaisers Wilhelm" hailed the Kaiser for telling the truth (*Neue Freie Presse*, 19 November). Paul Kruger (1825–1904) was the Boer leader; Frederick Roberts (1832–1914), the British supreme commander.

2. *John Bull* (*John Bulls andere Insel*) and *Doctor's Dilemma* (*Arzt am Scheideweg*) were in process of publication by Fischer.

3. *Arzt am Scheideweg* had opened at Reinhardt's Kammerspiele on 21 November 1908, with Alexander Moissi, Tilla Durieux, and Paul Wegener. Felix Holländer directed. The play was greeted with "polite coolness" (*Berliner Tageblatt*, 22 November) and "painful confusion" (*Vossische Zeitung*). Yet thanks to the fine cast, *Arzt* succeeded, running 82 times in the Kammerspiele and three times in the large Deutsches Theater. It was Reinhardt's first success with Shaw and in time the most popular of his Shavian productions.

10 Adelphi Terrace W.C.

25th February 1909

What is Gagliardi[1] dreaming of? I should have lost my rights in Italy if I had waited until now to have Helden translated into Italian. The only country in Europe in which I have not a translator is Portugal—except, of course, Holland & Russia, where they pirate me to my heart's content, as there is no copyright.

I hear that I have lost my case against Ledermann. No particulars have come to hand yet. If it is true, they will pirate all the novels.[2] As I was appealing against a former adverse decision, I suppose I cannot carry the case further.

I am writing to Gagliardi.

If you have to pay extra postage on this card, let me know.[3] I send it as an experiment.   GBS

Apcs.

   1. Maria Gagliardi, a translator from Italian associated with S. Fischer. Shaw had already contracted with Antonio Agresti to be his Italian translator.
   2. Ledermann had already published the remaining Shaw novels.
   3. Shaw, expecting that his card would be readdressed to Trebitsch in Berlin, wondered if extra postage would be required, as in England. It was not.

10 Adelphi Terrace W.C.

28th June 1909

My dear Trebitsch

There has been a great fuss here over the enclosed play Blanco Posnet [*The Shewing-up of Blanco Posnet*], which was announced by Beerbohm Tree for performance at His Majesty's Theatre, and forbidden by the Lord Chamberlain (our Censor) on the ground that it is blasphemous. Nevertheless, on Friday last, the 25th, the King made Tree a knight. On the same day the Lord Chamberlain forbad the performance of another play of mine called Press Cuttings which I also enclose. This time the objection was that it contained political personalities.[1]

This morning I have been approached by Reuter's Telegram Company and by the Correspondent of the Berliner Morgenpost. It has become known that Press Cuttings contains a passage relating to Germany, and to the war scare which certain people here are fomenting.[2] Reuter and the Morgenpost want me to give them the passages relating to Germany. I do not see, however, why I should not give them to you. If you translate the dialogue on pp 12–15, some Berlin paper will probably pay well enough for it to make it worth doing; and it will be a valuable advertisement for us anyhow. Besides, if I give it to Reuter now, he will telegraph it straightaway; and the English papers will retranslate it from the German, spoiling it in the process, and publish it here before the performance on the 9th. I want it timed so as to make this impossible: that is, it must not appear sooner than the 8th July.[3] If there is anything in the passage that puzzles you, send me your translation and I will set it right.

I have taken advantage of the Blanco Posnet affair to write a tremendous series of letters to The Times; and the result has been that the Prime Minister has promised to appoint a Select Committee of both Houses of Parliament to enquire into the whole question of the Censorship.[4] All this will give you material for an article of which the dialogue can form part. Do not give it to the Neue Freie Presse. It must appear in a Berlin paper.[5]

yours ever

G. Bernard Shaw

Tls.

1. *Press Cuttings* caricatures Prime Ministers Asquith and Balfour and General Redvers Buller (Mitchener).

2. General Mitchener in the play declares that England rules the seas "by nature" and must prepare for a German invasion.

3. Trebitsch's translation of the passage appeared in the *Berliner Tageblatt* (8 July), a day before the special private performance of *Press Cuttings* at the Court Theatre. The full play, *Zeitungsausschnitte*, appeared in *März* (July 1909).

4. The letters to the *Times* began on 29 May and continued through June. Subsequently, a Parliamentary Select Committee on censorship disallowed Shaw's statement, later included in the preface to *Blanco Posnet*.

5. Trebitsch did not write an article on the controversy.

10 Adelphi Terrace W.C.

3rd July 1909

Both plays [*Blanco Posnet* and *Press Cuttings*] are one-acters about an hour long. The program you suggest ought to be quite feasible at a theatre like the Grand Guignol; but I do not believe much in these scrappy programs in ordinary theatres . . . .

In haste,

G.B.S.

Tpcs.

Ayot St Lawrence. Welwyn

1st November 1909

My dear Trebitsch

What an awful thing to send Concordia! You forget that my fatherland is IRELAND, and that it has received Blanco Posnet with frantic enthusiasm, as it received John Bull's Other Island before.[1] I should be utterly damned in Ireland if I called England my fatherland, or accused Ireland of England's stupidity. I enclose a proper Shavian message.

I shall certainly not tell you the name of the Berlin lady. She will probably be introduced to you & perhaps entertain you some day. To reconcile you to her, I will tell you one thing more. She said that Meyerfeldt's translations of Wilde were infamous.

If you are a Jew (which is very interesting) what have you done with your nose? Meyerfeld is a real Jew: you can recognize him a mile off. But you have got mixed up with Germanic Christianity. Since 1809 there must have been several Trebitsches. The 1809 man was your great grandfather. Where did he come from? Then there was your grandfather & father. Did they marry Jewesses & eat "Kosher" meat & go to the synagogue, or did they marry German Christians? I want to know all about it. I want to know how your peculiar type, which is certainly neither vulgar Jew nor vulgar Austrian, is produced.[2]

I told the lady I had seen a photograph of your wife, and that she was an extraordinarily good imitation of a princess. But the lady would have it that Madame sold old clothes in the Ghetto of Cracow, and that the photograph was a portrait of a real princess which you bought to deceive me.[3] This being so, I insist on seeing the original next April.—I have not much hope of Barbara's success. Berlin is not religious enough for it.[4]

G.B.S.

Als.

1. Trebitsch had drafted a statement to Concordia, a journalists' club in Vienna, about the censoring of Shaw in his "fatherland." *Blanco Posnet*, after being banned in England, was promptly produced at the Abbey Theatre, Dublin, on 25 August, despite official British complaints.

2. Trebitsch's great-grandfather had emigrated from Moravia to Vienna. Trebitsch's parents were Jewish, but he did not receive any religious training.

3. Tina Trebitsch was a non-Jewish Viennese and, as mentioned, the widow of a Russian nobleman.

4. *Major Barbara*, which had its premiere at the Deutsches Volkstheater, Vienna, on 27 March 1909 and failed after four performances, was to open at Reinhardt's Kammerspiele on 5 November, with Lucie Höflich, Paul Wegener, and Alfred Abel. Felix Holländer directed. The play had been cut to soften its radical thrust and was poorly received, the *Vossische Zeitung* (6 November) noting that disciples and skeptics were disappointed with this poorest of Shaw's plays. The *Vorwärts* attacked Shaw's admiration for the self-made capitalist, whose talk about selling arms to the poor serves only to "salve the author's revolutionary conscience." *Major Barbara* ran 28 times in the small Kammerspiele.

Ayot St Lawrence. Welwyn
14th December 1909

The editor of the N.F.P. must be a hopeless idiot. I sent him an article which could not possibly be improved on, though it contained only 5 words. He now wants me to spoil it by adding 995 words of the sort of twaddle he can get from any hack journalist. Tell him to announce it exactly as if it were an ordinary article & put it in just as it stands. Charge him 1000 marks for translating it. And say that I am so disgusted by his stupidity that I will never write for the N.F.P. again, but send all my contributions to Die Zeit, which worries me daily for articles.[1]

G.B.S.

Apcs.

1. Shaw's unidentified statement to the *Neue Freie Presse* was not published, nor did Shaw carry out his threat to bypass the paper in the future.

Edstaston. Wem.
28th December 1909

. . . Bab is tremendous. What has he done besides this book on me?[1] . . .
I have just sent my new play [*Misalliance*] to the printer. If you can translate it in three weeks & rehearse it in another three, Reinhardt can produce it in Berlin *before* the London production.[2]

G.B.S.

Antoinette ("Tina") Trebitsch, 1910.

Apcs.

1. Julius Bab, eager to present Shaw with a copy of *Bernard Shaw*, dispatched an uncorrected proof copy. His pioneer study disputed the view of Shaw as nihilist and stressed the constructive moralist with roots in English puritanism.

2. Shaw's offer of a world premiere in Berlin of *Misalliance* was unrealistic in the time allotted.

10 Adelphi Terrace W.C.

7th February 1910

My dear Trebitsch

The prospect of Hermann Bahr's arrival terrifies me.[1] I have not read one of the books he has sent me; and as I do not speak German and he does not speak English, I do not see what we can do except shake hands and contemplate one another in friendly silence. However, I will do what is possible under these distressing circumstances to demonstrate my friendly disposition.

I enclose a copy of my new play [*Misalliance*]. If you are going to write an article about it, remember that it must not appear until the 24th February. The play will be produced on the 23rd; and I have undertaken that no description of it shall appear in the papers before it is produced. Already trouble has been made by an unauthorized and unfounded description which appeared in an American paper, and was immediately copied by the London papers. If you were to publish anything in Germany before the production, it would be immediately translated and spread all over the place here.[2] . . .

I note your cheerful remark that you are very ill. What is the matter with you? You really must manage to survive somehow. Your disappearance or disablement would be a most fearful misfortune for me.

yours ever

G. Bernard Shaw

PS The Stage Society is going to do 3 short plays by Felix Salten in one evening.[3] As no decent translations are available, I have undertaken to translate 10 pages of one of them whilst the rest is being translated in sections by 3 other people.

Tls.

1. Bahr was coming to England with his opera-star wife Anna von Mildenberg (1872–1946), who was to sing Klytemnestra in the London premiere of Richard Strauss's *Elektra*.

2. *Misalliance*, directed by Shaw, was to open at the Duke of York's Theatre as part of a repertory season produced by the American impresario Charles Frohman. Speculation about the play arose when the *Daily Mail* (31 January) reported rumors that there would be no intervals and the audience would decide when the curtain would fall.

3. Salten's three one-act plays, *Von andern Ufer* (English title, *Points of View*), opened at the Shaftesbury Theatre on 20 March 1910.

[10 Adelphi Terrace W.C.]

[c. 15th March 1910]

[My dear Trebitsch]

. . . The more you forget your English, the better you translate. The producer (régisseur?) of Blanco Posnet in Düsseldorf wrote to me asking whether I had any special instructions to give him.[1] I told him that I had nothing to add to the stage directions; but if there was any slang word current in Düssel-

dorf to express contempt and dislike—the coarser the better—he might substitute it for nichtswurdiger.[2] Nichtswurdiger sounds to me too literary; but
of course everything depends on how far it has been vulgarized by common
use. What is wanted is an equivalent to the French *sale*.

I was so alarmed by your account of Bahr's ignorance of English, that I decided to wait until he learnt it sufficiently to be able to meet me without the
risk of our staring at one another in helpless silence. At last he wrote to me
himself—in English! I then wrote him a long letter, and hope to entertain
him here soon. His wife refuses to come; but perhaps I shall be able to coax
her. Elektra has made an enormous success here.[3] I was present at the performance which Strauss conducted on Saturday [12 March] at Covent Garden in
the presence of the Queen. I have hardly ever seen such a demonstration in
an English theatre. The moment the curtain fell, the audience burst into a
roar of applause, and kept it up for a long time. The Queen sent for Strauss;
and the unfortunate man had a hard time of it with the audience roaring for
him to come repeatedly before the curtain and the Queen commanding his
immediate presence in her box.

We are looking forward to seeing you in May.

yours ever
G. Bernard Shaw

P.S. You have asked Miss Gillmore how the curtain can fall on pages 42
and 55.[4] I do not know how it *can*: all I can tell you is that it does. This
makes the 2nd Act only 20 minutes long. It cannot be helped: there are no
other places at which the curtain can fall. It would be much better for it not
to fall at all; but as the piece plays for over 2½ hours, it is absolutely necessary to provide intervals somewhere.

Tls.; incomplete.
1. *Blanco Posnet* and *Press Cuttings* opened on 4 March at the Schauspielhaus, Dusseldorf, and
ran three nights with an added performance in Duren.
2. Trebitsch had rendered Blanco's favorite epithet "rotten" as "nichtswürdiger"—vile, base.
3. *Elektra*—the first Strauss opera to be performed in England—opened at Covent Garden on
19 February. (A debate over Strauss's music between Shaw and Ernest Newman erupted in the *Nation* on 12 March and continued through 9 April.)
4. Georgina Gillmore, Shaw's half-cousin and secretary, had informed Trebitsch (24 February)
that the curtain in *Misalliance* came before the announcement of the airplane and after Lina leads
Tarleton off.

Tulle[1]
24th April 1910

Only by a series of forced marches will it be possible for me to get to London on the 2nd May, when I have a public engagement which I must keep.[2]
Therefore Paris is out of the question, though it is just possible that my wife
might go there to see you and Rodin & Brieux[3] & Chantecler.[4] I look forward
to seeing you and your wife in London. If Sorma can speak English I will try
to have a talk with her.[5] Getting Married is useless without a perfect en-
chantress in the part of Mrs George & a very charming bishop.[6]

G.B.S.

Apcs.

1. The Shaws along with Charlotte's sister, Mary Cholmondeley, were on holiday in France.

2. Shaw returned to London on 2 May to chair a lecture by Sidney Webb on "The Prevention of Destitution."

3. Charlotte was an admirer of Brieux, the French playwright, and had translated his *Maternité*.

4. Edmund Rostand's play *Chantecler* opened in Paris on 7 February and was a huge success.

5. Agnes Sorma did not meet Shaw.

6. *Getting Married* (*Heiraten*), produced by Otto Brahm—his only production of Shaw—opened on 9 April at the Lessing-Theater, with Else Lehmann and Emanuel Reicher, and closed after three performances. Critics blamed the play's feeble plot, characterization, and wit and implied that Shaw's powers had declined.

Ayot St Lawrence. Welwyn
17th May 1910

Bab is right. Walpole is not subtle enough for that; and it would be a frightfully brutal thing for him to say in Jennifer's presence as a mere guess.[1] Dubedat is in full possession of all his faculties until he dies. His mind is active; his hearing is so sharp that he overhears Ridgeon's remark about the dying actor; but he is too weak to turn his head to look at anything. He is quite conscious of the fact that he is dying splendidly as an artistic spectacle (note how thoroughly he understands Ridgeon's allusion to "the dying actor & his audience"), and he wants the world to hear about it. The newspaper man is the world: it is the presence of that spectator which has nerved him to the scene. His last anxiety is to be assured that he is still present.

I am writing to Constable about Bab. That book must be published somehow.

Our love to your very nice lady.[2]

G.B.S.

Apcs.

1. In *Doctor's Dilemma*, Walpole, bending over the dying Dubedat, reports: "He wants to know is the newspaper man here." Trebitsch couldn't credit that the artist's final thought was on the press.

2. The Shaws finally met Tina Trebitsch that May in London.

10 Adelphi Terrace W.C.
21st December 1910

My dear Trebitsch

I enclose the Preface, such as it is.[1] The General Election has been a frightful misfortune for me. I had to speak in public for ten nights running; and the physical effort, coming on top of the work of getting my new volume through the press, not to mention half a dozen other things, has left me good for nothing.[2] I am therefore starting on a voyage to Jamaica next Friday. I shall stay there about a week, and come back, arriving in England on the 25th January.

This has forced me to finish the Preface by a violent effort as best I can. As you will see, it all goes to pieces at the end; but I must send it as it is, as it will be too late when I come back.

I have not had time to look at the proofs, except for a hasty glance here and

there. I fully expect that there are ten mistakes in it for every one that occurred in the old version; for I do not believe a bit in your schoolmasters and
professors and people.[3] I notice that they do not know that when an Englishman names an hour with a "the" before it, he always means a train. Thus,
when Frank Warren says that his mother has gone up to town by *the* 11.15,
he means that she has gone to catch the 11.15 train. However, it does not
matter. I sampled the dialogue in one or two places; and it seemed to me to
have a distinct style, and to be not only accurate in the schoolmaster's way,
but artistically expressive.

We leave on Friday evening. If you get this on Friday morning, there will be
just time for you to wire to me in case I have forgotten anything of importance.

Do not be infuriated by the allusion to Sudermann.[4] We must not give ourselves the airs of a superior coterie. Sudermann has a good substantial talent; and we should be on friendly terms with him.

yours ever
G. Bernard Shaw

Tls.

1. "What I Owe to German Culture," to be used as a preface to the collected edition of Shaw's
plays that was in preparation. The essay appeared first in *Neue Rundschau* ("Was ich der deutschen
Kultur verdanke," March 1911; English version, *Adam*, 1970).

2. From 28 November to 7 December, Shaw campaigned for R. C. Phillimore and George
Lansbury. He was also preparing a sixpenny edition of *Man and Superman* with a new foreword.

3. To assist in revising the translations for the new edition, Trebitsch had hired a teacher of
English, Wilhelm Lehmann, who was instructed to concentrate on errors, not style. The first three
volumes of *Dramatische Werke*, purged of many blunders, appeared in May 1911.

4. In his essay, Shaw approvingly cited Sudermann's *Song of Songs* (*Das hohe Lied*) as a realistic
exposure of bohemianism.

10 Adelphi Terrace W.C.
23rd December 1910

The Sudermann book which I called The Song of Songs is Das Hohe Lied.
It has had a great success in America; but when it was announced here the
publisher [John Lane] was threatened with prosecution on the ground that it
is an obscene book. He asked me to read it, and advise him: that is how I
came to know about it.

G.B.S.

Apcs.

10 Adelphi Terrace W.C.
7th March 1911

My dear Trebitsch

I do not understand this Hungarian business. It seems perfectly clear
that I got the 500 kronen, and that if anybody is to pay it back, it must be
me. I am writing by this post to my Hungarian agent, Teleki, to ask him
what the deuce it all means.[1]

Do you know geography enough to be able to tell me whether Cracow is in
Austrian Poland or not. Ordynski, whom you probably know as one of

Rheinhardt's lieutenants, has just told me that he stage managed several productions of my plays at Cracow,[2] and that royalties on these were paid to Dr
Eirich. Is Eirich acting for Fischer?[3] If so, possibly Cracow is included in the
accounts that Fischer has sent me. But if not, then it would seem that the
wily Doctor believes himself to be the author of our plays. Can you throw
any light on this off-hand?

yours ever
[G. Bernard Shaw]

Tl.
    1. Fischer had sold rights to *You Never Can Tell* to a manager of the National Theatre, Budapest,
under the mistaken idea that it was to be performed in German. Meanwhile, Joseph Teleki, Shaw's
agent for Hungary, had negotiated with another manager of the same theatre for *You Never Can
Tell* and *Caesar*. Teleki advised Shaw to break Fischer's contract and return the 500 kronen
advanced.
    2. Richard Ordynski (1878–1953), one of Reinhardt's stage directors, was also associated with
theatres in Poland, where he ultimately settled.
    3. Eirich, the Viennese agent, acted for Fischer in the non-German portions of the Austrian
empire, which included Cracow.

Ayot St Lawrence. Welwyn
29th May 1911

My dear Trebitsch

The enclosed [*Fanny's First Play*] has just come from the printer.

Remember that this play is not yet published, and that the most frightful
copyright complications may ensue if you publish in Germany before I have
effected simultaneous publication in England & America.[1]

Performance does not matter, as pirates cannot get at the text.

My wife is planning motor tours in the Tyrol & talks of dropping into
Vienna, Munich, & the Italian towns in July & August, as if the weather
would be bearable or anybody would be in town. Please let her know about
Vienna: she wont believe me.

G.B.S.

Als.
    1. Beginning with *Doctor's Dilemma*, most of Shaw's new plays appeared in German transla-
tion before publication in English. *Fanny* was not published in English until 1914, but Shaw could
technically effect publication and copyright in England and America before actual publication.

10 Adelphi Terrace W.C.
2nd June 1911

My dear Trebitsch

Here is the end of Fanny. I do not see how the Induction and Epilogue can
be performed in Germany without a special adaptation of the critics to the
journalistic personnel of each town.[1] . . .

In haste,
yours ever
G. Bernard Shaw

Tls.
    1. Shaw's parody of well-known English theatre critics in the Induction and Epilogue to *Fanny*
could hardly be adapted to local conditions in Germany, and no such attempt was made.

10 Adelphi Terrace W.C.

3rd June 1911

My dear Trebitsch

Charlotte is very anxious that we should go to Munich to see Caesar and Cleopatra.[1] I have just been told, however, that the actress who plays Cleopatra is going to Vienna. Do you happen to know if this is true, and, if it is, at what date she is to leave Munich? If I go, I shall have to keep my presence a secret, or the play will be advertized by torch-light processions, serenades, banquets, and possibly a Te Deum in the Cathedral, of all of which I shall be the victim. I shall go incognito. . . .

yours ever

[G. Bernard Shaw][2]

Tl.

1. *Caesar*, unproduced in Germany since Reinhardt's venture in 1906, had opened at Munich's Residenz Theater on 10 February 1911, staged by Albert Steinrück of the original Berlin production, with Steinrück and Johanna Terwin in the title roles. Although reserved about the play, the press enthusiastically welcomed the production, which ran 24 times.

2. Signature cut out.

10 Adelphi Terrace W.C.

10th June 1911

My dear Trebitsch

When you stand on an English stage facing the audience the prompter's box is on your left; and that side of the stage is called the prompt side. Therefore the side to your right is called the opposite prompt side. This is shortened into P. and O.P.

I expect in about a week or ten days from now to cross the Channel and travel in the direction of Munich through the Vosges and the Black Forest. I shall not hurry; but I do not see how I can delay my arrival at Munich until the middle of August. However, we can arrange later on about meeting one another.

I have not had time to study the three volumes [*Dramatische Werke*]. I did read through my preface, which seemed to me to be all right; but probably Meyerfeld could discover plenty of errors in it.[1] . . .

I am sending you a volume of translations from Brieux, with a preface by me. The worst of giving papers like the Neue Freie Presse scraps from these prefaces is that it makes it impossible later on to publish the preface as a whole in any magazine. For instance, this Brieux preface would have made a considerable sensation in Paris if it had been published there in full. But my translator allowed himself to be seduced by the editor of L'Illustration into giving him two or three columns extracted from the preface; and after that none of the magazines would touch it.[2] . . .

yours ever

G. Bernard Shaw

Tls.

1. The three volumes of *Dramatische Werke* consisted of *Unpleasant Plays, Pleasant Plays,* and *Plays for Puritans.*

2. *Three Plays* by *Eugène Brieux* had recently appeared with Shaw's preface, written two years earlier, a copy of which—Shaw forgot—had been sent to Trebitsch, who published excerpts in *Zeitschrift* (1910–11) and *Schaubühne* (18, 25 May 1911). A segment in French had appeared in *L'Illustration* (7 May 1910), in honor of Brieux's pending election to the Académie Française.

[Grenoble]
postmarked 20th July [1911]

We are crossing & recrossing the Alps in our car by roads of this sort, which give plenty of practice in driving.¹ We are staying at Grenoble, Hotel Moderne, and making our excursions therefrom. In a few days we shall turn north again, and make for Munich through Switzerland and the Tyrol. After Munich we shall return through the Tyrol to the north of Italy & thence across France to Brittany, where I hope to have a month of seabathing, comparative quiet, & work. I am sorry the voyage fell through: *all* cabins look like that at first sight; but in two days one gets used to anything. More when we meet.

G.B.S.

Apcs.
1. The Shaws left London on 19 June.

Baur au Lac. Zürich
4th August 1911

My dear Trebitsch

Married people should never travel together: they blame one another for everything that goes wrong; and very soon each feels that the other is dragging him (or her) round Europe under pretence of benefiting his (or her) health, and really driving him (or her) mad.¹ It ends in Lahmann's [Sanatorium].

Why not hire a motor car for a month for 3,500 kr., and drive it over all the passes in the Tyrol. That is the only thing that reconciles me to these worrying holidays. I have driven over scores of passes in the Savoy & Dauphiny. In the valleys, in the towns, in the hotels, in the hideous heat, I have been wretched; but on the mountains I revive.

As you told me in your last letter that you would be in Munich early in August, I gave up my plan of avoiding Switzerland, and have come from Aigle by the Col de Pillon & the Saanen-Möser pass, Thun, Lucerne & here (Zürich), where I must stay for a few days to get some clothes washed and receive and attend to a budget of letters. When I leave this—probably on Monday morning—I shall go to Feldkirch & through the Arlberg pass into the Tyrol. I have not yet planned my movements after that; but roughly I intend to go north to Munich by the most mountainous roads I can find; and this ought to land me there not very far from the 15th. . . .

If Teleki is still at Lahmann's when you arrive there, be kind to him for my sake.² He believes in doctors, and is a wreck, accordingly.

We look forward to meeting you.

yrs ever
G. Bernard Shaw

PS My visit to Munich must be kept secret. If I am found out I shall have the car out and fly instantly. It is specially important that the actors should have no suspicion of my presence. I dont want to see how they act when the author is in the house: I want to see an ordinary performance in the regular routine, like the one I saw of Candida.

PPS I will telegraph you my addresses from time to time until we meet, provided I can ascertain them myself beforehand. What is the most comfortable hotel in Munich? When we were there before we stayed at the 4 Seasons.

Als.

1. Charlotte had insisted on a Tyrolean tour after Shaw had an attack of neuritis and was prescribed rest. The Shaws arrived in Zurich on 4 August.

2. The previous fall, Joseph Teleki, Shaw's agent for Hungary, had told Shaw that Trebitsch's version of *Blanco Posnet* was full of errors. In rebuttal, Trebitsch offered 100,000 marks (£5,000) to anyone who would find a mistake in the translation. Teleki promised to examine the play "line by line" and prove that Trebitsch had failed: "There will be no wriggling out of it for Mr. Trebitsch, and he will have to crawl down" (L. S. E.). Shaw tried to arrest the dispute by demanding of Teleki: "Why on earth should you waste your time and damage the great European firm of Bernard Shaw Unlimited. . . . Naturally being a Hungarian, you loathe all Austrians; but do not let the battle of Hungary and Austria be fought over my body" (*Collected Letters*, II, 953). Unknown to Shaw, Teleki, long unwell, had recently collapsed and died.

Baur au Lac. Zürich
7th August 1911

My dear Trebitsch

What do you mean by this erratic & extraordinary behaviour? First, on my announcing my intention of visiting Munich, you start for the North Pole. Then, when I turn south to Savoy, you return from the north & say you will be in Munich early in August. When I double back to catch you there, you retreat to Vienna, and tell me that as your mother is very ill you must go to her on the 16th! Did any man ever before say "My mother is dying: I must hasten to her bedside 12 days hence"? I am to leave Munich on the 14th; and you are to arrive there on the 28th! Finally you tell me that as you are in splendid health and quite able for work, you will go for 3 weeks to Lahmann's lunatic asylum!!

What am I to think of all this? You are running away from me, or else you are out of your senses.

My program is as follows. I leave Zürich early tomorrow morning. A day's journey will bring me to the Austrian frontier somewhere near Feldkirch. Another day will take me across the Arlberg pass, & two days more to Munich over the Fern pass and through Ober Ammergau. I shall therefore be in Munich on the 12th & 13th, after which there is nothing for me to do there unless Charlotte gets a fit of Wagnerizing and Mozartizing. But this could not last fourteen days, even if there were the least hope of your not changing all your plans again.

The only suggestion I can make is that we should go from Munich to Salzburg, and from Salzburg make an excursion to Ischl[1] and back to see you. The disadvantage of this is that either we shall not see your gnädige Frau, which we should very much like to do, or else she will have to come with you and endure your whole ten days of filial duty, which is out of all reason, as one mother is quite enough for anybody, and she has probably had enough of her own. She might, however, come to Salzburg to nurse a dying father, and, having decently buried him, go back to Ischl & pick you up there. These family complications are frightful.

The alternative of our going to Vienna is rather a severe one. I would face it if you were not both coming west to Salzburg & Munich; but as it is, I hesitate. By the shortest and ugliest route it is 253 mortal miles from Munich to Vienna. By Salzburg it is 286. People think that this is nothing to a motorist; but as a matter of fact if you travel 80 miles in this weather for 3 days in succession (and Charlotte can do no more; for it is useless to ask her to start at 7 and do 5 hours before noon) you are fit only for Dr Lahmann's at the end of it. East of Lambach there is nothing but hard work on a bad road until one reaches Vienna, which is, I suppose, hideously hot. Even calculating from Salzburg only, as we shall go there anyhow, the distance is 197 miles—practically 400 there & back. And we should not find you in Vienna after all; and Madame would be packing for her journey to join you. No: it is clear that Vienna is out of the question both for you and for us: we must meet at Ischl or Salzburg, unless you now run away again & avoid us by some new manoeuvre.

I have no idea of what hotels I shall stay at, or indeed what towns between this & Munich. The most probable seems the Wittelsbacher at Ober Ammergau. I will telegraph as soon as I have completed my plans. I understand that you recommend the Regina Palace at Munich.

auf wiedersehen
G. Bernard Shaw

Als.
   1. Where Trebitsch's ailing mother was in seclusion.

Regina Palast Hotel. Munich
13th August 1911

My dear Trebitsch

We shall have to stay here until Thursday. Why not send your heavy luggage to Ischl; come on Wednesday to Munich; stay the night; come with us in the motor to Salzburg on Thursday; and either go on to Ischl by train, or stay a night at Salzburg and let us drive you over to Ischl the next day? The car holds four people comfortably.

I have not pressed you to come to Munich because you would have nothing to do except see things that you are tired of—be bored out of your senses, in short—but a motor trip would amuse you and freshen you up.

I am in despair at missing The Philanderer, as the London production, through the sudden illness of Mrs Barker [Lillah McCarthy], fell to pieces so completely at the last moment that I have never really seen it played; and I am specially curious about it because nobody in England believes in it.[1] I had no idea that they had played it here. I am half disposed to let you tell the manager that I am here *incognito*, and would certainly go if he put it on.

So long as they do not find me out at the Residenz tonight I do not care what happens afterwards.

A Dr Maurice Ettingshausen, a Daily Mail correspondent, recognized me & called on me this morning. Also, at Tristan u. Isolde[2] at the Prinz Regenten, I was hailed by Percy Anderson, a famous London costume designer (he designed the Caesar costumes for London); but I have sworn both of them to secrecy.

In haste

yrs ever

G. Bernard Shaw

Als.

1. *Philanderer* had not been revived in England since its production in 1907 by Vedrenne-Barker. In Trebitsch's translation it had been staged for short runs in Berlin, Vienna, and other cities. Shaw missed by a month the Munich production of the play, which opened on 1 July at the Lustspielhaus for 13 performances, with Anton Edthofer in the title role.

2. Besides *Caesar* and *Tristan und Isolde*, the Shaws also saw *Die Meistersinger* in Munich.

[Hotel Tyrol. Innsbruck]

postmarked 22nd August 1911

Quite desolate without you. Why didnt you come on with us?[1]

I expect to be at the Imperial Hotel Trento, Trient, somewhere about the 27th. I have arranged a tremendous mountaineering tour for the next ten or twelve days.

We really were & are quite disconsolate at losing you.

G.B.S.

Apcs.

1. The Shaws finally caught up with Trebitsch in Salzburg on 17 August and drove with him to Ischl. Tina remained in Vienna. On 19 August, the friends parted, and the Shaws proceeded to Innsbruck and then to Italy.

[Courmayeur]

postmarked 6th September [1911]

As Charlotte, who got a swamping cold at Bergamo, insists on stopping here in Courmayeur for a day to rest, I have seized the opportunity to send a few lines about Press Cuttings to the N.F.P.[1]

The inundations in the Valtellina knocked all my plans to bits. The Stelvio[2] was unattainable. I had to return to the frontier on the Tonale pass to get my papers cleared & come round by Bergamo to Milan instead of by Como.

G.B.S.

Apcs.

1. *Press Cuttings*, acquired by Theater in der Josefstadt, Vienna, had been banned, perhaps because of its satire on the military. Shaw protested in a letter to the *Neue Freie Presse*, which reported the affair and Shaw's letter (10 September).

2. Stelvio Pass (2,758 m.), in the central Alps, connects the Valtellina with the upper Adige River Valley. It is the highest road in the Alps.

[Port Blanc]
postmarked [1]6th September 1911

Quite right, of course, about Reinhardt. Make it a rule to hurt his feelings frightfully at least twice a year, and he will never be happy without a play from you.

Just like me to forget to acknowledge the book. It arrived safely; but I want to read the play first.[1] I have neither read nor written anything on this tour: my idleness appals me.

TELEKI IS DEAD!!![2]

G.B.S.

Apcs.
    1. Trebitsch had sent Shaw his novella *Des Feldherrn erster Traum* (The General's First Dream; Frankfurt, 1910) and his play *Ein Muttersohn* (Mother's Boy; Berlin, 1911).
    2. Shaw's mail having caught up with him, he learned of Teleki's death.

[Ayot St Lawrence. Welwyn][1]
postmarked 23rd October 1911

In the Times of today it is announced that Fanny was a disappointment and a failure in Berlin, and that it was announced as a play by me.[2] Why did you let them do such a silly thing? The whole prologue & epilogue become absurd if the authorship is announced. Also the announcement of my name makes people expect a big & serious play instead of a trifle—"a little play for a little theatre." And according to The Times, the actors were puzzled & dull, & did not know that the piece was a wildly comic one in the first act & most of the third.[3] Tell me what really happened.

G.B.S.

Apcs.
    1. The Shaws returned to England on 4 October.
    2. *Fanny's First Play* (*Fannys erstes Stück*), which had been presented in London anonymously, opened at the Kleines Theater, directed by Barnowsky, on 21 October, with Mathilda Brandt and Alfred Abel.
    3. The *Times* (23 October), echoing the *Lokal-Anzeiger*, which faulted the production for pompous seriousness, reported that the audience and actors were puzzled and that the performances failed to create a recognizable milieu. *Fanny* ran 17 times.

[London]
[November-December 1911]

My dear Trebitsch
    . . . I have asked a Dr Szalai of Budapest to be my Hungarian agent. On looking into the matter I came to the conclusion that it would be a mistake to appoint an Austrian. Szalai has not yet answered; so I have said nothing to Eirich as yet.[1]

G.B.S.

Als.
    1. After Teleki's death, Otto Eirich, of Vienna, had renewed his request that Shaw appoint him agent for the non-German languages in Austro-Hungary. But Hevesi, Shaw's Hungarian translator,

alleged that Eirich withheld royalties from Ibsen and once tried to extort payment for a performance of Sophocles' *Electra* by claiming to represent the author! Hevesi recommended Dr. Emil Szalai (1874–1944), a Budapest lawyer.

10 Adelphi Terrace W.C.
7th March 1912

My dear Trebitsch

Do not let anybody who has been connected with the Munich performance [of *Caesar*] near the Burgtheater;[1] and do not allow them to cut the play except by cutting out the 3rd act. If they insist on having the 3rd act, they must play the whole thing through, even if it does not finish until 3 in the morning. But if they are wise they will omit that act altogether. In Munich they did half of it in the most stupid fashion possible because the people laughed when Caesar jumped into the water; and then they cut the climax out of the next act—the centre of the whole play—partly to gain time and partly because the Caesar [Albert Steinrück], who was also the producer, was such a hopeless imbecile that he had not intelligence enough to recognize his own best opportunities in the part. You will have to be stern about it, because they will tomfool with it if they can. If they do, tell them that I will come to Vienna and do what I did at Munich: denounce the whole thing to the press as an inartistic infamy.[2]

April 22nd is not the best time to come to London, because the Easter holidays will not be over, and if I am much run down at Easter, Charlotte may insist on dragging me away somewhere. However, it seems probable that I may have to remain here to rehearse a play.[3] In any case, I shall do my best not to miss you.

There is no particularly good news here. The coal miners are on strike;[4] the feminists are smashing windows in all directions (that is the only way to get attended to in England);[5] and it seems possible that the theatres may have to close for want of coal to keep the electric lighting works in operation.

I have written a new play [*Androcles and the Lion*] quite unlike any of the old ones. It would make quite a good opera book for Strauss. One of the principal characters is a lion. The rest are Christian martyrs and gladiators and Roman emperors. The final scene is in the Coliseum and requires a revolving stage. Rheinhardt had better build a big circus and produce it.[6]

I wish you would let me know before you do anything concerning the English rights of those plays of yours. You know that Trebitsches do not grow on gooseberry bushes, and that it is next to impossible to get people who can really write to undertake translations. I therefore think that if I were to give your plays to an ordinary commercial translator to be literally translated for a fixed sum, and I were to correct and polish up this translation myself, the result would be no worse than if you were to part with half your rights to somebody else.

Mrs Warren is raging violently in Paris just now.[7] If there is any place in Paris where they sell the Parisian illustrated papers, spend a franc on Comoedia Illustré for the 1st of March 1912, number 11. It contains several flashlight pictures of the production and some other pictures that may amuse you.

yours ever

G. Bernard Shaw

Tls.

1. The Burgtheater had finally yielded (see 18 June 1906) and *Caesar* was set to open on 28 March, with Albert Heine, who also directed, and Iphegenie Buchmann. It ran successfully 28 times.

2. This alleged denunciation has not been traced.

3. *Man and Superman*, which was being revived by Robert Loraine at the Criterion Theatre. It opened on 8 April.

4. The Miners' National Strike was won by the end of the month.

5. On 1 March, crowds of suffragettes with hammers attacked fashionable London shops and pelted the Prime Minister's home.

6. Reinhardt had used circuses for several Greek classics.

7. *Mrs Warren*, Shaw's second appearance in Paris, opened at the Théâtre des Arts on 16 February and provoked serious debate. Critics found the play powerful if disconcerting, and the production ran over 80 times.

10 Adelphi Terrace W.C.

10th April 1912

My dear Trebitsch

If your wife is not coming over, and you have no other reason for coming to London than to see me, I think you had better give it up. Charlotte will be away in Rome;[1] and she would very much rather you came when she was here. I shall have to go away for 3 weeks or so, not only to get a holiday, which I need very badly, but to allow the house to get its "spring cleaning," and to give some of our servants a rest, as we have had some illness in our domestic staff and consequently a good deal of overwork and worry for the rest who were not ill. I shall spend part of the time motoring about the country, and part of it staying with the Barkers or with some other friends of mine who have invited me to visit them. Altogether, circumstances are unpropitious for your visit, though I should be very glad to see you all the same.

Now comes the question of Charlotte's return from Rome. I have no idea as yet whether her health will improve there, or whether, in any case, she will find it enjoyable enough to tempt her to make a stay of any length; but it is just possible that I might fetch her back in the car; and in that case we might, instead of coming straight back home, come up north through the Tyrol and visit you in Vienna before Caesar is dead.[2] All this is very vague, and depends a good deal on times and seasons, as there would be no use going to Vienna in the hottest of the summer, when the theatres are shut and you are away. Still, I suggest it as a possibility.

There is another possibility. If you and your wife are coming to Paris, I might take the car over for a few days; and we might go and see Mrs Warren's Profession together at the Théâtre des Arts. Or if you are going to any pretty part of France, not too far off, I might go there; and we might have a few drives together.

I am sorry that all my arrangements are in such a mess that I cannot say anything more definite than this. I should not discourage you from coming to London if you had any other business except to see me; but as it is, I really do not think it would be worth your while.

> In haste,
> yours sincerely
> G. Bernard Shaw

PS If you came to England, you would probably have to come to some place in the provinces where I could pick you up in the car & rush you about for a few days through the English lanes—which would, I am afraid, be pretty dull for you.[3]

Tls.

1. Charlotte Shaw, complaining of ill health, insisted on a holiday in Italy, but Shaw refused to go, and Charlotte, furious, sailed alone.

2. Charlotte had fallen ill aboard ship. She remained in Rome until late May, but Shaw did not need to travel to Italy to fetch her home, and so the potential trip to Vienna, where *Caesar* was still playing, did not occur.

3. Shaw left for a month's motor tour of England on 20 April, two days before Trebitsch's scheduled arrival in London.

[Windermere]
30th April 1912

My dear Trebitsch

Here I am several hundred miles north of London with a bad back—lumbago, I suppose. To get to London would take at least three days. Two days there to get my custom house papers & do some other necessary things would make five days. Two days to Paris from London would make seven days. Thus even if I sprang up & rushed straight away (and one cannot start up with lumbago—it hurts too much) I could not reach you before the 8th May (I have an important engagement in London on the 9th, by the way), by which time you would be on your way back to Vienna probably. I am afraid I shall not be able to meet you after all, unless I follow you to Vienna. For I cannot cut this tour short: I am tired out myself; and I am giving a young lady (Miss [Georgina] Gillmore, who is going to get married & leave me) a holiday which she too needs very badly. How long do you intend to stay in Paris.

Charlotte writes as if she intended to join you & meet me; but I do not want her to leave Rome until her cough is better. Things have fallen out unluckily for our meeting: everything seems against it.

I detest the chateaux: they are fit for Americans only; but I should like to have gone to some of the cathedrals: there is no architecture like French Gothic.

I hear that the new revue at the Theatre des Arts is a failure & that they are putting up Mrs Warren again.[1]

Ow-ow-ow-ow!!! Have you ever had lumbago?

Letters to Adelphi Terrace will be sent on.

I am really desolate at missing you and your wife.

Ow-ow-ow-ow-ow-ah-ooh-ow!!!!!

It catches you just in *les reins*.

GBS

Als.
1. A satiric revue, *Mil neuf cent douze,* opened on 18 April at the Théâtre des Arts, Paris, and failed; *Mrs Warren* was hastily revived and ran from 4 to 20 May.

The failure of Shaw and Trebitsch to meet in England in May and the ensuing gap in their correspondence led Trebitsch to complain of neglect and changed feelings, which Charlotte denied by assuring Trebitsch on 7 October that she and her husband were very fond of him whether they wrote or not (Berg).

Ayot St Lawrence. Welwyn
13th November 1912

My dear Trebitsch
   The enclosed article on Rodin is of sufficient international interest to be worth translating. I daresay some of the German or Austrian papers would give us a few kronen for it.[1]

yrs ever
G.B.S.

Als.
1. Shaw's review article "Rodin" (*Nation,* 9 November) recalled his sitting for the sculptor; the German version appeared in *Zeitschrift* (4 January 1913).

Ayot St Lawrence. Welwyn
21st November 1912

My dear Trebitsch
   Here's a ridiculous thing! I have received the enclosed letter from Kellner. My secretary has thrown away the envelope with the postmark; and I dont know whether he is in Vienna or in Berlin or in München (as Karl Ludwig St suggests).[1]
   Do you know, or can you find out; and if so, will you send my reply on to him for me? I have left it open so that you may read it in case you have any curiosity about the questions he asks.

yours ever
G. Bernard Shaw

Als.
1. Helene Richter, a Viennese theatre historian, who was preparing a monograph on Shaw, had sought the aid of Leon Kellner, then visiting Vienna and staying at the Karl Ludwig Strasse. Kellner queried Shaw about the Zetetical Society, Shaw's poetic output, and the title *Widowers' Houses.* (Richter duly acknowledged Kellner's and Shaw's help in "Die Quintessenz des Shawismus," *Englische Studien,* 1912–13.)

[10 Adelphi Terrace W.C.]
postmarked 27th November 1912

I dont know Kellner intimately enough to treat him badly.
I will send you Overruled as soon as I get the printed copy corrected. I had
to change the title at the last moment as I found it had been already used.[1]

GBS

Apcs.

1. Shaw's one-act *Overruled* was originally titled *Trespassers Will Be Prosecuted* and appeared
as *Es hat nicht sollen sein* in *Neue Freie Presse* (23 March 1913).

10 Adelphi Terrace W.C.
29th January 1913

My dear Trebitsch

There is no legal difficulty about performing an English play in Germany
before it is performed in England. Your lawyer is wrong—lawyers always are
wrong—in supposing that an English play cannot be copyrighted in America
until it is printed and bound there. That regulation applies only to books.
Dramatic compositions were exempted from this regulation in the Copyright Act because very few plays are printed and published: they are almost
all performed from typewritten copies. Therefore all that has to be done is to
deposit a typewritten copy, or even a copy printed in England, at the Library
of Congress in Washington, with a small registration fee; and the trick is
done. Consequently, there is no difficulty on the score of copyright provided
you give me sufficient notice. What you have usually done in the past is to
publish the play as a literary composition, without giving me any notice at
all, and without securing the American copyright, with the result that it
would be possible for an American pirate to treat your translations as a noncopyright work, to retranslate it into English, and treat the translation as his
own property. Hence my urgent adjurations to you never under any circumstances to deal with any unpublished work of mine without giving me
ample warning before hand.

I am much puzzled at your not having received Overruled. I thought I had
sent you a copy with a letter about various things. The proposal to produce
Androcles had nothing to do with Reinhardt. The idea was that Granville
Barker was to visit a few German towns beginning at the Kunstlertheater in
Munich, with an English company playing in English, and that the first performance of Androcles was to be one of the attractions of this tour. Barker
was very hot on this when he was at Partenkirchen at Christmas. But now
the proposal seems to have dropped; and even if it be revived, it is hardly
likely to be carried out before October next.[1]

I have no general objection to Pygmalion making his first début at the
Burgtheater; on the contrary I should rather like the English production of
one of my plays to be anticipated abroad. But it is very important that a foreign production of this kind should not be a failure. Pygmalion is not suited

to a large theatre; and the Burgtheater is a very large theatre; besides, Pygmalion is essentially a star play: unless you have an actress of extraordinary qualifications and popularity, failure is certain. There is another very serious objection. It is my intention to produce Pygmalion here anonymously. The part of Eliza is to be played by Mrs Patrick Campbell; and the play will be announced as "By a Fellow of the Royal Society of Literature." This will give the idea that it is a classical play, and that Mrs Campbell is to appear as Galatea. As she has never appeared in a low life part, the surprise will be complete. But of course this would be all spoilt if the play were first produced in Vienna with my name on the program. This objection seems to me to be fatal: I see no means of getting round it.[2]

Androcles is just the sort of play for Reinhardt to produce; and if Barker's project is dropped, Reinhardt had better have the refusal of it. But I think you ought to make him give up Misalliance. He has lost interest in productions of that sort; and if he produces it now, he will do it half-heartedly, and aim not at making it a success but simply at preventing anybody else from getting it. Therefore I think you had better tell him to tear up the Misalliance contract, and that if he doesnt, he shall not have Androcles. Do not reproach him or quarrel with him: there is no use in that; and he and I are personally on friendly terms which I dont want to disturb; but tell him quite frankly that he is not serious about Misalliance and must give it up.[3]

As far as I can foresee at present I shall be in London at the end of April; and I shall certainly be very glad to see you then or at any other time.

yours ever
G. Bernard Shaw

P.S. I will send you a copy of Androcles as soon as I can get one printed. At present there exists only one imperfect and uncorrected copy, without any stage directions, and with the dialogue quite unfinished. Until I complete it and get it printed it would be of no use to you, even if I had a second copy to send.

Tls.

1. Barker's plan to tour Germany with *Androcles* was abandoned, and the play had its premiere the following September at the St. James's Theatre, London.

2. Shaw, despite these objections, gradually inclined toward chastising his English critics, and the following May, during Trebitsch's visit, gave his consent to the Burg premiere. Shaw quietly drops the name of Mrs. Patrick Campbell (1865–1940), whom he was rapturously pursuing at the time.

3. Reinhardt did give up *Misalliance*, which had failed in Vienna, and turned to *Androcles*, which appealed to his sense of spectacle.

[Dresden]
postmarked 30th June 1913

Here I am until Thursday, probably. I came at a moment's notice with Barker. His wife was coming with him; but she had a sore throat; and the doctor forbad her to travel. So I have never been to Dresden before, and as I wanted to see the Dalcroze school at Hellerau, I took Lillah's place. Barker must be back in London on Friday evening; and I shall most likely return with him, though it seems a pity not to visit Berlin, Prague & Vienna, especially Vienna.[1]

G.B.S.

Apcs.

1. Shaw and Barker attended a festival at the Academy of Eurythmics, Dresden-Hellerau, founded by Émile Dalcroze (Jaques-Delacroze, 1865–1950), Swiss composer, who taught music through bodily rhythms. Shaw returned to London on 4 July after visiting Leipzig and Weimar, but not Vienna.

10 Adelphi Terrace W.C.

12th July 1913

My dear Trebitsch

I received the translation of The Muttersohn, and have gone very carefully through the first act, reading the German original and using the translation as a dictionary. I will tell you more about it when I have had time to finish it; but I can tell you already that it is a difficult play to translate and a very difficult one to cast. Nothing would be easier than to make a straightforward slapdash translation into good vernacular English; but in doing so the poetic quality of the original would be lost. In fact, to get its mood and atmosphere perfectly, a good deal of it ought to be set to music. The casting difficulty arises over the part of the Mother. All the other parts require only such ordinary good acting as presentable actors can be coached into by a good producer; but for the Mother an actress of quite peculiar personality and attraction would be indispensable; for the play would be nothing without it. That is all I can tell you so far.[1]

I now enclose you a report of a speech which I made lately at the National Liberal Club here. It is a really important utterance of mine, because whilst all the other Socialists declare that they are practical men and that they do not dream of levelling everybody down to the same income, I maintain that equality of income is the sole object and the sole reality of Socialism.[2] I am sending this pamphlet to America and to France as well as to you for publication in some newspaper or magazine. In the meantime the publication here will be held back. Let me know as soon as you can whether you think you can do anything with it.

Hellerau was very interesting, but I daresay you know as much about it as I do. . . .

yours ever

G. Bernard Shaw

Tls.

1. Trebitsch had a literal translation made of his *Ein Muttersohn* so that Shaw could adapt it. The lugubrious play concerns a neurasthenic son, who fails as son and lover until enlightened on his relation to his mad mother.

2. In his speech on 1 May, "The Case for Equality," Shaw argued for equality of incomes on moral, political, economic, and biological grounds. In later years, under the impact of Soviet experience, Shaw qualified his stand by stressing basic rather than exact equality of income.

10 Adelphi Terrace W.C.
19th August 1913

As I am selling the Case for Equality to an American Magazine [*Metropolitan Magazine*] which offers 6000 Marks [$1,500] for the exclusive right of first publication in its columns, it is important that no publication should take place in Germany until *after* the American publication.[1] In fact, I am pledged to return the money if this occurs.

It was indiscreet of Kerr to repeat what I said about Hamon & Anatole France.[2] Fortunately Hamon does not read German. As to you, you have "given your proofs": besides, I am going to translate a play of yours; so we shall both be tarred with the same brush. I had no idea that Kerr was interviewing me, or I should have been on my guard.

G. Bernard Shaw

Apcs.
   1. The article appeared in the December issue of *Metropolitan Magazine*, which also ran a contest for the best answer to Shaw. The German version, "Ein Plädoyer für Gleichheit," appeared in *Neue Rundschau* (August 1914).
   2. Alfred Kerr, the noted Berlin critic, described meeting Shaw and reported Shaw's comment that "he would have preferred to have had Anatole France translate his works (instead of Hamon). 'But whoever has something to produce himself doesn't translate'" ("Ausflug," *Neue Rundschau*, 1913).

Ayot St Lawrence. Welwyn
27th August 1913

. . . My study of your play has been ruthlessly interrupted by Androcles, and by a sudden emergency in which I had to complete within a fortnight a new and worthless play (only an hour long, as it is to be produced at a variety theatre in Nov.) entitled Great Catherine, meaning Catherine II of Russia.[1]

G. Bernard Shaw

Apcs.
   1. *Great Catherine*, written for Gertrude Kingston, opened at the Vaudeville Theatre, London, on 18 November 1913, in tandem with Hermon Ould's *Before Sunset*, and ran 30 times.

10 Adelphi Terrace W.C.
1st September 1913

My dear Trebitsch

. . . Great Catherine is not yet ready for translation, as I have not revised the dialogue or worked out the stage business. If I sent it to you now you would translate the rough draft as it stands, and it would never get corrected. It is in four scenes, each lasting about fifteen minutes. The characters are Catherine, Patiomkin (a part for a big, powerful actor of heavy parts who is also a good comedian), an English officer (young and handsome, but not sentimental), an ingenue, a pretty Russian princess, Patiomkin's pet niece, a

Cossack sergeant, and two other parts—a court lady and a Chamberlain, which dont matter: anyone can play them.

The costumes will be expensive; and there must be a magnificent bed for Catherine; but the scenery must be done with painted cloths and curtains and not with built up sets, as it must be changed immediately: any delay between scenes would be fatal.

I implore you to leave Munich at once, and inform the Residenz, with regrets, that I cannot afford to have Pygmalion murdered as Caesar and Candida were, and that whilst I greatly enjoy their representations of Mozart's operas, I intend in future to have my plays handled in Munich by managements which have some gleams of artistic conscience and a few modern ideas. I am quite serious about this: I know they will make a mess of Pygmalion: they dont care how scandalously they throw things on the stage, as they can always talk about a great success when they have performed twenty times to empty houses, and then get "only £10,000 this year" from the court to make up the deficit.[1]

All right about Karpath:[2] I shant be here when he comes. I start for Mont Dore at the end of this week to pick up Charlotte and have a little tour.

G. Bernard Shaw

P.S. I wish you were here to see the first night of Androcles.[3]

Tls.

1. Despite Shaw's objections, *Pygmalion* opened at the Residenz, Munich's court theatre, on 22 November, after the Viennese and Berlin premieres. The production, directed by Albert Steinrück, who played Higgins to Helene Ritscher's Eliza, was well received and ran 39 times.

2. Ludwig Karpath (1866–1936), Viennese music critic with a special interest in Wagner and a penchant for geniuses.

3. The play had its world premiere on 1 September at the St. James's Theatre. Barker directed, and the cast included Lillah McCarthy, O. P. Heggie, Ben Webster, and Edward Sillward.

[Garunne]
postmarked 29th September 1913

I am arranging to have Pygmalion & Androcles published in America & England at once: that is, technically. Heaven only knows what mischief may come of your publication of Misalliance & Fanny. And I lose all the money I might get from Russia for advance copies: they pirate your confounded translations instead of paying me for copies of the play. However, it cant be helped; so tell Fischer to be ready when the performance takes place.[1] On the first of October I expect to arrive at the Grand Hotel, Biarritz. I shall stay there at least a week, perhaps longer.

G. Bernard Shaw

Apcs.

1. *Pygmalion* was to open in Vienna in October, *Androcles* in Berlin in November. Fischer then promptly issued the plays, three years before their English book publication.

My dear Trebitsch

Metropole & Excelsior Hotel. Bordeaux
11th October 1913

I have received a formal invitation from the director of the Burgtheater to attend the last private & first public rehearsal of Pygmalion. I cannot answer it, because I cannot read his name (it looks like Hugo Thinnig) and do not know whether he is a Count or a General or merely a common hochwohlgeboren [Hon.].[1] Will you tell him that if I came to the last dress rehearsal I should upset it from beginning to end, and that it is extremely fortunate for him that I am travelling in France, out of reach of Vienna.

I have to cross the channel on the 17th, and must travel more than 100 miles a day to reach it. Today I have come 140 miles; burst three tyres; and been 11 hours on the road. I left Biarritz this morning. Charlotte has gone on to London by train. How can I possibly write an article under such circumstances? If I could get a day's rest I should do it for you; but I cannot put off my return, as I have to deliver a lecture in London; and I am about 1000 kilometres from Boulogne. . . .

In great haste
G. Bernard Shaw

Als.; postscript omitted.
1. The Burgtheater was now under Hugo Thimig (1854–1944), distinguished actor and progenitor of a celebrated acting family. "Public dress rehearsals" were commonly held in German theatres for invited guests before official openings.

My dear Trebitsch

Ayot St Lawrence. Welwyn
20th October 1913

I am very strongly opposed to the publication of Androcles before its performance has started a discussion in the German press & roused public curiosity. Besides, the publication of the play beforehand would utterly destroy the surprise of the first performance, and might quite fairly be held by Reinhardt or any other manager to be a virtual breach of faith with him. On the other hand there is nothing whatever to be gained by immediate publication. Therefore hold it up until the play is actually produced.

I have left a mountain of letters unopened at Adelphi Terrace: among them probably one from you with a photograph of Liza, forwarded from Biarritz. Charlotte tells me you sent one. I return to London today & will begin to look through my arrears of correspondence at once.

My journey of 4000 kilometres by car, supposed to be a holiday, has left me a wreck. How long it will take me to recover from it—if I ever recover—heaven alone knows.

I shall send my congratulations to the Burgtheater on the 500th night of Pygmalion.[1] I take no interest whatever in first nights. Every play has a first night. The success of the play, if it really prove a success, calls for no comment. I meant it to be a success. As to the Emperor, I shall rub the importance of his share in the business into England, where Androcles is being withdrawn after 8 weeks because it draws only 20,000 kronen a week, and the unsubsidised, rackrented fashionable theatre costs 25,000 kronen to keep open. The Burgtheater would close next week if it had to pay rent.

yours, in the lowest spirits
GBS

Als.

1. *Pygmalion*, directed by Hugo Thimig, with Max Paulsen and Lili Marberg, had its world premiere at the Burg on 16 October, and, as the press noted, Shaw finally conquered Vienna. Critics foretold a triumphant success but pointed to the play's lightness, lack of challenging social content, and familiar comic situation. The play ran 25 times, a decided success for the elite Burg that soon was repeated in Berlin at Barnowsky's Lessing-Theater and elsewhere and marked a turning point in Shaw's popular acceptance in Germany. (Reinhardt had first refusal of *Pygmalion* in Berlin but relinquished the play because he had contracted for *Androcles* and did not want to schedule two new Shaw plays in one season. *Pygmalion* opened at the Lessing on 1 November with Tilla Durieux and Albert Steinrück and ran over one hundred times, a windfall for Barnowsky.)

10 Adelphi Terrace W.C.
14th November 1913

My dear Trebitsch

. . . The real disaster about Androcles is not Ordynski, who will produce it just as well as Reinhardt (he always does five sixths of Reinhardt's work) but the production at the Kammer instead of in the big circus.[1] This shews that Reinhardt accepted it solely to prevent any other manager getting it. However, it may possibly have some sort of success even in the Kammerspiele; but none the less Reinhardt's object will be attained if it be killed. Next time we shall have the theatre specified in the contract. But if I do another big spectacular play I shall think twice before letting R. have it on any terms. I dont blame him: les affaires sont les affaires; but he is evidently not very friendly to us.

Jethro Bithell[2] has not yet presented his introduction. I have neglected the Mother's Son [Trebitsch's *Muttersohn*] disgracefully; but someday I will finish it.

The story about my writing a book of travels in Germany is a canard.

My statement about the managers asking for a first performance in Germany was quite a proper one, though the suggestion began with you.[3] I was fighting the critics here, not doing justice to you. Why should I do you justice? I never stand on ceremony with you. One gets justice from strangers, not from intimate friends and collaborators.

You may assure the public that the gentlemen who are, as usual, declaring that your version of Pygmalion is not a faithful one have overreached themselves this time,[4] as the original has not yet been published; and yours was the only copy sent to Germany.

I am told that the Polish and Russian theatres procure, through agents, copies of German translations from the Viennese & Berlin theatres. Is this true? If so, it is a gross breach of faith on the part of the regisseurs.

In haste, ever yours
G. Bernard Shaw

Als.

1. *Androcles* (*Androklus und der Löwe*), staged by Richard Ordynski, opened in the Kammerspiele on 25 November with Victor Arnold as Androcles and Mary (Marlene) Dietrich as Lavinia. Only the *Berliner Tageblatt* (26 November) thought the play "extremely humorous"; otherwise critics found it "sophomoric horseplay" (*Lokal-Anzeiger*) and "unbearable" (*Vorwärts*). The play ran 18 times.

2. Jethro Bithell (1878–1962), a scholar-translator, whom Trebitsch had asked to translate his new play *Gefährliche Jahre* (Dangerous Years).

3. In the *Observer* (2 November) Shaw explained why he had given the premiere of *Pygmalion* to Austria and Germany before England: "It is the custom of the English press when a play of mine is produced, to inform the world that it is not a play—that it is dull, blasphemous, unpopular and financially unsuccessful. The news is duly telegraphed to Berlin and Vienna, with the result that the managers there have been compelled to postpone productions. . . . Hence arose an urgent demand on the part of the managers . . . that I should have my plays performed by them first. I have at last complied with this . . . demand."

4. A reviewer in the *Berliner Tageblatt* (2 November) had referred to the "pompous, imprecise translation" of *Pygmalion*.

Ayot St Lawrence. Welwyn
15th December 1913

Catherine is such boyish rubbish that I am half inclined to suppress it. It must not be announced as an important new play by me or it will deal a blow to my reputation. It is a music hall sketch, and utter slosh at that.[1]

Pygmalion is my last potboiler. In future I will write plays that will not be understood for 25 years, if ever.

I havnt written a line in The New Statesman for many months. I never write for it now.[2]

The New York Times has published long extracts from your Pygmalion, translated into the vilest American.[3] This will cost me £500, probably. Has Fischer got the certificate of registration in Washington?

G.B.S.

Apcs.

1. Trebitsch placed *Great Catherine* (*Die grosse Katharina*) with a large variety theatre in Vienna, the Apollo.

2. In April 1913, the Webbs launched the *New Statesman*, to which Shaw contributed unsigned articles, several of which Trebitsch translated and published. Shaw withdrew from the journal because of differences between him and the editor, Clifford Sharp.

3. On 30 November, the *New York Times* published an article on *Pygmalion* ("Bernard Shaw Snubs England and Amuses Germany"), with lengthy excerpts based on the published German text. Shaw considered suing, but in the end demanded only that the *Times* acknowledge its error and pledge not to repeat it. The paper apologized.

10 Adelphi Terrace W.C.
3rd March 1914
My dear Trebitsch
I cannot with any sort of decency prevent Miss Kingston[1] from playing Catherine in Germany. I wrote the play expressly for her; and the possibility of her playing the part in Germany, and even in the German language, was discussed between us. I can plead your contracts as far as the German language is concerned, though even as to that I think it would be bad policy on

George Bernard Shaw, 1914.

our part as well as ungenerous on mine if we closed any town against her without a definite contract from the Bolland [Roland] and Durieux[2] entrepreneurs to play in those towns. Long ago I set my face against the absurd practice of giving managers exclusive rights throughout a whole country; and I now never authorize the performance of a play except in a specified town within a specified period and on condition that I am to be paid damages if the play is not performed in that town and within that period. If the Bolland and Durieux managements will not give us such a contract, then a bird in the hand is worth two in the bush: let us license Miss Kingston. As to the ruin which will ensue, I have heard all that before in England and America and dont believe a word of it.

However, Miss Kingston is not at present proposing to play the piece in German: she wants to play it in English; and she does not insist on Vienna and Berlin: she wants to do a little trip along the Rhine. It would, however, be good business for us if she could give some performances of it in English in Vienna and Berlin *after* the appearance of Miss Bolland and Miss Durieux, as people would go to both performances to compare the English acting with the German. The comparison would make a considerable réclame; and many German people who do not know English would see it first in German and then in English. To say that this would not be good for both the English and German performances is manifest nonsense. Of course all artists and all managers strive furiously to prevent anyone else touching their parts or their plays; but the prudent author does not concern himself about that.

If Fischer collects the fees for both the English and German performances, he will have nothing to complain of; and you and I had better share the fees as usual.

Miss Kingston cannot tour with nothing but a short play like Catherine; and I do not at present know what other play she proposes to take out.[3] It may be that the whole affair will fall through, though Sydow[4] seems to be pretty keen on it. Meanwhile, if you happen to be writing to Sydow, be careful not to make any disparaging references to Miss Kingston, because your letters would not be held to be legally privileged; and Miss Kingston, who is a very clever woman, and is already not at all pleased at being stopped by a café chantant contract, will seize any advantage you may be unwary enough to give her.

I am very sorry to have to interfere with your arrangements in any way; but I cannot, without treating Miss Kingston very badly, meet her with a flat non possumus.

Tree now talks of putting off the production of Pygmalion from the 20th March until April; but nothing is settled as yet.[5]

Where will you be between the 8th and 13th of March? We are looking forward to meeting you.

yours ever
G. Bernard Shaw

Tls.

1. Gertrude Kingston (1866–1937), British actress-manager, painter, author, and political speaker. Kingston had suggested the idea of *Great Catherine* to Shaw, whom she thereafter addressed in the Russian manner as "little father."

2. Ida Roland (1889–1951) and Tilla Durieux (1880–1971), Viennese-born German actresses. Both had contracted, according to Fischer and Trebitsch, to play Catherine.

3. Miss Kingston planned to do *Brassbound*, to which Trebitsch also objected. But Kingston threatened suit if that "blighter" interfered with her plans, hinted that Trebitsch feared her exposing his flawed translation, and said that the Apollo Theater, Vienna, was a music hall restaurant, which no critic would attend, and that its proprietor was an ex-hotel thief who had spent three years in Sing Sing: "It really looks," she wrote to Shaw on 28 February, "as if you and I were all being made to dance to the pipe of the hotel thief and his leading lady! Will you ask to see T's translation of 'Catherine.' I think it would be as well." (B. L.)

4. Paul Sydow, who was managing the projected tour. The whole affair did fall through because of the war.

5. The English production with Beerbohm Tree and Mrs. Patrick Campbell opened on 11 April.

10 Adelphi Terrace W.C.
13th March 1914

Will you come to lunch tomorrow at 1 o'clock (not 1.30, as we have to go to an afternoon concert) and bring Jethro Bithell. Charlotte will be delighted to see you: she is désolée to have missed you this afternoon.

G. Bernard Shaw

Apcs.

10 Adelphi Terrace W.C.
8th May 1914

My dear Trebitsch

I enclose two documents. The first is a preface to a volume of Humanitarian essays, entitled Killing For Sport. It is not too long for a single article; but if a single word of it is published in any language before the 14th August next I shall forfeit three hundred pounds. The other is the great and long promised preface to Misalliance and Fanny's First Play, entitled Parents And Children. It must not be published before the 25th of this month. As it is 116 pages long it might be published as a book. It is certainly too long for a magazine article. However, there is one suggestion that may be worth considering. English daily newspapers sometimes publish a series of articles on some particular subject day by day. Perhaps the Neue Freie Presse might be disposed to publish the preface as a series of articles. But I am afraid it is too long for that: it must contain between forty and fifty thousand words.[1]

Rodin wrote to me a little time ago, saying that he had had an order from Vienna for a plaster cast of my bust, and asking me whether I thought he ought to comply. I told him to do so by all means as far as I was concerned. I take it that the enquiry came from you. I make only one condition about it, and that is that you accept the bust as a present to you and your wife from me and my wife. But as I do not wish Rodin to know about this lest he should refuse to allow me to pay for it, I send the cheque to you.[2] I have read your play [*Gefährliche Jahre*] in Jethro's translation, which is far too literal and literary for use on the stage. It is a quite grammatical translation; but it is not English dialogue: it is very much as if you were to translate Liza Doolittle's famous expletive by *nicht blutig wahrscheinlich*. The worst of it is that I dont know how to set about getting it right. I must read it in the original, because I cant get the movement of the scenes properly. I have not quite got hold of the characters. Why did you let the mother drop out of the play so soon? I am really afraid to touch it; I should tear the whole thing to pieces. I must read it again and see what I can make of it. One of its great difficulties is that the actress has to act an actress, and she has not only to act a piece of acting, but to repeat it. It seems easy to shew on the stage the difference between the way an actress plays a scene when the man she is playing with can make her really feel it, and the way she plays it when he is antipathetic to her; but it is really a very difficult matter: the better the actress the less difference there would be. What is more, many actresses could play a love scene very well indeed with a man for whom they did not care a rap personally, and could hardly bring themselves to play it at all with a man whom they really loved; and I am not at all sure that for the purposes of stage effect, it would not be better to make the woman break down hopelessly when she was in earnest and play brilliantly when she was indifferent. But no matter how you do it, such scenes will always be difficult. I never could bring myself to introduce actors and actresses as characters in plays: it goes dead against my instinct.[3] A little while ago I was talking to Sir John Hare[4] on the subject; and I found he had exactly the same repugnance.

I dont think your characters explain themselves clearly enough. In writing for the stage there are two points on which all ordinary probability and naturalness must be thrown to the winds. You must make reckless use of coincidences; and you must make your characters understand themselves and describe themselves much better than any real human being ever does or can. In Pygmalion, for instance, Doolittle paints a perfect and skilful portrait of his own character. The character is true to nature; but the ability to describe it to the audience is characteristic, not of a good for nothing dustman, but of Balzac. Just the opposite occurs with Higgins. Higgins is so absolutely unconscious of his own character, that he is in a state of continual complaint and surprise because people have such unreasonable notions about him. This is another way of making a character describe himself; and it is a more natural and probable way; but natural or not, the description has got to be effected somehow: either by self-portraiture or self-betrayal every character has to be defined to the audience. I daresay I shall find on further study that your characters do this: in fact, I already feel that there is an interesting contrast between the two young women, and between the father and son; but I am still a little puzzled by them.

Charlotte returns from America next Friday.[5]

yours ever
G. Bernard Shaw

Tls.

1. *Killing for Sport*, edited by Shaw's friend Henry Salt with a preface by Shaw, appeared that year as did Shaw's latest volume of plays with a "Treatise on Parents and Children," but the war intervened before Trebitsch could publish either essay.

2. Shaw's generous gift to Trebitsch was paralleled by Rodin's offering the plaster bust to Shaw for 900 francs instead of his usual 2,900.

3. In *Gefährliche Jahre*, Anny, an aspiring actress, is employed by a concerned father to play-act loving his sickly, infatuated son, Fritz. On two occasions she rehearses a love scene with Fritz: once her coldness shows through and arouses the youth's suspicions; the second time she discovers that she truly loves Fritz and plays the scene passionately. Shaw did not adapt the play.

4. Sir John Hare (1844–1921), prominent actor-manager.

5. Charlotte Shaw, hoping to improve her health, had gone to America with Lena Ashwell and the spiritualists Dr. and Mrs. James Mills. She also thereby avoided the London opening of *Pygmalion*, starring her rival for Shaw's attentions, Mrs. Patrick Campbell.

At last it seemed that the Shaws would visit Trebitsch in Vienna, where the International Socialist Congress was to open on 23 August. But on 28 July war broke out between Austria and Serbia and swiftly involved Germany against Russia and France, joined by England on 4 August. The Trebitsches, on holiday in Ostend, were caught in the panic and slowly worked their way back to Vienna, where Siegfried, a reserve officer, had to report. Shaw's telegram, sent to Ostend, did not reach Trebitsch until January 1915.

Salcombe
4th August 1914

YOU CAN DO NOTHING BUT REPORT YOURSELF BY TELEGRAPH AS RETURNING AT FIRST OPPORTUNITY WHAT A HIDEOUS SITUATION CIVILIZATION TEARING ITSELF TO PIECES INSTEAD OF STANDING SOLID AGAINST THE COMMON ENEMY IN THE EAST YOU AND I AT WAR CAN ABSURDITY GO FURTHER MY FRIENDLIEST WISHES GO WITH YOU UNDER ALL CIRCUMSTANCES

BERNARD SHAW

PART TWO

War and Politics

19 January 1915 through 28 December 1915

For the international Socialist movement, which had struggled to avert the clash between rival imperialisms that it saw was coming, the outbreak of war in August 1914 presented a clear if difficult choice: proletarian internationalism or bourgeois nationalism, however rationalized. With notable exceptions, socialists, more or less quickly, supported their nations' war efforts. Among the very first, German Social Democrats voted for war credits. British socialists soon followed. Although Labour M.P.s declared that balance-of-power diplomacy had precipitated the war and that Foreign Minister Sir Edward Grey was as culpable as Russia and Germany, defections from this stand began almost immediately and absolved England of any responsibility for the conflict. Only the Independent Labour Party for a time resisted the onrushing chauvinism.

Shaw, years earlier, had ridiculed British fears of a growing German navy (Preface to *John Bull*, 1906), and in 1905 he had drafted a manifesto on English-German friendship, welcoming German naval power as "an additional guarantee of civilization." Early in 1913 he had proposed a collective security pact between England, France, and Germany ("Armaments and Conscription," *Daily Chronicle*, 18 March). But England, Shaw later concluded, was bent on a showdown with its rival.

Like other British socialists, Shaw, though condemning the conflict as a "Balance of Power war and nothing else," and in spite of his disdain for British moral posturings, quickly announced his pro-war position. In "The Peril of Potsdam" (*Daily News*, 11 August), he pronounced the "Germany of Bismarck" the chief peril in Europe unlike the "Germany of Goethe and Beethoven, which has not an enemy on earth." Prussian militarism had thrown down the gauntlet, and "if Militarism is to be struck down the mortal blow must be aimed at Potsdam."

Shaw then withdrew to study the war in depth, while the English literati declared to the neutral world that Britain had "labored . . . to preserve peace" but was honor-bound to defend Belgian neutrality, French liberty, and Western ideals against the "rule of blood and iron" (*N. Y. Times*, 18 September). In contrast, Shaw emerged with a socialist analysis of the war as imperialistic and militaristic: England, guided by balance-of-power theory, not morality, had long prepared for war while deluding encircled Germany into believing that Britain would not join a continental struggle. By discrediting the English ruling class, Shaw's *Common Sense about the War* (*New Statesman*, supplement, 14 November 1914) sought to give the British working class—whose frank challenge to German militarism is contrasted with official hypocrisy—a claim to postwar power. And by focusing away from imperialism to militarism and onto popular antimilitarist aims, Shaw paradoxically enlisted socialist internationalism and "human solidarity" in a war against "Potsdamnation." Since the "heroic remedy" of revolution in both camps was unavailable, he said, the war against German Junkerdom must go on, but the ensuing peace must not be vengeful nor should despotic Russia be allowed to dominate Europe: "As against Russian civilization, German and Austrian civilization is our civilization."

Common Sense became the "talk of the town"; resolutions of support from labor bodies poured in; Fabian audiences crowded to hear Shaw. But such was Shaw's scornful indictment of British foreign policy, exposure of English Pecksniffery, and sympathy for Germany's dilemmas, that even the labor press rose to the attack. Protests poured in to the *New Statesman*; the *Westminster Gazette* editorialized about "Bernhardi" Shaw; a cartoon drew Shaw as half Irish terrier, half German dachshund wearing an Iron Cross; *Punch* (25 November) accused Shaw of comforting the enemy; and the *Express* (17 November) derided him as a man without a country, whose success in Germany explained his sympathies and should keep his royalties flowing in. The next year, "Dangle" in the Manchester *Daily Chronicle* (26 October 1915) declared that Shaw's spiritual home had always been Germany: "His sneering perversity is evidently of the same family as Goethe's Devil. That is probably why his popularity has been far greater in Germany than in his own country. . . . high-browed Teutons have established Shaw among the prophets, have made an aureole of his flaming whiskers, and enshrined his snuff-coloured Jaegers in metaphoric stained glass." Naturally, Shaw reciprocated.

German reaction to "The Peril of Potsdam" was largely angry. The most impassioned was that of Herbert Eulenberg, author and playwright, who castigated the British intellectuals for not opposing their government's betrayal of "European culture and morals" and urged Shaw to exert his talents to break the anti-German alliance ("Entgegnung an B. Shaw," *Vossische Zeitung*, 20 September 1914). The liberal *Berliner Tageblatt* (12 September), however, calling attention to the article's full text, quoted Shaw on English hypocrisy and Russian despotism and italicized Shaw's comment on the need to sustain German civilization.

"The Peril of Potsdam" withheld full criticism of Grey's crafty diplomacy, which had entrapped Germany. Not so *Common Sense*. Shortly after the appearance of Shaw's pamphlet, *Vossische Zeitung* (26 November) cited Shaw's contribution to *Nash's Magazine* ("One Thing to Be Done Besides Fighting," September), which skirted German militarism and called the war a "crime against civilization for the benefit of Russia," an "insane cause." The *Neue Freie Presse*, quoting the same excerpts, lauded Shaw as a brave, lonely truth-teller ("Bernard Shaw kein Uebermensch, aber ein Mensch," 28 November). Even the conservative *Tägliche Rundschau* (27 November) welcomed Shaw's restored perspective, and the *Münchner Neueste Nachrichten* hailed Shaw as England's "guilty conscience" (1 December).

Early the next year, *Vorwärts* (19 January 1915) declared that Shaw had been "misjudged": "Shaw belongs to those against whom our German press early in the war directed the most furious attacks . . . because he was suspected of being an English patriot, but . . . now, Shaw, this fellow without a fatherland, is among the chief witnesses of the entire German press." *Vorwärts* also published Shaw's telegram to Trebitsch, sent when war was declared but only recently received.

Still the ultras could not forgive Shaw or his defenders. In "Zum Kapitel Shaw" (*Bühne und Welt*, February 1915), Robert Walter inveighed: "Millions have been paid out for his snobbish plays; his image in bathrobe, at writing desk, and out walking has appeared in all the picture-papers; books and innumerable articles have been written about his witty plays, and literary clowns have even poetized him," but that Shaw was "a scoundrel was clear to many of us before." Hatred of all things English in the German theatre had, according to Walter, made Shaw, the "most cunning of literary businessmen," nervous. He was being whitewashed in complicity with those in the theatre who stood to gain and who had counseled him: "Write otherwise; in God's name, you can do it! . . . or you'll be bankrupt." And soon "Mrs. Warren will again ply her profession on the boards." But a day of bitter reckoning, he warned, awaited those who let themselves be spat on for profit.

Nevertheless, Shaw continued as a friendly witness in the liberal-left press. *Common Sense* was not published in Germany, but German intelligence used it to influence neutral opinion. In Dresden, a "Neutral Observer," who was handed a copy as a "truthful and unbiased" survey of England, reported that while Shakespeare, but not Shaw, was still staged in Dresden "most Germans" seemed to believe that Shaw's portrait of the modern Englishman was "more satisfactory and truer" (*Times*, 19 February). And indeed early in the war, Napoleon's speech on British hypocrisy in *Man of Destiny* was quoted in the *Frankfurter Zeitung* (28 August).

Trebitsch's response to the war was a fierce declaration: "Hass" (Hate; *Vossische Zeitung*, 4 December 1914), in which he reflected on productive and unproductive hate during this "terribly beautiful time." Swept away by patriotic fervor, Trebitsch concluded: "Today we all stand under the impress of the most powerful example of creative, terribly combat-ready hate that will not rest until its goal is achieved. It is the hate of the Germans, who are striving for light and free development against the treacherous, despotic, profit-addicted, sober English, against the bathing barbarians, who, because of their laudable need for cleanliness, have gained the unjust reputation of being civilized. This hate . . . will blessedly inspire Germany . . . and so long sustain and lend her wings in battle until the foe lies harmless on the ground."

Trebitsch certainly did not count the Irish Shaw among the "bathing barbarians" and sought to reestablish communications with England. But the disrupted mail prevented the delivery of his letter as well as Shaw's telegram. The telegram and a second letter by Trebitsch finally got through, and the correspondence resumed through neutral channels, allowing Shaw, by way of Trebitsch, to address the German press. But the uncertain mail, Shaw's preoccupation with the war, and the censor's knife curtailed the exchange of letters, and communication ceased altogether in 1916 after a hint to Shaw against "trading with the enemy." News reports of Shaw's opinions and activities, however, continued to appear in Germany.

Meanwhile, Trebitsch attempted to restore Shaw as a friendly witness to the German stage, not only by releasing Shaw's telegram and explanatory letters but also by alleging that Shaw was being persecuted because of his friendship toward the German people and imprudently hailing Shaw on his birthday as a spiritual son of Germany. In March 1916, *Devil's Disciple* reappeared in Vienna (Deutsches Volkstheater), clearly for its anti-British satire, and was warmly welcomed by the *Neue Freie Presse* (14 March), which avowed Germany's unaltered regard for Shaw. But an effort to exploit *John Bull* in Berlin the next season failed (see 22 August 1919), and except for *Mrs Warren* (Berliner Residenztheater, 1917–18) Shaw disappeared from the German capital. In Vienna, Trebitsch had some success in placing *Man of Destiny* (October 1916), *Widowers' Houses* (October 1917), *Mrs Warren* (February 1918), *Doctor's Dilemma* (April 1918), and *Fanny's First Play* (September 1918) in minor theatres. However limited, Shaw was the sole "enemy" playwright to appear with several works in wartime Germany.*

[10 Adelphi Terrace W.C.]
[begun 19th January;
completed 4th February 1915]
[My dear Trebitsch]¹

[Your letter of 27th December has just reached me. It is the first word that I have received from you since the war began. My wife's last letter to you at Ostend was returned after a long delay; and the letter of eight weeks ago which you mention (it must now be closer to twelve weeks) never reached me.]

Everybody in England is just as mad about the war as everybody in Germany and Austria. Berlin talks just the same nonsense as London. Germany is the standard bearer of Culture; Britain is the champion of Liberty. Ger-

*Gorky's *Lower Depths* (*Nachtasyl*) was successfully revived at the Volksbühne, Berlin, on 7 October 1916, no doubt to convey a negative image of Russia.

many has worked for peace for years and years; Britain never had a thought of war until Belgium was invaded. Germany must be annihilated; Britain must be disabled and disarmed; every Frenchman who makes a speech finishes every sentence with "jusqu'au bout" [to the death]. Grey[2] is a compound of Machiavelli and Judas Iscariot; the Kaiser worships Wotan and reads nothing but Nietzsche; the Crown Prince steals the forks and spoons from the chateaux he sleeps in. As to the atrocities committed by "the enemy," and the diaries found in the possession of prisoners shewing that all the armies are on the point of surrender, they are a steady source of income to the journalists who invent them. It is all too ghastly for words; but we are already passing out of the first and worst phase. When Commonsense came out, I was appearing every week at large public meetings in London; and when the papers found that instead of being torn to pieces I was more popular than ever, the notion that patriotism consists in frantic lying began to give way to the discovery that telling the truth was not so dangerous as everyone had supposed. By this time hardly any of the leading papers seriously dispute my assertion that the war is an Imperialist war to maintain the balance of power in Europe on the part of your and our Junker-diplomatists, and a popular war only as all wars are popular for a time, the solid basis of its support by the mass of the people being the conflict of Democracy with Junkerism all over the world. But I need hardly say that if Grey had announced that we had formed an alliance with Germany and Austria, and were at war with France and Russia, there would have been just the same patriotic fervor, and just the same democratic anti-Prussianism with the P left out, and the Kaiser hailed as our king's cousin and our old and faithful friend. And the Germans would have been embracing us in the name of Houston Chamberlain[3] as their natural allies in the eternal war of the Teuton with the Latin and the Slav.

As for me, I am not what is called pro-German, nor would the Germans have the smallest respect for me if I did not play for my side now that all questions of culture are dropped and nothing is going on but mere stabbing and shooting and bombarding. And neither am I an anti-German. There are no longer Germans and Englishmen, Austrians and Russians: there are only the men in a certain uniform who are trying to kill you, and the men in a certain different uniform who are trying to save you. And you must try to save the men who are trying to save you and to kill the men who are trying to kill you even if the saviours are Turks and the killers countrymen of Shakespear and Shaw, or the saviours Senegalese, Gurkas, Arabs and Sikhs and the killers countrymen of Goethe and Beethoven and Trebitsch. War reduces us all to a common level of savagery and vulgarity whilst it pretends to distinguish us by our respective greatnesses. Any London costermonger can shove a bayonet through Strauss's entrails much more easily than Strauss can shove one through his. Any Viennese Apache can knock my brains out. [Militarismus has just compelled me to pay about a thousand pounds in war tax in order to aid some "brave little Serb" or other to cut your throat or some Russian muzhik to blow your brains out, although I'd rather it cost me twice as much to save your life or to purchase in Vienna a fine painting for our National Gallery, and although I'd grieve far less over the deaths of a hundred Serbs or muzhiks than over your death.] That is what militarismus means; and can anything be more ghastly, more foolish, more intolerably oppressive? We cannot escape from it or prevent it just now; but at least we can shew how foolish the whole business is even from the point of view of British and German Junkerdom. And it was Junkerdom and not the tradesmen who made this war. Of course the tradesmen are making all they can out of it; but as nothing saved them all from ruin here except an unprecedented Socialistic assumption by the State of all their financial responsibilities, they were terrified out of their lives by the war. That is why Sir Edward Grey had to persuade the nation up to the last moment that we were not going to war at all.

The notion that Ireland could be of any use to Germany in a war with England was a wild delusion. My wife warned the Princess Lichnowsky[4] most earnestly against attaching any importance to the efforts the anti-Home Rulers were making to persuade the English electorate, for party purposes, that Ireland was on the brink of civil war. It was all bluff. It is odd that you, an Austrian should suppose that Prussia could do anything with the Irish. There would perhaps be a chance for Austria in Ireland because Austria is Catholic, and has made her rule popular in Poland where Protestant Prussia has failed as badly as England failed to conciliate Ireland. But Prussian rule in Ireland would be more unpopular by far than English rule; and the extreme Irish nationalists, who declare themselves on the side of every enemy of England, have quite failed to shake the position of Redmond,[5] the official parliamentary Home Rule leader, who offers England the support of the whole Irish Nationalist movement. And only the wildest misunderstanding of the political situation in Ireland could suggest that any other course was possible, even for Irishmen who dislike the English far more than they dislike the Germans.

[In your letter you say that every German will hate England until it is destroyed. Two days before you wrote these words, German and English soldiers alarmed their officers by leaving their trenches and chatting, smoking and playing football together. In a year's time after the war's end you will travel first to Paris, then to London where you will find many friends with whom you may breakfast and lunch although you would turn a Viennese bootblack who invited you to breakfast with him over to the police.] It is all hallucination, this war spirit: we all talk nonsense. German papers, French papers, English papers write the same articles word for word (except for the names); tell the same lies; believe the same impossible stories. The speeches are all the same: the French orators are all what I call Jusquaboutists, and the Germans Bisamendists, and the English Tothedeathists. And one thing that is certain is that "we" must win. There is never any doubt about that.

[My "unjust and unfriendly" words about Potsdam and militarismus ought to be honored with a memorial in Berlin's Siegesalle.[6] Three enraged Englishmen sent me iron crosses because of them. In the first wave of war-madness it was not easy to assert that all our official declarations were non-sense and our air of moral superiority groundless. Perhaps I will write an article for the "Revue des Nations." But if I do so, you may depend on it that all the war leaders will scream for my blood. The only person I envy nowadays is the Pope. If I were in his position I would excommunicate the entire society and then fill Europe so with my thunder that all would come running to Canossa and accept my adjusted map of Europe.

[I am, quite apart from myself, sorry for your sake that my plays are no longer performed. Why doesn't the Burgtheater play the Man of Destiny? Napoleon's speech about English realpolitik would have an unprecedented success. If the English should win, I shall call upon Sir Edward Grey to add a clause to the peace agreements obliging Berlin and Vienna to produce at least one hundred performances of my plays annually for the next 25 years. But don't tell this to the Neue Freie Presse, they will only see in this a new proof of our wish to conquer German trade.⁷

[I began this letter on 19th January and it is today 4th February. Perhaps it won't reach you because our censors refuse to read long letters, and if they do they may perhaps assume that it will so encourage you that you will immediately rush to the front and singlehandedly conquer the entire British and French army. Nevertheless I want to dispatch it on the possibility that it will be censored by an exceptionally intelligent official and get through.]

In London last August the usual series of nightly cheap orchestral concerts called Promenade Concerts announced patriotically that no German music would be performed. Everybody applauded the announcement. But nobody went to the concerts. Within a week a program full of Beethoven, Wagner and Strauss was announced. Everybody was shocked; and everybody went to the concert. It was a complete and decisive German victory, with nobody killed. A nation which can win victories like that should make a present of all its weapons and ammunition to its neighbors, and continue calmly to rule Europe in spite of all the idiots and jackboots who believe in no pre-eminence but pre-eminence in homicidal efficiency.

[Be assured that my wishes for you are most cordial and unpatriotic,

yours ever

G. Bernard Shaw]

Tls.; Texas.

1. This letter was translated and released by Trebitsch and appeared with some deletions softening the comments on Democracy versus Junkerdom in the *Münchner Neueste Nachrichten* (18 April) and the *Frankfurter Zeitung* (21 April). The present version is reconstructed from an incomplete typed copy of the original and the German texts. Retranslated portions are bracketed.

2. Sir Edward Grey (1862–1933), head of the Foreign Office.

3. Houston Chamberlain as a Germanophile living in Germany sided with the Central Powers.

4. Princess Mechtilde Lichnowsky (1879–1958), a writer, and wife of the German ambassador in London, was a friend of the Shaws.

5. John Edward Redmond (1856–1918), Irish M.P.

6. Shaw's article "The Peril of Potsdam" (*Daily News*, 11 August 1914) bore down on Prussian militarism ("Potsdam") and was attacked in the German press.

7. *Man of Destiny* was not staged in Germany at this time, but Napoleon's speech on British imperialism was cited in *Frankfurter Zeitung* (28 August 1914) and the *Neue Freie Presse* (17 January 1915).

10 Adelphi Terrace W.C.
9th June 1915

My dear Trebitsch

I have just had my breath taken away by an announcement in the Liverpool Daily Post and Mercury [6 June] that you have written to the Vossische Zeitung to say that I am being threatened and persecuted in London; that my life is no longer safe; that my doors remain closed to all visitors; and that my correspondence is being watched. This, it adds, you have received "from an absolutely reliable source."[1]

This makes me deeply ashamed of not having written to you; but, as you know, I have always been a bad correspondent, and I am now worse than ever, because I am writing a new pamphlet[2] on the war; and I find this so absorbing, and am in such a hurry to get it into shape and finished that I put off every other activity except matters of business which positively must be attended to. Besides, how can I write to you freely? If I were to tell you all the stupid things the German Government are doing, and what they ought to have done instead, I should be making myself the Kaiser's Prime Minister and enabling him to defeat all Europe, including England. And if I were to tell you all the stupid things the English Government does and what it ought to do instead, I should be giving away valuable information to the enemy. And there is really nothing else to write about except the stupidities of both Governments. All I will tell you now is that an English journalist, Cecil Chesterton,[3] brother of the famous Gilbert Chesterton, and himself a very able writer, says that we ought to offer Silesia to Austria to compensate her for the Slav provinces and Italia Redenta. That is the only original suggestion that has been made since the war began. You might mention it to the Emperor next time you take tea with him.[4]

The story of my persecution is wildly wrong. I never was so popular in my life. When my pamphlet appeared I was addressing big meetings in London every week, and inviting questions about the war. Some of the papers sent down to see me hissed and mobbed; but there was not a sound of disapproval: the meetings were crowded; not a single hostile question was asked; and I was applauded with special warmth at the last meeting. At a revival of Fanny's First Play, an attempt was made by a London paper to organize a demonstration against me on the first night;[5] and I went to it prepared to address the audience. There was not the faintest sign of hostility: I never had a friendlier audience. In the provinces and in America my plays have been in greater demand than ever before. Before Easter I went to Ireland—just when the German submarines were sinking everything in the Irish Channel, by the way—and I returned with the survivors of the Lusitania, which had just been sunk.[6] Thus I came back to England at the moment when the feeling against Germany was at its bitterest, and the shops of the bakers with German names were being looted (they will all be compensated; and the looters have had their heads broken and been sent to prison); and instead of going home I travelled about the country, first from Holyhead to London and then from London to the Lake District, where I attended a [Fabian] conference on the war [at Derwentwater, 21–25 May], and went on a tour over the mountains. This means that I stayed at several hotels—ten or twelve altogether. During all this time I never received the smallest incivility; and when I returned to London I found my portrait, painted in Ireland by Augustus John, exhibited in one of the principal shows.[7] Meanwhile my pamphlet continues to sell steadily; and the Jingo papers abuse me every day; so there is no question of my pamphlet being forgotten. In short, the only risk I am running is from your confounded Zeppelins, which drop bombs about without considering that one of them may fall on the head of "the upright man."[8]

Our newspapers have lately been behaving in a way which must puzzle you in Austria. After the usual daily announcements, month after month, of deeds of heroism and victories by the dozen for our troops, they suddenly began to declare that our army was on the verge of destruction. The Bishop of Pretoria [Michael Furse] wrote a long letter to The Times [25 May] describing the British lines as being held by a handful of outnumbered and weary men, desperately holding their last trenches whilst England was full of ablebodied men refusing to do their duty to their country. The explanation of this is that The Times and the party it represents want to introduce conscription into England, because the conscript soldier is much cheaper than the person you call the mercenary soldier. The opponents of conscription point out that we are doing very well, and that we have got as big an army as conscription would have raised for us. The advocates of conscription declare, on the contrary, that nothing but conscription can save us from defeat. That is why you have in England a thing impossible in Austria: namely, the Imperialist section of the press doing everything they can to terrify the nation by declaring that our army is doomed to destruction, and the Liberal and Labor papers declaring that we have the most splendid army in Europe, and that they hurl back the German conscripts as the rocks of the British coast hurl back the waves of the Atlantic. In other respects our press is very much like yours; and we are going on here just as you are no doubt going on in Vienna. We have our spiteful people and our frightened people and our innocent people who believe all the stories of atrocities and so forth; but I believe the mass of the nation feels about the war very much as you and I do: that is, they feel it to be a frightful failure of civilization that there should be a war at all between civilized western powers. There is plenty of good humor. We tell funny stories about the war, and make burlesque versions of Lissauer's hymn of hate[9] in which the word England is replaced by "Sauerkraut" or some such nonsense. Down at the lakes I heard a man who could not get his bell answered exclaim "Gott strafe this hotel!"[10] And so on and so forth.

I am writing another essay on the war, as long as the first. I hope to have it ready for publication before very long.

I hope they have not yet sent you to the Carpathians. Soldiering would be simply waste of your time: you can serve your country much better by telling it what you think of it with your pen than joining a cavalry regiment for a campaign in which horses are of no use.

I send this through our friend Leipnik.[11] If you have time let me have a line from you: your letters are always very welcome. Charlotte is always imagining that you are in a trench with shells bursting all around you and your clothes all over mud, and that you are not having proper food and have not washed your face or changed your clothes for a month; and it is a great relief to her that you are still safe and clean and comfortable.

yours as ever

G.B.S.

Tls.

1. On 28 May 1915, Trebitsch, not having heard from Shaw for some time, published the following statement in the *Vossische Zeitung*: "I have learned from an absolutely reliable and unimpeachable source that my dear friend Bernard Shaw, because of his *friendly attitude towards the German people*, is threatened and persecuted in London and his life is no longer safe. His door is closed to all visitors because of well-founded fears of assassination; his correspondence is watched and that accounts for my not having received any sign of life from him—by way of Holland or Switzerland—for many weeks. Only because there remain some in Germany who cannot forgive Shaw the few unfriendly words he expressed early in the war, when he was not yet oriented, do I communicate this news." Trebitsch's "source" is unidentified.

2. *More Common Sense about the War*, defending Shaw's version of how the war had started and calling on the belligerents to seek a mediated settlement. The pamphlet, submitted to the *New Statesman*, was rejected and remained unpublished except for portions that, in modified form, appeared elsewhere.

3. Cecil Chesterton (1879–1918) was the founder and editor of the *New Witness*.

4. The Trebitsches lived opposite the imperial park of Schönbrunn and through a friend of Tina Trebitsch had access to an intimate friend of the Emperor.

5. Three days before the Granville Barker–Lillah McCarthy revival of *Fanny* at the Kingsway Theatre, the *Daily Express* published a letter that, in effect, encouraged public protest against "this anti-British author" ("Effrontery. Protest Against a Coming Shaw Production").

6. Shaw stayed with Sir Horace Plunkett and also with Lady Gregory at Coole Park, near Galway Bay. The Cunard liner *Lusitania* was torpedoed off the Irish coast on 7 May 1915, with the loss of 1,198 lives.

7. The portrait of Shaw by Augustus John (1878–1961), Welsh-born anti-academic painter and etcher, was one of three that John painted during Shaw's stay at Coole. It was exhibited by the New English Art Club at the Royal Society of British Artists, and purchased by Shaw.

8. The first German zeppelin attack on London occurred on 1 June.

9. Ernst Lissauer (1882–1937), German author and poet, won an imperial order for his war poem "Hassgesang gegen England" ("Hymn of Hate against England").

10. *Gott strafe England!* (God punish England!) was a popular anti-British pamphlet published by the Munich satiric journal *Simplicissimus* (February 1915).

11. F. L. Leipnik was a Dutchman, who, as a neutral, forwarded mail between Shaw and Trebitsch.

10 Adelphi Terrace W.C.

28th July 1915

My dear Trebitsch

I must send you a hasty line or two; for I find that the result of putting off writing to you until I have time to write you a long letter is that months pass by, and you hear nothing at all from me.

The radio telegram you received from New York, about which I knew nothing, now turns out to be an extravagance of Granville Barker's. When he was in New York your story about my being shut up in my house to save me from assassination reached America, and made a great sensation there. Barker thought that it would stir up feeling against me by confirming the belief that I am a pro-German. He therefore asked a German friend of his to send you a warning; and the radio-telegram was the result.[1]

I am full of remorse on Leonhard's account. I suppose what happened was that he sent me the introduction from Zangwill with a request for an interview; and I was too busy to answer it instantly.[2] As you know, unless I answer a letter the moment it reaches me I never answer it at all, as it gets snowed under and forgotten in the heap of letters which I am forced to neglect.

Do not suppose that I believe the English papers. I would as soon think of believing the French or German or Austrian or Italian or Servian or Turkish papers, or the papers of any nation that is at war. One has to be guided by one's knowledge of human nature and by such facts as can be neither suppressed nor misrepresented. We know all about your victories here, and are expecting every hour to hear that you have captured Warsaw. In fact, we probably greatly exaggerate the capacity of the Prussian military machine. But we are as confident of victory as you are.

As to my own attitude, it has not changed since I wrote Common Sense About the War. I sometimes feel tempted to write Common Sense for Germans about the War; but it would certainly not please the Court of Berlin or the Junker party. Consequently, it would not help to restore my plays to the German stage. However, if you are bent on the desperate enterprise of having my plays performed in Vienna in October, you had better try Press Cuttings. It makes a British Commander in Chief sufficiently ridiculous to please the patriotic section of Vienna; and if the actor makes up as Admiral von Tirpitz,[3] the Social-democratic section will be equally pleased.

You must also bear in mind that the Germans would very properly lose all respect for me if I betrayed my neighbors. I hate this war; and, as you know, I have criticized the English Government very severely for not taking the steps which, as I believe, would have prevented it. But if I were a German, I should criticize the Berlin Government with equal fierceness for having made the war.

You may well ask how can England offer you Silesia when she has not got it. If that were the only difficulty, we would offer you the moon without hesitation. You must not, however, suppose that the English would like to see the war continued for four years. We also really count the days to the end as much as you. But how can we stop until Berlin stops, believing as we do that we can hold out longer than Berlin both in money and men? I cannot criticize the Austrian point of view, because we do not know in England what it is. It seems to us that by the ultimatum to Servia you dragged Berlin into the war, and then left Berlin to conduct it as best Berlin could. We may be quite wrong; but the news we get is all about Berlin and what the Kaiser is going to do. We are led to believe that you are as completely in the hands of Prussia as Bavaria is. The Emperor is never mentioned except as being able to walk about still in spite of his great age—105 or thereabouts according to English notions.[4] Berlin has played Vienna off the stage, in fact, as far as the English press is concerned; and of course the English nation knows nothing of Austria except what it learns from its press. In America it is the same. There are plenty of German agents there influencing the American press for all they are worth; but there are no Austrian agents. The curious result is that since the war began Austria has been talked about less than Ireland. We hardly realized we were at war with Austria until the entry of the Italians into the war reminded us of it.[5] One good consequence of this is that there is no feeling against the Austrians: all the hostile feeling is aimed at the Germans.

Our feeling about Prussia now is that she has tremendous industry and discipline, but no brains. We thought she was on the point of gaining the sympathy of the United States over the Chinese difficulty, as she certainly could have done had she played her cards well. At that very moment she sank the Lusitania.[6] After that, it was clear that Prussia had no diplomatic cunning, and could only win by conquering the world by force of arms. [Section deleted by the censor.] Prussia, it seems, cannot get rid of Admiral von Tirpitz; so, unless Prussia can conquer the world, she will not conquer England. That is what the people think here who are capable of thinking at all: what the papers say does not greatly matter. Why on earth do not the Austrians assert themselves in the diplomatic part of the business? You can let Potsdam manage the fighting; but you should say to the Kaiser "My military friend, you can look after the trenches and the batteries; but you must leave the diplomatic business to us, as it requires brains rather than jack boots." All this may seem very absurd to you; but it will give you an idea of what we are thinking about over here.

For my own part I still say that unless there is peace between England, France and Germany there can be no peace in the world; so we shall have to make up our minds to stop fighting sooner or later.

Charlotte is by no means as patriotic as your dear Princess. She has never gone near a hospital, and loathes the war too heartily to assist in it in any capacity except that of a reluctant taxpayer. I have great hopes that the Austrian authorities will not waste you on the trenches. But as there is such a shortage of intelligent officers in all the belligerent countries, I suppose you will presently be called upon to drill recruits, or to do some official administrative work.

On Saturday this week (31st) we go down for a couple of months to Torquay, where I made the acquaintance of our friend Leipnik last year. Until the end of September my address will be The Hydro, Torquay, South Devon.

Charlotte sends all sorts of affectionate messages.

yours ever
G.B.S.

Tls.
   1. Barker wrote to Shaw (19 February) from New York that *Common Sense* had created many enemies for Shaw in America (B. L.).

2. Rudolf Leonhard (1889–1953), German author, translator, and radical pacifist, was a friend of Israel Zangwill (1864–1926), English author, playwright, and pacifist.

3. Alfred von Tirpitz (1849–1930), German admiral and politician, influenced German foreign policy before the war.

4. Franz Joseph, born in 1830, died in 1916.

5. Italy, long a claimant on Austria, entered the war in May 1915.

6. Relations between Japan, an ally of Britain, and China had been tense since the beginning of 1915; Germany attempted to exploit American sympathies for China, but the sinking of the *Lusitania*, with a loss of 128 Americans, turned American opinion strongly against Germany.

The Hydro. Torquay

8th August 1915

My dear Trebitsch

I have written to Lord Haldane[1] about Dauthendy;[2] and Lord Haldane has written to the Foreign Office. He is doubtful as to whether any sort of Passierschein [pass] is possible; but I daresay his intervention will have its effect, as he is a close personal friend of Sir Edward Grey. At all events, this is the very best and utmost that can be done for Dauthendy as far as I know. Please let Fischer know. It is not clear from the correspondence whether the Imperial Chancellor took any action upon the recommendation from the Embassy at the Hague. It is desirable that he should do so; for then the Foreign Office will have something formal to act on.

A letter from me to you crossed yours from Carlsbad. I hope the Carlsbad people will examine you thoroughly and report you entirely unfit for service. I am prepared to swear, if necessary, that you faint on the slightest severe exertion and that you cannot see objects further off than five yards, and even then see them double.

There is a fearful scandal here about a certain Ignatius Trebitsch who got into parliament as member for Darlington, and who is in danger of being extradited from New York for forgery. As he glories in having been a spy, his case is much noticed in all the papers; and I am in daily expectation of being accused of having had my works translated by him. He is a Hungarian Jew. Do you know anything about him?[3]

yours ever

G. Bernard Shaw

Als.

1. Richard Burdon Haldane (1856–1928), Liberal leader and former Secretary of State and Lord Chancellor.

2. Max Dauthendey (1867–1918), German poet, painter, playwright, and world wanderer, was one of S. Fischer's authors. At the outbreak of war, he was interned in Java, then under Dutch control. Efforts to secure his release and safe passage through the British fleet failed and he succumbed to tropical disease.

3. Ignatius Trebitsch (I. T. Trebitsch-Lincoln, 1879–1943), Hungarian-born adventurer and naturalized Englishman, had entered Parliament in 1910 and was now in America purporting to be a German spy. The claim was spurious, but the British demanded his extradition for forgery. In 1916 he was returned to England, where he was imprisoned, denaturalized, and later expelled. He then turned spy in earnest. Born a Jew, he became a Christian and later a Buddhist monk; as such, he sought to become the Dalai Lama.

The Hydro. Torquay
27th August 1915

My dear [Trebitsch]

If the Censor meddles with my letters, I must stop writing about the war. I dont object to his returning a letter as inadvisable, but when he takes to blacking out sentences and sending you selected passages, making the letter, in effect, his letter and not mine, I had rather not be made responsible for the effect they may produce on you, and, through you as an influential journalist, upon the Vienna press. I am always extremely careful both in what I say and how I balance it; and it is quite evident from your reply to my last letter that the balance has been destroyed. The difficulty about the censorship is that nobody knows who the actual official who handles the letter is. He may be a much wiser man than I, and a better judge of what should be said and left unsaid. But on the other hand he may be a duffer who imagines that anyone who tells the truth to a German or Austrian, especially the truths that all Europe knows, is opening the gates of Buckingham Palace to the Kaiser. Or—and this is the most likely alternative—he may be an official censoring by simple rule of thumb, carrying out rules as to what may or may not be mentioned in an entirely senseless manner; and as I dont know what the rules are and cannot adapt my letters to them, there is nothing for it but to drop the subject.

I have a most desolating piece of news for you. Great Catherine will be produced in America with a *lever de rideau* entitled The Inca of Perusalem, by a Fellow of the Royal Society of Literature; and the Inca will most certainly be identified with the Allerhöchst [the Kaiser].[1] This appalling Majestäts beleidigung [lese majesty] will possibly ruin my already shattered prestige in Germany and Austria. Would it be possible to produce a play in Germany—a comic absurdity—in which the Kaiser was recognizably caricatured? Keep this a dead secret until the production takes place. Nothing is finally arranged yet; for the contract for the production of Great Catherine was in the Arabic, which your ungovernable naval commanders have sent to the bottom of the sea.

In Italy Emma Grammatica, without my knowledge, committed the gross blunder of producing the Schlachtenlenker [*Man of Destiny*]. It provoked a riot, though Napoleon's speech about the English was omitted.[2] Possibly it would please an Austrian audience as much as it displeased the Italian one.[3]

Tell the recruiting authorities that if they send you to the front it will get into all the English papers, and persuade us that Austria is exhausted and calling out her very last reserves; for everybody will believe that you are as old as I.

Barker is in France, reporting to the Government on the organization of our Red Cross work. Masefield[4] has gone to the Dardenelles, also on hospital work. By this time you will have received my letters about Dauthendy.

The Germans must put up as best they can with what you call my "disdain." The English complain of it far more bitterly. If the human race wishes me to respect it, it must behave very differently. The war leaves me exactly as the war against Philip II left Shakespear, and the war against Louis XIV left Swift. It is so horribly mischievous, and yet so horribly childish. We all boast of it as a great war because it has shed more gallons of blood than any previous one. In reality, it is the most trivial folly in history; and its chief enduring product will be The Inca of Perusalem: the worst play ever written.

immer und ewig yours

G. Bernard Shaw

Als.; Texas.

1. The two plays opened 14 November 1916 in New York's Neighborhood Playhouse. Gertrude Kingston played Catherine.

2. Emma Gramatica (1875–1965), Italian actress and proponent of Shaw, produced *The Man of Destiny* at Milan's Olimpia Theatre on 14 July. Luigi Carini played opposite her. Part of the audience, affronted by the portrait of Napoleon and ridicule of their British ally, demanded the play stop, but Gramatica cut the most incendiary speeches and the evening staggered to its end (*Corriere della Sera*, 15 July).

3. *Man of Destiny* was revived during the war in Vienna's Theater in der Josefstadt (27 October 1916) for 11 performances.

4. John Masefield (1878–1967), English poet, playwright, and novelist, became poet laureate in 1930.

The Hydro. Torquay

14th October 1915

My dear Trebitsch

Your letter dated the 7th Sept. did not reach me until this morning!!!!! It gives me unbounded joy by its news of your having failed to pass the doctor. Gesegnet sei dieser Arzt! er muss ein ganz geschickter Kerl sein [Blessed be this doctor! He must be a very clever fellow]. He is quite right. Anyone can see that you have a marked aneurism of the aorta, that your mitral valves are all wrong, and that you suffer from chronic pericarditis. You will die prematurely at the age of 98 in a hotel lift, from ascending too rapidly. If you attempted to do military service, you would fall from your horse in the first charge, the horse would stumble over you, all the other horses would stumble over it, and the whole squadron would be disgracefully annihilated.[1]

I wonder why on earth the Censor kept your letter for a month. Probably the military authorities were inquiring about those mysterious new generals on the staff of Hindenberg: Bach, Beethoven, Mozart and Wagner.

Your escape from glory is the best news; but I am also greatly pleased to hear that Moissi is safe as a prisoner of war.[2] I shall certainly do nothing to get him released: I would not exchange him for ten generals. Do you suppose I want him to be killed, or to sail about in the air dropping bombs on Adelphi Terrace? He will escape all dangers here and be well treated. Our ultra-patriots here are furious because we spend thousands of pounds fitting up country houses with billiard tables for the German officers whom we capture. Have you never heard of Donnington Hall and its luxuries? We think here that nothing proves the heroism of the German officers so well as the fact that they dont all surrender and have a pleasant time in England at our expense. But all the same I shall try to find out where Moissi is when I return to London next week.

Szalai, my agent in Budapest, writes that they are going to play Man &
Superman there. So I am no longer on the Magyar *index expurgatorius*.[3]

I must not say anything about politics or Heaven knows how long the
Censor will delay this letter.

Charlotte's heart is much comforted by the military doctor's view of
yours.

> ever
>
> G. Bernard Shaw

Als.
   1. As Austrian casualties mounted, Trebitsch's age group was called up. But the army doctor
found that Trebitsch had an enlarged heart. On private consultation, it turned out that he had only
a displaced diaphragm. Subsequently, Trebitsch served as a hospital orderly near his home.
   2. Alexander Moissi (1879–1935), born in Trieste, was the leading male star in Reinhardt's
company. The previous month, Moissi, now a German air force pilot, was shot down and interned
by the French. He was later found to suffer from tuberculosis and in July 1917 was exchanged and
returned to Berlin.
   3. Shaw was not produced in Hungary during the war, but he was revived immediately thereafter under the revolutionary regime of Béla Kun.

[Trebitsch to Shaw]

> Wien.
>
> 23rd October 1914 [1915]

My dear, dear Shaw!

Your kind letter from October 14 has reached me this moment turning a
dull and gloomy day into sunshine and pleasure.

But I do not understand a word, nor your joy about my 'escape.'

I told you, as far as a know (if I have not been drunk) *that I have been
taken* as fit for service *nevertheless* the military doctor found out I had a
bad "heart-neurose."

I am not free and shall have to enter the army when the recruits of my year
will have their turn. They say: not before January.

A lot of people believe that the war is going to end in 3 months. My wife is
very unhappy about my possibilities......[1]

I wished the german stages would follow the example of the Magyar play
houses. But, I am unhappy to say, there is no such hope.

Have you written a new play? If so, please let me have it. I should like to
adapt it *before* January.

Thousand hearty greetings and wishes from both of us to both of you.

> Yours ever
>
> Siegfried Trebitsch

Als.; Texas.
   1. Trebitsch's ellipsis.

> 10 Adelphi Terrace W.C.
>
> 9th November 1915

My dear Trebitsch

Can you tell me exactly what corps or regiment Alexander Moissi served
in? We have here a Society for aiding German prisoners; and through it I have

made enquiries; but the official answer is "cannot trace."[1] Lord Haldane is dining with us this week; and I shall ask him whether there is any better way of finding Moissi; but in the meantime the secretary of the Society tells me that there would be a better chance if I could give particulars as to Moissi's regiment. I said he was a flying lieutenant.

Edmund Gosse wrote a letter to The Times about Dauthendy—not a very gracious one.[2] He seemed to think that Dauthendy is lost; but I gather that he is still in Java; and if he is a wise man he will stay there and get used to the climate until the war is over.

I have two short plays, one of which will ruin you if you translate it; but I cannot send them to you because the Censor will not allow books to pass, as people have used books to convey military information. However, the publishers are allowed to send them; and I will try to get Constables to send copies to Fischer through our invaluable friend Leipnik. They do not matter much, I am afraid, as they are both topical: one [*O'Flaherty V.C.*] being the experiences of a Victoria Cross hero on returning from the trenches to recruit in Ireland, whilst the other [*The Inca of Perusalem*] introduces an Exalted Personage [the Kaiser] with moustaches like this— .[3] The authorship of the latter must remain a dead secret; and I hereby put the Censor on his honor not to betray it. Both pieces are short, lasting only 40 minutes.

Your respite until January is welcome news. Be sure you faint publicly at least twice a week in the meantime. You owe it to the doctor to bear out his diagnosis.

immer und ewig

G. Bernard Shaw

Tls.

1. Though Moissi had been shot down by the British, he was in French custody.

2. Edmond Gosse (1849–1928), noted man of letters, wrote to the *Times* (3 November) on behalf of the missing Dauthendey, but admitted that "however blameless and elderly a German poet may be, his fate at present leaves me cold."

3. *O'Flaherty V.C.*, offered to the Abbey Theatre as a "recruiting pamphlet," was opposed by the English authorities and withdrawn. *The Inca of Perusalem*, spoofing the Kaiser, was identified as by "A Member of the Royal Society of Literature" to avoid hurting Shaw's standing in Germany. Shaw sent signed rehearsal copies of these playlets to his publisher Otto Kyllmann, to be forwarded to Trebitsch. Kyllmann laid them aside, and over thirteen years passed before they resurfaced (see 14 May 1929).

Ayot St Lawrence. Welwyn
28th December 1915

My dear Trebitsch

Thank heaven you "have been" very ill. That means that you are no longer so, doesnt it? Just keep ill enough to be unfit for military service, and well enough to celebrate the peace with us when it comes. I spend all my evenings in the country here singing *Dona nobis pacem* in Beethoven's and Mozart's masses.

I cannot say anything about the revival of The Devil's Disciple.[1] I have just refused to allow it to be played in America, as this is not the moment in which I can gracefully remind the world that Britain has not always been on the side of liberty. But I have no control of the Austrian stage now: and though I cannot in any way sanction the performance I console myself with the hope that it may bring you in tantièmes, and that it wont make the smallest difference in the military situation.

The reports you allude to were not altogether unfounded.[2] I was addressing an audience which contained several well known people who were agitating for peace. The news of our evacuation of Servia had just come in; and I told them that it was quite useless to dream of peace at such a moment, as it was a moment of defeat for us. I said that if the Kaiser were intelligent enough to withdraw all his armies within the German frontier, and tell the world that he was content to shew that he could beat us, and that he now left the quarrel to the arbitration of the Pope or President Wilson, we should be placed in a very embarrassing situation, because we could not possibly accept the position of a beaten nation, and should have to insist on marching through Berlin just to shew that the Kaiser could *not* beat us, although that would place us in the shocking moral situation of fighting in mere pugnacity and pride. Naturally our silly papers reported me as having debited the usual clichés about "fighting to a finish," pushing on to Berlin, und so weiter.

It is curious how it encourages everybody to say that this war must be fought to the end—jusqu'au bout. I always say that I quite agree that it must be fought to the end, as I do not see how a war can finish before the end. It is like saying that we are all heroically determined to live until we die.

I am just passing through the press the sheets of my new volume containing Androcles, Overruled, & Pygmalion. Its chief new feature is a tremendous preface on Christianity.

I have just written a long letter to Maxim Gorky[3] on the relations between England and Russia. It will be published probably in America.

When will it all be over? What a Christmas!

Our love to you and your lady.

Auf Wiedersehen
G. Bernard Shaw

Tls.

1. *Devil's Disciple* was revived at the Deutsches Volkstheater, Vienna, on 18 March 1916 and ran 14 times. Shaw's reappearance was warmly welcomed by the *Neue Freie Presse*, which declared, "our relationship with Bernard Shaw has not changed even during the war."

2. On 2 December, Shaw spoke before a women's group on "The Nation's Vitality" and reportedly argued that peace at that point was impossible. In Berlin and Vienna, Shaw's views appeared as urging continuation of the war ("Shaw als Chauvinist," *8 Uhr Abendblatt*, 8 December; *Neues Wiener Journal*, 15 December). To correct the impression, Trebitsch released Shaw's letter to the *Frankfurter Zeitung* (23 January 1916), which defended Shaw and cited the letter.

3. Maxim Gorky (1868–1936), eminent Russian author, extolled Shaw for standing above the passions of the "senseless war" and solicited an article for the journal *Letopis*. Shaw's answer appeared in *Metropolitan* ("Shaking Hands with a Bear," May 1916) and declared that Russia's despotism undermined the moral position of the Allies and threatened neutral sympathies. Although he was above the mad passions of war, he was not, Shaw wrote, indifferent and wished his nation to win or at least not lose.

PART THREE

The Aftermath
24 December 1918 through 6 December 1932

As the war dragged on, Shaw despaired of a just peace and, after the outbreak of the Russian Revolution, concluded that the best solution from a proletarian view—barring revolution in the West—would be a stalemate that would prevent a vindictive peace that would merely lead to another war (letter to A. N. Thompson, 22 December 1917, *Collected Letters*, III; "The Falling Market in War Aims," *Daily Chronicle*, 12 January 1918). But by the fall of 1918, blockaded Germany was overcome.

On 3 November Austria capitulated; on the 11th an armistice with Germany, convulsed by revolution, was signed. On 9 November a Republic was hastily proclaimed; the rebellion was crushed; and the Weimar Republic arose on the shaken but surviving base of landowners and industrialists.

With the Treaty of Versailles, Shaw's fears were confirmed. Germany was held solely responsible for the war, and the penalties imposed were huge reparations, loss of colonies and foreign holdings, and a drastically reduced army and merchant marine. Unbalanced by reparations and restricted trade, the German economy plunged into raging inflation. The prewar rate of four marks to the dollar dropped to 7,000 marks in 1922, to 160,000 in 1923, and then to an inconceivable 4,200,000,000 marks to the dollar. Revolution threatened, but the government invoked emergency powers and in 1924 issued new currency. For a time, liberalized reparations and foreign loans further eased the strain. But as the Great Depression spread worldwide, these advances crumbled. German production fell more than 40 percent and unemployment rose to almost 45 percent of the work force. The nation was split, and the militant right found a Leader.

Truncated republican Austria, under Socialist rule, was even more luckless. Sustained by charity and credits, Austria's economic crisis persisted and deepened. Political dissension erupted violently in 1927 and offered a pretext for conservative authoritarian rule, followed by civil war and the defeat of the Socialists.

From the start, Shaw had reasoned against a punitive peace and called on England not to be "prostituted" by an "ignoble clamor for plunder and vengeance" (Bedfordshire *Express*, 3 January 1919). Instead, he pleaded for a humane, rational, and just treatment of the defeated nations and in *Peace Conference Hints* (1919) denied England any moral right to punish or quarantine Germany and urged again a supranational body, including Germany, to enforce the peace. If vengeance won out, Shaw warned, Europe would mark time until the next war or overthrow democracy for radical social forms, and he appealed for Christian chivalry and doing away with falsehood, unreason, hatred, and hardheartedness, which are war's most lasting depredations.

In Germany, Shaw's views were welcomed as "Bernard Shaw gegen die Pharisäer" (Bernard Shaw Against the Pharisees; *Neues Wiener Tagblatt*, 27 December 1918) or "Bernard Shaw gegen den Rachefrieden" (Shaw Against a Vindictive Peace; *Neue Freie Presse*, 15 June 1919). Excerpts from *Hints* appeared in conservative and liberal papers (e.g., *Deutsche Allgemeine Zeitung*, 21 May 1919; *Vossische Zeitung*, 22 May; *N.F.P.*, 15 June). A complete version followed (*Winke zur Friedenskonferenz*, 1919) and was favorably reviewed. But as Shaw later remarked, his essay had "about as much effect on the proceedings at Versailles as the buzzing of a London fly has on the meditations of a whale in Baffin's Bay" (*What I Really Wrote about the War*, 1930).

A month after the Armistice, Shaw gingerly felt his way back into corresponding with Vienna. Trebitsch, in turn, plunged into restoring Shaw in Germany. An augmented edition of *Dramatische Werke* appeared in 1919, and before the year's end *Heartbreak House*, Shaw's major war play, was placed with the Burg, which, shorn of imperial trappings,* had revived *Pygmalion* on 3 May 1919 and shortly added *Candida* to its repertory.

Unsettled conditions prevented the friends from meeting until the fall of 1923, when Shaw presented Trebitsch with *Saint Joan*. The following spring, *Joan* opened in London to unprecedented acclaim for the Irish playwright. News of the triumph flashed abroad, and Reinhardt, who had withdrawn to Vienna, returned to Berlin with a personally staged *Joan* that took Berlin by storm, raised the star of Elisabeth Bergner, and propelled Shaw, whose reputation had suffered from the trifling *Great Catherine* and the failure of *Heartbreak House*, to popular veneration. Uncannily, it occurred just as the German mark stabilized.

In 1926, as Shaw approached seventy, Germany, led by Trebitsch and S. Fischer, prepared to celebrate with tribute and greetings. That fall, Shaw received the Nobel Prize, and two years later, Leon Feuchtwanger, discussing Shaw's impact in Germany, observed: "He is regarded as a classic in the provinces as much as in Berlin. Every one of his plays, even the poorest, is rehearsed to the minutest detail and staged . . . in every possible style. Every

---

*With the dissolution of the Central Monarchies, court theatres became state theatres, and the municipal theatres, which had largely been leased to private companies, were now true municipal undertakings. But the majority of theatres remained private enterprises, fallen on evil times and facing a formidable rival: the movies.

letter is weighed, numbered, and commented on. . . . While . . . Sudermann has long disappeared from the stage; . . . while even Hauptmann occupies a very limited space in the . . . German theatre, Bernard Shaw since the war reigns supreme." (*Literary Digest*, 7 January 1928.) The following year Alfred Kerr, doyen of Berlin theatre critics, declared Shaw a "German classic" (*Neue Rundschau*, 1929).

Sanctions on "trading with the enemy" still obtained until peace was formally ratified. The following letter, cleared by the authorities, was forwarded to Trebitsch by the Dutch intermediary Leipnik.

Ayot St Lawrence. Welwyn
24th December 1918

Sir

Can you as my translator, give me any information as to the state of my affairs in the Central Empires. In England, the tantièmes due to German authors are held by the Board of Trade pending the final settlement. Is there a corresponding arrangement in Germany and Austria; and if so, is it still in operation? I understand that performances of my works in your translation have taken place during the war.[1]

As your personal circumstances have an obvious bearing on your capacity to act for me in business, I am particularly anxious to hear from you on this subject.

You will understand that as I have to obtain an official authorization to send you this letter, it must be confined strictly to business, and expressed in terms suitable to the existing political relations between our respective countries.

yours faithfully
[G. Bernard Shaw][2]

Tl.

1. During the war, Shaw could receive no prewar earnings from Germany. Royalties accrued during the war in Germany need not have been paid at all.
2. Signature cut off.

10 Adelphi Terrace W.C.
26th May 1919

Sir

I have received your letter dated the seventeenth of April. It relieved my mind considerably, as the telegram sent me from St Gallen had caused me some anxiety.[1]

The works which await translation into German are a very long play in three acts entitled Heartbreak House, and five short plays. Three of these

[*O'Flaherty, Inca, Augustus Does His Bit*] are topical jeux d'esprit concerning the war. The longest, called "The Inca of Perusalem" introduces the German Kaiser as the principal character. Of the other two, one, called Great Catherine (Catherine II of Russia) I may have sent you before the war. The other is a mere variety theatre "turn," called Annajanska, or the Bolshevik Empress. I enclose proof sheets of these plays.

I have received some enquiries on behalf of Georg Stilke, a Berlin publisher, from Saarbach of Köln, and also from the Swiss "information Telegraphique" as to the translation into German of my Peace Conference Hints. I have referred these enquirers to you. This book appeared first as a series of articles in the American papers, and was thus brought to the notice of the German-American press.[2] It has since been translated into Swedish. There is therefore no possibility of preventing its being quoted and made use of for propagandist purposes in Germany. But if a complete authorized translation of the full text as revised by me for publication in London can be published in Germany, a good deal of mischief that may be done by partial and garbled quotations can be avoided. Accordingly, I enclose a copy for your consideration.[3]

There are several passages in your letter which must be deferred until the conclusion of peace makes it possible for us to correspond without reserve. Meanwhile I need only say that they are entirely satisfactory to me and to my wife. We are both in excellent health.

yours faithfully
G. Bernard Shaw

Tls.
1. The Trebitsches were on holiday in Switzerland and had suffered some minor ailments.
2. *Peace Conference Hints* was serialized in Hearst's *New York American* during January–March 1919. A detailed summary with commentary appeared in the *Neue Zurcher Zeitung* (23–25 April) and then as a pamphlet. Selections, stressing Shaw's call for chivalry toward the Central Powers and incriminating England for the war, also were printed in *Deutsche Allgemeine Zeitung* (21 May) and *Vossische Zeitung* (22 May).
3. Fischer published Trebitsch's complete version of *Hints* (*Winke zur Friedenskonferenz*).

Parknasilla. Kenmare
20th July 1919
My dear Trebitsch
At last I have got you in a country which I can write to without being shot at dawn. You can judge how difficult my position has been from the fact that E. D. Morel, for simply sending a copy of his book about the war to Romain Rolland (an ally!), was imprisoned for six months.[1] Quite early in the war a certain paragraph in the Neue Freie Presse[2] brought on me a friendly warning from an official of my acquaintance that I had better not correspond with Vienna. As it seemed to me that I might get you into trouble as well as myself, I took the hint. My recent letters, as you must have guessed by their ridiculous formality, were passed through the Trading With The Enemy branch of the Treasury, as I explained in my letter to Leipnik. I did not make

use of him before because he was himself in a delicate position as an occasional visitor to England.

However, now that the war is officially over, I have applied to the Board of Trade for a license to "trade" with you. I doubt whether I shall get it before Austria ratifies the treaty and puts an end to the state of war between us.

I shudder to think of what the blockade must have meant to you.[3] It did not hurt me: I used honey instead of sugar and nut butter instead of real butter; and that was all. But of course prices have doubled or trebled; and the war taxation is six shillings in the pound Income Tax, four and sixpence Super tax, and Insurance against Death Duties—well, I simply dont insure. *Après moi le deluge!* You will laugh at this, as your lot must have been ruin and starvation. Do not dream of sending me any money, or letting Fischer do it: the drain on Germany will recoil on ourselves here in England, though we are not intelligent enough to see it, and are thinking of nothing but plunder. Let us wait—for years if necessary—until the exchange improves. Meanwhile you know through Leipnik the wishes I was unable to convey to you when their fulfillment would have been a breach of the blockade.[4] Better still, an English cheque would be of more use in Zurich than Austrian money. Have you anything to suggest in that direction?

I enclose a set of proofs of the preface ["Heartbreak House and Horseback Hall"] to the volume of plays I sent you. It will tell you a great deal that I should otherwise have to write to you. No doubt Vienna behaved very much as London did; so that it will all be only too familiar to you.

Charlotte's heart bled frightfully for you: nothing that I can write could express her feelings when the papers here wrote about the state of things in Vienna.

We are here at the seaside in the south of Ireland, and shall remain until late in August. It is impossible for me to go to Switzerland: I cannot afford it. Travelling is still very troublesome. I spent a week at the front in Flanders at the end of January 1917 at the invitation of the Commander in Chief [Sir Douglas Haig]; and even as a Government guest, the business of getting passports &c was wearisome in the extreme. I wrote three articles describing the Somme battlefields, Ypres, Arras &c &c.[5]

I am working at a huge tetralogy (like Wagner's Ring) called Back to Methuselah. First play, the Garden of Eden. Second Play, the present day. Third Play, 300 years hence. Fourth Play, a thousand years hence. The first three plays are already written. I am at work on the fourth. A colossal affair, with, alas! no money in it. I must stop now, to catch the post here; but there is still much to be said when I hear from you in reply to this. How has your wife sustained the trials of the war?

Our love to you both

G.B.S.

PS Glad you are at the Baur Lac. It shows that you are not utterly ruined yet.[6]

Als.

1. E. D. Morel (1873–1924), Labour M.P. and writer, had blamed the war largely on France and Russia, abetted by England, and in 1917 was convicted of evading censorship by sending his

Tsardom's Part in the War and other pamphlets to Romain Rolland (1866–1944), the French writer, then in neutral Switzerland.

2. Trebitsch's wartime birthday greeting to Shaw, calling Germany Shaw's "spiritual home" and praising Shaw as a "son" and "friend" who boldly defended Germany once he could gauge the lies directed against her. It was published on 26 July 1916 in *Neue Freie Presse* and badly translated in *Westminster Gazette* on 2 August 1916 ("Curious 'Tribute' to 'G. B. S.'").

3. The horrors of the Allied blockade were known to Shaw through Lina Richter's *Family Life in Germany under the Blockade*, issued that month with a preface by Shaw.

4. Shaw presumably means that Trebitsch was to retain Shaw's royalties for his own needs.

5. "Joy Riding at the Front," *Daily Chronicle*, 5, 7, 8 March 1917 (also with different heading in *New York American*, 25 March, 1, 8 April).

6. Baur au Lac was a first-class hotel in Zurich, where the Trebitsches were on holiday.

Parknasilla. Kenmare
4th August 1919
My dear Trebitsch

I have now at last received quite definite instructions from the Board of Trade as to my relations with Germany and Austria; and it is of the greatest importance that I should carry them out strictly. My head is in the lion's mouth; and I shall give him no excuse for snapping his jaws.

1. I may enter into *new* arrangements with persons in Germany and Austria for the performance and publication of my works in those countries.

2. Debts due to me by persons, firms, or companies *in Austria* may be received by me.

3. I may not receive debts due to me by Germans resident in Germany (Fischer z.b.) in respect of pre-war transactions or contracts, as these must be dealt with in the Clearing House scheme, which means, I suppose, that they must all be collected by the Allied Governments and redistributed by them to the individual creditors pro-rata.

I received from you a Post Office Order for £17 in an envelope without a letter. A few days before I received your letter saying that you were sending me 750f. But the exchange with Switzerland is about 24.50 = £1; so I expected only £15.[1] I can only say, with Cyrano, "Quelle geste!" But to send me money thus punctiliously is to treat me as an enemy. Do not be so haughty: spend my money: *steal* it: do anything you like with it as if it were your own until you are in easy circumstances once more.

I greatly doubt whether the Tetralogy will be played either on the English or the German stage. Still, one never knows. It is called Back to Methuselah. But I told you all about it, did I not? The length of the plays is the main difficulty. They are not the right length for a theatrical performance. Two of them would make the evening too long, one of them too short.

Is Germany too royalist still to stand The Inca of Perusalem? Here several people wanted to hang me for flattering that monster, that murderer, that Nero, Attila, submarine, superzeppelin archfiend! At present of course it would be impossible as long as he is threatened with a trial in London, a folly against which I have levelled all my powers of ridicule & invective.[2] But later on I can conceive a state of things in which the play would be as harmless (and as obsolete) as the old jokes in Simplicissimus.

As to Augustus being English, surely you had plenty of Augustuses in Berlin and Vienna.

However, none of these trifles is worth translating.[3]

Granville Barker fell in love with the wife of an American millionaire in New York. His wife had to divorce him; and the millionaire had to divorce *his* wife. So now the two are happily married, and living at 12 Hyde Park Place, London W.2.[4]

I must stop now, as communication is so slow that I must not miss the courier. Our love to you both.

G.B.S.

Als.

1. Shaw's figures, exchange rate, and arithmetic are faulty: Trebitsch remitted the value of 450 francs, about £17, from the Swiss publisher Max Rascher for *Common Sense*, finally issued in German, and a pending volume of Shaw's prewar essays: *Die Geliebte Shakespeares und andere Essays* (1920).

2. Shaw campaigned against demands to "Hang the Kaiser" ("What to Do with the Kaiser," *Sunday Evening Telegram*, 6 July).

3. Trebitsch did not publish Shaw's war playlets.

4. Barker divorced Lillah McCarthy and married Helen Huntington, former wife of A. M. Huntington, American railway scion. Mrs. Huntington, angered by Shaw's attempts to reconcile Lillah and Barker, effected an estrangement of the old friends.

Parknasilla. Kenmare
22nd August 1919

My dear Trebitsch

. . . I enclose an article from The Nation, edited by my friend H. W. Massingham. It could hardly be stronger if it were written for a Viennese paper.[1] The difficulty about the coal is that we here, in the classic coal country, victorious and triumphant, are paying enormous prices for coal, and are threatened with a coal famine next winter. Our miners strike; get larger wages; strike again; get still larger wages and shorter hours; and the price not only of coal, but of everything that depends on coal, goes up with leaps and bounds. The Conservatives think it right that the enemy should freeze; and the Liberals clamor for Free Imports, which means freedom to English people to buy up all the food and fuel in the world and leave the others to starve. My taxation for war alone is six shillings in every pound up to two thousand, and ten and sixpence after that. Money is depreciated to less than half its value; and prices are much higher than even the depreciation accounts for. I pay American Income Tax as well. The Chancellor of The Exchequer admits that we are bankrupt: his "Victory Loan" was a failure. Everybody expects a ruinous crash next year; and consequently everybody is spending recklessly whilst there is anything left to spend, crying "Let us eat and drink; for tomorrow we die." And this, if you please, is Success, Conquest, Deathless Heroism &c &c. The serious side of it is that we are too poor to be generous. If I plead for coal for Vienna, people say "I sat all last winter in my overcoat; and my wife died of pneumonia." However, like The Nation, the decent men & women go on pleading; and Hoover goes on warning;[2] and nothing is done.

As to Potsdamnation, I *meant* it.[3] I never believed in the effectiveness of the Prussian military system. I was more afraid of the easygoing Austrian system than of the Potsdam system. From the moment when the Germans attacked Liège (which they should have reduced in three hours in order to win the war) with regiments at peace strength and without siege guns, and took eleven days to capture all the forts after borrowing guns from Austria, I knew that the Kaiser's preparations were as delusive as Napoleon III's in 1870, and that he had already lost the war. It was quite literally a case of Potsdamnation. You must remember that I am a Socialist, and the sworn enemy of Junkerthum, both English and German. The only statesman left in Europe who interests me is Lenin. Besides, my own position was a difficult one. When the German papers were denouncing me as a Vaterlandslose Geselle [man without a country], the English papers were denouncing me as a pro-German, a traitor, and deuce knows what not! The German Junkers can hardly complain that I did not flatter them when I was equally unsparing of our British Junkers. In fact I criticized the British Junkers much more freely than the Germans. If my Common Sense About The War, published in Nov. 1914 under a heavy fire of Chauvinism, had been fully translated in Germany, it would have been clear that "Potsdamnation" was a very mild scrap of Majestätsbeleidigung addressed to the military and diplomatic entourage of the Kaiser, and was a reproach to the German people only for not having overthrown the militarist system, as they have done since. This system was never popular in Germany, and was endured only because its military efficiency made the Germans feel secure and respected. My contention was that the security was a delusion, and that the respect was fear, which always means hatred. Germany & Austria ought to have been invincible and impregnable, self-supporting economically and fully equipped militarily. But under the Kaiser's system Germany had become helplessly dependent on imports; and the invasion of Brussels & France was bungled and badly prepared, bungled at Liège, delayed at Antwerp by wrong information about phantom forces, and very badly bungled indeed by Von Kluck,[4] who rushed on actually without provisions. By the time the commanders who had attained their position by flattering the Kaiser were all relegated to the dust bin by the stern realities of war, it was too late: the war was lost by Germany. And in any case the blockade and the hostility which the Kaiser had provoked all over the world would have beaten Germany in the long run when the first rush on Paris had failed. These autocratic systems are imposing in theory, and make a fine show on parade; but they gradually push out the able and honest men and promote the courtiers and humbugs, who become the mere puppets of the commercial brigands; and the end is Smash. Exactly the same thing will happen to England if she is not very careful and very lucky.

The performance of John Bull was a silly mistake.[5] The play cannot succeed unless Tom Broadbent is popular and genial in spite of his absurdities. You might as well produce Le Bourgeois Gentilhomme with a melodramatic villain as the hero. But in any case, would anyone but a theatre manager be such a simpleton as to imagine that he could make a success of an enemy play before the war was over? Why, in 1915, the London Times was inserting letters denouncing Goethe—actually Goethe!—as a bad man and a worse poet. As to Nietzsche, he was a Prussian whose works were the favorite reading of Wilhelm-Attila.

As to Vol V of the Gesamtausgabe [collected edition], the publishers must be mad to cram three such prefaces and three such plays into one volume.[6] The readers will die of indigestion. I do not think John Bull's Other Island would be either uninteresting or specially unpopular in print, mainly because of the preface on the Irish question. That preface has been very largely quoted *partially*: it ought to be published *in extenso*. However, if Fischer insists on overloading his volumes, the Big Three had better be called Comedies of Science and Religion or something of that sort; for there are no neue Menschen [New Men] in them; and though Barbara and Lavinia are a bit gesteigertes [advanced] two swallows do not make a summer.

By the way, if you or Fischer send me money due in 1914, it will do me no good, as the Board of Trade will get every penny of it. Better wait.

The Gesamtausgabe is a colossal achievement for you & me; but what about your own plays? You have not sent me one for five years. You are becoming famous as a playwright, are you not.[7]

I must break off, as I have to pack for my departure.

G.B.S.

Als.

1. The lead article in the *Nation* (16 August) condemned the harsh terms imposed on Austria.
2. Herbert Hoover (1874–1964), director of European relief and future American president, denounced the blockade and warned against Europe's dependency on America (*Times*, 13 August).
3. The recent German edition of *Common Sense* (approved but not translated by Trebitsch) led Trebitsch to question Shaw on German militarism ("Potsdamnation").
4. Alexander von Kluck (1846–1934), German general.
5. On 20 January 1917, Barnowsky premiered *John Bull* at the Lessing-Theater, as anti-British satire, with a Prologue drawn from the preface and stage directions. But the intent backfired when the audience applauded the smug Englishman, Broadbent, addressing the Irish. Critics, excepting Alfred Kerr, found the production inopportune, and it was withdrawn after four nights.
6. The new edition of Shaw's *Dramatische Werke* (1919–21) added *Man and Superman* and a volume entitled *Komödien des Glaubens* (Comedies of Religion), consisting of *Major Barbara*, *Doctor's Dilemma*, and *Androcles*. The preface to *Androcles* was omitted and issued separately in 1925 (*Die Aussichten des Christentums*).
7. Trebitsch had written little during the war; his latest work was a play called *Frau Gittas Sühne* (Gitta's Atonement).

10 Adelphi Terrace W.C.
10th December 1919

My dear Trebitsch

The letter of which I enclose a copy has only just reached me. I waited for it before answering your letters. There is, I am afraid, very little comfort in it. The Lady Scott to whom it is addressed is the widow of Captain Scott who died on his trip back from the South Pole. She is a friend of mine and a friend of Cunninghame's; and I sent her a very strongly worded description of your services to English literature and asked her to send it on to Cunninghame with her good word. This letter is the result.[1] Possibly if you wrote to C. mentioning Lady Scott's name, and asking for an interview, he might see you and tell you anything that there is to be told.

In this country people are simply bored when they are told that Europe is starving. They know it and feel uncomfortable about it; but they can do nothing. Long before the armistice I and others warned the Government that unless Europe was rationed after the war, the rich countries would buy up all the food and fuel and leave the others nothing; but our statesmen had neither the ability nor the courage to grapple with the problem; and now we go on buying up everything, or exporting coal at colossal prices, with quiet selfishness. The victims are too far off to trouble us much.

Your letters sometimes come quickly, and sometimes three weeks after their date. What I have said above is the answer to your letter of the 20th September. It has taken all this time to get anything done.

Now as to your letter of the 3rd November. No doubt the credit of my reception at the Burgtheater is due to you, and not to Franz Joseph; but if I had said so, it would have quite spoilt my point. The Burgtheater is a public institution; and Franz Joseph used to represent the public. Schlenther told me that the theatre was part of the emperor's household and that I must not presume to bargain with the Emperor over the agreement. I told Schlenther that F. J. was only Emperor of Austria-Hungary, whilst I was, dramatically speaking Emperor of Europe, and that my terms were *à prendre ou à laisser*. So the poor fellow made no agreement at all. Thus I am able to reproach the British Empire with the inferiority of its culture to Austria, because though the king keeps racehorses he does not keep a theatre, and because we have no municipal theatres of any kind. The fact that you had a great deal of trouble in imposing me on Schlenther, and had to sacrifice your own interest to succeed, is one which I quite appreciate; but it does not excuse British barbarism. After all, if it was hard for you to get my plays into the Burg, at least the Burg was there for you to get them into, and you succeeded at last; whereas in England you could not possibly have succeeded because there is no Burgtheater in existence, or anything like it. Franz Joseph is therefore a very good stick to beat the English with; and I lay it on accordingly. A tribute to your devotion would not have produced the smallest effect on them.

As to the old story about the translations, the author of the paragraph is quite right as to his facts, though not as to the complexion he has put on them. I used to say that to all the Germans who began talking to me about your translations. I say it still to all foreigners who begin the same tale. It is always the same song: Trebitsch, Vallentin, Brouta, Hevesi, Hamon, Agresti are all infamous impostors: how can I possibly allow my works to be so horribly misrepresented? I always cut this sort of thing short exactly as the Viennese journalist describes, by saying "I know what you are going to tell me. I have heard it all before. Every living German thinks that he, and he alone, should translate my plays; and therefore every living German agrees that Trebitsch's translations are atrocious. No doubt they are not translations at all. He writes original plays, and puts my name to them. But as they seem to please the German public, and make money for me, I let him have his own way." I cannot argue with a German about his own language; and so I make fun of it. . . .

You may tell the Burgtheater that Heartbreak House will not be available until they have produced Frau Gitta.[2] As they will not accept a sentimental reason for this, you had better say that it is important to me that the translation of my play should be by a playwright of the first importance. . . .

Tomorrow night Arms and The Man is to be revived at the Duke of York's Theatre with [Robert] Loraine as Bluntschli. I am worn out with the rehearsals. Now that everyone has had a taste of military service the play will for the first time have a chance of complete success or furious failure.

I wish I could feel sure that you were as warm and well fed as I am; and yet it is abominably cold here. Take such care of yourself as is possible under the circumstances.

Auf wiedersehen
G. Bernard Shaw

Tls.

1. Lady Kathleen Scott, later Lady Kennet (1878–1947), sculptress, widow of the Antarctic explorer Captain Robert Falcon Scott, was involved in aid for Austria. At Shaw's request, she wrote to Sir Thomas Cuninghame, the British Military Representative in Vienna, on Trebitsch's behalf. Cuninghame's response (a copy of which Shaw enclosed) was that he would see the "food people," but that there was little that could be done.

2. Shaw's suggestion (at Trebitsch's hint?) that production of *Heartbreak House* be conditional upon the Burg's producing Trebitsch's *Frau Gittas Sühne* bore fruit. *Gitta* opened at the Burg on 3 February 1920 for a brief run of seven performances. *Heartbreak House* opened the following season (16 November 1920) after the Burg, no longer under conservative court control, moved rapidly to restore Shaw by staging *Candida* and reviving *Pygmalion*, both in 1919.

10 Adelphi Terrace W.C.
12th December 1919

My dear Trebitsch

Fischer has not sent the volumes [of the collected edition]: at least if he has, they have not yet reached me. I sent you a registered letter yesterday, which you have no doubt received by this time. This morning the packet of notes arrived from Professor Ferrière.[1] By the same post came your letter of the 30th.

I wish you had kept the money: it would have been much more useful to me keeping you alive than lying unused in my bank waiting for the exchange to improve. Oh, die Ehre [Honor], die Ehre!

The revival of Arms and The Man seems to have been a great success.[2] I was not present, as I had to address a political meeting elsewhere. It has taken a European war to make the critics and the public understand the play.

As I have opened an account with the Anglo-Oesterreichischen Bank in Budapest, I am sending the 17,276 Kronen there. They allow me 2% interest; and I may as well lodge the notes there as hoard them in my own cashbox. I should have told you all this before, and saved you the trouble of making use of Dr Ferrière.

ever
G. Bernard Shaw

Tls.

1. Trebitsch had remitted through a Swiss friend, Dr. Louis Ferrière, accumulated royalties of over 17,000 kronen and 100 marks, which had declined to a mere £22. Dr. Ferrière was in charge of food aid in Austria by the Red Cross and lived as Trebitsch's house guest.

2. The performance on 11 December at the Duke of York's was greeted with "prolonged applause" (*Daily Telegraph*, 12 December) and favorable notices. Several reviews noted that the war lent new pertinence to the play, which ran eight weeks.

10 Adelphi Terrace W.C.

15th January 1920

My dear Trebitsch

. . . It is stated in the English papers that a tax of 57% on capital has been established in Vienna. I enclose a proof of an article of mine on that subject, which Die Neue Freie Presse might be glad to have from you.[1] I cannot give the figures for Austria; but the argument applies *a fortiori*, as England is richer than Austria; and there is the further interesting point that it comes, not from a reactionary, but from an avowed Socialist, Communist, Bolshevik &c. &c. As I have no other copy, will you send me back the proof when you have done with it.

A great sensation has been made here by Professor [J. M.] Keynes of Cambridge, who was at Versailles as economic expert, and resigned that position and came home as a protest against the peace terms. He has now published a book [*Economic Consequences of the Peace*] in which he demonstrates that the indemnity demanded from Germany is an economic impossibility; and nobody ventures to dispute this.

We have an uneasy conscience here about Vienna. A Sunday collection was made the other day for the Viennese children in all English Churches. In our tiny little village in Hertfordshire the collection was the biggest ever known. It was not all made in the Church. My neighbor Cherry Garrard, famous as an Antarctic explorer,[2] does not go to Church; but he offered to double the collection. Then I doubled the total; and the rector was able to challenge the others to keep up the game. But of course these collections are a drop in the ocean; and those of us who are capable of understanding the situation are horribly afraid that the war has destroyed the machinery necessary to feed Europe.

By the way, in the matter of Cunninghame and Lady Scott, I acted with the most careful regard to your dignity. I did not present your case as that of a starving man, but simply as that of one who had rendered distinguished service to English literature, and had safeguarded the interests of British authors. The suggestion was that if there were any facilities available for privileged persons it would be a graceful act to extend them to you.

The Neue Freie Presse has got me into a terrible row here by printing portions of the preface to Heartbreak House as if they were an article specially contributed by me to "the enemy press." All the papers here quoted it with flaming headlines; and for a whole week I was execrated by the Chauvinists as a traitor. Of course the laugh was on my side when I explained that they had all been quoting a book which they reviewed at great length a few months ago, and that it was a pity that political journalists never read books, and literary journalists never wrote political articles.[3] But my explanation

was naturally not reproduced by the papers which had made fools of themselves; and the incident did me much more harm than good.

By the way I may now tell you that one of the reasons why I had to stop
writing to you rather abruptly during the war was that Die Neue Freie Presse
printed something about my devotion to Germany which very nearly got me
shot.[4] I had official friends who warned me privately that I must stop writing
to Austria at all hazards.

ever

G. Bernard Shaw

Tls.

1. The Austrian government proposed a steeply graduated tax on capital, something Shaw had
argued in "The Economics of Bedlam" (*Daily News*, 15 November 1919) was not possible. Trebitsch's version appeared in *Neue Freie Presse* on 1 February ("Die einmalige Vermögensabgabe").

2. Apsley Cherry-Garrard (1886–1959) was a member of Scott's expedition.

3. On 25 December 1919, the *Neue Freie Presse* published two excerpts (both bitingly critical of
the English) from Shaw's preface to *Heartbreak House* ("The Rabid Watchdogs of Liberty" and
"The Next Phase") as "Die nächste Entwicklung," without mentioning the source and thus leaving the impression that it was newly written for a German paper. Shaw's response to the resulting
attacks appeared in the *Observer* (4 January).

4. Shaw is referring to Trebitsch's birthday paragraph of July 1916. See Shaw's letter of 20 July
1919.

10 Adelphi Terrace W.C.

26th February 1920

My dear Trebitsch

Your request for "a little article on the reconstruction of the world" for the
Tagblatt is very flattering to me; but do you really think I can settle the fate
of Europe with half a dozen scratches of my pen? It would take me about two
months to produce anything but twaddle on such a subject.

Do not let the Deri incident worry you.[1] Deri thoroughly understood the
situation; and my Machiavellian letter amused him very much. But I am a
little anxious about that letter, all the same. It is quite safe for *me*; and if the
authorities are complaisant it may effect its purpose. But if they are not, and
insist on investigating the case *au fond*, Herself may be placed in a very difficult situation. (By the way, "Herself" is peasant Irish for the mistress of the
house, and Himself for the master; and I use it because I do not know whether
Frau Tina is polite, and feel that Madame Trebitsch is too distant to express
my feeling). It is, as you say, not easy to make a lady understand exactly
where it is necessary to draw the line in resisting what she knows to be an
unbearable injustice; but it is one thing to trifle with passports and ration
cards, and police regulations, and another thing [passage canceled by Tre-
bitsch]. However, you know this as well as I do, and will act accordingly—if
Herself is controllable.

I enclose receipt for the money; but you are wasting these Austrian notes
on me: I cant cash them. Fischer proposes to open an account for me at
the Deutschen Bank in Berlin; and I already have one opened at the Austro-
Hungarian Bank in Budapest. Why not send your Austrian notes there if
your confounded punctiliousness obliges you to deprive yourself of money
which you could use for the sake of giving me money that I cannot use? Of

course I could get a penny or even three halfpence for each korona if I were starving; but I am still able to keep two houses and a motor car. It would be a crime to make the smallest draft on Austria or even Germany under such circumstances.

I send this to Vienna, but presume you are in Berlin. If Frau Gitta's Transgression gets printed, send me a copy.[2]

ever

G. Bernard Shaw

Tls.

1. Hermann Deri, Viennese exporter, apparently interceded between Tina Trebitsch and Shaw in getting some of Tina's valuables out of Austria and safe from the tax collectors.

2. Trebitsch's play *Frau Gittas Sühne* was published that year by S. Fischer. By confounding the word *Sühne* with *Sünde*, Shaw mistranslates the title as Gitta's "Transgression" instead of "Atonement."

[Ayot St Lawrence. Welwyn]
26th May 1920

I have read Gitta, though most of your words are not in the dictionary. And I am waiting for a moment when I can write to you. Be patient: I am not wasting my time; and when Methuselah is finished I shall write fully. Gitta might suit Mrs Minnie Maddern Fiske.[1]

GBS

Ans.

1. Minnie Maddern Fiske (1865–1932), leading American actress, known for her performances of Ibsen.

Parknasilla. Kenmare
15th September 1920

My dear Trebitsch

I have been here on the Irish coast since the 19th July, working like ten negroes at my *magnum opus* Back to Methuselah. At last I have sent the entire work (five plays and a colossal preface) to the printer; and I can now turn to your letters and answer them.

However, I have not been neglecting you wholly. From time to time, when I had a spare moment in the evening, I devoted it to you by translating scraps of Gitta; and I am sending a complete English version of the first act to my secretary to type out from my shorthand notes. I do not know what you will say to it; but it will amuse you anyhow; and you can decide whether I am capable of finishing it. The difficulty has been partly that I do not know German, and mainly that apparently you do not know it either; for not one of your words could I find in the little pocket dictionary I travelled with (you have invented a language of your own) and I had to guess what it was all about by mere instinct. It is therefore possible that you may find the whole thing absurdly wrong from beginning to end. I have made some changes purposely because I have had to substitute things that the British and American actresses can do for the things that the experts of the Burgtheater can do. You have to give an English actress "business" and words all through. She can do the business; and she can speak the words if you suggest the proper tone to her; but there is no use asking her to convey by pure expression of face and plastique all that you ask the actress for at the end of the act: the scene would be unintelligible on the London stage as it stands. Consequently I have had to make it easier than you have made it. I hope my tricks wont make you furious. Also, it will disgust you to find Gitta called Jitta; but nothing else would prevent her being called Ghitta. I dont know what Sühne means: it isnt in the dictionary; so I have called the translation provisionally Jitta's Atonement, though it may be that I should have called it Jitta Expiates. If you think my version of the first act possible, I shall go on to the end and see whether it would tempt some star actress.

I was horribly tempted to make Haldenstedt sit up after Gitta's departure, and make a comedy of the sequel; but I shall resist all such temptations for the sake of trying my hand on a genuine Trebitsch play.[1]

Now as to your letters. They go back to the 1st May. You speak of "the Burg where next October Heartbreak House, wonderfully cast and produced, will reach the footlights." Ha! ha! Well, I will enclose with this a separate letter to you, a translation of which you must send to Director Albert Heine.[2] As you say Back to Methuselah is my Ring; but I cannot send you the plays by degrees because it is only within the last two months here at the seaside that I have reduced them to their final form. As to translating them, wait until you read them: you are not likely to be troubled by an application from Bayreuth; and the Burg will hardly devote five nights to them . . .[3] Cromwell has now been written by John Drinkwater: I have given him up.[4]

14th May. I dont know what to do about your friend's Shakespear article. No editor will now countenance the German claim to *unser J'expire*. To get over this difficulty at present the article should be as important as Einstein on Relativity; and, alas!, it *isnt*. You must tell Dr Kraus[5] that the moment is not propitious. Also, I am a very bad introducer for an article; for what the editors want from me is an article *by* me; and it infuriates them when I try to put them off with a substitute.

28th May. Haus Herzenstock should be Haus Herzzerreissen. Heartbreak is a chronic complaint, not a sudden shock.[6] But I doubt whether there exists any German equivalent for heartbreak. A disappointment in love is called a broken heart. Carlyle said that Free Trade was "heartbreaking nonsense"; and there are lots of gradations between these extremes; but usually the word implies deep pathos in the affliction it describes. . . . *Did* you go to Franzensbad[7] for steel baths? Utter humbug, all these cures.

22nd June. Sympathy concerning my sister.[8] Why does everybody assume that I was devoted to her, though when she was alive nobody ever asked me how she was. I saw her at intervals of months—sometimes many months. She was never at Adelphi Terrace in her life. It was by chance that I was with her when she died. As she left a will to say that there was to be no funeral, no flowers, no mourning, and as, nevertheless, several people turned up at the crematorium, I had to improvise a sort of funeral service of my own in the shape of an oration, as it was really impossible to throw her into the furnace like a scuttle of coals. What killed her was the war: her tuberculosis had stopped. But there was an aircraft gun quite close to her house on the southern heights, and during the air raids this gun shook and shattered everything near it. All the other guns were going too, varied only by the crash of the bombs. I dont know whether you had this experience in Vienna; but London had a great deal of it; and it was very unpleasant, and got worse as it went on. At first people were excited and curious; but when that passed, and they saw what the bombs could do to them, there was nothing but sheer funk. I was not a bit frightened in Ypres or Arras; but in London, though I was too lazy to get out of bed and take refuge in an underground shelter, and dropped off to sleep between each burst of firing, my heart tightened in the most disagreeable manner in spite of all arguments as to the uselessness of bothering about it. Well, Lucy had to leave London; but it was too late: she could not eat, and died of slow starvation. And—here is a dramatic contrast which I exploited in the funeral oration—whilst the German aces were doing their best to kill her she was kept alive by the devotion of her German nurse.[9]

[Section cut out.]

23rd July. You say I have 85,000M. with Fischer. At the present rate of exchange this amounts to a couple of shillings less than £436, the interest on which is more than £20 a year. Naturally I want either to invest this in some German industrial concern or place it on deposit account (interest bearing account) in a Berlin bank. You object on the ground that it will be taxed. But will it? I am not a German citizen; and it is a simple debt due to me. It seems ridiculous to leave things as they are. I already have a bundle of blue Marks in my bank here, quite useless; and if I had an account with a Berlin bank I could place them there at interest.

5th Sept. The Kr.3275 (which I shall have to declare for taxation here as £4 or thereabouts) I shall send to the Austro-Hungarian Bank to await the resurrection of the valuta [exchange value]. There is a very poor German lady here who brings me Marks and makes me cash them for shillings. Her brother, a German officer, sends her the Marks. She buys things for him in London for 3d that cost 2M.5opf in Hamburg. Those things are imported from Germany! . . . . . I think this is all. I will now add the formal letter for exhibition to Director Heine. My wife sends all sorts of messages to you both. By the way, Miss Murray, the daughter of Gilbert Murray,[10] who is in Vienna doing relief work (16 Singerstr.) wrote to me that Moissi was ill and destitute. I sent her £10 for the fund she was collecting for him. She then sent it back and said it was a false alarm, as he has plenty of money and is acting vigorously. But she gave me a harrowing account of the economic situation in Vienna. I picture you and Tina eating your boots. Is it very bad?

ever

G.B.S.

Als.

1. *Gitta* concerns the illicit love of Gitta (pronounced, in fact, with a hard "g") Lenkheim for Professor Bruno Haldenstedt, and the consequences that ensue after Bruno dies and Gitta's hus-

band learns about the affair. Shaw's trial first act introduced light touches and elaborated the stage directions: the trysting flat is erotic, and the "noble almost tragic" Gitta becomes a commonplace woman. In the original play, Bruno drops dead as he is drawn toward the bedroom; and Gitta sobs beside the body before rushing out to avoid a scandal. In Shaw's version, the partly undressed Jitta discovers her dead lover, dashes into the bedroom to retrieve her blouse, and leaves. A touch of remorse brings her back to place flowers on the corpse, but remembering that a dead man "cannot scatter flowers on himself" she makes the sign of the cross and flees.

2. Albert Heine (1867–1949), director of the Burg since 1918.

3. The ellipses in this letter are Shaw's.

4. Shaw had long considered a play on Cromwell. John Drinkwater (1882–1937), poet-playwright and a founder of the Birmingham Repertory Theatre, wrote popular chronicle plays.

5. Karl Kraus (1874–1936), noted Viennese satirist, editor, author, and Shakespeare devotee.

6. Trebitsch's title for *Heartbreak House* was *Haus Herzenstod*, which Shaw misread as *Herzenstock* (a non-word) and interpreted as heart failure.

7. A Czech spa, whose waters contained iron.

8. Shaw's only surviving older sister, Lucy, died on 27 March 1920.

9. Lucy Shaw's housekeeper-companion was Eva Maria Schneider, to whom Shaw left an annuity in his will for "devoted service to my sister."

10. Gilbert Murray (1866–1957), distinguished classical scholar and model for Cusins in *Major Barbara*. His younger daughter, Agnes, died in 1923.

[Parknasilla. Kenmare]
My dear Trebitsch[1] 16th September 1920

I was greatly touched by your promise of a production of Heartbreak House at the Burg, "wonderfully cast and produced." I must, however, warn you not to be too sanguine, and even to prepare for a complete disappointment. It would be much easier to secure the right cast in London than at the Burg, not because our actors are better, but because they are chosen solely with a view to their fitness for the parts, and engaged at high salaries for the run of the piece only. All this is changed when you transfer the play to theatres where there is a permanent company playing repertory. In such a company there is an etiquette which governs the distribution of the parts; and the more famous the theatre, the stricter the etiquette, the ci-devant Imperial theatres being the strictest of all. According to this etiquette the company consists of a Juvenile Lead (Erster Liebhaber?) and Ingenue, first and second Light Comedians and Singing Chambermaids (Soubrettes), first and second Low Comedians, Heavies (both sexes, for villainy, tragedy, blood & thunder &c), père noble & père bourgeois or first and second Old Man and Old Woman, Walking Gentlemen, Walking Ladies, and Utilities. These are the names which survive here from the traditions of the XVIII century; but the divisions, under whatever names, always exist in a stock company. And they must exist at the Burg.

Now what will happen? Just as I, in London, would say to the manager, "I must have Mrs Patrick Campbell for Hesione and Miss Ellen O'Malley for Ellie," you will go gaily to the Burg Director and say "I want Frau So & So for Hesione and Fraulein So & So for Ellie," selecting them because they have the right personalities and will give the right color & atmosphere to the parts. But the Director will hold up his hands in horror and exclaim "Impossible, my dear sir. Hesione is the Heavy Lead; and therefore it must be allotted to our Heavy Lead Frau Grimmigen [Mrs. Grim], whose Lady

Macbeth you admire so much. Ellie is the Juvenile Lead, and as such belongs to Fraulein Schönaugen [Miss Pretty-Eyes], whose success as Fedora and Froufrou and Magda² have given her a position which it is impossible for you to ignore." You will reply in despair "But, good God! Ellie must be utterly virginal and Hesione utterly voluptuous. Fraulein Schönaugen is forty; and if Frau Grimmigen (who must be fiftyfive if she's a day) is to look twenty years older than her she will have to look sixty and make the whole play ridiculous, as the scenes in which she fascinates Mangan will be turned into kitchen farce." But the Director's life will be easier if he quarrels with you and makes the play a failure than if he quarrels with his company. He will say, "Herr Trebitsch: I stand here to preserve the sacred traditions of the Burg Theater and of the Apostolic Empire under which it became great, and which will be restored as soon as the present revolutionary madness has passed. Bernard Shaw is a Bolshevik; and you will pardon my saying that you are very little better or you would not stain your pen by translating the infamies which a depraved public taste obliges me to produce here. But they shall be produced in the Imperial manner, not in the Bolshavian-Trebitschesque manner. H. H. may fail: I trust it will: it deserves to fail; but its chances will not be improved by anarchic methods of production. It will be cast by me, not by you. If the dialogue is unsuitable to the cast, it will be rewritten by the call boy, whose competence is unquestionable, as his uncle has had a farce performed with success in a leading beer cellar. If these arrangements displease you, we shall be very happy to dispense with your attendance at the rehearsals. Good morning."

You will be quite helpless in the face of this official attitude, as you must not, in your own interest, quarrel with the Burg. I am equally helpless. It is true that I can do without the Burg as easily as it can do without me; but if the play fails—as I fear it must—I cannot prove that it is not a failure on its merits: at least not until the productions in New York, Stockholm & Berlin enable me to judge whether the conditions or the play are at fault. But I shall not quarrel with the Burg anyhow. I have a great deal of sympathy with the repertory system, having suffered so much from the defects of the London system. Most of my plays will stand any sort of casting if the company is a good one and the direction reasonably artistic. I should be ashamed of my workmanship if they would not. But H. H. is a peculiar play, as dependent on atmosphere and on subtleties of personality in the performers as any of Tchekov's. Therefore the Burg system *may* smash it. I am quite prepared for that; and I want you to be prepared too. So do not be angry with them if the worst happens: they mean well; and it is very difficult to make what the artists will feel to be an unfair distribution of roles.

ever

G. Bernard Shaw

Als.

1. This letter was enclosed with the letter of 15 September 1920 and was intended for Director Heine.

2. Popular star roles in plays by Sardou, Meilhac & Halévy, and Sudermann.

Ayot St Lawrence. Welwyn
28th September 1920

My dear Trebitsch

The enclosed is a rough draft [of *Jitta's Atonement*, Act I]. There is no use getting it properly typed until you have corrected it. Charlotte says I have made it brutally realistic; but this is an unintended result of making the stage business more explicit for the sake of the actress; for, as I explained in my last letter, you must give our people something to do or to say: it is no use leaving it to them to express what you mean. The stock joke of the London stage is a fabulous stage direction "Sir Henry turns his back to the audience and conveys that he has a son at Harrow." However, you may be able to think of something nicer than I have suggested.

One of my suggestions is that Jitta should cross herself and the body at the end. This would be much more effective (ironically) if in the course of the previous scene she had said something to indicate that she was a sceptic. She could reproach him not only with bourgeois morality but with an attack of Christianity.

I have confined myself in furnishing the room to the things actually used by the actors. The British "property master" would not understand being ordered to provide a tea set when nobody has any tea. Also, I have introduced a tray with a siphon, as you instructed poor Mrs Billiter to produce a glass of water out of nothing by a conjuring trick.

Do not hesitate to tear the thing up if it is impossible. But dont tear it up merely because it is disappointing. Any translation you get will be that. I should even say that you were not likely to get anything much better if it were not that I must admit that it might be an advantage for the translator to know the language the piece is written in.

It may be that you have already made a contract with some English or American translator. In that case there is no harm done: just chuck my effort into the waste paper basket.

ever

G. Bernard Shaw

Tls.

[Trebitsch to Shaw]

Wien
1st October 1920

My dearest Shaw

Since I have met you 1914, I had the first great joy this morning, when your version of "Yittas[1] Atonement" reached me. It is much better than the original and I beg you by all means to continue and finish your version. The end of the act is grand and proves again your stage-genious. But please do put your name on the version, nobody will produce, without that important name, a play from a german author!

I was so free to write at page 3, 5 and 23 some remarks, more or less important. The last-will affair is much clearer convincing and better with you. I feel a childish delight reading Trebitsch in English. Of course I am not bound at all to no sort of translater. Please handle that play like your own. With thousand thanks again and again

Yours ever
Siegfried Trebitsch

Als.; Texas.

1. Trebitsch alters Shaw's "Jitta" to "Yitta" to accord with its German pronunciation. (German "j" equals English "y.") "Jitta" pronounced with an English "j" would not be a German name.

10 Adelphi Terrace W.C.
13th November 1920

. . . You are frightfully mistaken about Methuselah. It is true that the manuscript is all at the printers; but the proofs are not corrected yet. And do you think I have nothing else to do but finish Methuselah? It will be months and months before I have time to write you a proper letter: I am scrawling this in frantic haste.

Scenery is Naturschönheiten (this is just right), *not* Bühnengerät.[1]

I have done a little more of Gitta; but the translation will progress slowly until I have cleared off arrears of work.

An excellent interview with you has appeared here in The Observer, one of our leading Sunday papers, on the 7th ["The Vogue of G.B.S."].

I think I must get you to lodge my money in the Budapest bank; for with the valuta at 2000 Kr to the £, the notes are useless here. I will write further about this when I have gone into the matter.

G.B.S.

Apcs.

1. In *Heartbreak House* (Act II), Trebitsch carelessly translated "scenery" as "stage scenery" (*Bühnengerät*).

10 Adelphi Terrace W.C.
postmarked 29th November 1920

I have not yet seen Simon,[1] as the earliest date on which we could have him to lunch is next Friday. We intended to have him last Friday; but were prevented by having to entertain a lady who has learnt Jujetsu, and can throw a man over her head as easily as look at him. She happens to be also fiercely pro-Italian. So as I did not want to risk having Simon thrown over her head I put him off until the following week.[2]

The best way to build up civilization again would be to sink the countries which were victorious in the late war beneath the surface of the Atlantic for ten minutes. This would not spoil the machinery if it were quickly dried and oiled; and it would effectually remove all the obstructions to a resumption of those cordial relations without which civilization is impossible.

G. Bernard Shaw

Pcs.; in Blanche Patch's handwriting. Blanche Patch (1879–1966) was Shaw's secretary from 1920 till his death in 1950 (see Patch, *Thirty Years with G.B.S.*, 1951).
 1. Perhaps Josef Simon, Viennese banker, once part-owner of the Theater an der Wien, and brother-in-law of Johann Strauss.
 2. On Friday, 26 November, Shaw had lunch with Diana Watts (1867–1968), physical culturalist and dancer, who featured in one of her acts the lifting of a heavy man. She was the author of *The Fine Art of Jujutsu* (1906). As a "pro-Italian," she might be expected to share strong feelings against Austria.

10 Adelphi Terrace W.C.

15th January 1921

Quite a mockery to send me Kr 5000. Please lodge it to credit of my a/c with the Anglo-Austrian Bank, Budapest Branch, *alias* Anglo-Oesterreichischen Bank in Budapest, *alias* Angol-Osztrák Bank, Budapesti Fióktelepe. They allow me 2% interest, I think. But why not buy a cigarette with it?

Simon came to lunch, and helped to make up a very pleasant party. Deri I unfortunately missed, as I was in the country.

I have had to lay Yitta[1] aside until Methuselah is off my hands. I have had a great deal of business to do lately besides my professional work. My sister's death and the disposal of her house & property, the revision of my will in consequence, and a host of other worries, not to mention writing articles for the American papers to get ready money enough to pay my January taxes (nearly £4000!) have run me very hard; but when Methuselah is finally passed for press I will try to get Yitta under way again.

[GBS][2]

Apc.
 1. Shaw here adopts Trebitsch's spelling (see Trebitsch's letter of 1 October 1920).
 2. Signature cut off.

Ayot St Lawrence. Welwyn

2nd February 1921

My dear Trebitsch

I have taken all my foreign money to Barclays Bank (Central European Department); and accounts have now been opened in my name at the Deutsche Bank of Berlin, and the Wiener Bank Verein; so that in future you can lodge all Austrian money for me with the latter, and all German money with the former. I am writing to Fischer to lodge the money he holds for me with the Deutsche Bank. . . .

What really happened to H[eartbreak] H[ouse] at the Burg? I take it that the Kr16,780 are the author's fees—my half of them.[1] Fees of 33,560 kr, equal to £1398-6-8 at par, would be 10% on, say £14000, which would mean in London seven weeks splendid business and eight or nine weeks good business. What it means at the Burg I dont know. I should like to be able to say positively whether the play has been a real success in Vienna or not.[2]

I have written some literary reviews for America, and one set of three articles on Ireland and British Imperialism for which I got £1000. Is it worth your while to translate things like these?[3] I delivered a speech about the

Webbs' book; but the only thing I wrote about it was not about the book at all, but a personal note about the authors.[4]

I will send you the formal receipt tomorrow. This is only a line scrawled in great haste.

[ever

G. Bernard Shaw][5]

Al.

1. Shaw's fees from *Heartbreak House* at the Burg, valued at about £12, would have been a considerable sum before the war.

2. *Haus Herzenstod* (*Heartbreak House*), staged by Albert Heine, opened at the Burg on 16 November 1920, with Max Paulsen, Rosa Albach-Retty, and Maria Mayer, and ran only nine times. The *Arbeiter-Zeitung* (17 November) faulted the production, but others blamed the play, which the *Neue Freie Presse* found bewildering if wondrous. Audience response was divided, and the *Times* reported a "very poor reception."

3. Shaw's articles on Ireland, "The New Terrorism" (*N.Y. American*, 5, 12, 19, 26 December 1920), attacked English policy and anti-Sovietism and urged that the U.S., Germany, and Russia join to secure the peace. The articles were not translated into German.

4. On 3 December, Shaw spoke at King's Hall on the Webbs' *Constitution for the Socialist Commonwealth of Great Britain*; his review, "The Webb Constitution," appeared in the *Observer* (8 August 1920).

5. Closing and signature cut out.

10 Adelphi Terrace W.C.

17th March 1921

My dear Trebitsch

If you have not yet received the finally corrected sheets of Methuselah they may come any day, as the printer has instructions to send them the moment he can get the job done.

I now want to know exactly what the Burg people did with Heartbreak House. I have learned that they played it in four acts instead of in three. Did they cut out any of the dialogue? In America, a wellknown German producer was engaged for it. He immediately said that the play must be cut. Fortunately I heard this in time. I at once withdrew the play, and terrified them so effectually that they did not dare cut out a single comma. Result: the play ran for three and a half months drawing £200 eight times a week.[1] Heartbreak House is a very delicately balanced play: I cut it down to the last line myself before I printed it; and I know that any attempt to mutilate it means certain failure. So please tell me whether they cut it, and how much they cut it, and how they treated you in the matter; and then leave them to me and may God have mercy on their souls.

An American wrote to me the other day asking whether he should get you to translate a play. I told him of course that he could not find a better translator; but if the poor devil pays you in dollars and gets his tantièmes in Kronen, he will be ruined.

You asked me last September whether Mr Shaw of Geneva is an impostor. I never heard of him: who is he? At all events he is not this Mr Shaw.

Have you seen [Schnitzler's] Reigen; and what on earth is it all about? They tell me it is a play in eleven seductions.[2]

The first performance of Methuselah must be a complete one; so do not make any arrangements for separate performances. It will take three evenings and two matinées; so that there can be only two performances a week. The first will probably be in New York, at the same theatre as Heartbreak House.[3]

Our love to you and Tina.

ever,

G. Bernard Shaw

Tls.

1. *Heartbreak House*, produced by the Theatre Guild, had its American premiere in New York on 10 November 1920 and ran 125 times. Before the opening, the Guild sounded out Shaw, through his friend St. John Ervine, about cutting the play but relented. The "wellknown German producer" with the Theatre Guild was Emanuel Reicher (1849–1924), formerly of the Volksbühne, Berlin, but Dudley Digges directed *Heartbreak House*, not Reicher, who was replaced after the first rehearsals.

2. Arthur Schnitzler's sexual round dance in ten scenes, *Reigen* (*La Ronde*, 1903), long withheld from the stage, had opened in Vienna the previous month and was at first banned; in Berlin, where it had opened on 23 December 1920, the producers were tried but acquitted.

3. *Methuselah* opened first on 27 February 1922 at the Garrick Theatre, New York, produced by the Theatre Guild. The cycle was distributed over three successive weeks.

[Trebitsch to Shaw]

Wien

My dear Shaw   21st March 1921

I have written to you saturday, and I received your letter this morning. Here is my answer about the Burg people and Heartbreak House:

1. They did *not* cut a single line! not even a word.

2. As we remarked at the general rehearsal that the audience could not stand so much and so long deep arguing and speaking, without a little pause for breathing, we left the curtain down just for a few seconds at page 72 before Mrs. Hushabye is sitting down saying: "So Billy Dunn was poor nurse's little romance"—thats all.

As they all were in love with that play, they tried to force it on the public even after a very doubtful first night; but the last performance, (a wednesday) was so empty, that it had to be *the* last one. But as long as a certain Dr [Stephan] Hock is "dramaturg" at the Burg (managing almost everything) I shall not cross the threshhold of this house again. "Heartbreak-House" failed because of the impossible cast of the parts of the 2 ladies (Lady Utterw. and Mrs. H.) who were not at all fascinating. I protested in vain; this Dr. Hock answered crossly and rude in a way, I cannot allow to be spoken to; what he did was "terror" but art is not a Bolschewik-affair. I had at the rehearsals to fight for every sentence; he altered my versions, made horrible mistakes, and insulted me, when I protested him that he was wrong, for instance when I got your card saying that what I knew, "scenery" ment beautiful "nature" but never "theatre" etc. etc. I dont want to bother you with all these very bitter moments that infamous man created me. He did the meanest thing of the world: he reproached me errors, committed in my beginning and said, *therefore* I shall never be an authority in his eyes; but I realy *am* now, working quite differently now of course, than I did in the old young days......¹ Yes it is not always sweet to be your apostle.

Concerning your wishes about Methusaleh, which I have not yet in hand alas, I have been speaking here and in Berlin about the possibility of 3 evenings and two matinées. Well, they say that would ruin any theatre besides all the living authors would strike, being turned out during the run of your masterwork!! But we shall see, I always arrived *for you* at the end I wanted.

I really dont know who was Mr. Shaw of Geneva; he seems to be your Trebitsch-Lincoln some impostor.

Your American is very interesting and how funy that he is not the first one, longing to have me for his rotten business.

Do you know Charles Sumner Hayes of Chicago and his "play" The Natural Law? He wrote to me (a perfect Idealiste) that he should so much like to see his play adapted by me at Vienna! only for the sake of honour!!

As I want heaps of "Kronen," the money you refuse, proud to have a better one, I answered that I was willing to undertake the job for $600.—I shall even try, as he accepted the bargain, to place it at the right stage; but I shall explain him later that my name has not to be mentioned at the programm or in the press, as this would create literaric ideas, one should suggest a new G. B. S. or at least a new Oscar Wilde. My name belongs to your work and to mine. Under the same conditions I should accept also the proposal of *your* American. Who is he?

Schnitzler will send you his "Reigen" 10 scenes, 25 years old, very nice and inoffensives dialogues.

Now at last a very important question: The well known editor "Gustav Kiepenheuer" at Potsdam has bought your 3 novels from *Ledermann*, who published them years ago, without having an other right than the runing short of your copyright. Now he is anxious to get your "autorisation" and without being compelled he offers you royalties on the books. (5–10 procents of each sold book. I think) Please drop him a line of agreement, or write to me that you consent;² he is a decent fellow and wants to compensate the robery of Ledermann. Thats all for to-night.

Our love to both of you.

Yours ever
Siegfried Trebitsch

Als.; Texas.
1. Trebitsch's ellipsis.
2. Shaw accepted Kiepenheuer's offer.

St David's Hotel. Harlech
9th April 1921

My attempt to save you trouble has only multiplied your sorrows. I am very sorry. You must only do just as you did before.¹ But as we are on the verge of a strike here which may develop into civil war, and will certainly upset the post and all the transport services for a time, you had better wait until things are quieter before risking any registered letters.[2]

I am trying to recuperate here from the exhaustion of finishing Methuselah. I shall be here until the 18th; but letters will be forwarded from London.

G.B.S.

Apcs.

1. Trebitsch had been remitting Shaw's Austrian earnings in kronen. Shaw suggested that Trebitsch send checks instead, which Shaw would transfer to his Viennese account. But Trebitsch thought Shaw wanted checks in English currency.

2. A general strike, launched by the militant English coal miners, was being organized but collapsed the next week ("Black Friday").

Harlech
19th April 1921

No, no, no, no, no, no, I dont want £s.d.: I want Kronen. Simon thinks I want to touch the money. I dont: I want to keep it *in Vienna* until the exchange improves. Therefore if I receive Kronen notes, or a cheque for Kronen on a Vienna bank, I can send it to Barclay's to be lodged to my credit in Vienna. I have an a/c there (through Barclay's) at the Bank Verein; but it may not be in my own name: it may be in Barclay's. Anyhow, explain to Simon that there is no question of his getting me a better exchange, and that I want Austrian, not English money.

Forgive all this bother. I am travelling and at this moment in great haste, packing. The rest of your letter must stand over. I have a round of political speeches to make in the north & shall not be home again until the 8th May.[1] What am I to do with the cheque you have sent? I dont understand it.

G.B.S.

Apcs.

1. Shaw on his itinerary criticized general strikes as national suicide in which the proletariat would starve before the capitalists. He also did some electioneering.

Ayot St Lawrence. Welwyn
2nd June 1921

Deri's disastrous remittance reached me safely. Tell him that at present rates of exchange nothing less than a thousand million Kronen is worth acknowledging, as the cost of postage and the stamp on the receipt and on the cheque swallows it all up.[1]

I have lots more to say to you, but no time today to write it. More presently. Bless you!

GBS

Apcs.

1. Deri transmitted royalties to Shaw for *Heartbreak House* and *Androcles*, but as the krone continued to plunge the amount came to only £11.

Touring in Yorkshire
23rd July 1921

Hamon, my French translator, says that it is announced that Lehar is making an operetta of Pygmalion. Lehar is an Austrian, is he not?[1] Can you warn him that he cannot touch Pygmalion without infringing my copyright, and that I have no intention of allowing the history of The Chocolate Soldier to be repeated.

Your card acknowledging my wire has just arrived, having crossed a letter of mine about the tiara.[2] I address this to Vienna, as I do not know whether Franzensfest[e] is now in Austria or Italy. All I do know is that the new frontier is as bad (the other way) as the old one.

G.B.S.

Apcs.
1. Franz Lehár (1870–1948), Hungarian-born operetta composer, spent much of his career in Austria, where he wrote the popular *The Merry Widow* (1905).
2. Tina Trebitsch had managed to get her tiara (through Deri?) to England where Shaw placed it in safekeeping.

Herne Bay
28th August 1921

My dear Trebitsch

At the end of July I was at a Hydro (Wasserkur Anstalt [a water-cure sanatorium]—really a hotel) on the Yorkshire moors. Charlotte got ill and could not travel on the day we intended to leave; and I had to make up my mind to stay there with nothing to do for four or five days. So I set to work hard at Gitta, and nothing but Gitta, and finished her. That is to say, I finished my first draft of the dialogue in shorthand. I have not yet seen the typed transcript; and I have yet to revise that and to put in all the stage business; but still the main job is done: the rest is only drudgery and routine. I have not done justice to your poetry and your love of intense unhappiness, which convinces me that you have never been really unhappy in your life. Lenkheim, though a very correct professor, with all the proper feelings of an outraged husband, struck me as being rather a dull dog (like a real professor); and though I have not exactly made him a *mari à la mode*, I have ventured to make him a little less oppressively conventional than he would be in Austria, where they still fight duels (or at least think they ought to fight them) and do not admire Lenin & Trotsky as much as their late Apostolic Emperor.[1] I have got a little mild fun out of Mrs Haldenstedt and left her really happy;[2] and, though of course I havnt dared to say so, I have great hopes that the audience will feel pretty sure that in spite of Gitta's broken heart she will have at least a dozen other delightfully tragic affairs to amuse her before she finally retires as too old for adultery, and takes to religion with a spiritual adviser of thirty.

That is the good news. The bad is this Pygmalion business, of which I solemnly swear I never heard a word until Hamon wrote to me about Lehar. Your letter must have been lost in the post; for neglectful as I am of business

I would never have let such a horrible disaster occur if I had known about it. Never again will I face the loss and disgrace the thrice accursed Chocolate Soldier brought upon me. Whilst its vogue lasted—even whilst the mere memory of its vogue lasted—Arms & The Man (Helden) was banished from the stage: nobody would touch it. Pygmalion is my most steady source of income: it saved me from ruin during the war, and still brings in a substantial penny every week. To allow a comic opera to supplant it is out of the question. I might possibly consider an offer of £10,000 English money; but as matters stand now, if they attempt to use a word of my dialogue, or to connect my name or my play in any way with their abominable opera I will let loose all the engines of the Copyright law to destroy them utterly. I have no choice in the matter: the manager who is touring with the play in the provinces could sue me for damages if I ruined his business by letting Lehar loose on him. Therefore tell them anything you please; but stop them. . . .

We must extricate ourselves somehow: a Pygmalion operetta is quite out of the question.

In haste, ever

G. Bernard Shaw

Als.

1. In Shaw's translation, Gitta's husband, Lenkheim, is changed from a moralizing, humiliated bourgeois to a carefree soul, who, after an outburst of wounded pride, laughs at his wife's tragic airs and wryly admits his own infidelity. Gitta, now the jealous wife, orders Lenkheim home.

2. Instead of being an embittered widow, Shaw's Mrs. Haldenstedt is a sharp, commonsensical woman, who drops all gloom when persuaded that Bruno's affair was a passing fancy.

10 Adelphi Terrace W.C.

2nd October 1921

My dear Trebitsch

I now enclose my version of Gitta complete as far as the dialogue is concerned. You will see that I have rescued Gitta from the hopeless gloom and despair in which you plunged her deeper and deeper all through the play, plunging everybody else along with her lest a ray of light should spoil the absolute blackness of her future. But not only would this be fatal to the play here unless an actress with an extraordinary genius for tragedy could be found to play Gitta (and we have no such actress), but life is not like that here, whatever it may be in Austria. People think that a death will plunge them in grief for ever, and that discovered adultery is the end of a marriage. But they find that it is utterly impossible for a human being, even with such artificial aids as black clothes, retirement from society, visits of condolence and all the rest of it, to avoid not merely forgetfulness of their sorrow, but a strong reaction against it into cheerfulness. And nine tenths of the adulterers end in reconciliations, and even at the connivance of the injured party at its continuation. I have therefore ventured to shew at the end of your play that the tragedy of the first act, and the melodrama of the second are not the end of the world, and that all the survivors will go on living very much as they would have done if Bruno had died respectably in his bed surrounded by his weeping family.

However, if the liberties I have taken are unbearable you can refashion it to your heart's desire, and I will translate your alterations.

By the way you said in a note on page 3 of the first act that Mrs Billiter[1] does not know who Haldenstedt is, as she would tell the police. But in the second act it is clear that she *has* told the police, as otherwise they would not have known where to take the body to. Therefore she must be represented as knowing Bruno, but not knowing Gitta, which is what I have done.

What do you say to making the university a Polish or Czeckoslovakian or Danish one? Both here and in America managers are still afraid of anything German, as patriots are still rampant in both countries. The war made all our biggest fools persons of importance. They have relapsed into obscurity since 1918; but they are still pining for a chance of waving the flag again; and it might help an actress to face Gitta if she could be a Polish beauty instead of a Hun. It goes very much against the grain with me to make such a suggestion; but I am bound to be worldly-wise for your sake.

Will you, when you are sending me back the MS, send me a ground plan of the scenes, showing where the doors are, and how the furniture is placed. I can then work at the stage business and get half a dozen prompt copies typed. I could send one to Mrs Fiske in America and another to the Liverpool Repertory Theatre here. Mrs Patrick Campbell is playing with them at present; and both they and she might try it for a week to see how the public would take it.[2] If it made an impression, then Mrs Campbell might possibly get a London production financed, though her age and her impossible temper now make things very difficult for her. I may be able to think of something better when I have the work quite complete. Have you any plans for it? Have you an agent in America? Don't send the play to anyone, whether agent or principal, without letting me know first. I do not believe any agent can do anything for us that we can't do better for ourselves.

Now as to Lenin and Trotsky. They are the only statesmen in Europe in whom it is possible for any intelligent politician to take the slightest interest. They have had a terrific job to do; and the fact that after four years they are still holding Russia together shows that they are men of extraordinary quality. I have just read a book by Trotsky, "Communism and Terrorism," a polemic against Kautsky,[3] which shows Trotsky to be the best super-pamphleteer Europe had produced since Karl Marx. He has all the realism of Bismarck with a brilliancy of style and an international grasp of fundamental conditions that Bismarck, with his Junker limitations, never possessed. All the Moscow leaders write and speak well: to turn from their frank and significant utterances to the worn out claptrap and empty journalistic clichés with which our bourgeois statesmen cover up their ignorance and bewilderment is like playing with tiresome and ill-behaved children after talking with supermen. Whether they are equally able in practical affairs is not yet so certain, because it is so hard to find out what is really happening. I have met only one of them, Krassin;[4] and he is beyond question a much abler and better educated man than any member of the British Cabinet known to me. His retinue did not make a favorable impression: they looked like the office staff of a provincial branch of the Credit Lyonnais in France. But the reports of the few competent observers who have come into personal contact with the Moscow leaders, from Gorky and H. G. Wells to the sculptress Claire Sheridan,[5] prove beyond all reasonable doubt that the half dozen men who are at the head of the Soviet Government, are first class in energy, ability, and character. On their plane it is impossible to think of poor old Franz Josef at all: he would have been in his proper place as Trotsky's gamekeeper, just as our Edward VII, in spite of the terribly severe education wasted on him by his German father, would have been quite happy and successful as a sporting publican. But it is not fair to compare these hereditary idols, who have crowns thrust on their heads without consulting them, with men who come to the top out of poverty and obscurity when society breaks up into chaos. If at such a moment Lenin soars to the top and the Kaiser sinks into the insignificance of any ordinary country gentleman, it is evident that Lenin is the abler man. The bourgeois theory that he is only a greater scoundrel is absurd on the face of it: there are thousands of superlative scoundrels in Russia, but only one Lenin.

Of course you must allow for my personal bias. I have been a Bolshevist all my adult life, and was bowled over by Marx as long ago as 1882 or 3. Capitalism is no solution of the problems of civilization; and the monarchical forms which it exploits are for simpletons, not for the intelligentsia to which you and I belong. If Franz Josef had come to you as a private man and asked you to employ him as your butler, you would probably have refused him after a short enquiry into his character. You can imagine what I would have said to him if he had proposed to translate my plays.

However, I enclose an article on The Dictatorship of The Proletariat which I have just written for a Socialist magazine here called The Labor Monthly which can't afford to pay me for it.[6] Happily an American newspaper Syndicate has bought what is called "the serial right" (the right to print as an article in the newspapers) for $1200. It will explain my position much better than I can in a letter. If you translate it, perhaps the Neue Freie Presse will pay you Kr12,000,000,000 for it. I have altered the beginning and end so as to make it easier for a capitalist newspaper to print it. I did this successfully for America. By the way, do not make the mistake of offering it to Die Zeit or to any of the Socialist papers. They are much more timid about such things than the Imperialist papers. The explanation of this you may gather from the English proverb: "One man may steal a horse while another may not look over a hedge." An Imperialist paper, being above suspicion, may print much more advanced things than a Radical one. It can always write a leading article pretending to refute my errors.

It was a great relief to hear that Fischer had saved us from the Pygmalion complication. My secretary wrote to you about the films, as I am so busy rehearsing Heartbreak House that I have no time to write. I could not write this if it were not Sunday. I was offered £20,000 a year for five years if I would give two of my plays to be filmed every year. But I have never consented to the filming of any of my plays, partly because if I go into the film business I shall either write for the screen *ad hoc,* or else make my own scenario from my own play, instead of leaving it to an American producer to fool with. Have you never thought of writing for the screen, or selling the film rights in your novels?

I think this is all I have to say today. Don't forget to send me the ground plan of the Gitta scenery. The roughest scrawl will do: just an outline of the stage showing where the doors come, and a few little squares and big squares to represent chairs and tables. Of course I could invent these and arrange the business accordingly; but it will save me trouble if I haven't to think of this.

I suppose there is no chance of your coming over here to see Heartbreak House.[7] We still have a disgraceful Aliens Act in force under which the Government are trying to expel Oscar Levy;[8] so it would be easier for me to go to Vienna. Travelling is still very uncomfortable, I am told; and now that I have passed my 65th birthday I shrink from any journey that I can't make in my car. But we should much like to see you again.

ever
G. Bernard Shaw

PS. 4th October 1921. I have just received from a Berlin autograph hunter a copy of your translation of Pygmalion in Fischer's edition. It is incomplete, lacking the prose sequel; and your name is not on the title-page. You ought to insist on your name always appearing on the title-page as well as in the foot-note on the back of it. . . .

Tls.

1. The landlady of Bruno's trysting flat.
2. Mrs. Patrick Campbell did not perform *Jitta.*
3. Karl Kautsky (1854–1938), leading German Marxist, rejected Bolshevism and proletarian dictatorship. His *Terrorismus und Kommunismus* (1919) was answered by Trotsky under the same title (trans. into Engl., 1921).
4. Leonid Krassin (1870–1926), Commissar of Foreign Trade, negotiated an Anglo-Soviet treaty.
5. H. G. Wells and Clare Sheridan (1885–1970), English sculptress and feminist, who was invited to sculpt Lenin and Trotsky, had visited Russia and reported favorably on the Soviet leaders in *Russia in the Shadows* (1920) and *Russian Portraits* (1921), respectively.
6. The article (*Labour Monthly*, October 1921) stressed universal compulsory labor and did earn a modest £29 from the new Marxist journal.
7. *Heartbreak House* opened at the Court Theatre, London, on 18 October, with Ellen O'Malley and Edith Evans (1888–1976).
8. Dr. Oscar Levy (1867–1946), prominent German Nietzschean scholar residing in London, was shortly expelled as an "undesirable alien."

[Trebitsch to Shaw]

Wien
11th October 1921

My dearest Shaw

Many hearty thanks for your letter, the writing for the Bank and "Yitta's Atonement"! Your version is as much better than mine as you are the greater poet of us two. I was puzzeled very much reading your bold alterations. Wonderful in the first act the comperation of the book left without father like an orphan left behind. It makes the last will much more comprehensible. The

III. Akt is in your version almost a comedy! I would not dare this towards a german audience. I only miss the "ritardando" in the scene between the two women, where Agnes says in my text: "I am happy to speake at last woman to woman" (page 58). How clever you introduced the names of Einstein, Goethe & Rousseau. I approve also fully the suggestion to give a Polish university! Please than instead of "Agram" say "*Warschau*." If this play, where I miss your name as the adapters one will reach the English-American footlights I shall owe it to your genious. I am often thinking why I became so poor, that a journey to London has become an impossibility for me; sometimes I am sick of longing to see you and now I have the hope to realize that dear plan. As soon as "Yitta" will have earned for my share the necessary sum for the journey and a week in London under the old easy conditions (comfortably) I shall come and see you and your dear wife. Why is it not to-morrow? Tina says she will come with me by all means!.....[1] About the Tiara there is not much to say: The owner [Tina] cried almost, that you could think, she would like to wear anymore again such a fossile. But it is almost the last real fortune left!! She hopes you will find some way to mark it as her property, perhaps she will even consent to sell it one day. How much could she get for it in London? By the way: I thought Mrs. Billiter did not know *who* his guest was, but the police and their physichians discovered soon, called at the place, who the dead man was. I have nobody, no agent whatever for America and England! I leave all that entirely to you as you trusted your work to me; please act with Yitta as you would with an own play, thats all I can request. Will you have printed and published it? I think you will much more agree with my new play [*Kaiser Diokletian*], which will soon come out in German. I enclose the perfect ground plan of the Burgtheater, which probably will satisfy you very much.

I have sent your article: "The dictatorship of the Prol" at once to the "Neue freie Presse" and I am wondering if they will print it.[2] All this is quite true and I am sure that Lenin and Trotzky have brain and sense and ability. But please answer one question: why do you not reply with one single word to my just accuse that they are the greatest murderers of the universe. They have slain and tortured ten times more men than the Czar in that terrible war!! They have not created happiness, they only killed and destroyed and only can go on by continuing killing and destroying. They made the *Chaos* they need for their mean plans. And they rule by that wreched Kapitalism they are right to condemn. They are sending heaps of money to all the other countries to get the similar revolution everywhere. Well, I only can bow to *examples* as all the great men have given, but not to *Terror*; this other sort of unjustice to the unjust (perhaps). I am your pupil and we must have a serious conversation about this question as soon as we meet again; one of the great moments I am still expecting in my life.

A book of mine "The woman without Tuesday" has been filmed (I received 20,000 Marks for it).[3] The book was a big success, the screen not; but all my novels are like made for that purpose. I am with you rehearsing Heartbreak House; Tina's pet-play. For to-day to reach the mail, our love to both of you.

Yours ever

Siegfried Trebitsch

Als.; Texas.
1. Trebitsch's ellipsis.
2. *Neue Freie Presse* did not print the article.
3. Trebitsch's novella *Die Frau ohne Dienstag* (The Woman Without a Tuesday), another tale of sexual guilt, had been filmed by Larus, Berlin, and released the previous year.

My dear Trebitsch   [late 1921]
This is quite impossible. The Weltverfilmungsrecht [world film rights] of Pygmalion is worth at least £10,000. If I had been willing to sell it I could have sold it in America, which is my proper market for such things, twenty times over. Of course I am open to an offer from the Gorron people; but how can they possibly compete with Los Angeles. Besides, these films kill the plays: that is why I have refused, in spite of enormous offers, to let my plays be filmed.

In haste—I shall write later about the other matters.

GBS

Tell Korngold[1] that I like his music, but that I will have no more Chocolate Soldiers. Let him lay a finger on The Devil's Disciple at his peril. The D's D. is grand opera, not operetta.

Als.
1. Eric Korngold (1897–1957), Viennese composer, who later emigrated to Hollywood, had produced an opera *Die tote Stadt* (1920), based on Trebitsch's translation of Rodenbach's *Le Mirage*.

10 Adelphi Terrace W.C.

17th February 1922

My dear Trebitsch
Is it possible that I did not write to you about Pygmalion? I have a distinct recollection of a letter explaining that I could at any moment get £10,000 for the film rights of Pygmalion from America, or for any play of mine, and that therefore the disposal of them in Germany is out of the question. Tell Fischer ganz genau [quite exactly] that he may tell all inquirers that the film rights of my plays are not available, as experience shows that a film kills a play, and that even if I should change my mind on this point, the rate of exchange, and the scale on which the business is done in Los Angeles, would prevent me dealing with any Central European firm. If Portens[1] wishes to compete with the Americans he must start with an offer of 9,000,000 Marks.

For some months past I have been engaged on two big jobs[2] which had to be finished within a certain time; and the only way in which I can now get anything finished at all is to keep steadily at them day by day and neglect everything else, business, correspondence, money, friends—absolutely everything. The two jobs are done; but the arrears of business and letters left are terrible. You have been one of the sufferers. I made a desperate effort the other day to finish Gitta; but I found that much more remains to be done than I thought. I have not only to work out the stage business, but to revise the dialogue a good deal, especially in the first half, which is too German in form to be quite natural and easy for English actors. I was forced to put it aside and have a turn at my business affairs, which are falling into ruinous neglect. But when I have put them into some sort of order I will tackle Gitta. I want, however, to consult you about printing my version when it is finally ready. Could I save anything by having it printed in Germany or Austria? Printing and paper are still very dear here; and big profits are being made by importing German goods and selling them at English prices.

They are rehearsing Methuselah in America.[3] It seems to me a mad enterprize; but it may succeed if they can persuade the New Yorkers that the play is the biggest thing on earth.

[Richard] Strauss wants me to go to Salzburg in the autumn to hear him conduct Mozart's Don Juan.[4] English people say they are well treated in Germany when they travel. In France and Italy their lives are hardly safe. Vive l'entente!

Our best love to you both.

ever

G. Bernard Shaw

Tls.

1. Franz Porten (1888–1932), German film producer and director, father of Henny Porten, Germany's first film star.

2. During December and January Shaw was occupied with a lengthy preface to the Webbs' *English Prisons under Local Government*; earlier he was busy with a series of articles on "The Limitation Conference," published in the *New York American* and *Nation* during November and December.

3. *Methuselah* opened in New York on 27 February and ran eight times in a three-evening sequence, spaced one week apart. Thereafter, 48 performances were given with variations in the sequence of plays.

4. Shaw had recently met Strauss at a luncheon given by the English composer Sir Edward Elgar. Strauss invited Shaw to the Mozart Festival in Salzburg, which had been launched in 1920 by Reinhardt, Strauss, and von Hofmannsthal.

Great Malvern (on a holiday tour)
21st April 1922

My dear Trebitsch

This Jugoslav business is very puzzling. Before the war I had to deal with about five languages of the existence of which I had never heard. At last I made an agreement with a translator in Agram [Zagreb]; but I have not heard of him or from him for years; and I have forgotten his name.[1] Agram was in the Austro-Hungarian empire; but now there is no Austro-Hungarian empire; and Jugoslavia is a new State—one of "the Little Entente," I suppose. I dont know whether it has joined the Berne Convention or not. If not, there is no copyright.[2]

Szalai has been my Hungarian agent; and he has been very capable and energetic. If any foreigner, Hungarian or German, has a moral claim to my Jugoslavian business, it is he. So you see I am in a difficulty. I cannot decently appoint Fischer over his head without consulting him as to the situation; and national sentiment is at present so very touchy (empfindlich) that it may be better for us to appoint a Jugoslavian agent, if such a phenomenon exists. I see nothing for it but to write to Szalai and to the long forgotten Croatian translator (if my secretary can hunt out his name and address among my papers) and then consider what is to be done. I doubt if there is much money to be got anyhow.

As to Schnitzler I thought I had written to you generally that I could not take on any extra jobs. I do not see why Arthur cannot turn sixty without my assistance:[3] when I turned sixty I did not trouble him. I think this business of playwrights sending testimonials to one another ridiculous. His plays are just a little *vieux jeu* [old fashioned]: life does not consist exclusively of amourettes; and he is a virtuoso in amourettes only. But I enjoy them, and think he ought to persuade Granville-Barker to translate Reigen as a pendant to Anatole.[4] But I am damned if I am going to celebrate his 60th birthday: any fool can be 60 if he lives long enough.

I leave this place tomorrow, and shall spend next week at the St David's Hotel, Harlech, North Wales, and the following week at the Shakespear Hotel, Stratford-on-Avon, Warwickshire, returning home on the 7th May. But letters will be forwarded from Adelphi as usual.

I have brought Gitta with me; but I cannot get to work on her: I came away because I was utterly worn out; and I am not quite ready to begin again; but at Stratford I hope to get something done. Age and its imbecilities are beginning to tell on me.

ever
G. Bernard Shaw

Als.

1. In 1912, Milan Šenoa (1869–1961), geographer and author from Zagreb, was appointed Shaw's Croatian translator, but he did not translate any of Shaw's works.

2. Translations based on Trebitsch's versions had recently appeared in Yugoslavia, which did not adhere to the Bern Convention, and Trebitsch, who felt entitled to share the Yugoslav royalties, had urged Shaw to appoint Fischer as agent for Yugoslavia. Shaw later agreed.

3. Schnitzler was to celebrate his 60th birthday in May.

4. Barker had adapted Schnitzler's *Anatol* (1911), but he did not translate *Reigen*.

Ayot St Lawrence. Welwyn
15th May 1922

. . . Since I returned home a week ago I have been working like a nigger at Jitta; and I am only half way through. Mrs Billiter and the flower girl and the planning of their business took me two whole days! I am now postponing everything to it; and I hope to send you the typed copy ready for Fischer's printer before the end of the month.[1] It is a devil of a job, but not at all uninteresting; and I hope I shall not spoil it.

Can you procure me a prospectus of the Salzburg Mozart Festival? I can find out nothing here about it.[2]

Mrs Patrick Campbell, who would have been a wonderful Gitta fifteen years ago, has published a lot of my letters in her autobiography.[3]

G.B.S.

Who played Gitta in Vienna; and what was the date of the first production? I want a list of all your works, and the date and place of your birth.

Apcs.; incomplete.
   1. It was cheaper to print rehearsal copies of *Jitta* in Germany through S. Fischer. But Shaw decided on typed copies, and *Jitta* was not printed until 1926 (*Translations and Tomfooleries*).
   2. The Salzburg Festival, scheduled for 13–29 August, presented four Mozart operas and premiered Hofmannsthal's *Das Salzburger grosse Welttheater.*
   3. To repair her fortunes, Mrs. Patrick Campbell published *My Life and Some Letters* (1922). Shaw, who advised her, forbade her publishing any of his intimate letters but let a harmless selection stand.

10 Adelphi Terrace W.C.
17th June 1922

My dear Trebitsch

At last I have received from the typist the prompt copies of Gitta, ready for the stage. By this post I am sending a copy to an actor-manager [Dion Boucicault] whose wife is one of the most popular actresses in London (Irene Vanbrugh), and who is himself the cleverest actor on the stage.[1] He would play Alfred [Lenkheim] very well: in fact I had him in my mind in translating the part.

I am also sending a copy to America, to the Theatre Guild, which produced Heartbreak House and Methuselah.

Of course it is late in the season for any immediate result; but at any rate I have set the ball rolling.

You will find that in this final acting edition of the play I have committed some fresh outrages. In one or two places you finished a scene, and then went back to it. This is a novelist's trick, not a playwright's. It occurs between Jitta and Alfred in Act II and between Agnes and Jitta in Act III. In both cases they take the audience back to a point already passed, and wallow in emotions already sufficiently expressed. I have cut these returns clean out and kept the play moving straight on with gathering momentum. Nothing has been lost by this except the characteristic Trebitschian brooding that is so deliciously sad and noble in your novels but that I could never reproduce. It would require a very special audience, in a theatre suitably draped and colored, with a mystically lighted stage and wonderful dark rich dresses. My method of getting a play across the footlights is like revolver shooting: every line has a bullet in it and comes with an explosion.

Still I really think I have kept the story of Jitta there just as it is in the original; so you must forgive me: I have done my best. . . .

I am afraid a trip to Salzburg will not be possible (Hermann Bahr says the place is full of Schiebers [profiteers])[2] but that, too, I shall not decide today.

ever
G. Bernard Shaw

Tls.
   1. The acting couple Dion Boucicault (the younger, 1859–1929) and Irene Vanbrugh (1872–1949) had scored successes in plays by Pinero, Milne, and Barrie.
   2. Bahr's remark reflects the postwar rise of parvenu elements in fashionable theatres.

Ayot St Lawrence. Welwyn
2nd July 1922

I am sorry to say that I have decided against Salzburg. We are going to Ireland instead, if the blown-up railways can be repaired in time.[1] William Randolph Hearst, the American newspaper king, wants me to go to Vienna and write him a series of articles protesting against the economic and political isolation of the city, and against the Balkanization of Central Europe generally; but I dont think I could produce anything good enough. Of course I should jump at the offer if I were a young journalist and could speak German and Jugo-Slavian (whatever language that may be) well. But *now*—!

Another annoying piece of news is that the actress [Irene Vanbrugh] on whom I was depending for Jitta is going to Australia & South Africa. However, Australian gold non olet [doesn't smell]; and if she likes to try Jitta on the natives, all the better.

Kissingen is all right if you avoid the doctors, the baths, the waters, and the rest of the hygienic swindlers.[2]

G.B.S.

Apcs.

1. In December 1921 Ireland was divided into a Free State and Northern Ireland, but struggles continued and the railways were raided.

2. Trebitsch was on a cure at Bad Kissingen, which the Shaws had visited in 1912.

Walton Park Hotel. Clevedon
15th July 1922

My dear Trebitsch

. . . I met Irene Vanbrugh the other day. She said that her Australian trip, if it comes off at all, will not be until next year. She had not read Jitta; so all she could say was that her husband (Dion Boucicault—Lenkheim) liked it, and she was curious about it and would read it soon.

Ireland is impossible: our hotel will probably be the last stronghold of the Republicans. But this does not mean that we can go to Salzburg, as I have made engagements in England from the middle of August to the middle of September. . . .

If the worst comes to the worst, remember that I am not absolutely destitute. You can share my last pound; and I can share Tina's last diamond.

This is just a hasty hotel scrawl.

ever
G. Bernard Shaw

Als.

Ayot St Lawrence. Welwyn
21st September 1922

My dear Trebitsch

I am cabling to New York to the Theatre Guild there to say that Berta[1] is in the field, and that the Guild must make up its mind at once whether it will produce Jitta or not. If they decide not to, then the lady had better negotiate with me, as I shall demand higher terms than those you mention. I enclose a blue paper shewing my usual charges; and I will certainly not let Jitta go for less, as it has to bear two authors instead of one.

The advantage of dealing with the Theatre Guild is that it will cast the play better than a star actress would. I believe the play will fail unless Lenkheim is played by a clever and popular actor; and nothing will persuade Berta that it matters twopence who plays Lenkheim as long as she plays Jitta: indeed she will go out of her way to find some worm whose powers will not enable him to compete with her. The T.G. does not stand any nonsense of that sort.

Lawrence Langner is one of the directors of the T.G.; and his press puff suggests that the Guild is going to do the play. You see his game: first to persuade the public that the play is a Shaw play and not a Trebitsch, and second, that it is a comedy and not a tragedy. On the last point he has overshot the mark badly: it is a blunder to send the people to such a first act expecting a comedy; and I will see that this is stopped. As to the first point, it is unfair to you, and a sacrifice of the attraction of novelty which you bring to the performance; and I will see that this also is better handled;[2] but I take it that you do not care very much what the Americans do if they pay for their follies in solid dollars. The performance will make an end of all their romancing, as it will be evident at once that there is another hand than mine in the work, and one that will not be forgotten as the preliminary paragraphs will be forgotten.

I am sorry to say that Dion Boucicault, the husband of Irene Vanbrugh, and the actor for whom I designed Lenkheim, has sent the play back saying that they both like it, but that he has no right to hold it up, as he has no theatre and may not have one until they go to Australia. If they go to Australia I doubt if they will ever come back, as they have both reached that point in their careers at which they can make much more money by touring on the strength of their London reputation than by continuing the hazards of London management in competition with younger people. However, if Jitta does well in New York, or in London in other hands, they may be glad to have it for Australia; and Australian fees will exchange at a handsome valuta. Non olet.

Meanwhile I am hesitating as to whom I should approach next. There are two or three possible Jittas; but the man is the difficulty.

I have given Beecher[3] the name of an American agent, Paul Reynolds of 70 Fifth Avenue, New York, who knows the market value of any stuff of mine better than anyone else. As the law stands the letters are yours and the copyright is mine.[4] That is, you can prevent publication by simply withholding the actual piece of paper which is your material property; and I can prevent anyone "multiplying copies" (that is, printing) of what is written on the piece of paper. Our control is therefore complete. I do not want any share of the price; but that is no concern of Mr Beecher's, who may fairly be asked to content himself with one third of the money, leaving two thirds to us— really to you. I shall have no trouble in the matter; and I shall not part with my copyright; so you need have no scruple about my getting nothing except the very lively satisfaction of knowing that you are getting some dollars as well as our unfortunate tantièmen-Kronen.

I must, however, revise the interview. Beecher has just sent me a letter 18 pages long!!!!! in which he explains to me that his discretion may be relied on, and then proceeds to quote as interesting matter for publication the most appalling remarks about Kellner, several details of our business arrangements with the theatres which it would be a gross breach of etiquette to make public, and a statement that my wife hates Germany, which would make her furious and be most painfully misunderstood after the war. In short, Beecher hasnt the least notion of what is fit for publication and what isnt. In other words, he is an American journalist. I am telling him to send me whatever it is he proposes to publish when it has been censored by you. Then I will do my own censoring. The result will, I hope, be presentable.

I will write again when I have brought the Theatre Guild to a decision about Jitta.

ever
G. Bernard Shaw

Tls.

1. Bertha Kalich (1874–1939), Polish-born actress, who starred in New York's Yiddish theatre but also performed in English.

2. On 30 September, Shaw wrote to Lawrence Langner (1890–1962) of the Theatre Guild, objecting to the publicity that stressed Shaw's part in *Jitta* and urging that Trebitsch's contribution of "HEART" be underscored.

3. Robert Beecher, American journalist then in Vienna.

4. With Trebitsch's assistance, Beecher had prepared an article consisting of 27 letters and cards from Shaw's early correspondence with Trebitsch, with running commentary by Beecher.

Ayot St Lawrence. Welwyn
2nd October 1922

I have seen Madame Kalich and her daughter. They came out here to Ayot, and enjoyed themselves very much, apparently. She will do very well for Jitta; and when I would not decide anything she and her husband[1] assailed me through the telephone (nine tenths inaudibly) until I was nearly distracted. They would have paid anything in advance if I had consented to decide the matter finally. But I must try to get a proposal from some responsible management and have her engaged at a salary. If I give the play to her she will cut it and ruin it. She will engage second rate serious actors for Lenkheim and Agnes instead of first rate comedians. She will end the play with Edith in her arms & a limelight on her upturned face. And the play will fail. It would be safer to give her your play and let her get an exact translation than to let her loose on our joint version. I must delay the affair until I see what can be done with the managers. I know the urgency of the money side of the affair, but I had rather make the advance myself than throw the play away in a hurry.

. G.B.S.

Apcs.
1. Leopold Spachner, president of the Kalich Producing Company; he counted among his authors Sudermann, Schnitzler, Maeterlinck, and Trebitsch.

10 Adelphi Terrace W.C.
4th October 1922

My dear Trebitsch

As to the $500 offer by Spachner, je m'en fiche [I don't give a hang]. I do not want $250, I can wait for it for a year if necessary. But, you say, *you* can't afford to wait. But you can. For the purposes of this play you and I are a Firma. Spachner wants the play very badly: that is our advantage. If we were in pressing want of money that would be *his* advantage; but though, like everyone else, I am ruined by the war, yet I have enough money lying at my bank to make a sum of £50 a matter of complete indifference to me, whether I pay it or receive it. You have at your disposal not only the rights in the play, but a diamond tiara worth £1,000,000,000,000,000,000, or thereabouts; and it is at my bank in my hands. Under such circumstances you must draw on me while the negotiations are proceeding. I enclose £50, and can let you have another £50 without the slightest inconvenience to myself as soon as you please.

I found out many things from Madame Kalich, among others that she did not propose to bind herself to a production before the 31st December; and there is still time for that. My objection to dealing with her instead of with a manager is that if she takes a theatre on sharing terms, she will get only half the money, and out of this she will have to pay our fees. Therefore my 15%, 10%, 7½% and 5%, which is quite reasonable, will become for her, 30%, 20%, 15% and 10%, which is quite unreasonable.[1] Jitta will not bear such percentages unless it has a colossal success; and its class is too high for that. But if the manager engages her at a salary, she is safe, and the undivided receipts will bear the percentage.

You ask whether a loss of money by Madame Kalich is our business. It is, very decidedly. If she makes money you may be able to dispose of the rights of your other plays in America. And in any case a bargain that is not good for both parties is a bad bargain. Failures damage everybody.

I have written a letter to Madame, and another to A. H. Woods,[2] who promised her the theatre. He is in London, but is returning to New York in the same ship which carries my letter to her. When he arrives next week they will discuss it; and it may be that she will induce him to undertake the production himself, giving her a salary and a percentage of the receipts above an agreed minimum, which is what I should prefer. If not, I may have to give her a contract; but at all events I have put the fear of God into her as to the casting and production. Spachner is naturally irritated and bewildered by my way of arranging the whole business over his head; but he will get used to that, especially as I can say lots of things to Madame that he dare not say himself.

Do not be uneasy: just put the affair out of your mind. If you don't, my proceedings will drive you almost as distracted as they have driven poor Spachner.

ever

G. Bernard Shaw

PS I did not see Spachner. But I invited Madame and her daughter out to our little country house, and drove them seven miles from the station in my smartest car. They were delighted.

Tls.

1. Shaw's theatre fees were on a sliding scale of 5 to 15 percent based on gross box-office receipts.
2. A. H. Woods (1870–1951), American impresario and theatre owner, who won and lost fortunes in popular entertainment.

[Ayot St Lawrence. Welwyn]
1st November 1922

My dear Trebitsch

I enclose the American contract for your signature. It explains itself, except on one point. It is my custom not to ask for an advance, but to ask for a guarantee that I shall receive at least £500 ($2500) unless the play is a complete failure. This is to protect myself in the event of the management taking off the play when it is doing fairly well and replacing it with some popular trash which he thinks will do still better. But in this case I want to get an advance of £50 ($250) for you, win, lose, or draw. . . .

I hope all will go through smoothly; but I never believe in the production of a play until the curtain goes up on the first night. A dozen things may happen to upset the apple cart; but we can do no more, and must now leave it to Shubert,[1] Bertha, and Luck.

ever

G. Bernard Shaw

. . . PPPS Your letter of the 28th has just arrived. Do not be too sanguine: if you are, Bertha Kalich will drop dead, or Shubert go bankrupt, or the theatre be burnt, or my solicitor will abscond with the advance. The sooner I get the Beecher interview the better. We are in the thick of an election here; and I shall have to travel about and make speeches;[2] so that it will be more difficult for me to write up the interview than it would be in quiet times.

Tls.

1. Lee Shubert (1873?–1953), American producer and theatre owner, who had earlier produced *Widowers' Houses* and *Fanny*. He had wired Shaw on 25 October that he would produce *Jitta* with Kalich immediately. Unknown to Shaw until much later, Spachner was half-partner in the venture (letter of Spachner to Shaw, 16 January 1924; Texas).
2. The British elections of 1922 brought the Labour Party to the fore as the official opposition.

10 Adelphi Terrace W.C.
3rd November 1922

. . . the cheque [from Shubert] has to travel from New York to Vienna or Berlin. It could not possibly arrive before the 20th: it may not arrive until the 30th. Meanwhile I have much more than £50 lying at my bank for the amusement of my bankers. You could exchange my cheque for £50 in Berlin for M1,240,000!! I offer to make you a millionaire without the cost of a single farthing to myself (the bank doesn't pay me interest on my current account) and you refuse. Why?

I have never drawn a Mark or a Kroner from Europe since the war. They await the Resurrection.

G.B.S.

Apcs.

Ayot St Lawrence. Welwyn
2nd December 1922

My dear Trebitsch

That Beecher affair was a terrible corvée. I could have written an act of a play—if not a whole play—in the time it took me to make the thing fit for publication; and even now it is so absurdly long that I do not see how even an American weekly paper can find room for it. I was forced to work at it because if I had sent it back to him he would have sent it to America on his own account, or kept repeating the statements in it in other articles; and as there was not a single bit of his history of my career in America that was not hopelessly wrong, my only way of avoiding endless annoyance and misrepresentation in future was to set it right.

I cut out bushels of his intolerable repetitions and twaddlings. I do not believe he read a word of it over to himself before sending it. However, I got it off at last; and now we must wait for Reynolds[1] to sell it as best he can to the Saturday Evening Post or any other paper which admires Beecher's style. I had no time to write a preface to it: I was distracted with the waste of time correcting it: besides, the 26 letters from me was sufficient. I cut out one of them [dated 18 December 1902] which was quite improper for publication. It gave away the secrets of rehearsal, which are as the secrets of the confessional. I also cut out a sentence of yours in which you said that Wiene was too old for his part. If Wiene is dead that would not matter; but as he may be alive for all I know, I thought it safer to cut the phrase out.[2]

I do not know what is happening in America about Jitta except that Shubert evidently does not demur to the terms of the agreement, because I have had a cablegram asking me not to insist on production before the New Year in New York, as he cannot get a first rate theatre so soon. I have cabled in reply that the exact date does not matter: any time in January will do. Meanwhile he wants to try the play out in the country, which is American for giving a few performances in the provinces to get it into trim before opening in the capital. Of this I strongly approve. We need not fear any avoidable delay, as both he and Bertha Kalich have the same interest in beginning in New York as soon as they can. Forcing them to keep the letter of the contract would have driven them to an inferior theatre, and would have been senseless and disobliging.

I am sorry to have had to worry you with contracts; but they are very necessary here and in America. In Germany and Austria, where the repertory system prevails, and there are no tours, and, above all, where managers never dream of trying to prevent other managers in other towns from performing plays which they nevertheless have ceased to perform themselves, one can depend on custom and verbal understanding; but here, where the manager wants a monopoly, and all the customs, as far as there are any customs, are survivals from an obsolete state of things in which the author's fee was fifteen shillings an act, and he often wrote the fifth act whilst the fourth was being performed, precise agreements are indispensable.

You have also to consider that I may drop dead at any moment; and you would have no end of trouble to establish your rights legally without documents.

As Jitta was not copyrighted in the United States, and is consequently in the public domain there, I have registered a copy of my version as "a dramatic composition by George Bernard Shaw" (these are the words of the Copyright Act) and just put a little note inside "founded on Siegfried Trebitsch's Frau Gitta's Sühne." This se[c]ures copyright for my version. It would not prevent anyone else from making a fresh adaptation, provided no use was made of mine in the process; but nobody would dream of doing that.

I grieve to say that I havnt the faintest recollection of Armand Carrel;[3] but Charlotte is searching for it; and if she finds it I will try to read it (dont forget that I really dont know German) and say something polite about it. I daresay it will be better than Beecher's Benjamin Franklin, which is also lying about somewhere.

Tell Robert that somebody has sent me the programme of the Devil's Disciple, and that I am furious because your name is not in it, and I therefore believe he has tampered with the text of the play.[4] It is of the greatest importance that our names should be *always* connected; so that in Germany people will always think of Shaw-Trebitsch, and not of Shaw. I refuse to write to Robert. I disown him. . . .

In great haste, ever
G. Bernard Shaw

Tls.

1. Paul R. Reynolds (1864–1944), pioneer American literary agent.
2. Karl Wiené, the Dick Dudgeon of the 1903 *Teufelskerl*, had in fact died in 1913.
3. A play (1920) by Moritz Heimann, reader for S. Fischer and Trebitsch's friend.
4. Eugen Robert [Weiss], Berlin director, produced *Devil's Disciple* at the Tribüne, which seated 296, on 31 October 1922, with a notable cast of Albert Bassermann (Dick), Kurt Götz (Burgoyne), and Else Heims (Judith).

Ayot St Lawrence. Welwyn
23rd December 1922

My dear Trebitsch

All right: when the Christmas holidays are over I will go to London and try my hand at diamond selling.[1] I have already made some enquiries from ladies with wedding presents to sell; and they have given me some addresses, and told me that sometimes the dealers will buy, and sometimes refuse to do anything but take the diamonds to sell if they can. It depends on the demand. . . .

As I said before, I never believe in the production of a play until the money is actually taken at the doors and the curtain up. I have written to Stern[2] to say that I dont care whether the production is delayed (within reason) but that I want the agreement signed and the advance paid at once. That is all that can be done. I daresay Spachner is a model husband; but I have no opinion of him as a man of business. My terms are not at all onerous; and Shubert is accustomed to them: he produced Fanny's First Play, and was glad not only to pay my percentages but to give a commission to Barker as well. Possibly I could have extorted an advance of more than $500 by taking advantage of Bertha's eagerness and Spachner's weakness; but I would as soon have thought of robbing two children in the street. I had to take care of them as well as of ourselves; and I have no reason to doubt that the affair will go through smoothly. It is true that you have not touched the money yet; but I have enough to be in no hurry. In war everyone has to go against the law of his nature; and the war is not over yet: it has been worse since the armistice than before. When it comes to your having to eat Tina or die of starvation I will dangle my dollars before you again; and you will yield. I have never hesitated to accept obligations from you and then neglect you scandalously for months. Well, why should I be the obliged party always? If Shubert hesitates I shall tell him not to sign if he has the smallest misgiving—that I will take the play off his hands with the greatest willingness, as I set no store by it, and will probably have no difficulty in disposing of it elsewhere. That is my way of doing business. You see, if he wont produce the play he wont; and nothing that we can do can make him. But if he will produce it nothing will hurry him so effectually as the possibility of its slipping through his fingers into those of a rival manager.

I hope you are bearing up against Christmas. It is bad enough here; it must be damnable in Vienna. However, cheer up: it comes only once a year, fortunately. And we always have our own souls to retire into.

hurriedly—this doesnt count as a letter—

G. Bernard Shaw

Tls.
1. That is, selling Tina's tiara. Shaw did not succeed in selling it.
2. Benjamin Stern, Shaw's American lawyer, who handled the contract with Shubert.

Hotel Metropole. Minehead
10th April 1923

Lenkheim—or rather the actor who played him with some success—died really, not dramatically, dead as mutton.[1] . . .

God knows where Beecher's article appeared! I never asked.[2]

Bertha seems to be going on with Jitta. I suspect Shubert has shoved it on to her, which perhaps explains the delay with the royalties.

G.B.S.

Apcs.
> 1. Francis Byrne, playing Lenkheim in Bertha Kalich's production of *Jitta*, collapsed and died on 7 February, only three weeks after the play opened at the Comedy Theatre in New York. Charles Richman took over, but the play, which had had mixed reviews, closed after 37 performances.
> 2. Beecher's article was not published at this time, but years later a shortened version appeared in *Plain Talk* ("Letters from George Bernard Shaw to Siegfried Trebitsch," February, March 1930).

10 Adelphi Terrace W.C.
[May 1923]

My dear Trebitsch

Under our agreement with Shubert we cannot license any other manager to perform the play until he has definitely forfeited his rights. Strictly speaking he has already done so by his delay in paying the royalties;[1] but it would not be reasonable to take advantage of that. Therefore, before letting the play go to the stock houses I must write to Shubert and ask him whether I may regard Jitta as off his hands. . . .

Did I tell you that I am working on a play about Joan of Arc?[2]

ever
G. Bernard Shaw

Tls.
> 1. Shaw did not receive his share of the royalties from *Jitta*—$2,507—until late in May.
> 2. Shaw began *Saint Joan* on 29 April and finished it on 24 August.

[Ayot St Lawrence. Welwyn]
11th June 1923

. . . Do not come too early in October as we all take holidays in August and September, and sometimes do not come back until the middle of October.[1] It would be too horrible to miss you.

GBS

Ans.
> 1. Trebitsch, having earned American royalties on *Jitta*, was planning his first trip to England since March 1914.

Ayot St Lawrence. Welwyn
27th June 1923

I have already told Die N[eue] R[undschau] that I cannot undertake any journalism until Joan is burnt. Tell all these people that it is no use asking me for these *pièces d'occasion*: I never write now unless I have something important to say.

Agatha is an English name, and not at all a bad one for a play, as it has not been used before as far as I can recollect.[1]

I dont understand about the preface. For once, your English is obscure. It suggests a hoax of some kind; but I cannot make out exactly what.[2]

Apc.

1. Trebitsch had written a new play and was exploring an English-sounding title. He finally named it, not after its heroine Agathe, but *Das Land der Treue* (Land of Constancy).

2. Trebitsch published *Das Land der Treue* (Berlin, 1924) as a "free adaptation" of an English play by the nonexistent W. Charles Lenox. When produced in 1927, the "hoax" was out. According to the *Berliner Tageblatt* (11 May) Trebitsch, having had little success with the German stage, decided to present his new play as by an English dramatist, since foreign authors had an easier time being produced than native playwrights.

The Malvern Hotel. Malvern

23rd September 1923

My dear Trebitsch

I must write briefly because when I was in Ireland I fell on the rocks and cracked two of my ribs, besides wrenching one of them nearly out of my spine; and though I have been up and about ever since, my hand feels a little paralytic when I write much.

We shall be at Ayot from Saturday the 20th October to Thursday the 24th. If you could come on Saturday, so much the better. We can put you up at Ayot, and send you up to London for the day to do any business you have there. If you want to go to a theatre and stay the night in London you could sleep in my bed at Adelphi Terrace; and our housekeeper there could give you breakfast in the morning. You need not bring evening clothes unless you have social engagements apart from us, as Ayot is a village where nobody dreams of dressing. Immediately before you arrive I will get the tiara from the bank and have it at Ayot for you. If you travel with light luggage and leave your colossal trunk behind you, you will be independent of dock strikes, which sometimes cause travellers inconvenience here: for instance when I went to Ireland I had to handle my own trunks and help to unload the ship!

If you smoke cigars, you will give Charlotte asthma; but except for that you will find Ayot bearable. I dont think you have been there: it must have been Harmer Green, a former residence, also at Welwyn, that you visited.

The Langham was the Ritz of London in the days of Queen Victoria: now it is passée. There are now cheap hotels—the Strand Palace and the Regent Palace—10s/6d a night and no tips—and still cheaper "temperance hotels" in Bloomsbury where bed & breakfast can be had for 8s/—, which are really just as comfortable as many of the more expensive ones; but I will say no more about them until I hear whether you need a hotel at all. At Ayot we shall let you alone when you are tired of being a guest; and you can come and go without ceremony. There will be a car at your disposal.

I hope to be able to give you printed proofs of Joan; but there is no other new play: Joan is *the* new play.

ever

G. Bernard Shaw

PS We shall be here (in Malvern) until the end of the month.

PSS I think the Piccadilly Hotel is one of the very expensive ones.

Als.; Cornell.

The Malvern Hotel. Great Malvern
25th September 1923

If you get up early and leave Paris (Nord) at 8.30, you will arrive in London (Victoria) at 15.45 (3.45 p.m.). My car can meet you there and take you straight down to Ayot: a run of 30 miles. You could then have a complete rest on Sunday, which is a dreadfully stupid day in London.

If you wish to spend Saturday night in London, you will have to catch the 10.30 train on Sunday morning from Kings Cross to Hatfield. There are very few trains on Sunday.

But you would be too tired to enjoy anything on Saturday after your journey. Much better make for Ayot.

G.B.S.

Apcs.

10 Adelphi Terrace W.C.
16th October 1923

Just get out of the train; and wait until I find you.

If I do not appear, it will mean that there has been an accident to the car. In that case take a taxi to 10 Adelphi Terrace, where they can telephone to Ayot St Lawrence for news of me; and tell you how to come down by train. If I am killed, you can console Charlotte or retreat to the Langham Hotel. But if nothing extraordinary happens I will be on the platform when the train arrives; and the car will be close at hand.

G. Bernard Shaw

PS All ladies who travel carry revolvers and have adventures. Tina can avoid them—if she really wishes to—by coming with you.

Apcs.

10 Adelphi Terrace W.C.
17th October 1923

Cook is wrong about the 10 train being the fastest: it is 15 minutes slower than the 8.25. The 8.25 has all the restaurant services &c. of the 10, the only difference being that it takes 3rd class passengers, whereas the 10 takes only 1st & 2nd. The advantage of the 8.25 is that it arrives at 15.20; so that we could drive down to Ayot by daylight. Also the 1st & 2nd class is probably less crowded. But it involves an uncomfortably early start; and as the 10 starts at a reasonable hour, and is undoubtedly the fashionable train, I will meet it at 17.10 (5.10 p.m.) at Victoria unless I hear from you to the contrary.

On Saturday morning I shall take the Stirnbinde [i.e., Tina's tiara] from the bank if you are quite sure that you can take it back with you safely.

The equinoctial gales are over; and the weather at the end of October is usually fine in England.

G.B.S.

Apcs.

Trebitsch arrived in England, without Tina, on Saturday, 20 October, and was met by Shaw. After spending Sunday at Ayot, Trebitsch left the next day with a copy of *Saint Joan* and Tina's tiara ("A Visit to Bernard Shaw," *Living Age*, 2 February 1924).

[Trebitsch to Shaw]

Wien
31st March 1924

My dear Shaw

I am just leaving for Florence but only *for a weeks* treatment at Dr Munari (please write *Savoy Hotel Florence*) who discovered a sort of mud which is said to cure all kinds of nerve-pains, neuralgies ec. ec. We shall see. I still like to hope....[1]

I am so happy about Joans big success in London,[2] we congratulate you of all our heart. I shall find it very difficult that time to beat London in Berlin and Vienna next octobre.

Is Archibald Henderson[3] a duffer like Robert Beecher? After his letters it must not be easy for you to work with him.

Have you saved me at last from Spachner by giving him your blessings concerning the Stock Comp. and film rights of "Yitta"? I am longing to hear that you *have* sent him *your* agreement.[4]

Our love to both of you

Yours ever
Siegfried Trebitsch

Als.; Texas.

1. Trebitsch's ellipsis.

2. *Joan* opened at the New Theatre, London, with Sybil Thorndike (1882–1976), on 26 March, and triumphed. Shaw and Lewis Casson (1875–1969) directed.

3. Archibald Henderson (1877–1963) was working on a revision of his 1911 biography of Shaw. He had also asked Trebitsch to place one of his "Dialogues" (which appeared in book form as *Table-Talk of G.B.S.*, 1925) in Vienna after engaging others to do the translation and placing it in Berlin.

4. In January, Leopold Spachner wrote to Shaw for permission to place *Jitta* with stock companies. He also mentioned an offer of $4,000 for film rights, provided Shaw's name appeared as adapter.

Ayot St Lawrence. Welwyn
14th May 1924

For Heaven's sake do not let St Joan get into print until you have the final corrected copy to work from. The one you have is only an early proof: I made several alterations, which are necessary for the stage business, at rehearsal. As to the Archbishop (of Rheims), read lines 17 & 18 on page 109. He and the Inquisitor appear during the vision of the statue.

The preface has cost me endless work; but I sent what I hope will be the last proof to the printer yesterday; and if the revise is finally satisfactory I will send you a copy at once.

I had to take an Easter holiday to recover from a horrible cold; but I had to work like the devil all the time. I haven't been able to write to anybody. I am sorry Tina was ill too.

[By the way "Charlotte Shaw Esq." . . .]¹ —is exclusively masculine. A married woman takes both her husband's names, thus: Mrs Bernard Shaw. Mrs Siegfried Trebitsch. Mrs Richard Strauss u.s.w.

                                                            G.B.S.

Apcs.
    1. Segment canceled by Trebitsch but partly legible.

                                             10 Adelphi Terrace W.C.
                                             12th June 1924
My dear Trebitsch
    . . . I do not know that it will be worth your while to come to London to see the production [*Saint Joan*]; but it would be no harm if some of the more important German managers or producers were to see it. The scenery and costumes, by Charles Ricketts, cannot be improved on by any artist in Europe. The incidental music, by Foulds,¹ is also just right for its purpose and modern in style. And the contrivance by which it has been made possible to change the scenes so quickly that the play can be finished in 3 ¼ hours with only one Pause of ten minutes ought to be seen by any producer who has no modern machinery on his stage. But these matters are for business managers and stage engineers: you would get only the fun of the performance, and perhaps some hints as to the acting; but I am so tired of the affair that I feel as if it would bore you beyond endurance, and therefore cannot urge you to come, especially as it is no use trying to get a German actor to act like an English one or to get his effects in the same way. Besides, you would have a good actor in the part in which I have a bad one, and vice versa, in which case nothing but mischief could come of handling them in the same way. It would really be more interesting for you to see my production *after* you had done yours. We should have the pleasure of seeing you again if you came; but as that would cost me nothing, and cost you a good deal, I shall not encourage you to come.

    As to the Spachner film business, the difficulty is that they want to "feature" me as the author of the film; and this I absolutely bar. Whether under these circumstances Spachner will be able to do any business for us, I doubt. I have no confidence in his business ability. I told him he might exploit the stock rights; but nothing has come of it in spite of his promises. I made a first rate arrangement for Bertha with Shubert; and he spoiled it all by letting Shubert persuade him that the play would not be produced unless he bought a half share in it. He fell to this bluff like a baby; and of course Shubert took no further interest in the affair, as, for reasons which I have not time to explain, his contribution did not cost him anything that he would not have had to pay anyhow, Jitta or no Jitta, to keep his theatres open.

Who is Allen W. Porterfield? Certainly I will read his translation of Der Geliebte if you will send me a copy.[2] . . .

What happened to The Admirable Bashville and Schmiede? Had the production any success? and why were you so angry about it when you wrote your letter of the 3rd January?[3] But you need not answer this question, as I have really no curiosity about it.

Tauchnitz wrote to me the other day saying that Joan was already published in German.[4] What did he mean by that? I find that you wrote to me on the 23rd February about the possibility of the Neue Freie Presse and the Rundschau publishing it in April and May. I was so busy with Joan that I did not answer any letters for months. Did the play appear in these papers? Or is Tauchnitz mistaken?[5] . . .

ever

G. Bernard Shaw

Tls.

1. John H. Foulds (1880–1939), English composer who wrote for the theatre.

2. Allen W. Porterfield (1879–1952) was the American translator of Schnitzler. His version of Trebitsch's *Der Geliebte* was not published or staged.

3. *Bashville* (*Der Boxkampf*) opened along with *Man of Destiny* on 24 May 1924 at the Deutsches Volkstheater, Vienna, and ran 11 times. There was no "Schmiede" in the production, but Shaw perhaps puns on the name of Jakob Feldhammer (which like *Schmiede* means *forge*), who played the boxer Cashel Byron and who, according to the *Neues Wiener Journal*, knocked the role "crooked and lame."

4. Bernhard Tauchnitz, Leipzig, published Shaw's English works for continental distribution.

5. Trebitsch published *Saint Joan* (*Die heilige Johanna*) in *Neue Rundschau* (June through September 1924) without Shaw's revisions, though they were later included in the book edition.

10 Adelphi Terrace W.C.

3rd July 1924

My dear Trebitsch

If the Bank Verein is in danger the surest way to bring it to the ground with a crash is for everyone to draw their money out of the bank. Since the war I have not drawn a farthing from the defeated countries; and I shall not do so now. It is very kind of you to warn me; but I am so disgusted with the "make Germany pay" business that I take a sardonic pleasure in demonstrating that the only effect of it has been to force Germany and Austria to inflate their currencies, and thereby make *me* pay. So do not worry any more about it but leave me and my bank balances to their fate.

I am horrified to hear that Reinhardt is to produce St Joan.[1] I look to you to prevent him from murdering and mutilating the piece if you can. Tell him that I was thunderstruck when I heard that he had performed The Doctor's Dilemma without the last act,[2] and that you have had the greatest difficulty in persuading me to allow him to handle Joan, as I do not believe he understands or likes my work, or that he has an idea in his head later than 1820.

I received Der Geliebte and also your translation of Bashville, but I have not had time to read either, though I could not resist a peep at Bashville to sample the verse, which seems to me excellent. Wormwood Scrubs [in *Bash-*

ville], by the way, is the name of a place and of a prison: there is no "bush" about it. [Section crossed out by Trebitsch.]

I do not know how to advise Fischer as to the rival biographies. Bab has written an essay: it is not really a biography.[3] Henderson has written a real biography, full of information about me; but it is out of date; and he is going to prepare a new edition.[4] Perhaps Fischer's best plan would be to publish Bab's book now, and wait until Henderson's new edition is ready before touching it. . . .

I know nothing of Diedrichstein;[5] but then I know next to nothing of the contemporary American stage, and not so much as I should of the British stage. My generation has passed away; and I shall soon have to follow its example.

We are going to take a holiday in Scotland presently.

ever
G. Bernard Shaw

Tls.

1. Reinhardt, whose star had dimmed in postwar Berlin, had moved to Vienna, but with the London success of *Joan* he quickly acquired the play and announced that he would return to Berlin to direct *Joan* personally, his first such undertaking with Shaw.

2. Shaw is mistaken here: Reinhardt did not omit the last act of *Doctor's Dilemma*, although Trebitsch proposed doing so in the published version (see 18 April 1908).

3. Julius Bab had revised his *Bernard Shaw*, but Fischer withheld publication until 1926 in honor of Shaw's 70th birthday.

4. Henderson's 1911 biography of Shaw was not published in Germany; his revised version appeared in 1932.

5. Leo Ditrichstein (Diedrichstein, 1865–1928), Hungarian-born American actor, also adapted German plays.

Die heilige Johanna (*Saint Joan*) opened at the Deutsches Theater on 14 October, a day after its premiere in Dresden's Schauspielhaus. Reinhardt's followers flocked to the theatre to greet the returned master, and the evening— working its Reinhardtian "magic"—went off splendidly, stirring audience and critics alike and raising the star of the young Viennese actress Elisabeth Bergner (b. 1898): "a great evening" (*Lokal-Anzeiger*, 15 October); "One of Europe's few sovereign brains speaks here and . . . even rarer a sovereign heart" (*Deutsche Allgemeine Zeitung*). *Johanna* ran 146 times that season and another 24 the next, a record opening run for Shaw in Germany and the zenith of his German fame.

Gleneagles Hotel. Perthshire
12th September 1924

My dear Trebitsch

I have been wandering about here in Scotland since the middle of July. The report about Moscow is a *canard*.[1] The Soviet would hang me for

Elisabeth Bergner as Saint Joan, Berlin, 1924.

Marxbeleidigung [crime against Marx]. I am the only living man who has shewn the exact error in Karl's theory of value, and traced the mental process which led him to it.[2]

Although St Joan is still filling the theatre every night, it must come off on the 25th October, because Miss Thorndike's lease of the theatre expires on that day, and she must have some rest and change. Therefore you must arrange your visit to London so as to arrive before that. You can then compare the London production with Berlin and Vienna. The sooner you come the better, as the weather will be getting wintrier all through the month.

We have had no summer here: only a few gleams of sunshine between oceans of rain.

I have a headache, and cannot write any more. We leave this hotel on the 17th, and will be back at Ayot St Lawrence three or four days later.

I wish we had a house in London where we could make you both comfortable; but we have no room at all in Adelphi Terrace; and you know what Ayot is like. Do you think Tina would stand Ayot? But we should be delighted to see you both.[3]

ever

G. Bernard Shaw

Als.

1. On 26 August, *Vossische Zeitung* reported Shaw would visit Russia in October.
2. Shaw traced Marx's "error" in value-theory to Marx's metaphysics, social sympathies, and imagination (review of *Capital, National Reformer*, 21 August 1887; also in *Bernard Shaw and Karl Marx*).
3. Tina did not accompany her husband to London.

Lincoln
23rd September [1924]

WE CANNOT BE IN LONDON ON FRIDAY BUT MY SECRETARY HAS BOOKED YOUR ROOM AT THE PICCADILLY WHY NOT TAKE THE ELEVEN THIRTY TRAIN KINGS CROSS TO HATFIELD ON SATURDAY MORNING AND STAY OVER THE WEEK END WITH US AT AYOT WE CAN GO TO JOAN TOGETHER ON MONDAY THE CAR WILL BE AT HATFIELD AT TWELVE ON SATURDAY TO MEET YOU UNLESS YOU WIRE TO THE CONTRARY YOUR VISIT IS MOST WELCOME

SHAW

Telegram.

10 Adelphi Terrace W.C.
9th December 1924

My dear Trebitsch

Tell the idiot that the battle of herrings was not, as he supposes, fought by the herrings.[1] It was fought on the 12th February 1429 at Rouvray, when Sir John Fastolfe, bringing a convoy of provisions, mostly salt fish, to the English troops in Orleans, was attacked by the Duc de Bourbon. The ease with which Fastolfe, with a handful of archers, defeated the French, is an example of the utter demoralization of the French before Joan came. This battle is always called the Battle of Herrings in England; and the people who have never heard of it have probably never heard of the Battle of Waterloo. The French call it the battle of Rouvray.

On the 26th of this month we sail from Southampton for Madeira, and shall not return until about the middle of February.

As I see no use in holding up Jitta for what is called a West End production, I am going to let Violet Vanbrugh,[2] who in her bloom was a leading London actress, and is still very handsome, try Jitta on tour. Her daughter, Prudence Vanbrugh, is just the right age [twenty-two] for Edith. They are taking a play by Violet's brother [*The Letter of the Law*, by Kenneth Barnes] round the provinces; and Violet wants to give two special matinées in each city of some other play. She likes Jitta; and I have told her she may have it for these matinées and make it part of her repertoire if it proves successful. But first she will try it at a rather nice suburban theatre at Putney Bridge, called the Grand Theatre, Fulham, playing it every night for a fortnight, and keeping another fortnight free before her tour in case the business at the theatre should make it possible to prolong this little suburban run.

I have spent the last four days in London in an almost black fog (artificial light all day) reading the play to the company and rehearsing and arranging it so that the producer will have everything settled for him when he gets to work in January in my absence. In the evenings I studied it and worked out the movements and cut out some irrelevancies and repetitions in my translation which would have no value with English actors and an English audience. My version is a perfectly shocking transposition of your poetic and imaginative fiction in[to] cheesemongering British fact; but nobody will know that; and there is enough of the interest and dignity of the original left to secure you a respectful reception from the press. And we shall make a few pounds in tantièmes.

If Miss Vanbrugh finds herself a success in the play she will play it in London again, at Putney Bridge if she can do no better, but possibly in a West End theatre if she can induce one to let her in on sharing terms. Then there will be a *grande première*, and you might seize the opportunity to pay us another visit, and see it.[3] . . .

Tell the editor of the N[eue] F[reie] P[resse], and the manager of the D[eutsches] V[olkstheater],[4] and all the rest of the people that want to take up my overcrowded time that I am dead, and not likely to recover.

Friend and wind do not rhyme.[5] Friend sounds like fremd with an n instead of an m. Wind is sometimes pronounced weind and sometimes winnd; but it does not rhyme to friend either way.

I think I prefer bereit [ready] to wert [worthy][6] because I might have written worthy instead of ready; but I didnt, because it introduces an idea quite foreign to my meaning: The world will be ready to receive the saints when it is strong enough and big enough, not when its moral character is reformed.

I have torn up my letter to the N.F.P. You can tell the editor you had a letter from me for him. That will console him—perhaps—for not getting a

Christmas message. I never send messages. He would never print any if he
had any sense.   ever

                                                    G. Bernard Shaw

A&tls.
   1. "Battle of the Herrings" is mentioned in the preface to *Joan*.
   2. Violet Vanbrugh (1867–1942) was an older sister of Irene Vanbrugh, whom Shaw had preferred for *Jitta*.
   3. No West End production was given.
   4. The Deutsches Volkstheater had successfully produced *Joan* after the Burg hesitated to challenge the censors who held up approving the play. *Johanna*, with Annemarie Steinsieck and Anton
Edthofer, opened on 24 October before a highly expectant audience and ran 58 times that season.
   5. In *Joan*, Dunois attempts to rhyme: "since I am a friend to thee, change thou the wind for
me," and adds: "No: it does not rhyme."
   6. Trebitsch had rendered Joan's final cry about the earth, "when will it be ready to receive Thy
saints?" as "be worthy" (*wert*). He corrected the error for the book edition (1925).

                                          10 Adelphi Terrace W.C.
                                          22nd December 1924

   An alarm from Paris. It is stated that a German company from Berlin has
undertaken to play St Joan in German in Paris at l'Exposition des Arts Deco-
ratifs, May to October 1925.[1]
   You must stop this at once. I should have to take costly legal proceedings
to interdict the performance if it were persisted in. It would be not only a
violation of my French contract for the first production of Joan in France,
but a breach of taste which would bring down the entire French press on the
play and on me. Just imagine the national saint of France introduced in a
German version by a German company! It would almost lead to a resumption of the war. Please act at once, and vigorously.[2]

                                                    G.B.S.

Apcs.
   1. Reinhardt had a plan to bring *Johanna* to Paris for the exhibit, which was to open 29 April
1925.
   2. Trebitsch did. A French version of *Joan*, produced by Georges Pitoëff (who played the
Dauphin) with Ludmilla Pitoëff as Joan, opened at the Théâtre des Arts on 28 April. The exhibit
also had on display the idiosyncratic designs of *Joan* in Tairov's Kamerny Theatre in Moscow (see
15 May 1925).

                                          Reid's Palace Hotel. Funchal
                                          6th January 1925
My dear [Trebitsch]
   We arrived here on the 31st after a voyage which included two days tempest
in the Channel and the Bay of Biscay. We were 11 hours late; and today's ship
has wirelessed that it will be even later.
   The place is a paradise that occasionally strikes you as a hell. Gorgeous
flowers everywhere, midday sunshine so powerful that clothes are unnecessary, and swimming in the Atlantic the only possible exercise, plenty of
fruit, exquisitely soft water to wash in, English money current, five or six
climates between pine and palm accessible within 20 minutes, a luxurious

hotel (£4-10-0 a day for 2 bedrooms, a sitting room, and well cooked food), all 3½ days out from Southampton, sound very tempting; but I should go mad if I hadnt some work to do.[1]

We expect to stay until the middle of February. . . .

Charlotte sends her love. She blooms in this climate; but getting away was a desperately fatiguing and worrying business; and the voyage—ugh!

ever

G. Bernard Shaw

PS The Honorable Ivor Ferguson [Montagu], a son of Lord Swaythling (a Jewish peer), says he is going to denounce Reinhardt's production as a monstrous misrepresentation of St Joan.[2] A lady whose signature I cannot decipher also writes protesting that Joan is represented in Berlin as a weak, fragile, snivelling Dame aux Camellias. Has Reinhardt been playing any tricks? A man who could produce The Doctor's Dilemma without the last act is *capable de tout*.

Als.

1. Shaw was at work on the foreword to *Imprisonment* and the introductory essay to "Dramatic Criticism" in *A Selection from the Writings of H. W. Massingham*.

2. Ivor Montagu (1904–84), a fellow Fabian who turned Marxist (Shaw slipped on the name), was interested in film-making, and while in Berlin had seen Bergner's Joan, whose elfin charm and heart-wringing intensity Montagu thought distorted Shaw's earthy visionary. Montagu so informed Shaw, but he did not publish his views.

10 Adelphi Terrace W.C.

13th March 1925

My dear Trebitsch

My long delay in writing to you about Jitta has been caused by two things. I have not yet seen the play, as I was in Madeira when it was produced, and second, I did not until yesterday succeed in getting the returns and the cheque for our royalties out of the management of the theatre. In the meantime I had two cheques from Miss Vanbrugh, who is playing Jitta twice every week on her tour through the provinces.[1] . . .

Of course things happened in my absence that would not have happened had I been in London. In spite of my most careful instructions, I found my name in larger letters than yours, and yours given, not as Siegfried Trebitsch, but as Stephan Trebitsch because Siegfried was too German. Yet at the same time the press was crammed with paragraphs giving my own history of the translation, making it clear that you are my German translator. Then paragraphs appeared ridiculing the theatre for trying to suppress the fact that you are a Hun, and ridiculing me for my vanity in having my name printed in larger letters than yours. Annoying as these things were, they kept the papers talking about the play and about you; so that the performances were well advertised more than most West End productions; and everybody here now knows the name of Siegfried Trebitsch almost as well as the name of Bernard Shaw. The same thing may be said about the press notices. They were exasperating in their patriotic assumption that all the parts they didn't like were yours and all the parts they did like mine; and this was made worse by the fact that the first act, being a conversation between two cultured people with some subtlety of motive and delicacy of feeling and character, was dull, for our critics are utter Philistines, and do not understand that sort of thing. But they were quite good notices from the box office point of view. A few critics complained that they could not procure the original text: these were the few who can read German. None of them succeeded in getting a copy: they were all guessing in the dark as to how far the translation was faithful; and it was more amusing to guess that it was not faithful at all; and there were suggestions that you should translate Jitta's Atonement as a new and original Shaw play. All this was extremely irritating; but as the editors put it in and the public promptly read with avidity, it was probably the best thing that could have happened to us.[2]

Nothing more is likely to happen to Jitta until the autumn, except that Miss Vanbrugh will give a couple of matinees of it in Leicester, Croydon, Bristol, Edinburgh, Brighton, Newcastle, Glasgow and Nottingham. At present my intention is to see the performance on Saturday the 21st at Leicester, as I have to go to Birmingham on that day to rehearse Caesar and Cleopatra,[3] and I may as well take Leicester on the way. Until then I can say nothing about the performance except that it is clear that the actor who played Lenkheim [J. Leslie Frith] had a great success.

I will write to Fischer about the money. I am forced to break off abruptly here and leave this letter to Miss Patch to send off. I will resume it after Leicester.

>   ever
>   G. Bernard Shaw
>   pp Blanche Patch
>   (Secretary)

Tl.

1. After two weeks at the Grand Theatre, Fulham, where it opened on 26 January, *Jitta* toured a dozen cities, earning small sums along the way.

2. Most of the ads and programs for *Jitta* featured Shaw's name prominently while printing "S. Trebitsch" in small type, a fact noticed by the *Evening Standard* (27 January) and commented on by the *Daily News*. Included in the program was Shaw's "Translator's note," giving the history of the collaboration. Reviewers supposed the first act to be Trebitsch's and the rest—above all the third act with its comic reversal—to be Shaw's, an "atonement," as the *Daily News* put it, for the "portentous dulness" of "S. Trebitsch's" play. Nevertheless, the audience came from all over London, according to the *Fulham Gazette*, which headlined *Jitta's* "Great Success" (30 January).

3. Barry Jackson's revival of *Caesar* at the Birmingham Repertory Theatre opened on 28 March with Cedric Hardwicke and Gwen Ffrangcon-Davies.

>   The Malvern Hotel. Great Malvern
>   16th April 1925

My dear Trebitsch

My correspondence is now a mere heap of bitter reproaches for urgent letters left unanswered for months. I saw Jitta at Leicester as long ago as the 21st March by stopping on my way to Birmingham to rehearse Caesar; but a string of unlucky circumstances prevented me from writing even to Miss Vanbrugh; and I had to rush from the theatre in such a hurry to keep an appointment with a wegweisend car outside Birmingham that I could not go round to the stage to see her.

Now that at last I *have* written to her she replies that I have "reduced her to *pulp*."[1]

The funniest thing about it is that I was very much struck with your play when I saw it on the stage. It held the audience in spite of a bad performance—not a very bad one, but still not right. Miss Vanbrugh was all wrong. She is a handsome woman and a lady; but she took the greatest pains to present Jitta as an unattractive *whore*, and succeeded only too well. I meant her to play it as what we call "a straight part": that is, to be herself. But she says she gathered from the book that Jitta was an improper person and a hypocrite, and played her accordingly. Accordingly, all your poetic refinement and all Jitta's feminine charm vanished; and the play was pulled through by Lenkheim, who was very effective, but made the mistake of playing to Agnes in the same violent way as to Jitta, and clowning the scene into the bargain, so that the audience got just a little tired of him at the end—or would have if the play had lasted another five minutes.

Agnes was played by a clever *young* actress with a strong American accent [Violet Clifford], *not* the one [Nancy Price] who played the part very successfully (I am told) in London. The first act tried hard to grip the audience and would have done so completely if only Jitta and Haldenstedt had got the dialogue across intelligibly; but they ululated instead of talking plainly; and the audience could only guess what they were driving at, and wait for the impropriety to begin in earnest.

I hardly know what to do about the play. Miss Vanbrugh thinks she can do what I want if I take the production in hand myself. I am not convinced of this, because she has been playing female Apaches and prostitutes for so long that I doubt whether I can get her back to her own quite nice self.

Her tour does not finish until the 4th May, when it will be too late in the season for a West End production. You understand, of course, that the production at Putney Bridge was a suburban affair of no importance—financially or theatrically. But already I have been offered a West End production by another actress, not, however, one for whom I could throw over Miss Vanbrugh.

Fischer sent me a lot of Jittas in the original. Also, by the way, a lot of money: the first I have received from Central Europe since the war.[2] I refused to sign the special edition [of *Die heilige Johanna*] because I have never consented to sell my signature in that way.[3] I have refused my American publishers and my London publishers; and they would be justly offended if I signed a German edition. I know of course that it is a common practice; but it is a very sordid one. Of what value would any of the copies I have autographed for my friends be if they could buy one at the nearest shop.

Fischer has sent me proofs of the illustrations. They are EXECRABLE— Boutet de Monvel[4] and water. If anyone sent me a copy of the play containing them I should tear them out and put them in the fire. The imbecile who perpetrated them might have put his dirty little starved Cinderella into a book of fairy tales and not thrust her into my strong St Joan. How could Fischer make such a choice? I am sending him back the proofs with comments that will make him jump. . . .

What on earth does Elastic Cans mean?[5] We have elastic water bottles (Gummiflaschen?) to warm our beds; but an elastic can is an impossibility. Do you mean Elastic Bands? It is most disgraceful of me not to have read the translation you sent me.[6] I shall do so on my return to Ayot; but I am rather afraid to, lest I should be unable to keep my hands off it.

Tell Elizabeth Bergner to write to me for an appointment when she arrives, so that she may not call and find that I [am] out of town, or be told that I am out, as everyone is unless my parlormaid has been told beforehand to admit them. Can Elizabeth speak English? Would she like to meet Sybil Thorndike.

I think this is all. Do not worry about your health: all that will go away when you pass sixty. 50 to 60 is the worst time of life; 60 to 70 is much better; and I am looking forward to my seventies eagerly. But do not tell Tina this.

ever

G. Bernard Shaw

Als.; postscript omitted.

1. The word "pulp" is underlined twice.

2. With the stabilization of the German currency (old marks were replaced by new Reichmarks at the rate of 1,000,000,000 M to one RM), Fischer remitted Shaw's accumulated earnings, which came to £1,166. He also sold off some shares purchased for Shaw and forwarded £67.

3. In honor of the 50th printing of *Joan* in German, Fischer issued a special edition, illustrated by George G. Kobbe. One hundred fifty copies were specially bound, numbered, and signed by the artist.

4. Boutet de Monvel (1851–1913), French painter and illustrator of children's books, including one called *Jeanne d'Arc*.

5. "Elastic cans" is probably a misreading of something Trebitsch wrote.

6. Almost a year earlier Trebitsch had sent Shaw the commissioned English version of his play *Der Geliebte*.

London

15th May [1925]

RUSSIANS TOTALLY UNAUTHORIZED EVEN IN RUSSIA FISCHER SHOULD STOP THEM EXCEPT IN TOWNS WHERE JOAN HAS ALREADY BEEN PERFORMED AND MAKE THEM PAY IN THE OTHERS.[1] YOU WILL SEE JOAN AT THEATRE DES ARTS IN PARIS.[2]

SHAW

Telegram.

1. An unauthorized production of *Joan* had opened the previous October in Moscow's Kamerny Theatre, staged by its theatricalist director Alexander Tairov on a multileveled platform with stylized and caricatured costumes and acting. Joan wore a kind of space-suit armor: heavy boots, broad belt descending between her legs, and massive breastplate, while the Dauphin was made up like a clown. Shaw thought it "a sort of feeble burlesque," which, he supposed, "we must expect from Russia" (*The Sphere*, 29 November 1924). When in Russia in 1931, Shaw was presented with a set of photographs of the Tairov *Joan*. The production was now on tour in Lithuania, Germany and Austria.

2. Pitoëff's *Joan* continued in Paris through June.

Passfield Corner. Liphook
7th June 1925

My dear Trebitsch

I am at last in a condition which may be described as well. At all events I am able to drive the car and to do some work. I am at this address for a couple of days only, taking a country holiday to prepare myself for a public appearance the day after tomorrow at the Savoy Theatre, not as an actor but as an orator.[1]

I seize the opportunity of the holiday to answer your letters.

[John] Masefield is a well known English poet and playwright. He has written a play called The Trial of Jesus, and given a performance of it in the big music room at his house in Oxford [9 May 1925]. I was present at this performance; and it completely confirmed my opinion that Jesus is an impossible subject for a play.[2] His story is just the opposite of Joan's. Joan's heresies and blasphemies are not heresies and blasphemies to us: we sympathize with them. And she defends herself splendidly, wiping the floor with her accusers every time. Jesus is convicted for asserting that he is the Messiah, and that he will rise from the dead after three days and come again in glory to establish his kingdom on earth. To us that is the delusion of a madman. Instead of defending himself he remains arrogantly dumb, only breaking silence occasionally to insult Pilate, who is trying to be reasonable and even friendly with him. The effect when it is brought to life on the stage is extremely unpleasant; and the cruelties and horrors of the scourging and so forth make it worse, as they are torturing, not a martyr, but a madman. In reading the gospels we do not realize this; but the stage brings it out mercilessly; and the spectacle is shocking to simple Salvationists and intensely disagreeable to the Intelligentsia.

Of Dr Coudenhove and his Ida I heard nothing.[3] Perhaps he wrote when I was in bed, and was put off by my secretary. . . .

Now as to poor Elisabeth [Bergner], who has taken a deadly revenge on me by giving me her influenza. We arranged a lunch for her with Sybil Thorndike and her husband [Lewis Casson] and a famous explorer [Apsley Cherry-Garrard] who is young and goodlooking. She could not come, poor child, as she was ill in her hotel. As I could not very well visit her in her bedroom, I asked Ivor Montague, a son of Lord Swaythling (one of our great Jewish bankers) to call and make enquiries. His mother is one of those charitable enormously rich great Jewish ladies who would come to the rescue at once if the case were serious. I did not dare to let Charlotte go, because she gets influenza too easily, though she fortunately did not catch it from me.

Now Ivor is a very remarkable young man: a Socialist of a very masterful and independent type, interested in the theatre, and especially in films.[4] He saw Elisabeth's Joan in Berlin, and declared that it was all wrong; and he was not at all overawed by her reputation. He arranged that she was to come to tea with us the day before she left London; and we had to come up from the country to see her. Ivor came to the tea too; and poor Elisabeth, still horribly ill, found herself treated like an infant in arms instead of being worshipped as a great genius. This was not what she expected; and I am afraid she was a little puzzled and disappointed.

She is a strange little animal; and her curious resemblance to the imaginary portraits of Joan which were made long after her death in the fifteenth and sixteenth centuries was very striking; but she did not look as if she could give the hardy *maitresse femme* of my play as well as the more touching *naiveté* of the character.

What she wanted was my consent to the filming of Joan; and I have since had a letter from the man who wants to make the film,[5] and who writes like a blind enthusiast. I have not been able to answer him yet; but the project is out of the question. There is no reason why he—or anyone else—should not make a film of the history of Joan of Arc with Elisabeth as Joan. I have no monopoly of her story, which is public property everywhere. What is peculiar to my version is just what cannot possibly be represented in pictures. But the public would not know this; and a film version with my name attached would simply kill the play. Therefore I shall not consent on any account, though I should be glad to see a good film of Joan going the rounds. Everybody who saw it would want to see the play to hear what Joan said as well as see what she did. But if they thought the film was the play, they would consider that they had seen it already, [and] would not come to the theatre. That is what always happens when a play is filmed; and that is why I never allow my plays to be filmed.

So you may tell Elisabeth to go ahead with her film, but that my name must not be connected with it; and of course the scenario must be quite different, with all Joan's feats of arms at full length, including her thrashing the prostitutes out of the camp with her sword, and lots of incidents which I have left out.

Tell her also not to be a little fool about myself and Montague. We were and are quite friendly, and are likely to be much more useful to her than her idolaters. . . .

I think this is all. I am experimenting with a new portable typewriter, and am now too tired of it to go on. . . .

ever
G. Bernard Shaw

Tls.

1. Shaw, recovering from the flu, was visiting Beatrice and Sidney Webb in Hampshire. On the 9th he was to debate Hilaire Belloc on "What Is Coming?"

2. After the success of *Joan*, Reinhardt suggested that Shaw write a play about Jesus.

3. Richard Coudenhove-Kalergi (1894–1972), an Austrian political thinker, founder of the Pan-European Union, and his wife, the Viennese actress Ida Roland, were friends and neighbors of the Trebitsches.

4. Ivor Montagu was only 21 and had just left Cambridge. Eventually he became a film producer, writer, and critic and worked with the Soviet director Sergei Eisenstein in Hollywood. He also served on the London *Daily Worker*.

5. Presumably Paul Czinner, Hungarian-born producer-director, who had directed Miss Bergner in the film *Nju* (1924) and married her in 1933.

Ayot St Lawrence. Welwyn
16th June 1925

My dear Trebitsch

You will see by the enclosed letter from Fischer that he has settled with Tairov.[1] Before putting the matter into the hands of your Viennese lawyers you had better find out from Fischer whether his arrangement does not cover Austria as well as Germany. . . .

Tell Tina that the equinoctial gales come at the end of September, and are the worst in the year, except the March ones. The end of October and beginning of November are usually fine in England. Besides, why not fly?

Violet Vanbrugh, whom I hope to see this week, has nothing to shew the West End people except a fortnight at a suburban theatre and 2 matinées a week in the provinces. That does not count as a tour success. The West End rents are frightful: £450 or £500 a week!

hastily
G.B.S.

Als.
1. Tairov's Kamerny Theatre performed *Joan* three times on tour, once in Vienna, and paid Shaw a royalty of £16. (In Cologne the production was banned because of religious objections.)

In the Orkney Islands—en voyage
13th August 1925

My dear Trebitsch

I received your and Tina's birthday message here in Scotland where I am travelling.[1] You should not remind me that I am now in my seventieth year: my infirmities keep it only too well before me. However, it was pleasant to hear from you, even on a painful subject.

I received the half-yearly statement of my account from the Bank-Verein the other day; and this time I have forced myself to study it, and to make up my mind to close it and have the balance transferred to London. . . .

I find that your shocking ignorance of the Bible has led you to translate a passage from the Gospel in the style of the Neue Freie Presse. At the end of the Tent Scene in Saint Joan, the Chaplain says "Es ist zweckmässig, dass ein solches Weib für die Allgemeinheit sterbe." It is the last sentence in the last speech but one. Look at Ev. Johannis, chapter XVIII, verse 14. "Es wäre gut, das ein Mensch würde umgebracht für das Volk." Or chapter XI verses 49–50: "Ihr wisset nichts bedenket auch nichts, es ist uns besser, Ein Mensch sterbe für das Volk, denn dass das ganze Volk verderbe."[2]

yours ever
G. Bernard Shaw

ps This was hastily written in shorthand more than ten days ago. The typed transcript has been following me about ever since. It reads rather grumpily; but my sentiments are as cordial as ever.

Tls.
1. The Shaws were out of London from 19 July to 12 October.

2. The Chaplain's line in *Joan*—"It is expedient that one woman die for the people"—echoes the King James Bible (*John*, 18:14). Trebitsch did not use the Lutheran German equivalent, but his version is actually closer to Shaw's English and was not altered.

Mackenzie's Hotel. Tongue. Lairg
23rd August 1925

My dear Trebitsch

For the past fortnight I have been travelling in the Orkney and Shetland islands, leaving my letters to accumulate in London until I could give a fixed address. On coming to anchor in this hotel, where I shall stay until the end of the month at least, I find your letter, or rather Fischer's, awaiting me with a great bundle of others. As it is by this time doubtful whether you are in Chamonix or Berlin, I send this to Vienna.

I am writing by this post direct to Fischer telling him not to listen to the wiles of the Hamburger Sender.[1] Broadcasting (Rundfunk) is death to a play. I have taken pains to find out all about this. I have had a four-valve radio set installed at Ayot St Lawrence, so that I could listen-in myself. I have consulted other owners of wireless sets. And I have broadcasted one of my short plays myself. The result admits of no doubt and no hope. The effect is so bad that nobody who has ever tried to hear a play by Rundfunk will ever be persuaded, even by free tickets, to endure that horror again in a theatre. The M150 from the Hamburg man would cost us at least M150,000,000,000,000,000,000,000,000,000, in future tantièmes. The English managers refuse to accept a play that has been broadcasted; and if the German managers were wise they would do the same. Therefore do not be tempted by the hundred and fifty pieces of silver.

My own broadcasting was a great success; but then I chose a short play (O'Flaherty V.C.) in strongly contrasted dialects specially suitable for the purpose, and read all the parts myself.[2]

You will have to keep a tight hand over Barnowsky, or he will do something foolish with Methuselah.[3] He will say that In The Beginning is too short, and will try to put two plays into one evening, or he will want to cut the long plays, or he will get rattled (frightened and fussed) over the whole business, and lose his head. You must make him do exactly what he is told. In America they tried to do the five plays in three evenings, and nearly killed their audiences, whom they had to keep awake with buckets of boiling coffee. In Birmingham and London they gave the work in sets of five performances on five successive evenings; and all went well.[4]

Barnowsky's people want me to write something somewhere to celebrate something about him. Tell all these people that I receive every week a dozen requests for messages to newspapers congratulating them on their fiftieth number or their fiftythousandth or the birth of their seventeenth baby or something or other, and that it is quite useless: their letters and telegrams go straight into the waste paper basket.

Henderson has arranged for the publication of his Table Talk of G.B.S. in a German translation by [Hermann] Scheffauer (or Sheffaur). He does these things without consulting me. The book contains a misstatement by him which has just cost me £123-3-0 to settle a libel action, though I am quite innocent.[5] He is a terror, is Archibald; but when he gets out his new edition of his great biography of me you will have to consider whether you should translate it.

We can talk further of these matters when you and Tina come over at the end of October.

ever

G. Bernard Shaw

Tls.

1. Fischer had informed Trebitsch that a Hamburg radio station was offering 150 marks per play for rights to Shaw. Trebitsch's note, forwarding the information, said: "This is of enormous importance! Please answer at once and give your consent."

2. The BBC broadcast, Shaw's first, was *O'Flaherty* on 20 November 1924.

3. Victor Barnowsky, who was to celebrate his 50th birthday the next month, was preparing the German premiere of *Methuselah*.

4. The cycle was produced by Barry Jackson at his Birmingham Repertory Theatre beginning on 9 October 1923 and ran four times before transferring to the Court Theatre, London, for an additional four cycles.

5. Henderson's *Table-Talk of G.B.S.* (1925), in which Shaw collaborated, contained a remark by Henderson linking Caradoc Evans's *My People* with the "pornographic novel." Evans threatened suit, and Shaw altered the passage for subsequent issues. The German version, *Tischgespräche mit Bernard Shaw*, was published by Fischer (1926).

North West Scotland

5th September 1925

It is always so: travelling wrecks the health unless it is full of hardships. Cold, hunger, exposure, hard beds, bad food, and contretemps of all sorts are indispensable. I hope you have recovered.

Let nothing persuade you to consent to allow Barnowsky to play Parts I & II on the same evening. "In the Beginning" makes a unique impression by itself: no audience dreams of wanting anything more. The Gospel of the B's B utterly destroys this impression, and turns a startling success into a wearisome puzzling failure. That was how New York made a mess of the cycle, which was a triumph in Birmingham. Tell B. that he must positively give the cycle on 5 nights or not give it at all. Imagine yourself a critic with Part I to write about at leisure after an early closing! Then imagine having to write hurriedly about Parts I & II both, after midnight! It is *asking for* bad notices and failure. Do not countenance it for a moment.

G.B.S.

Apcs.

Strathpeffer

5th October 1925

We are just starting homeward; but it will take us more than a week by car. We then have to get everything right in London before we settle in at Ayot; so I am wiring you to fix the 19th as the earliest safe date for Ayot. If you come by way of Venice(!) you can attend the first night of Johanna there with Emma Gramatica as la Pucelle.[1] I hope the weather will be favorable for Tina's crossing. We are looking forward to seeing her.

G.B.S.

Apcs.
   1. The Italian version of *Saint Joan* (*Santa Giovanna*) opened in Venice on 17 October at the Goldoni Theatre, with Gramatica as the Maid and Giuseppi Sterni as the Dauphin.

10 Adelphi Terrace W.C.
[c. 13th October 1925]

Just back from a tour in the provinces and in Scotland, where I have been making terrible speeches about the indemnities. The delivery of ships has thrown all our shipwrights out of work; and they are all wishing the indemnity at the bottom of the sea.[1]

Too tired to write a letter
GBS

Ans.
   1. An unprecedented depression had hit English shipbuilding. Conservatives attributed the collapse to high labor costs, but Shaw blamed it on the reparations exacted from the German merchant marine.

Ayot St Lawrence. Welwyn
[late October 1925]

My dear Trebitsch
I feel sure from a long experience that Tina will not be ready at 10-30 unless she hurries her packing quite unnecessarily. I shall therefore tell Day (our chauffeur) to be at the Ritz at 11. As you will be ready at 10 you will have time for a walk about St James's. This will warm you up before you start on the drive to Ayot, which will take from 60 to 90 minutes.

I intended to come into town myself and meet you; but on reflection you will be freer, and Tina will be less fussed if she is a bit late, if I leave you alone until you arrive here: besides, I shall be able to deal with my letters before you come, and thus be entirely at your disposal for the rest of the day.

If you want to communicate with me before you come, you have my telephone number above; but when the exchange answers you must say "Toll, please." They will then switch you on to the Toll exchange. When Toll answers, ask for Codicote-one-eight. Toll will ask you for your number, which will be Ritz Hotel, so-and-so. But perhaps the best plan is to ask the hotel porter to get you on to Codicote 18 through Toll: a trunk call. They usually get the calls through pretty quickly; but it is easier after 7 in the evening than in the morning. If all is well, do not bother to phone: I tell you about it only in case something goes wrong: for instance a black London fog, which would make it impossible for the car to reach you, and would imprison you in the Ritz until it clears away.

I am happy to say that up to now the weather looks quite promising.

There is only one thing that troubles me. It seems nothing short of barbarous to make Tina come all the way to London only to bury herself in a tiny village which is just like any Austrian village, with nobody to talk to except an old man and his wife, and see nothing of London. You think the house very nice because it is just big enough for you; but Tina will think it a wretched little hovel without a private boudoir for her to take refuge in when she is bored to distraction. That is the difference between a man's view of a house and a woman's. So it must be understood that she may order the car and take flight to the Ritz at any moment, without the least ceremony. She will go mad unless she feels that she can escape.

I have a camera; and she can take as many photographs of us as she likes.

Do not dream of going to see the performances of my plays at the Regent Theatre.[1] I never go myself. If you are dead tired after your journey, but do not want to go to bed, go to the London Pavilion (in Piccadilly Circus, quite close) and see On With The Dance, a very jolly revue[2]—the best thing of the kind in London—which will not call for the smallest mental effort, and will amuse you. You will also see Thesiger,[3] who made a wonderful success as the Dauphin in St Joan, and now gets a much bigger salary for pretending to be a lady undressing for bed. You can sleep in the Pavilion stalls as comfortably as at the Ritz if you are too tired to keep awake.

Arnold Bennett writes to me that he is interested in Jitta, and would like to speculate in it: I will shew you his letter when you come.[4] I have not yet answered it.

We lunch here at 1-30. If there is anything you would like to do in London before you come down, remember that the car is at your disposal exactly as if it were your own.

ever

G. Bernard Shaw

Tls.

1. The Macdona Players, formed in 1921 to tour the provinces in plays of Shaw, were offering a season of Shaw in London, popularly priced, at the Regent Theatre.
2. By Noel Coward; it contained two ballets, one created and danced by Leonide Massine.
3. Ernest Thesiger (1879–1961).
4. Arnold Bennett (1867–1931), novelist and playwright, had seen Jitta and recorded in his Journal (31 January 1925) that Shaw's transformation of the play was "simply electrical." He now considered producing the play with his wife, Dorothy Cheston, in the title role.

10 Adelphi Terrace W.C.
7th November 1925

. . . Tina is quite wrong about the sea making her ill. Perhaps it did not make her ill enough. I know a man whose wife was dying. He took her to America; and she was violently sick all through the voyage. But her health was so improved that when they got ashore he continued making her sick with emetics until she was completely cured. All their friends then came to him when they were ill to be made sick; and he achieved so many cures that he has now set up in practice and makes a large income. Tina must go to

Venice and pay us another visit by long sea through the Mediterranean and the Bay of Biscay.

When we were crossing the Pentland Firth to Orkney I was talking to a lady with a dreadful leaden complexion, very ugly. Suddenly she rushed down into the cabin, and (as Charlotte saw) was frightfully sick. I saw her again as she landed, and her complexion was clear and rosy, her eyes sparkling, and her ugliness changed to the liveliest good looks.

Buy Tina an ounce of ipecacuanha lozenges as a beginning.

G.B.S.

I am frantically hurried, and cannot write a letter today.

Als.

On 19 September, a "first evening" of Parts I and II of *Methuselah* opened at Barnowsky's Tribüne and later transferred (on 19 November) to the Theater in der Königgrätzerstrasse. A "second evening" of Parts III–V was about to open on 26 November. The whole work was extensively cut.

London
20th November 1925

MONSTROUS TOMFOOLERY IT FALSIFIES THE WHOLE CYCLE STOP IT RUTHLESSLY.

BERNARD SHAW

Telegram.

Ayot St Lawrence. Welwyn
6th December 1925

My dear Trebitsch

I enclose the negatives, which will perhaps be better reproduced for your purpose in Vienna than in London. They should be enlarged to at least half plate size on a glossy bromide paper giving the maximum contrast. In the case of the picture with the bust[1] in it, a skilful retoucher could improve it greatly by going over the wall behind us with a fine pencil. The wall would then print white, and our faces and that of the bust would come out against it in much higher relief instead of being almost lost in it as at present.

Send me back the negatives at your convenience. They might be useful here for Jitta. Arnold Bennett's inquiries were on behalf of Nancy Price, who made a success as Haldenstadt's widow. But I cannot let it go into her hands, as she objects to Miss Vanbrugh, which I suppose means that she wants Jitta to be obliterated so as to make Agnes supreme. And that would be asking for failure.

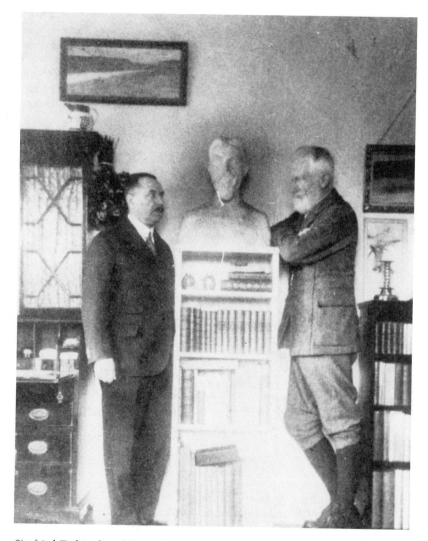

Siegfried Trebitsch and Bernard Shaw beside Rodin's bust of Shaw, Ayot, 1925.

As to Herr Direktor Schickaneder [Mr. Chicanery] Barnowsky, tell him
that as he gets his ideas and takes his instructions from America he had
better get his plays there too. Every person who has suffered the intolerable
infliction of Parts III & IV[2] of Methuselah on the same evening will warn his
friends not to go. You will find that Barnowsky cut down the first act of the
Elderly Gentleman to nothing the moment your back was turned. He has
done what they did in America; and the result will be the same: empty
houses when the Shaw-at-any-cost little public is exhausted. He has broken
faith with me and spoilt my Methuselah debut in Berlin; and I hope you will
never let him have a chance of doing that again. The press notices are no
consolation for empty benches.[3] Please convey my sentence of excom-
munication to him with bell, book, and candle, blast him! . . .

G. Bernard Shaw

Als.
  1. Rodin's bust of Shaw.
  2. Actually Parts III–V.
  3. Notices of the "first evening" were very favorable: *Berliner Tageblatt* (22 September) praised
Shaw for producing a monumental work in advanced age; *Vossische Zeitung* (23 September) took
pleasure in a crowning work of intellect by Europe's leading playwright; and the *Deutsche Allgemeine Zeitung* lamented the need to go abroad for worthwhile drama. The "second evening" was
also welcomed but was less successful, running 15 times whereas the "first" ran 92.

[Ayot St Lawrence. Welwyn]
8th December 1925

. . . I have been trying to talk German today to Ernest Toller,[1] ein sehr
liebenswurdig Kerl [a very nice fellow].

G.B.S.

Ans.
  1. Ernst Toller (1893–1939), German expressionist playwright and left-wing revolutionary, was
introduced to Shaw by Ivor Montagu at the home of his parents, Lord and Lady Swaythling.

Ayot St Lawrence. Welwyn
18th December 1925

Toller came down to Ayot for lunch after we had met him at Lady Swaythling's. We liked him very much indeed. He is the only man I ever met who
seemed the better for five years imprisonment.[1]
  Bartsch[2] may lasciar ogni speranza [abandon all hope]. I tolerated that
wretched opera [*The Chocolate Soldier*] because they all implored me not to
ruin them by stopping it. It brought money to the poor devil of a librettist,
and to the composer, and gave employment to a lot of poor singers and
choristers. Of course they broke faith with me; but I winked at it.
  But these film magnates have no such claim ad misericordiam. I wired to
Bartsch to Budapest to tell him that the Theatre Guild in America, now hav-

ing a great success with Arms & The Man, would probably stop a film, and that I could not undertake not to do so myself.[3]

ever

G.B.S.

Apcs.

1. In 1919, Toller was arrested and sentenced to five years' imprisonment for his part in the short-lived Bavarian Soviet Republic. In jail he barely escaped assassination and composed *Masse-Mensch* (English title, *Masses and Man*), his most famous play. After Hitler came to power Toller emigrated to America. He committed suicide in 1939.

2. Hans Bartsch (1884–1952), German-born American theatre producer, owned part interest in *The Chocolate Soldier*, which he now wanted to film.

3. *Arms and the Man* was currently running in a Theatre Guild revival (14 September 1925) with Alfred Lunt and Lynn Fontanne.

Falmouth Hotel. Falmouth
27th December 1925

For Heaven's sake stop your sculptor if he is coming to London hoping to sculpt me. Tell him that I positively will not sit to him. These poor devils think that if I can be induced to sit to them they will become well known and will be able to sell the bust. Nobody takes the slightest notice of them or of the bust; and in the end they come to me starving and begging me to buy the thing for £150, for £100, for £50, for £5, for five shillings, and shew by their disappointment at my refusal that they were counting on me all the time. Tell Ernesto[1] that now that you have told me what he wants there is no chance of his even seeing me: I will avoid him like the plague.

Cramp in the stomach is the deadliest sort of Wadenkrampf, much more than cramp in the leg. It doubles you up; and down you go.[2]

I havn't yet read your Chesterton article, but will muster up my German and tackle it presently.[3]

Who is Herbert Eulenberg, author of Gegen Shaw: eine Streitschrift, published by Reissner in Dresden?[4]

GBS

Apcs.

1. Ernesto di Fiori (1884–1945), Italian (part Austrian) artist, well known in Germany, had recently sculpted Elisabeth Bergner, Jack Dempsey, and Benjamino Gigli.

2. The He-Ancient's remark in *Methuselah* that the body can be drowned by a "cramp in the stomach" puzzled Trebitsch, who thought it should be "cramp in the leg" (*Wadenkrampf*).

3. A German translation of G. K. Chesterton's *George Bernard Shaw* was reviewed by Trebitsch in *Vossische Zeitung* (18 December; also *Neue Freie Presse*, 21 December).

4. Aroused by Shaw's acclaim, Herbert Eulenberg (1876–1949), neoromantic German playwright and author, wrote a slashing polemic *Gegen Shaw* (Against Shaw, 1925), calling Shaw a "jellyfish" and "weathervane" who was inspired by Mammon and denigrated the heroic.

The Falmouth Hotel. Falmouth
3rd January 1926

I do not remember the passage about cramp in the stomach. I have not a copy of Methuselah here. But it *cannot* mean the drowning of a person on dry land. In Part III the Archbishop describes how he pretended to have been drowned; and there is the American inventor's discovery of how to breathe under water; but where does the cramp come in?[1] There must be some misunderstanding.

All sculptors are poor devils; and the Italians are the poorest and most rapacious of the lot. The last one to whom I fell a victim (after the solemnest protestations that it was all right) was an Italian, well known and very skilful.[2]

G.B.S.

Apcs.
  1. Trebitsch still could not credit that one could drown from stomach cramp. Years later, when revising his translation (1947), he altered "drowned" to "choked."
  2. Probably Prince Paul Troubetskoy (1866–1938), of Russian descent but born and reared in Italy. After seeing Rodin's bust of Shaw, Troubetskoy demanded a half-hour's sitting which turned into two sittings and three hours. Later he made a statuette and a full-length statue of Shaw.

[Falmouth Hotel. Falmouth]
14th January 1926

We leave Falmouth tomorrow; so cancel the address. We expect to reach Ayot on Sunday.

Of course the Jitta film rights are yours: I have no share in or claim on them whatever.[1] But as the Americans are quite capable of announcing the film as by me, you had better make it clear that if this is done my agents will immediately stop the performances. . . .

I hope the lecture tour will be lucrative; for it will be very tiresome.[2] I never speak in public now if I can help it. I have had enough of it, and am too old for it. On the last occasion I spoke for 80 minutes, and was quite exhausted next day. I used to hold big audiences for 110 minutes without turning a hair.

G.B.S.

Apcs.
  1. Since a silent film of *Jitta* would not reproduce his dialogue, Shaw renounced any claim to cinema rights.
  2. In honor of Shaw's approaching 70th birthday, Trebitsch undertook a lecture tour on "Bernard Shaw's Rise to Fame in Germany" ("Der deutsche Aufstieg Bernard Shaws," later published in *Weltbühne*, 1926; reprinted in a shorter version as "How I Discovered Bernard Shaw," *Bookman*, April 1931).

Without consulting Shaw, S. Fischer and Trebitsch began planning a celebration of Shaw's 70th birthday to include an album of autograph tributes. Shaw, who preferred not to be reminded of his birthdays and who scorned such public ceremonies, at first objected. On 1 March Charlotte wrote to Trebitsch: "You appall and horrify me! *Don't*, we pray you, think of such a thing. *Stop* it: smother it, in every way you can . . . *G.B.S. is really vexed about this.* I have seldom seen him more so." (Berg.) Trebitsch, crestfallen, offered to withdraw from the festivities and had to be reassured: "We do not wish to cause you pain in any way," Charlotte wrote on 9 March. "We are very fond of you, and very grateful to you for all you have done." Shaw, who was ill with the flu, dictated his letter to Charlotte.

Ayot St Lawrence. Welwyn
My dear Trebitsch   (Dictated)   19th March 1926

You must not let this birthday business worry you. If the German Nation, which celebrated neither my youth nor my prime, wishes to celebrate my dotage by all means let it enjoy itself in that strange fashion as much as it pleases. Perhaps it is desirable that the world should be reminded that I am old & past my work, though I certainly need no such reminder myself. The only condition I make is that they shall not ask me to join in the festivities. I have done the work, but I positively refuse to do the shouting.

There is no reason whatever why you should not be as prominant in the affair as you please. Nothing could be more against my wishes than that all the gentlemen who have been assuring me for the last 30 years that your infamous translations have ruined my reputation in Germany & that they themselves are the true high priests of the Shavian culte, should now gorge themselves at public banquets in my honour from which you are absent, and send me albums of autographs from which your own is missing. Even honest devotees like Julius Bab must not be allowed to take your place in the sun. It must be a case of "Trebitsch, Trebitsch über alles." So do not step an inch out of the limelight under the mistaken impression that I desire your effacement. So you, & the faithful Fischer, may make the most of the occasion.

This is all I have to say for the moment. I have been in bed for 10 days & am ten feet long in consequence. When I have recovered my natural stature & activity I can attend to business.

Meanwhile give my love to Tina & tell her not to let you overdo the banquets. My health should be always drunk reverently in Billin wasser[1] after a simple vegetarian meal.

ever
G. Bernard Shaw

Als.; Charlotte Shaw's handwriting.
1. A sparkling mineral water from the springs of Bilin (Bilina), a spa in northwest Bohemia.

Ayot St Lawrence. Welwyn
3rd April 1926

I am still far from well. Did I tell you that the attack came after seeing a film called Nju?[1] The moment I saw Elisabeth I said to Charlotte "she has given me influenza again."

I am in a difficulty about Jitta. I have to print it to make up a volume entitled *Translations, Trifles, and Tomfooleries,* for a special edition of my complete dramatic works for sale by weekly installments.[2] I find it practically impossible to separate the cost of manufacturing Jitta from that of the rest of the volume or to ascertain what the profit on it will be. Will you sell me the English literary right for a lump sum. Fischer could value it for you, if you find it difficult to fix a sum yourself. This will not touch the performing right, which will remain as before.

The printing will make it much easier to obtain performances.

G.B.S.

Apcs.
1. *Nju*, a German film based on the Russian expressionist play by Ossip Dymow, produced and directed by Paul Czinner, with Elisabeth Bergner, Emil Jannings, and Conrad Veidt.
2. This Pocket Edition in twelve volumes—the first collected edition of Shaw's plays in English—was published by Globe. The price was £5.10.0 in monthly installments of 6 shillings. Volume 12 of the edition contained six playlets and *Jitta*.

Ayot St Lawrence. Welwyn
17th May 1926
My dear Trebitsch

I am very much bothered about this business of Jitta. Why did you not ask Fischer about it? I cannot fix the price when I am the purchaser: it is clearly a case in which some third party who knows the market should make a valuation. When you leave it to me you are virtually saying "Make me an offer." This is reasonable enough; but you add that you will accept whatever I offer, which of course makes it impossible for me to make any offer. You really must not be sentimental about business.

As far as I can ascertain there is no market price here. If I ask my publisher what he would have paid for the translation rights of Jitta apart from any question of my translating it he will reply that he would not have paid anything at all, as there is no market here for foreign plays, and even Hauptmann is only available in a bad American translation of his complete works.

The simplest plan would be to publish Jitta and give you half royalties, as in the case of my books in Germany. Unfortunately there are no royalties available. Here I manufacture my books myself and send them to the publisher, who publishes and sells them, and hands me over the proceeds less 15% commission for himself. If I were publishing Jitta as a separate volume it would be possible by keeping careful accounts to find out exactly what the profits (if any) on the Jitta volume were, and to give you an agreed share. But I am publishing it in a volume which contains four or five other plays or rather playlets; and it would be quite impossible to distinguish the profits on Jitta from those on the rest. To save all these complications I want to buy you out once for all as far as the publishing rights in Jitta are concerned. This is the more important as I may die presently; and arrangements that may go very easily between us may be very troublesome as between our widows and executors.

I do not want an *exclusive* right to translate and publish Jitta in English. I have altered my preface as you desire about the husband, and added that my translation is so inadequate that the play ought to be read in the original.[1] Possibly you may, like Hauptmann, some day find an English or American publisher willing to undertake a complete edition of your plays, in which case my Anglicised and vulgarized and stagey adaptation should be replaced by a faithful and poetic one. You would still retain your power to authorise this; and of course your performing rights and film rights and so forth would not be affected at all.

As I see we shall never get on unless I make a move I will make a proposal. I offer you one hundred pounds (£100) . . .

Before you accept this, send . . . to Fischer and ask him whether he considers it fair. If he says No, ask him what he would consider fair. Do not, I beg you, be sentimental about this. If you cannot make an estimate yourself you must consult somebody with some experience.

I enclose the cheque, as you say it will be useful; but this need not commit you to accepting it if you are advised that it is insufficient.

Charlotte got your letter this morning. We are very sorry to hear that Tina is not well. She will probably get much worse if she tries to live on fruit exclusively. Tell her to eat what she likes, take no baths nor treatments of any sort, and see how Carlsbad agrees with her. The fruit gospel has been dangerously overdone of late.

I wish you would stop those fools at the Volkstheater from meddling with my plays. There are only two policies likely to succeed with the hell scene from Man & Superman. One—quite easy—is to let it alone. The other is to play it as it is written. To cut it is fatal.[2]

Do not let them broadcast Candida. Nobody who hears a play broadcast ever goes to see it; and they talk for days afterwards about how it bored them. It is the surest way of killing a play I know.

ever
G. Bernard Shaw

P.S. As to my health, all I can say is that I am not well yet, and am desperately but not very successfully trying not to work much. But what can I do? The work won't wait.

Tls.

1. In the revised "Translator's Note" Shaw stresses the temperamental differences between the German and English versions. Gitta's husband is no longer a man "who hardly escapes . . . from the strict Spanish tradition of jealousy," but "a character-study much subtler and more elusive than . . . my frankly comedic" one. Shaw also avers that he was "shamefully unable to do justice" to the original play.

2. On 5 May, the Deutsches Volkstheater, Vienna, revived *Man & Superman*, in a new staging by Karlheinz Martin, which included a shortened Hell Scene and starred Anton Edthofer and Margaret Koeppfe. The play ran sixteen times as against seven performances there in 1907.

[Ayot St Lawrence. Welwyn]
18th June 1926

I saw Violet Vanbrugh the other day, and am (with your permission) getting a literal translation of Gitta, by someone who knows German![1] made to give her a better notion of the part. I have spoiled the play horribly.

GBS

Ans.
1. Alma von Bank, who occasionally helped Shaw with German correspondence.

10 Adelphi Terrace W.C.
25th June 1926

My dear Trebitsch

The story about my having finished two one act plays is, as usual, a flat lie. I am still struggling to get my book on Socialism finished; and until it is out you may contradict all tales of new plays.

I enclose a proof of the first act of Gitta with the preface as modified. Will you read it and tell me whether you would like it still further modified? Do not hesitate to pull it to pieces until it is quite right.

What about my description of the play as a tragi-comedy? Shall I retain that?[1]

The sole use I propose to make of the literal translation is to let Miss Vanbrugh read it, so that she may see that though Gitta met a gentleman in an apartment hired for the purpose she did not smoke cigarettes and dress and behave like a cocotte. Unless she reads the original she will misrepresent the character.

Tell Fischer there are no child photographs of me. I paid the reproduction fee on the one I sent you as for reproduction in Bab's book;[2] but it does not matter.

Our July movements are not settled. We may be here for a part of the month; but Charlotte wants to get away soon and return earlier than usual; so it may not be necessary to wait until October.

In haste, ever
G. Bernard Shaw

Tls.
1. The description was dropped.
2. A revised edition of Bab's *Bernard Shaw* was issued by Fischer in honor of Shaw's seventieth birthday.

Ayot St Lawrence. Welwyn
1st August 1926

I hope the cure has not killed you.[1] Dont ever have a 70th birthday: skip from 69 to 71. I had to accept a dinner from the Labor Party; and I managed to make a fine speech;[2] but what am I to do with all the congratulations, and with that gorgeous album?[3] I havnt time to look at it, much less write to everyone. Dr Stresemann sent me official congratulations through your Botschafter [Ambassador] Friedrich Sthamer; and I have acknowledged it in a letter which is already published in the London Sunday papers.[4] It will be more popular in Germany than in England.

On Wednesday the 4th we go to the Hotel Regina Palace, Stresa, Lago

Maggiore, Italy. I have had to do three months work in the last 6 weeks, and am all over neuritis with overwork when I needed complete rest to get well.

How did your very dangerous cure come off?

Tina's telegram was the nicest of all.

My printers will send you proofs of the volume containing Jitta and a lot of trash, including two little plays that you have never seen [*The Glimpse of Reality* and *The Fascinating Foundling*].

I have struck out Hugo & Gautier.[5]

Let me have a line to Stresa. What is your new play[6] about?

G.B.S.

Apcs.

  1. Trebitsch had gone to the Bircher-Benner Clinic, Zurich, which pioneered raw vegetarian diets. Modified fasting on fruit juice was part of the regimen.

  2. The dinner, on 26 July, was at the Hotel Metropole.

  3. The album, made of specially prepared paper and bound by S. Fischer, contained autograph tributes from eminent Germans, including Einstein, Spengler, Hauptmann, Schnitzler, Mann, Richard Strauss, and Arnold Schönberg. It remains in the library at Shaw's Corner, Ayot.

  4. Gustav Stresemann (1878–1929) was the German Foreign Minister. Friedrich Sthamer (1856–1931) was the German ambassador in London. Shaw in his reply contrasted the cordiality of the German government with that of England, which had canceled the broadcast of his birthday speech, and contrasted also English barbarism with German culture, to which he owed his European reputation (*Observer*, 1 August).

  5. In his preface to *Jitta*, Shaw had compared Vienna to the France of Victor Hugo and Théophile Gautier; on Trebitsch's prompting he now described Vienna as "romantic in the manner of Verdi's operas and modern in the manner of Maupassant and Baudelaire."

  6. Trebitsch's new work, *Der Geheilte* (The Man Who Was Cured), was a novella, not a play.

10 Adelphi Terrace W.C.
2nd August 1926

Yesterday I posted a card to you from Ayot, addressed to Vienna.

Galsworthy did not refuse the invitation: his place was reserved for him; but he was too ill to come.[1]

Tomorrow we start for the Hotel Regina Palace, Stresa, Lago Maggiore.

We stayed at the Miramonte once before the war, just after we parted from you that day on the road after Salzburg.[2]

We are not taking the car: the drive across France would take too long. We go straight through by the Orient luxe.

I am nearly dead; and the journey will probably finish me.

If that other card does not overtake you, let me know: it contained a scrap or two of news.

Our love to Tina.

WHAT a birthday!!! Thank God it cannot occur again.

G.B.S.

Apcs.

  1. John Galsworthy (1867–1933), British novelist and dramatist. Arnold Bennett and the playwright James M. Barrie also sent their regrets.

  2. The Trebitsches were on holiday at the Hotel Miramonte, Cortina d'Ampezzo, Italy.

[Regina Palace Hotel. Stresa]
postmarked 27th August 1926

Collect all the medical advice you can get as to what NOT to eat, and stuff yourself with it until you have recovered. What is wrong is simple starva-tion, probably; but you dont tell me what your "attacks" are. Be more ex-plicit: we are quite anxious about you. I very nearly died of my birthday; and if anyone ever proposes to celebrate a birthday of mine again I shall prose-cute him for constructive murder.[1]

We shall not remain away from home so long this year as last; but I doubt whether we shall return and put our house in order before October.

Send me another bulletin, however brief, from Salzburg.

GBS

Apcs.

1. "Constructive murder": a legal concept involving straining the law to include otherwise nonpunishable acts.

Regina Palace Hotel. Stresa
28th September 1926

My dear Trebitsch

I should have written sooner; but I first had to fix the date of our return and secure berths in the Orient Express; and when this was at last done Charlotte suddenly collapsed with violent pains in her inside (only a chill; but I was terrified lest it should be appendicitis), and could not leave her bed until today. Now, however, I think her complete recovery in time for our journey is certain.

We shall leave Stresa, then, on Monday next, the 4th, in the evening, and reach London late in the afternoon on Tuesday the 5th. Then there will be the unpacking and getting the two houses in order after 2 months absence, with other matters that will keep us a good deal occupied during the rest of the week. Charlotte doesn't think she could attend to you properly and make you comfortable until Monday the 11th at Ayot.

On the other hand, that may be inconvenient for you; and you are too inti-mate a friend to mind it being a bit of a scramble if you would rather come earlier and rush away again. We could see you at Adelphi Terrace on Friday the 8th. We go to Ayot on the 9th. They have been putting in new stoves and things there; and Charlotte will not feel settled in until the Monday, to say nothing of the heap of letters and books that are waiting for me there; but if you don't mind our being a bit distracted with all this, and leaving you to make the best of it, you could come down for the week end—or say from Sunday morning—and get away (if you must) on the 11th. The alternative is to come on the 11th & stay as long as you like (at Ayot). We shall be de-lighted to see you anyhow and anywhen.

It is a great relief to hear that Tina is mending. Your first account was so heartrending that we really had nothing helpful to say, and could only wait for a time when condoling letters would not be a mere worry. Besides, I was

getting much better myself, and could not bring myself to flourish my recovery in poor Tina's face. Gallstones are damnable things. I know a man
who says he can prevent them from recurring by curing the tendency which
produces them. I'll talk to you about him when we meet.

I should dissuade you from bothering about Berlin if it were not likely to
be a change that will do you good.[1] That absurd fruit cure might have killed
you (a fast on water alone would have been the real thing); but as it did not,
there may have been some good in it. We are all the more anxious to have a
look at you.

Let us hear what you decide. Do just what you like best.

ever

G. Bernard Shaw

Als.
    1. Trebitsch planned to attend the Berlin revival of *Superman* at the Lessing-Theater, on 5 Oc-
tober, with Eugen Klöpfer and Carola Neher. Unlike the Reinhardt production that failed in 1906,
this production included a cut third act and ran 78 times.

[10 Adelphi Terrace W.C.]

postmarked 9th October 1926

The train leaves Kings Cross at 11.30. That is where you tell the taxi to
drive you to.

Neither the Club nor the lady are important, though she makes a great
fuss about them.[1] You had better stay until Thursday morning, when I must
go up to town until Saturday.

Your destination is Hatfield, where the car will meet you.

G.B.S.

Apcs.
    1. Trebitsch wanted to meet Mrs. Dawson-Scott, poet and novelist and founder in 1921 of
the P.E.N. Club, which Trebitsch, a founding member of the Austrian branch, enthusiastically
supported.

Belatedly, on 3 November, Shaw wrote to Fischer acknowledging the birthday album:

"You must have been surprised by my long silence concerning the magnificent tribute you sent to me on the occasion of my 70th birthday, signed as it
was by so many names eminent not only in Germany but in Europe and indeed throughout the civilized world. . . . But the effect was as if you had
hung a massive gold chain round the neck of a goose, and, with the best intentions, sunk the poor bird to the bottom of the pond.

"Had I been in perfect health and in the fullest vigor of my prime, I should
have recovered from the avalanche sooner; but I was 70, and, as it unluckily
happened, only half recovered from a long and serious illness. What was I to
do? I could have thanked you with a cordial handshake as I do now most

heartily thank you for your friendly labors in organising the tribute. I could have embraced Trebitsch, to whom I owe my reputation in Germany. But how is one to shake hands with a range of mountains, or embrace Valhalla? Picture the old man wagging his overwhelmed head and mumbling Bitte, bitte, sehr verbunden, tausend Dank etc. etc. until he falls asleep exhausted!

"I confess I got out of the difficulty by simply running away. A speech at a banquet, a letter to Herr Stresemann which provoked the most gratifying expressions of jealousy in the London press, and I fled to Italy and gave instructions that all journalists and all persons who looked as if they intended to congratulate me were to be informed that I had been drowned that morning whilst bathing in the Lago Maggiore.

"On my return I hoped that everybody had forgotten all about my seventieth birthday; but the remonstrances of my wife, who has to see that I behave properly, and a visit from Trebitsch, awakened my lulled conscience, and made me feel that I must write to you and beg you to do what you can to convey to the signatories of the tribute that not a line of it was lost on me. Apart from the warm personal gratification it has given me I shall treasure it as an unchallengeable certificate of my success as a servant of European literature. If when I come to the final judgment I am reported—as I certainly shall be if the Recording Angel happens to be an Englishman—for having presumptuously thought myself a writer of some merit, I shall reply 'Germany thought so,' and that will settle the case." (Private Collection of Mr. & Mrs. B. Lenowitz.)

Fischer circulated a German translation of Shaw's letter to the signatories of the album.

10 Adelphi Terrace W.C.
4th November 1926

My dear Trebitsch

I have written the letter to Fischer: it was posted last night, and will be in his hands before you receive this.

Miss Violet Vanbrugh, who created the part of Jitta here, has shewn the play to Cyril Maude, one of our star comedy actors, who has just retired, but has a good ten years more work in him if he chooses, as he probably will, to emerge from his retirement. I enclose the passages from his letters to Miss Vanbrugh which deal with the play. There is no doubt that if he played Lenkheim he would do more to secure a success than anyone else on the English stage. You must not build on this; but it may interest you to know his opinion of the play.[1] . . .

Our love to Tina, and congratulations to you on your recovery.

ever
G.B.S.

Tls.
    1. Nothing came of the attempt to interest Cyril Maude (1862–1951), the retired actor-manager, in *Jitta*.

The Hydro Hotel. Torquay
13th January 1927

My dear Trebitsch

The report about filming St Joan is a lie, as usual; but it is true that I have been investigating the phono-film, and think it may have a great future.[1] You should do all you can to encourage it, because it makes the translator as indispensable as the author. If St Joan was filmed in the ordinary way you would be, as you say, ruined; but if it were phono-filmed there would have to be a special film of your translation for all the German speaking countries.

I do not know what this new "Mein Freund Bernhard Shaw" of Henderson's is: he has told me nothing about it; but he is selling the serial rights; and editors are writing to know whether I approve. I echo your comment.[2]

Cyril Maude is returning to the stage, and is announced to appear in a new play [*The Wicked Earl*, by Walter Hackett], not Jitta. I have very little hope of his interest in Lenkheim ever coming to anything.

I am in Torquay at present working hard at the book on Socialism.[3] Only by neglecting everything else shall I finish it; but it is almost complete now.

Is Tina quite well?

In great haste,
G.B.S.

Tls.; postscript omitted.
 1. The *Neue Freie Presse* had reported on 30 December 1926 that Shaw intended to film *Saint Joan* with Sybil Thorndike and would appear in a prologue to the movie.
 2. Archibald Henderson, again bypassing Trebitsch, published a two-part article in *Neue Freie Presse* (1, 9 January), "Mein Freund Bernard Shaw," based on conversations with Shaw. Other articles followed in various German papers.
 3. *The Intelligent Woman's Guide to Socialism and Capitalism*, begun in 1925, had grown into a massive volume.

10 Adelphi Terrace W.C.
26th March 1927

Sybil Thorndike wants to know whether a season of plays in English (she being the star) would have any chance of success in Vienna this summer. She is engaged here until the 12th June. It seems to me that the weather will be too hot then for theatregoing; but I promised her I would ask you.

How is Tina; and how are you?

GBS

Apcs.

The Malvern Hotel. Malvern
12th April 1927

I cannot hunt out what I wrote about Max Liebermann in 1890 or thereabouts.[1] I was then writing little paragraphs about picture exhibitions every week for The World, at five pence a line. Only half a dozen times a year did I write a regular full dress article—not so often, indeed. Even if I could find what I wrote without some days searching, it would probably be only 12 lines or so, not worth resuscitating at this time of day.

GBS

. . . L'affaire Bernstein est raccommodée [is patched up]: he has just visited London; and we have drunk Blutbrüderschaft [blood-brotherhood].[2]

Apcs.

   1. Liebermann, the leading German impressionist painter, was approaching his 80th birthday.

   2. A year or so earlier, Henry Bernstein (1876–1953), popular French dramatist, known for his temper and dueling, became embroiled with Shaw in *Le Temps* after Shaw attributed his cool French reception to the provincialism of Paris (10 August 1925). Bernstein, defending France's honor, condemned Shaw as a bad-mannered, boastful self-advertiser, who even laughed at his mother's cremation ("G.B.S. et Paris," 7, 14 September). Shaw in an "Open Letter" (16 November) declared that Bernstein as a romantic Jew did not understand the half-savage French Gentiles, who would see Bernstein's flag-waving as a Jewish plot to exploit French feelings. Responding in the same issue, Bernstein impugned Shaw's socialism and, offended by Shaw's mentioning his Jewishness (like Max Nordau earlier, see 4 August 1907), scoffed: "dear Socialist, multimillionaire, and anti-Semite." In a "Postscript," published in *Der Jude* (Berlin, January 1926), which reproduced his letter, Shaw declared that he had been misunderstood; that as an English author, in a country relatively free of anti-Semitism, he felt no constraint to treat Jewish matters with the greatest delicacy, that he was sympathetic to the Jews but against exaggerated nationalisms, and found it absurd for Jews to side with imperialist jingoism (retranslated from the German in the *Jewish Chronicle*, 12 February 1926).

Ayot St Lawrence. Welwyn
29th April 1927

Nothing passed between myself and Rheinhardt that called for any remark.[1] He looked extraordinarily well and open-airy, as if he had never been near a theatre in his life. I never saw a man less spoilt by his profession.

As to The Land of the Leal, how can I help? What does the title mean? Is it heaven or the fatherland?[2]

I congratulate you on being young enough to travel all the way to Berlin to see one of your own plays. I shouldnt go half the distance to see one of mine. Well, success—!!!

GBS

Apcs.

   1. On 10 March, for the first and only time, Max Reinhardt visited Shaw.

   2. Trebitsch's *Das Land der Treue* (Land of Constancy, see 27 June 1923) was to have its premiere at Reinhardt's Kammerspiele on 10 May 1927. The title, rendered by Shaw as "Land of the Leal" after an old Scottish song, refers to marriage. *Das Land* was tepidly received as a "product of the museum" (*Berliner Tageblatt*) and ran only eight times.

Ayot St Lawrence. Welwyn
12th July 1927

My dear Trebitsch

You may take it for granted that all the stories about me in the papers are lies. But this time they have accidentally hit on the truth. Yes: we ARE leaving Adelphi Terrace after thirty years; and Charlotte and I are up to our necks in Ewigschmutzigkeit [endless dirt], rooting out and selling off millions of books and prints and pictures and rubbish of every sort accumulated during that period.

As to the address, it is not changed yet. On the 24th we leave London for Stresa where we expect to arrive on the morning of the 26th. Our address then for at least six weeks if not more will be Regina Palace Hotel, Stresa,

Lago Maggiore, Italy. Our furniture will be moved during our absence; and when we return we shall go into 4 Whitehall Court, London S.W. 1. So until the 24th we shall be at the Adelphi; then at Stresa; and finally at Whitehall Court.

I cannot advise you about Shubert without fuller information.[1] Have you exercised your translation rights soon enough (within ten years) to prevent them from falling into the public domain? However, the lapse of the translation rights does not involve lapse of performing rights. Did you register a copy of the play at the Library of Congress and pay a dollar? Did you dispose of the translation rights to any person who might have sold them to Shubert subsequently?

Read the enclosed prospectus of The Dramatists' Guild of America. I have joined it, though I should never dream of signing a contract without reserving all rights except that of stage performance. You will see, however, that if you are a member ($37 a year), or an associate (which is cheaper) it will be difficult for Shubert to treat you badly. He must want the film rights: and this means that no matter whether you have any rights in America or not he must obtain your licence for the British Empire, where you certainly have rights, and indeed for the whole civilized world. Rights within frontiers without the right to cross them are no use for the film.

As to what you can get I have no notion. I ask £20,000! For Gitta Berta Kalich's husband said he could not get more than £400. You had better ask for an offer, and make it clear that you know quite well that Shubert *must* have your consent or give the play up. And if you join the Guild you have of course the right to ask their advice and protection.

I must break off hastily to catch the post.

G.B.S.

Tls.

1. Trebitsch suspected that Lee Shubert was out to pirate *Das Land*, but Shubert did not produce the play.

10 Adelphi Terrace W.C.
21st July 1927

My dear Trebitsch

I do not think that Shubert will venture to use your play unless he has a good title. The risk of your taking an action against him is too great. America is full of lawyers who make a speciality of actions for infringement of copyright; you will see some mention of it in the paper I sent you about the Guild of Dramatists. My personal interference would do no good: I have no *locus standi* in the affair; and there is no reason why Shubert should be afraid of me.

As to the book [*The Intelligent Woman's Guide to Socialism and Capitalism*], it is not yet complete. I will send you a copy as soon as it is in its final shape. I hope to send my corrected proofs to the printer before I leave for Stresa; but the corrections are so extensive that it will take him some time to make them.

Is Tina carrying a red flag in Vienna?[1] I hope the revolution has left her unharmed. I think you had both better keep out of Italy until that frontier on the Brenner Pass is rectified.

I note your address at Cabourg, which should be Cabourg-sur-mer, Calvados, France. Why don't you sit naked in the sun on the banks of the Danube, as all the other Austrians are doing instead of going to a sanatorium?

In haste
G. Bernard Shaw

Tls.

1. On Black Friday (15 July), the workers of Vienna attacked the Palace of Justice after three fascists were acquitted of killing two Socialists. Police fired into the crowds, killing 85 and wounding hundreds. Dispatches raved of "Communist" insurrection and Red dictatorship; those implicated in the revolt were arrested, and Italy's command at the Brenner Pass threatened to intervene.

[Regina Palace Hotel. Stresa]
postmarked 29th August 1927

You will remember that we are at Ayot from Saturday afternoons to Wednesday only, and that we have no spare bedroom at 4 Whitehall Court, our new flat. Therefore you should aim at a week end—the 15th, 22nd, or 29th Oct. [Any] of the three would suit us; but if it is all the same to you, select the 22nd. You will find Ayot as dull as usual; but if you can stand it we shall be delighted to see you.

The printer has just sent me the first 6 sheets of the book. Fischer will lose the advertisement of the notices of the English edition if he publishes simultaneously.

G.B.S.

Why not come to see us here instead of trudging all the way to London? As our guest, of course. Much better for your health.

Apcs.

Charlotte also wrote to Trebitsch inviting him to visit in Stresa rather than London. Trebitsch interpreted the suggestion as implying that his London visits were a strain on Charlotte's nerves. On 11 September Charlotte wrote reproving Trebitsch for such ideas and explaining that she invited him to Stresa for the scenery and warm weather but that she preferred his visiting at Ayot. (Berg.)

Regina Palace Hotel. Stresa
7th September 1927
My dear Trebitsch

At last I have something definite about Gitta.

Miss Dorothy Cheston (Mrs Arnold Bennett) has taken the Royal Court Theatre in London with Theodore Komisarjevsky[1] as her producer, and proposes to open her season there with (1) Merejewsky's Paul I,[2] and (2) Jitta. The terms will be those in the enclosed blue paper; but as the theatre is a small one, and when crammed to its utmost capacity holds only about £160, the 15 percent at the top of the sliding scale can never be reached. We shall be lucky if we reach the 10%, and this has to be divided between us; so that for each of us it must be reckoned as 2½ and 5% according to the money in the house.

On receiving this offer I sent Miss Vanbrugh (the original English Jitta) an ultimatum, asking what she could do for us. The best she can promise is a series of matinées at the West End *or* a production at one of the suburban theatres where nothing runs longer than a fortnight at most, although a success sometimes gets transferred to the West End if it is something new and startling either as a play or as a part for a new actor or actress. Both conditions have been made impossible in the case of Jitta by the previous production at Fulham. There can be no question whatever that the Cheston-Komisarjevsky offer is the better, though it remains to be seen whether Miss Cheston, whom I have never seen act, and who is comparatively young and untried, can carry the part with the authority and distinction of Miss Vanbrugh. However, she has had some experience, and received very flattering press notices, especially as to her voice and diction, which are of the first importance in a play which can have no success unless it is clearly understood from start to finish. The worst of it is that she is quite mad about the part, and has been trying to buy an option on the play from me for years through Arnold Bennett, who also believes in it. I say "the worst" because this craze (she says she *is* Jitta, though she quite obviously isn't) makes her judgment worthless. On the other hand it makes her willing to submit to any conditions I like to make, and secures for us a consideration very different from that which was all we could expect from a commercial management like that of Shubert in America, half-reluctantly producing the play as a *pis aller* [last resource].

Above all, Komisar is *facile princeps* [easily the first] as a modern artistic producer. His Tchekov and Pirandello productions were superb; and next to Granville-Barker or myself you could not possibly do better in London. The relief to me of being able to entrust the work (a month's slavery) to someone else, and to retain only some supervision of it, is enormous. The smallness of the theatre is not a disadvantage. It means a low rent, and consequently a longer run with moderate receipts than would be possible at a big central theatre with an enormous war-inflated rent. And the place has a certain artistic prestige. It is the Vedrenne-Barker Theatre, and had been the Pinero theatre before that. It is the Barry Jackson—Methuselah theatre. I am sorry to have to add that it is an abominably uncomfortable theatre, on and off the stage, and that Heartbreak House drew only £500 a week at it. . . .

The biggest fly in the ointment is Komisar's confounded project of producing Paul I before Jitta. I could insist on Jitta coming first; but for many reasons I do not like to prevent the production of a play by a distinguished Russian author, even though I think the conditions at the Court Theatre are all against its success there. I have pointed out the difficulties to Mrs Bennett; but I must not go beyond that. Consequently I cannot give you a date for the production. If Paul I fails, it will come off in a fortnight, which is the shortest time for which actors can be engaged in London. In that case Jitta would be produced on the 17th October. If Paul proved worth a longer run the date would be deferred accordingly. It is still possible for Mrs Bennett to change her mind and begin with Jitta on the 3rd. I will let you know her final decision as soon as I know it myself.

Now as you have a curious taste for witnessing productions of your own plays instead of thanking God you are out of their reach, all this affects the question of your visit. Would you like to wait for the first night at the Court? You know that in London they do not call the author before the curtain 17 times after each act. At the end of the play, they call the actors two or three times. Then some idiot bawls "Authorrrr!", and a melancholy anomaly in evening dress makes a loutish attempt at a bow, and vanishes. That is all at most. When the play is mine, somebody appears and says "The author is not in the house." The audience utters a baffled yowl of disappointment, and goes home. Foreign authors, accustomed to ovations, find this very depressing; but it is the utmost that the most popular playwright expects in London.

ever

G.B.S.

ps I am in bed with a colic.

Als.

1. Theodore Komisarjevsky (1882–1954), Russian stage director and designer who had emigrated to England in 1919.

2. Dmitri Merejkovski (1866–1941), Russian author and religious thinker, also emigrated after the Revolution. His play *Paul I* opened the "International Season" at the Court Theatre, produced by Dorothy Cheston Bennett on 4 October.

[Regina Palace Hotel. Stresa]
[c. 10th September 1927]

I have never seen the present set of Macdona Players act. The company is a provincial one, and is not up to the standard of finished West End London productions; but their continual practice in my plays must give them a certain quality that has its value. They sometimes play in London. Foreign companies always get much more praise than they deserve; and a week at the Lessing could do no harm.[1]

The Court people have consented to make Jitta their second production.

G.B.S.

Apcs.
    1. The Macdona Players, touring with *Getting Married* and *You Never Can Tell*, did not perform in Berlin's Lessing-Theater.

[Regina Palace Hotel. Stresa]
postmarked 14th September 1927

As usual, the settlement of the affair is only the beginning of trouble. Mrs Bennett now writes that they have settled to make Jitta their *third* play,[1] and that Komisarjevsky has been run into by an automobile and had his leg broken.

I have accordingly withheld the agreement, and said that unless and until they obtain the extension of their lease of the Court Theatre to Easter we shall not engage ourselves for third place.

There will be all sorts of bothers like this until the play is actually produced, until when you had better dismiss it from your mind and from your arrangements.

G.B.S.

Apcs.
    1. Dorothy Cheston decided to follow *Paul I* with *Mr. Prohack*, adapted from Arnold Bennett's novel.

4 Whitehall Court S.W.
17th October 1927

I have just ascertained that Mrs Bennett must give up the Court Theatre on the 8th Jan, and that the Merejovsky play is drawing enough money (about £100 a night) to keep it going for a while. Further, I have realised that the wonderful Lenkheim they propose is a young man of 24[1] whom I remember at the Royal Academy of Dramatic Art as a born low comedian and funny fat man, not a bit what we need. What is worse, a very clever critic and an experienced manager both tell me that Mrs B. cannot act, though I shall suspend my judgment until I see her on the stage and can decide for myself as to whether her defects are curable by coaching.

On the whole I think there is no chance of Jitta coming on this year; and I conclude that we had better leave her out of the question as far as your visit is concerned. When could you come? The sooner the better.

G.B.S.

Apcs.
    1. Charles Laughton (1899–1962)—actually 28 at the time—who was later to achieve great success as a tragic as well as comic actor.

4 Whitehall Court S.W.
23rd October 1927

I have sent a few lines for Kerr to Fischer.[1] It is a mistake to do this sort of thing. If you do it for one you have to do it for all the rest; and no matter how much you say they never forgive you for saying too little, whereas if you flatly refuse them all impartially and tell them to go to the devil the wound is cured, like a lump on a fallen child's head, in a day or two. Besides, what is the value of a *solicited* testimonial? Do you suppose I have ever looked at that blue album of Fischer's? I don't even know where it is.

In your telegram you transposed our movements between town and country. We are at Ayot from Saturday afternoon to Wednesday afternoon. We can put you up there; but it is horribly dull and wretchedly cold. In London we cannot put you up; but we can see you as much as you please; and you can look at all the things that are going on in London. There is nothing to do in Ayot but work, work, work. But do just as you please. We are at your disposal for the week 5–12 Nov. Next year you must come in summer and drive about in the long evenings with us.

G.B.S.

Apcs.

   1. In honor of the 60th birthday of Alfred Kerr, doyen of Berlin theatre critics, Joseph Chapiro prepared a study *Für Alfred Kerr*, to be published by Fischer (1928) along with a section of tributes. Shaw's contribution read: "I never heard of anything so absurd as congratulating a man on his sixtieth birthday. They will be congratulating our babies in their cradles next. Why, man, you have hardly begun to live yet. I expect you to go on writing for a quarter of a century longer at least."

Ayot St Lawrence. Welwyn
7th November 1927

My dear Trebitsch

Saturday will not do: we do not arrive at Ayot until late in the afternoon; and you would have a wretched journey back in the dark.

All your business in London can be done on Thursday, Friday & Saturday. Come down tomorrow (Tuesday) and spend the night here, coming up to London with us on Wednesday afternoon. Then we shall have time for a talk. Go to Kings Cross terminus and take a ticket to Hatfield. The train leaves Kings + at 11.30, and arrives at 12 at Hatfield, where you will find our car waiting for you with a warm overcoat in it.[1] . . .

ever
G.B.S.

Als.

   1. Trebitsch described his visit to the Shaws in "Wiedersehen mit Shaw," *Berliner Tageblatt*, 9 December; translated as "New G.B.S. Book for Women," *Daily Chronicle*, 10 December.

Cliveden. Taplow
3rd January 1928

Madame de Kubie must be a naïve sort of creature to imagine that Pitoeff can dispose of *your* play on *my* instructions.[1] He has no right to let anyone even see your play without your express authority or that of your agent. And how can she possibly know that the other manager would read, accept, & perform the play at once? The woman's a simpleton.

Jitta is still in a condition of suspended animation. I do not know whether Mrs Bennett has secured a new theatre or not; but I have great misgivings about the cast: the Lenkheim she proposes [Charles Laughton] is too young and is not of the right type.

The great book [*Intelligent Woman's Guide*] is being indexed. I will send you the final proofs at the earliest possible moment.

If your Kubie woman can propose any sensible way in which I can help, I will; but I cannot commit an idiotic impropriety for her.

G.B.S.

Apcs.

1. Georges Pitoëff (1887–1939), a proponent of Shaw in Paris, did not produce a French version of *Gitta*. Madame de Kubie remains unidentified.

4 Whitehall Court S.W.
27th January 1928

My dear Trebitsch

The difficulty about this 30 years business is that the 50 years is too long.[1] Compare it with the 14 years allowed to the inventor of a machine, and it becomes ridiculous. And as the great majority of books published die at the age of 18 months the question affects only a very few authors.

The arguments in the Entwurf [draft] you sent me are quite beside the point. The difference between 30 and 50 years has absolutely no effect whatever on the book trade: a change to 50 would not change the prices of books or the profits of publishers or the remuneration of authors by a single Pfennig. In America the term is so short [28 years] that I have had to renew the copyright of Plays Pleasant and Unpleasant for a further term by paying a new registration fee; and America is one of the biggest book markets in the world. I get higher royalties in America than in Germany, where the term is much longer.

There are only two arguments that are likely to have any weight. One is the desirability of uniformity for its own sake. All the recent changes have been to 50 years, and Germany ought to come into line with England, France, and Italy merely to prevent the anomaly of books being copyright in one country and not in the others. The other is that except in the case of classic works whose authors have been dead for at least a century it is almost impossible to induce a publisher to print a book unless he can secure a right of exclusive property in it from the author or his heirs. Tolstoy dedicated his works freely to the people of all nations; and the result was that until the Countess Tolstoy intervened and asserted his rights in spite of him, there were no good editions of his works to be had in England or America, and even still the absence of legal copyright with Russia obstructs the circulation of his works instead of helping it. Much of my early writing is noncopyright in America; but publishers there will not touch it because it is available for their competitors as well: they insist on copyright.

These two arguments could be used by the Societies of German authors in an appeal for an extension of copyright to 50 years; and it is from them that the appeal should come, not from me. I am a Socialist, and cannot plead for an extension of property on principle. As to you, what does it matter to you what happens 30 years after your death? Tina will not survive you so long; and you have no children. . . .

As to the article you sent, I wrote it years ago for a trade union of clerks.[2] It appeared in their magazine and was forgotten until last year, when a new and energetic secretary dug it up and, without my leave, sold it in England, America and on the Continent for the benefit of the Union. I have no remedy: the mischief is done. I am sorry you are worried by these things; but they are exceptional, and do not imply any indifference on my part to your interests.
[ever

G. Bernard Shaw][3]

Tl.
    1. Preparations were under way for an International Copyright Conference in Rome to revise the Bern Convention and extend the period of copyright in Germany to 50 years.
    2. Shaw's preface to J. H. Lloyd and R. Scouller's *Trade Unionism for Clerks* (1919) was reprinted in *Tit-Bits* (5 November 1927) as "If I Were a Clerk Again." An unauthorized German translation came to Trebitsch's attention.
    3. Closing and signature cut out.

4 Whitehall Court S.W.
9th March 1928

My dear Trebitsch

The enclosed two sheets 2F and 2G are to be substituted for those sent you by the printers. Please take the old sheets and destroy them at once, so that there can be no possibility of your translating from the wrong ones. They contain important alterations referring to Syndicalism.

As to the film Dawn, I refused to say anything about it until a special private exhibition of it was given at which the only persons present (except the film people) were myself, Sybil Thorndike, and her husband Lewis Casson.[1] If it had been an attempt to stir up war feeling against Germany I should have done my utmost to prevent its public exhibition. But I found that the film was scrupulously fair to Germany: in fact the incident which Austen Chamberlain complained of as false and insulting *to Edith Cavell*, represented a German soldier as refusing to take part in her execution and being shot for his refusal. At the end his grave and Edith's are shewn side by side. His name, Rammel, is given; and the film people maintain that the incident actually happened. They even shewed me a photograph of his dead body; but a photograph of a dead soldier proves nothing. The point is that this sympathetic person is a German. All the rank and file Germans are represented as behaving very sympathetically, and Edith Cavell is made to say "Everybody has been very kind to me." Even [General] Von Bissing and the Oberst, though of course stiff, official, and inexorable, are not vilified in any way.

What is more, the film makes it quite clear that Edith Cavell did all the things she was shot for doing and that she was quite aware that the penalty was death. The general effect is to exhibit her not as an Englishwoman murdered by brutal Prussians, but as a woman who put the law of God as she understood it above military law, and helped fugitives to escape simply because they were in trouble just as she nursed men who were wounded, without asking what their nationality was. The film is an anti-war film, not an anti-German one. Also it is a wonderful piece of acting by Miss Thorndike: one of those artistic achievements that cannot be suppressed for long.

In my opinion the attempt to suppress it has been a great mistake. The moment it became known that the German Government had remonstrated a furious article appeared in one of the Sunday papers [*Sunday Express*, 12 February] headed "Are the Germans to be allowed to kill Nurse Cavell again?". The absurdity of objecting to make her the heroine of a film when we have a monument to her in the middle of London was capped by an article in The Jewish World [5 January 1928] protesting against the film called "The King of Kings (Jesus Christ)" as an attempt to raise prejudice against the Jews. A situation was thus created in which the suppression of the film was doing far more harm than an exhibition of the worst possible anti-German film could have done. I declared that the opposition to the film was a mistake, and that it ought to be and would be exhibited. Charlotte was distressed at this, because we had just been lunching at the German Embassy with the Sthamers, who, not having seen the film, were trying to stop it. But their opposition only made matters worse. A censorship exercised by a Jingo-Imperialist English statesman does not hurt the national amour propre; but a censorship by Germany is not so easy to bear. We were at once reminded that plenty of ultra-nationalist films had been exhibited in Germany.

I hope to get the book [*Intelligent Woman's Guide*] out before Easter. Fischer will be a bit late with it if he waits until October. The discussion of it in the press will have lost its interest by then.

[ever
G. Bernard Shaw]²

Tl.

1. *Dawn*, starring Sybil Thorndike, was based on the life of Edith Cavell (1865–1915), an English nurse who served in Brussels during the war and was arrested, tried, and executed by the Germans for aiding the escape of Allied prisoners. A statue of her was erected in St. Martin's Place, London. The film was banned after the German ambassador, Friedrich Sthamer, and the British Foreign Secretary, Austen Chamberlain (1863–1937), protested that it was contributing to international discord. Shaw defended the film (*New York Times*, 19 February). (The ban was lifted in April.)

2. Closing and signature cut out.

4 Whitehall Court S.W.
20th March 1928

My dear Trebitsch

The price of the book [*Intelligent Woman's Guide*] is to be fifteen shillings. Later on, when the sale of the first edition has paid for the cost of producing it a cheap popular edition may follow. Probably Fischer will have to do the same for Germany.

As to the film rights of Jitta M 6000 [£300] seems a very small price. If they are worth buying at all they ought to be worth more than that. The last offer I had from Ufa[1] for the film rights of Arms and the Man was M 250,000. You say that the transaction would leave America untouched; but this is a mistake: films go all over the world; and the sale of a German film will put an end to the possibility of an American firm making a bid for my translation. However you decide, do not sell the film rights for more than five years; and let the M 6000 be an advance on account of a royalty and not a final lump sum.

I think a better bargain ought to be possible. You say you want money; but that is not a business reason: everybody wants money. You will want it just as badly when you have spent the M6000.

As to the date of publication for the book, we have the same tradition here about July and August being bad months; but I believe people read more during their holidays than at more busy times; and I have had books published right in the middle of the holiday season with very good results.

ever

GBS

Tls.
    1. Universum-Film A.G., giant German film producing and distributing company.

4 Whitehall Court S.W.

16th April 1928

"grobe Hausmanns Kost" [coarse plain fare] is probably right. To come down to tin tacks is to stop talking idealistically and come to practical business—to come down from the clouds to the solid earth. When a man tells a girl's father that he adores her and will die if he does not marry her, and the father replies "That is all very fine, young man; but how much money can you settle on her? and what is your income?" the father is coming down to tin tacks. "Tin tacks" only means something hard and sharp and practical: it is not to be taken literally. Tin is introduced for the sake of alliteration, just as when Mussolini or Bismarck are said to be "as big as blue beef." I dont remember the passage in The Guide; but no doubt it means "to come from the abstract to the concrete" or from the general to the particular.

G.B.S.

Apcs.

Ayot St Lawrence. Welwyn

8th May 1928

How much will the Radio people pay for the broadcasting? If it is well done it may assist ordinary theatrical representations. If badly done it is disastrous. I have tried a little here; but I thought the effect abominable.[1] And I had the trouble of rewriting the passages which are unintelligible without visible action.

I have just received descriptions of a performance of "Man kann nie wissen," altered so as to seem the work of a depraved madman, with Gloria as a vamp (vampire harlot) with obscene dances.[2] I have mislaid the letters and forget the place; but when I find them I shall, I think, ask Fischer to threaten withdrawal of license. . . .

In haste
GBS

Apcs.

1. Shaw authorized the BBC to perform *Passion, Poison* on 13 January 1926. On 28 March 1928 the Macdona players performed *The Man of Destiny.*

2. *Mann kann nie wissen* (*You Never Can Tell*) opened at the Schauspielhaus, Frankfurt, on 27 April, with Kundry Siewert as Gloria, described in one review as an "Amazon" (*Frankfurter Zeitung,* 28 April).

Ayot St Lawrence. Welwyn
16th May 1928

My dear Trebitsch

I protest in the strongest manner against any kind of tampering with St Joan in Vienna. I was astounded when I learnt that Vienna was classed, not with the great European capitals, but with the Fundamentalist villages of Ohio, as a place where the inhabitants were too childish and superstitious to endure the presentation on the stage of passages from the history of The Church. If the Deutsches Volkstheater attempts to revive the play without the scene in which the fate of Joan is decided between the Feudal chiefs and the princes of the Church, then I beg you to make public the fact that the play so presented is not my play, and that these ridiculous mutilations have not, and never have had, my sanction. My native capital, Dublin, is intensely and jealously Catholic; but the play was received there without a breath of protest; and the particular scene in question was one of the most successful moments of the performance. Am I to be persuaded that Vienna is three centuries behind Dublin in culture?

There! Will that do for publication if necessary?[1]

The Intelligent W's G. has not yet been published, and will not be until the first of June.

For purposes of local government London is divided into 28 boroughs, one of the poorest of them being Poplar. The Poplar Guardians (of the poor) who have to relieve destitute persons out of the rates, it being the law in England that every destitute person must be fed and housed, are popularly elected; and so it came about that there was a majority of Socialists among the Guardians. Instead of giving the barest minimum of relief under the most degrading conditions, as the capitalist practice is, they gave a full subsistence wage to all applicants without requiring them to go into the workhouse. The rates went up enormously in consequence; and there was a tremendous row about it, in the course of which the word Poplarism came into general use to denote the policy of generous "outdoor relief" (relief outside the workhouse) by Socialists.[2] Parliament has since legislated against it.

I should certainly not advise the omission of the chapters on religion and children in schools; but there is no reason why you should not put a note saying that the conditions spoken of are of course those prevailing in English schools.[3] But you must be careful how you put this, for unless the German schools have been Bolshevized since the war there is no essential difference between the German and the British system. My main proposition, which is that schools are prisons in disguise, their real purpose being to save parents the trouble of bringing up their children, holds good everywhere.

The disgraceful performances of Man Kann nie Wissen were at Frankfurt.

Surely Sweden and Holland are in the Berne Convention. I get royalties from them and make contracts. What you must mean is that the Radio people there are trying to claim that broadcasting is not a violation of copyright. If Fischer can find out the date of a broadcast of any of my plays either from Amsterdam or Stockholm I will set the Society of Authors to work to claim fees.[4] . . .

Tell Fischer that 50,000 copies of the I.W.G.S. have already been sold in America *before publication*, and that the 10,000 I ordered to be printed here are not sufficient to meet the orders. The printers are at work on an additional supply as hard as they can. Even Sweden offers me £100 for an edition of 3,000.

Ich glaube dass ist Alles [I believe that's all].

Our loves to Tina.

ever

GBS

Tls.

1. The planned revival was dropped.

2. "Poplarism" appears under "Sham Socialism" in *Intelligent Woman's Guide*.

3. The chapter "Socialism and Children" was included in the German edition without comment.

4. Authors' rights over radio performances were implied in the Bern Convention but not spelled out until twenty years later at Brussels. Several of Shaw's plays, most recently *Pygmalion* (on 12 February and 25 April, respectively), had been broadcast in Sweden and Holland without payment of royalty.

Ayot St Lawrence. Welwyn

21st May 1928

. . . I have sent a copy of the Guide to Fischer so that he may see the style in which it has been published here. I have sent a copy to Tina. It may not have arrived yet, as when I say I have sent it I mean that I have instructed the publishers to send it; and they have until the 1st June (the day of publication) to dispatch it.

Lest you should take Tina's copy to Berlin to shew to Fischer I write this to let you know that he has one already.

GBS

Apcs.

Ayot St Lawrence. Welwyn
2nd July 1928

I object most strenuously to the title "Was ist Socialismus &c &c." There are a thousand books in the world with that title. There is not one book called The Intelligent Woman's Guide. Your first version of the title was right: this one is disastrously wrong. At least 80,000 of the English edition have been sold with The Intelligent Woman in the forefront. If it had been called What is Socialism? not 8000 would have been sold. How stupid those people are! Give them a good thing and their first idea is to change it into some banality or other.

On the 15th Charlotte and I intend to go to the French Riviera—to Beau-vallon sur Mer (Var) between Marseilles and Cannes—for six weeks or so for sun baths and sea baths.

What sort of place is Tarasp?[1] It is such a pity that we cannot meet in the sun instead of dragging you across the Channel to Ayot in chill October.

G.B.S.

Apcs.
1. A Swiss spa, where Trebitsch was on holiday.

[Hotel Beau-Site. Cap d'Antibes]
24th July 1928

My dear Trebitsch

We could not find rooms at Beauvallon, and after wandering for a week in the frightful heat, which drove us both quite crazy (we are all right now) we settled in this little hotel, where they make us very comfortable.

As to Freissler,[1] I presume you are paying him a fixed sum for technical help, revising his chapters if necessary to secure continuity of literary style. This hardly entitles him to appear on the titlepage as joint-translator; but you should put in a foreword acknowledging his assistance in the technical detail.[2]

Fischer ought to pay him and deduct the money from your royalties; but a still better plan would be to let me pay (I have plenty of money at the bank and can do so without the least inconvenience) and settle with me as and when you please, or preferably not at all unless the profits of the book are enormous. How much?

Do not reproach me for letting you hear all the news about my new play &c &c &c from the newspapers. The papers tell you; you tell me; and that is the first I hear of these things.

Why do you believe all those silly stories? They are all lies.

ever
G.B.S.

ps. The title is all wrong. Von C[apitalismus] u. S[ozialismus] is worse than ever. The whole point of the title is that it is a *long* one, and that it begins with Guide and Intelligent Woman. Who on earth at this time of day would buy or read a book Von C.u.S.? The length of the original title is unusual, *purposely*. Does Fischer want people to believe that there is nothing unusual about the book? Your original version of the title was right; and if F. doesn't like it he must lump it.

Als.

1. Ernst Freissler, novelist and translator, who was helping Trebitsch with the German version of *Intelligent Woman's Guide*.

2. Neither Trebitsch nor Freissler appeared on the title page, but they were credited as co-translators on the verso.

Hotel Beau-Site. Cap d'Antibes
24th August 1928

My dear Trebitsch

Why worry about my not answering letters? Do I ever answer them promptly? Your nerves have been shattered by that book.

As to Freissler I am quite willing to pay half the 3500 Marks, or the whole, if you think better of your refusal. (To think better of any thing is to change your mind about it.)

As to the title I still tell you obstinately and dogmatically (because I *know*) that if you call it Kapitalismus & Socialismus you will lose 90% of the sale that it would have if you put The Intelligent Woman's Guide first. Der Arzt am Scheideweg [The Doctor's Dilemma] is right because it is exact and follows the sequence of my title; but if you had called it The Opsonin Theory: a dilemma for doctors" you would have killed both the book and the play stone dead. Only three or four medical students would have bought it. People will not buy dry treatises on political economy: they *will* buy a book about women by Shaw. I tell you again and again that, grammar or no grammar, lengthy title or short title, Capitalism & Socialism must come last and The Intelligent Woman's Guide must come first. Your original Leitführer [Guide] was right; and those who persuaded you out of it were damned fools. You may, if you like, imagine that every idiot knows better than you; but if you imagine that they know better than I you will be a bankrupt before Christmas.

I cannot find the letter in which you mentioned a plot. But a plot is no more use to me than a beefsteak. I dont use them. You do. So you must keep it for yourself.

We are thinking of going to Geneva for a week or so before we return to England, which, owing to our servants' holidays and housepainting and so forth we must not do until about the 10th Sept.[1] The attraction held out to us is the League of Nations!

This Riviera is hell on earth with the scum of the earth stranded on the beach. Bathing and driving through the mountains keep us from going mad. Hence my bad temper. It seems a mockery to send affectionate messages to Tina. I hate the whole human race. So does Charlotte mostly.

G. Bernard Shaw

Als.
1. The Shaws visited Geneva from 4 to 16 September and returned to London on the 18th.

[Hotel Beau-Site. Cap d'Antibes]
3rd September 1928

Your letter arrives just as we are starting. I wrote to Baur au Lac to explain that your wonderful title is much too wonderful, and would not only lead people to think that the book was not written by me, but that it is a Führer to Capitalism in the German sense: that is, an inducement and exhortation to it.[1]

Forgive my mulishness.

The auto waits: farewell.

G.B.S.

Als.; postscript omitted.
1. The final German title for the *Intelligent Woman's Guide* followed the original: *Wegweiser für die intelligente Frau zum Sozialismus und Kapitalismus* (1928).

Ayot St Lawrence. Welwyn
2nd October 1928

. . . The title need not say anything about the interview being authorized. That part of the affair is between you and the purchaser. *Siegfried Trebitsch Interviews Bernard Shaw* is sufficient and quite good. You should write a short introduction describing Ayot and me in the usual manner: otherwise it would be not an interview but a catechism.[1]

Charlotte hopes you had a good crossing. We are glad you had a fine day here, and sorry Tina was not with you to see Ayot looking really nice in the sun.

G.B.S.

Apcs.
1. Trebitsch, who arrived in England on 26 September, visited the Shaws in London on the 27th and at Ayot on the 29th and was now preparing an interview for publication. The interview appeared on 15 November in *Vossische Zeitung* ("Interview mit Shaw") and the *Evening Standard* ("Mr. Bernard Shaw on Topics I Cannot Resist") and then in the *New York Times* ("Questions That Shaw Could Not Resist," 18 November).

Ayot St Lawrence. Welwyn
14th October 1928

I have expanded the reference to Mussolini considerably, and made several other important alterations in the interview.[1]

I have sent it to Raymond Savage,[2] asking him to have an extra fair copy made and sent to you. Do not let it appear in the German papers until you have incorporated the changes.

I have written a letter to Karel Capek which he will probably publish, as it contains a reference to the Tyrol frontier.[3]

G.B.S.

Apcs.
　1. Shaw's alterations expanded his remarks on women in England and on the conditions that led to Mussolini's dictatorship: liberal ineffectualness and the outrage of veterans at disorder and denigration of the war by Socialists and Syndicalists (Texas).
　2. Raymond Savage (1888–1964), London literary agent whom Shaw used to place the interview.
　3. Shaw's letter to Karel Čapek (1890–1938), the Czech dramatist, novelist, and journalist, appeared in *Lidové noviny* on the 10th anniversary of the Czech Republic (28 October) and contrasted the favorable treatment of Hungarians in Czechoslovakia with that of Czechs in Hungary and wished that Italy would adopt the Czech example in the Tyrol. (Shaw clarified his remarks in *Pester Lloyd* [Budapest, 14 November] after Emil Szalai, his Hungarian agent, suggested that Shaw might have hurt his standing in Hungary.)

Ayot St Lawrence. Welwyn
11th December 1928

Nothing is settled with Pola Negri. Why do you believe all these newspaper tales? She would of course be an ideal Jitta; but I cannot see in the play a film that would be tempting enough to catch so big a fish—certainly not until it makes a success on the English stage.[1]

Sir Barry Jackson wants to produce it at his Repertory Theatre in Birmingham in March. That means only a week in the provinces; but if it makes anything of a hit, and B.J. takes a fancy to it, he might try it in London later on. He is planning a summer season—a Shavian Bühnenfestspiel—at Malvern, à la Bayreuth. . . .

G.B.S.

Apcs.
　1. Pola Negri (b. 1894), Polish-born, German-American film and stage star, was famous for her flamboyant life and style. On 30 November, she lunched with Shaw and announced prematurely that she was to be the first to star in a film of a Shaw play: *Caesar.*

Ayot St Lawrence. Welwyn
20th March 1929

The London General Press is not a newspaper, but a news agency that plagues me by sending me ridiculous interviews about me for my approval. It did not send me the one you mention.

You have no remedy except against the N.F.P. for publishing the interview; and as you would have (in English law) to prove damage or defamation, and would incidentally antagonize a friendly newspaper, your only resource is to send them a polite repudiation of the interview and ask them to publish it.[1]

It is no use asking the L.G.P. for an indemnity. I have no reason to suppose that it is an opulent concern; and in any case your legal remedy is not against it (as it did not publish) but against the N.F.P.

The printer promises me the revised Apple Cart on Friday. I will post it to you on that day, I hope.[2]

G.B.S.

Apcs.
　1. The purported interview in the *Neue Freie Presse* has not been traced.
　2. *The Apple Cart*, written in November and December 1928, was intended for the opening of the Malvern Festival in August 1929. Reinhardt had telegraphed his interest, and Trebitsch was impatiently awaiting his copy.

4 Whitehall Court S.W.
22nd March 1929

My dear Trebitsch

Here you are at last. [Florian] Sobieniowski, my Polish translator, has just called and carried off his copy [of *The Apple Cart*] to prepare for Warsaw; but with this exception you have the first cut at the joint.

ever

G. Bernard Shaw

PS What is the German equivalent for "upsetting the apple cart"? It means spoiling a project or wrecking an enterprise.

Ans.

Ayot St Lawrence. Welwyn
31st March 1929

If the première of The Apple Cart will be in October there is no hurry about the preface (if I write one). Probably I shall publish the play here in August simultaneously with the first performance at Malvern.

The verses[1] are from Byron's Childe Harold; but as poetry in that form is untranslateable you had better find some passage in a German poem about Einsamkeit [solitude] and substitute it.[2]

On the 7th I go with Charlotte to an island in the Adriatic (Brioni, close to Pola in Istria) to shake off the effects of the flu. If we like it we shall probably spend a month there.[3]

G.B.S.

All my copies of the play are gone. I shall have no more to spare until I make a further revision.

Apcs.

1. Declaimed by Pamphilius in Act I of *Apple Cart*.
2. Trebitsch substituted the German version of Otto Gildmeister, which followed Byron's stanzaic form.
3. Shaw planned a long holiday in Brioni with his new friend Gene Tunney, the retired Irish-American boxing champion.

Hotel Brioni. Brioni
18th April 1929

My dear Trebitsch

We did not arrive until yesterday.[1] When, after a long journey, you expect to find yourself in an Italian hotel and do actually find yourself in a German Irrenanstalt [madhouse], you need a few days to get over the shock before you feel sure enough of staying another day in the place to commit yourself to having a visitor for the week end. When Charlotte, lightly clad in her evening things, and expecting to get a good dinner downstairs in a warm dining room, found that she had to walk quarter of a mile in the open air with the bora blowing its worst, it seemed impossible that we could be here next Sunday or indeed ten minutes longer than we could help.

However, today the sun shines and the sea is very blue, though the wind is still icy (we have brought far too light clothing) and the climate acutely irritating. We shall stay a while to explore the coast (including Laurana) and settle whether we shall move or not. Then we shall give you the word to start. I myself would not undertake a double 17 hours journey to spend a day with le bon Dieu himself; but you seem positively to enjoy such horrors. But then you are a thoroughly mobilized man, whereas I am a born immovable. All I can say is that if the abominable bora is still blowing when you come, don't curse me for it. I understand that the alternative, the scirocco, is still worse. What will Tina say if the expedition knocks you up for a month? Instead of giving you a warm invitation I warn you solemnly against the adventure, which will be all right for us, but possibly fatal to you. Why run risks to see whether an old man and his wife have developed three more wrinkles since last autumn?

The best hotel in Malvern is the Abbey. Address: the Abbey Hotel, Great Malvern, Worcester, England. The hotel we stay at is full for August already; and in any case I don't think it would suit you. If you really mean to come all that way to see the première of The Apple Cart you must secure rooms at once. You will find it much more amusing than Ayot St Lawrence; so I will not discourage you. But do not come for one night and run away again. Malvern is within reach of some very pretty bits of England.

The title of The Apple Cart must have some German equivalent. To defeat a project of any sort—to produce a catastrophe which makes an end of any plan—is to upset the apple cart. There must be a popular phrase to express this. If not, the play might be called simply Checkmate. The title should somehow express the situation of the king parrying the thrust of Proteus and winning the bout.

When I came here I heard nothing but German. I said to the porter "I see that here one must speak German." His reply was "Oh nein, nein, nein, nein: italienisch, italienisch. Guten abend."[2]

A devil of a place. Nothing to do for an old man who does not play games. Ugh! I cannot write cordially, even to you.

GBS

Als.

1. The Shaws left for the Adriatic on Sunday the 14th, a week later than planned.

2. The Istrian peninsula had formerly been under Austrian rule, hence the prevalence of German.

Hotel Brioni. Istria
22nd April 1929

If the Jolly Joker (it sounds dreadful in English) is the equivalent of The Ace of Trumps, then it would not be a bad title. King's Comedy—no. How have you translated the speeches in the last act which mention the apple cart? On page 71 Nicobar says "You cant upset the apple cart like this." On page 77 Magnus says "So I have not upset the apple cart after all." Nicobar cannot say "You cannot play the jolly joker like this." An exact translation ought to give the clue to the title.

You must secure your rooms at the Abbey Hotel instantly or it may be full up. If you mention my name they will give you the worst rooms in the house, because I never stay there.

Tina will find Malvern as good a Kurort [health resort; spa] as any in Germany. The waters are famous: one glass destroys my digestion for a week. But the air is first rate, and the views from the hills wunderschön. She certainly must come.

G.B.S.

Apcs.

Hotel Brioni. Brioni
25th April 1929

My dear Trebitsch

Here at last is a serious performance of Jitta. I wish I had been in England to see whether it was good enough to justify me in urging Sir Barry Jackson to transfer it to London. However, he will know his own mind about it. I will talk to him when I go back. I do not know whether you can remember the girl who gave a remarkably firm performance of the part of Zoo in the Tragedy of an Elderly Gentleman (Methuselah IV) at Birmingham, and who also played the flapper in Barnabas (M.II); but she was Eileen Beldon, the Jitta of the enclosed notices.

By the way some desperate little venture in Glasgow gave a couple of performances of Jitta some months ago; and they must have paid a few shillings for royalties. Did Miss Patch send you your half?

ever
G. Bernard Shaw

Als.

Hotel Brioni. Istria
27th April 1929

1. Crown Derby is a famous kind of English pottery, like the French Sévres.[1]

2. The date is sufficiently indicated by the remark of Sempronius that his father died in 1962. Give no further clue.

3. Yes: the palace *is* Buckingham Palace; but it must not be called so. Simply the Royal Palace.

GBS

Apcs.

1. In this card, Shaw replies to Trebitsch's queries about *Apple Cart*.

Hotel Brioni. Brioni
1st May 1929

My dear Trebitsch

I return the press cuttings [on *Jitta*] with one new one, as I never keep such things. Tear them up if you do not want them.

The Balance of Power is not an attractive title: nobody would buy tickets. The Odd Trick (meaning the seventh trick in whist when both sides have already won six) would do if people still played whist; but unfortunately they now play nothing but bridge. The Ace Up the King's Sleeve, The New Kingcraft, The King's Last Stand,[1]—No: I can't think of the right title tonight; and it is time to go to bed. But I find it very hard to believe that there is no German equivalent for upsetting the apple cart. Both Snowden and the German Chancellor nearly upset the apple cart the other day on the questions of reparations and the American debt.[2] What did the Germans say about it?

We have got used to Brioni because something happened to a friend of ours which obliged us to give up all intention of leaving until the danger was over.[3] But we shall probably go on to Ragusa for a while before returning to England.

If a title occurs to me I shall let you know.

GBS

Als.

1. Shaw ran a wavy line through the rejected titles.

2. A conference to reduce German reparations was deadlocked when Germany rejected Allied demands as excessive and Philip Snowden (1864–1937), former Labour chancellor of the exchequer, threatened to repudiate the Allied position as insufficient, should Labour win the pending elections.

3. Gene Tunney's wife, Polly, had an attack of acute appendicitis and was narrowly saved by a noted German surgeon who by a remarkable coincidence appeared on the island in time to operate.

Hotel Brioni. Istria

8th May 1929

Emperor of America is not bad; but it throws all the emphasis on a mere episode.[1] The Return of The Prodigal would have the same drawback. There is a Gräfin here (Schaumberg-Lippe, I think)[2] who thinks The Jolly Joker an ideal title, and says it would be understood perfectly all over Germany. But somehow I do not feel that we have found the right name yet. . . .

G.B.S.

Apcs.

1. Trebitsch had suggested *Kaiser von Amerika* as a title for *Apple Cart*. The idea came to him from a statue of Ferdinand Maximilian that stood a short distance from Trebitsch's home and bore the legend "Kaiser von Mexico."

2. Countess Schaumburg-Lippe was a remnant of the princely pre-Weimar days.

[Hotel Brioni. Istria]

[14th May 1929]

No: the title won't do. It will make people believe that the action and place and characters are American, which will not attract Berlin; and it is utterly misleading as to the main theme of the play. . . .

I have just heard that a correspondent of mine has in his possession a rehearsal copy of O'Flaherty and one of The Inca of Perusalem, both inscribed by me "to Siegfried Trebitsch from Bernard Shaw, 9th Nov. 1919 [1915]." He asks my permission to sell them! He cannot remember how they came into his hands. This is a complete mystery to me. Can you throw any light on it? [1]

Tomorrow we move to the Imperial Hotel, Dubrovnik, Jugoslavia. If we are comfortable there we shall stay four or five days at least.

G.B.S.

Apcs.; postscript omitted.

1. In 1915, Shaw sent inscribed copies of *Inca* and *O'Flaherty* to Otto Kyllmann, of Constable, to be forwarded to Trebitsch (see 9 November 1915). Kyllmann put them aside and forgot them. Though Shaw did not permit Kyllmann to sell the copies, Trebitsch, to whom they were sent, secretly disposed of them—along with his inscribed copy of *Apple Cart*—in the booming market for Shaviana.

[Dubrovnik]
postmarked 21st·May 1929

Undoubtedly the right title for The Apple Cart is The Ultimatum; but it is very prosaic. I have given your Schalek lady a long talking-to.[1] I never heard of your Diocletian. How long ago did you write it? Was it ever acted? [2]

I shall be at Split (Spalato) from Friday to Sunday; but you had better address to Hotel Danieli, Venezia, where we expect to arrive on Monday at midnight.

G.B.S.

Apcs.

1. The interview by Alice Schalek (1874–1956), Viennese journalist, novelist, and travel writer, appeared in *Dresdner neueste Nachrichten* on 19 July.

2. Trebitsch's blank verse drama *Kaiser Diokletian*, written during the war, was unsuited for production, but later in 1929, in honor of Trebitsch's 60th (actually 61st) birthday, the play was read by an actor at the Theater in der Josefstadt, Vienna.

Venice
29th May [1929]

ALL REPORTS FALSE I COME NEITHER TO WARSAW VIENNA NOR BERLIN [1] THANKS FOR DIOCLETIAN

Telegram.

1. Productions of *Apple Cart* were pending in Berlin and Warsaw, and the International P.E.N. Congress was to open in Vienna on 24 June.

Hotel Danieli. Venezia
4th June 1929

I presume you mean that you will not be let return from England unless you are revaccinated at every frontier.[1] In that case do not dream of coming. Revaccination will make you horribly ill for a week or more at best; and at worst it may leave you an invalid for the rest of your life or kill you. I know all about vaccination; and if other people knew as much it would be declared a criminal practice. Cancel your order for rooms at once and give up all intention of visiting England until this ridiculous scare is over. Vaccination kills more people than smallpox in civilized countries.

All the letters that went to Brioni have been sent on. The PEN Club business was of no consequence to me, as nothing would induce me to go to their congresses. On the 11th I start for London and expect to arrive there on the afternoon of the 12th.

G.B.S.

Apcs.; Texas.
1. Smallpox had appeared among the crew of an English ship returned from Bombay, and France took measures to protect itself.

Ayot St Lawrence. Welwyn
26th June 1929

The smallpox scare is over; and the French have withdrawn their demand for the revaccination of persons entering France from England. As there have been several deaths from encephalitis following vaccination you will see that my warning was not unfounded. The Terry correspondence, if printed at all, will appear in a private collector's edition and sold at £10-10-0 a copy.[1]

If Reinhardt is discouraged by the German press notices [on *Apple Cart* in Warsaw] tell him that if he wishes to be released from his contract we will tear it up at once. If he has paid an advance I will repay it.

If you are interviewed by the German papers tell them that they have disgraced themselves; that the Warsaw production has been a brilliant success;[2] and that not one word will be cut for the German production: on the contrary, I may add another half hour to it.

G.B.S.

Apcs.
1. Ellen Terry died the previous year, and her executors undertook a volume of the Terry-Shaw letters. The "private" edition was dropped, but the letters appeared in 1931.
2. The world premiere of *Apple Cart* went to the Polish producer and Shavian, Arnold Szyfman, who pleaded for the honor and argued that the play was best suited for Poland where the struggle between Marshal Pilsudski and parliament paralleled the play. As *Wielki Kram* (Vanity Fair) it opened on 14 June at the Teatr Polski, Warsaw, with Junosza-Stepowski as Magnus. Nothing was spared for the world premiere before a distinguished audience. But the *Berliner Tageblatt* (15 June) reported only a "modest succès d'estime" and anticipated failure in Germany unless the play was cut. In London, however, the *Observer* (16 June) reported a "splendid" production and "great ovation": a "triumph" for producer, cast, and director, if dubiously for Shaw.

Ayot St Lawrence. Welwyn
29th July 1929

. . . An invitation to Liesl sent to the address you gave us has produced no response whatever![1]

An.
1. Trebitsch had asked Shaw to invite Elisabeth Bergner (Liesl), who was in England, to visit him.

Ayot St Lawrence. Welwyn
30th July 1929

Liesl has just answered. She has been to Berlin and back; and the invitation followed and reached her too late. But as she is now in Cornwall, hundreds of miles off, we shall not see her unless she comes to Malvern.

By the way, a further letter from the Warsaw manager [Arnold Szyfman] amply confirms Sobieniowski's assurances that the Apple Cart has been brilliantly successful. So Reinhardt need not be discouraged. . . .

G.B.S.

Apcs.

Ayot St Lawrence. Welwyn
4th August 1929

. . . On Tuesday we go to The Malvern Hotel, Great Malvern, Worcs. It is within a hundred yards of the Abbey Hotel—turn left when you come out. Is Tina coming?[1]

GBS

Ans.

1. Tina did not come.

The Malvern Hotel. Malvern
9th August 1929

You cannot send your trunk from Victoria to Malvern. What you had better do is to drive with all your luggage from Victoria to Paddington (the Great Western terminus from which the Malvern trains start) and stay the night at the Great Western Hotel which forms part of the station. Then you will be on the spot for your train next day, luggage and all.

If, however, you have rashly engaged a room at another hotel, and do not wish to cancel the order, you can drive from Victoria to Paddington and leave your trunk in the cloak room there; then take your handbag to your hotel, and pick up your trunk next day when you start. The porter will get it for you if you give him the scontrino [baggage claim check].

G.B.S.

Apcs.

The Malvern Hotel. Great Malvern
16th August 1929

I have a ticket for you for every performance from the 27th to the end of the Festival.[1]

The article about Sobieniowski is very amusing, because the *facts* are very largely correct; but the construction put on them is comically wrong.[2] However, I can explain better when we meet.

He is coming down here, I believe; so you may have the joy of meeting him. Hans Rothe[3] is coming, I hear; and they tell me that the Fischers[4] have taken seats.

G.B.S.

Apcs.
1. The Malvern Festival opened for two weeks on 19 August with *Apple Cart*, starring Cedric Hardwicke and Edith Evans. *Methuselah*, *Heartbreak House*, and *Caesar* were also presented. All were directed by H. K. Ayliff (1872–1949). Trebitsch actually arrived on the 26th.
2. On 28 April 1929, the *Observer* had published an interview with Shaw's Polish translator, Sobieniowski, in which Sobieniowski described *Apple Cart* as being from the "same mind as [Shaw's] first novel, but [showing] proofs of his growth and . . . more of the knowing and loving smile of the sage."
3. Hans Rothe (b. 1894), German dramaturg, translator of Shakespeare, and foe of Trebitsch's translations, was now on Reinhardt's staff.
4. This was the first meeting between Shaw and Fischer.

The Malvern Hotel
26th August 1929

Please come straight on to the theatre without changing your dress. The performance begins at 8; and you must be in time for the prologue [of *Caesar*]. The theatre is just round the corner—turn left as you leave the hotel, and then left again. You will find me in the seat next to yours.

GBS

Ans.

[The Malvern Hotel. Malvern]
1st September 1929

. . . Hans Rothe says that the word by which you have translated Breakages means hernia or intestinal rupture.[1] I have only just heard this, and don't know whether it is serious or only a joke of the coulisses [backstage].

I hope you have had an easy and pleasant journey.

G.B.S.

Apcs.
1. "Breakages, Ltd."—Shaw's symbolic name for corporate England in *Apple Cart*—was rendered by Trebitsch as *Bruchschadengesellschaft*. *Bruch*, i.e., "breakage," is also the medical term for "hernia."

Ayot St Lawrence. Welwyn
29th September 1929

My dear [Trebitsch]
There is nothing to be said about the London production except that so far it has been a colossal success: over M6000 at every performance.[1] On the first night Ramsay MacDonald[2] & General Dawes[3] were present.

Cracow has repeated the Warsaw success.[4] The prophets of evil have been utterly abashed. The preliminary fortnight in Birmingham drew crowded houses.

I am so pressed with work on my Collected Edition (a terrible job which I have now bound myself to finish within six months)[5] that it is only in the evenings after dinner that I am able to read a few pages of your translation. You must make the best of my corrections in view of my ignorance of your language.
                 In haste—the village post is early on Sundays.
                                                                    G.B.S.

Tls.; Texas.
    1. *Apple Cart* was a remarkable success not only at Malvern and Birmingham but also in London, where it had 258 performances, a longer run than any previous Shaw production except *Fanny*.
    2. Ramsay MacDonald (1866–1937), prime minister in the first Labour government, 1924. In June 1929, after a Labour victory, he again became prime minister.
    3. Charles G. Dawes (1865–1951), American banker, vice-president, and ambassador to Britain, author of the Dawes Plan for postwar Germany and Nobel Peace laureate (1925).
    4. *Apple Cart* opened in Cracow's Teatr Miejski on 7 September and ran nine times.
    5. *The Works of Bernard Shaw: Collected Edition* appeared (1930–32) in a limited edition of 30 volumes (in America it was issued as the "Ayot St. Lawrence Edition"). The "standard edition" then appeared (1931–32) and ultimately was expanded to 37 volumes.

                                                   4 Whitehall Court S.W.
                                                   29th November 1929
My dear Trebitsch
    I have had to put off answering your letter until I had ascertained the full extent of the changes made by Reinhardt in The Apple Cart.[1] My first intimation of the affair came from the pictures in the illustrated papers, which shewed an arrangement of the stage with a huge table, and a flapper-cocotte make-up for Orinthia, utterly incompatible with an honest attempt to carry out my design.[2] I then discovered that my text has been so barbarously cut that the performance lasts only 2 hours and 10 minutes, in spite of the fact that about 80 speeches have been interpolated, no doubt by the young theatre poet [Hans Rothe] we met at Malvern, whose business it was to translate your versions into good Berliner German. A lot of scandalous business, with a bed on the stage, has been introduced so as to get a vulgar laugh when the king speaks of the "strangely innocent relations," and to contradict that very serious passage flatly. The ending has been cut out, and an idiotic "Bist du allein?" "Ja" substituted.[3]
    It is impossible for me to leave these changes unexposed. And you must tell Fischer that Reinhardt must be struck off his list of managers eligible for contracts with me. We need not quarrel with Reinhardt about it: no doubt he sincerely believes that his changes are improvements, and that the king's speech about the orbits of the stars, which is the top note of the serious side of the scene, is made interesting by the two nibbling the same stick of chocolate. But that is not how I want my plays handled; and he will not get a chance of doing it again if I can help it.
    I enclose a letter which you can give to the press. The postscript, without being offensive to Reinhardt and his tame poet, makes it clear that R's Apple Cart is not my Apple Cart.

"Kingly Recreation: German Version—Herr Werner Krauss as the King, with Fraulein Maria Bard, who hardly suggests the professedly platonic love between this 'strangely innocent woman' and her Royal master." (*The Graphic.*)

I am—for a wonder—almost surprised, though I thought that no extremity of folly, vulgarity, and disloyalty on the part of a manager-producer could surprise me. How could Reinhardt be such a damned fool! Why did you let him?

ever

G.B.S.

Als.

1. This production (*Kaiser von Amerika*), the second and last Shaw play Reinhardt directed personally, opened at the Deutsches Theater on 19 October with Werner Krauss as Magnus and Maria Bard as Orinthia.

2. A picture report in *The Graphic* (16 November) showed a bedizened, flirtatious Orinthia, on her knees, leaning against Magnus and stroking his hair. In contrast was a picture of the English production with Miss Evans seated sedately, back to Magnus, who leans on his arm toward her. Reinhardt's set also included a poster bed.

3. From Sobieniowski Shaw learned that *Kaiser* had been cut, speeches added, and the ending altered so that the queen, instead of leading Magnus off to dinner, asks: "Bist du allein?" ("Are you alone?"), and he answers, "Ja," thereby stressing the loneliness of genius. *Kaiser* was a huge success with its eminent first-night audience. Critics were more reserved—not about the production, but about Shaw's apparent stance against democracy. Alfred Kerr sadly reflected that Shaw's past followers would have to part with him (*Berliner Tageblatt*, 20 October); the liberal-left *8 Uhr Abendblatt* (21 October) was shocked and concluded that either Shaw was joking or his brain "through the appearance of Mussolini, has become inflamed and a bit cracked." *Vorwärts*, more aware of Shaw's intent, noted the malicious delight of the elite audience in the stupidity of the parliamentary ministers, underscored in the production, and declared that Shaw reaped more than he bargained for. *Kaiser* ran 197 times that season and an additional 14 times the next, the longest run for a Reinhardt premiere of Shaw.

4 Whitehall Court S.W.

29th November 1929

My dear Trebitsch[1]

I have read with some amusement the articles in the German press on The Apple Cart, especially those which declare that I have executed a complete political *volte face*, and that the writers, who have followed me faithfully up to 1929, must now regretfully part company from me. I am afraid I have been unintentionally imposing on them all these years in the character of a good old 1848 Liberal. Can it be possible that my vogue in Germany, of which I have been so proud, has been all a mistake? Or is it merely that theatre critics in Germany, like theatre critics in England, never read anything, never know anything, never understand anything, never do anything except go to the theatre and write about it without having had time to think over what they write? For when in all my life have I ever taught that all kings are necessarily fools and scoundrels, and that all that is needed to produce an infallibly right and infinitely wise government is to give Hans and Gretchen a vote? If that is what Republicanism and Democracy mean in Germany then God help Germany! But if I say this I shall be reported as believing that to make Hans omniscient all that is necessary is to put a steel helmet on him. Now the value of a steel helmet depends on whether there are any brains inside it; and people with brains are usually sensible enough to prefer a more comfortable headgear. In Germany as in other countries there are several well known groups of idealogues with set programs of opinions which have for the most part no reference to fact or to human nature. I cannot write a word without some attempt being made to assign to me either a membership of one of these groups or a hostility to it. Rash journalists will have it that I must be some particular sort of German idiot, whereas the truth is that I am not an idiot at all—or rather, that I am an entirely unique idiot, quite outside the common political assortments.

As to democracy in Germany, my old relations with the Social-Democrats have left me without any illusions as to its hopeless futility. They were wonderful talkers—Bebel[2] was the greatest talker the world ever produced—and wonderful organizers. Wilhelm Liebknecht[3] was an inveterate parliamentarian. The rise of the party, the multiplication of its votes from election to election, its newspapers, its ubiquitous branches, its marvellous discipline were the pride and glory of proletarian politics. Bebel tried to crush Jaurès with a recital of them on one famous occasion; but all Jaurès said was "If we had all that in France, something would happen."[4] Something did happen: the war. If German-Social Democracy had been worth tuppence the war would have been a war between Russia and Austria-Germany, without a single German soldier east of the Oder, and Russia's allies paralyzed by Western democracy. After what actually occurred is it to be wondered at that The Apple Cart is not exactly the sort of play that Bebel would have written; though Liebknecht, a thoroughly disillusioned old parliamentary fox, would have understood it well enough.

The Apple Cart is a warning to those who are still dreaming the old dreams and listening to the old speeches. When King Magnus says that democracy, having destroyed responsible government and given the political leadership to neither king nor minister as such, but to the strong men and the adroit humbugs, without giving them any real power over the organized might of private capital, sensible Germans will ask themselves whether this is happening or not instead of wasting time discussing whether I have changed my mind or not. Is democracy as we have it at present anything more than a device to give the nation what King Magnus calls a sensation of selfgovernment whilst it is really being driven hither and thither as helplessly as it was driven into the trenches in 1914 and out of them in 1918?

I will say nothing about the annexation of the British Isles by America: let it pass for the moment as a joke. But let Germany not forget that jokes, especially my jokes, have a way of turning into earnest.

faithfully
G. Bernard Shaw

PS You will understand, of course, that in my allusions to The Apple Cart I am writing of the play as written by me and produced under my direction in London. The version produced in Berlin must be regarded as a collaboration, involuntary on my part, between myself and my friend Reinhardt and his literary lieutenants, who have invented many new features, including a new ending and the transformation of the king's lady friend into a cocotte, for which I can accept no responsibility. I do not think, however, that these changes affect the political lesson of the play.

Tls.
  1. Shaw enclosed this letter in the preceding one of 29 November 1929. It was published in *8 Uhr Abendblatt,* 16 December 1929, without the postscript.
  2. August Bebel (1840–1913).
  3. Wilhelm Liebknecht (1826–1900), co-founder, with Bebel, of the German Social-Democratic Party and like him a member of the Reichstag.
  4. Within the Party, Bebel opposed the revolutionary left and reformist right, a position that the French socialist Jean Jaurès (1859–1914), in a celebrated debate, argued condemned the Party to passivity.

4 Whitehall Court S.W.
19th December 1929

My dear Trebitsch

Something will have to be done about this travesty of Reinhardt's. It is evidently very much worse than it was when you saw it. The particulars of the changes and interpolations sent to me could not be invented; and there is hardly one of them that does not indicate how the whole play has been vulgarized in the stupidest and coarsest way.

I wrote to Tina about it, intending, of course, that she should shew you the letter; but she is persuaded that you will drop down dead if anyone throws a rose leaf at you. You both believe as much in doctors as if you had never read The Doctor's Dilemma; and naturally they do all they can to persuade you two robust people that they are keeping you alive with the utmost difficulty. What am I to do now that you have both deserted me?

In Berlin the mischief is done. My disciples there, expecting a worthy successor to St Joan, have been presented with a pornographic Jew baiting farce, with all my best strokes missed and filled up with dirt.[1] And you tell me, in effect, that the changes are the improvements by which Reinhardt has changed my bad play into a good one.[2] How am I to prevent all the other cities from copying Reinhardt's changes? You refuse to help me and repeat all the baby talk of the London and American Reinhardt's as if I had not learnt it by heart forty years ago. Why have you not challenged him, shot him, sabred him, buried him in unconsecrated ground for contemptuously disregarding your translation in the face of Berlin? Why do you tell me that I should be only too thankful to him for treating me as if I were hired by him to supply him with scenarios to dress up according to his own fancy?

In the postscript to my letter for publication I made it clear in the most moderate way that Reinhardt's version of the play was not mine. You suppressed this. I shall therefore have to take other steps to clear myself. But if you refuse to associate yourself with me in this, and take Reinhardt's part against me, you will put me in a very difficult position; for I must treat you either as sharing my grievance or as conspiring with Reinhardt to misrepresent me. That is, you must either quarrel with Reinhardt or quarrel with me. Clearly you must quarrel with Reinhardt.

I suggest that you write to R. to the following effect. 1. That I have found out how he has treated the Apple Cart through his colossal stupidity in altering the end. This was reported in the papers; and I then sent a compe-

Caricature of the cast in Act I of *The Apple Cart* in Reinhardt's production, Berlin, 1929. Kurt Gerron is Boanerges.

tent person [Sobieniowski] who knew the play thoroughly to Berlin and obtained a circumstantial report of the changes made. 2. That by making these changes he has produced a very serious breach between you and me, as I naturally hold you responsible for them. 3. That my first step was to send Fischer peremptory instructions not to entrust any plays of mine in future to the Deutsches theatre for production. 4. That my letter published in the Abendblatt contained a postscript declaring with perfect good humor that the play as produced in Berlin was the product of an uninvited collaboration of R and his lieutenants with the original author, and that I must not be held responsible for it; that for R's sake you had suppressed this postscript; and that I had taken this suppression as a final act of approval by you of R's proceedings, thus making your position very much worse, and producing a situation in which you must either disavow the changes or break off relations with me. 5. That your attempts to persuade me that the changes were necessary to secure the success of the play could not convince me in the face of the great success of my version in Warsaw and London (it has succeeded in Prague also),[3] and that I consider that whereas these successes greatly advanced my reputation in political and official society as well as attracting the general public, the Berlin perversion has disgraced and degraded me. 6. That I cannot for your sake, or rather for the sake of your banking account, make any public protest until the run of the Rheinhardt version is over, but that I am threatening to ask some other manager to follow up that run with some performances of the real Shaw play so as to give the Berlin playgoers a chance of proving that their taste is not so low as Max supposes. 7. That whether I have any serious intention of doing this you cannot say; but that there can be no doubt that I regard R's version as an open expression of his contempt for my professional ability, his conviction that he understands the theatre better than I do both before and behind the curtain, and his belief that it is his own powers as a dramatic poet and his adroitness as a producer that enable him to transform my works from hopeless ineptitudes to overwhelming popular successes. He may be right; but that is not the understanding on which I entrust my plays to managers; and in future the relations between me and R., however personally friendly, will not be professional.

You can put this to R. in any framework of your own that pleases you, as I do not want to interfere with your private attitude towards him. But some-body must make him thoroughly aware of his sins; and if you finally decide to take his side in the matter, tell me so frankly and I will find some way of getting at him without implicating you. You must, however, be prepared for his defence, which will be, probably, that he had your consent to the changes, and that you were my representative.

Let me know whether the play is still doing good business or whether the end is in sight, as I must time my thunderbolt accordingly.[4]

G.B.S.

Als.

1. Drawings and photos of the Reinhardt *Apple Cart* (especially the drawing in *8 Uhr Abend-blatt*, 21 October) showed Boanerges (Kurt Gerron) as fat, potbellied, and long-nosed, boorishly dressed in a striped peasant blouse, and looking like a caricature of a Jew. Gerron played the part as a thorough vulgarian.

2. Trebitsch was not alone in arguing that Reinhardt had improved Shaw's play. The *Abendblatt* praised Reinhardt's adaptation as masterful, and the *Observer* (10 November) reported the decisive German opinion that without Reinhardt's direction, *Apple Cart* would have been boring.

3. *Apple Cart* (*Americký císar*) opened at the National Theatre in Prague on 7 December. It had nine performances there and four more at the Burgher Theatre. Karel Čapek wrote to Shaw in January that the play was a "great literary success" (B.L.).

4. Shaw, sensing the trepidation with which Trebitsch must await his next thunderbolt, wrote on the outer flap of his next letter: "Sein Sie nicht nervos. Geschäftspapier only." ("Don't be ner-vous. Only a business-document.") The letter was from a would-be translator with Shaw's routine note on Trebitsch's prior rights.

Ayot St Lawrence. Welwyn
31st January [December] 1929

The moment I saw that sublime "Bist du allein?" "Ja-a-a-a-a!"—rideau très lent [very slow curtain], spotlight on King, orchestra plays Einsamkeit [solitude] music, I knew what that double-distilled quintessence of a Schafskopf [blockhead] was doing with my play. That motif is completely exhausted in the first act; and the recurrence to it at the end is the blunder of an idiot who thinks he knows the author's business better than the author. But to miss the echo of the scene with Orinthia, the king going like a lamb with his unpretentious wife after fighting like a lion with the goddess—the most popular stroke in the whole play with the wives who drag their hus-bands to the theatre (men always want to stay at home) was a miracle of ig-norant maladresse, of utter incapacity for handling serious work or even of understanding the public taste. It has been all a stupid blunder: there was the same bad press here, the same reasons and the same fools to be trampled on. Do you think *I*[1] don't know? Tell Tina that unless she forgives me at once I will write you such letters as will drive you to murder Max and then commit suicide.

                                                                    G.B.S.

Apcs.
    1. The word "I" is underlined three times.

                                                    4 Whitehall Court S.W.
                                                      21st January 1930
My dear Trebitsch

What! Reinhardt again in Vienna![1] And you more than ever convinced that his version is far better than mine, and that mine would have been a failure! And to pacify me you and he have agreed to restore the ending! And Max, who believes that I am a fool as well as a bungler, explains that the ending would not have suited Kraus but is just the thing for Waldau. Even if such a silly tale had any sense in it I should still ask what right he had to give a leading part to an actor who could not make an effect that any English actor earning five pounds a week could make. But of course it is shameless nonsense.

I take it that he has altered nothing else, since you mention nothing else. His silly telephone scene, his disgusting bedroom scene with the two munching chocolate, his Boanerges baited as a Jew and dressed as a racegoer's bookie, his interpolated jokes and omissions, his last scene with its carefully planned open air effect spoilt by shewing the palace on the stage to make a door for the Queen to peep through, his ridiculous big Reichstag table, his blunders piled on stupidities—Oh, why am I not in Vienna to talk to him myself and teach him his business?

Do the German theatres, like the English and American ones take what are called flashlights of their productions: that is, photographs of the scenes and characters to distribute to the press? If so, could you order for me from the photographer a German set and a Vienna set? I will pay for them of course. But without them I cannot judge the full atrocity of Max's travesty. When he called on me here last time he looked so healthy and young and bucolic that I hardly believed he had ever seen a theatre in his life. Now I know the explanation: he has ceased to be an artist. Tell him to give up the theatre and grow turnips.

We met the German ambassador yesterday. When Charlotte spoke of The Apple Cart he looked very grave and shook his head. He had heard all about it.

The London production is still playing to full houses. Max will be very sorry to hear it. Count M-P must be a most appalling vulgarian if he really prefers my decencies to Max's obscenities.[2] But probably he was drunk when he went to sleep.

And now, is Max to produce the play *everywhere* in Germany? Am I to be degraded to the rank of a third rate *opéra bouffe* librettist throughout the entire Fatherland?

                                                                    ever
                                                                    G.B.S.

PS I think I will write an article for the Tagblatt entitled Max Rheinhardt before and after Hollywood.[3]

Tls.

1. Reinhardt's production of *Apple Cart* opened on 11 January at the small, ornate Theater in der Josefstadt, Vienna, which Reinhardt acquired in 1924. Gustav Waldau (1871–1958) was Magnus; Paula Wessely, Orinthia; and Hans Albers, a revue and operetta star, Boanerges. The Viennese production did not repeat the Berlin triumph, but it ran 40 times. Felix Salten praised the production but thought the costumes too revue-like (*Neue Freie Presse*, 13 January). The socialist *Arbeiter-Zeitung* faulted Reinhardt for turning the political comedy into operetta—a form recently cultivated by Reinhardt in his acclaimed *Fledermaus*—and regretted that Shaw, despite his anticapitalist thrust, had played into the hands of the bourgeois audience, which missed the socialist spirit of his sallies against democracy.

2. Shaw's idea may be inverted. Trebitsch most likely mentioned a Count M-P, who fell asleep at the London production but not at Reinhardt's.

3. Reinhardt had gone on a fruitless quest to Hollywood in late 1928.

Ayot St Lawrence. Welwyn
23rd February 1930

All the villainy of the affair is in that abominable poster. Orinthia, the proud, the aristocratic, the goddesslike, the woman of lofty enchantments and "strangely innocent relations" an unscrupulous little kiosk mamsell letting Magnus play with her as with a kitten! Boanerges a dirty bargee! Proteus a bilious fool! All the rest typists and clerks round an office table! Magnus the average sensual man! Vulgarity wallowing drunk in a suburban ditch! How can I ever expect a decent German to speak to me again?

In Milan they omitted the last scene reluctantly because R. had put a statement in the papers that I approved of his doing so. It was at once restored when I protested. The Italian papers said that the play contained nothing of interest to Italians; but it succeeded for all that.[1] The Baltimore production promises an enormous New York success.[2] As to the failure in silly old Vienna, it serves R. right for trying to drag Mozart down to the level of vulgarized Offenbach. May he perish everlastingly!

How is the Riviera looking? Is Tina still angry with me? Here the cold is hideous.

G.B.S.

Apcs.

1. *The Apple Cart* (*L'Imperatore d'America*), produced and directed by Febo Mari, opened at the Teatro Filodrammatici, Milan, on 1 February to very qualified reviews and ran only through the 11th.

2. The Theatre Guild production had a successful tryout in Baltimore, but the New York opening on 24 February at the Martin Beck received mixed notices, and the play ran only 88 times.

The Palace Hotel. Buxton. Derbyshire
23th April 1930

My dear Trebitsch

At last a spare moment to write to you. After working 7 days a week for 6 months I have been forced to take a few days holiday.

The report that I am coming to Vienna for the Sexual Reform Congress is, as usual, a canard.[1]

A Viennese music publisher has written to me about Great Catherine, proposing a division of 60-40 between myself and Lilien.² I have replied that the publication of the score (Partitur) and the giving of performances in the theatre are two quite separate transactions; that the theatre tantièmes will be dealt with by Fischer, who will deal directly with the theatre on the one hand and with me on the other; that both tantièmes and book royalties must be divided 50-50 between composer and authors & translators; that Dr Maril should be paid a lump sum by the publishers for his work as part of the expenses of production, leaving a clear 50% to be divided 25-25 between you and me; and that I must know the price at which the vocal scores (scores for voices and piano accompaniment) will be sold in the music shops before I can judge what royalty the sales will bear. In no case will I pay two commissions.

If you approve of this, you can reply in the same terms when they approach you. They have not yet answered me. Probably the shock of discovering that I am a man of business as well as an author has been too great. . . .

Barry Jackson was of course very civil to Max [Reinhardt], who received him *en grand seigneur* and treated him with distinguished consideration. It was not his business to make mischief between Max and me; nor could he say anything that implied that his production was better than Rheinhardt's. But his report to me confirmed everything that I had heard before. You must remember that Max's version and production is not bad *of its kind*. Some of my friends, including even Charles Ricketts³ avow shamelessly that they prefer the Berlin Apple Cart to the London one. They are delighted by Maria Bard's acrobatic feats; by her clever playing of jazzed Bach & Chopin; by her antics in the bed; by her making Orinthia a whore and Magnus a libertine. Naturally, when the play is transposed into that amusing and popular but utterly vulgar key, everything that establishes my own higher key has to come out. For instance my little overture for Sempronius & Pamphilius, which at once establishes the tone of the palace as refined and quiet, and gives the utmost relief and effect to the violent intrusion of Boanerges, is utterly incompatible with the atmosphere of a rowdy brothel; so Max has to cut it out and begin with a vulgarized Boanerges waiting for a vieux marcheur [old rake] king, a male Duchess of Gerolstein.⁴ Then one bit after another comes out; and the holes have to be stuffed with rubbish. No doubt the result is quite homogeneous: the piece is perfect in its genre, and a complete success. Rheinhardt has lost his courage and his conscience; but he has made money, and confirmed his new reputation as a connoisseur in garbage. And the public thinks that it is I who have lost my courage and conscience, and who have become its courtesan. I have made money which I do not need, and lost caste in Germany, or at least in Berlin. Everywhere else I am congratulated on having taken a new step forward. Germans write to me as if I had taken to drink.

In future Rheinhardt must find other authors to drag through the mud. I will have nothing more to do with him: I cannot afford to be reduced to the ranks after all these years for his amusement and enrichment.

It does not greatly matter; for all these theatre specialists are being superseded by the triumphant Talkies. I have at last consented to let Arms & The Man be filmed and microphoned;[5] and this first experiment will be repeated, I presume, in Germany in your version. And for that we need no Maxes, nor Jessners,[6] nor Barnowskys. Also we had better save up Jannings for the talking film, though Major Barbara is too long—*as yet,* for the screen.[7] But do not forget that the film producers are just as bad as Rheinhardt, and must be as ruthlessly kept to their own business and not allowed to meddle with ours, which they think they understand and dont.

Note, by the way, that the 150 performances of Max's Apple Cart in Berlin are completely beaten by the run of *my* Apple Cart in London. The end of the London run is not yet in sight.

For my Collected Edition I have written a preface to The Apple Cart, and made some important little changes in the earlier plays. I am compiling a volume of my writings on the war [*What I Really Wrote about the War*]. There is my first novel [*Immaturity*] (1879) never before published, with an autobiographical preface. And tons of old articles—criticisms, essays, polemics &c &c &c.

G.B.S.

Als.

1. The Fourth International Sexual Reform Congress was to meet in Vienna in September. The previous year, Shaw delivered a talk at the Third Congress in London on "The Need for Expert Opinion in Sexual Reform" (*Sexual Reform Congress: Proceedings,* 1930).

2. With the aid of Konrad Maril (1889–1956), a Fischer editor, Trebitsch prepared a German libretto of *Great Catherine* for the Dutch composer Ignace Lilien (1897–1964). The resulting opera, *Die grosse Katharina,* was performed two years later at the May Festival in Wiesbaden and then issued by Universal-Editions, Vienna.

3. Charles Ricketts (1866–1931), painter and stage designer.

4. The inconstant heroine of Offenbach's operetta bearing her name.

5. Earlier, Shaw had granted the Theatre Guild an option to film *Arms and the Man,* but the Guild withdrew and Shaw now negotiated with Associated Radio Pictures.

6. Leopold Jessner (1878–1945), leading postwar German producer-director, famous for his use of steps and platforms.

7. Emil Jannings (1884–1950), German stage and film star, had recently returned from Hollywood to join the Deutsches Volkstheater, Vienna, where he played the financier in Mirbeau's *Geschäft ist Geschäft.* Trebitsch presumably thought Jannings would make an excellent Undershaft in *Major Barbara.*

The Palace Hotel. Buxton
24th April 1930

My dear Trebitsch

Tell the [Fox] Movietone people that if they attempt to film The Chocolate Soldier I will proceed against them instantly for infringement of my performing right. As I told you in my last letter I have decided to try Arms & The Man as a Talkie. A Chocolate Soldier film would kill the play stone dead. The American film companies have been trying for months past to buy the performing right in Arms & The Man so that they may make a Chocolate Soldier film without fear of my stopping it.

Is there any German firm that you can trust to make a really artistic film of Helden at full length *exactly as it stands*—NOT of a scenario founded on it and lasting 40 minutes? If there is, I am prepared to consider a proposal;

and when such a film has exhausted its vogue, then perhaps we might tolerate the Chocolate Soldier for an enormous sum.

I am writing to Miss Patch to send you the program of the Malvern Festival. I ought to write a new play to give it a genuine raison d'être; but I am afraid that is impossible in the time at my disposal.

I am sorry you will have to refuse the Movietone money; but you must be content with the infamous gains of the prostituted Apple Cart. You are as bad as Max: you would sell my soul for gold. The Chocolate Soldier is a filthier travesty than Der K[aiser] von A[merika].

By the way, that title brings us up against Sax Rohmer's novel [*The Emperor of America*, 1929].[1] We shall have the Movietone people filming the novel and exhibiting the film all through Germany as an Apple Cart film.

ever
GBS

Jitta will be performed for one week at the Arts Theatre in London, beginning Wednesday 30th April & ending Tuesday the 7th May, just to remind the managers of the play's existence, with the old cast: Miss Violet Vanbrugh &c. This is not, I am afraid, very important; but it *might* lead to something better if the press notices are good.

Als.

1. Sax Rohmer (1883–1959), popular English-born American writer, creator of the Dr. Fu Manchu stories.

4 Whitehall Court S.W.
1st May 1930

My dear Trebitsch

All these stories of my coming to Warsaw in June, for Pen Club and Sexual Reform Congresses and the like are false.

As to The Chocolate Soldier I thought I had made it clear in my last letter that until Arms and the Man has been filmed as a Talkie and its vogue thoroughly exhausted I will not allow The Chocolate Soldier to be performed either in the ordinary theatre or in the cinema. I could get $100,000 = £20,000 = M.400,000 for giving way on this point. Who is it that is tempting you? How much are you offered? Is it for the German language only? I shall not accept in any case, as I have already promised to let an English firm make a Talkie of Arms and the Man; but I like to know exactly what I am refusing.

Jitta was produced last night at the Arts Theatre (legally only a private club to which members and subscribing associates only are admitted). I was not satisfied with the performance and doubt whether it will lead to anything; but Sir Henry Norman[1] came to me twice between the acts, and expressed himself with such enthusiasm about the play as a play full of interesting ideas which left him at the end of each act keenly curious to hear the next, that I began to wonder whether my misgivings were justified. I will write further about it when I send you the press notices. So far I have seen only that in The Times, which says that I "have made the play a travesty of what it must have been and made the task of Miss Violet Vanbrugh, as Jitta, quite impossible." In short, that *I* have spoilt your play, which I am afraid is true. Serve you right for letting M[ax] R[einhardt] spoil mine!

ever

G. Bernard Shaw

Tl.; signature typed.
    1. Sir Henry Norman (1858–1939), author, journalist, industrialist; associated with the *Pall Mall Gazette* and then with the *Daily Chronicle*.

Ayot St Lawrence. Welwyn
23rd July 1930

British International Pictures are making a Talkie of How He Lied to Her Husband. As they have some German actors here, they want to make a German version at the same time. I have warned them that they must use your translation and purchase your consent; so be prepared if they write to you.[1] . . .

G.B.S.

Apcs.
    1. Shaw had turned from Associated Radio to British International Pictures with *Arms*, but first a trial film was to be made of *How He Lied*. No German version was produced.

4 Whitehall Court S.W.
1st August 1930

My dear Trebitsch

I do not know what Hevesi has published: the visit was a private one, and he did not tell me that he was interviewing me; but I tell everybody that Rheinhardt's Der K. von A. is not my play, nor anything like it, as they can find out from reading your translation.[1] As Max interpolated no less than eighty speeches of his own, the time of performance tells me nothing as to the extent of his crimes. These manager producers are all the same: they begin well and get a great reputation thereby; and they end by believing that they, and not the authors, have made the success (and sometimes they are right) and then it is all over with them: there is nothing to be done but find young men who have their reputations still to make.

The Collected Edition of my works and the Malvern affair, involving the rehearsal of five plays, has so overworked me, and certain changes that we are making at Ayot so overworked Charlotte also after her illness,[2] that we must get a rest of some kind when Malvern is done with. It is therefore possible that we may not be at home at the end of September; but I will let you know our movements as soon as I know them myself. We shall be back later in October in any case. May we expect Tina this time?

If Max intends to play any tricks with Johanna you must stop him.[3] I have been kinder to him than he deserves (merely for your sake) in making no public protest about The Apple Cart; but if he concludes that I shall be equally forbearing next time, Heaven help him.

ever

G.B.S.

Tls.

1. Alexander Hevesi, Shaw's Hungarian translator, published an article "George Bernard Shaw gegen Reinhardt und schöpferische Regie" (*Berliner Zeitung am Mittag*, 23 August, but presumably earlier in Budapest) in which he reported that Shaw expressed no pleasure in the success of the Berlin *Apple Cart*, that he believed the play was cut since it ran only two hours, and that he was dubious about "original creative" direction.

2. Charlotte Shaw had been ill with scarlet fever.

3. Reinhardt was celebrating his 25th anniversary with the Deutsches Theater and apparently there was talk of his reviving *Joan*.

The Malvern Hotel. Malvern

23rd September 1930

My dear Trebitsch

You know our routine: Saturday afternoon to Thursday morning at Ayot St Lawrence: Thursday morning to Saturday afternoon in London at 4 Whitehall Court.

You have seen enough of Ayot to realize that it wastes your time to vegetate there when you might be in London. Therefore I take it that you would greatly prefer to come at the London end of the week and stay, a free man, at your hotel, looking in at Whitehall Court when it suits you.

Your dates can be Oct 9-11, or 16-18, or 23-25. I have an engagement for the 30th which makes that date less convenient. Let me know to 4 Whitehall Court, London S.W.1—when we may expect you.

The equinoctial gales have been frightful: the coast is strewn with wrecks; but they are over, and your chance of a Meerestille [quiet sea] is now reasonably fair.

Lose no opportunity of studying the picture-talkie theatres in Germany: they are going to be far more important than the stage.

We shall have left this hotel by the time you receive this; so do not address your reply to Malvern.

ever

G. Bernard Shaw

Als.

Ayot St Lawrence. Welwyn

8th October 1930

Of course you will be most welcome at Ayot whenever you care to come. You can come down with us on Saturday afternoon and return on Monday morning by train, or you can drive down for a few hours on Sunday just as you please. Our only desire was to spare you the damnable dullness of our village and enable you to spend all your nights in London to see what there is to be seen at the theatres.

The Hyde Park Hotel is much more pleasantly situated than the Carlton or Claridges, and probably more comfortable. We shall expect you at 4 Whitehall Court to lunch at 1.30 on Thursday the 16th.[1]

G.B.S.

Apcs.

1. Trebitsch was in England from the 16th, visiting the Shaws in London, then on 19 October at Ayot. On 27 October Shaw wrote to his neighbor Apsley Cherry-Garrard, the explorer, who had invited the Shaws to lunch along with Trebitsch: "Trebitsch did not put up at Ayot: he motored down for lunch only; and he had such a lot of business to settle, and Charlotte was so determined to have it out with him about the Rheinhardt-Berlin travesty of The Apple Cart (a thing impossible under the protection of your roof) that we thought it better to cry off lunch at Lamer. She certainly took it out of him ruthlessly: I had to rescue him several times." (Texas.) Charlotte's concern may well have arisen from her being the prototype of the Queen in *Apple Cart* and foil to Mrs. Patrick Campbell–Orinthia. Any suggestion of sexual intimacies between Magnus and Orinthia would therefore personally offend her honor.

4 Whitehall Court S.W.
23rd October 1930

My dear Trebitsch
Will this do?[1]
Had you a good journey back?

ever
GBS

Ans.

1. That year the Burgtheater formed a Studio for young actors, directors and designers. Shaw, at Trebitsch's request, sent a statement strongly endorsing the project and offering the Studio—whose participants were unpaid—free use of *Androcles*.

4 Whitehall Court S.W.
15th November 1930

The prefaces to the Terry letters and to Immaturity must not be published until the two books are ready: they must not be published separately beforehand. The Terry letters are not likely to be on the market until late next year; but Immaturity may appear this year or early in the spring.[1]

Charlotte has had a bad accident—a fall in the street—bruises and broken bones; but she hopes to be on her feet again, none the worse, in a few weeks time.

GBS

Apcs.

1. *Immaturity*, Volume I of Shaw's *Works*, had already appeared in the limited Collected Edition (1930) but was not published in the Standard Edition until the next November. Trebitsch's version (*Junger Wein gärt*) was issued by Fischer in 1933.

4 Whitehall Court S.W.
7th February 1931

My dear Trebitsch
My correspondence with Ellen Terry (we exchanged hundreds of letters) will be published this year. An American gentleman, Mr Elbridge L. Adams,

has purchased the Terry copyrights and the letters I wrote to Ellen (that is, the bits of paper on which they are written, *not* the copyright). In due course we shall be seeking a publisher in Germany; and presumably Fischer will be able to offer Adams as much as any other publisher, and you will do the translation.[1]

The German papers seem to have settled into a habit of reporting everything I do as a failure. All I can say is that the film [*How He Lied*] is the opening item in the program of the Carlton, which is a first rate London cinema.[2] Although the principal film, to which mine is only a *lever de rideau*, attracts the wrong sort of audience for my work, the people laugh at it as much as cinema audiences ever laugh (or perhaps a bit more) and it is kept in the bill. It has just been produced in America, with what result I know not.

It has been a hazardous experiment, because there is no change of scene, and the dialogue is absolutely continuous from beginning to end except during the fight. As far as I know such a thing has never been attempted before. Also the dialogue is English, not American, and pre-war, not post war. Consequently the illiterate reporters who have never heard any language but Hollywood American, nor any colloquialisms, except post war ones, and who were mentally incapable of sustained attention, complained bitterly and just hated it. The qualified literate critics were all quite civil.[3]

I don't understand about Pabst and Mrs W's Prof. Who is Pabst?[4] Anyhow I have settled nothing about Mrs W. with Pabst or anyone else. . . .

> In great haste: I am much overworked
> and will die presently unless I take
> a holiday
> GBS

Als.

1. *Ellen Terry and Bernard Shaw: A Correspondence*, edited by Christopher St. John, was published jointly in 1931 by the Fountain Press (New York), owned by Adams, and Constable in a special edition of 3,000 copies. American and English trade editions appeared the same year. Fischer decided against a German edition, and none appeared.

2. *How He Lied* was directed by Cecil Lewis, with Edmund Gwenn, Vera Lennox, and Robert Harris. The double bill, which opened on 12 January, also included Ernst Lubitsch's *Monte Carlo*.

3. *How He Lied* was dismissed as "extremely artificial and stilted" (*Daily Telegraph*), as a "melancholy entertainment" (*Times*), and as a "trifle" (*Daily Herald*). Its failure was reported in Berlin by the *Vossische Zeitung* (14 January).

4. G. W. Pabst (1885–1967), prominent Austro-German film director associated with the realistic German cinema. His *Tagebuch einer Verlorenen* (Diary of a Lost One, 1929) dealt with prostitution in bourgeois society in a way that partly recalled *Mrs Warren*.

[Trebitsch to Shaw]

Vienna
My dear Shaw   In wilde haste!   27th April 1931

Working at your "Immaturity" I discovered a very funny and great mistake: At page 4 line six from below you say "Robert Smith was a youth of eighteen" and at page 23, line three from below you say: "He was only twentytwo" and later on he is again eighteen.

Please correct this as I did and answer my last letter, I implore you, if you have not answered it yet.
Yours ever
Siegfried Trebitsch

Tls.; Texas.

Hotel Lotti. Paris
28th April 1931
My dear Trebitsch

These accursed films are complicating life beyond endurance. I will not license The Chocolate Soldier under any circumstances. It would absolutely kill Arms & The Man for the screen; and it has done me quite harm enough already without that climax of injury. I have tolerated two productions of it [in Vienna and Berlin], and had another revival made without my knowledge [in New York]. I have had to defend an action taken against me by an American purchaser of the rights which, though I won it triumphantly, cost me about £1000.[1] Attempt after attempt has been made to induce me to sell the film rights of Arms & The Man with the object of shelving it and producing The C.S. with impunity. I have defeated them all, and have steadily told them that they must provide Strauss's score with a new libretto bearing a new name—exactly what you tell me they are at last threatening to do. It is no threat to me: I am delighted (having urged it myself); for when it is done we shall be rid of The Chocolate Soldier forever; and Arms & The Man will have a chance. So cable O[scar] S[traus] to go ahead with the new libretto *and the new title*, as there is nothing I desire more, and there is no chance of my consenting to the abominable C.S.

I have been on the continent since the 3rd March. When I was in Venice I seriously considered flying to Vienna; and if I had been alone I should certainly have done it; but Charlotte refuses to fly. In February I was too overworked and exhausted to attend to anything but my Collected Edition, which will be the death of me; and now I am too heartily sick of vagabondizing to think of anything but getting back.[2] Charlotte is in bed with a bad cold; my own inside is upset; I am tired beyond words; The Apple Cart at the Theatre des Arts (Pitoeff) is ugly, silly, and incompetent;[3] and I am in the worst of humors.
G.B.S.

Als.

1. In 1925, Jesse Levinson, an American lawyer, bought world film rights to *Chocolate Soldier*, but Shaw forbade the project. Levinson sued unsuccessfully in America and then in England, where he was assessed Shaw's court costs, but he left without paying.

2. Since leaving Ayot, which was undergoing repairs, the Shaws had been in the Middle East and the Greek islands and were on their way home by way of Venice and Paris.

3. Pitoëff's production (*La Charrette de Pommes*), with Pitoëff as Magnus and his wife, Ludmilla, as Orinthia, opened at the Théâtre des Arts, Paris, on 14 April and ran until 29 May.

4 Whitehall Court S.W.
15th June 1931

Make the Immaturity young man 18.

There is a popular locution to express incredulity as to good news: "It's too good to be true." I am at work upon a new play which I call, provisionally, Too True to be Good. I have written the first draft of two acts and part of the third. It is shockingly farcical, and deals with the break-up of European morals by the war.

This is *all*. The journalists are adding inventions of their own; but you may disregard them.

GBS

Apcs.

Ayot St Lawrence. Welwyn
30th November 1931

My dear Trebitsch

I know quite well that everybody in Vienna is stony broke, and that you and Tina are desperately trying to live on a mere million or two of Schillings per month. I know also that it would be a great relief to you if I were to sell the talkie rights of all my plays to Ufa to be remanufactured into pornographic farces by producers who dont know the A.B.C. of their business and therefore think they know more of it than I do. I see quite plainly all the magnificent opportunities these duffers think I have thrown away: the girl undressing, the girl in her bath, the girl buying her new underclothing at the modiste's and trying it on, the girl flying from the advances of the two old satyrs and being rescued by the jeune premier. I also fully appreciate the almost miraculous theatrical stupidity of making the housekeeper speak as vulgarly as the girl and being corrected accordingly, and dragging in an extra lady for a lesson in phonetics, on the principle that you cannot do a good thing too often.

Tell Ufa that I am not a purveyor of raw material for their amateurs to spoil, and that I do not sell my name to be attached to other people's bad work. When they learn their job they can come to me. But probably I shall be dead long before that; and so will you. At present Germany *seems* to be obsessed with post war pornography;[1] but the truth is that the Germans must be getting heartily sick of underclothing and nakedness and the sort of thing that Reinhardt imposed on the mutilated corpse of The Apple Cart. Our turn will come, if it comes at all, when the German public realizes that looking through bedroom keyholes is neither comfortable nor exciting, and will accept nothing but the book of Job, the second part of Faust, and the Russian films, which have no sex appeal in them and are much more interesting than anything that Hollywood can turn out. . . .

On the 24th December I sail with Charlotte for the Cape of Good Hope, which means that I shall be away for about three months.[2] The new play [*Too True to be Good*] will not be produced until August, at the Malvern Festival. I am at work at its final revision for the stage, and hope to have a copy in your hands before I leave. But it must not be published nor any account of it given to the Press before its production here. I do not object, however, to a Berlin production as soon as you can arrange one; only, this time I will have none of Reinhardt's pornography. I lost caste very seriously last time through his handling of The Apple Cart in Germany; and I cannot afford another such disgrace, nor can you.

You must not think of publishing your novel at your own expense. If any publisher does not believe in it enough to venture on it, have nothing to do with him. June Head should try Gollancz, who has just published a Russian novel, or Jonathan Cape, or some of the young publishers, of whom there is now quite a large group. What about the film rights? For screen purposes a murder should not be committed in the darkness of a fog; but I daresay that could be got over if the story is thrilling enough.[3]

I have been continuously overworked ever since I came back from Russia.[4] You and all my friends revile me because I have not answered their letters; but how can I? Now that you are growing old you are becoming frightfully grob [uncouth]: you will end by persuading yourself that I am your worst enemy. Tina will run away with a younger man if you are not more amiable.

ever

GBS

Tls.

1. Postwar Germany, under the freedoms of the Republic, was flooded with pornographic films.
2. The Shaws sailed for South Africa and remained there through February.
3. Trebitsch's novel *Mord im Nebel* (Murder in the Fog), published by Fischer, concerns a guilt-ridden hero, who in momentary madness commits murder in a London fog. Trebitsch approached June Head, an established translator, for an English version, without success.
4. In mid-July, Shaw, accompanied by Nancy Lady Astor, M.P., and the Liberal statesman Philip Kerr, Marquess of Lothian, had traveled to the Soviet Union, where Shaw was feted as a friend of the Revolution, celebrated his 75th birthday, and met Stalin.

Ayot St Lawrence. Welwyn

3rd May 1932

. . . You must be adamant on the question of the third act of Too True. These duffers will never learn that audiences get tired of laughing, and *want* something heavy after two acts of it.[1] In spite of a bad press the American production has triumphed.[2] Warsaw will probably again get in ahead of Berlin.[3] Sobieniowsky is at work there.

G. Bernard Shaw

Why not come to Malvern?

Apcs.

1. Act III of *Too True* consists of "talk" and a long sermon.
2. The Theatre Guild production opened at the Colonial Theatre in Boston on 29 February, with Beatrice Lillie and Leo G. Carroll. Notices were unfavorable, but the *New York Times* (13 March) reported an intense controversy, which "makes for a smiling box office." The New York opening on 4 April was better received, but the play ran only 57 times.
3. The European premiere took place in Warsaw on 4 June at Szyfman's Teatr Polski and scandalized the Home Secretary when the audience applauded the play's comments on the military. The censor who passed the play was fired, and Szyfman was ordered to suppress the third act. After lengthy negotiations some 72 lines were cut. The production ran only 37 times.

Ayot St Lawrence. Welwyn
3rd May 1932

Zu wahr um schön zu sein [Too True to be Good] will do very well. It is untrue that I have made any changes for Barry Jackson or for America, where the third act carries everything before it as I expected it would. Do not expose me to a repetition of the horrible disgrace of The Apple Cart à la Reinhardt.

I did not write a novel in South Africa: I wrote a sort of Voltairean pamphlet about 15000 words long entitled The Adventures of The Black Girl in her Search for God.[1] I think of publishing it as a little book with illustrations—if I can find the right artist. I will send you a proof. Do you think Fischer would care to publish it?

Too True will be produced at Malvern in August, just like The Apple Cart; and then, after a week or so in Birmingham, will go on to London at B[arry] J[ackson]'s theatre: the Queen's.

G.B.S.

Apcs.
1. Shaw's plans were upset in South Africa by an auto mishap in which Shaw depressed the accelerator instead of the brake pedal and sent the car he was driving into the fields. Charlotte was severely bruised and laid up for weeks. During the enforced idleness, Shaw wrote his pamphlet.

Ayot St Lawrence. Welwyn
15th May 1932

None of these artists dare I trust for the Black Girl.[1] They are all ironical, derisive, clever, and ugly. They would produce something like the old French Comic Bible,[2] and make the story a hideous mockery.

I want something as simple and serious as Holbein's Bible pictures but with modern beauty. I am trying a young and unknown Englishman[3] who works on the wood and is both designer and engraver, and who will design the picture as part of the book and not as an "illustration" stuck into it. If he succeeds his work can be reproduced everywhere.[4]

Keep Fischer quiet until I report the result.

G. Bernard Shaw

Apcs.
1. Fischer had suggested several postwar German artists, presumably expressionists.
2. *La Bible Amusant,* a notorious illustrated work by the anticlerical ex-seminarian Léo Taxil.
3. John Farleigh (1900–1965).
4. Working from Shaw's rough sketches, Farleigh produced a series of woodcuts that established his reputation.

Ayot St Lawrence. Welwyn
25th May 1932

I assure you Grosz[1] is precisely the wrong man. I want a *religious* artist, not an anti-clerical satirist. I have found an English draughtsman and wood engraver who will do; and now I can settle nothing until he has finished his work (which may take some months) and the book is ready for press.[2] I have of course no objection to simultaneous publication in England and Germany; but there must be no serial publication in the Rundschau or anywhere else. Fischer must be crazy to propose such a thing: it would kill the book.

H[eartbreak] H[ouse] is doing very badly at the Queens, drawing less than half its expenses.[3]

I will write to you about one or two things in Zu Wahr, of which I have as yet read only the first act. It seems to me to be a very vivid and brilliant translation: quite as good as the original if not better.

GBS

Tpcs.

1. George Grosz (1893–1959), leading postwar German artist, famous for his mordant, grotesque antiwar and anticapitalist paintings. He later fled Nazi Germany for the United States.

2. On 24 May, Shaw wrote Farleigh: "The Germans are pressing me hard to let them have a German illustrator, especially one who has been imprisoned for blasphemy, and richly deserved it for his hideously clever work. We must show them how it should really be done" (Farleigh, *Graven Image*, 1940). Grosz, arraigned in 1928 for blasphemy, was finally acquitted in December 1931.

3. The Barry Jackson production, with Eileen Beldon, Cedric Hardwicke, and Edith Evans, opened at the Queen's on 25 April.

Ayot St Lawrence. Welwyn
1st June 1932

All I can do about the Helden [*Arms and The Man*] film is to put a clause in the agreement disclosing that I have an authorised translator in Germany (or rather for the German language) and that the manufacturers must use his translation and procure his consent at their own expense. I have done this; and the rest is up to you if and when a German version of the film is made.

As to the accursed Chocolate Soldier I will not license it until the new film is exhausted and utterly dead.

Tell the managers that all their troubles are due to their belief that because audiences can laugh for two acts they can laugh for three. In America the last act of Zu Wahr is *more* successful than the first.[1]

GBS

Apcs.

1. German managers resisted *Zu wahr* because of the sermonizing third act. In America, some critics preferred the third act, the *New York Times* calling Aubrey's speech "one of [Shaw's] grandest utterances."

Ayot St Lawrence. Welwyn
22nd July 1932

My dear Trebitsch

When I wrote Zu Wahr I quite forgot that measles is a disease for which no microbe has been discovered.[1] I have therefore had to alter page 9 of the prompt book. You can tear pp 9-10 out of your copy and stick in the enclosed (folding up the tail to make it fit). I have marked the altered parts in red ink. . . .

I go to Malvern the day after tomorrow. Address The Malvern Hotel, Great Malvern, Worc.

ever

G.B.S.

Als.

1. In the original version of *Too True* the Monster identified himself as a sick bacillus, whose brother had been observed under a microscope.

The Malvern Hotel. Great Malvern

16th August 1932

Do not grieve for the failure. It is quite imaginary. The play, so far, is an enormous success.[1]

Klein[2] did not come: he sent a telegram at the last moment.

GBS

Ans.

1. *Too True*, directed by Ayliff, with Cedric Hardwicke, Leonora Corbett, Ellen Pollock, and Walter Hudd, opened at Malvern on 6 August, to very poor notices. Headlines read: "Too Dreary to Be Good," "Too Poor to Be Shaw," etc. But the audience was "devotedly cordial" (*Morning Post*), and Shaw, in the *Evening Standard* (8 August), insisted that despite the critics "my play is a tremendous success."

2. Robert Klein (1893–1958), formerly with Reinhardt but now director of the Theater in der Stresemannstrasse. He was to produce the German premiere of *Too True*.

Malvern

5th September [1932]

FIRST NIGHT CHANGED TO TUESDAY THIRTEENTH NOT FOURTEENTH WE COME FROM MALVERN TO LONDON THAT AFTERNOON DINE WITH US AND SEE THE PERFORMANCE FROM OUR BOX   SHAW[1]

Telegram.

1. The London premiere of *Too True* took place before a distinguished audience at the New Theatre on 13 September: "the most brilliant 'first night' for a long time" (*Daily Telegraph*). But the critics did not alter their views, and the play ran only 47 times. Trebitsch joined the Shaws for the occasion and later described his visit in "Frühstück mit Bernard Shaw" (*Vossische Zeitung*, 18 October).

Ayot St Lawrence. Welwyn

11th October 1932

Ask Klein what he thinks my life would be worth if I spent it in gadding all over Europe and America attending first nights of my plays.[1]

To spend a day or two with you and Tina would be quite another matter; but if I had time for that I should go to Vienna and most carefully choose a time when there were no plays of mine being performed. But I have no time for anything just now except work.[2] . . .

GBS

Als.

1. Robert Klein, who had attended the London premiere of *Too True*, had invited Shaw to the German premiere, starring Alexander Moissi, Erika von Thallmann, and Mathias Wiemann, which took place on 21 October at the Theater in der Stresemannstrasse. Notices of the premiere reflected the sharpened ideological splits in Germany. The antiliberal press indicted Shaw of nihilism (*Lokal-Anzeiger*, 22 October), whereas *Vorwärts* heard a positive note below the "pathos" of this "wise comedy," and the liberal press stressed the "deep melancholy of old age" (*Vossische Zeitung*): "a great souled Prospero wrote it" (Kerr, *Berliner Tageblatt*). The audience was enthusiastic, but a few hissed the remark that daughters should declare their independence, the conservative *Deutsche Allgemeine Zeitung* noting that Germans no longer put up with attacks on the family. *Zu wahr* ran 55 times.

2. Trebitsch, alert to public relations, released this letter from Shaw to the press but dropped the reference to himself, Tina, and Vienna and substituted Berlin, where *Zu wahr* was playing (*Neue Freie Presse*, 29 October).

Ayot St Lawrence. Welwyn
1st November 1932

My dear Trebitsch

Am I a god, to perform miracles? Fischer must wait until the pictures [for *Black Girl*] are ready: the artist is at work on four more, which will be the last.

I will send you presently a few last corrections and additions to Zu Wahr, for the regular printed edition: they dont concern the performances. And I suppose there will be a preface.

The German papers know more than I about Warum Imperium?[1] I never heard of it.

On the 17th Dec. Charlotte and I are to embark at Monaco for a trip round the world ending at Southampton in April next year. I hope to get a new play written on the ship.

ever

G. Bernard Shaw

Als.

1. Shaw's misreading of "Sacrum Imperium," the old Latin title for the Holy Roman Empire. On 12 October, the German Chancellor, Von Papen, created an international stir by a speech calling for a Greater German Reich and invoking the old Latin name.

Ayot St Lawrence. Welwyn
23rd November 1932

My dear Trebitsch

You are without exception the most complete heathen I have ever met. Not only have you no religion yourself: you cannot believe that anyone else has any. When you say that nobody will understand my postscript [to *Black Girl*] because nobody in Germany reads the Bible or cares about it you forget that if this were so the story would be as unintelligible and uninteresting as the postscript.[1]

I assure you that Luther's Bible is the same work as the British Bible; only the translations are into German instead of into English. The thirty years war was all about the Bible; and the war of 1914–18 was led by generals who go to church every Sunday to hear the Bible read, and by the Kaiser, who never reads your novels and constantly reads English sermons. He probably sleeps with a Bible under his pillow.

The Black Girl is not intended for pagans like you, who know nothing and care nothing about the Bible, but for the millions of people who were brought up on it and regard it as the revelation of religion to mankind.

Your notion of using the postscript as a preface to Too True is beyond words. There is not the faintest connection between them. You might as well use the Methuselah preface for St Joan.

The English edition, which was announced for the first of December, may be a few days late, as some of the covers have been badly printed and are having to be redone. I will send a copy to Fischer and one to you the moment I can lay hands on them; but simultaneous publication is hardly possible. There are 19 blocks to be made for the pictures.

The book must be a cheap one: in England it will be only half a crown; and unless I can sell 25,000 almost at once I shall be out-of-pocket by it.

I write in great haste: the preparations for my cruise and all the jobs I have to finish before I leave are crushing.

ever

G. Bernard Shaw

Tls.
1. The postscript essay to *Black Girl* deals largely with the evolving theology of the Bible. For the Penguin edition (1946), Shaw turned the postscript into a preface.

Ayot St Lawrence. Welwyn
6th December 1932

Fischer must have copies made of the stereos. My printers, Messrs R. & R. Clark, Brandon St, Edinburgh, Scotland, have the original plates in constant use at present. Fischer can order duplicates from them or get a German firm to make plates by photographing the impressions in the book.

I await Ayliff's account of the Viennese Zu Wahr.[1] He has just sent me a postcard.

GBS

Apcs.
1. *Zu wahr* opened at the Deutsches Volkstheater, Vienna, on 2 December with Luise Rainer, Paul Wagner, and Franz Schafheitlin. H. K. Ayliff of the Malvern production was present. Trebitsch sent Shaw a program with a note: "It was a huge success, press very favorable, Aylif will tell you all the details." The production ran 17 times.

PART FOUR

In the Shadow of Hitler
12 May 1933 through 9 March 1938

O<small>N</small> 30 JANUARY 1933, German parliamentary paralysis ended with the chancellorship of Adolf Hitler. The burning of the Reichstag in February provided the pretext for the government's assumption of emergency powers and suppressing the left, while the Enabling Act, which followed, yielded powers of decree to the administration, thereby removing parliament as a force. In May, trade unions were incorporated into a state-directed Labor Front, and shortly thereafter all political parties except the Nazi were dissolved.

The next year, the economy was put under state regulation; in 1935, labor service by youth became compulsory and later was extended to adults. Step by step, German Jews were barred from civil service, teaching, and the professions; Jewish enterprises were pressured into "Aryanization" by forced sale; and in 1935 the Nuremberg Laws in effect deprived German Jews of citizenship and forbade them to intermarry.

Internationally, Hitler annulled the Versailles Treaty by reuniting with the Saar, restoring compulsory military service, and remilitarizing the Rhineland.

Shaw, when asked about Hitler on his world cruise, declared that anti-Semitism was a "disgrace" that "destroyed any credit the Nazis might have had" and exposed their lack of program. Of Hitler Shaw was circumspect: "I know nothing about him"; but anyone who based his career on persecuting Jews was like "an officer in the army who begins his career by cheating at cards" (*New York Times*, 4, 13 April 1933). The situation, for Shaw, was dismaying since Hitler's power demanded statesmanship and sanity. Moreover, Shaw had compromised himself with the left by not rejecting Italian fascism out of hand but rather accepting Mussolini's seizure of power and suppression of Liberal opposition as the alternative to chaos and defending his organization of public services and state control of the economy as popular and socialistic, even though fascism's underlying capitalism—"middle-class Bolshevism"—could, Shaw early realized, degenerate into plutocratic dictatorship ("A Dialogue on Things in General between Bernard Shaw and

Archibald Henderson," *Harper's Magazine*, May 1924; also *Fortnightly Review*, 2 June 1924). Hitler's anticommunism was thus, for Shaw, a basic incongruity in National *Socialism*. Anti-Semitism was even more alarming: madness or opportunism, a foreboding peril and moral blight.

On returning to England in April 1933, Shaw prepared an interview in which he disarmingly expressed sympathy for many aspects of National Socialism and even claimed Hitler as a disciple (presumably on Labor Service), but then decried Hitler's Judophobia as a "sort of insanity," "a very malignant disease," an "incomprehensible excrescence" on the "great Nazi movement" that must be "something nobler" than pillage. And Shaw urged the Nazi leaders to quarantine their rabid followers ("Halt, Hitler!" *Sunday-Dispatch*, 4 June).

As a friend of Germany, Shaw hoped to bring the Party heads to reason. But by the end of June, he ruefully observed that his interview had achieved nothing (letter to J. Bab, 29 June 1933; Leo Baeck Institute). Still it was too soon to take Hitler's full measure. But that fall, when Hitler withdrew from the League of Nations and tore up the Versailles Treaty, Shaw thought him "perfectly right" (*New York Times*, 13 October 1933); his move was a masterstroke. But Shaw confessed to personal grievances against Nazi Germany: he was indebted to German-Jewish enterprise and artistry; exiled Einstein was his friend; the Nazis were attacking his plays with cries of "Down with Jew Shaw!"; and he, Shaw, was a Communist (*Europäische Revue*, November 1933).

On 23 November, in a Fabian lecture, Shaw called Hitler a "very remarkable man," recommended from the start by his look of "intense resentment" but mad on anti-Semitism and anti-Marxism and professing a bogus racialism that would lead to stock degeneracy ("The Politics of Unpolitical Animals," reprinted in Shaw, *Practical Politics*, 1976).

In time, Shaw defended Germany's right to rearm, and when in 1935 Hitler renounced further claims on France, Shaw declared it "nice to go for a holiday and know that Hitler had settled everything so well in Europe" (*New York Times*, 22 March). Yet "I am not a Fascist," Shaw insisted to Sylvia Pankhurst, but a Communist; the Corporate State was preferable to laissez-faire capitalism, but "the ideal Corporate State could be achieved only through Communism" (*Sunday Referee*, 21 July 1935). And in mid-1936, with the pretenses of fascism to transform capitalism increasingly hollow, Shaw wondered where Mussolini was going "so fast": "He is like an old-fashioned automobile—a wonderfully awesome thing to watch, and the explosions are thrilling, but it never took you where you wanted to go. . . . Mankind is dreadfully stupid. The biggest thing we produce is trouble." (*New York Times*, 26 July 1936.) By then Shaw had composed *Geneva*, hailing the fascist dictators before the bar of world justice.

The next year, in a chapter added to the *Intelligent Woman's Guide to Socialism and Capitalism*, Shaw diagnosed fascism as suffering the fatal vice of capitalism: "The organization of popular ignorance and romantic folly may be trusted to upset incompetent governments, idolize a Leader, go mad with patriotic excitement . . . and above all, rob, batter, imprison and slaughter the little scattered organizations of the poor as presumptuous, seditious and dangerous. But this is not the way to save civilization: it is the broad path to its destruction." For capitalist maldistribution "there is no remedy in Fascism," which as long as it maintains private property must end in a "morass of general poverty and exceptional riches . . . with the ever present threat of proletarian revolution held off by grudging doles that seem much less attractive than the Bread and Circuses of the ancient Roman Fascism which perished and dragged down the European civilization of that time with it, precisely as modern Fascism will if it remains only the latest mask of capitalism."

In Germany, Shaw's comments defending German policy were reproduced; those rebuking Hitler's Judophobia, scornfully rebutted. No monolithic stand on Shaw, even in the Party, emerged. Alfred Rosenberg, Nazi theoretician, had placed Shaw among the "army of half-breed 'artists'" that opposed the importance of "revived racial spirit" (*Der Mythos des 20. Jahrhunderts*, 1932). Yet Shaw could not be easily dismissed. On the one hand, Shaw could be accused of antiheroism, antinationalism, Bolshevism, intellectualism, individualism, pro-Semitism, and antiracialism. But he could be praised for sympathy with the German people; criticism of Marx, liberalism, and parliamentarism; instinct for life; call for leaders; and perhaps fellow-traveling with National Socialism (e.g., E. Scheiner, *G. B. Shaw Nationalsozialist?*, 1934; Karl-Hans Galinsky, "G.B. Shaws Auseinandersetzung mit dem Deutschtum," *Zeitschrift für Neusprachlichen Unterricht*, 1935). A Party hack might boast that the Nazis were "barbarous" enough to find Pirandello and Shaw "snobbish trifles" (V. Braumüller, "Von den Aufgaben nationalsozialistischer Theaterkritik," *Deutsche Bühne*, January 1936), but that year on Shaw's eightieth birthday high if qualified tributes were paid to Shaw's intellect, moral earnestness, wit, humanity, reformist spirit, and honesty (*Germania*); concern for justice (*Berliner Tageblatt*, 26 July 1936); and embodiment of the life force (*Deutsche Allgemeine Zeitung*). Yet Shaw was faulted for being more preacher than activist, more destroyer than creator, and for failing to grasp the new order.

Throughout the period, Party leaders saw no reason to proscribe Shaw, and even during the war Goebbels rejected banning Shaw, whom he justified as "antiplutocratic," Irish rather than English, and satirist of Britain (*Kriegspropaganda 1939–1941*, 1966). In 1934, he cited as "very clever" Warwick's ironic definition of "traitor" in *Joan* as one not wholly devoted to his nation's interests (*New York Times*, 19 November). And in December 1936, he attended the Berlin premiere of *Millionairess*. In 1939, Hitler, in Munich, attended *Caesar* (*Times*, 6 February); the year before, a German minister requested that the recently filmed *Pygmalion* be sent to Hitler (Valerie Pascal, *The Devil and His Disciple*, 1971); and in his "secret conversations" Hitler, citing Joan of Arc, added, "portrayed, incidentally, much more faithfully by Shaw than by Schiller" (*Hitler's Secret Conversations*, 1953). Shaw was *persona grata*, but within limits.

Goebbels might attend *Millionairess*, but its preface, speculating on Hitler's Semitic forebears, was unacceptable. Shaw's new plays were produced and published, except for *Geneva*, which placed Hitler (Battler) on stage. And Goebbels distinguished between Shaw the playwright and Shaw the political commentator. The latter Goebbels himself monitored and, when at odds with German war propaganda, suppressed. In turn, Shaw did not deny his plays to Nazi Germany, and when queried by Trebitsch replied, "Why shouldn't they be played before cannibals?" (Trebitsch's *Chronicle* gives a fuller reply, but Alfred Kerr reported Shaw's answer "verbatim" from Trebitsch much earlier in "Bei Bernard Shaw," *Pester Lloyd*, 23 February 1936.)

Freed from "worm-eaten liberalism" and Jewish "anti-völkisch" cosmopolitanism, German theatre was thrown open to disaffected native writers. Production of foreign plays sharply declined from over 30 percent of premieres before 1933 to less than 3 percent in 1933–34 and never more than 6.6 percent in the Nazi epoch. Of contemporary foreign playwrights, Shaw led in productions and performances, with *Pygmalion* the apparent favorite before the war and *Joan* thereafter. Only *Arms* was avoided as antiheroic and of course *Geneva* (Ilse Pitsch, "Das Theater als politisch-publizistisches Führungsmittel im Dritten Reich," unpubl. diss., Munster, 1952). Yet the vogue of Shaw was in decline: none of his new plays was performed first in Berlin; *The Simpleton of the Unexpected Isles* (1935) did not reach Berlin at all. The result was a dramatic fall in Shaw's German earnings with a temporary resurgence in 1935–36 (thanks to the movies).

Trebitsch, as an Austrian, was for a time spared the Nazi scourge, and until late 1935, when the Nuremberg laws were effected, he attended select productions of Shaw in Germany. His name as translator was at times expunged from programs, but his reduced income cut more deeply. Still, worse lay ahead.

4 Whitehall Court S.W.
12th–15th May 1933

My dear Trebitsch
    I have not had a moment free for private correspondence since I landed until today (the 12th).[1]
    My first impulse was to write you a long and fierce letter for publication in the German press, bringing all my guns to bear on Hitler's stupid mistake in trying to make political capital out of the Judenhetze [Jew-baiting],* and on his attempt to cover up the essentially Communist character of his proclamation of compulsory labor and his nationalization of the Trade Unions (the first being pure Bernard Shawism and the second borrowed from Russia) by a senseless denunciation of Marxism. For in such a crisis as the present you have either to hit back and hit hard, or else accept the situation in an attitude of complete submission.

But on reflection I saw that I could not involve you in such a controversy, not only because you would run all the risks of it and I none, but because your sympathies, except to the extent to which they are Bohemian artistic sympathies, are Junker sympathies. You believe all the rubbish the newspapers print about Russia.† Although the 1914 war began by the mobilisation of Imperialist Russia against Germany, and the Bolsheviks stopped that war by the peace of Brest Litovsk and were denounced for it by their Allies, who accused them of being in the pay of Germany, you would, if you could, restore the Imperial government in Russia and go back to the anti-Russian situation of 1914. If the Junkers were wise and far-sighted instead of being blinded by class prejudice and dread of losing their properties they would say that as they have nothing to fear diplomatically from a Communist Russia and everything to fear from an Imperialist Russia, it is their interest that Russia should remain Communist even if Germany remains Capitalist. But they are not wise; and the consequence is that they have made a combination with Nazi Hitlerism, which derives all its electoral strength from the sentimentalized and Chauvinized Socialism of the city proletariats. They have made Hitler dictator for four years only to find themselves left out of his councils and his distribution of public posts, and the situation dominated by Colonel Goering, a Socialist who is determined to break up the big Junker estates in the east and give them to the peasants (just as Lenin did) to secure their support for Fascism.[2]

You have not analyzed the position because you hate politics, and are quite unaccustomed to and inexpert at the sort of political controversy in which I am as practised as I am in playwriting. You had better keep out of the melée as much as possible. If you are pressed as to why you translate me, who am a notorious Communist, and a strenuous upholder of the present regime in Russia, you must say that you are not concerned with all that— that you have introduced me to Germany as a great artist, and that all you know about my present attitude is that though I may have expressed the greatest contempt for the Judenhetze I have been the first to applaud Hitler's two great steps as to compulsory labor and the trade unions when the whole British press are denouncing them savagely, exactly as I supported Mussolini when he too was being denounced as the most infamous of usurpers and tyrants. But you are not committed to my opinions: all you know is that I have a right to be heard, and that to pretend that my artistic works should not be read in Germany because of my opinions is as ridiculous as to make the same objection to translations of the works of Tolstoy or of the Koran. But whatever you say or do, you must be careful not to shew the least sign of being intimidated, or of caring one snap of your fingers what anybody thinks or threatens.

As to silencing me, that is not possible. I can neither refuse to receive the press when I visit a foreign country nor educate them to report what I say correctly. If the consequences prove ruinous to both of us I cannot help it; but let us wait until we really are ruined. My ruin has been announced so often that I am no longer afraid of scarecrows. If they worry you about it say

"All I know is that Shaw is the greatest man who ever lived and everything he says must be right." They wont shoot you: they will treat you as a privileged lunatic.

On the voyage I wrote a comedietta for two persons [*Village Wooing*], which would occupy about one hour in performance, and a very long political play of the Apple Cart kind [*On the Rocks*], which I still have to finish and cut down into reasonable length. I shall not take any trouble to have them performed, but publish them in the same volume as Too True.

By the way, what has happened to that play [*Too True*]? Is it true that the Nazis interrupted performances with shouts of "Down with the Jew Shaw!"?[3]

Tell dear Tina that Vichy water, though no use in bottles, is radio-active when you drink it straight out of the ground. It does wonders for livers, but may be good for other organs as well.

In haste, as usual
G. Bernard Shaw

P.S. 15th May 1933. Rosenburg has just returned to Berlin overwhelmed by the avalanche of execration brought down on Hitler by the persecution of the Jews.[4] Meanwhile I receive piteous letters from Jews, notably Alfred Kerr and Julius Bab,[5] asking me to help them. But how can any private purse help in a wholesale catastrophe like this one?....[6] Another matter. Tauchnitz wants to publish The Black Girl in English. Ordinarily I should not permit this until Fischer had had a long start with the German edition. But if Fischer dare not publish your translation there is no longer any reason for stopping Tauchnitz. What is the present situation? Is the boycott lifted? Rosenberg's report will not encourage it.[7]

All this is written without reserve as you are on French soil. Is there any risk in Austria of your letters being opened, or of your being boycotted? I dare not write a line frankly to anyone in Germany.

How much are you a Jew? I know that you are a practising heathen; but do any of your kinsfolk go to the synagogue?

Excuse all the marginal scrawlings; but the situation changes almost from hour to hour.

*All through my tour the first question put by the press at every port was about Hitler. I said that a statesman who began by a persecution of the Jews was compromised as hopelessly as an officer who began by cheating at cards. But I approved of the subsequent edicts. I admitted that the Germans had as much right to exclude non-Germans from governmental posts as the Americans to reserve the presidency for Americans, but insisted that displaced Jews should be compensated and not driven out penniless by hounding on the mob to attack them.

†The Russians, in their desperate struggle to civilize their hundred million peasants, have been forced to spend recklessly on education, and they have probably overcapitalized in machinery, with the result that they may have run short of food for the moment. But the stories told by the runaways when they find that there is a good market for anti-Communist lies are quite

worthless as evidence of the collapse of Communism, though some of the tales of individual and accidental hardships may be true enough. But even these are trifles compared to what is happening in England and America. In New York well dressed gentlemen are begging in the streets desperately and shamelessly.

Tls.

1. Shaw had been busy, since his return, composing the interview "Halt, Hitler!" (*Sunday-Dispatch*, 4 June), attacking Hitler's anti-Semitism.

2. Hermann Goering (1893–1946), Hitler's chief aide and premier of Prussia, in a draft-law declared peasant lands inalienable but did not in fact break up the Junker estates as demanded by the Party's left wing.

3. In February, *Too True* opened in Mannheim with Alexander Moissi (not a Jew) in the leading role and was disrupted by Nazi shouts of "Jew Moissi," "Jew Shaw" until police intervened.

4. Alfred Rosenberg (1893–1946), Nazi ideologist, had just finished an exploratory visit to England where he faced hostile demonstrations and a bad press.

5. Kerr and Bab both later emigrated from Germany.

6. Shaw's ellipsis.

7. On 1 April, Hitler had declared a boycott of German-Jewish businesses, but it lapsed after some days. Fischer, who was a Jew, was uncertain whether he should publish the fable, whose religious views would offend the clericalists. Tauchnitz did publish the English text in 1935; the German version did not appear until 1948.

Malvern Hotel. Malvern

9th August 1933

My dear Trebitsch

I really have nothing fresh to tell you. I am working as hard and fast as I can to get the new play, called ON THE ROCKS, ready for production in London by Charles Macdona (not Barry Jackson) at the Prince's Theatre, where Macdona has now done what I have been urging for years: the reduction of the prices of admission to from one shilling to five, including entertainment tax.[1]

I was greatly astonished by the publication of the letter I wrote to Dr Haiser from Stresa years ago.[2] I had forgotten all about it; but it does credit to my political prescience that it read as if it had been written yesterday.

As you see, we are at Malvern, and shall probably remain until I have to return to London to produce ON THE ROCKS. A production at the end of September is not absolutely impossible; but nothing is settled. A successful play in London may run for six months; and if Macdona had such a success on hand I should have to wait. That, however, is not very likely to happen. All I can say is that ON THE ROCKS may be produced any time between the last days of September and the end of the year. I hope for your sake that it will be sooner rather than later so that you may have fine weather for your visit.

As for the short play called A VILLAGE WOOING I have not touched it since I landed in April: it is merely a first rough draft. As nobody wants a play for two characters only, and lasting only an hour, it will be useful only to pad out my next volume, which will contain TOO TRUE and ON THE ROCKS as well.

It would certainly be most unwise of you to visit Germany until Hitler is thoroughly intimidated both as to Israel and Austria. Meanwhile I will neglect no opportunity to convince him that if he burns you as a Jew I will blow the fire hard enough to scorch him very unpleasantly. He has just had to climb down before Italy's remonstrance as to Austria; and Italy got in only five minutes before England, with the League of Nations behind her.[3] This suggests that he can be bullied; but I repeat that I have not yet taken his measure and am only guessing.

I am afraid ON THE ROCKS may prove as little use abroad as JOHN BULL'S OTHER ISLAND, as it is all politics and very English politics at that.

Robert Klein (?) is in London vigorously asserting that TOO GOOD was not a failure in his hands in Germany, as it ran over 100 nights.[4] Is there any truth in the story that Moissi got into trouble over an attempt to get some obstetric experience in a hospital for some play in which he was interested?[5]

Glorious weather here. Is there any chance of Tina coming with you this year?

                                                                GBS

Tls.

1. Charles Macdona (1860–1946) had in fact initiated "Shaw for the Million" at reduced prices back in 1925. His production of *On the Rocks* opened in London on 25 November 1933 at the Winter Garden Theatre (not the Prince's), directed by Lewis Casson, and ran 41 times.

2. Dr. Franz Haiser (1871–1945), a Viennese Nietzschean and racialist antidemocrat, assumed that Shaw shared his views about a "new race aristocracy," but he was disabused in a letter by Shaw either in 1926 or 1927 and now reprinted in *Time and Tide* ("Bernard Shaw expounds 'Hitlerism and the Nordic Myth,'" 22 July). Shaw dismissed Haiser's racial theories as "pseudo-Nietzschean nonsense" and called for social equality, a scientific means of determining human capacity, and popular elections of qualified candidates.

3. Italy, which had its own designs on Austria, had resisted Hitler's plans for annexation, whereupon Germany undertook to avoid frontier incidents and cease its propaganda assault on Austria.

4. Klein's Berlin production of *Too True* ran 55 times.

5. In the fall of 1931, Moissi, actor turned novelist, was writing a scene in which a woman gives birth. He persuaded some doctors in Salzburg to allow him to witness a birth in the guise of a physician. When the truth was out, the woman's family brought suit, religious circles were outraged, and the Nazis condemned the hospital administration.

                                                    Ayot St Lawrence. Welwyn
                                                    1st October 1933
My dear Trebitsch

Your letter of the 20th Sept. came into my hands ten minutes ago for the first time through a mistake in sending my letters to the country!!!

We are at Ayot at usual; and our routine still is to come up to London on Thursday mornings and return on Saturday afternoons. Charlotte usually comes up before me on Wednesday and has a day at her club.

Will you come to lunch on Thursday at 1.30. And will you bring with you Elizabeth Bergner and her husband and Wernher Kraus and his wife (if he has one).[1] I believe he does not speak English; and as I have forgotten all my German you will have to interpret. Let Miss Patch know as soon as possible whether this will suit you. If the rest cannot come, no matter: come yourself.

We shall be delighted to see you always, no matter how long you stay.

                                                    always
                                                    G. Bernard Shaw

Als.
1. On 5 October, Trebitsch lunched with the Shaws along with Werner Krauss (1884–1959) and Maria Bard (1900–1944), Krauss's wife, who played Orinthia to Krauss's Magnus in Reinhardt's *Apple Cart*. Elisabeth Bergner and her husband, Paul Czinner, did not join the group, perhaps because of Hitler's friendship for Krauss, who shortly became vice-president of the Theatre Chamber under Goebbels.

4 Whitehall Court S.W.
21st October 1933

My dear Trebitsch

You must keep your head clear about this Nazi business. Hitler's withdrawal from the League of Nations and the Disarmament Committee is a masterstroke; and no German, whether he be Austrian or Prussian, can refuse his hearty approval without placing himself in a hopelessly false position. You, as an Austrian, must be in favor of the repudiation of the Treaty of Versailles, and the refusal of any German or Austrian government to remain in any league or international committee in an inferior position. It is by taking this stand that Hitler has rallied the whole German nation to him, and made such an impression in Austria. And on these points you should support Hitler without reserve. It is only by making this clear that you can repudiate Hitler's Judophobia, and his persecution of Social-Democrats and Communists as such, and declare that an Ausgleich [settlement; i.e., coordination with Germany] is impossible until the German Nazis discard this irrelevant and discreditable side of their program.[1]

Whatever you say, dont treat the question as if Hitler and Dollfus were two gamecocks, and you were backing Dollfus.[2]

The enclosed may amuse you. I have to make it clear that in Hitler's last big move I am entirely on his side and against English anti-German Jingoism.

I hope you have arrived safely in Vienna and that Tina finds you looking the better for your journey.

always

G. Bernard Shaw

PS Hollywood seems to be in earnest about The Devil's Disciple (with Barrymore). They also want St Joan with Katharine Hepburn; but their limit of 80 minutes is impossible for that play.[3]

Tls.
1. In May, Hitler accepted a call for disarmament, but when by October it became clear that the Allies would not grant Germany parity, he withdrew from the Disarmament Conference and the League of Nations. Approached by the *Europäische Revue* (Berlin) for a comment, Shaw wrote a brief statement (see 22 December 1933), a copy of which he apparently enclosed for Trebitsch.
2. Engelbert Dollfuss (1892–1934), the authoritarian Austrian chancellor, opposed unification with Nazi Germany for conservative-clerical reasons. He was assassinated by Austrian Nazis the next year.
3. Katharine Hepburn (b. 1907) had made her film debut the previous year in *Bill of Divorcement* (RKO) with John Barrymore (1882–1942). Nothing came of either proposal, however.

4 Whitehall Court S.W.

22nd December 1933

My dear Trebitsch

I am very uneasy about this business of On The Rocks and Reinhardt. If he is let go within ten miles of the play, he will turn it into an intrigue between the Prime Minister and his secretary, and use the table as a cover for indecent liberties between the Duke and Aloysia. My reputation suffered greatly in Germany from his version of The Apple Cart. You must just tell W[erner] K[rauss] that I will not have On The Rocks produced by Reinhardt.[1] Tell him I have too much respect for his great talent and dignity as an artist to allow him to be placed under the direction of our friend Max, who revels in pornographic farce and has no respect for actors and actresses.

The final revised version of On The Rocks was sent to you a few days ago. The most important change in the dialogue is the omission of the letter of resignation to the King, which I discarded after the first performance. The changes in the stage business are considerable; so please go carefully over the directions and over the description of the scene. When the Downing Street Cabinet room was reproduced on the stage I found it had three doors instead of two. This altered almost all the secretary's entrances. I had to put in another chair at the table, and also an armchair to accommodate Aloysia and the Duke, and to reverse the position of the Admiral and Glenmorrison. Unless all these changes are made in the stage directions the producer will be hopelessly confused.

Now as to politics. I tried to dissuade you from going to Berlin; but I guessed that you would go; so I fired my shot in the Europaisches Revue just in time.[2] I am informed that Colonel Goebbels, on being asked why my plays were out of favor, declared that I am *persona gratissima* in Berlin, and that my plays are welcome "when they are not opposed to Nazi principles."[3]

You must bear in mind that Hitler began his career as a strong pro-German and anti-Slav, all for the Ausgleich [*Gleichschaltung*: "Coordination" with Austria] and against Jugo Slavia and Czechoslovakia and the rest of the non-German elements. This was hopeless under Franz Josef and the Archduke; but when the war cut off the Jugoslavs and Czechoslavs, and left Vienna like a starving shepherd whose sheep had all run away, the case for the Ausgleich— Hitler's case—was enormously strengthened. Mussolini objects because his Brenner frontier is an ethnological outrage, easier to maintain against poor crippled Vienna than against a united and belligerent German Reich. Hitler, who needs Mussolini's friendship just at present, does not want to stir up this question; but it will arise inevitably sooner or later. I think if I were in your place I should advocate a union with Germany, which would please Berlin, though I should denounce anti-Semitism and all the nonsense about Nordics and Latins as bogus ethnology and bad biology.

Fascism, or the organisation of the State as a hierarchy of industrial and professional corporations, is right as far as it goes; but what real power will the corporations have unless they own the land and control the industries—

unless, that is, the State is Socialist as well as Fascist? Therefore the persecution of Socialists as Socialists is even sillier than the persecution of Jews *qua* Jews; for if Fascism is to come to anything it must come to Communism finally. The alternative is a bourgeois republic in which the Corporations would be the tools of the financiers and their industrial allies just as the parliamentary Cabinets are. If you meddle in politics at all, keep these leading considerations in your head. You may be challenged to explain my views, if not your own. . . .

> always
> G. Bernard Shaw

. . . You suggest Mrs Baker-Eddy as a future heroine. But she is in On The Rocks as the lady doctor![4]

Tls.

1. Reinhardt, who was a Jew, had left Germany in March 1933 and in April he was removed from the Deutsches Theater. In June, he wrote to the Nazi government, pointedly ceding his theatres to the German people. In theory, Reinhardt was free to return to Germany—loss of rights by Jewish emigrants came later—and Werner Krauss, as vice-president of the Theatre Chamber, may have felt able to sponsor Reinhardt to direct *On the Rocks*.

2. In his comment to the *Europäische Revue* (November 1933), Shaw praised Hitler's withdrawal from the Conference and League but attacked his persecution of the Jews.

3. In practice, established artists who did not challenge the "cultural will" of the state were tolerated by Joseph Goebbels (1897–1945), Minister of Propaganda.

4. Mary Baker Eddy (1821–1910), founder of the Christian Science movement, stressed the spiritual basis of illness; so too the lady doctor in *On the Rocks*: "It is the mind that makes the body: that is . . . the secret of all true healers."

> 4 Whitehall Court S.W.
> 30th December 1933

. . . Congratulations on the professorship.[1] What a lark!

How can I possibly trust Max with On The Rocks? He will turn it into a filthy intrigue between the Prime Minister and his secretary. He knows nothing about politics. I must have a respectable producer. [Robert] Klein is here, and wants to go to America. But if Max can produce in Germany now, why not Klein?[2]

> GBS

Apcs.

1. On his 65th birthday, Trebitsch received an honorary professorship from the Austrian government for his services to Austrian literature.

2. Reinhardt did not return to Germany but retired to Austria where he turned his Theater in der Josefstadt over to associates. In all he had introduced nine of Shaw's plays to Berlin, produced another five and added two others in Vienna for over 1,300 performances, second only to Shakespeare in Reinhardt's repertory. In October 1937, Reinhardt emigrated to America where his career was eclipsed. He died in New York on 31 October 1943.

[Trebitsch to Shaw]

Wien
24th January 1934
My dear Shaw:
 It is a very hard work to reach the footlights of a German stage for "On the rocks." All the Nazi-managers want the title "England erwache!" Please tell me at once, if you would give your consent to that title.[1]

Yours ever
Siegfried Trebitsch

P.S. Are you still in London? When will you start your cruisade?[2]

Tls.; Texas.
 1. The revolutionary song "England, arise!" which ends *On the Rocks*, was translated as "England, erwache!" and inadvertently echoed the Nazi slogan, "Deutschland erwache!" Under pressure from some managers, Trebitsch adopted the cry as subtitle to *Festgefahren* (Run Aground) in several programs but not in the published version.
 2. The Shaws were preparing for a cruise to New Zealand.

[Ayot St Lawrence. Welwyn]
5th February 1934

 Yes: I think "England, erwache" a *much better* title than On The Rocks, though it seems odd that it should be preferred in Germany. So by all means adopt it.
 We start for N[ew] Z[ealand] this week: on Thursday the 8th. The voyage will take 4 weeks; we shall be a month on shore; and then 4 weeks return voyage will land us back again in England about the middle of May.
 Miss Patch will remain on duty meanwhile.
 I am in a fearful hurry packing.
 Our love to Tina.
 Auf wiedersehen!

GBS

Als; written at the bottom of Trebitsch's letter of 24 January 1934.

4 Whitehall Court S.W.
2nd June 1934

 I am just concluding an agreement for the production of On The Rocks in Amsterdam. In it I undertake that this performance shall be the first in Holland in *any* language, meaning that there shall be no prior performance in German.[1] There was a fearful row over a German performance of a former play [*Too True*]: I had to offer to return part of the advance made for the Dutch production.[2]
 Is Fischer fully aware that he must not touch Holland? Your very surprising announcement of the success of On The Rocks in Germany makes my

Dutch agent nervous about this new agreement.[3] I promised him I would warn you again about it. More presently.

In a hurry as usual
GBS

Apcs.
 1. The Dutch premiere of *On the Rocks* (*Vastgeloopen*) took place at the Vereenigd Rotterdamsch-Hofstad Toneel on the following 20 November.
 2. In January 1933, Moissi on tour in Amsterdam with *Too True* anticipated the Dutch premiere.
 3. *On the Rocks* (*Festgefahren*) opened simultaneously on 17 March in Hamburg, Stuttgart, and Königsberg and then on 21 March in Berlin's Volksbühne, directed by Heinz Hilpert, with Ernst Karchow, Oskar Sima, and Roma Bahn. It was generally welcomed as an attack on parliamentarism and support for a "leader." The *Schwäbischer-Merkur* (20 March) pointed to the subtitle "England, erwache!" as a summons to follow Germany and Italy and accepted Sir Arthur's program of compulsory labor, etc., as "national-socialist." Berlin notices followed the same line with some reservations about Shaw's ambiguous "Leader-idea" (*Lokal-Anzeiger*, 23 March), liberalism, and failure to distinguish communist, fascist, and national-socialist dictatorships (*Deutsche Allgemeine Zeitung*). *Neue Literatur* (May 1934) hoped the play would be widely produced abroad and add to an understanding of Germany. *Festgefahren* ran seven times each in Hamburg and Stuttgart, and 25 times in Berlin.

[Trebitsch to Shaw]
Wien
6th June 1934

Many thanks for your card. Amsterdam is quite safe as far as the Dutch production is concerned and it shall be no prior performance in German be quite sure of that, please. But your manager ought to know that "On the rocks" has been done March 20/22 in Berlin, Hamburg, Königsberg, Frankfurt, Bremen and Stut[t]gart. Very successful everywhere, without a very long run. I have sent programs ec. ec. long ago to Miss Patch for you. About what is your agent nervous then?

Please let me know at least the plots of the new plays you have written during your crusade.

Yours ever
Siegfried Trebitsch

Apcs.; National Library of Ireland.

4 Whitehall Court S.W.
15th June 1934

My dear Trebitsch
 ... As to this film business it is very difficult.[1] Naturally an offer which would put M 15000 [about $3,600 or £730] into your pocket at once is very tempting; but it would be a bad bargain for me. The usual course is to sell the world rights to Hollywood. But this is really a relic of the days of the movies, when there was no question of speech. Now that we have talkies I am inclined to deal with the different countries separately. My standard terms are ten per cent on the sums received from the exhibitors by manufac-

turers without any advance; and of this you could claim half as usual. But if you are desperately pressed for ready money you could license the use of your translation for five years for a sum down, leaving me to take 5% instead of 10%.

I think Pygmalion a very bad choice; and I should make it a condition that there was to be no sentimental nonsense about Higgins and Eliza being lovers. Eliza married Freddy; and the notion of her marrying Higgins is disgusting. But, as I have said, the play is not a very good one to film, as it is too long, and the character of Doolittle is so important in it and so unsuitable for the screen.

It is a pity that this Judophobia craze makes it impossible for the moment to have a film of Johanna with Liesl Bergner.[2]

faithfully

G. Bernard Shaw

Tls.; postscript omitted.

1. The German film company Klagemann in association with Fox Film was angling for rights to *Pygmalion*.

2. Elisabeth Bergner, barred from the German stage as a non-Aryan, had emigrated to England in 1933.

Ayot St Lawrence. Welwyn

26th June 1934

They may Viennify the names in Pygmalion at the Raimundtheater as much as they please. I forgot to say so in my last letter. . . .

One of the three new plays is a brief trifle—historical—called The Six of Calais. I will send you a printed copy in the course of the week. The others are full length, or will be when I have finished arranging them for the stage.[1] One is an ultra-fantastic oriental modern (or futurist) play [*The Simpleton of the Unexpected Isles*], the other a contemporary comedy [*The Millionairess*]. No plots, and contents indescribable.

G.B.S.

Apcs.

1. All three plays had been composed during Shaw's recent cruise.

4 Whitehall Court S.W.

3rd July 1934

Had you not better put Dr Koretz into direct communication with me? The agreement as drafted is not sufficient: I shall propose a much longer and more exact one. But first I want to know where Klagemann comes in? Dr Koretz represents the German Fox Film. I am prepared to deal with F.F. or with K.; if you can assure me that K. is a solid firm. But why am I to deal with both?[1] . . .

I am sorry to delay the transaction; but the film business is frightfully complicated. And we have no scenario submitted to us.

In haste

G.B.S.

Apcs.

1. Dr. Paul Koretz (ca. 1885–1980), a Viennese lawyer specializing in copyright, had initiated the scheme for a German-language film of *Pygmalion* with Fox Film as guarantor of Shaw's royalties and Klagemann Films, of Berlin, as producing company.

Ayot St Lawrence. Welwyn

20th July 1934

My dear Trebitsch

I go to Malvern on Sunday the 22nd. Address The Malvern Hotel, Great Malvern. Worc. They are performing You Never Can Tell there.[1]

On Tuesday last [17 July] Androcles was revived and my new sketch The Six of Calais produced at the open air theatre in Regents Park. I will send you a copy of this as soon as I get it back from the printer with all the stage business completed and filled in.

I am in correspondence with Loretz [Koretz]; but I cannot fight him with both hands tied behind me by Tina. I am haunted by the thought of her starving on the top floor of the Park Hotel instead of wearing all her diamonds on the *piano nobile* [first story]. So if you are resolved to sell your film rights in Pygmalion for 20,000 Schillings (about 730 pounds sterling), I will buy them from you for that sum; Tina will astonish Karlsbad with her expenditure; and Koretz will be at my mercy. What say you?

I have committed myself to a Joan-Bergner film for the English language. She has been extraordinarily successful here, playing to full houses every night.[2] And in spite of her childlike charm she is a clever woman of business, refusing baares Geld [ready cash] and insisting on a percentage, like me.

I now have two American firms and one French and one Italian clamoring for Pygmalion. I do not know how it will end;[3] but it is clear that I shall be badly worsted unless I am prepared to say No, and to wait for the right moment, which is another way of saying that I must acquire your rights instead of letting Fox Films acquire them. A line or a wire to Malvern will bring you a cheque without further delay.

always yours

G. Bernard Shaw

Als.

1. *You Never Can Tell* opened at Malvern on 27 July, directed by Herbert Prentice, with Godfrey Kenton, Joyce Bland, and Stanley Lathbury.

2. The previous December, Elisabeth Bergner created a sensation in London as the madcap mistress in Margaret Kennedy's *Escape Me Never*, which ran for eight months. On 8 February 1934, Shaw wrote to Bergner asking her to star in a movie of *Joan*.

3. Nothing came of any of these offers.

Malvern Hotel. Malvern
4th March [August] 1934

My dear Trebitsch

The enclosed cheque ought to realise the requisite number of schillings and a little over.

I enclose also a form of receipt. It is not only a receipt for the money but an assignment of your film rights to me. You must translate it into your best German and have it stamped and witnessed (or whatever legal ceremonies are necessary to make it legal in Germany—if any) as I must have a document to convince Koretz and secure my 10%.[1]

I shall have to make a rough scenario for him, including some new scenes: the play cannot be filmed as it stands.

I enclose The Six of Calais. The other plays (both full length) are The Simpleton of The Unexpected Isles and The Millionairess. The latter is not completed: I have altered its plan since I drafted it on the ship.

ever
G. Bernard Shaw

Als.
  1. Trebitsch had accepted Shaw's offer to buy his rights in a film of *Pygmalion* for £750.

4 Whitehall Court S.W.
22nd September 1934

My dear Trebitsch

We shall be at home all through October pursuing our usual Ayot-London routine; so any time that will suit you for your visit will suit us.

I see no reason for a visit to Berlin unless you really like Berlin and want to see that old play again. As you have been in Berlin so often before, and are too old now to fall in love with Paula Wessely,[1] I should advise you to go anywhere else on earth—preferably some place you have never visited before.

I cannot write to congratulate Frau Fischer until her husband is actually dead. Besides, I liked the old boy and was indebted to him for his friendly and honest management of our business. This persecution falling on him so late in life was a hard bit of luck for him.[2]

I am cutting Pygmalion to bits for Koretz and have sent him a draft agreement;[3] so the affair is in train, and he need not trouble you further about it. . . .

The weather is changing and the days are shortening. An early date for your visit in October will be better than a late one. Will Tina come?

always
G. Bernard Shaw

Tls.
  1. Paula Wessely (b. 1908), Austrian actress, was also associated with the Deutsches Theater, Berlin, where she performed *Joan* the next month.
  2. Samuel Fischer, who remained in Germany, was critically ill and died on 15 October, largely ignored. Shaw's remark about congratulating Mrs. Fischer is idiosyncratic Shavian humor.

3. Shaw's scenario for *Pygmalion* tried to accommodate the cinema by breaking the play into scenes, omitting some parts and interpolating others.

4 Whitehall Court S.W.
27th September 1934

O.K. We shall expect to hear from you on the morning of the 15th to say where you are. . . .

O.K. (now universal in America) means Oll Krekt = All Correct = Ganz gut = Agreed = Quite all right = anything that signifies assent. It has even grown into a verb "to okay." It is more than 60 years since I first heard it; but it is quite fresh in America.[1]

GBS

Apcs.
  1. Shaw is mistaken: "O.K." originated in America and was popularized in 1840.

4 Whitehall Court S.W.
12th October 1934

My dear Trebitsch

We go down to Ayot St Lawrence . . . tomorrow afternoon (Saturday) and shall be there until Thursday the 18th. On Saturday the 20th I have to travel to Oxfordshire, 70 miles off, to consecrate a hall to the memory of the poet William Morris;[1] and I shall probably have to spend the night in Oxford.

Except for this engagement we shall be accessible whenever it suits you to come to us. As you know, we cannot put you up at our flat in London. There is a spare bedroom at your disposal at Ayot; but the village is so dull that it would be a waste of your precious time in England to spend much of it there. But do exactly as you please. We shall not worry you; and you need have no fear of worrying us. Just let us know what will suit you.

I hope they were civil to you in Berlin.

GBS

Als.
  1. The dedication was part of the centenary celebration of Shaw's friend William Morris (1834–1896), poet, artist, and socialist, who is buried near his home, Kelmscott Manor, in Oxfordshire. Shaw spoke of Morris as a saint who did not gain his knowledge or wisdom through a university: "Oxford can do many wonderful things, but it cannot turn out a man like Morris, except in the sense of turning him out of the door."

Ayot St Lawrence. Welwyn
15th October 1934

You got busy very early this morning. I rang you up at 10.15 to suggest your coming here to lunch, and, if you wished, to dine and sleep. You could leave Kings Cross at 11.30 for Hatfield, where the car could meet you; and you would be back in London at 5. However, now we had better wait until Thursday, as you no doubt have plenty to do in London.

I am afraid Oxford is impossible as we are going down as guests and sleeping in a private house.

GBS

Apcs.

4 Whitehall Court S.W.
2nd November 1934

Here are the photographs—not so bad.

I hope you reached home safely.

Charlotte is remorseful about our last evening: she says our wireless must have bored you horribly.

I am still working at the St Joan scenario.[1]

GBS

Als.

1. Shaw completed his scenario of *Joan* for Elisabeth Bergner on 13 November. Bergner objected to the script as uncinematic, and Shaw then prepared a second script, but new obstacles arose (see 27 August 1938).

Ayot St Lawrence. Welwyn
22nd December 1934

People have been writing to me about L[eopold] J[essner]; but Robert K[lein] was beforehand with him by some months. I have replied politely; but I never give my name as patron (not protector) of anything. If all the exiled managers rush to London to take theatres here there will be trouble. I cannot do for them what I have refused to do for any English commercial manager. However, I will be as friendly as I can.[1]

As to the Censorship, the Burg had better find out what its attitude will be before committing itself to the production, making it clear that the play will not be cut or altered, and that the Censorship must either approve of it or else take the full responsibility of preventing its performance in Austria.[2] What about the Wessely Joan? Is it to be mutilated to please the priests?[3]

GBS

Apcs.

1. Leopold Jessner, the noted German producer-director, who was both Jew and socialist, had fled Germany for England and was trying to salvage his career by directing a company of Jewish actors in German repertory. (Both Klein and Jessner later emigrated to the United States.)

2. The Burgtheater was interested in Shaw's comedy *Simpleton of the Unexpected Isles* (*Die Insel der Überraschungen*). But the play's evolutionary ideas, marital experiments, and strange divinities caused the Austrian censors to ban production.

3. Paula Wessely's *Joan* had ended in Berlin after 46 performances and she was hoping to recreate the role in Vienna, but the play was still having problems with the censors (see 16 May 1928). Two years later, Wessely did perform *Joan* at the Burg.

Ayot St Lawrence. Welwyn
1st January 1935

Everything is in perfect order as far as I am concerned. I have drafted the agreement with all Koretz's points included and sent it to London Fox Films for approval and execution.

Now, however, London F.F. declare that they want to exhibit the film in Holland, Poland, and *London*!!![1] and that it is out of the profits obtained in these and other places outside Germany that they propose to guarantee the German royalties.

I have replied that, if so, the bargain is off, and the German firm must wait until the export of royalties is no longer illegal.[2]

Koretz and I understood what we were doing: F.F., being Americans in the film business, are incapable of understanding anything. So all our time is wasted.

GBS

Apcs.
   1. The word "London" is underlined three times.
   2. Shaw had negotiated with Fox Film for the English as well as German versions of *Pygmalion*, but the problem was to guarantee that German royalties would not be withheld, since only Aryan movie firms were permitted in Germany and export of currency was strictly regulated. Fox refused a flat guarantee.

4 Whitehall Court S.W.
9th January 1935

Decidedly our luck is out. Charlotte has suddenly become so seriously ill that it is doubtful whether we shall not have to cancel our voyage.[1]

Eberhard Klagemann writes to me in great disappointment and distress about the Pygmalion film. But I am puzzled by his letter heading. He is Klagemann Films. Koretz acted for Fox Films (the German branch). Are they the same?[2] . . .

GBS

Apcs.
   1. The Shaws were planning to tour South America.
   2. Fox Film was no longer a partner to the negotiations, and the German film producer Eberhard Klagemann (b. 1904), who was "Aryan," turned directly to Shaw and came to terms with him shortly.

4 Whitehall Court S.W.
10th January 1935

The Irish Free State has repudiated the British citizenship of the Irish people. The question then arose, what is the status of Irishmen living in England? The press asked me whether I intended to take out papers of naturalization to make me legally an Englishman. I said that I had the whole world to choose from and could just as easily become a Peruvian as an Englishman. I said if I changed at all (which of course I have no intention of doing) I should choose the country where I was most highly appreciated. I warned England that Russia might win in that competition. I made no allusion to Maxim Gorky. The joke seems to be taken seriously by some of the German journalists.[1] It does not matter: Russophobia is a folly that will soon pass.

My journey has been put off until the 26th by a sudden illness which has prostrated Charlotte. I had to cancel the South American trip, and engage for another tour round Africa to the Dutch East Indies. I hope she will recover in time for it. What a world of mishaps!

GBS

Apcs.
    1. On 8 January, the *Neue Freie Presse* reported: "It is confirmed that Bernard Shaw has requested Soviet citizenship and that this has been granted him on the proposal of Maxim Gorky."

4 Whitehall Court S.W.
16th February 1935

I am posting this by ordinary mail, and posting another card (about Klagemann) by air mail.

Let me know how much sooner (if at all) the air mailed card reaches you. I want to find out how much time is saved by air.

GBS

Apcs.

4 Whitehall Court S.W.
16th February 1935

I have sent Klagemann his contract.[1] He can now go ahead as fast as he likes.

It is reported here that The Simpleton is to be produced in Hamburg. What about Berlin?[2]

GBS

Apcs.
    1. The agreement with Klagemann stipulated that Shaw's script be followed meticulously.
    2. *Insel* opened simultaneously in Hamburg and Leipzig on 30 March. No Berlin production followed.

4 Whitehall Court S.W.
22nd June 1935

My dear Trebitsch

. . . On my voyage I got through a lot of work. I have finished The Millionairess, which was only half completed. I have written two prefaces, one of which will get you into trouble if you translate it, as it contains an exposure of the silliness of Anti-Semitism. I have offered to prove that it would have been better for the world if the Jews had never existed, and then to prove exactly the same thing of the Germans or any other human group.[1]

The Millionairess is a play with a very strong part for a female star, and, if you can get the right woman, it will be a moneymaker and cover Tina with diamonds. I hope to get it printed and to send you a copy in the course of the next few weeks.

Hans Rothe has sent me photographs of the Leipzig production of The Simpleton, with which I am greatly pleased.[2] If only the German producer had been in America the horrible failure in New York would have been impossible.[3]

The Malvern Festival, of which I enclose a program, will not begin until the 29th July, and will last until the 24th of August. Is there any chance of seeing you there, or would you prefer to wait until later on, on the chance of seeing The Millionairess? It is only a chance so far, as I have made no arrangements for its production yet.

I did not get your last two letters until we landed on our return from South Africa.

What is the new book? A novel?[4]

ever
G. Bernard Shaw

Tls.

1. In the preface to *The Millionairess* Shaw dealt with Hitler's Judophobia as an "appalling breach of cultural faith," "a craze, a complex . . . one of those lesions which sometimes prove fatal." *Die Millionärin* appeared (Fischer, 1935) without the preface.

2. The Leipzig production of *Simpleton* at the Schauspielhaus, staged by Otto Werther, with sets by Franz Nitsche, was highly praised, but the play's fantasy and experiment in race-improvement were dismissed (*Leipziger Neueste Nachrichten*, 1 April). The play ran eight times. (In Hamburg, the Party paper, *Hamburger Tageblatt*, stonily reported that part of the audience burst into applause when Vashti declared that "Obedience is freedom from the intolerable fatigue of thought" and when Prola remarked that the ancient divine emperors reappeared as fascist dictators and that people gladly gave up their freedom to leaders who forbade them to think: "National Socialism appears to those who have not grasped it just as Shaw's passages declare. . . . But the applause of those eternally behind the times neither surprised nor frightened us. . . . And just as little can Shaw upset us.")

3. The Theatre Guild *Simpleton*, which opened on 18 February, was poorly received and ran only 40 times.

4. Trebitsch's novel *Heimkehr zum Ich* (Return to One's Self), which was published in Vienna in 1936 (Trebitsch could not be published in Germany), was about a homosexual's struggle with his fate.

4 Whitehall Court S.W.
27th June 1935

My dear Trebitsch

When I was in S. Africa, the Minister for Transport, Mr Pirow (note the Teutonic name) made a public appeal for white immigrants to keep up the white population.[1] If the Germans are offended by the charge of sterility implied in this appeal, it is to Mr Pirow they must look and not to me.

It is alleged in certain quarters in Africa, Australia, and New Zealand, that white families become degenerate and extinct in the third generation. This is certainly not true of all white families under all circumstances; but Mr Pirow's appeal proves that, as in New Zealand, the white people do not multiply as the colored people do. I at first attributed this to Birth Control, but was assured that the white natives *want* more children.

One day, in conversation with an able public man, a doctor by profession, I remarked on the fact that although the day was one of unbroken sunshine, the sun went down at 5.15, almost without twilight, and left us in darkness until 7.30 in the morning! "We are glad of it" he said. "We get too much sunshine."

It immediately occurred to me that the effect of excessive sunshine on white skins might have something to do with white sterility.[2] If so, the remedy is clearly pigmentation, which can be brought about most easily by interbreeding with the colored races. Germans in Africa do not object: there are plenty of half breeds in what used to be German Africa.

Talk about "the negro" is mere ignorance. The colored races are as different as Prussians from Bavarians, or as Baltic Celts from Viennese. German "poor whites" (for instance, the only half human charcoal burners) are shockingly inferior to Zulus.

In Hawai, in New Zealand, and in Jamaica, there are hardly any pure bred natives left. The white man, however "Nordic," cannot resist the very attractive native women. Even in the United States the fanatical boycott of "the tar brush" is being relaxed to an extent which astonishes old Americans. We may live to see a Reichskanzler [chancellor of Germany] with a Zulu, Bantu, or Hawaian wife.

Tell Colonel Goering with my compliments that I have backed his regime in England to the point of making myself unpopular, and shall continue to do so on all matters in which he and Hitler stand for permanent truths and genuine Realpolitik. But this racial stuff is damned English nonsense, foisted on Germany by Houston Chamberlain.[3] The future is to the mongrel, not to the Junker. I, Bernard Shaw, have said it. And if Germany boycotts me, so much the worse for German culture.

ever

G. Bernard Shaw

PS Give this to the press, but not until you are safely back in Vienna. It will be a magnificent advertisement if they dare print it. If not, send copies privately to Goering and Hitler.[4]

Tls.

   1. Oswald Pirow (1890–1959), South African Minister of Defense, was pro-Nazi.
   2. Shaw's intuitions on sunlight and reproduction bear on animals, but light's impact on human fertility is largely unexplored; moreover, light works on animal ovulation through the eyes and brain, rather than the skin.
   3. Houston Chamberlain's pro-Teuton racial theories won a following in Germany, including Hitler.
   4. Trebitsch translated Shaw's letter and filed it with the original, but he did not publish it, let alone mail it to Goering and Hitler.

[Trebitsch to Shaw]

Vienna
18th September 1935

My dear Shaw:

The German "Millionairess" is ready in all its brilliancy and I shall read this tempting play this week to the managers of the Burgtheater. If they want to take it up they might have the ambition to get what we call "Welt-urauffühung," that means to produce it before any other stage can do so. But this might interfer with your arrangements and possibly with the contract you have already signed with a Londoner stage.

For this reason I beg you to send me a wire informing me about the first night in London and giving or refusing your consent.[1]

I hope to leave Vienna October 1st or 2nd for Paris, and looking forward to seeing you both October 10th or some days later in London.

I am longing for this meeting, once happy to see the days passing so very quickly.

Our love to both of you.

Yours ever
Siegfried Trebitsch

Tls.; Texas.
1. On the face of this letter Shaw drafted a wire: "Go ahead let Vienna get in first I have no contracts Shaw."

Ayot St Lawrence. Welwyn
19th November 1935

I have no news. Korda[1] came to see me, and wanted to come again *with a lawyer*; but I told him that if there were any law business *I* would do it, and that he must wait until I had a scenario of C[aesar] & C[leopatra] ready. I have said the same to Klagemann; so there is no immediate prospect of any business being done or any money accruing to us before 1937 or thereabouts.[2] I doubt whether C & C is any use at all for the screen, because the grand catastrophes of their deaths are not arrived at.

The National Theatre of Prague demands the world première of The Millionairess for February. I have told them that the race is open to all comers, and that Vienna and Warsaw would get in first unless they hurried up.

G.B.S.

Apcs.
1. Alexander Korda (1893–1956), Hungarian-born English film producer.
2. Klagemann was again tempting Trebitsch with a lump payment for Trebitsch's rights in *Caesar*.

Ayot St Lawrence. Welwyn
15th December 1935

My dear Trebitsch

Klagemann must wait. I sail for the Pacific on the 22nd January;[1] and it is utterly beyond my possibilities to complete a scenario of Caesar and Cleopatra before then. Even if I had nothing else to do it would be difficult: as it is, I have about two months work to jam in by hook or crook. Besides, I have not made up my mind about C. and C.: I may decide on another play. Anyhow there can be no question of a scenario or an agreement until my return in April. And whether the agreement will be with Klagemann I cannot say until I have seen the Pygmalion film.[2]

I have disposed of the English film of Pygmalion to Gabriel Pascal,[3] whom I think you have met. He has been trying to get the Klagemann film over for me; and one was actually sent; but it was so badly worn—so "rainy"—that Pascal sent it back. He expects to have a new one to shew me on Thursday next. Until I see this I cannot judge whether I can depend on Klagemann to understand my artistic planning for the screen.

Korda is out of the song: I shall see no more of him now that I have closed with Pascal. He is too busy on other jobs to be of use to me in the way I want. He would certainly not entertain Jitta at present.

The film business has not so far proved very lucrative. Klagemann sends me elaborate accounts and says that the money is enclosed with them; but this part of the affair is wholly imaginary: not a rap has reached me. I daresay this can be explained; but meanwhile I am heavily out of pocket by the transaction.

For the moment you and Tina must starve. Shall I lend you £500 on account pending some transaction between us for your translation rights? If so, send me a wire with the single word Yes; and I will remit.

as ever

G. Bernard Shaw

Tls.

1. The cruise was to take the Shaws to Miami, Havana, Honolulu, San Francisco and the Grand Canyon, and Mexico.

2. Klagemann's *Pygmalion*, with Jenny Jugo and Gustav Gründgens, directed by Erich Engel, had been released in Berlin in September.

3. Gabriel Pascal (1894–1954), Hungarian-born film producer, who had been working in Italy and Germany, had recently returned from the Near and Far East convinced that his destiny was linked with that of Shaw. He so charmed Shaw that he quickly secured Shaw's contract and thereafter, during Shaw's lifetime, was exclusively authorized to film Shaw's plays.

Ayot St Lawrence. Welwyn
30th December 1935

My dear Trebitsch

I am appalled at your unhappy bargain with Klagemann.[1] You will get nothing, because in the film business [it] is not the manufacturer who makes the profit but the distributor. The manufacturer is ruined unless he has shares in the distributing company, which of course he takes care to secure before he does the work. As Klagemann is no novice he must have known perfectly well that he was taking advantage of your innocence when he offered you a profit sharing agreement—unless indeed you asked him for one, in which case he is entitled to plead Caveat Emptor.

A notice of The Millionairess has appeared here in The Observer and made me rather nervous, because, though its quotations from the text prove that the writer had access either to the prompt book or to the rehearsals, his account of the plot is extraordinarily confused and incomplete.[2] Are you sure they are not tampering with it? If you allow them the smallest latitude they will spoil it and the play will be a ghastly failure. If they have found the right woman for Epifania, and she sticks faithfully to her part as I have written it, it will be a success; and you will make some money. But if you let them talk you into accepting the smallest variations, the danger of failure will be very great. The play is not like the Apple Cart. Infamous as Reinhardt's travesty of that play was, it at least made money, though it dragged my reputation through the mud. But this cannot happen with The Millionairess. Unless it is pure Shaw, it is doomed.[3]

I have not yet seen the Pygmalion film: the exhibition has been put off until next Friday the third January. Pascal has told me some things about it that make me uneasy. I have your solemn assurance that it follows my scenario exactly; but Pascal denies this. If Klagemann has betrayed me, and humbugged you into believing that his changes dont matter, I shall not trust him again.

All film adventurers denounce one another as crooks, mostly quite justly. To my great surprise Pascal made an exception in the case of Klagemann, who is, he says, a gentleman. He claims to have met you, but no more. He is a Hungarian, apparently a man of birth and education, and an extraordinarily clever and dramatic talker. He reminds me of Frank Harris,[4] though he has certainly been better brought up. I am taking a big chance with him; but I should have to do that with anybody. Artistically he is vehemently Antisemite, which just suits me; for it is always the Jew who thinks he knows better than I do how to put a play on the stage or screen. He is equally vehemently pro-Jew in business. He says "In the studio, no Jews. In distribution and exhibition, all Jews." So I have given him a Pygmalion contract for the English language; and now, advienne que pourra, as Baudricourt said [in *Joan*].

I hope to write a new play on my voyage (22 Jan. to 6th April).[5] It would pay me better to turn my old plays into scenarios: but that takes as long or longer. I wish you could write scenarios: then we could retrieve your shattered fortunes.

How, exactly, was your income cut off? On what ground can the German government pillage an Austrian subject?[6] I want to know this politically as well as personally.

Be sure you tell the Academie management that if they alter a single word or incident in The Millionairess they shall never have another play of mine to murder.

ever
G. Bernard Shaw

Tls.

1. For his services in preparing the script for Klagemann's *Pygmalion*, Trebitsch was to receive a share in the producer's profits.

2. On 22 December, the *Observer* reported from Vienna on the pending world premiere of *Millionairess* at the Akademie Theater, a small house managed by the Burg, and gave a garbled version of the play.

3. *Die Millionärin*, with Maria Eis, opened at the Akademie on 4 January to generally favorable notices. The *Neue Freie Presse* (5 January) found it an "astonishing performance" for an old man and wondered why the Burg did not choose its main auditorium. The *Neues Wiener Tagblatt*, however, was puzzled and finally bored with Shaw's "glittering dialectical feats." The play ran 29 times.

4. Frank Harris (1856–1931), editor, author, and adventurer, for whom Shaw worked as drama critic on the *Saturday Review*. Shaw retained affection for Harris and delighted in his scandalous tales.

5. During his cruise Shaw began *Geneva*.
6. In lamenting that his income from Germany was cut off, Trebitsch referred to the decline in his German royalties rather than to seizure of funds.

4 Whitehall Court S.W.
16th January 1936

My dear Siegfried

You will certainly drive me crazy with your changes of front. You assured me repeatedly that I need have no fear; that Klagemann was a perfect gentleman and that my scenario was being faithfully followed in every particular. And all the time, as you now tell me, you were in Berlin in a nest of scoundrels fighting to prevent them from making changes even more monstrous than those they have actually made! If you had given me the smallest hint of this I could have tackled K. before it was too late.[1] But you kept patting me on the back and telling me not to worry—that it was all right—and that the film would be just what I wanted it to be. And this, you say, was to save me from being disturbed by your conflicts with K!

Klagemann very wisely says nothing. He has sent more money: that is his best argument.

Why should not the hundred stages of Germany produce The Millionairess? If the Pygmalion film is not banned, why should The Millionairess be banned?[2] In any case persecutions do not last for ever. What I feared was that you had property which had been confiscated.

Since writing the above I have received your letter of the 14th, in which you promise me that when you come to London in October you will tell me how you have been deceiving me for the last 30 years.[3] But the present trouble is about your deceiving me for the last 30 weeks. Why dwell on your past crimes?[4]

I must make my own scenarios to avoid intolerable complications. You forget that I have to deal with all the countries on earth, with authorised translators in several of them. If I had to arrange for a rake-off for you in all these countries in addition to what my translators could claim the transaction would be impossible. But it does not matter, as Klagemann is the only bidder for C & C; and I do not propose to trust him with another film.

If Koretz will give me the name and address of any film producer who is not a crook (according to all the others) I shall be obliged to him. This particular one [Klagemann] has deeply engraved on his frontal sinus the vertical wrinkles which are made by the human conscience. What a contrast with you, who have no conscience whatever!

your long suffering
G. Bernard Shaw

Tls.

1. Despite Shaw's proviso, Klagemann's *Pygmalion* took liberties with Shaw's scenario, each a blunder, according to Shaw: a horse-race, ping-pong contest, etc. Scenes that Shaw deliberately omitted, e.g., the party dance, were added.
2. *Millionairess* was not banned in Germany. Like *On the Rocks* and *Simpleton*, *Millionairess*

had its premiere in a German provincial theatre, opening in Munich's Kammerspiele on 15 August 1936 and then on 17 December in Berlin's Volksbühne, with Goebbels in attendance. The Berlin press, though more ideological than the Viennese, treated the play largely as light entertainment, but the Party *Völkischer Beobachter* (19 December) found that Shaw had exposed "Capital itself in womanly guise." The Berlin production, directed by Richard Weichert, with Flockina von Platen, ran over 50 times.

3. A note is added here in Trebitsch's handwriting: "Bezieht sich auf Striche die ich zugelassen habe, um den Erfolg zu sichern und die Aufführungen durchzusetzen. [This refers to the cuts which I permitted in order to assure success and to achieve productions.] Siegfried Trebitsch   Zürich. 19 Oktober 1953."

4. Trebitsch, who helped with the script of *Pygmalion*, now confessed that he had permitted changes in Shaw's plays throughout the years.

4 Whitehall Court S.W.
22nd June 1936

My dear Trebitsch

These translations which infuriate you cannot be prevented. The right of translation lasts only ten years. If it is not exercised within that time it lapses, and anyone can translate without asking my leave or yours. Consequently the translation of A Sunday in the Surrey Hills, which was published here in a newspaper in the eighteen-eighties, is in the public domain in Germany. Nothing can be done about it. But the other one—the dialogue in a solicitor's office called Beauty's Duty—though it was written many years ago, was not published until my volume of short stories appeared in 1931. Its translation and publication is therefore a flat piracy; and you can, if you think it worth while, demand damages from the newspaper for infringement of your rights and mine. The thing is so trivial that there is not much money in it; but if you could make the editor publish an apology for the infringement (it need not be in humiliating terms) it might be useful in intimidating other pirates.

As to the suppression of your name as translator in Germany, that is such a tiny drop in the ocean of persecution that any complaint on your part would be like Sganarelle's "Mes gages! Mes Gages!" after Don Juan's damnation. Provided they pay you your tantièmes you must touch your hat and be thankful.[1] What puzzled me is that Fischer used to publish editions of our books without your name as translator. I called your attention to this once; but nothing came of it as far as I can remember. . . .

I saw Dr Maril, and have since given him a recommendation for a job he was seeking; but it is evident that he misunderstood my political conversation hopelessly.[2]

To what extent is the Fischer firm broken up? Can they carry on in Switzerland or must we find new publishers?[3]

faithfully
G. Bernard Shaw

Tls.
1. The suppression of Trebitsch's name on programs to Shaw's plays in Germany was uneven but noticeable.
2. Konrad Maril, formerly of S. Fischer's Theatre Division, had emigrated to England, where he sought to join a literary agency.

3. Under duress to sell out to "reliable" hands, S. Fischer's heirs at the end of 1935 turned the Verlag over to a new corporation, managed by Peter Suhrkamp, a devoted Fischer employee, who hoped one day to return the firm to the Fischers. Dr. Gottfried Bermann, who had succeeded his father-in-law, S. Fischer, planned to reopen in Switzerland. When it developed that Swiss regulations would not allow Bermann to open there, he established the Bermann-Fischer Verlag in Vienna, and Trebitsch transferred Shaw's publication and agent's rights to that firm.

> Ayot St Lawrence. Welwyn
> 16th September 1936

By all means come on the 1st October. You will be welcome at any time.[1]

> GBS

Apcs.
1. Trebitsch arrived in London on 30 September. The following week he lunched with the Shaws along with Elisabeth Bergner.

> 4 Whitehall Court S.W.
> 3rd February 1937

After seven weeks at His Majesty's Theatre (a very large one) The Boy David has been withdrawn; and C. B. Cochran, the manager, in a letter to The Times, has described it as a failure.[1] He need not have done so: all that it was necessary to say was that the theatre had been let to another manager and that all the other theatres were let. When I saw the play the house was full. Elizabeth's acting was extraordinary: the scenes between David [Elisabeth Bergner] and Saul [Godfrey Tearle] were beautifully written to suit her; and she got the very last drop out of them and a little more to boot. But the other characters are mere lay figures, with names taken from the Bible story; and London West End playgoers heartily dislike the Bible. Barrie has used the St Joan device of a dream to shew David's future in a series of visions; but they are ugly and quite dull except for the death of Saul, which enables David to recite a famous Bible passage. The scenery quite fails to realize Augustus John's designs: it is ugly and depressing.

Warum reisen Sie nach Amerika [Why are you traveling to America]?[2]

> GBS

Apcs.
1. *The Boy David*, written for Elisabeth Bergner by James M. Barrie and produced by Charles B. Cochran (1872–1951), famous English impresario, had opened on 14 December 1936 and recently closed.
2. At the urging of the American ambassador to Vienna, G. Messersmith, Trebitsch undertook a lecture tour of the United States and departed at the end of March, but the project was aborted in New York when Trebitsch fell ill and had to return home.

> Victoria Hotel. Sidmouth
> 14th May 1937

The cheque does not matter; but the agreement with Colin, who has just sent me a copy of it, is absolute madness.[1] Colin is to produce the play himself as manager; and for introducing the play to himself as agent he is to have 15% commission on the fees: a thing never heard of on this earth before.

But this is a trifle compared to his claiming 50% of the film fees, which may amount to thousands of pounds, his proper remuneration being 10%. Were you sober when you signed this? or did he pay you a huge advance on a/c of your share?

Fortunately my letter to you of the 11th October 1933 refers to filming only. He cannot produce the play in the theatre in my version without my consent, which I shall refuse. My sympathies are now all with der Führer. 50%! G[ott] in H[immel]!

GBS

Apcs.

1. Saul Colin (1909–1967), Romanian-born producer, critic, and Hollywood agent in Paris, had first sought film rights in *Jitta* in 1933. To facilitate the project, Shaw appointed Trebitsch his agent for licensing the film, but nothing happened. Colin was now an emigré producer in New York, where he and Trebitsch apparently met.

On 1 June, Colin wrote to Shaw, "Why are you torturing our friend Siegfried Trebitsch?" Colin explained that his terms were standard in America, that a film company would not buy *Jitta* unless it were first revived on the stage, and that his 50 percent fee would go to repay costs of revival (Texas).

[Trebitsch to Shaw]

Vienna
4th June 1937

My dear Shaw:

Last night one of the owners of the Century Fox in Hollywood (his name is Julius Steger) told me *privately* that the filming of "Jittas atonement" has been forbidden by the censorship.[1] They don't allow the plot. So this does not matter any longer.

Please try by all means to give Colin your consent with the production on the stage in New York. I am sure he will do his very best to meet you.— Consider that it is one of my last chances to earn some money and make a living again.

Are you my friend or not? Sometimes I am quite upset when I observe that you refuse to help me as soon as a favourable opportunity comes.

Please wire a few words in the moment the agreement is perfect.

Yours ever
Siegfried Trebitsch

Tls.; Texas.

1. A scenario of *Jitta*, submitted to Century Fox, was found censorable on grounds of adultery. The reader, reporting on the script, suggested that instead of having Bruno die during the assignation in a clandestine apartment, he should die in a private room in a Budapest cafe to the strains of a gypsy band during his very first rendezvous with Jitta! The reader also commented that Shaw's

refusal to lend his name to any film of *Jitta* might be overcome since Shaw was strongly obligated to Trebitsch.

4 Whitehall Court S.W.
7th June 1937

My dear Trebitsch

I am writing to Colin offering my usual terms for a stage production of Jitta, the terms to include your consent. When I get the royalties I can give you half of them. You will have nothing to do with Colin.

The Catholic censorship of the films will not remain effective very long. It is absolutely ignorant and crude and it has no authority except what it gets from Hollywood's fear that if the priests ban a film, the twenty million Catholics in the U.S.A. will not go and see it. That, of course, is nonsense: the priests have been telling their flocks since the world began that they must not do this, that, and the other. But they do it all the same.

I have told Colin that I regard your agreement as evidence that when you signed it you were incapable of managing your affairs properly. Can I do more?

ever
G. Bernard Shaw

Tls.

[Trebitsch to Shaw]

Vienna
9th June 1937

My dear Shaw:

Many thanks for the good will you seem to show in order of coming to an agreement with Colin. May it please to God that this important affair will be settled soon. I am only happy if you get all the royalties and pay the compliments back by sending me my half. But what a shame for me if Colin will believe now that I was signing contracts being incapable of any responsibility!

Our love to both of you.

Yours ever
Siegfried Trebitsch

P.S. If poor Colin will act not only as a manager but as an agent too who is collecting fees as well—what will you grant him in that case? You don't mention a single word about this possible duplicity [i.e., duplicate role].

Tls.; Texas.

4 Whitehall Court S.W.
26th June 1937

For the moment I have only laid Colin in ruins. My interest in filming Jitta is the same as yours; but as I am not pressed for money I am not so hopeful about getting anything done just now. If the Pygmalion film now being manufactured [by Pascal] proves a success it will put me on the map in the film world, where at present I am regarded as impossible. In that case the film firms will run like sheep after anything with my name on it.

A theatrical revival of Jitta would absolutely kill its film rights unless it had a first rate success; and for that we should need a Wessely and a Kraus[s]. Without them the risk would be too great. We must wait.

GBS

Apcs.

Blackhill. Malvern
24th July 1937

My dear Trebitsch

You must root out of your mind the notion that Colin is offering you a golden opportunity of making a lot of money out of Jitta, and that I am preventing you from embracing it. Why should I? My interest in it is the same as yours. The truth is that the opportunity is imaginary. Matters stand exactly as they did before Colin went to America except that he has induced you to sign an agreement which you should never have signed, and given you absolutely nothing for it.

The only excuse for Colin is that he is a complete novice in America and imagines he can do things which are quite out of his power. The excuse for you is your illness and the fact that you also have not grasped the American situation.

The situation is this. The American film people will not touch Jitta until they have done their worst with Pygmalion, The Devil's Disciple, and all my more popular plays. When I have had a great screen success they will rush to exploit it; and those who cannot get anything else of mine will take Jitta as a *pis aller*. In this way and in no other I may be said to be standing in the way of Jitta; but I cannot help it and neither can Colin.

As to a stage revival of the play, it is of course possible that a first rate tragic actress and a first rate character comedian could make a success of it. If Colin could find such a pair, and had money enough to take a theatre and try his hand at management, then we could deal with him as with any other manager; but we have no reason to believe that he has any such resources. A secondrate performance would not only fail: it would kill the film rights. However, the field is open to Colin or anyone else, either as agent procuring a performance of the play and receiving 10% commission on the royalties, or as a manager producing the play at his own risk, but not as both. And a stage production would be quite independent of the film rights.

But really, unless Colin renounces that agreement that he made you sign, I should hesitate to deal with him or through him at all. Fortunately for you, if he comes into the affair at all he will have to come in on my terms.

As to my withdrawal of the unofficial Power of Attorney I gave you in 1933, a Power of Attorney is always revocable except when it has been given "for a consideration": that is, only if you had bought it from me. As it was, I only made you my agent; and when an agent goes mad his Power of Attorney has to be revoked.[1]

I hope you are recovering your wits, and am very sorry that your trip to America proved fruitless. Why did you undertake it without a lecture engagement?[2]

This letter has been delayed an unconscionable time by pressing engagements of many kinds, and perhaps in the hope that I might think of some way of making it more cheerful for you.

I must do what I can to create interest in Jitta, which has been most undeservedly neglected.

I am staying with Barry Jackson at Malvern for the production of The Millionairess and the revival of The Apple Cart at the Festival;[3] but this time I shall not make my usual long stay: I shall return home on the 3rd of August and take my holiday on the south coast in September.

as ever

G. Bernard Shaw

Tls.

1. Shaw had revoked the authorization granted Trebitsch to license the filming of *Jitta*.

2. As mentioned, Trebitsch's American lecture tour was aborted.

3. *Millionairess* opened at Malvern on 26 July (Shaw's 81st birthday) and was followed on 28 July by *Apple Cart*. Both plays were directed by Herbert Prentice and starred Elspeth March.

On the same day, Trebitsch wrote to Colin: "That 'Yitta' will not reach the footlights now next winter makes me unhappy and sick! I shall never forget Shaw this break of friendship. Please sell Yitta for the film, and let this be our small revenge." (Cornell.)

4 Whitehall Court S.W.

4th August 1937

My dear Trebitsch

I dont object to your grasping whatever you can get; but in this case you didnt grasp anything. You should have grasped Dr C.'s neck and given him a good shaking. It seems comic that I should have made you my agent for dealing with your own play; but legally I could make you my agent to negotiate my rights as translator as well as your own rights as author.

Barry Jackson is tired of west-end London management: he wont touch Jitta. Nobody will, unless some very brilliant actress takes a fancy to the part and induces her pet manager to produce it. That may happen; but there is no sign of it as yet.

As you see, we have come back to London. I stayed only as long as was absolutely necessary. After eight Festivals I was tired of Malvern. I get no rest there. We shall spend September at the seaside—probably at Sidmouth—

coming back home in October, when we hope to see you sheltering your poverty at the best hotel [the Dorchester] in Park Lane. We want to hear about the Odyssey.

ever

G. Bernard Shaw

Tls.

Victoria Hotel. Sidmouth
9th September 1937

My dear Trebitsch

I should have sent you the enclosed correspondence a month ago; but I was busy and distracted with other things and so put it off from day to day until I forgot all about it.

You will see that I have carefully cut the attested signatures out of the agreement. Having cut them out, I burnt them. I did this because I feared you would immediately send the agreement back to Colin with an apology for my wicked ill treatment of him. Now, however, you are safe until you go back to America.

Poor Colin has been a whole month expecting two pretty letters from us, hailing him as the most chivalrous of our friends and clients. Certainly we have now no reason to complain, and can welcome him as The Prodigal Son. I acquit him of anything worse than acquisitive naïveté; but you must not sign any more agreements with him or anyone else without letting me have a peep at them first.

Koretz always comes to see me when he is passing through London; and of course I shall be glad to talk to Mayer and the great Schenck (they call him Skenk in America) to their hearts' content.[1] Their colossal plans never come to anything; but they are endlessly amusing to watch. I will tell them that Jitta is a curiously underrated masterpiece.

You must not mind the vagaries of this typewriter: I am too old to do anything properly. Yesterday Charlotte and I tried to climb over a hedge. We both fell flat on our backs into the ditch. However, since we came here Charlotte has fallen downstairs only once.

In any future agreement about Jitta you must be careful to stipulate that in all affiches and "sub-titles" your name shall not appear in smaller letters than mine. The worst clause in that infamy of Colin's was the clause enabling him expressly to advertize the play as by

BERNARD SHAW
& SIEGFRIED TREBITSCH

Affectionate salutations to Tina.

We shall be here at the seaside for the next few weeks.

GBS

Tls.

1. Louis B. Mayer (1885–1957) and Joseph Schenck (1878–1961) were major Hollywood producers.

4 Whitehall Court S.W.

9th October 1937

My dear Trebitsch

We are at Ayot St Lawrence as usual; but we shall return to London on Wednesday. Will you dine with us at Whitehall Court at 7.30 on Wednesday evening? If we do not hear from you to the contrary we shall expect you then.[1]

In arranging in this way we are assuming that Ayot would bore you to tears and that you have enough business in London to fill up your time until Wednesday evening. . . .

We are looking forward to seeing you. . . .

GBS

Als.

1. Trebitsch arrived in London on Sunday, 10 October. He dined with the Shaws on Wednesday and lunched with them the next day, and on 21 October brought Paul Czinner and Elisabeth Bergner along to lunch.

4 Whitehall Court S.W.

15th December 1937

My dear Trebitsch

I have answered every letter of yours for months past with electric promptitude.

The Devisenreichsstelle is now paying me £200 a month to wipe out the arrears due to me on the Pygmalion film.[1] . . .

I have not had time to tackle your novel yet.[2] When I do I will let you know at once. Meanwhile I have a terrible job in hand which has obliged me to read several books and taken up every moment I can spare for reading.[3]

I am glad you are throwing off your fevers; but you must not do it by handing them on to Tina. Has she ever tried fasting for a month on bread and butter and lemon juice? Or on prayer? You have tried every quackery in Europe. Havent you found one for her?

as ever

G. Bernard Shaw

Tls.

1. After initial payments of £2,845 from Klagemann, Shaw's film royalties were blocked, then released piecemeal for an additional £2,100.

2. Trebitsch's novel *Der Verjüngte* (Rejuvenated), issued by Bermann-Fischer, dealt with the current interest in sexual restoration through glandular operation.

3. Shaw was working on a preface to a reissue of Frank Harris's *Oscar Wilde* (1938).

4 Whitehall Court S.W.

12th January 1938

My dear Trebitsch

Miss Cooper has had a bad failure on her return to London in a play which ran for four nights only.[1] As it happens I do not know her personally; but I discussed the matter with Miss Nancy Price, who played the old woman [Agnes] in the original production of Jitta, and would like to play it again. She thought a revival as suggested would be an excellent idea; so I left it to work in her mind. She is in a very strong position just now, having had an enormous success in a play which is still running.[2]

I am not sure that Barbara is a good choice for Frau Wessely, because in the last act Barbara is supplanted by Undershaft; but I am writing to "Vienna" to say that I am quite open to a proposal.[3]

Tell Colin that it is for him to make a serious proposal as soon as he has the means to produce Jitta or any other play of ours. If Miss Cooper should take up the play and make a success of it in London she would probably take it to New York, in which case we should have no difficulty in obtaining a film production. But we shall not in that case need Colin; so be very careful not to entangle yourself with him again.

G. Bernard Shaw

Tls.
1. Gladys Cooper (1888–1971), popular English actress, after an absence in America, failed in *Goodbye to Yesterday* and was scouting suitable plays.
2. Nancy Price's great success was in *Whiteoaks*, by Mazo de la Roche. *Jitta* was not revived at this time.
3. *Major Barbara* was not revived in Vienna at this time.

4 Whitehall Court S.W.
12th February 1938

My dear Trebitsch

For the last ten years I have been inundated with letters asking me to use my commanding influence to obtain the release of some political prisoner in Germany, Russia, Spain or Italy. Of course I have no commanding influence and can do nothing helpful. My experience is that foreign interference does more harm than good to the prisoner. I therefore take care not to meddle in such matters.

As to the letter of Koretz, what do you want me to do? You induced me to speculate in your share of the Pygmalion film royalties by buying your rights in 1934 for £750. After this I paid you only the half of Fischer's royalties, not of Klagemann's. Now that the speculation has turned out better for me than for you, you want me to restore your Pygmalion rights and give you half the royalties as if the £750 transaction had never taken place, treating that sum as an advance on account of royalties. Is this correct?[1] . . .

ever
G. Bernard Shaw

Tls.
1. Trebitsch relented on his sale of rights in the Klagemann *Pygmalion*.

Ayot St Lawrence. Welwyn
9th March 1938

My dear Trebitsch

I have not had time to translate these letters, full of business terms. What does Arisierung mean?[1] I can't find it in the dictionary.

If they will not pay your shares unmittelbar [directly] can you not direct that they are to be paid to me. I can then send you your half.

In great haste & bewilderment

G. Bernard Shaw

Als.

1. *Arisierung* ("Aryanization") was the Nazi policy pressuring Jews to transfer their properties to "Aryans." That process overtook S. Fischer Verlag, now managed by Peter Suhrkamp, who, with Bermann-Fischer's consent, acted as Shaw's agent for Germany but could no longer remit funds directly to Trebitsch, a Jew.

PART FIVE

Anschluss, Exile, and War
15 March 1938 through 5 May 1945

On 12 MARCH 1938, Hitler entered Austria and on the 13th he proclaimed its Anschluss (annexation) to the Reich. The following day, before the jubilant crowds of Vienna, he announced: One Reich, One People, One Führer. For Austrian Jews it was a disaster, and almost from the start they faced forced emigration.

Trebitsch and his wife, Tina, fled soon after the Anschluss, abandoning home, personal belongings, and assets. Siegfried was approaching seventy; Tina was one year younger.

As Trebitsch recounts in his *Chronicle*, he had mentally prepared himself and Tina for possible flight. On the 13th, he and Tina, on the way to their lawyer, were stopped by an S.A. officer, who demanded to know why their chauffeured automobile had no swastika. Trebitsch's answer that he was nonpolitical was brushed aside. The officer got into the car and while waiting for a military column to pass began questioning Trebitsch's chauffeur and making notes. With the officer occupied, Trebitsch opened the car door, drew Tina after him, and fled. Hours later, the chauffeur returned home, the worse for a beating. The car was never seen again.

Through a friendly Czech official, the Trebitsches obtained Czech passports, which offered tenuous security in light of Hitler's claims on Czechoslovakia; they also had reserved plane tickets for Prague, where Siegfried was scheduled to lecture at Masaryk University on 16 March. Thus provided, the Trebitsches left Vienna and after a short stay in Prague moved to Zurich, which, except for a broken interlude of a year and a half in France, became the couple's new home.

Shaw's immediate concern at the Anschluss was to counter the peril facing Trebitsch. Toward that end, he sent an Aesopian postcard (15 March) to Trebitsch in Vienna and publicly supported the Anschluss, which he had long advocated, as good in itself and inevitable in the wake of Versailles: "And so, Heil Hitler!" ("Heil Hitler," *Evening Standard*, 17 March; with different headlines, *New York Daily Mirror* and *Journal-American*.) But when Hitler pressed claims on Czechoslovakia, Shaw rejected the concept of a

Greater Germany and warned of the consequences if Hitler provoked war (*New York Times*, 10 July). And in a rejoinder to his critics, Shaw disclaimed admiring dictatorship and insisted the issue was getting things done: "I don't really want to see a Hitler in this country, but I am not sure that it would be a bad thing. It might be an improvement on a so-called democracy that is not really a democracy at all. . . . I am tired of the way in which the newspapers, bribed or persuaded . . . by the dictators, continue to make it appear that I am an admirer of dictatorship. All my work shows the truth to be otherwise." (*Star*, 4 August.)

In September, Czechoslovakia was threatened with invasion, and Britain and France mobilized. Shaw urged the Trebitsches, then in France, to return to Switzerland, although he wasn't "VERY apprehensive" about Hitler's threats. And after the Munich Agreement was signed on 30 September by Great Britain, France, Italy, and Germany—giving Hitler the Sudetenland— Shaw declared that Hitler and Mussolini were "highly capable revolutionary and proletarian leaders who are giving their people as big a dose of Socialism as they can stand." He couldn't predict whether the settlement was the end or the beginning of trouble, but it appeared satisfactory since it avoided war (*Sunday Referee*, 2 October).

The Trebitsches, concerned to obtain more secure nationality than that of Czechoslovakia, returned to Paris in the spring of 1939, just as Hitler occupied what remained of the Czech republic. A month before, Shaw predicted that there was not the "least chance" of imminent war, although wars would occur unless perhaps man suppressed his insane pugnacity and learned that modern warfare produced no winners. In that "single redeeming feature" one might find "some particle of hope" ("Never Another World War," *Rotarian*, February 1939).

Meanwhile, on the night of 9 November 1938 (Kristallnacht), anti-Semitic terror swept through Germany in vengeance for the assassination of a German official, in Paris, by a distraught Jewish emigré. A huge Penance Tax was imposed on the German Jewish community, Aryanization became compulsory, and emigration policy passed to the Gestapo. As outrage against Germany spread, Shaw denounced Hitler's anti-Semitism as an intolerable phobia that dumped tens of thousands of destitute Jews on overcrowded neighbors, threatened to exterminate a part of the human race, and raised questions about Hitler's sanity: "Will civilization stand for this? . . . We talk about a Jewish problem. There is no problem: there is only the crude fact that Herr Hitler is plundering the Jews." And Shaw adds, "I have almost damned myself politically by defending the German and Italian leaders against the silly abuse heaped on them by the spokesmen and journalists of our pseudo-democracy; but now that they have let me down by condescending to anti-Semitism, I must really disown all sympathy with that anachronism, and point the way to stop it." The way? A League of Nations' committee staffed with psychiatrists to determine if fascism's anti-Jewish measures were legitimate or pathological. ("How to Deal with the Jewish Difficulty," *Time and Tide*, 26 November 1938.)

Hitler, bent on his own course, turned on Poland with demands and out-maneuvered England and France by a nonaggression pact with the Soviet Union in the summer of 1939. Shaw, who attacked Britain for not playing the Soviet trump against Germany, hailed the "joyful news" as Hitler's going to Canossa: "Hitler is under the powerful thumb of Stalin, whose interest in peace is overwhelming." Why then were others terrified? "Am I mad? If not, why? Why? Why?" (*New York Times*, 28 August 1939.)

The answer came with stunning swiftness. On 1 September, German troops invaded Poland. World War II had begun.

In "Uncommon Sense About the War" (*New Statesman*, 7 October 1939), after the fall of Poland, Shaw argued that there was "no further excuse for continuing the war." As for Hitler's presumed drives for world conquest, it would be wiser to wait and see and then join with Russia and the United States to crush such an attempt. But peace or not, he said, the world would go on without devastated Europe and would experience "immense gratification of the primitive instinct that is at the bottom of all this mischief . . . to wit pugnacity, sheer pugnacity for its own sake."

With the fall of France in June 1940, Shaw saw no choice for England but continued struggle for its own and humanity's sake. Hitler's Judophobia threatened other races, and "We ought to have declared war on Germany the moment Mr Hitler's police stole Einstein's violin." But he continued to find Hitler "one of the curiosities of political history"—a man of courage and sagacity who had managed the "triumphant rescue" of Germany from Versailles—and to dismiss arguments against Hitler's dictatorship as such. Shaw's remarks prepared in June 1940 for the BBC were banned ("The Unavoidable Subject," *Platform and Pulpit*, 1961). His rejoinder, "The Cops Won't Let Me Talk" (*Living Age*, September 1940), added the caution against Churchillian anti-Bolshevism and the temptation to join Germany to crush the Soviet Union.

When in the summer of 1941 Hitler struck east on his own, the astonished Shaw found the news "too good to be true" for the Allies, who "owing to the inconceivable folly of Hitler" had only to "sit and smile while Stalin smashes Hitler," who, he said, didn't have a "dog's chance": "Either Hitler's a greater fool than I took him for or he has gone completely mad" (*New York Times*, 23 June). On reflection, Shaw admitted that he had mistaken his man but speculated that Hitler may wrongly have feared an attack from Russia ("My Mistake," *New Statesman*, 5 July); and when Hitler did offer that excuse, Shaw concluded that it exposed National Socialism as a "plutocratic sham" ("From the Führer's Mouth," *New Statesman*, 11 October).

To the Union of Soviet Writers, which asked for a statement on "Fascist Barbarism," Shaw wrote on 17 July: "Never mind the barbarism: all war is barbarous, and to squeal is childish. Let us rather apologize for the terrible things we must do to our German comrades before the Führer loses his glamor for them. When two mighty ideas clash millions of lives count for nothing. It is as champion of an idea that Adolf Hitler has flung down his glove to Russia. Russia picks it up as the champion of a far mightier idea. When she strikes down Adolf's idea she will become the spiritual center of the world. And with that task before her she may not heed the cries of the wounded or the tears of the bereaved . . . we are at a corner that civilization has not yet got around. Russia is pledged to get us round at this time or perish, SO ONWARD RUSSIA FOR THE LEADERSHIP OF THE WORLD, FOR THE SICKLE, THE HAMMER, AND THE SWORD OF JUSTICE."

Once again Shaw was diverted from playwriting. *Everybody's Political What's What?* was not completed until 1944. By then the defeat of Germany was all but certain, and Shaw warned against a punitive peace as wrong in itself and an encouragement to German resistance (*New York Times*, 6 January 1944). Bitter struggle continued. Then on 30 April 1945, Hitler shot himself. A week later Germany surrendered unconditionally.

With the circle full drawn, Shaw in his Preface to *Geneva* (1945) balanced the ledger on the late dictator: Hitler was a failed bohemian turned beer-hall orator, who mixed sound political insight with fanciful racism; a "born leader," who came to terms with Germany's plutocracy, was given the Chancellorship, and through popular idolatry gained great personal power, although "his whole stock-in-trade was a brazen voice and a doctrine made up of scraps of Socialism, mortal hatred of the Jews, and complete contempt for pseudo-democratic parliamentary mobocracy." After combating unemployment and restoring German self-respect, Hitler, his head turned by power and worship, became a "mad Messiah" who believed he was destined to conquer the world for the Chosen Race of Germans. But miscalculating on Western support for his attack on the Soviet Union and mistreating the captive peoples, Hitler raised mighty forces against him, and along with Mussolini—"poor devils"—was scrapped as a failure and nuisance.

Although the Trebitsches managed to escape France after its fall and reach safety in neutral Switzerland, they were short of funds, and exile told on Siegfried's nerves. He repeatedly expressed his desperation to Shaw. He could no longer visit England, and Shaw could not transfer funds abroad. Finally, Shaw, despairing in the fall of 1942 of doing anything more for his friend, buried himself in his work and wrote few letters to Trebitsch.

Ayot St Lawrence. Welwyn
15th March 1938

The glorious news did not reach us (by wireless) until after I had closed and posted my last letter to you.

As you may remember I have always been in favor of the Anschluss; and I have spent the whole day writing a strong article in support of it for general circulation at home and abroad. As an Austrian and compatriot of der Führer you are much to be congratulated.

If Tina's health obliges you to travel, why not come to England, where we are having an extraordinarily fine spring?

. AYOT ST LAWRENCE, WELWYN, HERTS. | STATION: WHEATHAMPSTEAD, L.&N.E.R. 2¼ MILES. | TELEGRAMS: BERNARD SHAW, CODICOTE. | 4, WHITEHALL COURT, LONDON, S.W.1.

15ᵗʰ March 1938

The glorious news did not reach us (by wireless) until after I had closed and posted my last letter to you.

As you may remember I have always been in favor of the Anschluss; and I have spent the whole day writing a strong article in support of it for general circulation at home and abroad. As an Austrian and compatriot of der ⚡ Führer you are much to be congratulated.

If Tina's health obliges you to travel, why not come to England, where we are having an extraordinarily fine spring?

I shall certainly take your advice about the Reichstelle. Many thanks.

G. Bernard Shaw

Postcard to Trebitsch, 15 March 1938.

I shall certainly take your advice about the Reichstelle [German Foreign Exchange Authority]. Many thanks.

G. Bernard Shaw

Apcs.

4 Whitehall Court S.W.
18th March 1938

My dear Trebitsch

We are glad to hear that you are safe in Prague. I have just instructed my bankers to send you a draft on Prague for the Czechoslovakian equivalent of 1200 German marks [c. £100]. Yesterday all London was placarded with "Bernard Shaw" "Heil, Hitler!" in the biggest capitals. At the same time I sent you a postcard congratulating you on the glorious achievement of the Anschluss by your fellowcountryman the Führer.[1]

And now you reproach me because I did not write letters pointing out that you are a Jew marked out for Nazi persecution.

You say that I am the only one of your friends who has not done this. In that case I am the only one of your friends who is not a mischievous fool. As for you, you have many merits and talents; but in politics you are the most thoughtless idiot in Europe. You are furious with me because I did not betray you to the police, who are pretty sure to read all your correspondence.

I hope my unfeeling conduct helped you to get a passport.[2] Let us hear about your adventures when you have time to write.

ever

GBS

Tls.; postscript omitted.
1. The Trebitsches flew to Prague on 16 March, before Shaw's postcard arrived, and it was forwarded to them there.
2. Actually, the friendly Czech ambassador in Vienna was able to provide Trebitsch with Czech papers thanks to the continued links of the Trebitsch family with Moravia, where their silk mills were located.

4 Whitehall Court S.W.
31st March 1938

My dear Trebitsch

As you have no doubt guessed, my telegram was sent in the belief that you had wired to me, whereas it was somebody else who wanted to know the address of a Mr Messerschmidt. Frau Salzer[1] made out its real meaning. I made a more serious mistake about the money I sent. When instructing my banker to send you M12800, I left out the last figure and made it M.1280.[2] This was quite unintentional. The exchange today is M 12.36 = £1 sterling. At this rate M.10.800 = £875-15s: at least Miss Patch says so. I enclose my cheque for £876. The Swiss bankers will be very glad to have a London cheque; and the odd shillings will cover their charges.

There are a hundred questions we want to ask—how you got your passports—what is happening to your house—have you any money except what I sent you—was your brother in Prague friendly—have you any foreign investments to live on out of Germany—is Tina recovering now that the first shock is over????? but they must wait until we meet.[3]

My Heil Hitler article came just in the nick of time; and the card I sent to Hietzing was everything that the Gestapo could desire. If I had written sympathetically you would probably now be in a concentration camp. Anybody else on earth except Siegfried Trebitsch would have understood this.

Tina was very wise to stop at Zurich.[4] It is just the place for both of you to recover in.

faithfully

G. Bernard Shaw

Tls.
1. Presumably the wife of E. M. Salzer, Viennese foreign correspondent, living in London.
2. Shaw slips in his figures: he intended to send Trebitsch M12,000 (£1,000) and wrongly dispatched M1,200.
3. As noted, the Trebitsches carried Czech passports. Their villa in Hietzing was left in care of their loyal chauffeur, Adolf Scharf, and Siegfried's accountant, Luise Siegl (who later married Scharf). Trebitsch's brother, Heinrich, an attorney, had earlier fled Vienna for Prague. Tina's jewels, which provided ready assets, were spirited abroad to Tina by the Czech ambassador's wife.
4. The Trebitsches had intended to go to Paris at once to seek French citizenship, but Tina, exhausted, urged the more restful Zurich. They were staying at the Dolder Grand Hotel.

4 Whitehall Court S.W.

8th April 1938

The 20th is all right as far as we are concerned, as we are not going away for Easter and shall be in London from the afternoon of the 20th to the afternoon of the 23rd. But as other people may be holidaying it would perhaps be better to wait until the 27th. However, it makes no difference to us: the sooner we see you the better we shall be pleased.

GBS

Apcs.

4 Whitehall Court S.W.

14th April 1938

We shall expect you next Wednesday to dinner at 7.30.[1] We shall be out-of-doors all the afternoon.

To have a British passport one must be a British subject.[2] To become one it is necessary to live in England for 5 years and to pay a fee of £10.

The alternative is a special Act of Parliament!!!!!

GBS

Tls.
1. Trebitsch arrived in London on 20 April and dined with Shaw that evening: "[Shaw] wanted to hear from me about our escape—which was in fact nothing of the kind, because we had, after all, not been pursued, about experiences with the Nazis, which I had not had, and, in short, a great deal more than I could tell" (*Chronicle*).
2. Trebitsch had apparently inquired about the possibility of getting a British passport.

Ayot St Lawrence. Welwyn
22nd May 1938

I have not written to Vienna for two reasons. 1. The case was so puzzling and the risk of doing more harm than good so great that I could not make up my mind what to say.[1] 2. I am rather seriously ill. My brain is clear and my organs sound; but I can hardly walk. At 82 this may mean anything.[2]

So I had a long talk with Koretz and gave him your address. He promised to write to you and advise you. He thinks you can escape the fugitive tax.[3] The rest he will tell you. Meanwhile I do nothing, being disabled and possibly moribund.

GBS

Apcs.
    1. After the announcement of the Reich Flight Tax to be assessed on emigrating Jews (amounting to one-quarter of their holdings), Trebitsch apparently sought Shaw's intervention with the authorities in Vienna.
    2. Shaw was suffering from pernicious anemia and slowly recovered.
    3. Paul Koretz, the Viennese lawyer, was also in exile. His belief that Trebitsch might escape the Flight Tax was probably based on Trebitsch's claim to Czech citizenship. In July, Trebitsch sent a declaration of his Austrian holdings to Vienna, amounting, along with Tina's assets, to M174,321 (£13,945). He also declared a share in the Czech branch of the family business, valued at M209,987 (£16,798) and noted his Czech citizenship.

4 Whitehall Court S.W.
20th June 1938

Are your affairs being competently handled in Vienna?[1]
The newspaper reports are very puzzling.
What do you think of Geneva? Would the Nazis tolerate it?[2]

GBS

Ans.
    1. On 14 June, the Reich Interior Minister had called for forced Aryanization of Jewish property, but the façade of voluntarism was kept until late that year. Trebitsch ultimately retained a Viennese lawyer, Dr. Indra, to represent him.
    2. Shaw refers to his satire on the fascist dictators. *Geneva* was not produced in Nazi Germany.

Ayot St Lawrence. Welwyn
19th July 1938

I don't quite understand. Does Bermann propose to publish Geneva in the German language or in Swedish?[1] If in German what will Fischer say?

Or has Fischer ceased to exist? I have received no acknowledgment of the document I sent him nor of the letter which accompanied it.

If Bermann contemplates a Swedish version it must be translated by Lady [Ebba] Low . . . directly from the English text. She is my authorized translator for Sweden.

GBS

Apcs.
    1. Bermann Fischer, fleeing Vienna, had reestablished his firm in Stockholm.

4 Whitehall Court S.W.
30th July 1938

My dear Trebitsch

The blunder about Geneva has been discovered and corrected. Just change it to "Gentlemen: you are at the Hague" and leave out the bit about the hotel and the lake.[1]

I am bothered about this business of Bermann and Fischer. I have no objection to the proposed publication in Stockholm; but how is that to be reconciled with the following clause in the agreement that Fischer wants me to sign:

Der Autor überträgt dem Verlag den alleinigen Bühnenvertrieb für seine gesamte dramatische Produktion in Deutschland, einschliesslich Deutsch-Oesterreich, *sowohl für die bisher erschienenen Werke,* wie für die künftig erscheinenden. [The author transfers to the Verlag exclusive theatre-agency rights for his collected dramatic production in Germany, including German-Austria. *This applies as well to his previously published works* as to those which will be published in the future.]

I shall not sign the Fischer agreement as it stands in any case; but I want to know whether Fischer and Bermann are now independent rivals or branches of the same business.[2]

G. Bernard Shaw

Tls.
1. Shaw had forgotten the scene shift in *Geneva* to the Hague and inappropriately referred to Geneva and its lake.
2. S. Fischer, Berlin (Suhrkamp), held agent's rights in Shaw through Bermann Fischer, but to get official approval to remit royalties requested direct authorization from Shaw to represent him. Shaw, unclear of the arrangements, was puzzled.

4 Whitehall Court S.W.
5th August 1938

My dear Trebitsch

Newcomer is a bother. Ankommling or Eindringling or Neuling are correct; but to me they suggest newly born babies.[1] Do they suggest this in German? Ein alt (or echt) Radikal might do, if Radicalism means what it does in England; but I am not sure that it does not mean a Conservative of the extreme Right, whereas here it means an old-fashioned supporter of what used to be the extreme left of Liberalism.

I am still muddled about Fischer. Are all the old agreements cancelled by the new legislation? If they are, will a new agreement be valid assuming that the Fischer Verlag is a Jewish one?[2]

It is easy to give Bermann a new agreement for Geneva if he is not a rival to Fischer. Meanwhile Fischer has full authority from me to collect all tantièmes &c due to me in Germany. I have to be careful about these legal documents because you are like an Englishman in being ready to sign anything that will bring an immediate return in cash. . . .

GBS

Tls.
1. The character Newcomer in *Geneva* became in Trebitsch's version Ein Neuling.
2. S. Fischer, Berlin, was, of course, Aryanized under Suhrkamp.

The Impney Hotel. Droitwich
25th August 1938

I wrote to you to Zürich about Liesl's [Elisabeth Bergner's] Joan. Shocking—the little devil![1]
May I take it that you are a fixture at Évian?[2]
Lohengrin was not my idea; but it comes off all right.[3]

GBS

Apcs.; Texas.

1. *Joan* with Bergner opened at the Malvern Festival, now managed by Roy Limbert, on 6 August.
2. The Trebitsches went on holiday to the fashionable spa Évian-les-Bains.
3. *Geneva* had its world premiere at Malvern on 1 August. In the production, the designer Paul Shelving dressed Battler (Hitler) in Wagnerian style as Lohengrin, since Hitler's identification with Lohengrin and his adulation of Wagner were well known.

The Impney Hotel. Droitwich
27th August 1938

My dear Trebitsch

The Press, though very kindly to Eliza's personal fascination, was practically unanimous as to her hopeless inadequacy as the Warrior Maid.

She not only cut out all the lines she promised me not to cut out, but a great deal more into the bargain. The end of the court scene fell quite flat because she would not say "Thou'rt answered, old Gruffandgrum" and grovelled like a hedgehog instead of kneeling with a radiant face to heaven. The cathedral scene was a complete failure as far as she was concerned. She cut out the final speech all but a few words, and walked out like a parlormaid answering a telephone ring. But for Dunois [Stephen Murray] roaring his way through the scene it would have sent everyone to sleep.

Her excuse was that she was sparing herself for the evening performance (I was at a matinée); but a careful account I received of the evening performance from someone who knows the play by heart shewed that she made just the same cuts and achieved just the same failures.

Ayliff has nothing to say in her defence. He could not persuade her to speak the rough soldierly lines or the religiously exalted ones. She cut the scene with the Dauphin to pieces. The truth is that not only has she not the physical size and strength for Joan; but she understands neither Joan's religion nor her politics, and wants only to be pathetic and little.

I wrote this to her briefly and bluntly though not at all angrily, and said she must drop the film. I have not heard from her since, nor seen her.[1]

Are you serious in asking me what I mean by uncircumsized?[2] You really are the most complete heathen I ever met. Ask the nearest Rabbi or consult a dictionary if you can find one.

But surely Tina knows. Charlotte shrieked with laughter at your innocence.

G. Bernard Shaw

Als.; Texas.

1. Ms. Bergner was bitterly unhappy with Shaw's reaction. She had, according to her memoirs, agreed on very short notice to perform at Malvern as a birthday gift to Shaw on condition that her role follow Reinhardt's cuts and blocking (she added cuts of her own), and that she concentrate on relearning her old part in English and attend only the final week of rehearsals. Ayliff, the director, agreed but then confounded her with a different text and staging. And Shaw broke a vow, which she demanded of him, not to attend any matinée. (*Bewundert viel und viel gescholten* . . . , 1978, pp. 178–89; Bergner also reproduces in German a stinging letter purportedly from Shaw.) Plans for a film with Bergner, which had lapsed in 1936 when Shaw refused to accommodate American Catholic objections, now ended. Shaw turned instead to Pascal and the English actress Wendy Hiller. But no film of *Joan* was made until 1957, when Otto Preminger, using a scenario by Graham Greene, produced *Joan* with the American Jean Seberg in the title role.

2. On 14 August, the *Observer* noted that despite Shaw's translator being Jewish, Shaw was performed and published in Germany. Shaw, concerned about repercussions against Trebitsch, replied (21 August): "Now Herr Trebitsch is an uncircumcised Lutheran German who has never . . . set foot in a synagogue. [Trebitsch was nominally a Lutheran since his Imperial army days, when he was pressured to declare a religion (see *Chronicle*).] . . . He may have a Jewish ancestor, but which of us has not." Trebitsch was not a "Jew in any separate sense" but must be classed as a citizen of his native land.

The Impney Hotel. Droitwich
30th August 1938

For liver the only place is Vichy, where you drink the water straight out of the ground in yellow glasses before it has time to lose its radio-activity or whatever else its secret may be. The bottled water is quite useless.

We shall look out for you on the tenth October.

I gave Fischer a complete authorisation to act as my agent in Germany. He can arrange with the theatres and collect tantièmes under this. I cannot give him an agreement which would prevent our authorizing Bermann to produce Geneva in Stockholm.

G. Bernard Shaw

Apcs.; Texas.

The Impney Hotel. Droitwich
13th September 1938

Pascal's address is 10 Bolton St, Piccadilly, London W.1. Do not run after him: tell him you will be in London in October and that if that is too late he must come to Paris. He has *diable au corps* and is always rushing all over the globe. With my agreement in his pocket he cannot be short of money. He is a demonic genius in his way. It is useless and frightfully expensive, to keep up with his meteoric movements. As he *must* deal with you, you need not worry.[1]

GBS

Apcs.

1. Pascal, whose *Pygmalion* was soon to be released, was licensed to distribute the movie in non-English countries with subtitles by Shaw's authorized translators.

The Impney Hotel. Droitwich
28th September 1938

My dear Trebitsch

You and Tina ought to be in Switzerland. I am not VERY apprehensive of Hitler going to extremities next Saturday;[1] but if he does, and the Czechs fight him, there will be war between Germany and France-plus-England-plus-Russia; and in that case you and Tina will be interned in a concentration camp as prisoners of war if you are on French or English soil. Probably there will be time for you to get out before a formal declaration of war starts the shooting; but you must be prepared for this. And unhappily your visit to London must be put off until the war ends, if it ever does end during our lifetime.

For the moment the value of my English rights in Germany is about two-pence halfpenny, which makes the value of your half share three farthings. But it would not pay me to buy you out even at that figure, as I know by experience that if I ever made sixpence by the film you would immediately denounce me as a swindler and a thief if I did not pay you half exactly as if you had never sold your rights.[2] Therefore no more such purchases for me. Pascal has not written to you because I told him to leave you to me. By this I meant that if you were in immediate need I would lend you what you required. That is all I can do. But you must tell me how much I must lend, as there can be no question of sale of rights in the existing political situation.

Pascal now says that he is arranging to have his money in Italian lire instead of marks; but as Mussolini has threatened an alliance with Germany in the event of a war, the lira is likely to [be] worth even less than the mark presently.

Your passport cannot be a Sudeten passport. There is no such thing: it must be a Czechoslovakian one; and Hitler does not propose to annex Prague. However, there will be no harm in getting a less questionable passport if possible; but I do not see how it can be done unless you become a naturalized citizen of the State issuing it. De Valera[3] could not do it to oblige me even if I knew him, which I dont. As a Protestant absentee landlord I am not *persona grata* in Eire.[4]

The whole situation is quite devilish for refugees.

Zweig is an idiot.[5] The word "uncircumcized" was the most important in my Observer letter, as circumcision is the diagnostic of Judaism; and he who is baptized "of the spirit and water" is a Christian, no matter whether he has a number six nose[6] (which you havnt) or not.

We return to London on Monday.

G. Bernard Shaw

Tls.

1. On 26 September, Hitler demanded that Czechoslovakia evacuate the Sudetenland by Saturday, 1 October, or face war. Britain and France began to mobilize, but Mussolini's intervention led to the Munich Conference on 29 and 30 September at which the English and French—without the Czechs or Russians—agreed to German occupation of the Sudetenland.

2. Trebitsch, who had complained when his sale of rights in Klagemann's *Pygmalion* turned out in Shaw's favor (see 12 February 1938), now offered to sell his rights in any German version of Pascal's *Pygmalion*.

3. Eamon De Valera (1882–1975), prime minister of Ireland.
4. The Trebitsches, in Paris, were working to obtain French citizenship and also speculating on Irish naturalization.
5. Stefan Zweig (1881–1942), Viennese biographer, poet, and novelist, was Jewish, and temporarily found refuge in England. He later emigrated to Brazil where he committed suicide.
6. The figure 6 resembles an aquiline nose in profile.

Ayot St Lawrence. Welwyn
29th November 1938

. . . They are playing Man & Superman at the Deutsches Theater in Berlin, with an actor named Heinrich Marlow, made up as ME, reading extracts from the preface.[1] What folly! . . .

I am deep in the writing of a new play, which is really a history lesson in the form of an educational film.[2]

Miss Patch will send you an article of mine which will mich verdorben [ruin me] as persona grata with Goebbels & Cie.[3]

GBS

Apcs.
1. *Superman* was revived at the Deutsches Theater on 6 September, by Heinz Hilpert, directed by Erich Engel, with Eva Lissa and Ferdinand Marian. A prologue was delivered by Bruno Hübner (not Heinrich Marlow) made up as Shaw and flanked by blackboards showing the evolution of man.
2. Shaw had recently begun *In Good King Charles's Golden Days*, as an educational film script for Pascal, but it ended as a two-act play.
3. Shaw's article "How to Deal with the Jewish Difficulty" (*Time and Tide*, 26 November) followed Kristallnacht (9 November) and the intensification of anti-Jewish measures and questioned Hitler's sanity.

Ayot St Lawrence. Welwyn
6th December 1938

It was unwise to call attention to the furs; but the incident proves that your goods are still untouched in Maxingstrasse and may be left there until the persecution slackens.[1]

Can you not sell the trunk to some kind Frenchman who will claim it at the frontier and then make you a present of it?

Furs are abominable things: they are far inferior in healthiness to wool; and the cruelty of seal hunting is horrible. But if Tina does not agree with me, Charlotte, who has, I regret to say, *two* fur coats, would be delighted to lend one of them to Tina for as long as she likes. . . .

GBS

Apcs.
1. The Trebitsches had left most of their personal effects in their house on Maxingstrasse in care of their chauffeur and his future wife, who, on Tina's instructions, managed at times to deliver items abroad.

4 Whitehall Court S.W.
7th December 1938

What has happened to Berman[n-Fischer]? You write that there has been some disappointment; but I dont know what it is.[1]

I can do nothing for Szekely:[2] I must stick to Pascal, who has made a magnificent success of Pygmalion, but will make next to nothing by it, whilst the financiers & distributors will make fortunes.[3] Pascal is going to do Major Barbara.

All the western world is abusing Battler [i.e., Hitler] frantically. The Jews want me to do the same. What good does it do? It only makes the mischief worse. My way is better.

GBS

Apcs.

1. Along with *Geneva* (*Genf*), Trebitsch had submitted a volume of his short stories to Bermann Fischer, but Bermann Fischer declined to publish them.

2. William Szekely (1897–1966), a Hungarian film producer who had worked in Berlin and Vienna and was now in exile.

3. Pascal's *Pygmalion*, directed by Anthony Asquith and starring Wendy Hiller and Leslie Howard, had opened in London's Leicester Square Theatre on 6 October to critical and popular acclaim but left Pascal with empty pockets, since to obtain financing for the film he had relinquished his shares to the financiers.

4 Whitehall Court S.W.
14th December 1938

I will not sign that agreement[1] under any circumstances whatever, not if your life and mine and Tina's and Charlotte's depended on it.

Fischer already possesses two agreements (or rather licences) the first from myself alone giving him full powers as my agent, the second doing the same with your consent.

But he persists, without a word of explanation, in demanding an assignment of copyright, which would transfer all our property to himself, and leave me with a mere charge on whatever he may make by doing absolutely what he likes with the plays, including sale of the film rights for anything he can get for them, and you with nothing at all.

NO.

G. Bernard Shaw

Apcs.

1. To satisfy the German Foreign Exchange Authority, S. Fischer (Suhrkamp) asked for a new agreement assigning agency rights to the reorganized firm, but Shaw misunderstood it as transfer of copyright.

4 Whitehall Court S.W.
5th January 1939

My dear Trebitsch

Fischer does not know his business or he would understand my difficulty about the agreement. It is a short document assigning my rights to him for two years. During that two years he, as proprietor of the copyright, could sell all the rights that are included in the copyright, film rights, translation rights, adaptation rights, in fact every right that a literary work can possess. That is why I have never parted with a copyright and never will. . . .

If Fischer cannot understand this he has had no legal training and is therefore unfit to be an agent. I know nothing about him, as he is not our old friend Fischer but an Aryan ersatz product.

What is Bermann doing with your translation [of Geneva]?[1] Do you know whether Hitler reads English? I have read somewhere that he does. If so, I think I shall send him a copy. If not, why should I not send him a copy of your translation? It is no use asking for official opinions: no censor dare pass Geneva.[2] But it is possible that Hitler might pass it, as it is really very flattering to him.

The cold here is horrid.

GBS

Tls.

1. Bermann Fischer objected to the lenient treatment of dictators in *Geneva* and declined to publish the play.

2. S. Fischer, Berlin, hesitated to publish *Geneva* without official sanction.

4 Whitehall Court S.W.
26th January 1939

My dear Trebitsch

. . . When I suggested letting Hitler read Geneva, I did not mean to reveal the name of the translator. I find it very difficult to get any credible account of the man. Emil Ludwig,[1] who has just lunched with us, believes as you do that H. is an illiterate semi-idiot; that Mein Kampf was written for him by other people; and that he knows no language except an Austrian dialect, and very little of that. This is quite incredible. A book entitled "I Knew Hitler" by an educated German who worked with Hitler from the beginning, and had to teach him how to dress for dinner, gives a very different account of him, and one fully consistent with his extraordinary career.[2] As the author had quarrelled with Hitler and was writing in exile, his book cannot be said to be written to order. Lloyd George, a shrewd judge of public men, was so impressed by his visit to Berchtesgaden that the article he wrote on his return to England in praise of Hitler and his social work in Germany had to be toned down before the News Chronicle dared publish it.[3] Chamberlain has not suggested that he was confronted at Berchtesgaden and Munich with an imbecile.[4] In spite of Hitler's crazy anti-Semitism and anti-Bolshevism, der Führer is a man to be taken very seriously. The pro-Semite abuse that is levelled at him is just as absurd as the anti-Semite scurrilities of Goebbel[s] & Co.

The actor who plays Battler in London is dressed as Lohengrin. I have just learnt that Hitler was greatly pleased by a picture of himself as Lohengrin.[5]

However, I have not sent him your translation. But if only he could read English I should be tempted to send him the original.

As to Bermann you must not think of making any concessions to him either in respect of Geneva or of your stories. I never believed that he could continue as a German publisher in Scandinavia: evidently you must find a Swiss publisher, and you must not be hampered in your approach by any engagements to Bermann. Simply drop him. If he has not paid you anything in respect of the Geneva translation, so much the better: you can get rid of him without having to repay him. As he is as anxious to get rid of you as you should be to get rid of him, you will be able to extricate yourself without difficulty.

Do not blame Bermann. What could he do, poor devil? His misfortunes and yours are bad enough without embittering them with useless recriminations or offers of concessions which would only make his situation worse. Of course he wants to get rid of us both; and he is quite right. . . .

June Head's translation of Emigrationsong is very tender and elegant; but what is wanted for a popular political song is crudity and violence: what can be sung by a lady in a drawingroom is useless in the streets.[6] The Marseillaise is the vulgarest tune in Europe: that is why it is so much better for a marching crowd than Haydn's very superior Deutschland Uber Alles. The vogue of such a song must begin with a favorite singer at a variety theatre, or a march to the frontier. In either case there must be plenty of big drum in the rhythm. You must turn it into a sailor's chanty.

Have I left anything unanswered?

GBS

Tls.

1. Emil Ludwig (1881–1948), German-Jewish author and outspoken anti-Nazi, had emigrated to Switzerland in 1932.

2. *I Knew Hitler*, by Kurt Ludecke, an early Nazi who abandoned the Party, had appeared the previous year.

3. Former prime minister David Lloyd George (1863–1945), after visiting Hitler, professed "admiration" for Hitler as "unquestionably a great leader," not a "mechanical moron" (*News Chronicle*, 21 September 1936).

4. Neville Chamberlain (1869–1940), British prime minister, had conferred with Hitler at Berchtesgaden and Godesberg before the Munich Conference that ceded the Sudetenland to Germany.

5. Hubert Lanzinger's painting of Hitler as medieval knight was shown at the Festival of German Art, Munich, opened by Hitler in July 1937.

6. Trebitsch hoped that his "Emigrantenlied" (Emigrants Song), which June Head had translated, would become a rallying cry for German refugees.

Ayot St Lawrence. Welwyn
31st January 1939

What a frightful experience![1] Next time you have to break a door open do not take Tina with you. Nowadays we are accustomed to read about such things and hear about them; but to *see* them upsets one for days. The effect will pass away, as such effects always mercifully do; but in the meantime dont talk to her about it: there is nothing to be done but rock her in your arms and kiss her. That is what I should do if Charlotte had such a shock.

Suicide, the last extremity of egotism, is sometimes justifiable and even obligatory. But under all ordinary vicissitudes of fortune it must be ruled out. One should not do it in a hotel, but in some place where the police will find the body and dispose of it. I am not sure that one should not commit half a dozen murders first, since it can be done with impunity; but the difficulty is to secure for the victims the fair trial to which they are entitled. Still, suicide is so unnatural that you will feel that Leopold's way out is not really open to sane men. It is mystically barred.

You see, I was right about Hitler. His speech was a wonderful performance:[2] nobody else in Europe could have made it. Of course the part about the Jews was stark raving nonsense: he is mad on that subject; but the rest was masterly. Naturally you have no reason to love him; but nothing is more dangerous than to underrate your adversary; and, believe me, it is childish to think of Hitler as E[mil] L[udwig] does: Adolf leaves the next ablest statesman in Germany nowhere.

Even if it were not so, what possible good can come of my reviling him as all the anti-Nazi papers and talkers are doing? If I joined in the vituperation I should do no good to you or anyone else; and I might do you a great deal of harm.

Now for the practical point. The outcry against the expulsion of the Jews has, it is said, so far chastened the Anti-Semites that they are allowing some of the fugitives to return and retrieve their personal belongings. Whether this is true I do not know, nor have I any particulars.[3] Have you found out anything about it? . . .

Charlotte is very much moved at Tina's distress; but, I repeat, it will not bear talking about. . . . GBS

Tls.

1. Early on 24 January, Mr. and Mrs. Leopold Lipschütz, Jewish refugees related to Trebitsch, committed suicide in Nice. Leopold Lipschütz (1870–1939) was editor of the Viennese *Kronenzeitung*. The Trebitsches, who had moved to Nice for the winter, were summoned to the couple's apartment after a relative rang their bell and received no answer. The concierge broke in and discovered the bodies. A note explained that they had received menacing letters from Austrian Nazis threatening cruel death.

2. On 30 January, Hitler gave an address, which except for its threats against Jews, opponents, and "warmongers" was relatively moderate and was on the whole well received in the West. He avoided claims in the East and urged equitable redistribution of colonies. He also scoffed at Western humanitarian pretenses by noting the reluctance to admit German refugees.

3. German Jewish emigrants could take their personal belongings except for gold, jewels, and art works, but they were hardly likely or able to return to claim their possessions.

4 Whitehall Court S.W.
21st February 1939

My dear Trebitsch

Writing is difficult. I have had another reaction after an injection[1] which has frightened Charlotte. Miss Patch has influenza and is disabled for ten days. Our servants here have also been stricken; and as to the domestic staff at Ayot they are all in bed with it. We have to scramble along as best we can.

As a rule I am against allowing my plays to be used as opera librettos. They are set to their own verbal music and are spoiled by being sung and orchestrated. The Chocolate Soldier has been a hateful experience; and nothing much has come of Lilien's Catherine. But of course if I could find anyone capable of playing Mozart to my Beaumarchais I should have to consider it. You had better tell them that it is quite useless to approach me with a proposal that does not mention the name of the composer. He would have to be a pretty big one for Caesar.

I think it would be better to get rid of Bermann altogether, and look for an Aryan publisher. At all events do not sacrifice your interest to a supposed necessity for having Geneva published. I can wait for Germany in the long run longer than Germany can wait for me. Meanwhile what is happening to all our books? They must be selling still, as the theatres are using them. I presume the deAryanized Fischer firm is still handling them. Then why can it not publish Geneva without the translator's name?[2]

No letters have been lost between us. I am always a bad correspondent because I find that if I write letters I write nothing else, and must let everything else go if I am to get on with my plays.

How are you getting on in Nice? Is Tina getting used to her exile?

GBS

Tls.

1. Shaw, slowly recovering from anemia, was receiving injections to stimulate his liver.

2. The problem with publishing *Geneva* in Germany was not that Trebitsch was Jewish but that the portrait of Hitler was unacceptable.

4 Whitehall Court S.W.
22nd February 1939

My dear Trebitsch

What is the use of looking at the accounts? All I learn is that Fischer has RM10,143,40 of ours gutgeschrieben [credited] in his books. They might as well be at the bottom of the sea as far as we are concerned.[1] He has collected these tantièmes as our agent and is safely possessed of them. What prevents his sending them to us just as he sends the Klagemann money?[2] What has our agreement with him to [do] with it now that he has received the tantièmes from the theatres without any question? I can get no explanation from him: neither explanation nor money; only a demand that I shall assign all my copyrights to him, which would entitle him to transfer the tantièmes to his own credit instead of to mine.

I am not unmindful of your need of this money; but what can I do? I have given him a complete authorization to collect; and so have you. And *he has collected*. It may be that there is some regulation which forbids him to send the money; but he does not say so. He simply sits on the cash and leaves us destitute. . . .

GBS

Tls.

1. S. Fischer (Suhrkamp) in fact had remitted installments on theatre royalties to Shaw, including Trebitsch's share, since receiving authorization in August 1938.

2. Royalties from Klagemann's *Pygmalion* were remitted by Klagemann, not S. Fischer.

4 Whitehall Court S.W.

6th March 1939

My dear Trebitsch

I am puzzled by the man being Hellmer on the first page of your letter and Mainzer on the second. However I have addressed a letter to Mainzer certifying that Hellmer is an honorable person.[1]

The 12th April is the Wednesday following Easter Sunday; so any of your friends who leave London for the Easter holiday may not be back. But as we shall probably be at home the date will probably suit us. You will be very welcome.

We must go into Fischer's accounts, because he has made some payments and I dont know whether any part of these belong to you.

G. Bernard Shaw

Tls.

1. At Trebitsch's request, Shaw wrote to Arthur Mainzer, formerly of the Neues Theater, Frankfurt, who had found refuge in England and was now trying to obtain admittance to England for Arthur Hellmer (1880–1961), also of the Neues Theater. Shaw, who knew neither of the men, was confused by the identical first names. The Hellmers were permitted into England the following July.

Ayot St Lawrence. Welwyn

13th March 1939

My dear Trebitsch

I hope you have got over the flu. Here all our domestic affairs and movements have been thrown into confusion by its ravages in our staffs. I write this from Ayot: my first visit there for a month.

The thousand pounds expected from Pascal is imaginary. He is not touring any play for me: he is preparing to film The Doctor's Dilemma.[1] Whether he will be allowed to exhibit this film in Germany and Austria with your translation "dubbed" on it is very doubtful. If not, we may find a German firm to undertake it. But it will be a long time before that is settled; and meanwhile there is no likelihood of your getting anything out of Pascal, who has been unmercifully plundered by the financiers over Pygmalion, though his prestige and consequently his credit has soared to the skies.

You say I think nobody wants money because I dont. But I do. The newspapers have stated that I have made £66,000 by the Pygmalion film; and this has brought down on me everyone on earth who wants money either because they are starving refugees or Utopians with plans for the regeneration of the universe needing only £15,000 to be set on foot at once. As to widows and invalids among my poor relatives, there seems no end to them.

The truth is that I have had from Pygmalion just £3000, which has gone straight into the hands of the Inland Revenue Office for taxes, with all my ready cash and several thousands which I had to borrow.[2]

As to you and Tina, I have not dared to make any inquiry as to what you were living on and how much you have left. I concluded that when you were at the end of your resources you would let me know how much you needed to go on with. I must find it for you somehow. Let me know how you stand.

Has Tina come with you to Paris, or does she stay in Nice?[3]
I have had to buy a *rente viagère* [lifetime annuity] of £144 a year for himself and his wife. I have lost money by France. Thanks to you Germany has
been a better bargain. "Himself" means my French translator Hamon.

I could not write until today at Ayot. You have no notion of how impossible it is for me to correspond punctually—or at all. I find that if I answer
letters my work stops. It is three or four weeks since I added a word to the
Newton play [*In Good King Charles's Golden Days*], or to anything else
that will bring me in a farthing.

Forgive all this grumbling; but that remark of yours about my doing
nothing but rolling in money provokes me to air my grievances.

G. Bernard Shaw

Tls.
  1. Reports of Pascal's next Shaw film varied from time to time: Shaw favored *Major Barbara*,
but Pascal inclined toward *Doctor's Dilemma*. Shaw won out, but the film was not completed
until 1941, when German distribution was ruled out.
  2. Shaw's windfall royalties from Pascal's *Pygmalion* did not come until the next year when he
received £25,000.
  3. The Trebitsches were again in Paris, seeking French citizenship.

4 Whitehall Court S.W.
25th March 1939

My dear Trebitsch

I enclose a letter which will enable you to prove that you have business
here which involves a visit to this country.[1]

You must come as a refugee and a victim of Hitler; for Nazi Germans are
not very welcome here at present. I am still very sceptical as to the likelihood of war; but the world is so stupidly governed that any folly is possible; and though you are in no greater danger here than in France, still it
might be better to keep very quiet within reach of Zurich until the atmosphere is a little less electric.

Anyhow, if you decide to come you have my letter; and you are always welcome chez nous.

GBS

Tls.
  1. On 15 March Hitler absorbed what remained of Czechoslovakia. He then occupied Memel,
forced an economic agreement on Romania, and demanded the return of Danzig from Poland. With
Czechoslovakia now a German protectorate, Trebitsch's Czech passport posed new problems of
entry into England. Shaw's enclosure addressed to Trebitsch was as follows:
       This business of my German rights, and your share of the royalties as my translator, is so
    complicated that it is impossible to settle it or even discuss it fully by correspondence. You
    cannot return to Germany to speak to our Berlin agent because you are a Christian non-
    Aryan. There is nothing for it but for you to come to London and go into our affairs with me
    personally.
       Will you therefore come to England as soon as possible and have a business talk with me?
    I will arrange for your stay at the Dorchester House Hotel.

Ayot St Lawrence. Welwyn
6th April 1939

I am writing to the Dorchester House Hotel to expect you on the 12th. Come to lunch at Whitehall Court on Thursday the 13th at 1.15.[1]

We shall be at Ayot until the evening of the 12th. If I can do anything to assist your journey let me know.

Geneva is dying of Passion Week, but may possibly revive after Easter Monday.[2]

GBS

Apcs.

1. While Trebitsch was in London, Shaw presented him with £1,000 from his earnings on Klagemann's *Pygmalion*, even though Trebitsch had sold his rights in the film (Texas). Presumably, Shaw also paid Trebitsch his share in the royalties remitted by S. Fischer.

2. *Geneva* opened in London on 22 November 1938 and ran until 17 June 1939 for 237 performances, one of the longest runs for Shaw in London.

4 Whitehall Court S.W.
24th May 1939

Do not come over for Jitta: it would be a wicked waste of money. The Embassy is a suburban theatre where plays are "tried out" (Probe unterziehen) for a fortnight. If they please any of the regular West End managers they are transferred to a West End theatre with a fashionable cast. Unless this happens you need not trouble yourself about the Embassy, where the tantièmes will be quite negligible. I have not seen the performance there yet.[1]

The Fischer agreement covers all the old arrangements with the old non-Aryan firm. Its purpose is solely to provide a new firm with a document which will satisfy the Devisencentral [i.e., Foreign Exchange Authority] and enable us to get our royalties sent to us from Germany. That is what Fischer has been bothering me about all these months. The only question now is, will the Dc accept this Vertrag [contract] and sanction the remittances? If not, the German version of Charles will have to go to a Swiss publisher. Tell Fischer I am becoming convinced that he is a hopeless Schafkopf [blockhead].

G. Bernard Shaw

Apcs.

1. *Jitta* was revived on 15 May at the "Q" Theatre by Jack and Beatrice de Leon, who produced many of Shaw's plays and whose productions ran alternately at the suburban Embassy Theatre. The production did not move to the West End.

4 Whitehall Court S.W.
13th July 1939

My dear Trebitsch

It is no use sending you copies of Charles until the text is finally decided on. I have submitted it to two famous astronomers with the result that I have had to make a budget of corrections. Not until after the production at Malvern will the book be ready for translation.

I shall not go to Malvern this year. I am quite tired of the place; and I am too old to work at the rehearsals. In the case of Geneva I left all that to Ayliff, and shall do so in future; so I shall not be wanted.

Pascal has changed his plans and is going to film Major Barbara before the Dilemma.

I gave a sitting to Mrs Freund, though her color photographs were quite execrable. She admitted it, but pleaded that they were not so bad when thrown on a screen.[1]

Julius Bab wants to know where you are living. He has failed to get a visa for London, but hopes to be more successful in September. His address is 21 rue du Marché, Neuilly sur Seine.[2]

As to naturalization I hear so much about German Jewish doctors being made "honorary Aryans" that I have been considering whether it would not be possible to have you added to the list.[3]

I always write to you when I have anything to say and when I have time.

Does Kantorovich[4] send you your half of the tantièmes? Miss Patch is assuming that he does.

G. Bernard Shaw

Tls.; Texas.

1. Gisèle Freund (b. 1912), Berlin-born photographer then in exile in France, specialized in portraits of writers and artists and in working-class life. Through H. G. Wells she gained access to Shaw, who demanded to see her experimental color shots and exclaimed, "They are pretty awful, don't you agree?" and proceeded to instruct her on taking his portrait. "Don't cut off a bit of my beard," he warned. Suddenly the lights went off, and Shaw suggested that he stand by the window in the moonlight. The result was a strikingly handsome Shaw, in blue-violet light, but with part of his beard cut off! (Freund, *The World in My Camera*, 1974.) Forewarned, Mrs. Freund never sent the picture to Shaw.

2. Bab, then in France, emigrated to America.

3. The plight of German Jewish doctors had in fact deteriorated, but isolated instances of privileged Jews—e.g., those who contributed to the Nazis before 1933—being made "honorary Aryans" probably occurred.

4. Michael Kantorowitz (1877–1961), Russian-born Swiss lawyer and theatre agent, and Shaw's representative in Switzerland.

England was now at war. On 1 September, German troops crossed into Poland. Two days later, England, followed by France, declared war on Germany. Shortly before, the Trebitsches, aided by influential friends, had obtained French citizenship and returned to the Dolder Hotel in Zurich.

[Hotel Esplanade. Frinton-on-Sea]
postmarked 7th September 1939

Our address until the 30th, when we return to Ayot St Lawrence, Welwyn, Herts, is

Hotel Esplanade
Frinton-on-Sea
Essex.

This is all I can say on this card, even now that you are a Frenchman and an ally. More later on.

G. Bernard Shaw

Apcs.

> Hotel Esplanade. Frinton-on-Sea
> until the 29th
> 22nd September 1939

I am not sure whether you are in Zürich or Versailles; and I have added a scene to Geneva including the declaration of war and the Russian intervention which you must add to your translation—about 600 words.[1] I will send it when you let me know where you are.

Charlotte has been very ill;[2] and it has been impossible for me to write. More when I know your address.

G. Bernard Shaw

Duplicate of this card to Paris, Hotel P. de Galles.

Apcs.
1. Shaw's updating of *Geneva* also predicted Battler's failure and condemned all parties for the war.
2. Charlotte Shaw, 81, was ill with crippling lumbago.

> Ayot St Lawrence. Welwyn
> 18th October 1939

I hear from Salten[1] that you have finished the naturalization business, and are at Zürich.

While you were in Paris I wrote a long letter to you; but the march of events in Poland[2] and at home was too quick for me; and I scrapped it all.

Charlotte's illness, which continues, has upset all my domestic arrangements. I have to remain in the country with her. That also spoilt my letter.

Meanwhile all my writing energy is expended on the war controversy. I am all for a suspension of hostilities and a conference.[3]

How is Tina?

Write to me and repeat all the questions you still want me to answer. My head is quite empty. I presume the war choked off Copenhagen.[4]

G.B.S.

Apcs.
1. Felix Salten, who had lingered in Vienna but was now safe in Zurich.
2. Hitler entered Warsaw on 5 October and the next day offered peace to the West.
3. Shaw's "Uncommon Sense About the War" had appeared in the *New Statesman* on 7 October.
4. Trebitsch was planning to attend the P.E.N. congress in Copenhagen, but the war forced its cancellation.

Ayot St Lawrence. Welwyn
2nd November 1939

Your card dated the 25th Oct. arrived this evening. Your letter dated the 27th came two days ago. The war has upset everything, including remittances from Germany.

Have you a bank account in Zürich?[1] If so, what is the name of the bank?

I am working at a new edition of Pygmalion which will contain some of the film scenes.[2] When it is ready Reiss[3] can use it as a scenario. But can you manage the Swiss dialect?

Charlotte's health is improving slowly. We may be able to go to London next week.

If only I could stop the war there would be no difficulty about your coming over as usual. As it is—!!!!!

GBS

Apcs.
    1. With the outbreak of war, Shaw's German royalties were placed in a blocked account in Leipzig.
    2. A new edition of *Pygmalion*, exploiting the interest aroused by the movie, appeared in 1941 with five scenes written especially for the film.
    3. Kurt Reiss (1901–1974), Swiss publisher and theatre agent, who proposed filming *Pygmalion* in Swiss-German dialect.

Ayot St Lawrence. Welwyn
3rd November 1939

. . . The war I am trying to stop leaves the gentleman you mention [Hitler] quite unharmed. His residence is the safest place in Europe; and the attack will rally all his countrymen round him, and possibly bring to his aid the most powerful State in the world [the Soviet Union].[1] Every day of the war makes a change of government [in Germany] more difficult.

Leave these political questions to me: I have studied them for fifty years.

Besides, it is the war that is keeping you away from London. Dont you want to come?

Copenhagen referred to the P.E.N. Club Conference.

GBS

Apcs.
    1. Trebitsch opposed Shaw's peace efforts and suggested that the Allies bomb Hitler's residence. An assassination attempt on Hitler the next week was, in fact, laid by German propaganda to British Intelligence and increased pro-Hitler sentiment in Germany.

Ayot St Lawrence. Welwyn
6th November 1939

My dear Trebitsch

It is hard news; but it was inevitable.[1] Now that you are legally a Frenchman you are an alien enemy to the German Reich. Your excuse is that this was not the case when you applied for French naturalization, and that the step was forced on you by your persecution as a Jew. If there is any way in which you can formally protest *on this ground* against the sequestration of your property it might be well to do so. Meanwhile the Reich may at least repair the roof. Someday you may be able to take the house again.

What is Tina's legal nationality?[2] Is it the same as yours, as in Britain? If she remains a Russian[3] why is she not an enthusiastic Bolshevik? I am. Holy Russia has saved the soul of the world, as Sasha Kropotkin[4] told me she would do years ago. That will cure Tina's heart.

The gentleman you write about [Hitler] has rendered such colossal services to his country that it is not wise to disparage him, especially as it can do no good.

What is your financial position? You must remember that I am quite ignorant of your resources, or Tina's over and beyond your share in my royalties.

Do not forget to answer my question as to your bankers.

Pascal believes that you are—or were—a millionaire!

On the 1st January I shall have to pay the British Government £11,000; but even that will not quite finish me. But what will happen in January 1941, heaven alone knows.

What prevents you moving to Nice *now*?[5] Prices, however, are rising everywhere, and will continue to do so.

G. Bernard Shaw

Als.

1. The previous month, the Viennese authorities sequestered the Trebitsches' villa on Maxingstrasse and all its furnishings, including bronzes and paintings and a Gobelin tapestry. These furnishings were later auctioned off to pay the Flight Tax, but the villa itself was spared since Tina, as half-owner, was Aryan and not subject to expropriation. During the war the villa housed a military court. Trebitsch's housekeepers—who shortly married—remained in two rooms with a separate entrance.

2. Tina had also acquired French citizenship.

3. Shaw alludes to Tina's first marriage to a Russian nobleman.

4. Sasha Kropotkin Lebedeff, daughter of the revolutionary anarchist Prince Peter Kropotkin. She and her husband, Boris, translated one or two of Shaw's plays.

5. As French citizens, the Trebitsches, still in Zurich, considered settling in France.

4 Whitehall Court S.W.
[c. early December 1939]

My dear Trebitsch

Hamon is still alive and active. But in any case your proposal to become my French translator is a crazy one. What would you say if I made Hamon my German translator and left him to find some German to do the work for him?

Hamon, with three daughters, has always been desperately poor. Years ago I had to buy his house in Brittany for him. And within the last few years I have had to buy him an annuity for his own and his wife's life, of £12 a month. And this enables him to live comfortably according to his standard of comfort. When the French film of Pygmalion materializes he will be, for awhile at least, a millionaire.

Now the difficulty with you is that you have never been poor. As far as I can gather from your letters you cannot live on less than £2000 a year, whereas Hamon can live on £144 a year and a house, with what else he can pick up as a revolutionary author and journalist. Probably your two brothers also need £2000 a year each, and expect you to provide it for them. And as the war and your predicament as a non-Aryan, and both our predicaments as alien enemies, has cut off all supplies from Germany, your assets are nil.

It is this situation which has made it difficult for me to write to you. I cannot buy you a joint annuity of £6000 for the joint lives of yourself, Tina, and your brothers: my own settled income (and I have several dependents) is less than that and is being reduced by terrific war taxation. You will have to play a mechanical piano in the streets with Tina exhibiting a hired baby to excite compassion. And that will not bring in £6000 a year. You and Tina would be not a bit less happy than you are now; but I could never persuade you both of that because you have never been poor.

However, this is not very helpful or consoling. But for the life of me I can think of nothing else to say.

I have been as civil to "the gentleman" [Hitler] as possible. Abusing him could do no good and might do you harm. It is still possible that a change of government in Germany and a conclusion of the war might end in some sort of recovery of your property (or at least some of it); but this would not have been helped if I had joined the imperialists who are bent on making a Punic war of it and vilifying the gentleman as the basest of scoundrels and playing for a second and worse Versailles. You have blown off steam quite enough in your letters to me. In future be careful not to do or say anything that could make your return to Wien and your resumption of German nationality difficult or impossible.

Meanwhile I do not see how you can make a living except in some German community under a foreign Government; and such communities do not exist except in America. You can translate into German French, but not into literary French; and the pay for such work is too small to be divided with another person. I wish I could bring about some performances of Jitta, or get it filmed. Are the plots of any of your plays or novels saleable for filming?

Have you got the Topolski edition of Geneva?[1] It contains the full text with all the additions that are not in the rehearsal copies. Miss Patch thinks you have it but is not quite sure.

Is Tina now with you in Paris, or have you still one foot in France and the other in Switzerland? Between Dolder and Paris and the Locarno banker, with ruined friends on all sides, and you, though apparently penniless, travelling as if you were richer than ever, I am quite distracted. Where do you get all the money you are spending? What about Nice?

G. Bernard Shaw

Tls.; Texas.

1. *Geneva*, illustrated by Feliks Topolski (b. 1907), had appeared the previous June with several substantive revisions, which enhanced the role of the Jew, muted criticism of the British, and deleted a speech on human pugnacity.

4 Whitehall Court S.W.
17th January 1940

. . . Over a thousand people are killed here every month in the black-out.
Only one British soldier has been killed on the western front![1] In October
every theatre in London was closed. Do you need any better reasons for staying away?

Colin[2] may make your fortune if he can. But he shall not make his own at
our expense.

Why does it amuse you to heap imaginary reproaches on me?

G.B.S.

Apcs.; Texas.
1. Hitler's offensive against the West was still some months away and the Western front was
quiet.
2. Saul Colin, the New York agent-producer, who after two years' silence had appeared again
with plans for *Jitta*.

4 Whitehall Court S.W.
postmarked 23rd February 1940

. . . I think I have had all your letters; but I am still bewildered at your
living at an expensive hotel[1] when you would be so much more comfortable
in an apartment with a friendly French family. You must have resources of
which I know nothing.

I should write if I had anything cheerful to say, but I havnt. I am always
glad to see your unshaken handwriting.

G.B.S.

Apcs.; Texas.
1. The Trebitsches had settled into the Hotel Winter Palace, Nice.

Ayot St Lawrence. Welwyn
11th March 1940

My dear Trebitsch

This is the first sensible letter you have sent me since the Dispersal. I have
been making inquiries, and find that "apartments" have disappeared from
London economy, and that people who formerly lived in them now live in
hotels or in "service flats" like mine in Whitehall. It is interesting to learn
that this is true of the Riviera also, and that you can patronize hotels and
save Tina the burden of housekeeping and finding servants with a good
conscience.

In London, however, you could have three weeks at a *good* hotel with all
meals included for what it costs for bed and breakfast at the Dorchester. You
would not have jazz bands and crowds of actresses and smart women every
night at supper: the company would be bourgeois and not all in evening
dress at dinner; but there would be solid comfort, entire respectability, and

good public rooms to write in. The Victorian hotels which were within my recollection famous as the best in London—the Langham and Charing Cross, for instance—are not "smart" (smartness was not considered respectable by the old Queen); but they are as good as ever; and you can stand up without knocking a hole in the ceiling with your head. Fifty years ago you would have thought them the last word in luxury. That is one of the advantages of being old: what was good enough for Franz Josef and Victoria is good enough for us.

We are now in summer time; and the black-out does not begin until half past seven. You can go to a cinema or a theatre matinée without being blinded or run over; and if you come when there is a moon the risks are negligible. In April there will be still more daylight.[1] As to the war, the Powers are still very wisely afraid to bombard each other's capitals; and London is the safest place in the west of Europe except perhaps Monte Carlo. But this security may not last: there is uncertainty enough about it to make it impossible to say whether you ought to come here next month unless you have more pressing business than to see two people whose united ages amount to 167. We cannot believe that we are interesting enough to make the journey worth while for our sakes alone. Still, it would be a change for you which would probably do you good. My only doubt is whether I may not have to take Charlotte away for a few weeks after Easter, as she also has had a hard time through a hard winter and talks of going to the Isle of Wight to recuperate. However, she is so much better now that she can hold out at home until the holidays are over. If you can afford the journey we must arrange it somehow. Pascal still assures me that you are a millionaire.

Is Monaco a neutral State like Switzerland from which you can communicate with Vienna? . . .

As to the word fluxions in Charles there may not be any German version of it. What happened was that Newton invented the differential calculus (an infinitesimal calculus) for his own convenience when he was a young man, and said nothing about it. He called this mathematical method Fluxions because it enabled him to determine the rate at which a continually changing quantity—a *flowing* quantity—changes. Later on Leibniz invented the same method independently; but his figuration (notation) was so much easier to work with that it was adopted by all the mathematicians and called the calculus, or the infinitesimal calculus, or the integral calculus, or the differential calculus, whilst Newton's word Fluxions was dropped. The Muret-Sanders dictionary gives for Fluxions the same word, for Equinox das Aequinoktium, and for Notation das Bezeichnungssystem. The ducking stool is a long plank on wheels with a chair at the end. Women who were scolds and shrews were tied in the chair and dipped into the pond or river until they were half drowned.

I received Krauss's visit but refused to sit to him.[2] There are too many portraits of me in the world. Foreign painters imagine that if they can paint Shaw their fortunes will be made. If I let them do it they find that they have wasted their time painting a picture that nobody will buy; and they come back to me begging me to buy it. Therefore I always refuse to sit unless the painter can produce a commission from some rich client for a portrait of me. Frau Krauss, who must have been brilliantly pretty when she was young, tried all her blandishments on me; but I was adamant.

You must not mind my hardheartedness. Charlotte and I are old and in our second childhood. We can no longer feel things (except little things) as you do, which is very fortunate for us, because human misery is so appalling nowadays that if we allowed ourselves to dwell on it we should only add imaginary miseries of our own to the real miseries of others without doing them any good. When the inflation of the German currency ruined the middle classes after the treaty of Versailles I received hundreds of heartbreaking letters from Germans telling me all about their wrecked lives and begging for sums from five shillings to five hundred pounds or even for an abusive postcard which they could sell as an autograph. I had to harden my heart until it was like that of a professional torturer and executioner; and I have not yet recovered from that anaesthetic, nor shall I dare to until this war is over. But I am none the less conscious of your misfortunes, and of how much more they afflict you than they would me, who have been really poor as you have never been.

I could live on £2 a week; but Tina could not, nor Charlotte, nor you.

I think I have now answered all your letters; and Heaven knows when I shall have time to write again. But we are always glad to hear from you.

G. Bernard Shaw

Tls.; Texas.
1. Trebitsch, temporarily in Monaco, planned to visit London in April.
2. Viktor Krauss was a Viennese painter and a friend of Trebitsch.

Ayot St Lawrence. Welwyn
17th March 1940

. . . Miss Patch is collecting the tariffs of the best Victorian hotels for you. . . .

G. Bernard Shaw

Apcs.; Texas.

4 Whitehall Court S.W.
28th March 1940

We shall be at Ayot on the 22nd April; but we shall return to London early on the 23rd [24th] (Wednesday) and shall expect you on that day at Whitehall Court for lunch.

I am sending you a formal letter for official use.

Pascal has just called, having received your letter. You must not quarrel with him:[1] he is a delightful creature, but quite outside all ordinary rules. Still, a Magyar and a man of honor.

We must talk about the Swiss film [of *Pygmalion*] when we meet.

GBS

Apcs.; Texas.
    1. Trebitsch's quarrel with Pascal is undetermined.

Ayot St Lawrence. Welwyn
7th April 1940
My dear Trebitsch

I cannot write to the Home Office instructing it to give you a visa: I wish I could; but things are not done in that way. I am not *persona grata* with the Home Secretary, possibly quite the opposite. All I can do is to give you a letter to produce as proof that you have pressing unpolitical business concerning payments due from the continent to England.[1]

You are mistaken in supposing that the highly respectable Langham Hotel is farther away from Whitehall Court than Park Lane. It is nearer, and *much* nearer to the theatres. For your purposes it is a more desirable address than the Dorchester. But as you are coming as my guest, and I shall pay your bill, you may dismiss all that from your mind and go where you please.

You must understand that Miss Patch, who, unlike Pascal, believes you to be a ruined man, is greatly concerned about your utter ignorance of how to live on less than several thousands a year, and is trying to instruct you in that art. She is not treating you as a pauper, but as a well-to-do professional man. I could tell you of no less than four grades of hotel much cheaper than the Langham, the Russell, and the Charing Cross (the latter within five minutes of Whitehall and ten of the theatres), all three first class Victorian hotels used by first class professional people, who would not be seen at the two you prefer. However, do not bother any more about your quarters: if you feel more at home at the D[orchester] go there by all means. DONT go to the other you mention.

Pascal offers you simple but luxurious private hospitality at his "old barn" outside London;[2] but I explained that you must be nearer to Whitehall.

As to Kurt Reiss it is for him to make the next move.[3] I have furnished him with the scenario. You say he accepts it; but he must tell *me*. Have you asked him for a lump sum, or will you be content with five per cent?

How can P[ascal] possibly blackmail you?[4] If what Elizabeth [Bergner] says is true you can blackmail him.

I am amused and delighted by the no-dinner cure.

G. Bernard Shaw

Tls.
    1. Shaw enclosed the following letter addressed to Trebitsch (Texas):

Is it at all possible for you to come to London for a week or so? You have done this for so many years past that the authorities can scarcely suspect you of being a suspicious stranger; and now that you have chosen and acquired French nationality you rank as a friendly alien.

Your business as the translator of all my works (I am the author of fifty plays, all well established on the continental stages) makes it necessary for us to confer personally at least once a year, especially now that correspondence is so slow and so difficult for the censor to pass in view of the fact that we have to discuss names of places and dates that might cover treasonable information. The war has mucked up our foreign affairs so hopelessly that I cannot disentangle them unless I can meet you. I am too old to go to you; so you must come to me if it is at all possible.

ps. You had better explain that our business concerns money coming from the Continent to England. In return I export nothing but my permission to perform my plays.

2. Pascal, now an English citizen, had bought a country home, the "old barn," in Buckinghamshire.

3. Nothing came of Reiss's plans for a Swiss-dialect film of *Pygmalion*.

4. Trebitsch's fears of blackmail are unexplained.

4 Whitehall Court S.W.

11th April 1940

My dear Trebitsch

I have just discovered Mayfair Court. It is not, as I thought, the Mayfair Hotel; and you must be careful to get the address right: it is Mayfair Court, Stratton Street, London, W.1.

It is not a hotel, but a great new pile of service flats (like Whitehall Court) in which, if they could find you a furnished apartment, you would be quite alone. It is nearer to us than the Dorchester. I know nothing about it. It is very fashionably situated, and therefore probably expensive; but you need not bother about that.

Remember that you will have to bring an electric torch in your pocket, as it is pitch dark in London at nine o'clock.

The events of Saturday[1] have not made London a pleasanter place for Germans, even when they are Jewish refugees; and though we shall be glad to see you I am not sure that I should advise you to come. And you may have some difficulty in getting the visa, as the regulations have been tightened up a good deal. So do not be too much disappointed if you find yourself unable to come after all. However, I daresay you will get through. You always do.

It is possible that Pascal might buy your claim on half the royalties from Germany on Barbara on the film of which he is at present at work. But as neither you nor I can get a penny out of Germany during the war you could not expect enough to make such a bargain worth while. A sale to anyone except Pascal is quite out of the question: it would complicate matters beyond endurance. And it would be irrevocable in any case.

Bear in mind too, that it will be difficult to take money out of England. I can get it neither in nor out. In fact the movement of money is hampered by the war just like the movement of persons. And the situation is much exacerbated by the latest news from the front. I doubt whether you will be able to do any business in England. If you do, it will be at a heavy disadvantage. I do not say this to discourage you from coming; but I am bound to let you know that the political crisis is all against it. At the same time I should like very much to have a talk with you; so do not imagine that if you get through you will not be welcome at Whitehall Court.

[G. Bernard Shaw]

Tl.

1. On Saturday, 6 April, a Norwegian vessel carrying English coal from Swansea to Oslo was torpedoed by a Nazi submarine without warning. Twelve lives were lost as the Nazi crew, so the English press reported, looked on. In response, the Allies decided to blockade the Baltic, but Hitler struck first by invading Norway and Denmark.

4 Whitehall Court S.W.
postmarked 18th April 1940

You need not bother about evening dress: the place [Dorchester Hotel] is full of men on leave in Khaki; and a black morning suit such as you ordinarily wear will be quite sufficient.

Tina need not worry about the black-out. If you stand on the kerb and keep calling Taxi, one will stop for you and miraculously carry you to your destination as if it were broad daylight. The drivers have developed eyes like owls': they can see in the dark.

I am telling the Dorchester to expect you on Tuesday.[1] Do not trouble to economize: you shall *not* share the cost.

GBS

Apcs.; Texas.
1. Trebitsch arrived the following week for what was his last visit to Shaw until the war ended.

Ayot St Lawrence. Welwyn
22nd May 1940

I have written to Colin to say that if, acting as *your* agent (not mine), he could obtain for your interest during the next five years a lump sum of, say, $50,000, and you consented to accept this, I would perhaps make my own royalties subject to a deduction of that sum and take my chance of there being anything left for me.[1] . . .

How did you find Tina on your return?

GBS

Apcs.; Texas.
1. Colin's plans for *Jitta* did not materialize.

[Ayot St Lawrence. Welwyn]
20th August 1940

My dear Trebitsch

I have to cut off the address from the top of this letter because my letters to Vichy[1] were returned after six weeks by the censors, who objected that they revealed the profound secret that I live in London and in Ayot, and might provoke a bombing raid on those places.

Your telegram got through; but it finds me powerless to help you. I am not allowed to send money abroad unless I can prove that it is in payment of a commercial debt. Charlotte tried to send £10 to a friend in Lausanne as a present, but permission was refused. Even this letter may reach you, or may not.

A certain Miss Traub, who has a sister in America named Lucy Tal,[2] claims to be a friend of yours, and says that your name has been added to a list of literary refugees for whom a fund has been started in Hollywood to pay their fares to America and support them for a year whilst they are looking for employment. But what could you do in America?

Here in England the laws against alien refugees have been carried to such an extreme that if you and Tina landed here you would both be arrested as you stepped off the gangway, and interned. That would be a way of providing for you; but it would not be up to your standard of comfort.

I should have written this letter several days ago; but two things delayed me. First, I tried to think of anything helpful to say to you or do for you, and could not. Second, your telegram got mislaid among Charlotte's papers. When we were in Ayot I concluded that it was in London, and in London after frantic searches I thought it must be in Ayot. And meanwhile I had not your address. Today it was found; and I hasten to write, though alas! I have nothing to say.

After the collapse of France things seemed very bad for us; but the escape from Dunkirk bucked us up; we were successful in the air; and now we believe that we have the upper hand on the Channel and are snapping our fingers at Hitler and his threat of invasion.[3]

We hope for better news of Tina, and any news at all of yourself.

G. Bernard Shaw

Als.

1. The Trebitsches had been living in Paris but managed to escape to Vichy before the German occupation, and from there went on to Switzerland, first to the Valmont Sanatorium at Glion and thence to the Dolder Hotel in Zurich.

2. Lucy Tal, the wife of Ernest Peter Tal, a Viennese publisher who had emigrated to America.

3. In May, Hitler's armies, striking through the Low Countries, entered France and pinned the Allied northern forces against the Channel. Some 340,000 Allied troops escaped through a massive sea effort at Dunkirk between 26 May and 4 June. On 14 June Paris fell, and France surrendered eight days later. In July, the French government, led by collaborationist Marshal Phillipe Pétain, moved to Vichy in unoccupied France. The Battle of Britain, launched by air on 13 August, succumbed to British air defenses, and the planned German invasion of England was broken off on 17 September.

4 Whitehall Court S.W.
9th October 1940

My dear Trebitsch

All your letters have been answered; but the war has knocked all the postal services to pieces: they are now only beginning to recover. I have just received a letter from Frank Harris's widow in Nice, in debt, and desperate. It is dated July 28!!! Even if it had arrived in time I could have done nothing for her, as I am not allowed to send money abroad except as part of some absolutely necessary commercial transaction. Possibly you may get all my letters before Christmas, except those which have been returned to me after 6 weeks delay because they had my address on them.

Meanwhile your friends in America have been busy trying to get your name on the list of an Emergency Fund for the assistance of literary refugees from the Nazi persecutions by paying their fares to Hollywood and finding posts as "writers" there for a year. A writer in Hollywood is an employee who adapts novels for the screen or supplies scraps of dialogue, or episodes (sequences is the Hollywood term) for films in the course of manufacture.

Miss Traub here in London and her sister Mrs Tal in America asked me to cable to certain ladies who were helping to get your name on the list, thanking them for their efforts on your behalf. Before I took any action news came that your name was on the list. Then came later news that the Emergency Committee had seen a picture of a sumptuous hotel at which you were living, and struck your name off on the assumption that you were not "destitute" but were in the most opulent circumstances. I am writing to Miss Traub to explain that these hotels which look so splendid on picture postcards are the cheapest places to live in nowadays, as even if the scheme would be quite unsuitable for you, it is better to leave no stone unturned in the present desperate circumstances. Your English is not Californian enough for Hollywood; but stories are always in demand there, and these you might be able to supply. But their taste in stories is hardly up to your standard.

Whilst all this was going on, messages were coming through from you from Vichy, from Glion, from Lausanne; and now it appears that you are back again at the Dolder in Zurich.[1]

That means, I hope, that Tina is well enough to leave Glion Valmont and resume her normal life.

We are well; but we are staying all the time at Ayot, as we can sleep here more quietly than in London, where every raid sets our guns thundering victoriously but noisily. Miss Patch is with us.

As the postal service is improving I am a little more hopeful of this reaching you than I should have been a month ago. Anyhow I must chance it.

G. Bernard Shaw

Tls.
    1. Shaw's letter of 20 August did not arrive in Glion until 7 October. By then the Trebitsches had moved to Lausanne and thence to Zurich, where they arrived on 15 September.

[Trebitsch to Shaw]

[Dolder Hotel.] Zurich
7th December 1940

My dear Shaw

I received today your letter dated October 9th! What a relief to read your well known writing and to hear that you are all remaining at Ayot. What would we give to join you there! Shall we see you again? This question is tormenting me so often. Please tell them in America with my love and thanks, that the wife of the Manager of the Dolder is an old friend of Tina being from Vienna (an austrian too.) We are here paying guests, but more guests than paying.....[1] besides we do not remain here so very long, living more in Lausanne which is a much cheaper town. Tina is still very ill, she has been cut twice by a surgeon. An infection was the reason after a cure of injections for the bad "neuritis" she acquired at Vichy.

It is of course a pity that the £650 are at the Westminsterbank in Paris![2] who could expect what happened?! If Tina will recover, I should like to go to Hollywood and earn money and make a living again in a new world. I have lot of friends there who would do their utmost to help me. Thanks for your excellent answer to Miss Traub, which she will forward to America, I hope.

It may become soon my last rescue, to be on the list of that Emergency fund. Please let me know at once your opinion and advice. Ought we to leave Europe??!! How long will last the war? after your idea? Elisabeth [Bergner] and Paul [Czinner] are in Los Angeles and they would do their utmost for me. Please invent soon an absolutely necessary commercial transaction between us.

I have wired to you from Lausanne a fortnight ago, asking dispatches from time to time, but I remained without answers. We should like to go to Niece, but what will happen there? that is the question. *Perhaps* I could get money there from the Westminsterbank? heaven knows. I have to wear my summer things. My wintercoat and cloths are in a trunk in *Paris*. We *cannot* get there. I should like to catch cold and die easyly, but this poor Tina, left quite alone......We are *not* among the french who lost their "naturalisation"!

Our love to both of you.

Yours ever
Siegf. Trebitsch

P.S. Please take the same kind of writing paper as I do; then I shall have your letters much quicker.[3]

Als.; Ayot.
 1. The ellipses in this letter are Trebitsch's.
 2. Shortly before the fall of France, Shaw had deposited £650 to Trebitsch's credit in the Paris branch of the Westminster Bank, but the funds were now blocked.
 3. Trebitsch used light airmail stationery.

[Ayot St Lawrence. Welwyn]
21st December 1940

My dear Trebitsch

Your letter dated the 15th November has just been delivered here, a month and three days after you posted it.[1] On such terms it is no use writing letters: I have given it up as hopeless. Besides, I have no consolation for you, and no news that you have not learnt from the papers. If I had, it would probably be unsafe to put it in writing. During war, one must be callous and laugh at destruction and ruin.

However, you must not let the newspapers and the German broadcasts persuade you that England is a desert of smoking ruins and decaying corpses. The extraordinary thing about this war is that though the weapons are more deadly and the bombardments more terrible than ever before, the number of people killed is extraordinarily small. The results are counted not in casualties but in prisoners. I drove for two hours yesterday through the northern environs of London without seeing a single house that was damaged. When the sirens sound the alarm nobody takes any notice until "extreme danger" is signalled; and even then the new shelters are sufficient for only a fraction of the people.

You know this little village where you used to stay with us until you found it too dull to be borne. Well, we have no shelters, no fire brigade, no protection of any kind; and on the 15th of last month we had a full dress bombardment: two bombs within a stone's throw of us and three more near enough to shake the house, not to mention a shower of incendiary shells. Yet not a window was broken nor a person hurt. At the highest rate of killing yet reached by the Blitzkrieg (now much reduced) it would take to exterminate all the inhabitants of England and Scotland 416 years! Where will der Führer be by that time? Where will the German Reich and the British Empire be?

So do not let this war make you too unhappy: you have lived through worse; and I am in greater danger of being run over by a motor car than of being bombed.

I am positively relieved to hear that Tina has only a bad leg. I pictured her with a bad heart. Charlotte is suffering torments from lumbago; but it is not getting worse and will pass.

I can say no more. This may never reach you. You may be in America by this time; but America too may soon be in the war.[2]

Auf wiedersehen
G. Bernard Shaw

Tls.

1. Shaw's letter, addressed to the Hotel Beau Site, Lausanne, did not arrive until 19 March, and was then forwarded to Trebitsch in Zurich.

2. American involvement in the European war increased after the fall of France, with aid to Britain and an undeclared naval war against German submarines.

Ayot St Lawrence. Welwyn
8th March 1941

Your letter dated 2nd Feb. has reached me today, the 8th March! Your telegram from The Winter Hotel [Gstaad] gave no address. I concluded that you were back at Nice, and telegraphed to you there; but the message was returned as undeliverable. I have answered your letters and telegrams again and again with no result. At last I have given up trying to correspond with the continent. An urgent letter from Frank Harris's widow took months to reach me too late. I wrote to Mrs Julius Bab and had my letter returned to me three months later without explanation. I have no hope of your getting this card. I dont know where Gstaad is. All is well with us, though Charlotte has been very ill and has not quite recovered.

G.B.S.

Apcs.

Ayot St Lawrence. Welwyn
2nd April 1941

Your letter from Montreux, dated the 15th February, has just reached me, having taken 44 days in transit.

Meanwhile your letter from Gstaad has arrived and been answered; but it is evident from your letters that my replies are never delivered.

Perhaps they will be when we are both dead.

I have no hope of this reaching you; but I send it so as to be able to assure you that *all* your communications have been acknowledged; and that my silence is only apparent.

At least I know that you are alive.

G. Bernard Shaw [1]

Apcs.; Ayot.

1. This card was returned undelivered.

Ayot St Lawrence. Welwyn
24th April 1941

My dear Trebitsch

At last letters are getting through with some regularity. Your last but two has just reached me *after* your last. The prisoners of war on both sides suffered so much from not getting their letters from home that the belligerents had to put their heads together to improve matters; and now letters marked Air Mail with a fivepenny stamp are getting through in a few weeks with some degree of certainty.[1]

I cannot possibly get a visa for you. I have no relations at the Foreign Office that would enable me to use private influence; but there are plenty of people there and elsewhere to whom I am known simply as a Communist and a propagandist of all sorts of sedition. You say that I know all they might ask in the way of dates etc etc; but I know absolutely nothing except your name, profession, and present address.

You must apply in person for a visa from the American Consul in Lausanne, and find out there how you are to get to America if the visa is granted, and what other visas you will need. If there are any others you must get them from the Consuls of the countries concerned in Lausanne. Your notion that my notoriety gives me a pull with the authorities in London and New York is wildly mistaken. It has just the opposite effect.

I do not see how you would be safer in California than in Switzerland; and in some respects, unless you have German connections there, your situation would be more difficult.

So far, the Barbara film promises to be as great a success as the Pygmalion.[2] If so, I shall be quite ruined, as the royalties will put me again in the millionaire class, which means that out of every pound I receive I shall only have about eighteen pence to live on after paying my war taxes.[3] If it goes to Germany there are several new scenes to be translated; but until the war is over I have no control, nor have you.

Here in Ayot your room is occupied by Miss Patch. I have not been in London since last September: nobody sleeps there now if they can possibly keep away.

I cannot imagine how you and Tina live. I almost believe Pascal's assurances that you have vast private means.

I have heard nothing about The Chocolate Soldier. I shall cable my American lawyer to warn Hollywood that I will stop any such film until Pascal has produced Arms & The Man.[4]

always yours
G. Bernard Shaw

Tls.

1. Airmail from England was routed through Lisbon and from there proceeded by surface transport.

2. Despite the war and bombings, Pascal completed filming *Major Barbara*, which he produced and directed. The film, starring Wendy Hiller, Rex Harrison, and Robert Morley, had its premiere away from beleaguered London in Nassau on 20 March and opened at the Odeon Theatre in London on 7 April. Neither critics nor audiences took to *Major Barbara* as they had to *Pygmalion*, and box office returns were disappointing.

3. Shaw had invested in *Barbara* and lost on the venture, but his fears that large royalties would ruin him through taxes were illusory. The English tax system imposed higher rates on *successive* portions of one's gross income, so the last segment of a very high income could be taxed at 19/6 in the £, but not, as Shaw stubbornly believed, one's total income.

4. M.G.M. had announced its intentions to film *Chocolate Soldier*.

Ayot St Lawrence. Welwyn

29th May 1941

My dear Trebitsch

Your letter from Zurich, dated the 9th, has just reached me here on the 28th.

At last I have provoked you to tell me how you have managed to live all this time. All I knew was that you had lost everything and that the money you had from me was locked up in the Westminster Bank in Paris: in short, that you were utterly without resources of any kind. Yet you were living in hotels and Tina in sanatoria representing on their picture postcards as palatial, and travelling between Lausanne and Zurich like an opulent tourist.[1] Charlotte and I wondered how you did it; but all we learnt from your letters was that you were, as we supposed, penniless. Even now, when, by playing off Pascal's joke on you, I have extorted from you the news that some bank is paying you a small income, you give me no explanation of this [un]accountable fact.

However, the fact is a fact, and relieves my anxiety for the moment; though whether your notion of a "small" income is £5 or £5000, I do not know. Anyhow, I assume that we were right here in assuming that you must be sorely in need of money. But that does not help, because I cannot send you any. I am not allowed to send money abroad, not even to Ireland or America. And I havent any to send. On the 30th June I have to find £8000 to pay to the British Government as the 2nd instalment of my taxes for 1940; and I have not half that sum in the bank. I have four destitute relatives to support, 5 employees to maintain, and two empty houses, bombed and uninhabitable, to pay rent and rates for. I shall not starve; but I have not a penny to spare: nine tenths of what I get goes in war taxation. I tell you this, depressing as it is for you, because you evidently think that I am rolling in money.

There is no harm in your having an American visa; but it would be madness for you to go there now. America is now practically at war with both Vichy and Berlin: your Czechoslovakian passport is now better than your French one. Switzerland is your sole neutral refuge. You have friends there, and must hold on there for the present.

[Pascal's film] Barbara is no use to you until the war ends and it can be translated and produced in Germany. The Chocolate Soldier production is cancelled. Pascal has succeeded in stopping it. There is no immediate hope in any of the old directions. The rich are bled white: it is the poor who are flourishing, with wages high and no [un]employment. As to the war, cities are being bombed and battleships sunk leaving both sides not a step nearer a decision: one almost hopes that the war will die of its own absurdity before America develops its full power or Russia takes a hand, when the game will be up.

But I must stop; for I have nothing to tell you that you have not already learnt from the newspapers except these dismal money matters, which I am ashamed to plague you with, and would not mention were it not that you think I possess resources and powers which are quite imaginary.

It may amuse you a little to reproach me with my apparent indifference to your troubles: if so, do it to your heart's content: it seems to be the only service I can do you.

Can you get any journalistic work to do in Switzerland? Or write a book about your adventures?[2]

Although I do not think it would be wise for you to go to America I should not oppose it on Tina's account; for I am not at all sure that the voyage and change might not renew your youth and cure all her ills.

always yours
G. Bernard Shaw

Tls.; postscripts omitted.
1. The Trebitsches were living at the luxurious Dolder Hotel in Zurich, but evidently let Shaw believe that they were based more modestly in Lausanne, at the Hotel Beau Site. For the next two years, Shaw addressed his letters to Lausanne, where they were forwarded to Zurich.
2. Trebitsch did attempt to write for Swiss newspapers and to join the literary life of Zurich, but he was dismayed by being regarded as "Shaw's translator," not as an independent author.

Ayot St Lawrence. Welwyn
16th July 1941

My dear Trebitsch

I cannot understand this Chocolate Soldier business. You have no claim on the English version. Neither of us can authorize a German film because that would be trading with the enemy. But if an Anglo-American film were made, there may be enough German picture theatres in the U.S.A. to make it profitable to "dub" a German translation on the film. Is it for this that you are offered $30,000?[1] If so, you will have to establish your right not only to translate Arms and the Man but Jacobssohn's travesty of it and the American translation of that travesty. This might be disputed. The cost of a lawsuit, prohibitive for you, is the merest trifle in production costs totalling up to perhaps 1¼ million dollars.

Koretz[2] has just written to me to say that Molnar[3] has been asked to provide a new libretto. If he does so we are both completely sidetracked.

Tell me as exactly as you can the legal nature of your claim for the $30,000, and what agreement you hold obliging the producers to pay it to you in the event of my consenting to a filming of the Chocolate Soldier as it stands at present. You have never told me anything about it. And I am obliged not to allow the C.S. to be filmed until Arms and the Man has been filmed and fully exploited.

Naturally it would be the greatest relief to me if you could by hook or by crook get hold of a sum that would enable you and Tina to live in America for the duration of the war; but I have too much experience of American "tall talk" about large sums of money to believe in anything but a cast iron legal document.

I have asked Koretz whether he can explain the situation to me; but it will be six weeks at least before I can have any reply from him. He enquires after you in a very friendly manner. His address for the moment is 344 South Peck Drive, Hollywood, California.

The war may now end sooner than seemed possible before Adolf, believing that Uncle Joe was waiting to attack him when he was fully engaged with Britain and America, began his desperate attempt to crush the U.S.S.R. first.[4] You may be back in Hietzing before you buy your passage to California.

G. Bernard Shaw

Tls.

1. M.G.M. had offered Trebitsch $30,000 to translate the scenario of *Chocolate Soldier* if he could get Shaw to allow the film.

2. Paul Koretz, who had emigrated to America, was now counsel to Louis B. Mayer of M.G.M.

3. Ferenc Molnar (1878–1952), the popular Hungarian playwright. He was to adapt his comedy *The Guardsman* into a libretto for Straus's score to *Soldier*.

4. On 22 June 1941, Hitler launched Operation Barbarossa against the Soviet Union. (Originally scheduled for 15 May, it had been postponed by the invasion of Yugoslavia in April.) Shaw greeted the news as "too good to be true" for the Allies and doomed to failure (*News Chronicle; New York Times*, 23 June).

Cliveden. Taplow until the 30th

17th August 1941

My dear Trebitsch

Your letter dated my birthday [26 July] and full of reproaches, reached me today, having taken 22 days in transit.

You think now that in the old days I wrote to you every week. The truth is that you were always complaining that I did not answer your letters, exactly as you are complaining now. But then I did often leave you unanswered for months, whereas I now answer every letter promptly. Only, you expect the answer in two days. It arrives—when it arrives at all—in three weeks, during which you curse me every morning for my neglect.

The worst of it is that though I have many things to say to you I may not write them, as the Censors would probably object. All I can say is that the end of the war seems much nearer than it did, and that it will be an end favorable to you personally.

The "cruel change" which you accuse me of is real enough: it is the change from the vigor of my prime to the callousness and impotence of old age. Has it not yet occurred to you that I am now a very old man? It is amazing how people who have read in the newspapers that I am 85 write to me asking me to do things impossible to anyone over 40. You are just as thoughtless as they are.

I know your difficulties and have thought a good deal about them; but as to compassion! what can you expect from an octogenarian with the world falling into ruins round him?

However, keep on reproaching me. It relieves your feelings and amuses me. *All* your letters have been and shall be answered. Our best regards to Tina.

G. Bernard Shaw

Als.

Cliveden. Taplow
25th August 1941

My dear Trebitsch

Disregard this address: we return home on the 30th. Your letter dated the 1st reached me today.

I have already explained The Chocolate Soldier business to you; but as my letters may miscarry I will explain it again.

It is out of my power to license the screening of The C.S. £100,000 ($500,000) has been raised for the filming of Arms & The Man on my pledge that I will not allow the C.S. to be filmed, or its title used until the vogue of the Arms film is exhausted. The expected profit is about £200,000 at least, of which I should take £20,000.

A C.S. film would kill this enterprise stone dead. Yet you think it would not cost me a penny!

And no capitalist would ever again risk a farthing on the strength of my pledged word and my common sense.

I have no doubt that Metro-Goldwyn would pay you or anyone else $30,000 to obtain my consent. Such a transaction would be ruinous to me and disgraceful to you.

However, my information from Pascal is that the C.S. music, in which I have no part, is now being fitted to Molnar's play, and that there is no longer any question of Jacobsohn's travesty. I therefore repeat all this only to convince you—if that is possible—that I have not heartlessly robbed you of your last thaler for the mere fun of injuring you to the extent of refusing to save your life.

I do not understand the situation as to your French naturalization. You say its days are numbered; but how? Was it a temporary naturalization only, or has Vichy cancelled it?[1]

If you will send me the necessary documents I can of course ask Masaryk[2] for a passport from the Cz-sl Government in London, which is not really a Government *in esse*; and probably both the British & American Governments would treat it as valid. But it would not secure your entry to the U.S.A. without a minimum of capital and a place in the quota. Still, if they admitted Julius Bab they might admit you.

But alas! Bab's friends are appealing to me to save him from destitution while he writes a History of Acting. They dont know that I should not be allowed to send money to America for such a purpose even if the war taxation left me any to send.

Tina need not regret my photograph: I can send her a dozen to replace it when Hietzing is in a federated State of the Reich and the present holder of my bust admiring it in St Helena.[3]

In my early days I was always anxious and unhappy when I had only sixpence in my pocket; but when the 6[d] was gone and I had nothing, my spirits went up at once.

Dont torment yourself with imagining that I am less friendly than when you were prosperous. I am not. But in the face of this war only a heart as hard as the nether millstone can survive.

G. Bernard Shaw

Als.

1. The French regime in Vichy collaborated with the German occupation in rounding up stateless Jews, and there was talk of relieving recently naturalized French Jews of their citizenship.

2. Jan Masaryk (1886–1948), Czechoslovak diplomat, now vice-premier of the Provisional Czech Government in exile. He knew both Shaw and Trebitsch.

3. Apparently, through his devoted housekeepers, who carried items abroad, Trebitsch had managed to get his copy of the Rodin bust out of Hietzing and into safekeeping in Paris, where he retrieved it after the war.

Ayot St Lawrence. Welwyn
16th September 1941

. . . You persist in treating me as a stingy millionaire just as Pascal treats you, though at present when I earn a pound the tax collector leaves me only sixpence to live on.[1]

The war has driven everyone mad.

Another brother gone![2] Have you any left? "In deepest misery" too! Schade! [Pity!]

Everybody's Political What's What is nearly finished.[3] I hope to get it published by the end of the year.

Pardon my callousness.

GBS

Apcs.

1. Shaw's persistent claim that the more he earned the less he retained was wrong (see n. 3, 24 April 1941).

2. Trebitsch's brother Heinrich died on 18 August in Nice.

3. Shaw's *Everybody's Political What's What?* continued to be plagued with difficulties and was not finished that year.

Ayot St Lawrence. Welwyn
27th October 1941

My dear Trebitsch

Koretz will find it hard to get any grip on The Chocolate Soldier. My people are objecting to the use of that title for the new version on the ground that though there is no copyright title as such, the dialogue of a play must not be quoted in a way likely to mislead the public as to the authorship. If my people succeed in this, the title will not be used and so your claim falls

Siegfried Trebitsch, 1942.

to the ground.[1] If they fail you fail too. And your title was Helden, which has not been borrowed. However, as the Hollywood people have no brains it is just possible that Koretz may frighten them into paying something for nothing.

I must not take refuge in Switzerland, as the great G.B.S. could not decently join the taxdodgers. I must face the music here.

The new book will not be ready for translation for perhaps a couple of months; and I doubt whether it would be of any use in Germany. It is concerned altogether with British politics. You would find it very tedious to translate and in some places it would hardly be intelligible. Only a few chapters would be interesting to Germans; and these it might not be easy to get published under Nazi rule. If only I could finish it and get to work on a new play then I could give you something interesting and hopeful to do, which I greatly desire.

Your stepbrother [Oscar Trebitsch] need not despair. Neither need you. The dream that began with Fichte[2] in 1800 will not be realized. When Bismarck's pro-Russian policy was abandoned in 1890, and the dream was left to the Allerhöchst and the Führer, the glories of 1870 became impossible. The future is to the dream of Karl Marx.

always yours
G. Bernard Shaw

Tls.
1. Despite Shaw's objections, M.G.M. released the Straus-Molnar operetta as *The Chocolate Soldier*.
2. Johann Fichte (1762–1814), German philosopher. Like the later Nazis, he inclined toward a nationalistic form of state socialism and called for a united and armed Germany to lead the world.

[Ayot St Lawrence. Welwyn]
7th January 1942

I WRITE BUT MY LETTERS DO NOT REACH YOU WE ARE WELL AND YOUR PEN SUBSCRIPTION[1] IS PAID WE DO NOT FORGET YOU THE WAR WILL NOT LAST FOR EVER COURAGE COURAGE   SHAW

Telegram.
1. International P.E.N. During the war and thereafter, Shaw paid Trebitsch's dues to the London headquarters.

England[1]
19th February 1942
My dear Trebitsch

Your letter dated the 25th January arrived on the 14th February. And a postcard which I sent to you on the 2nd April last, addressed to a hotel at Montreux, has just been returned to me, though it was passed by the censor. In the face of such dates you must not blame me when you get no reply to your letters. The replies are on the way, and will arrive perhaps when the war is over.

Do not torment yourself with the delusion that you should have remained in England. You would have been interned in a concentration camp in the Isle of Man; and though you would have been released after some months your situation would have been much more difficult than it is in Switzerland even if you had escaped the Blitz. On the whole you are better off in Lausanne[2] than you would be in London.

I have done all I could to obtain a permit to send you £100 through United Artists or through my bankers. I pleaded that you had been the means of transferring a good deal of money from Germany to England; that you were not a Nazi but a Jewish refugee; that an exception should be made in your favor etc etc; but it was all in vain: the Treasury was obdurate and maintained that any action which would have the effect of transferring money to you would be against the defence regulations.

In any case I could do very little; for my own financial situation is difficult enough, as you may judge from the fact that when the enormous success of [the] Pygmalion film put £29,000 into my pocket, the Chancellor of the Exchequer took £50,000 out of it. Another such "success" and I shall be poorer than you are.[3]

As to The Chocolate Soldier my lawyer maintained that though there is no copyright in titles yet the three words were a plagiarism of the text of Arms and the Man. But it was impossible to claim that your title "Helden" or the words "praliné Soldat" had been used in the English version. I could not in any case have started an expensive and very doubtful lawsuit on such a point. Finally they did what I myself advised them to do. They took an entirely different and very good comedy by Molnar as their libretto, and made the hero and heroine sing Oscar Strauss's musical numbers, in which I have no copyright whatever.[4] This new version has been performed in London; and not one of the press notices said a word about Arms and the Man. So the affair is closed as far as I am concerned. It is still possible that the old German version may be revived; and in that case, when the war is over, you could claim a royalty; but there is no present help nor much future promise in this. I never believed that you could get anything out of the business. The only way I could have helped you in it was by consenting to the filming of the old version on condition that the bribe they offered you to persuade me was paid to you; but I was pledged to Pascal not to allow such a filming, and anyhow it would not have been a decent transaction.

I could say much more; but the uncertainty of this ever reaching you and the pressure on my writing time on my new book and other matters obliges me to stop. Your miseries, which I dare not think about, may end sooner than we expect. If they dont, we shall be companions in misfortune.

always yours
G. Bernard Shaw

Tls.

1. Shaw omits his Ayot address to avoid possible censorship.
2. As noted, Shaw believed that the Trebitsches were in Lausanne, although they were in Zurich.
3. Shaw's total taxable income for the period involved (1938–39, 1939–40) exceeded £66,000, however.

4. The M.G.M. film of the Straus-Molnar operetta, released as *The Chocolate Soldier*, starred Risë Stevens and Nelson Eddy.

[Ayot St Lawrence. Welwyn]
8th August 1942

My dear Trebitsch

I am afraid nothing can be done. I have written to Kantorowitz asking whether he can suggest any step I can take beyond authorizing him to collect all fees due to me for plays and books in the German language; but your authorization is as good as mine: that is to say no good at all. If you cannot get money from me in England, nor from your bankers in France, what chance is there of getting it from Berlin?

An unfortunate lady at your hotel, Mrs Leonie Plesch,[1] writes to me to help her, evidently in the belief that I have unlimited power and political influence in London. I have none: my intervention would do her more harm than good. Do try to make her understand this. Even you seem to think that I must be in favor as a notorious Red now that London is in league with Moscow. Sancta simplicitas!!! Do you really believe that Churchill is now a Bolshevist or Stalin a British Imperialist? The lady gives me a string of names of friends of hers in London any of whom could help her—if help were possible—better than I can. Try to make her understand this. She says you are one of her best friends; so perhaps she will believe you.

I cannot bring myself to write these heartbreaking letters—even to you— to say that I can do nothing. It is better to work away at my book, and at my business affairs, and leave myself no time to attend to the endless misfortunes brought by the war on people whom I know, and people whom I dont know (like Mrs Arpad Plesch) but who in desperation appeal to me as if my reputation made me a sort of political and financial Providence.

Charlotte is still an invalid; and the latest medical examination, a very thorough one, establishes the fact that she is incurable,[2] though her life is not in immediate danger except in so far as both our lives at our age (we are both 86) are in daily danger and cannot in the course of nature last much longer.

My financial condition is appalling. For the first time in my life I have had to overdraw my bank account. The overdraft runs to four figures. People think I am a millionaire, forgetting that millionaires are now taxed 95% in income tax and surtax alone, to say nothing of all the other imposts.

You see, when I write to you I have nothing to say except what will depress you more than my silence, adding my troubles to your own. Be thankful when I do not write: it is the kindest thing I can do for you.

Impossible to discuss politics: our letters would be censored.

However, the war cannot last for ever.

Our love to Tina. Is she getting used to living on the brink of abyss? After all, people live on the slope of Vesuvius or Etna as if they were living at Hietzing. The volcanos are safer nowadays.

always yours
G. Bernard Shaw

PS I omit my address, as it may be objected to by the censors. But a letter addressed George Bernard Shaw, Wellknown author, England, will reach me. It is often used by Americans.

Als.

1. Mrs. Leonie Plesch, wife of Arpad Plesch (1889–1974), Hungarian-born financier and lawyer, who had gone into exile.

2. Charlotte Shaw's chronic lumbago had been diagnosed as osteitis deformans, the result of an accident in her teens.

Ayot St Lawrence. Welwyn
28th September 1942

My dear Trebitsch

My correspondence with the authorities here has come to an end, without, I fear, any result. They have been attentive and sympathetic; but nothing has come of it but the letter to Fischer which has just been approved and sent to you by the Board of Trade. Fischer cannot act on it without the sanction of the German Exchange Control; and there is little hope of that sanction being granted. You can but try. . . .

As to your hotel bill, my guarantee would be worthless.[1] I have just received from the Inland Revenue a demand for £10,000 surtax. I have at the bank £1100. How can I honestly guarantee your subsistence, or even that of my servants and destitute relatives under such circumstances, to say nothing of my age, which makes my death a daily possibility? I do not understand your difficulty about giving Dolder a cheque on the Westminster Bank. The money is there to your credit, is it not? Of course you would tell Dolder that the cheque would not be paid. He would lodge it in his Swiss bank. The Swiss bank would present the cheque to the Westminster. The Westminster would return it unpaid with an explanation that payment was forbidden by the German authorities. But this explanation would prove to Dolder that the money was there to your credit and that the cheque would become valid when the war was over. It could be held by him as proof of the debt and security for its payment; for if there were no funds to meet it he could prosecute you for the serious crime of trying to pass a worthless cheque. This would give him an effective hold on you, whereas on me his hold would be very insecure and cost more to enforce than it was worth, if indeed he could enforce it at all. At all events you might offer him the cheque as the best you could do for him.

You had better let Kanto[rowitz] know what I have done. It is possible that the German Exchange Control might sanction payment to a neutral Swiss agent which they would refuse to you. You must formally authorize him to act as your agent. I have formally authorized him to act as mine and undertaken to recognize his receipts as if they were signed by myself.

I am afraid I can do no more, *advienne que pourra* [come what may]! I strongly deprecate veronal: it is much wiser to die of starvation, because somehow one *doesnt*. We shall both survive this bloody business.

always yours
G. Bernard Shaw

Tls.

1. Trebitsch, pleading desperation, asked Shaw to guarantee his debt to the Dolder Hotel for the duration of the war. Shaw, as noted, had lodged £650 to Trebitsch's credit in Paris through the Westminster Bank. Shaw now attempted through the British Foreign Office to have his German royalties, collected by S. Fischer (Suhrkamp), released to Kantorowitz, his neutral Swiss agent, and credited to Trebitsch as a French citizen. On 10 November, Shaw wrote to R. D. Blumenfeld of the *Daily Express*, who had met Trebitsch some years earlier (Texas):

Trebitsch and his wife are still in Lausanne at the Hotel Beau Site.

They are in desperate circumstances, all the worse because T. has not the faintest notion of how people with small incomes live. And he has no income at all. The last of his wife's jewels are now sold. He has £600 to his credit at the Westminster Bank; but . . . he cannot touch it. I have exhausted every dodge to help him . . . but without success; and I cannot make him understand the difficulty.

His first step, which was to become naturalized in France, was only an additional complication. His project of going to America came to nothing. He has laid in a store of veronal to poison himself and Frau Trebitsch; but even that does not come off.

I give him up: I can do no more.

Actually, the Trebitsches were in Zurich, and Tina retained some jewels.

Ayot St Lawrence. Welwyn
5th October 1942

Shew this letter to Dolder.¹ It proves (a) that you have £650 sterling in the Westminster Bank, and (b) that it cannot be drawn out *even by you yourself* until the war is over.

GBS

Ans.

1. Shaw enclosed a letter from the manager of the Westminster Bank.

[Ayot St Lawrence. Welwyn]
15th November 1942

TRANSLATION RIGHT BELONGS TO PEARSON¹ NOT TO ME HE WILL NEGOTIATE ONLY WITH SWISS-GERMAN PUBLISHER YOU MUST INDUCE ONE TO BUY THE RIGHTS AND EMPLOY YOU TO TRANSLATE² STOP YOUR LETTERS HAVE BEEN RECEIVED AND ACTED ON HAVE YOU RECEIVED MINE BERNARD SHAW

Telegram.

1. Hesketh Pearson's biography *Bernard Shaw: His Life and Personality* (American title, *G.B.S.: A Full Length Portrait*) had recently appeared.

2. No publisher was found for a German translation.

Ayot St Lawrence. Welwyn
1st December 1942

My dear Princess Tina

I have delayed answering your letter in the hope that I might have some good news for you; but alas! all the steps I have taken have led nowhere. I have done everything possible only to be met with polite regrets that nothing can be done. At last, in desperation, I have written to the British

Minister in Bern to ask him whether he can suggest any way in which the blockade can be pierced. No reply yet. Letters take so long to reach their destination that I never know what letter of mine Siegfried is answering.

The worst of it is that as Siegfried is no diplomatist everything I do seems wrong to him. He thinks that I can get money due to myself from Berlin, but that the mention of his name would be fatal. The case is just the reverse. I am "the enemy"; and payment to me is out of the question. Our Foreign Office could not ask the German Exchange Control to sanction it or connive at it without being obliged to reciprocate in other cases; and this it cannot do. It suggested my trying the Board of Trade, which I did; but that broke down also.

I authorized Fischer to make all payments to Kantorowitz, and authorized Kanto to act as our agent; but nothing came of it. Neither of them answered my letters.

Meanwhile Siegfried is legally a Frenchman no longer at war with Germany; and as he was living in a neutral country Fischer could send him money without "trading with the enemy." Unfortunately Siegfried is a non-Aryan. Still, he is legally a Frenchman; and it was at least worth trying whether the German Exchange Control would raise that objection. Siegfried was *frantic* because his name was mentioned; but how could it be concealed? I could not go to the Foreign Office and the Board of Trade without giving our names. I could not authorize Fischer and Kanto anonymously. Our names are as well known as those of Hitler and Churchill. Secrecy was utterly impossible. Far from vainly trying to escape from his reputation and mine, he ought to take every opportunity of shouting his grievances to the four corners of heaven and making himself the most famous victim of tyranny in Europe.

Now as to the Westminster Bank. Siegfried will have it that his £600 has been confiscated. But what evidence has he of this? The Bank closed its Paris branch when the Germans came in, and transferred the credits in its books to its London head quarters. I wrote to the manager of the branch at which I keep my own account, and sent his reply to Siegfried. Whether it has yet reached him I do not know; but it said nothing about confiscation: it said only that the money could not be touched during the war. Still, the money is there and can presumably be touched when the war is over. Siegfried can at least shew the manager's letter to Dolder to prove to him that he has some real security for the debt. Siegfried has not told me what the amount of that debt now is: he only asks me to guarantee "some of it." But I cannot guarantee anything. On the 31st of December I have to pay £12,000 to the Exchequer; but I have not half that sum in the Bank to pay it with. Siegfried treats me as a rich man. I was fairly rich before the war; but now—however, I must not bother you with my money troubles: you have too many of your own.

Charlotte, I am sorry to say, is painfully but not dangerously ill, and the doctors can do nothing for her. She sends her kindest regards. We are both terribly old: our united ages are 172!

always affectionately yours
G. Bernard Shaw

Tls.

Ayot St Lawrence. [Welwyn]
29th April 1943

My dear Trebitsch

I am certainly a bad correspondent; but I find that if I write private letters my work on my book stops. And I hate writing to say that I have nothing to say, and that all my attempts to help you have failed.

After trying the Treasury and the Foreign Office in vain I finally wrote to the British Minister in Bern. He was very polite and sympathetic; but he said that he must abide by the decision of the Foreign Office, which was that it could not ask the Exchange Control (the German one) to do you a favor without incurring an obligation to grant similar favors to German subjects; and this it must not do. I asked the Bern man whether he could suggest any means of sending you money. He replied that he could not: it is not possible. He said too that he had tried to get into communication with you at the address I gave him (the Lausanne one) but that you were not there.

This Minister has since been transferred to another post; and his successor knows nothing about us.

If the war ends well for the Allies it is possible that you may recover some of your Austrian property; [1] and as far as I can make out you still have your money locked up in the Westminster Bank, though it is not now touchable. I sent you the manager's letter bearing this construction, as it should help you to obtain credit from Dolder. Whether you received it or not I do not know: the postal arrangements are hopeless. Our letters cross each other so often that I never know which letter I am answering nor whether you have received my last one.

Pascal has just returned to England after two years in America and nothing done. [2] I do not understand what you are claiming from United Artists. If anything is due to you it can be collected far more easily by Kantorovich than by me, as I am a belligerent and he a neutral. I have no relations with U.A., and no means of influencing them. I have given K the fullest authorization to get anything he can for you. What he cannot do, still less can I do. My direct interference makes matters worse.

You will see by the enclosed press cutting that Pearson's book is banned in Germany. I will make a final effort to have a copy sent to you by my London bookseller; but I doubt whether it will get through.

I am in all sorts of difficulties myself; but as your own are quite enough for you to bear I will not plague you with them.

You see, I have nothing cheerful to tell you; and yet you wonder that I do not write oftener. I think of you much too often; for there is so much misery and horror in the world today that only by forgetting it can we keep sane. The war would be unbearable if it were not so interesting that we cannot help being curious to see how it will end. Meanwhile we must grin and bear it.

as ever

G. Bernard Shaw

Miss Patch is away on her Easter holiday; so I have had to type this myself. Everything I do now is full of blunders.

Tls.

1. A turning point in the war had occurred the previous November with the Allied breakthrough in North Africa and the decisive Soviet counteroffensive at Stalingrad, which forced the surrender of the German Sixth Army in February and raised hopes for Allied victory.

2. Pascal, because of the war situation, turned to Hollywood to finance his next film, but Shaw's refusal to allow changes in his scenarios led to a break in negotiations, and Pascal returned to England.

Ayot St Lawrence. Welwyn

21st July 1943

My dear Trebitsch

Do not torment yourself because Pearson's book is not entitled *Shaw in Germany* with Siegfried Trebitsch as its hero. Pearson, an English author writing for British readers, knows nothing of the adventures of my works on the Continent. Trebitsch in Germany, Hugo Vallentin in Sweden, Hamon in France, Agresti in Italy, Hevesi in Hungary, Brouta in Spain, mean nothing to him.[1] If he had known all about them and done justice to them in his book there would have been no room left for me, and nobody in England or America would have read it. There is only one person living who could write *Shaw in Germany* and that person is yourself. I could not write it because except for Fischer's accounts, which I seldom looked at, and for our talks during your visits and your letters, I know very little more than Pearson of what actually passed. I know what I owe to you in the lump, but not in biographical detail.

I did not plan Pearson's book. He sent it to me when it was written; and I corrected it as to the facts and filled in his narrative to some extent: that was all.[2] I could not advise him to spoil it as Goethe spoilt his Dichtung und Wahrheit by writing at great length about everyone except himself.

You still think that you should have settled in England for the duration of the war.[3] I did not think so, and do not now think so. To begin with, you would not have been allowed to stay. If you had been allowed you would have probably been interned. In going to a neutral country where German is spoken you made the best choice. All my correspondence about the advisability of your going to America came to nothing.

In describing you as an Austrian, Pearson has done you a service. Possibly I suggested it. Germans are not popular just now in England; but Austrians are sympathized with as victims of Nazi aggression.

In short, dear Trebitsch, your letter is all nonsense: you have much to suffer and complain of; but blame the war, not me, for it.

Pearson's book is having an enormous sale: why dont you volunteer for the German translation?

G. Bernard Shaw

You give me no address. As the postmark is Zürich, I address this to the Hotel Dolder.

Tls.

1. Of Shaw's translators, only Trebitsch is mentioned in Pearson's biography in connection with Shaw's service to his "Austrian translator" in adapting *Jitta*.

2. Since Pearson acknowledged ("Acknowledgments") the active collaboration of Shaw, Trebitsch was offended by his virtual omission from the book.

3. Trebitsch was also unhappy with his literary reception in Switzerland. (See letter of Herman Ould to Trebitsch, 28 March 1943; P.E.N., London.)

Ayot St Lawrence. Welwyn
8th September 1944

My dear Trebitsch

At last a letter from you dated the 8th August. Not hearing from you for so long I was getting anxious about you. I rejoice to see by your handwriting and by your Empfindung that you are in better health and spirits than you were before you got used to exile and poverty. It looks as if you will soon be back in Hietzing[1] unless, like so many refugees, you prefer to stay where you are for the rest of your life. Life in Zürich must be easier than it will be in Wien for a long time to come.

As Bermann has never been of any use to us I am quite in favor of establishing Amstutz and Kantorowitz as our publishers and agents;[2] but have you considered the possibility of the old firm re-establishing itself in Berlin? In that case they would expect our support. But I think they are too old to begin again.

I am now on the best of terms with Arthur Rank, the British film monopolist, magnate, and millionaire.[3] The Pygmalion film you mention is a reissue of the old one under a new agreement with Rank's chief film financing company which restricts his licence to the English language and obliges him to use your version if he extends his operations to the German language. You do not say in your letter whether the film was exhibited in English, or "dubbed" with German explanations, or in a completely German version. If no German words are spoken or dubbed, then you have no claim. But if any of the dialogue has been translated and quoted Kantorowitz should write to the secretary of General Cinema Finance Corporation Limited, 53 New Broad Street, London, E.C.2. and make a claim on your behalf for royalty or compensation. He must be careful not to mention Pascal, as Pascal under the new agreement is a regisseur pure and simple: he has nothing to do with the financial side of the affair.

The new agreement came into operation at the beginning of this year. Before that date the Pascal Film Company was responsible; but as it is now extinct, and Pascal was not personally responsible for its debts, it would be waste of time to attempt to recover anything from it.

My new book called Everybody's Political What's What will be published on the 15th September, a week hence. As it is not *belles lettres*, but a treatise on political economy like The Intelligent Woman's Guide, you may not care to translate it, partly because political economy is not your subject, and partly because, as it deals almost entirely with English institutions and affairs, you might not be able to find a publisher for it.[4]

Genug [enough] about business. I am pretty well: in fact my health has improved since my wife's death;[5] but in my 89th year I am no longer the Shaw you knew. I am very old, and have so much business to get through to leave my estate and Charlotte's in a settled and solvent state, and so many changes to make in my household,[6] that I have had no time for any literary work except occasional articles on the war and a long postscript to a new edition of Back To Methuselah.[7] My windows have been blown in and some doors and walls damaged (I must not say where or when) but I have not been hurt.

Give my love to Tina. She also must now be so accustomed to your changed way of life that she may not want to go back.[8] Capitalist prosperity is not so happy as it pretends to be.

G. Bernard Shaw

Tls.

1. Allied victory seemed assured. The relentless Russian offensive had swept from the Soviet Union through the Balkans and was poised to attack Germany itself. In the west, the Allies had opened a second front in June at Normandy and were racing toward Germany.

2. Relations with Bermann-Fischer were broken, and S. Fischer, Berlin—renamed by order of Goebbels the Suhrkamp Verlag—had been closed after Suhrkamp's political arrest in April 1944.

3. Pascal's new agreement with J. Arthur Rank (1888–1972), English producer and head of General Cinema Finance Corp., provided that Rank finance the next three Shaw films. *Caesar and Cleopatra*, the first of the planned films, was in production with Vivien Leigh and Claude Rains, directed by Pascal. Rank had served as distributor of Pascal's *Pygmalion*, which played in Switzerland with subtitles not supplied by Trebitsch.

4. The book eventually went to Amstutz und Herdeg, Zurich, and was translated (with Trebitsch's consent) by Franz Fein (*Politik für Jedermann*, 1945).

5. Charlotte Shaw had died the year before, on 12 September 1943.

6. Shaw's housekeeper and gardener had both recently retired.

7. *Back to Methuselah* was to appear in the Oxford "World's Classics" series.

8. Trebitsch at last provided Shaw with a Zurich address: Kurhausstrasse 65. Unknown to Shaw, the address was that of the Dolder Hotel, not a modest apartment.

Ayot St Lawrence. Welwyn
22nd February 1945

My dear Trebitsch

I am in the dark about these Swiss publishers. Two of them, Artemis[1] and Anstutz & Herder [Amstutz & Herdeg], claim to have contracts with you. I have assured Artemis that our old contract is still valid, and have received its reply thanking me. Anstutz & Herder have written to me for a portrait, which I have sent them. Neither of them has raised any difficulty as to your authority to deal with my works in the German language. What more do you want me to do?

Kantorowitz is authorized to collect all German theatre fees for us, as, being a neutral, he may "trade with the enemy," which I may not. But now you tell me that you have given this agency to A. G. Reis of Basel,[2] presumably also a Swiss. Apparently you have given Reis and Kanto the same job. How do you reconcile their interests?

I am sorry to be so bad a correspondent; but you must try to grasp the fact that I am on the verge of my 90th year, and that the settlement of Charlotte's affairs[3] and the need for leaving my own estate in order for my death, which in the course of nature cannot be far off, has overwhelmed me with a mass of business that would tax a man in the prime of life. I have not forgotten you and Tina in the least; you are very much on my mind at times; but whenever I want to write to you there are a dozen urgent businesses to be attended to besides my literary work, for which I have hardly any time, and at which I make many senile blunders.

So be patient and forgive; and write to me when you have time and feel disposed. Whether your letters are answered or not they are always welcome.

G.B.S.

Tls.; signature typed.

1. Trebitsch had contracted with Artemis Verlag, Zurich, for a new collected edition of Shaw's plays in German to include the unpublished *Genf* (*Geneva*) and *Der gute König Karl* (*King Charles*) and some previously omitted prefaces.

2. In February 1943, Trebitsch, in a vain attempt to get royalties out of Germany, transferred agent's rights from Suhrkamp (formerly S. Fischer, Berlin) to Reiss A.G. (meaning Inc., not Reiss's initials) of Basel, while retaining Kantorowitz for Switzerland.

3. Charlotte Shaw left a considerable fortune inherited from her parents, and there were many tasks involving death duties, sales of stocks, and administration of legacies.

Ayot St Lawrence. Welwyn
5th May 1945

My dear Trebitsch

This very important letter has just been found among my old papers. I am keeping it and sending you only this copy, as we had better not risk the loss of the original in transit.[1]

I cannot tell you whether I have received all your letters and telegrams because I do not know how many you have sent. Those that I have received I have answered. The only point that is not cleared up is your undertaking not to publish in Switzerland, apparently as a condition of your entry visa. Have you since naturalized as a Swiss citizen and thus cancelled the undertaking?[2]

I fear we must make up our minds not to meet again; for I am too old to be recognizable, and you cannot afford the journey. You have not yet learnt how to live on less than £1,000,000 a year, and would go straight to the most expensive hotel in Park Lane, not knowing that there are cheaper places quite as comfortable.

I gather from your last telegram that there is a letter from you on the way; but it has not yet reached me.

Alas for Vienna![3] Love to Tina.

G. Bernard Shaw

Tls.

1. Shaw enclosed Suhrkamp's letter to Trebitsch of 10 January 1939, explaining that he sought only agent's rights for Germany (see 14 December 1938 and 5 January 1939).

2. As an alien, Trebitsch's right to work in Switzerland was formally limited, but finding a publisher was harder than gaining permission to publish.

3. The Russians had entered Vienna on 13 April and there were reports of widespread damage to the city and its famed buildings.

PART SIX

The Last Years

28 September 1945 through 7 September 1950

With the fall of the Third Reich, Germany was split into four occupation zones under the Allied Control Council. Twenty-four Nazi leaders were tried before an International Military Tribunal in Nuremberg; twelve were sentenced to death. Goering, the most prominent of the defendants, escaped hanging by swallowing poison just before the scheduled executions on 15 October 1946.

Shaw, who remarked on the ordinariness of the prisoners, urged that they be released into obscurity (*Daily Herald*, 3 October), and when consternation greeted Goering's suicide, Shaw declared that he would have provided all the condemned men with morphine to spare "us the disgusting job of hanging them" (*Times*, 21 October). Shortly after, he joined in calling for amnesty of all war and political prisoners (*New York Times*, 20 December).

As tensions rose between the Western Allies and the Soviet Union, Shaw warned against Churchill's call for an anti-Soviet Anglo-American alliance (*New York Times*, 7 March 1946), censured the Labour Party's anti-Communist foreign policy, and suggested a political lexicon to help resolve international disputes (*Times*, 19 and 30 August 1946).

Finding expansive analysis too tiring, Shaw, now past ninety, turned again to playwriting, composing a new act and preface for *Geneva* and wrestling with his last full-length play, *Buoyant Billions*. "Is it not a serious sign of dotage," wrote Shaw in his "prefacette" to *Buoyant Billions* (1947), "to talk about oneself . . . ? Should it not warn me that my bolt is shot, and my place silent in the chimney corner? . . . yet I cannot hold my tongue nor my pen. As long as I live I must write. If I stopped writing I should die for want of something to do." Alert to the "resources of decivilization" in atomic war, Shaw, while not sanguine that mankind would escape destruction, did not despair of man's instinct for survival and capacity to learn.

The German theatre, which had been shut down by Goebbels in September 1944 as part of a "total war" effort, quickly revived under the occupation despite huge destruction. On 27 May 1945, Schönthan's farce *Der Raub der Sabinerinnen* was staged in the Western sector of Berlin. On 26 June,

Schiller's *Der Parasit* reopened the Deutsches Theater, in the Soviet sector, with Russian officials in attendance, and Berlin resumed its leading theatrical role until the cold war separated the rival sectors.

Within two months of Germany's surrender, Shaw reappeared with a Burgtheater production of *Candida* at the Akademie Theater (the Burg itself had been severely bombed) on 3 July 1945. The following month (27 August), the first act of *Androcles* appeared in Berlin at the Jürgen-Fehlings Theater in a triple bill that included Goethe and Kleist. *Candida* heralded the full return of Shaw to Berlin on 26 September at the Volkstheater Pankow (Russian sector). *Pygmalion* followed on 19 March 1946 at the Rheingau Theater (Western sector). On 11 May, a member of the Hamburger Kammerspiele informed Shaw of the "enormous success" of *Mrs Warren* and added, "The German public is very glad to see your plays after not having this chance for such a long time" (Texas). And on 4 October, the Kammerspiele of the Deutsches Theater, Berlin, reopened with *Captain Brassbound*.

Shaw was again the most favored modern "classic" in Germany, with the possible exception of Hauptmann, who for a time in Berlin exceeded Shaw in number of productions, if not in number of plays.*

The outpouring of tributes on Shaw's ninetieth birthday in 1946 further demonstrated the playwright's celebrity in Germany. Nazi strictures on Shaw as antiheroic, nihilistic, and intellectual vanished. Instead, Shaw was lauded as an intellectual dramatist who humanized greatness (*Tagesspiegel*, 25 July), and the Christian Democrat *Neue Zeit* (1 August) declared that Shaw's best works were his antiheroic histories. In East Berlin, the non-Party *Berliner Zeitung* (25 July) hailed Shaw as the "Voltaire of the decadent Bourgeoisie," whose cynicism grew from love of humanity, and added, "It is presently a simple fact that no repertory company can afford to go for long without producing Shaw." The Red Army *Tägliche Rundschau* (26 July) welcomed Shaw as a yea-sayer, who acknowledged Marx's power and was a friend of the Soviet Union. But the German Party paper, *Neues Deutschland*, condemned Shaw's Fabianism, scorn of the working class, and expectation that the evolution of a superman would effect his goals, which led him to praise Mussolini and not decisively reject Hitler.

That same year, the Swiss firm of Artemis launched the new collected edition of Shaw's plays, *Gesammelte Dramatische Werke*, which appeared between 1946 and 1948, in twelve volumes, containing thirty-four plays and their prefaces, including the previously unpublished *Geneva* and *Good King*

---

*Surveys of postwar German repertory are lacking. But that of Berlin, East and West, from 1945 to 1970, reveals that only Hauptmann, of the modern "classics," outranks Shaw with 54 productions of 20 plays to Shaw's 49 productions of 24 plays. Chekhov follows with 31 productions; Kaiser, 22; Ibsen, 21; Gorki, 19 (mostly in East Berlin, where he exceeds Shaw by 1 production); Hofmannsthal, 15; Strindberg, 13; Pirandello, 12; Wedekind and O'Neill, 11; Wilde, 10. *Pygmalion* leads in popularity, followed by *Joan*, *Candida*, *Androcles*, *Heartbreak House*, *Mrs Warren*, *Widowers' Houses*, and *You Never Can Tell* (H. Reichardt et al., *25 Jahre Theater in Berlin. Premieren 1945–1970*, 1972). A review of German productions, exclusive of East Germany, from 1964 to 1974 reveals Shaw as the only modern "classic" among the five most frequently produced playwrights in any of these years (Michael Patterson, *German Theatre Today*, 1976).

Charles. Revised with the aid of an assistant, the edition impressively crowned Trebitsch's services as "Shaw's translator."

In the spring of 1946—six years after last seeing Shaw—Trebitsch reappeared at Ayot. He was seventy-eight, Shaw eighty-nine. "When I visited him in the later days," Trebitsch told an interviewer, "[Shaw] did not express his strangely naïve opinions about Hitler and Stalin any more. And gradually we did not even write to each other [about politics]. . . . He surely is the greatest writer of many generations, and the encounter with him and his personal charm represent, of course, the greatest event of my life—his political carelessness, however, grieved me very much for years."* And in his *Chronicle*, Trebitsch recalled: "I . . . had long talks with him. . . . But even at that time he turned out to be failing, in a strange way. He was impatient, was afraid of falling asleep when he leaned back in his chair, and at the same time too, was afraid of showing this understandable weakness even in front of as familiar a visitor as I was. Intellectually he was as fresh as ever, and to my astonished delight his hearing had not suffered in any way at all. The difference in relation to the old days lay chiefly in the fact that he no longer walked so far beyond the house in order to accompany me to the taxi that had brought me, after a farewell that was kept light and airy, as he had always been so deft in doing."

--------------◄●►--------------

Ayot St Lawrence. Welwyn
28th September 1945

My dear Trebitsch

The prostrate operation[1] is a horribly painful operation; but three of my best friends are recovering from it, and I cannot write to them every day to sympathize and ask how they are; so I dont write to them at all. I cannot write any letters now, as I am overwhelmed with literary work and the business connected with it and with the arrangement of my affairs after my death, which may occur at any moment. I am in my 90th year; and you write as I were in my 19th. I cannot walk more than a mile, very unsteadily and leaning on a stick. I make many mistakes, and hardly dare go to London for a few days at very long intervals, though I keep my flat there. I am greatly relieved to learn that you have given up your mad project of coming to London for nothing but to see me. I dont want anyone to see me as I am now; and I dont want to see anybody. My regard for you and Tina is undiminished; but you must write me off as dead. Write as often as you please; but dont expect replies.

G.B.S.

Apcs.
1. Trebitsch, nearing 77, underwent a prostate operation and recovered.

*Ernest Mandowsky, "European Encounters," *Jerusalem Post*, 10 November 1950.

Trebitsch requested that Shaw write a brief preface for the planned collected edition of Shaw's plays.

Ayot St Lawrence. Welwyn
[c. 21st February 1946]

SORRY PREFACE IMPOSSIBLE IT WOULD COST ME A MONTHS WORK   SHAW
Telegram.

[Ayot St Lawrence. Welwyn]
13th March 1946

My dear Trebitsch

An amazing misunderstanding between us has just come to light. I have just received a long letter from you explaining your circumstances in great detail, and asking me to guarantee your hotel bill for the duration of the war as I had guaranteed Troubetskoy's, with other matters which seemed strangely out of date. I thought your mind must be giving way.

I looked at the date of the letter. It was August 1942! I looked at the official postmark on the envelope. It was March 1946!!

As the Swiss Post Office is 3½ years behind time heaven knows how many letters you have written to me that I have not yet received. I now understand why you complained so often that I did not answer your letters. I never got them.

By the way, I did not guarantee Troubetskoy's hotel bill. But when it was 18 months in arrear I bought a statuette from him which enabled him to clear it.[1] As to guaranteeing your income I cannot even guarantee my own. Do you realize that for six years the war taxation has left me only sixpence out of every pound I earn, and that I have six people entirely dependent on me, to say nothing of my having to keep an expensive flat in London as well as my villa in Ayot Saint Lawrence? I am solvent for the moment; but I cannot answer for the future. So, no guarantees. However, I shall not see you starve if I can help it.

Now as to your last up-to-date letter. You are to be sent to one of the three most expensive hotels in London.[2] When I was last in Venice the best hotel begged me to occupy their best suite for nothing as long as I liked. On other occasions my bill has been so ridiculously small that I have had to return it and insist on being charged full prices.

Why was this? Because as a noted journalist I was expected to write up the hotel in the press, and as a celebrated author to make it known and fashionable by choosing it to stay in. This is why you are offered rooms in the Dorchester or Brown's (very select) at estaminet prices. If you accept, in common honesty you have to get an interview into the papers as taking place in the hotel, and say something very nice about it.

But I cannot go up to Whitehall Court. You must come down here to Ayot for a couple of hours and have a talk with a damnably old man. I shall be quite glad to see you; but it will not be worth your while to come so far for so little; so I still do not advise you to come unless you really have other business and enough money to spare.   G. Bernard Shaw

Your last letter has arrived promptly. By all means send me a written questionnaire, and do not be restrained by any of these delicacies and sentimentalities which are quite thrown away on me. What do you suppose I care about last meetings at my age? I never see anyone now without being conscious that it is probably our last meeting; and it does not trouble me in the least. When the cat leaves the room it may never see me alive again; but I dont cry about it.

Do you still write for the [Basler] Nationalzeitung? [3]

Visas are easier to get now.

I also had migraines every month. They stopped 20 years ago. Probably yours will stop *now*.

Tls.
1. Paul Troubetskoy's statuette of Shaw was sculpted in 1926 while Shaw was vacationing in Stresa.
2. Trebitsch was preparing to arrive in London on 24 April, and Shaw was arranging for his stay in a prominent hotel as a visiting dignitary.
3. The *Basler National-Zeitung* had published poems, short stories, and feuilletons by Trebitsch.

[Ayot St Lawrence. Welwyn]
[late March 1946]

You must write your questions and leave them to me to answer, whether we actually meet or not. [1] And they must not be questions that are answered in my books already and would take me two years to answer over again. Our conversation will be far too private and intimate for publication. I am not going to make speeches to you.

I am assuming that you now have important business to do in London, and are to be well paid for it. Otherwise I beg you not to come. Food is rationed here; and you cannot buy clothes without coupons. Everything purchable is dear and adulterated. Life is much less pleasant and healthy than in Switzerland. To come merely to see me is sentimental nonsense. I am now an old dotard of 90, not fit for anyone to see. I cannot entertain you in London, where I have not been for two years, nor in this village, which as you know is unbearably dull. I can still correspond with friends; but I dont want to see them or to see anyone. You dont know what it is to be 90.

Anyhow you now know what to expect if you can afford to come and have something else to do than contemplate my decay.

G.B.S.

Als.

   1. This letter was written on one of Shaw's printed cards dealing with interviews. Shaw required submission of written questions on current topics that could be answered in 20 words or less.

Ayot St Lawrence. Welwyn
6th April 1946

These questions are quite hopeless. They are all about literature, fifty years out of date. It is quite that time since I read novels or short stories. I know nothing about the young lions of the present moment; and they know nothing about Maupassant. And you know less than nothing about politics, which is the subject on which people want to hear what I have to say.

You finish your literary questions with "All this from Shakespear's time to up-to-date."

Are you quite mad? Do you think I can write an encyclopedia in a week?

I am being pressed from all sides for an article on my birthday. Perhaps I shall write it. If so, it will be about political and sociological developments during my lifetime, and will take the place of the interview you contemplate.[1]

I look forward with dread to the 24th. What shall I do with you?

G.B.S.

Apcs.

   1. Shaw did not write a special political article for his approaching 90th birthday, but he did grant several interviews.

Ayot St Lawrence. Welwyn
17th April 1946

My dear Trebitsch

Your letters are childish in the face of a starving world. You must really consider the situation seriously and stop whining about my no longer liking you. All that is babytalk with which I have no patience.

Nothing that you have written to me has convinced me that there is the smallest excuse for your coming to England by air and putting up at a hotel *de luxe* for a fortnight. If you have all that money to throw away you should spend it on a holiday with Tina on the mountains or the lakes, and buy her some new clothes with it. Spending it on a perfectly useless, expensive, uncomfortable, difficult, unhealthy journey to Ayot Saint Lawrence to see a very old man to whom you have nothing to say that cannot be said by letter, and who should be written off as dead, seems to me such a monstrous waste of time and money that I cannot pretend to look forward to it with any satisfaction. Do think it over. Ask Tina whether she really likes being left out of your holiday. Have you not yet ceased to be a bachelor husband?

We must give up the interview. Every set of questions you send me are more impossible than the earlier ones. Each of them would take six months to answer. My only possible reply is Read my books. You are no journalist. You had better induce some publisher to take up an important book about me [*G.B.S. 90*] by several eminent English writers and now in the press waiting for my birthday. The editor is S. Winsten, Ayot Saint Lawrence, Welwyn, Herts (same as mine) and the publishers the Hutchinson firm. You should try to be engaged as translator.

Suhrkamph has written to the British Council, claiming to be still my authorized publisher as the successor of Fischer, and saying that he has a lot of money of mine. He was of course unable to have any dealings with us during the war; but now that the war is over he can settle up. As far as I can ascertain his claim is valid, though I can get rid of him at six months notice. But why should I if he is now established in Berlin?[1] I am told that Swiss publishers and agents cannot operate in Germany. Is this correct?

In haste to catch the village post—

G. Bernard Shaw

Tls.

1. Suhrkamp, licensed by the British authorities to reopen his Verlag, now claimed rights in Shaw, based on Shaw's May 1939 authorization, and contested Trebitsch's arrangements. Suhrkamp collected Shaw's wartime royalties amounting to 209,930 marks.

Ayot St Lawrence. Welwyn
28th April 1946

My dear Tina

Siegfried arrived here yesterday in high spirits, none the worse for his journey; and we talked for two hours. I was very glad to see him, though I still think the money the journey cost should have been spent on new clothes and a holiday for you. However, our talk was most useful to me, as I have never had time to attend seriously to my foreign affairs. Siegfried has clarified them for me.

He is coming again on Thursday next, and yet again for a farewell visit before he leaves for Paris.

His visit is an outrageous extravagance in money, but a very enjoyable incident for both of us, and a healthy change and holiday for him. I wish you had come with him.

G.B.S.

Apcs.

Ayot St Lawrence. Welwyn
30th April 1946

My dear Trebitsch

Come on Thursday by the same train: the car will meet you as before. As it will be the 1st May the trains may be changed; but there is sure to be one at or near the same hour. Still, you had better look at the hotel ABC (if they have one for May) to make sure.

If you want to secure topical interviews for the Zeitung you must be prepared with written questions.[1] Here are a few suggestions.

1 As Federal Republics have now taken the place of monarchies as the typical form of government, Switzerland as the oldest of them should take a very prominent place in the U[nited] N[ations] O[rganization] councils. Can

you explain why it is less considered and consulted than many minor States from which nothing can be learnt?

2 Do you believe that reparations and security can be included in the aims of the conferences without converting the peace into an armistice and in effect continuing the war under Cease Fire orders until it is resumed again in twenty years time or less?

3 What prospect is there of the British Commonwealth admitting that it must do all it can to repair the terrific damage it has done not only in Germany but in France and Italy, and take its chance of a rebuilt Germany regaining its position as a European Power?

4 As Switzerland is inaccessible except overland through foreign States have you any views as to the problem of wayleaves for foreign armies through neutral countries?

If you can get answers (written if possible) to the first three of these questions it will be more than enough. The 4th is superfluous. You should try them on all the Cabinet Ministers and Opposition leaders. But as that is impossible try Bevan, Bevin, Dalton, Churchill, Eden and Truman.[2]

It is no use talking to any of them about literature or fine art in any form.

G. Bernard Shaw

Als.

1. Trebitsch now planned to interview British political figures for the Swiss press.

2. Aneurin Bevan, Ernest Bevin, and Hugh Dalton were members of the Labour cabinet; Churchill and former foreign secretary Anthony Eden were, of course, in the opposition; and Harry Truman was the American president, as the nonagenarian Shaw momentarily forgot.

Ayot St Lawrence. Welwyn
21st May 1946

My dear Trebitsch

Read the enclosed letter carefully and send it back to me.

I knew nothing of the Control Commission. Neither did you. It has deadlocked us in Switzerland as completely as we were deadlocked in Germany.[1]

I see nothing for it except to make Suhrkamp our publisher and agent, like Fischer, in the British zone. But the Control Commission will grab the money anyhow. . . .

Now as to the Artemis agreements. They are both impossible for me to confirm. The one for The Black Girl is for the whole term of the copyright: fifty years![2] I have never in my life signed or approved such a surrender of my copyright: my utmost is a license for five years, renewable thereafter at six months notice if both parties are willing to continue.

The other agreement [for the collected edition of Shaw's plays] has the five years limit; but the money terms are absurd. . . . The royalty should be *at least* 15% on *all* copies, but not unless and until they are sold. No advances. . . .

I am sorry to have to worry you with all this. I still think your visit an extravagance; but I was glad to see you, and enjoyed our chats thoroughly.

G. Bernard Shaw

Als.

1. The British Control Commission for occupied Germany informed Shaw that his Swiss publisher (Artemis) and agent (Reiss) could not operate in their zone.

2. In addition to the collected edition of Shaw's plays, Artemis undertook the still unpublished German version of *The Adventures of the Black Girl* (*Ein Negermädchen sucht Gott;* see 12–15 May 1933, n. 7). The book appeared in 1948 with a foreword by Walter Nigg and the original illustrations by J. Farleigh.

Ayot St Lawrence. Welwyn

14th June 1946

My dear Trebitsch

The enclosed letter is a copy of one which I am this day sending by registered post to Berman[n] Fischer, whose address in Stockholm (Stureplan 19) I have only just obtained. I have had to give it a good deal of consideration before drafting it; and you have been naturally impatient because you sign any paper that is put before you without giving it any consideration at all.[1]

The agreement with Artemis I cannot confirm: I must redraft it completely. Clause 4 says 'Der Ubersetzer erhält 15% vom Ladenpreis des broschierten Exemplares fur jedes vom Verlag verkaufte Exemplar" [The translator receives 15% of the retail price of the paperbound copies for each copy sold by the publishers]. 15% on a broschierten Exemplar would be a penny or thereabouts. Under this clause Artemis can fix the retail price [of the clothbound copies] at twenty Swiss francs and pay us a penny royalty instead of three shillings.

A man who would sign that would sign anything.

A publisher who would slip it into an agreement would be practising pretty sharply. But I do not think Artemis intended this. They were thinking of The Black Girl as a pamphlet only.

The second clause, strictly interpreted, would give Artemis exclusive rights for all languages.

I will send you a new agreement covering both the collected edition and The Black Girl next week, I hope.

I note your remark that IF I do not settle all this business for you instantly you will regard your trip to London as an extravagance. It WAS an outrageous extravagance: I told you again and again that you could not afford it. And now you tell me that you are looking forward to repeating it next year! You are incorrigible and impossible.

My letter to Tina requires no answer. Do not let her worry about it. It must madden her to see all the money that should have been spent on her spent on me.

I wish we could make Suhrkamp our German publisher. I do not believe that this Four Zone arrangement of Germany will last.

GBS

Tls.

1. Dr. Gottfried Bermann Fischer had reestablished relations with Peter Suhrkamp in Berlin in expectation that the former S. Fischer Verlag would be returned to the Fischer family. As heir to the firm, Bermann Fischer claimed rights in Shaw, but Shaw denied that his license was heritable and canceled any agreements with Bermann-Fischer Verlag, not as an "unfriendly act" but "imposed on me by political conditions." Bermann Fischer withdrew.

Ayot St Lawrence. Welwyn
26th June 1946

My dear Trebitsch

I enclose the agreement which I offer to Artemis. Read it carefully before you submit it to them. It gives them all your translations, including the eight volumes [*Dramatische Werke*, issued by S. Fischer, 1911–31] and the Black Girl, subject to a royalty of 15%. . . .

A German Protestant gets no sympathy as such.[1] Therefore you must submit for the present to be a Jewish refugee. Besides, it was as a Non-Aryan that you were robbed and exiled from Vienna.

Mrs Fischer has written to me from New York begging me to help her in her poverty.[2] I have told her that I have no money to spare, but that if Berman[n-Fischer] has any funds of mine I might make her a grant-in-aid out of it. . . .

Excuse the mess I have made of typing this letter. I should have handed it over to Blanche Patch; but by letting it go as it is I shall save a post. It is legible though slovenly.

G. Bernard Shaw

Tls.

1. Trebitsch, seeking restitution of his house in Vienna, was thinking of applying as an exiled Austrian Protestant (which he nominally was since his army days). The villa, which had been sequestered but not sold (see 6 November 1939), was returned to Trebitsch the following month. He then sold it to the Czech embassy. (As for his personal effects, loss of business, forced taxes, personal damages, etc., Trebitsch did not lodge any claims until shortly before his death in 1956.)

2. Mrs. Samuel Fischer, widow of the publisher, had remained in Germany until early 1939 before joining her daughter and son-in-law in Stockholm and then in New York. The trauma of displacement had affected her, and she anxiously dreaded poverty.

Ayot St Lawrence. Welwyn
5th July 1946

. . . You *misled* me completely. You made me believe that they (A[rtemis] and R[eiss]) could deal with the whole of Germany and made me give notice to Surkamp and Berman to that effect. You never mentioned the British Control, which has just come down on me and declared all my proceedings mistaken and *invalid*. I shall have to place the affair in their friendly hands. . . .

G.B.S.

Apcs.

Ayot St Lawrence. Welwyn
13th July 1946

Siegfried, Sigfried,

You will drive me crazy with your sentimental nonsense about terrible blows and going to bed and all the rest of it. Damn it, man, do you imagine that I am a pretty girl of 17 and you a blithering adolescent of 18? Drop it; and help me to straighten out this business.

First, are those agreements which I sent you in your hands or in those of Artemis. If in yours send them back to me; and leave it to me to substitute new ones, which will be quite satisfactory to them. If not—if Artemis has got them and is sticking to them, let me know at once. Until you do I can do nothing.

I quite understand, and always have understood, that Reiss is an agent and not a publisher. What I did not know was about the British Control.[1] You said you told me about it; but now you admit that you never thought it worth mentioning. Ashley Dukes, an old friend and fellow-Fabian, and an official of the Control, enlightened me.[2]

Now as to the original agreement with Fischer. I have no recollection of ever signing it. What is yours? Your copy is lost; but Berman may have the counterpart. Are you sure that there was ever any agreement on paper?

Let me have an answer on these two points. And no more Sorrows of Werther.[3]

G. Bernard Shaw

Tls.

1. The Control Commission questioned Trebitsch's right in 1943 to cancel Shaw's 1939 agreement with Suhrkamp and thus recognized Suhrkamp as Shaw's agent. Trebitsch's agreement with Artemis was complicated by Suhrkamp's not being advised of the intended rival edition. But Artemis, satisfied of its rights, proceeded with the new edition (*Gesammelte Dramatische Werke*, 12 vols., 1946–48).

2. Ashley Dukes (1885–1959), English author, was Theatre and Music Adviser to the Control Commission and handled Shaw's case.

3. *The Sorrows of Young Werther*, Goethe's epistolary romance (1774).

Ayot St Lawrence. Welwyn
28th July 1946

Stop worrying yourself and me about this publishing business: I understand it all perfectly, and will settle it as far as it can be settled while the British Consul refuses to recognize as valid any agreements or notices to cancel agreements dated after 1939.

Put the whole affair out of your head and get well.[1] There is nothing wrong except with your nerves. Nobody is quarreling with you.

My birthday has been indescribable; another such would kill me. Hundreds of letters and telegrams by every post: I am the world's Great Man for the moment.[2]

Send me no more complaining letters. Enjoy yourself (the Hotel looks expensive) and cease pitying yourself.

In great haste
G.B.S.

Tls.

1. Trebitsch, wounded by Shaw's comments, had gone to Bad Tarasp, a spa in Switzerland.

2. Besides the tributes and honors, Shaw's birthday was marked in London by an exhibit of Shaviana at the National Book League, a performance of *Don Juan in Hell* at the Arts Theatre, and special publications.

Ayot St Lawrence. Welwyn
1st August 1946

Not a word to Suhrkamp until the political question is settled. He is enjoying the interest on our money and has nothing to complain of.

The word is schweig [Silence!]. Above all, no promises or commitals to anybody. Put business out of your mind; and make the most of your dolce far niente [pleasant idleness].

GBS

Apcs.

Ayot St Lawrence. Welwyn
7th September 1946

There is no changed last act of Geneva. There is a new act: the third.[1] It is now a play in four acts.

GBS

Apcs.

1. For the Standard Edition of *Geneva* (1947), Shaw added a new preface and new third act, in which he again criticizes Britain, attacks both liberal-democratic and messianic-dictatorial governments, and expresses greater hope in human capacity, freed from ignorance, to evolve politically.

[Ayot St Lawrence. Welwyn]
21st October 1946

My dear Trebitsch

I have just had a letter from an agent named Dr Kolb, claiming all the Fischer rights for Bermann.

I have replied that I do not admit that my relations with the extinct firm of Fischer were negotiable, heritable, or in any way transferable, or that Bermann of Stockholm can possibly represent Fischer of Berlin as a German publisher.

This must be our position. Reiss must not recognize Bermann as having any rights now or formerly.

As to British control it is impossible to say just now what the end of it may be. Ashley Dukes is a friend of mine and will not work against us; but nobody can foresee how the zone arrangements will finally settle.

I am recovering from a fall in London which disabled my left hip and has kept me in bed for a week.[1] I am now back at Ayot crawling about on two sticks but mending slowly.

G. Bernard Shaw

Tls.; postscript omitted.
1. While in his London study, Shaw turned to greet Sobieniowski and slipped from his revolving chair.

[Ayot St Lawrence. Welwyn]
postmarked 23rd October 1946

A[shley] D[ukes] is an old friend and Fabian colleague of mine. Can you not bear the thought of my having any friend in the world except yourself?

Pull yourself together; and stop plaguing me with the complaints of a jealous child.

A. D. will be very useful behind the scenes at the zone complications.

GBS

Apcs.

Ayot St Lawrence. Welwyn
3rd December 1946

My dear Trebitsch

I enclose 3 copies of the Artemis agreement executed by myself. . . .

This agreement cancels all previous ones and puts all the books on a 15% royalty, which is very reasonable for the high prices charged to the public by Artemis.

I leave the business of procuring Artemis's signature in your hands.

Note the latest political news. The British and American zone Controls are now merged. This is an admission that the separate Controls have been a failure. Their regulations will probably be changed.

Pascal claims that he has bought your half share of Caesar & Cleopatra for a lump sum.[1] If this is so have you stipulated that your translation shall be used and acknowledged by your name in all the advertisements?

Or do you sign anything that brings you ready money?

GBS

Als.

1. Pascal had gone abroad after the failure of *Caesar*, which opened in London on 13 December 1945, and had recently returned to England. *Caesar* had incurred huge expenses, and Pascal was denounced for wartime extravagance. His contract with Rank, who lost heavily on the film, was broken, and he could no longer obtain financing in England.

[Ayot St Lawrence. Welwyn]
26th December 1946

My dear Trebitsch

I have never corresponded with Suhrcamp but I told Ashley Cooper [Dukes] that when it became necessary to appoint a German publisher as Fischer's successor, I should consider Suhrcamp favorably provided he was not acting for Berman nor for anyone but himself.

As to Mrs Fischer I forget what passed. I certainly gave her no claim on any future royalties; but no doubt I told her that I should not ask her to return any payments she had already received.[1] . . .

I hope Tina's flu has passed. I scribble this in great haste. My Christmas correspondence is an avalanche.

G.B.S.

Als.
1. Any promise of future royalties to Mrs. Fischer could be construed as acknowledging Bermann-Fischer's claims.

Ayot St Lawrence. Welwyn
20th January 1947

My dear Trebitsch

Reiss is coming to London to confer with Ashley Dukes and the Control. He claims to have advanced you M. 25,000 (£2000) on your half share of our roya[l]ties. Is this so?

It is no use my repeating that I have made no agreement with Frau Fischer, nor with Suhrkamp. But no matter how often I tell you you keep on complaining that I have made all sorts of agreements with all sorts of people. I have made *none*, except with Artemis and Anschutz.

I do not recognize any claims of Berman or Suhrkamp or anyone else to succeed to the Fischer Verlag. My licenses are not heritable, negotiable, nor transferable in any way.

I am willing, however, to make Suhrkamp my publisher and agent for Germany by a new agreement if he will accept my terms.

I do not hold myself bound by any war agreements of yours, because they were made under duress without consulting me. You also must take this legal position.

Have you left Kürhausstrasse? Your last letter is from Dolder.[1]

GBS

Als.
1. Shaw was still unaware that Trebitsch's address, Kurhausstrasse 65, and the Dolder Hotel were the same, nor apparently did Trebitsch enlighten him.

Ayot St Lawrence. Welwyn
10th February 1947

My dear Trebitsch

Isolnay [Zsolnay], like all agents, finds it more profitable to make several easy rapid bargains with the publishers than to stand for the highest terms for the authors.[1]

How are Swiss authors to live when the publishers can get the best English books for 10%?

Books sold at more than 2.50 can bear roya[l]ties of 15% or 20%. I have had 25%.

Anyhow I will not accept less than 15%. . . .

. . . You are only wasting your time and mine in going against me on the percentage figure. Tell them they must sign at once, and that Mr Isolnay is not my agent and "cuts no ice" with me.

GBS

Als.
1. Paul Zsolnay (1895–1961), a Viennese publisher who had gone into exile in London and become a director of the William Heinemann publishing company, was not an agent but may have

advised his old friend Trebitsch in his dealings with Artemis, whose normal author's royalty was 10 percent.

Ayot St Lawrence. Welwyn
19th February 1947

My dear Tina

What are they saying about me?

I am well fed, well warmed, comfortable, and in first rate health. The cold weather agrees with me: I like snow. I sleep well under eiderdo[w]ns and with hot water bottles galore.

And all over Europe people are starving and shivering to death!

Much as I value your sympathy it is thrown away on me.

Look at my latest photograph! Did you ever see a man of 90 look better?

Tell Siegfried not to bother about the Suhrkamp business. I will look after it.

G.B.S.

Als.

Ayot St Lawrence. Welwyn
20th April 1947

Answer Mr Spiro[1]

NO

There are enough portraits of me in existence by famous artists.

To do justice to a painter one must sit for him (a day's work) from 12 to 30 times, though he always begins by asking for 2.

At 90 this is out of the question. He probably thinks I am 40 or thereabouts.

G.B.S.

Apcs.
1. Eugene Spiro (b. 1874), German portrait painter and landscape artist, exiled during the Nazi era.

Ayot St Lawrence. Welwyn
22nd April 1947

I have been disabled badly for a fortnight past by a very unexpected attack of muscular rheumatism, which is now called fibrocitis; and I have to go every day at noon to the hospital for short wave electric treatment, after which I must rest. But you can come any day after 3.30 if you phone in the morning to say you are coming.[1]

G.B.S.

Apcs.
1. Trebitsch had arrived in London and was at the Dorchester Hotel.

Shaw in his nineties. Sent to Tina Trebitsch on 19 February 1947.

Ayot St Lawrence. Welwyn
6th May 1947

I find that as I need a little rest after lunch, and have then to catch the village post at 4, the arrival of anyone before that hour upsets me considerably. I was the worse for it on Monday.[1]

Will you therefore come by the train that leaves King's Cross at 3.10? Day[2] will meet you at Welwyn Garden City at 3.49. You will arrive here a little after 4; and we shall have just an hour to talk, which is just the right time for both of us.

GBS

Apcs.
  1. Trebitsch had been to Ayot the previous day and reappeared on Friday, the 9th.
  2. Frederick Day, Shaw's chauffeur and gardener.

Ayot St Lawrence. Welwyn
4th July 1947

I have changed my mind about the new play. I am writing an additional act, and altering the title to *A World Betterer's Courtship: a Comedy of Manners*.[1] Do not make this public; for I may change my mind again, or die, or put the play in the fire.

At all events you must wait until the new version is finished and printed. I have not yet the least notion of how it will end.

I wish I knew what to advise about your arthritis. The registered doctors cannot cure it. Try the Nature Cure treatment. Keep changing until you get some result.

G.B.S.

Apcs.
  1. This play, originally called *Old Bill Buoyant's Billions*, was one that Shaw began in 1936 while in the Far East and took up again in 1945. Shaw abandoned the new title and settled on *Buoyant Billions: A Comedy of No Manners*. "The World Betterer" became the title of the first act.

[Trebitsch to Shaw]

[Zurich]
16th August 1947

My dear Shaw

I finished the translation of your wonderful preface to "Geneva." And I discovered some errors which you ought to rectificate in the next edition.

  1. Dünkirchen [Dunkirk] was not *1941*, but *1940*.

  2. Hitler came not *1930* to Munich but already about *1920*.

  3. When the war started at Poland the English did not longer try to appease.

  4. page 8: *Meanwhile* the British and American armies were "liberating" french cities.....ec. ec.[1] That was never "meanwhile," but much later! It is rather difficult to alter this.[2]

Schinznach did not cure me, but the pain is now a little easier and in the whole neck, all around and not as before at one spot. We suffer enormously from the heat and I am swimming every day.[3] We hope you are well. Our love to you.

Yours ever
S. Trebitsch

Als.; Texas.
1. Trebitsch's ellipsis.
2. The dates corrected by Trebitsch were altered but not the statement about appeasing Germany or the word "Meanwhile."
3. Schinznach-Bad in Switzerland offered thermal baths for rheumatism and skin diseases.

Ayot St Lawrence. Welwyn
3rd September 1947

. . . Herr Muck is impressive: if I were you I should try his diet for your arthritis, as the other cures have failed.

Tell him that though I have been a vegetarian for 60 years I was poisoning myself all the time; for I had headaches every month to get rid of the accumulated gift [poison]. The headaches stopped when I was 70. My health has improved since I gave up eating cooked pulse (haricots and lentils) and maccaroni, and substituted uncooked vegetables, chopped or grated.

But I cannot walk. I can only hobble for short distances with a stick.

G.B.S.

Apcs.

Ayot St Lawrence. Welwyn
22nd November 1947

I have managed to get a copy of the Wagner Brevier for Richard Strauss and am having it bound for him.[1]

What is his address?

GBS

Apcs.
1. After the war, Richard Strauss, facing charges of Nazi collaboration (he was later cleared), retired to Switzerland where he and Trebitsch, long acquainted, became friends. While awaiting denazification, Strauss was in financial difficulties, and his possessions in Germany were blocked.

Ayot St Lawrence. Welwyn
11th January 1948

There is no such book as The Authors & Writers Who's Who. There is The A. & W's Year Book, of which my bookseller will send you a copy.[1] Who's Who is an enormous directory of celebrities of all sorts, of no use to you, and very costly. The Jahrbuch contains all you need.

GBS

Pascal is in Rome, married to a woman 30 years younger, but fairly clever.[2]

Apcs.
1. Shaw confuses two reference works. Trebitsch properly inquired about *The Author's and Writer's Who's Who*, a directory of authors, markets, agents, etc. *The Author's Year Book* was an early reference work.
2. The previous September, Pascal, 53, married the Hungarian actress Valerie Hidveghy and shortly after introduced her to Shaw.

Ayot St Lawrence. Welwyn
5th March 1948

My dear Trebitsch

It will be a good thing for us if Surkamp buys out Reiss.[1] A Swiss publisher for Germany is ridiculous. Surkamp must succeed Fischer as our agent and publisher.

I do not know how much Surkamp has paid to the British Control on your account; but I have had none of it.[2] I have sent in my claim mentioning S., but being unable to name any definite sum. We shall probably both be dead before they settle whether Germany is to be Bizonia or Trizonia or Federal or Communist, and which of them owes us the money.

I enclose a card my housekeeper has just found unposted. It is now of no importance; but I thought you had had it.

I am going to publish a volume of autobiographic sketches. It is now in the press. When will you have time to translate it?[3] Did I send you my new play called [Buoyant Billions:] a Comedy of No Manners? I cannot remember anything longer than ten minutes.

G. Bernard Shaw

Tls.
1. Reiss eventually yielded agent's rights for Germany to Suhrkamp, but he retained them for Austria.
2. After July 1938, Suhrkamp credited all of Shaw's earnings, including Trebitsch's share (which could no longer be sent to Trebitsch), to Shaw's account. Shaw's wartime royalties were placed in a blocked account; his postwar earnings went to the Control Commission and as of July 1948 amounted to RM503,564.
3. Shaw's *Sixteen Self Sketches*—originally titled *Autobiographic Scraps and Sketches*—appeared the next year. Trebitsch's translation, *Sechzehn selbstbiographische Skizzen*, was published by Artemis in 1950.

Ayot St Lawrence. Welwyn
11th March 1948

Emil Ludwig writes to me that you think I have written new prefaces to my plays. This is a mistake. I have written a postscript to Methuselah: that is all. . . .

"World betterer" is my translation of Weltverbesserungswahn [world-reforming madness] invented by Tolstoy's children to describe his politics.

The Autobiographic Sketches are not ready for you yet. You shall have them as soon as possible.

GBS

Tls.

[Ayot St Lawrence. Welwyn]
26th April 1948

DO NOT COME[1] I CAN DO ABSOLUTELY NOTHING FOR YOU BECAUSE OF THE
CAPITAL LEVY AND THE EXPENSE OF YOUR JOURNEY AND RISK TO YOUR HEALTH
ARE QUITE UNNECESSARY   SHAW

Draft wire, s.; Texas.
    1. Trebitsch was planning his annual pilgrimage to Shaw. In his engagement book for this day,
Shaw wrote: "Trebitsch wants to come twice before May 3. Put him off."

On the same day, Trebitsch wired Shaw: VERY UNHAPPY BUT CAN ONLY DE-
PART NEXT FRIDAY LOVE TREBITSCH. On the face of the wire Shaw wrote:
"This seems to have been sent before he received our cable." But the expla-
nation came the next day: DID NOT SHOW YOUR HARTLESS TELEGRAM TO
YOUR SUFERING OLDEST FRIEND DISAPPOINTED   TINA. To which Shaw re-
plied: NEVER MIND THE HEARTLESSNESS DO NOT LET HIM COME. (Texas.)

Ayot St Lawrence. Welwyn
23rd May 1948

It was a great relief to hear that Tina is not to be Walpoled.[1] These breast
operations are troublesome for a year (my old housekeeper Mrs Higgs had
one). I wish you could find a Naturopath or psychiatrist or some unregistered
genius to look after you. Official medicine is apparently unable to cure you;
but it goes on with its useless treatments all the same. . . .

Anyhow you are not coming; and that also is a relief. You dont understand
the British dislike of Empfindlichkeit [sensibility] and Sentimentalität. I
have had to forbid Pascal to kiss me, as he did at first to the scandal of the
village. As to [Sidney] Webb, he was my oldest and best friend as well as my
political partner. You think I saw him every day. As a matter of fact, though
he lived within a three hours motor drive from me I did not see him for years
before his death; and we exchanged very few letters. But our feelings were
quite unchanged, as mine are towards you. I never shook hands with Webb in
all my life; and I dont want to shake hands with you nor to contemplate your
wrinkles. You want to shake my hand and contemplate my wrinkles and my
infirm steps so badly that you think it worth while to visit London at a cost
that you can afford no more than you can keep a steam yacht just to satisfy
your Empfindlichkeit. You must understand that in England this is sentimental nonsense: I have no patience with it; and if we cannot remain good
friends without it we had better not pretend to be friends at all.

Of course Tina does not notice your wrinkles: she sees you every day. But
you are not a bit like your old self; and neither am I. However, you are still

Siegfried Trebitsch; and I can keep my regard for you without seeing you for a hundred years.

Now do you understand?

G.B.S.

Tl.; signature typed.

1. "Walpoled": surgically operated on—Shaw's neologism from Cutler Walpole, the ever-ready surgeon in *Doctor's Dilemma*.

Ayot St Lawrence. Welwyn
7th June 1948

The British dislike of sentimentality has nothing whatever to do with literature or art. It is as strong in a turf bookmaker as in the most sentimental poet. Dickens's early novel called the Old Curiosity Shop is sickeningly sentimental; but Dickens would never have dreamt of travelling a thousand miles to kiss you or shake your hand. He would have considered personal endearments between males as unmanly and homosexual. An essay about Galsworthy and the rest would only prove how utterly you misunderstand the subject. . . .

If Dr P. wants the film rights of any of my works why does he not apply to me for them? My shop is open: it is not necessary to come in by the back door. However, it does not matter, as I am reserving Candida for Pascal.

What is Woman without Tuesday? an extraordinary title. Is it a play or a new novel of yours? Can you make a scenario of it?[1] Can I help?

I have just found among my old papers a very abusive letter about your translations. I send you the specific objections made in it in case you have not yourself revised them. You are sometimes misled by the dictionary. Your most persistent mistake is to translate the word "wit" as always meaning Scherz or Spass [joke].[2] In English a wit means an amusingly clever person, never a joke. Oscar Wilde was a famous wit; but when I write that So-and-So was "at his wits' end" I mean that he was at the end of his mental resources and could not understand. "Out of his wits" means simply mad. You may say that I made a witty remark; but to say as you often do that I "made a wit" is nonsense.[3] Wit means wisdom: humour implies fun.

The trip to Paris was quite excusable. The change has probably done you a lot of good. But you had business there.[4] You did not go so far merely to shake somebody's paw.

G.B.S.

Tl.; signature typed.

1. "The Woman Without a Tuesday" (*Frau ohne Dienstag*), Trebitsch's 1919 novella, had recently been reprinted in Zurich. Years before (see 11 October 1921), Trebitsch mentioned it and its failure as a movie.

2. Trebitsch's mistranslations of "wit" concern largely his early version of *Candida* and were later corrected.

3. Trebitsch's "ein Witz machen" is normal German for "to make a joke" and not the nonsensical "to make a wit."

4. Trebitsch's trips to Paris were required to maintain his French citizenship.

Ayot St Lawrence. Welwyn
22nd June 1948

My dear Trebitsch

. . . I return the invitation of Clarence Sadd, which is not in the least sentimental. It is a quite ordinary cordial invitation to you to come and play chess with him, not to weep in your arms.[1]

Some years ago a millionaire shopkeeper[2] died and left a great sum to found a colony for old people who had saved a little money but not enough to support them. It was a beautiful estate; and they lived there in comfort and even luxury. Soon something unexpected and puzzling happened. They all went mad. They bored one another out of their senses.

They were cured by inviting all the young people in the district to visit the colony and play lawn tennis and take tea there.

Make friends with young people or you will go mad too. Forget Bahr and Schnitzler: they are dead. Forget me except for business matters. I am more than half dead, and belong to your past. I may die before September, or even before you receive this letter. In that case write me off without wasting your time on vain regrets. Do not say that you are not built that way: the world is built that way; and you must live in the world, not in a *pays de Cocagne*.

I will not give you one of my plays:[3] you are too old. If I did such a crazy thing I should give it to a young man. Actually my plays will go to living and ageless public institutions when I die.[4]

Loewenstein[5] should not have sent you my Tribune polemic: it is topical and quite unsuitable for publication in Germany.[6] But not a copy of my books the less will be sold in Germany. In politics you are out of your depth. Hitler's Judenhetze exiled and robbed you; but you are amply revenged, though not yet compensated. Spitting on his grave is not a policy.

If the film companies were not such sheep they would jump at Jitta instead of begging for stale Pygmalion. I have done all I can to convert them.

This is enough for one day.   G.B.S.

Tl.; signature typed.

1. Trebitsch, vexed with Shaw's not wanting him to visit, enclosed a letter from Clarence Sadd (1883–1962), British financier and president of the British Chess Federation, inviting Trebitsch, who was an ardent chess player (his father founded the Vienna Chess Club), to London.

2. William Whiteley (1831–1907). He endowed the Whiteley Homes for the Aged Poor in Surrey.

3. Trebitsch presumably asked for one of Shaw's dramatic manuscripts.

4. Shaw's dramatic manuscripts went to the British Library.

5. F. E. Loewenstein (1901–1969), a German-Jewish refugee, who was now Shaw's bibliographer and assistant.

6. A sharp debate between Shaw and Michael Foot, left-wing Labourite and co-editor of the *Tribune*, followed Shaw's attack on Labour's anti-Sovietism and his praise of Stalin ("Front Bench Nonsense," *Daily Herald*, 13 May). Foot dismissed Shaw as having "stopped thinking about fifteen years ago" and called his views on Mussolini, taxes, and communism "gibberish" and nonsense (*Tribune*, 21 May). Shaw retorted that since he was at least thirty years ahead of his time even if he had stopped thinking he was still fifteen years ahead of Foot, and he restated his positions on fascism, communism, and democracy (*Tribune*, 28 May). Further exchanges followed (4, 11, 18 June).

Ayot St Lawrence. Welwyn
8th July 1948

My dear Trebitsch

I have revised B[uoyant] B[illions] drastically, cutting out Thirdborn alto-gether as he has no character and says nothing that cannot be said by the others. Also I have greatly improved the mathematician, and deleted much superflous dialogue.[1] I will send you the revised version as soon as it is printed. What do you intend to call it? In English the word buoyant means not only floating in water as a cork does, but, when applied to a human being, energetically highspi[ri]ted, gaily superior to misfortune. And Bil-lionen is a familiar and quite intelligible German word which came into use during the inflation after 1918. I am assured of this by Loewenstein who, as an echt Berliner, maintains that you do not know a word of German, and speak and write a barbarous Austrian dialect. His suggestion of DER BIL-LIONEN SPRUDEL seems to me acceptable.

As to your change of address I told you years ago that this was inevitable, and that you and Tina could no longer afford to live in hotels of the Dolder class and put up in Park Lane in London instead of Bloomsbury.[2] But you have not yet learnt the lesson: rich habits are hard to shake off. Tina cannot imagine I have not unlimited money.

But it is astonishing how soon one gets used to cramped flats. On a sea voyage one has to live in a cabin no larger than a pantry on shore. In two days one feels quite at home in it. In Hietzing you were never unhappy because your house was not a royal Schloss; and you will not be unhappy in your new flat because it is not a Dolder suite. Here in England there is such a shortage of houses and servants that ladies like Tina are scrubbing and cooking, sleeping and eating, in single rooms; but they seem all the better for it. If only you were both younger I should not pity you.

If you have made Diocletian[3] sufficiently topical (Stalin or Tito in dis-guise) this may prove the moment for it.

G.B.S.

Tl.; signature typed.
   1. The revised *Buoyant Billions* was more compact and less abstract, and Secondborn, the mathematician, was given an eloquent speech on intellectual ecstasy.
   2. The Trebitsches had moved into a "modest, rather cosy little apartment" (*Chronicle*) on the well-situated Dufourstrasse, Zurich. It was actually a small double apartment—so that Tina could have her own bath—and Tina had to do some housekeeping.
   3. Trebitsch's play *Kaiser Diokletian* (1922), on the Roman emperor who seized power and was an able reformer, was never produced.

Ayot St Lawrence. Welwyn
14th July 1948

My dear Trebitsch

The new version will be very welcome to the Schauspiel[1] because it will save them a salary and greatly improve the stage effect without costing the theatre a farthing, or making any serious difference in the length.

WELTVERBESSERER [World Betterer] will not do for a title. There are two Weltbesserers in the play. The central figures are Old Bill, who is constantly in question even when he is not on stage, the mathematician who is Einstein, and the women. None of them are Weltbesserers. The subject of the play is Old Bill's money. For the present, until we find a title, it can be announced simply as A COMEDY OF NO MANNERS. This might be our final choice, like Shakespear's COMEDY OF ERRORS, if we can find nothing better.

What name have you given Buoyant?

TOO MUCH MONEY would be short and possible.

If Artemis has printed the play it must reprint it. But surely it has not yet got beyond proof sheets. You will not find the revision very arduous; and the improvement will convince you of its necessity and please you. It amounts only to what I should have done at first; but you must blame my old age for that. Besides, it was the new life of Einstein by Dr Frank Philipps [Philipp Frank][2] that made me reconsider the play.

There is no question of a performance in Malvern this year. The Festival, if it is ever revived, must wait until next year,[3] as the authorities, under a new law, insist on a rebuild of the theatre. The Zurich Aufführung seems likely to be the first in the world.

Never mind Loewenstein. To a Berliner Austrian is a dialect. To a Viennese, Berlinese is a dialect. As long as your translations are in your own style I care nothing about Grillparzer[4] & Co.

Do not let Tina undertake the demenagement [moving]. Have it done by a furniture remover during your holiday. Or leave it to your secretary if you have one. That is what I did when I moved from Adelphi to Whitehall.

G.B.S.

Tl.; signature typed.
    1. The Schauspielhaus in Zurich, which gave the world premiere of *Buoyant Billions*.
    2. Philipp Frank (1884–1966), physicist and author of *Einstein, His Life and Times* (Engl. trans., London, 1948).
    3. The Malvern Festival, suspended during the war, was reopened in 1949.
    4. Franz Grillparzer (1791–1872), classic Austrian playwright.

Ayot St Lawrence. Welwyn
17th July 1948

Ask the Schauspieldirektor[1] what he thinks of ZU VIEL GELD [Too Much Money] as a title for B.B. I expect he will be delighted with it; for WELTVERBESSERERS is certainly the worst title in the world. . . .

G.B.S.

Tpc.; signature typed.
    1. The artistic director of the Schauspielhaus, Zurich, was Oskar Wälterlin (1895–1961).

Ayot St Lawrence. Welwyn
22nd July 1948

Zu viel Geld is easy to say. Zu viel zu viel is a worse tongue-twister than Weltverbessers.

I give them a good title; and immediately they set to work to spoil it. It must be ZU VIEL GELD ganz einfach [quite simply].[1]

Tolstoy's children made fun of his ways as Weltverbessererswahn [world-betterers-madness]. That was one of my reasons for discarding the word. It suggested a different sort of play.

If Tina has done the moving she may be tired; but it will cure her when she has rested.[2] Housework is healthy for women.

I have begun a new play: a political one.[3]

G.B.S.

Tpc.; signature typed.

1. The German title for *Buoyant Billions* became, as Shaw insisted, *Zu viel Geld* (Too Much Money), but a problem with the subtitle, *A Comedy of No Manners*, remained.
2. The Trebitsches, to recuperate from the effort of moving, had gone to Bad Ragaz, Switzerland.
3. On 17 July, Shaw began *Farfetched Fables*, a short play in six scenes.

[Ayot St Lawrence. Welwyn]
30th July 1948

My dear Trebitsch

. . . I think the play must be called "eine ungebrauchliche Komodie" [an unusual comedy]. The English "no manners" does not mean *bad* manners.

Tell the manager of the Schauspielhaus that the play must not be announced and produced as a heavy highbrow profound dramatic poem. Nobody would go to see it. Everybody will go to see it as a Volkstück. It is essentially a light comedy. He may introduce as many comic songs as he likes.

It has been hellishly hot here for 3 days, but will presently finish up in a thunderstorm. Thinking of the past will make you sleepless: the present is far more interesting.

G.B.S.

Als.

[Ayot St Lawrence. Welwyn]
5th August 1948

My dear Siegfried

You may be an epic poet; but nothing will ever make you a playwright. You think a play is a string of splendid sentences and epigrams, with every speech a poem that Goethe might have been proud of. You could not make a greater mistake. You might string a thousand splendid sentences and exquisite poems together without making a play. On the stage every speech must provoke its answer and make the audience curious to hear it. Every word that digresses and breaks the chain of thought, however splendid, must be ruthlessly cut.

You should have made the cuts yourself and told me that my old hand was losing its cunning. They will not shorten the play more than a few minutes, easily compensated by adding one minute to each interval. If the program is too short, one of my shorter plays, Village Wooing or The Six of Calais can be played without extra fees.

As to reading the preface, it is a silly outrage which I absolutely forbid. Do not countenance it for a moment. You are really losing your wits to suggest such an imbecility. The Burgtheater [the Schauspielhaus] will have more sense than to object to my improvements.[1]

If you can sell your copyrights for a sufficient joint annuity payable by a responsible Insurance Company and not dependent on a millionaire who may become bankrupt at any moment, you certainly ought to do it.[2] The millionaire can buy such an annuity for you.

As "a comedy of no manners" is untranslatable, it had better be dropped. In England it depends on the fact that "a comedy of manners" denotes a special genre as "comedy of Arts" does in Italian. It has nothing to do with misbehaviour.[3]

G.B.S.

Tl.; signature typed.
1. Despite Shaw's objections, the Schauspielhaus extended *Buoyant Billions* by reading parts of the preface from the stage before a projection of Shaw.
2. Trebitsch was considering selling his Shavian royalties to the London publisher William Heinemann, one of whose directors was the "millionaire" Paul Zsolnay, Trebitsch's friend.
3. Shaw's objections were overruled and the German subtitle became "Eine unmanierliche Komödie" (An Unmannerly Comedy).

Ayot St Lawrence. Welwyn
3rd September 1948

My dear Siegfried

I note that in Lucerne you chose the most expensive hotel there, and one of the worst.

In London you are returning to the Dorchester.[1]

You are incorrigible; and if you sell out for an annuity you must budget for at least the equivalent in Swiss francs of £3000 a year.

It is no use telling me that you want an allowance per month: the insurance companies pay by the year or half year. I do not know what securities may be available in Switzerland. My own annuity is from a Canadian Company, and was negotiated for me by Stanley Clench, of 44 Duke Street, Saint James's, London W. 1. He acts as agent for the Canadian Companies, and is a sound financial adviser.

I have no engagements at present on or after the 10th. I shall be free any afternoon after 4. Let me know when to expect you as soon as possible.

I have nearly finished a new play [*Farfetched Fables*].

G.B.S.

Tl.; signature typed.
1. Trebitsch arrived on 10 September for a fortnight in England. It was the last time the two friends met.

Ayot St Lawrence. Welwyn
20th September 1948

My dear Trebitsch

Your crazy telegrams shew that you do not understand the situations in spite of all my explanations. You will get nothing from Rank: he owes you nothing. You assured me that he never paid you anything; but it now appears that he did pay you. You persist in asking him for five per cent of the royalties. He has nothing whatever to do with your share of my royalties, which is a matter between you and me; and as my royalty for the current five years is only one per cent and is heavily surtaxed, your share on the C&C film is only ½%.[1]

It is clear to me that you will go away with your pockets empty unless I make you an advance (which I can ill afford) on account of your ½%. I therefore enclose my cheque for £100. As it is a crossed cheque it cannot be cashed across the counter, and must be presented by a bank. The hotel will cash it for you if you pay your bill with it: if not, your friend who pays the bill can do it. Failing him you can take the cheque to Zürich to your own banker.

You can now drop your claim on G.C.F.C., and go home happy.

G.B.S.

Tl.; signature typed.

1. Trebitsch, still in London, claimed royalties from the Rank Organization (General Cinema Finance Corp.) for the German distribution of *Caesar* despite Pascal's claim that Trebitsch had sold his share (see 3 December 1946). Shaw's film royalty was 10 percent of gross receipts, but to avoid taxes Shaw had arranged to defer his royalties, and was taking only 1 percent.

Ayot St Lawrence. Welwyn
29th November 1948

My dear Trebitsch

I do not know how you can establish the value of your copyrights. The war has so upset everything that your income for the last ten years can prove nothing as to what it will be for the next ten. Not only is the number of my plays changing as I write new ones, but the number of performances and copies sold varies with the fluctuations in my vogue in Germany. I have just written that Stalin should have the vacant Nobel Peace Prize.[1] That may destroy for months the vogue I may have gained by my recent verdict that neither the Russians nor the Americans nor the French nor British have any right to be in Germany except the right of conquest, and that they must clear out sooner or later.[2] After my death, which is imminent, there will be a slump in Shaw which may reach oblivion for many of the fifty years of my copyright. You have no certainty to sell: your friend must back his fancy as if he were backing a horse. At most all you can do is to ask *Ashley Dukes* how much money of mine the British Control has, and what period it covers.

You must not expect me to get excited about Zu Viel running for sixteen nights at the Schauspielhaus.[3] Man and Superman has been running in

America for sixteen hundred, and has yet to finish in London. As usual the only notices in the press here reported it as being very coldly received.[4]

I have been frightfully busy writing a big preface for Far Fetched Fables. I have to revise and piece together again and again to delete my senile blunders and produce anything coherent and stylish.

Tina's photograph is charming. This is more than can be said for ours.

G. Bernard Shaw

Tls.

1. Shaw praised Stalin as having "the best right" to the Nobel Peace Prize in his preface to *Farfetched Fables*.

2. In a letter to the *Times* (19 August 1948), Shaw cited Britain's "right" to be in Berlin as confusion between alterable arrangements and human rights.

3. *Buoyant Billions* (*Zu viel Geld*), which had had its premiere in the Schauspielhaus, Zurich, on 21 October 1948, ran 15 times. The play was directed by Berthold Viertel, and the cast included Will Quadflieg, Maria Becker, and Therese Giehse.

4. The *Neue Zürcher Zeitung* (23 October), while temperate about *Zu viel Geld*, reported strong applause, but the London *Times* noted "polite but unenthusiastic reception."

Ayot St Lawrence. Welwyn
6th January 1949

My dear Trebitsch

I shall most certainly not pay a farthing for you to that Pen Club Fund. The woman [E. Arnot Robertson] for whose benefit it has been got up, sued a newspaper for criticizing her, and lost her action after incurring heavy costs, as she richly deserved.[1]

By English law every adverse criticism except in Parliamentary debate is a libel; but between authors and critics there is a tacit understanding that neither of them is to go to law about it. An author who does is never criticized again: that is, never mentioned in the press, which means virtual extinction. Without this understanding there could be no criticism at all. The Pen Club should not have countenanced its violation by getting up a fund to pay the costs of the lost action. I refused to contribute, and will not help you to do it. So put the Pen appeal in the fire and forget it.

The South of Europe can be horribly cold in winter. You should fly to Los Gatos in California, where it is always summer. That will cost you a lot of money; but you never seem to be at a loss for millions.

But why do you persist in these treatments that never cure you? There are several alternatives: osteopathy, homeopathy, vegetarianism, Nature Cure, psychotherapy, Christian Science, etc. Try them all; and stick to the one that will cure, if such a thing exists.

I will let you have the new play [*Farfetched Fables*] when I get it from the printer.

Never mind what Pascal tells you. He has a new programme every day. His description of my new play is utter nonsense. Nothing is yet settled about his next filmings.[2]

Loewenstein is writing to you about South America.[3]

G. Bernard Shaw

Tls.

1. E. Arnot Robertson (1903–1961), English author and critic, had sued Metro-Goldwyn-Mayer for writing to the BBC barring her from M.G.M. previews and requesting that she be removed from reviewing M.G.M. films because she was out of touch with the public. Ms. Robertson published the letter in the *Times* (4 October 1946) and took action for defamation. A jury found for Ms. Robertson, but the verdict was overturned on appeal. Now the P.E.N. was raising funds for a final appeal to the House of Lords. (It was rejected.) Shaw gained a misleading impression of the case.

2. Pascal, still without a studio, had negotiated unsuccessfully for productions of Shaw in Hollywood, Ireland, and Italy.

3. The German market in South America offered some income for Shaw-Trebitsch.

Ayot St Lawrence. Welwyn
16th February 1949

My dear Trebitsch

You were simply eating too much: that is the only Fava secret. All you needed was a month of fasting. As you were probably suffering also from excessive protein, you will do still better if you cut out the eggs and the spaghetti from Fava's bill of fare, and have the spinach chopped up with turnips, carrots, tomatos and watercress, and eat it UNCOOKED, with salad dressing and chutney to your taste. You will find this quite satisfying and surprisingly eatable and digestible; and you can add as much fruit as you like. Drink tomato juice. No flesh, fish, fowl, *nor eggs.*

The Malvern Festival will begin in August with Buoyant Billions,[1] which is already disposed of as far as you are concerned by the performance at the Schauspielhaus. You can leave it to be dealt with by Kantorovich.

Farfetched Fables is a series of six short plays to be performed by the same half dozen players in different costumes and characters in postwar ages. It is suitable only for little groups of amateurs, and is useless to regular commercial theatres. However, you can judge for yourself when you read it. I will send you a copy as soon as it is printed.

There is a marionette theatre in Malvern. The puppetmaster sent me two puppets representing myself and Shakespear, and asked [me] to write one of my famous plays for them, to last ten minutes in performance. I did so.[2] It took me two days. Is there a puppet show in Zurich?

Pascal is not yet filming. The Irish project has fallen through;[3] and he has had to go to Malta, where a great banking firm has undertaken to supply the needed capital. But the films will be made in England. The transaction is not yet concluded, and may never be, as Pascal announces a new enterprise three or four times a week, ending in smoke.

He tells me, by the way, that you have a fixed delusion that I am immensely rich, and that I am holding back millions, half of which belong to you. You had better read the enclosed pink card,[4] though it will probably make no impression on you. Pascal says he did his best to enlighten you, but that you evidently did not believe him. If imaginary riches make you happy, by all means imagine them; but they will never materialize.

GBS

Tls.

1. The Malvern Festival, managed by Roy Limbert, opened on 8 August with *Apple Cart*, followed by *King Charles*, and on 13 August by *Buoyant Billions*, directed by Esmé Percy, with Denholm Elliott, Frances Day, and Dermot Walsh.

2. *Shakes versus Shav*, written for the Waldo Lanchester Marionette Theatre, Malvern, was performed on 9 August.

3. Pascal had attempted to establish an Irish film industry, but he failed to raise sufficient capital. His Maltese project also collapsed.

4. The pink card, one of Shaw's famous printed cards, answered begging letters and declared that while all assume that Shaw is a multimillionaire, his income is largely confiscated by taxes for public benefit. He doesn't complain, but "it is useless to ask him for money: he has none to spare."

[Trebitsch to Shaw]

[Zurich]
18th February 1949

My dear Shaw

Does the name Dr Rudolf Kassner great Viennese Philosopher, very celebrated, tell you something? And who on earth was Harry Cust who wanted to have you at lunch with Kassner.[1]

Please ask Dr Loewenstein to translate to you the enclosed [passages from Kassner].

Yours ever
S.T.

P.S. I should like to send Kassner your reply.

Als.; Texas.

1. Dr. Rudolf Kassner (1873–1959), Viennese cultural philosopher and physiognomist, in his *Umgang der Jahre* (Zurich, 1949), reprinted a memoir of encountering Shaw in a one-piece knitted garment and of Harry Cust (1861–1917), editor and occasional poet, trying to bring Kassner and Shaw together at lunch.

Ayot St Lawrence. Welwyn
21st February 1949

I once took a walk through the west end of London in a knitted woolen suit invented by Jaeger;[1] but this had nothing to do with Cust, with whom my acquaintance was very slight, or with Dr Kassner, of whom I have no recollection.

Your notion about my income tax is utter blodsinn [nonsense]. I cannot by any means evade taxation; but if I could what claim would you have on it? You are entitled to half the royalties received by me for performance of your translations; but the British Control has not paid me anything; and you have drawn on me during your visits to London for more than I am likely to get from South America.[2]

Many years ago I contributed £100 to the National Theatre Fund, on the Committee of which I served until my retirement. I have contributed nothing since, nor have I bequeathed anything to it in my will. Are you suggesting that I should make a new will leaving my entire property to you?

I am not complaining; but your letter shews that you believe that I am holding back from you large sums for which I am heavily in debt to you, and am spending on myself or paying away in avoidable taxation.

There is not the smallest foundation for this. Get it out of your mind, or you will end by ranking me as a first class

CROOK

(Schurke)

GBS

Maugham[3] and the estates of Kipling & Galsworthy are as hard hit by the war taxation as I am.

Tls.

    1. Dr. Gustav Jaeger (1832–1917), German hygienist.

    2. Trebitsch apparently suggested that Shaw could reduce his taxes by sharing his income. Shaw had previously advanced Trebitsch £300 on unrealized royalties from German productions in South America.

    3. W. Somerset Maugham (1874–1965), highly successful, wealthy English author.

Ayot St Lawrence. Welwyn
22nd March 1949

My dear Trebitsch

Stop bothering me about Far Fetched Fables: I will send you a proof when I get one. Pascal knows only what I told him about it. I have answered all your letters.

What is upsetting your health is your indulgence in sentimental grievances. Get rid of your old friends and make young ones. Old people who have no other company than themselves go mad, that is why you are going mad and trying to drive me mad too. We are both back numbers, not boys, and should drop one another and never speak or write to anyone over 40.

G.B.S.

Tls.

[Trebitsch to Shaw]

Dufourstrasse 121. Zurich
27th March 1949

My dear Shaw,

After a few days which seemed to clear up my life a little, I had a disagreeable news. I knew that I had soon again to go to Paris, to show myself to the authorities and explain again and again why I am forced to live in Switzerland, but now they try the same game on poor Tina. They want to see her and to reproach her behavior to her: to run away with a french "passeport for 11 years without showing herself again." They want to try to persuade her to return to france.

Well, a trip to Paris is not so bad, but we cannot afford it, hardly for one.

Now Tina wants me to ask you, if you could perhaps put to her disposal some film-royalties, which are laging there and which you cannot or will not fetch to London. She gives you her love and thanks in advance but pretends that Caesar & C was filmed in Paris very successful, which I do not remember.

Please dont be angry and drop me a line on this disagreeable subject.

Yours ever
Siegfr. Trebitsch[1]

Als.; Texas.

  1. On the face of this letter Shaw noted for Loewenstein to write to Trebitsch:

There is no money in Paris over which I have any control or which belongs to anyone except to S. T. himself. If he cannot get it, how can I?

  If the authorities demand a visit let them pay for it. The reply to them must be that a personal visit is beyond the means of Frau Trebitsch, but she will give any evidence of her existence that she can afford. Anyhow, suppose they cancel her passport and her French nationality, what harm will that do her?

  You may say as from yourself that S. T's continued assumption that I have money of his which I am holding back from him makes our personal relations very difficult. *In fact* he is in my debt.

Ayot St Lawrence. Welwyn
22nd April 1949

Utter nonsense!

S[hakes] v. S[hav] is a play for puppets, lasting less than ten minutes and playable only in a marionette theatre.

I have ordered some rehearsal copies, and will let you have one when they arrive. I always do.

Why bother me and yourself with these foolish or mistaken proposals?

GBS

Apcs.; Texas.

Ayot St Lawrence. Welwyn
23rd May 1949

Why should I interfere in this affair? Your Maries have got what they want. When the B.B.C. asks me to authorize the broadcast I will consent; that is all.[1]

But however successful the whole play may have been, it does not follow that detached scenes or speeches will be either intelligible or effective. I never advise them, and mostly forbid them. I do not consider the selection a wise one.

GBS

Apcs.

  1. Maria Fein, German-Swiss actress, and her actress daughter, Maria Becker, had toured after the war in *Mrs Warren*. They now proposed readings, in English, from *Mrs Warren* over the BBC, but nothing materialized.

Ayot St Lawrence. Welwyn
30th July 1949

My dear Trebitsch

I send you the reply of the Control to my inquiry.

What it comes to is that all our money is "blocked" in the hands of Fräulein Getrude Gowze, Veerstucken 3E, Hamburg, who has been appointed my agent, and takes a commission of 4%.[1] Not even if you go to Germany and live there for a time can you touch a penny of it, because you are not related to me.[2] 70% of it has been "cancelled":[3] that is, confiscated. No reason given. We can do nothing but wait until the Control makes up its mind to pay us, and when, and how, or not at all. The matter is under consideration. For another 4 years perhaps, when we shall both be dead.

Ashley Dukes thought you could perhaps get your share if you went to Germany. He was wrong. You are blocked as completely as I am.

Send the document back when you have studied it, and made a note of the total figures.

If I am ever paid you will probably have to come to London to get your share. Until then there is nothing more to be said or done.

Winsten's book [*Days with Bernard Shaw*, 1949] is a tissue of misunderstandings and spoiled stories. But he writes pleasantly; and his fictitious Shaw is better liked by many readers than the real one.

G.B.S.

Als.

1. Fräulein Gertrude Gowze was the Custodian for Foreign Authors.

2. Foreign-owned funds were being gradually unblocked in the Western zones, permitting some uses within Germany but not their transfer abroad. Since all of Shaw's German royalties, including Trebitsch's share, were credited to Shaw, Trebitsch could not draw on them.

3. Suhrkamp reported that 35 percent, not 70 percent, of Shaw's earnings had been "extinguished" by the Control after the currency reform of 1948.

Ayot St Lawrence. Welwyn
11th September 1949

My dear Trebitsch

Rubber stamps are not valid (giltig) in England.

I now enclose an Urkunde [deed] with a ten shilling Government embossed stamp, which makes it what is called a *deed poll*, and gives it legal validity. The signature is witnessed by a solicitor who is also a Commissioner of Oaths. He assures me that nothing more can be done to satisfy Surkamf and the Control.[1]

As to the matter of selling your interest in my copyrights I cannot advise you either for or against it. You must judge the situation for yourself. On one point however you must be adamant. Accept nothing but a life annuity for yourself and Tina jointly from a first rate Insurance Company. Without this you would have no security; for your friend [Paul Zsolnay] might go bankrupt and leave you penniless (Kreutzerlos).[2] And there must be no reduction on the death of either of you. If Tina survives you she will need *more* money, not less, for your obsequies and the settlement of your affairs, and must not have to live more cheaply.

I foresee difficulties; and I do not know whether 6000 Swiss francs per month (£4,500 a year?) subject to Income Tax, will enable you to live in comfort. I can say no more at present.

G. Bernard Shaw

Als.
> 1. Shaw executed a formal deed attesting to Trebitsch's half-share in Shaw's German royalties.
> 2. As noted, Trebitsch was negotiating with William Heinemann Ltd., through Paul Zsolnay.

[Ayot St Lawrence. Welwyn]
postmarked 29 September 1949

Call it *Phantastischen Fabeln*. Weltweite is quite wrong.[1] There is no German word corresponding exactly to farfetched, which has nothing to do with distance. It means too far reasoned, supersubtle, too ingenious to be convincing.

Why do you let the surgeons cut you to pieces? There is a first rate Nature Cure Clinic in Zürich.[2] Try my diet.

Let me have your address in Wien.[3]

Apc.
> 1. Trebitsch, misunderstanding "farfetched," proposed *Weltweite Fabeln* (Worldwide Fables), but he corrected it to *Phantastische Fabeln* (*Neue Schweizer Rundschau*, March 1950).
> 2. Presumably the Bircher-Benner Clinic, which pioneered raw food diets. (Earlier, Shaw had found the cure "very dangerous"—1 August 1926.)
> 3. For the first time since his exile, Trebitsch agreed to visit Vienna, where he was feted by the P.E.N. and Concordia (Press) clubs, but he declined to resettle in Austria.

Ayot St Lawrence. Welwyn
3rd November 1949

Be careful. I cannot advise you. Do not accept any money, and do not come to London to be talked into a bad bargain after three bottles of Burgundy, nor have any private friendly relations with Zsolnay until the question is finally settled one way or another.

If you accept a single Swiss franc or even a railway ticket you are committed and lost.

No payment except an annuity for your life and Tina's from an Insurance Company. . . .

If you come to London as Z's friend and at his expense I shall refuse to see you. You MUST be businesslike.

G.B.S.

Apcs.; Texas.

Ayot St Lawrence. Welwyn
12th November 1949

Very well. Go your own way; disregard my advice; and die a pauper.[1] . . .
I have told you what to do. You will not do it. I have nothing more to say,
except to ask you not to visit me if you come to London. The friends by
whom you intend to be guided will no doubt entertain you and pay your expenses. I WONT.

G.B.S.

Apcs.; Texas.

1. Trebitsch was considering selling his rights in Shaw for a private annuity from Heinemann
instead of one from an insurance company.

Ayot St Lawrence. Welwyn
18th November 1949

My dear Trebitsch
Good.
And now, who has been your best friend? Without my Schimpflexicon
[scolding words] you would have dug yourself a Bettler's [beggar's] grave.
Postcards are a penny cheaper than letters.[1] Only in villages are they read
by postmistresses; in Zürich there is no time to read dozens of cards every
day, even if they were in the German language. And who cares anyhow?
You must not dream of coming to London. You cannot afford it. You have
had two holidays this autumn already: Kaiserhof[2] and Wien. Above all, you
must not see any of your old friends until you are safely insured. You are too
sentimental. And I have no money for you.
The weather here is schreklik: terrible fogs and floods: Arctic cold. Two
days of it would kill you.

GBS

Als.; Texas.

1. Trebitsch was mortified that Shaw would discuss his business and upbraid him in an open
postcard.
2. Before his visit to Vienna, Trebitsch and his wife went to Bad Gastein (the Kaiserhof) to test
the atmosphere in their former homeland.

Ayot St Lawrence. Welwyn
21st November 1949

. . . You must not go back on me now. You must positively NOT come to
London to be talked over. The weather is terrible: it would kill you. When
the days are long and warm, and you have the insurance policy safe in your
pocket I will see you, *but not before*.

G.B.S.

Apcs.; Texas.

Ayot St Lawrence. Welwyn
23rd November 1949

My dear Trebitsch

You will drive me mad with your misunderstanding of my suggestions and of the whole affair.

I never dreamt of such nonsense as your going to an Insurance Company and asking them to buy your copyrights. That is not their business. What I told you, and now tell you again for the fifty thousandth time, is that the security of any private friend of yours or of Heinemann for your livelihood is no security at all; and to prove it I have told you repeatedly that I, who was rich before the war, have now barely enough to live on myself.

Therefore your friends, if they wish to buy your interest in my works, must put down the price—200,000 Swiss francs or whatever it may be—of a life annuity for you and Tina from an Insurance Company, and give you the policy. You need have no trouble at all in the matter except to name your price. You do not deal with the Insurance Company: that is the business of the purchaser: and the Company has nothing to do with your copyright: it simply sells the annuity in the ordinary course of its insurance business. There is nothing for you to come to London for; nothing to discuss: you just get the Policy and the trick is done. I mentioned Clench only because he might get better terms *for the purchaser* from one of the Canadian Companies, which are very safe. You just do nothing, nothing, nothing, nothing, nothing, NOTHING, *NOTHING.*[1]

If you cannot understand this I must give you up as gehirnlos [brainless]. My urging you not to come to London is because I can see no object in the invitation except to talk you out of your demand for Insurance. You can send me your book:[2] I do not want to see you or to see anybody. Especially I do not want to see you until this insurance business is settled, because I doubt whether the baares Geld [cash] will be forthcoming. Your visit would be a senseless waste of money, and in your present state of health would be dangerous.

For heaven's sake let us stop this correspondence, which is costing me more time than I can afford. I have said all I have to say, and I cannot keep saying it over and over again. If you cannot understand it, or will not take it, you must go your own way and take the consequences.

In desperation
GBS

Tls.; Texas.
   1. The last "nothing" is underscored three times.
   2. *Die Heimkehr des Diomedes* (Diomedes' Return), a lyrical prose tale based on the Homeric myth, shortly published by Artemis. Its theme was the suffering hero doomed to be a satellite.

Ayot St Lawrence. Welwyn
28th November 1949

I see you are determined to come, no matter what I say. The flying will not hurt you: on the contrary it will probably be good for you. I agree with the pilot and the doctor so far. But do not come to Ayot. The fogs here have been so terrible that all over the country cars have been abandoned in hundreds, and their occupants left to get to their destination in the dark and the cold as best they could. Even when there is no fog it is dark at four o'clock; and the lanes here are dangerous. You have been here only in summer, and do not know what it is like now. All my would-be visitors are put off until after Easter.

In any case I do not want to see you. I have given you all the advice I can; and you will not take it, and only half understand it. We should waste time talking about it; and I am too old to have any time to waste. Clench need cost you nothing. He is an insurance agent, getting his commission from the insurance company when he secures a client for it. All he can do is to induce the purchaser of an annuity to deal with one of the companies for which he acts by quoting better terms, or the greater security of the Canadian companies. You might thus have the choice of the company; but you have nothing else to do with Clench.

I repeat, your negotiations will either come to nothing or end in your being humbugged into taking much less than your film prospects are worth, and having no security.

However, you will not be warned, and will probably die *sur la paille* and leave Tina to starve.

When I was rich I provided for my French translator Hamon by buying an annuity for him. He is dead; but he did not die destitute, nor is his widow penniless. But if she had my security only, she would now be a pauper.

So again farewell; and go your own way. I wash my hands of the affair.

GBS

Tls.; Texas.

Ayot St Lawrence. Welwyn
29th November 1949

Tina is quite right: I know all about it, and have been trying to knock it into your Schafskopf for weeks past. But why then does she conclude that I am a Til Eulenspiegel making mischievous fun of you?

But now I must tell you that you ought not to accept any money from Zsolnay or Heinemann or anyone else concerned. You know at last that the business will take much longer than a week, and that you can do nothing but stick to your demand for a secure annuity for your life and Tina's. If they cannot find the money to purchase the annuity they will say that you had no right to take their money unless you intended to negotiate and compromise.

And if you do this you are lost; and so is Tina. If you stand by your guns they will say that unless you return the money you will have cheated them out of a pleasure trip at their expense.

To minimize or avoid taxation I have during the last 20 years bought annuity bonds, sinking fund policies, deferred annuities, and a life annuity for Charlotte and myself jointly to the amount of £125,000 from the Canadian Insurance Companies by Clench's advice (given gratis). They pay in dollars, the soundest currency in the world. All these speculations have turned out well. Of course I had to put down the cash to start.

Clench tells me that this game is up, as the companies are fed up with deferred annuities and the like: but still it is part of the business of insurance to sell annuities to all purchasers as a baker sells loaves, the price varying with the current rate of interest and the age of the annuitant. You and Tina are old enough to make your Lebensversicherung [life insurance] comparatively cheap.

Refer Zsolnay & Co to Clench for advice, expressing your preference for dollar securities (which means Canada); but do not come to England; and do not accept a farthing from Z & Co on any pretext whatever.

G.B.S.

Tl., signature typed; Texas.

Ayot St Lawrence. Welwyn
1st December 1949

The Artemis pronouncement about Anglo-saxon rights is blödsinn: there are no such rights. For your own original works you have copyright practically everywhere in Europe except in Russia for your life and 50 years. In the U.S.A. you have only half that term, unless you renewed it, and had it registered in the Congress Library in Washington when the book was first published. As you probably neglected these formalities, I take it that your copyrights are limited to the European countries within the Convention.

As to my works you have nothing but copyright in your translations; and this copyright is not exclusive: I could authorize another translator to make a new translation if I chose.

This is all you have to sell. You can sell it for the rest of your life plus 50 years for an insured annuity if you can find a purchaser. But you can also assign it for any shorter period for an agreed sum.

Consequently if, as Artemis says, (and I agree) an insured annuity is out of the question for the present you can tell Heinemann that he can have all your literary earnings for one year for, say, 36,000 Swiss francs baares Geld. At the end of the year he can consider whether it is worth his while to renew for another year; and you will have found out whether you can live decently on 3,000 francs [£250] a month.

This needs no journey, no solicitor, no negotiation that cannot be conducted on a couple of postcards. It is simply Yes or No, how much and how little, trial and error. The law is not in question: it is as plain as a pikestaff.

No more of your gottverdammt Schwarmerei [damned gushings].

I do not want to see you.

I do not want to see you.

I do not want to see you.

I do not want to see you.

I DO NOT WANT TO SEE ANYBODY!

GBS

Tls.; Texas.

[Ayot St Lawrence. Welwyn]
6th December 1949

Your letter is utter nonsense, and shews that you do not understand a word of what I have written to you. If you have nothing to offer what has all our correspondence been about? What are you coming to England for? Do you suppose you can "negotiate" H[einemann] into giving you a pension for nothing?

What you have to offer is the income from your copyrights. It is so uncertain that nobody is likely to pay you enough for you to live on if you sell it ganz und gar outright for its whole duration. But you need not sell it for its whole duration. You can sell it for a day, a month, a year, five years, any period for which you can find a buyer.

I suggest that you sell it for a year to H. (or anyone else who will buy it) for X francs cash down in advance. This needs no security nor annuity nor Insurance nor any other precaution against loss or devaluation. At the end of the year you will have found out whether X francs is enough for you to live on; and H. (or another) will have found out what your copyrights are worth at present.

You can do this without coming to England. If H. pays your expenses they will be deducted from the price whether they are mentioned in the accounts or not.

But I am wasting time writing you all this over again. You will not understand. Your journey will come to nothing, and will empty your pockets of your loose cash.

G.B.S.

Tl., signature typed; Texas.

Ayot St Lawrence. Welwyn
postmarked 12th December 1949

Why did you not tell me all this before? [1]

Not a word of it!

All your stocks should have been converted into annuity years ago.

I never knew you had any.

G.B.S.

Apcs.
   1. Trebitsch had arrived in London and was at the Dorchester Hotel. At Shaw's insistence, he did not visit Ayot but wrote to Shaw from London.

Ayot St Lawrence. Welwyn
20th December 1949

My dear Trebitsch

   I have nothing more to say. I gave you the best advice I could after the most careful consideration. I told you to stay at home and do nothing, leaving all the necessary contacts with solicitors and their cost to Z[solnay] and H[einemann]. All there was for you to do was to fix your price for yourself and Tina jointly and to stick to it.

   You have done exactly the contrary in every point. You have gone to London. You have consulted an expensive firm of solicitors who will no doubt send you a bill of costs for making a very bad bargain for both parties. You have not stuck to your 6000; and you have let down Tina, who, when you die, will have to pay your doctor's fees and your funeral expenses, move into cheaper lodgings, dress like a washerwoman, and half starve. You have made no attempt to find out from Clench whether it would not be possible to circumvent the Bank of England by a Canadian dollar annuity to make up the shortage. H. has only had to jingle a handful of Swiss francs under your nose and you have snatched at it like a child at a sugar plum without a thought for Tina or for your own future.[1]

   Well, that is [the] sort of man Siegfried Trebitsch is. There is nothing more to be said. What is done cannot be undone by me. It will probably undo itself after a year's experience.

G.B.S.

Tls.; Texas.
   1. Trebitsch had agreed with Heinemann to accept monthly payments for himself and Tina during their lifetimes, in return for which Heinemann, after Trebitsch died, was to receive Trebitsch's royalties from his translations of Shaw. No Austrian or Swiss earnings were involved. These, Shaw had earlier arranged, were to go entirely—including the playwright's share—to Trebitsch.

Ayot St Lawrence. Welwyn
29th December 1949

   The Diomedes[1] arrived safely. I have not had time to read it yet. It will be a big undertaking; for I cannot really read German without a dictionary, except begging letters, which are all the same.

   The pictures do not interest me. They do not illustrate the story nor belong to the book. I know this because they could not possibly illustrate any story nor belong to any book: they are a portfolio of quite irrelevant drawings stuck in between the leaves, and are very far from equalling the work of Dürer, Altdorfer, or Delacroix. They are only pretentious, and can add nothing to the value of your work, as to which I can say nothing until I have read it.

G.B.S.

Glad you enjoyed your trip.

Apcs.; Texas.

1. Trebitsch sent a copy of his *Diomedes*, which had just been issued by Artemis in a limited edition of 450 copies, illustrated by Hans Ernie.

Ayot St Lawrence. Welwyn
10th January 1950

My dear Trebitsch

Loewenstein is an echt Berliner, and will not admit that you, being Wiener, can speak or write German. I must read Diomedes for myself as best I can.

I also have been informed by the British Control that my war royalties have been collected, and that they will be lodged to my credit in any bank in Amsterdam I choose to name. Why Amsterdam I do not know. The money seems as far from my pocket as ever.[1]

Can you explain why you, a champion chess player, are unable to understand the simplest matter of business, and I, a world famous author, economist, and biologist, cannot play chess because I cannot foresee two moves ahead and am checkmated in three?

I know quite well that I could avoid British taxation by living abroad for seven months every year, and all taxation by living all the year round at the South Pole. This idiocy of [Clarence] Sadds convinces me that people who have brains for chess have no brains for anything else.

You still think I am a millionaire and that when you die Tina can live in luxury by marrying me. That would be charming; but how if I were to die before you do, as I almost certainly shall?

G. Bernard Shaw

Tls.; Texas.

1. The next month, Shaw's ledger showed a payment in Dutch florins, amounting to £143, from the Custodians of Deutsche Revisions & Treuhand A.G. But whether any war or postwar German royalties were paid directly to Shaw during his life is undetermined.

Ayot St Lawrence. Welwyn
18th January 1950

My dear Trebitsch

The English Insurance Companies pay annuities of about £9 a year for every £100 cash to persons aged 70; but the Canadian Companies pay only £7.10.0 or thereabouts. These payments are for life; but of course you can buy an annuity for one year or any other period, though short periods are mostly insured by guaranteed bank overdrafts. What I suggested was that you should ask for an annuity of 6000 for the year or for a guaranteed overdraft, which would have given both you and H[einemann] time to find out whether you could live comfortably on that sum and H. could find out equally whether he could make a profit by the transaction, or at least "break even." But I could not make you understand.

Maugham presumably likes life on the Riviera[1] and leaves his affairs to be dealt with by agents and solicitors and the Society of Authors. I have so much business to do here that I work seven hours a day, Sundays and all. I could not live on the Riviera any more than you could live in the crater of

Stromboli. At this moment I am in a difficulty because I owe £12,471 to the Treasury and I am owed £77,000 by a Film Corporation, out of which I shall have to pay £75,075 Surtax.[2] All the writers of begging letters in Europe think that if I can pay such taxes I must be very rich. And you say the same. That is what comes of wasting your brain on chess. The truth is that I have not a penny to spare.

Who is translating Diomedes?[3]

GBS

Tls.; Texas.
1. Somerset Maugham lived in southern France from 1930 on.
2. Shaw's deferred film earnings, which he was compelled to receive and declare that year, finally totaled £88,234.
3. *Diomedes* was not translated.

Ayot St Lawrence. Welwyn
8th March 1950

There was nothing to write about. If I were not well I should be dead. . . .

As to the £600 stamp duty it does not concern me.[1] You would not take my advice. You need not have had a written and stamped contract: only a "gentleman's agreement" to try your plan for a year experimentally. The £600 contract gives you no security whatever against default by H. Serve you right: if I were a billionaire I would not contribute a farthing to your folly.

GBS

H. should pay the whole £600: which is his gain and your loss.

Apcs.; Texas.
1. Trebitsch in having a formal contract drawn up with Heinemann had incurred an expense of £600.

Ayot St Lawrence. Welwyn
13th March 1950

I have never recognized B[ermann] as my agent nor countena[n]ced him in any way; and I have reaffirmed that S[uhrkamp] is my sole German agent, not "for ever" but until further notice.[1] . . .

I think Arms & The Man (Helden) has been performed in France. St Joan certainly has. None of the others.[2]

GBS

Apcs.; Texas.
1. A settlement between Suhrkamp and the Fischer family was pending: the offices of the "Peter Suhrkamp Verlag, formerly S. Fischer" were to go to Bermann Fischer and be revived as the S. Fischer Verlag; Suhrkamp was to establish his own company. Authors were free to choose Suhrkamp or S. Fischer. Shaw chose Suhrkamp as agent; his publisher remained Artemis.
2. Shaw's productions in France included at least 16 plays.

[Ayot St Lawrence. Welwyn]
[early June 1950]

My dear Trebitsch

I have written to Bernauer [Bermann]; but what possible excuse have I for writing to Oskar?[1] and it would not make a penny difference to you if I did. Everywhere I meet the same delusion: people think that if they can connect my name with their enterprises their fortune is made. The truth is that as I am a very controversial author my name repels as many people as it attracts: sometimes more.

There is no reason, however, why you should not ask Oskar why he has never produced my Hell Scene. You can tell him that it is about to be toured in the U.S.A. with a cast of stars.[2] When Man and Superman is played in its entirety with the Hell Scene, the performance lasts over five hours; but the theatre is always full. The only reason for not playing it every night is that no actor could stand the strain.

The costumes, seen against a dead black background, make a superb picture: Doña Ana as a Velasquez Infanta and the Devil in a mantle stuck all over with little red hearts.[3] Talk to Oskar about it; but dont drag me in.

G. Bernard Shaw

Tls.; Texas.
    1. Oskar Wälterlin, of the Schauspielhaus, Zurich; Trebitsch was negotiating with him for a production of *Man and Superman*.
    2. Shaw had just authorized Charles Laughton to tour in "Don Juan in Hell," but the production—a dramatic reading by Laughton, Charles Boyer, Agnes Moorehead, and Cedric Hardwicke—was delayed until February 1951.
    3. The description recalls the 1907 production at the Court, designed by Charles Ricketts.

Ayot St Lawrence. Welwyn
13th June 1950

The mistake about Berman's name was caused by your writing the letter M thus *u* instead of *m*.

I have not kept a copy of my letter. I told him that the Fischer connexion ceased in 1914–18 (the Judenhetze [Jew baiting])[1] and that Surkamp has since been my agent, appointed by the British Control. I added that you desired the situation to be made clear to him.

The English Standard Edition of Buoyant Billions, Farfetched Fables, and Shakes v Shav, with their prefaces, is in the press and will soon be published.[2]

G.B.S.

Apcs.; Texas.
    1. Shaw means of course the Hitler era when S. Fischer was "Aryanized" (1935) and Suhrkamp confirmed as Shaw's agent (1938).
    2. The volume appeared posthumously in March 1951.

[Ayot St Lawrence. Welwyn]
[c. 21st July 1950]

My dear Trebitsch

I can throw no light on this. The only explanation I can think of is that Heinemann is trying to sell your rights and using Fischer as his agent.[1] I do not know what the terms of your agreement with Heinemann are; but I gathered from what you told me that the agreement gave you no security whatever. Now in English law copyright cannot pass without a consideration: that is, unless you executed a deed of assignment of your rights and were paid for it, Heinemann has no rights to sell.

Löwenstein has gone away for the week-end and left your letter for me to deal with. He always assumes that I am a master of the German tongue which I am very far from being; so I may not quite understand Suhrkamp.

Next Wednesday I shall be 94. Last Monday I began a new play called SHE WOULD NOT.[2] Only a comedietta. I cannot write any big stuff now because I have already said all I have to say on that scale.

G.B.S.

Tl., signature typed; Texas.
   1. Trebitsch had forwarded a letter from Suhrkamp about some "mysterious business" from New York, offering agent's rights in Shaw to Bermann Fischer. The "Shaw" later turned out to be the American writer Irwin Shaw.
   2. Shaw's last dramatic effort, finally titled *Why She Would Not*, was begun on 17 July and a draft completed in six days.

Ayot St Lawrence. Welwyn
31st July 1950

For all dates and memoranda ask Loewenstein. No use asking me.

The play [*Why She Would Not*] has gone to the printers; and when they send proofs you shall have one unless I tear it up; for it is a pitiable little old man's drivel.[1]

G.B.S.

Apcs.; Texas.
   1. The promised copy of *Why She Would Not* was never sent, since Shaw suffered his fatal fall and was hospitalized before the proofs were received. The comedietta, presumed unfinished, was not released for publication until 1956.

Ayot St Lawrence. Welwyn
23rd August 1950

My dear Trebitsch

This news of your health is very distressing.[1] There must be something wrong with your habits and diet.

Do you still eat meat? If I were to eat it, my evacuations would stink; and I should give myself up for dead. They are entirely odorless. Are·yours? They ought to be. Why not try my diet?

I learnt only lately that the original performance in German of Man & Superman included the Hell scene (Act III) and that the whole play was cut to pieces to get it within the ordinary time limit.[2] That must not occur again. The third act must be omitted, and the other three played uncut. That is how it is played in England, and how I intended it to be played. Sometimes it is played in its entirety on one night every week, when the performance lasts 5½ hours with an interval for dinner, as at Bayreuth. On that night the house is always crowded.

In America the third act is performed as a separate piece called Don Juan in Hell.

See to it that no tricks are played this time.

G.B.S.

Tl.; signature typed.
  1. Trebitsch, past 80, was experiencing angina chest pains in addition to his migraines and arthritis.
  2. Shaw was misinformed; the 1906 production omitted the third act.

Ayot St Lawrence. Welwyn
31st August 1950

Tell the silly man to use his brains if he has got any. He changes your diet by cutting off your alcohol. He cuts off your coffee. He cuts off your tobacco. He cuts off half your other victuals. And then he says if you cut off what is left of your meat at 80 you will die.

Why do you let yourself be imposed on by such blodsinn?

A spoonful or two of coffee in your milk will prevent it from constipating you and do you no harm.

However, as you never believe what I say or take my advice I will worry you no farther. So go on with your anginas and arthritis and all the ills you prefer just as Charlotte did with her osteitis deformans and died of it.

As to Man & Superman you have absolute power to control the production. You have only to say No and they must do what you dictate. If they cut a line or try to drag in the third act the fault will be yours; and you will betray me.[1]

What is this about Suhrkamp and Artemis? Artemis has no power to sublet his license. It is not possible to have two publishers for my works in German or any other language: they will not bear any division of the profits. You must stop any such transaction at once.[2] When subletting is allowed the sublessees sublet again and again until there is so little left for the actual publisher that he has to write my works off as a failure or go bankrupt.

If Artemis has had enough of Shaw and throws up his license I shall consider a proposal from Suhrkamp to become my *sole* German publisher; but there must be no dealing between them: Artemis has nothing to sell to Suhrkamp nor to anybody except his already printed stock of my and your books.[3]

G.B.S.

Tl.; signature typed.
  1. The Schauspielhaus production of *Superman*, which opened the next spring (7 April 1951), was a cut version that included part of the hell scene. Eleven performances were given.

2. Artemis had entered into a licensing agreement permitting Suhrkamp to publish select works of Shaw.

3. Shaw failed to stop the agreement between Artemis and Suhrkamp. That year, Suhrkamp issued a volume of Shaw's plays: *Klassische Werke*, consisting of *Mrs Warren*, *Candida*, *Caesar*, *Major Barbara*, *Pygmalion*, and *Joan*. Subsequently, Suhrkamp published two volumes of Shaw's prefaces (*Vorreden zu den Stücken*, 1952–53) as well as reprints of *Black Girl* and *Sixteen Self-Sketches*. In 1968, all publishing rights were transferred by the Shaw Estate to Suhrkamp, which undertook to issue new translations of Shaw's plays.

Ayot St Lawrence. Welwyn
7th September 1950

My dear Siegfried

We must stop squabbling and appoint an agent to transact our literary business. At present you are the Dictator; and a Dictator who cannot say No nor resist an offer of a handful of Swiss francs is of no use to me. It took you three years to negotiate a production at the Schauspielhaus. A competent agent could have done it [in] three weeks. I should have done it in three days. You have explained nothing about Suhrkamf: you simply do not understand.

I will say no more about your health. An invalid who thinks it "coarse" to mention his bowels is impossible.

Is Kantorowitz still in business? If so I can refer all business matters to him.

If you can afford your annual visit to London you can please yourself; but to come only to see me would be a senseless extravagance; so keep away from Ayot Saint Lawrence. Keep to your younger friends; and leave me out of the question.

All you need reply to this is Yes or No about Kantorowitz.[1]

G.B.S.

Tl.; signature typed.

1. M. Kantorowitz continued as Shaw's agent for Switzerland until 1957, when those rights went to Suhrkamp.

EPILOGUE

ON 10 SEPTEMBER 1950, three days after writing his last letter to Trebitsch, Shaw fell in his garden and fractured his thigh. News of Shaw's fall and hospitalization flashed abroad. Trebitsch anxiously inquired after his friend from F. E. Loewenstein but was not to hear from him directly again. Early in October, Shaw returned to Ayot, but weakened by infection and unable to care for himself, he declared he would write no more, and on 2 November, in his ninety-fifth year, peacefully died.

Tributes poured in. In Germany, East and West, notices hailed the "fanatical fighter for truth" (*Nacht Express*, East Berlin, 2 November), the "Voltaire of the Twentieth Century" (East German Cultural Association), the "modern Diogenes" (*Frankfurter Allgemeine Zeitung*), "our greatest teacher" (Independent-Socialist *Telegraf*). In East Germany, Shaw was mourned as the greatest contemporary author and playwright, who, a thorn to his class, preferred Stalin to Churchill and ceased to amuse when he opposed the atom bomb and supported the Soviet Union (*Berliner Zeitung*). *Neues Deutschland*, hitherto critical of the Fabian Shaw, now stressed the playwright's stand on peace and the Soviet state. For an unhappy few, Shaw remained a suspect "bourgeois," and Arnold Zweig, resettled in East Berlin, cautioned that only time would tell which of Shaw's works suited the "new life" of socialism (*Manchester Guardian*).

Trebitsch's eulogy was an address in the Schauspielhaus, Zurich. Two months later, Trebitsch completed his memoirs, *Chronik eines Lebens*, placing Shaw on stage among a huge cast of characters and scenes. In his possession were the letters of Shaw (all but a few that were sold) and the copy of Rodin's bust of Shaw, somehow rescued from Vienna. In 1956, having arranged to sell Shaw's letters, which he had guarded as a treasure, Trebitsch went to his bank, retrieved the heavy bundle of correspondence, and suffered a heart attack.* He was in his eighty-eighth year. On 3 June, Siegfried Trebitsch—felled by the hand of his dead friend—died, having outlived Tina by two years. The bulk of his estate came to 500,000 Swiss francs ($115,000); Shaw had left £367,233 (over $1,000,000).

*Private communication from Mrs. Katharina Wyler-Salten, daughter of Felix Salten and close friend of Trebitsch.

INDEX

Italic page numbers indicate identifying notes.

demned Nazi leaders, 370, 425; on oc-
cupation of Germany, 451. *See also*
Hitler; Russia (Soviet Union)
Wotan, 183
Wright, Sir Almroth, *112*
Writing, 32, 71

Yeats, William Butler, 69n; *Land of
Heart's Desire*, 77
Yugoslavia, 231–32, 338

Zangwill, Israel, 189, *191*n
Zeit, 21, 23f, 40, 42, 48, 58, 146, 227

Zeitungsausschnitte, see under Shaw,
works of, *Press Cuttings*
Zetetical Society, 162n
Ziegel, Erich, 129
Zieler, Gustav, 68, *69*n
Zsolnay, Paul, *438*, 457–64 *passim*
Zulus, 350
Zu viel Geld, see under Shaw, works of,
Buoyant Billions
Zu wahr um schön zu sein, see under
Shaw, works of, *Too True to be Good*
Zweig, Arnold, 471
Zweig, Stefan, 5, 378, *379*n

Library of Congress Cataloging-in-Publication Data

Shaw, Bernard, 1856–1950.
 Bernard Shaw's letters to Siegfried Trebitsch.

 Includes index.
  1. Shaw, Bernard, 1856–1950—Correspondence.
 2. Dramatists, Irish—20th century—Correspondence.
 3. Trebitsch, Siegfried, 1869–1956.   4. Shaw, Bernard,
 1856–1950—Translations, German.   5. Shaw, Bernard,
 1856–1950—Appreciation—Europe.   I. Trebitsch,
 Siegfried, 1869–1956. II. Weiss, Samuel A. (Samuel
 Abba), 1922– .   III. Title.
 PR5366.A484 1986   822'.912 [B]   84-40329
 ISBN 0-8047-1257-3 (alk. paper)